HELSINKI

COPENHAGEN

MOSCOW

NORTHERN

BERLIN

CENTRAL

KIEV

SOUTH
EAST

ROME

ATHENS

The New York Times

36

HOURS

EDITED BY BARBARA IRELAND

The New York Times

HOURS
EUROPE

TASCHEN

Contents

NORTH ATLANTIC

SOUTHWEST

CENTRAL

SOUTHEAST

NORTHERN

Foreword

Packed with history, art, diverse culture, and natural beauty, Europe challenges the traveler with its density of riches. How even to comprehend it, much less experience it all? But hop across Europe one weekend at a time, and it comes down to size. No, you can't take in all the wealth and vibrant life of a Dublin or Krakow, much less Paris or Rome, in 36 of the widest-awake hours. But with a well-crafted itinerary, you can come surprisingly close. String those weekends together as leisure and opportunity allow, and eventually you will have your own grand tour.

Since 2006, when the popular 36 Hours feature in The New York Times expanded its scope beyond North America, it has taken readers on uniquely designed, meticulously researched Friday-to-Sunday excursions all over Europe, from Reykjavik to Istanbul. The New York Times 36 Hours: Europe, first published in 2012, gathers together the best of these weekend trips from around the continent. In this second edition, itineraries in several cities are substantially revised to take into account significant new developments or wider viewpoints. Six new destinations are added. And all 130 articles are updated and refreshed to reflect current conditions and travel opportunities.

As 36 Hours has done from the beginning, each of these itineraries lays out a practical, achievable trip that gets to the heart of a destination in limited time. Whether a 36 Hours is serving as a guide for actual exploring or as a source of new ideas to dream on, it lives in the realm of the possible and accessible. Rather than recounting a trip the writer took, it offers up a trip the reader can take.

The work of hundreds of writers, photographers, graphic artists, designers, and editors, combining their talents over many years, has gone into 36 Hours. Europe has provided these creative people with a bounty of material. The itineraries on these pages will take you to great world capitals like London, Berlin, and Moscow; into tiny countries with big personalities, like Georgia and Slovenia; and through eye-popping landscapes from the Alps to the Isle of Skye. They trace the footsteps of Bach and the Beatles. They explore the grandeur of the Parthenon and the quirks of a K.G.B. spies' nest.

There's plenty to see and do. Sip coffee in a Viennese cafe, bike in Amsterdam, party all night in Ibiza, get up early for the best produce at a market in Provence. But might you also care to go mudlarking in London? Ride a dry-land toboggan in Madeira? Kayak in Gdansk? Search for the spot along Lake Geneva where Mary Shelley dreamed up Frankenstein?

Your guides are seasoned New York Times journalists and savvy travel writers. Elaine Sciolino, a longtime foreign correspondent, offers three separate tours of Paris and a side trip in southern France. Frank Bruni, the Times op-ed columnist and food writer, advises on pizza and priceless art in Rome. Seth Sherwood, one of America's liveliest and most prolific travel writers, lays out a dozen weekends from Copenhagen to Bodrum, home of the Turkish jet set. And the former Times travel editor who created 36 Hours, Stuart Emmrich, brings his inventive touch to itineraries in London, Edinburgh, Oslo, and Barcelona.

This book is not a conventional guidebook, and 36 Hours intentionally does not replicate the guidebook formula. It works as a selective summary. Travelers who have more days to spend may want to use a 36 Hours as a starting point. Others may want to juggle an itinerary, staying longer at the beach and skipping the art gallery, or kayaking in the morning rather than in the afternoon.

There are no rules. The weekend is yours, and Europe is waiting. — BARBARA IRELAND, EDITOR

PAGE 2 In a swirl of light, Rome's frenetic traffic streams past the Colosseum, the city's ancient symbol of empire.

OPPOSITE The Matterhorn, challenge to climbers and landmark for skiers, pierces the Alpine skies on the border of Switzerland and Italy.

Tips for Using This Book

Plotting the Course: Travelers don't make their way through a continent alphabetically, and this book doesn't either. North Atlantic, Southwest, Central, Southeast, and Northern — each section is introduced with a regional map, begins in a prominent city or destination, and winds from place to place the way a touring adventurer might. Alphabetical indexes appear at the end of the book.

On the Ground: Every *36 Hours* follows a workable numbered itinerary, which is both outlined in the text and shown with corresponding numbers on a detailed destination map. The schedule is practical: it really is possible to get from one place to the next easily and in the allotted time, although of course many travelers will prefer to take things at their own pace and perhaps take some of their own detours.

The Not So Obvious: The itineraries do not all follow exactly the same pattern. Some recommend a restaurant for lunch; some don't. Night life may or may not be covered. The destination dictates, and so, to some extent, does the personality of the author who researched and wrote the article. In some large cities, where it is impossible to see everything in a week-end, more than one itinerary is offered. Readers are assumed to have some knowledge about traveling; that for example, it is always wise to make a reservation at a popular restaurant, and that in seasonal destinations, some businesses close in the off-months.

Travel Documents: Citizens of the European Union travel freely between countries within the Union. Others must have passports. EU citizens must have passports when traveling outside the EU. Some European nations still require visas from some travelers. Travelers are always wise to check on the requirements before planning journeys to countries where they have not been before.

Finding Your Way: Addresses, telephone numbers, and website addresses are provided wherever possible for the locations recommended within each destination. However, businesses that serve travelers are changing with the times. Some shops now rely more on their Facebook pages than on websites. Some restaurants no longer take reservations at a telephone number, but rely on customers to use the Internet or reserve through a hotel concierge. Savvy travelers everywhere use their GPS-equipped smartphones to help them stay oriented, and tourist sites increasingly cater to that trend with mobile apps. Travelers should also note that because of differences in Internet browsers, some websites cannot be reached without the use of the "www" prefix.

Updates: While all of the articles in this volume were updated and fact-checked for publication in 2016, it is inevitable that some of the featured businesses and destinations will change in time. If you spot any errors in your travels, please feel free to send your corrections via email to 36hourseurope@taschen.com. Please include "36 Hours Correction" in the subject line of your email to assure that it gets to the right person for future updates.

OPPOSITE St. Basil's Cathedral in Moscow.

THE BASICS

A brief informational box for the destination, called "The Basics," appears with each *36 Hours* article in this book. The box provides some orientation on transportation for that location and recommends three reliable hotels or other lodgings, with contact information and a price range.

PRICES

Hotel room, standard double:
Budget, under $125 per night: $
Moderate, $126 to $250: $$
Expensive, $251 to $375: $$$
Luxury, $376 and up: $$$$

Restaurants, dinner entree:
Budget, under $15: $
Moderate, $16 to $30: $$

Expensive, $31 to $45: $$$
Very expensive: $46 and up: $$$$

Restaurants, full breakfast or lunch entree:
Budget, up to $10: $
Moderate, $11 to $20: $$
Expensive, $21 to $30: $$$
Very expensive, $31 and up: $$$$

the Highlands & Isle of Skye 80

Glasgow 74

EDINBURGH 6

DUBLIN 84

GUINNESS

Dublin for Readers 88

Liverpool 58

Birmingham 54

Cork 94

South Wales 62

Oxford 44

Brighton 40

NORTH ATLANTIC

Hampstead
34

London 12

literary London
24

East
London
18

London with
Children 28

Haarlem
118

AMSTERDAM
112

Cambridge 50

LONDON

Bruges 108

Antwerp 104

BRUSSELS 98

London

London is not a city that dazzles on first viewing. It doesn't have the majestic boulevards of Paris, the towering skyscrapers of Hong Kong, or the breathtaking sweep of Sydney's famed harbor. But if the evening skies are clear, stroll across Waterloo Bridge right off the Strand, stop about midway, and look around. In front lie the sprawling National Theatre complex and the fanciful London Eye. To your right, bathed in a soft golden light, are the Houses of Parliament and Big Ben. To your left, the brightly lit dome of St. Paul's Cathedral emerges from the shadows, much as it did during World War II, when the cathedral remained standing while the rest of the East End was in rubble. And below, a few slow-moving boats float by, recalling the days when the Thames was one of Europe's most important commercial waterways. It's at this quiet moment, with this historic, shimmering city stretched out before you, that London wins you over. — BY STUART EMMRICH

FRIDAY

1 *Shaken or Stirred?* 5 p.m.

For more than 80 years, the **Dorchester Hotel** on Park Lane (44-20-7629-8888; thedorchester.com) has been home to one of the best cocktail bars in London. In particular, the martinis (including the house specialty, the Martinez, made with Old Tom gin, re-created from an early 18th-century recipe) are excellent at this elegantly furnished watering hole, with its lacquered mahogany walls and Dale Chihuly-like glass installations. The place bustles in the early evening with businessmen stopping in for a drink before heading home to surrounding Mayfair and hotel guests having a quick one before going out on the town. For traditionalists, an expertly prepared gin and tonic, offered with a selection of house-flavored bitters (try the cardamom or ginger), is worth even the sticker shock of the bill.

2 *Bacon After Dark* 8 p.m.

Evenings are a great time to take in the **Tate Modern** (Bankside; 44-20-7887-8888; tate.org.uk/modern), which is open until 10 p.m. every Friday and Saturday. The galleries are less crowded — meaning you don't have to elbow your way through other spectators to get a decent look at works like Francis Bacon's *Reclining Woman* — and there are evening talks, films, and events throughout the year. Last admission to the galleries is at 9:15 p.m.

3 *East End Hot Spot* 9:30 p.m.

The ethnic melting pot that is London is awash in top-notch cuisine from throughout the world. In the up-and-coming area of Clerkenwell, the Spanish-Moorish restaurant **Moro** (34-36 Exmouth Market; 44-20-7833-8336; moro.co.uk; $$$) draws fashionably dressed trendsetters from around the city for dishes like beetroot and almond soup or charcoal-grilled bream with winter tabbouleh and pistachio sauce.

4 *Last Call at Leicester Square* 10:30 p.m.

Anyone turned off by the charmlessness of Times Square in New York, best regarded as a place that you hurriedly pass through on your way to somewhere else, might be amazed at the late-night vibrancy of **Leicester Square**, in the heart of the West End. Though the specific elements don't amount to much — a Burger King, a Pizza Hut, a couple of movie theaters, and nightclubs with doormen who are alternately entreating and threatening — it all comes together to create a lively gathering spot for 20-somethings spilling out of nearby pubs by around

OPPOSITE The heart of London: Big Ben and the Houses of Parliament.

BELOW Follow the Thames Path to pubs and Shakespeare's Globe theater.

11 p.m., most of whom clearly don't want the night to end. It's a sometimes-chaotic party scene that lasts until 2:30 a.m. or so, when everyone starts heading home on the early-morning buses that fan out from central London.

SATURDAY

5 *A Trip to the Market* 11 a.m.

On Saturday mornings, join what at times feels like the entire population of London and head across the Thames to **Borough Market** (8 Southwark Street; 44-20-7407-1002; boroughmarket.org.uk), London's oldest covered fruit and vegetable market. (Closest Underground stop: London Bridge on the Jubilee and

Northern lines.) It's a perfect spot for grazers looking for a late breakfast or an early lunch. You can get freshly fried fish and chips at one stall and grilled sausages at another, plus olives imported from Turkey, handmade chocolates, and freshly made apple cider. Or join the line of people at the **Hobbs** stand (9 Bedale Street) for succulent roasted beef served in a tortilla wrap or freshly baked baguette. Or maybe just pop into the neighboring **Globe Tavern** (8 Bedale Street) for a cold one to start the day.

6 *A Walk Along the River* 12:30 p.m.

Walk off those Cumberland sausages (or that beer) with a stroll along the **Thames Path**, where you'll pass Shakespeare's Globe theater and the National Theatre complex, plus a series of inviting restaurants and pubs. There's a good chance your journey will be serenaded by young musicians playing under acoustic-perfect covered walkways. One Saturday, the offerings ranged from Mozart and jazz to reggae and "If I Were a Rich Man" played on a xylophone. (Better than it sounds.)

7 *Westminster, Unplugged* 5 p.m.

Music of a different sort can be found at the Evensong at **Westminster Abbey** (westminster-abbey. org), sung by the highly skilled Boys' Choir and attended by a few hundred people each afternoon (weekdays; not held on Wednesdays). It's a thrilling

experience, and a perfect way to see the abbey itself without having to battle the crowds, as the church is closed to normal tourist traffic about an hour before Evensong begins. (Enter through the main west doors, and try to get there by around 4:45.)

8 *Curtains Up* 7:30 p.m.

Though some have complained about the Broadway-ification of the London theater scene, with its increasing reliance on bloated musicals and empty-headed revivals, the **West End** still remains a place to find compelling, original theater a year or two before it heads to New York. (In recent years, such Tony Award-winning shows as *Billy Elliot*, *Frost/Nixon*, and *Jerusalem* all got their start in London.) And prices are generally far lower than in New York. (Cheaper tickets, still, can be found at the TKTS Ticket Booth in Leicester Square. Hours: 10 a.m. to 5 p.m. every day except Sunday, when it is open from 11 a.m. to 4:30 p.m.) A good planning tool is the London Theater Guide Online (londontheatre. co.uk), which has up-to-date news on the city's productions, including the West End and the Fringe, with links to newspaper reviews and online ticket agencies.

9 *A Bit of Paris in Mayfair* 10:30 p.m.

There was a time when Shepherd Market was best known as the place where well-to-do British businessmen could go for discreet trysts with upscale prostitutes. Now the neighborhood's louche reputation has given way to trendiness as a number of intimate, fashionable restaurants have moved into this tiny Mayfair enclave. Among the most inviting is **Le Boudin Blanc** (5 Trebeck Street; 44-20-7499-3292; boudinblanc.co.uk; $$$), a bustling two-story French bistro with a menu heavy on traditional offerings — beef with bordelaise, lemon sole, duck confit — along with some unexpected touches, perhaps monkfish cheeks roasted with butter beans, mussels, leeks, and chorizo. If the weather is nice, try to reserve one of the restaurant's outdoor tables.

SUNDAY

10 *Strings and Sherry* 11:30 a.m.

There is perhaps no better cultural bargain in London than the hourlong classical music concerts at **Wigmore Hall** (36 Wigmore Street; 44-20-7935-2141; wigmore-hall.org.uk). Every Sunday morning, for an admission price easy on anyone's budget (and including a postperformance glass of sherry), you

OPPOSITE ABOVE An art exhibit along the Thames Path.

OPPOSITE BELOW A choice of cheeses at the Borough Market, a perfect spot for grazers.

ABOVE The interior of the Tate Modern.

sweep views of the London skyline. Sunday brunch is served until 2:45 p.m. and includes offerings like grilled mackerel, potatoes roasted in goose fat, and Stornoway black pudding. Reservations essential. Afterward, head around the corner to the stately **National Gallery** (Trafalgar Square; 44-20-7747-2885; nationalgallery.org.uk) with its spectacular collection of European old masters, including Rembrandt's *Self-Portrait at the Age of 34* and Caravaggio's *Supper at Emmaus.*

can hear up-and-coming chamber music groups in a cozy venue. Most performances sell out, but it's usually possible to get a ticket if you arrive by 11 a.m. and wait for returns.

11 *A Picture-Perfect Lunch* 1 p.m.

After strolling through the **National Portrait Gallery** (St. Martin's Place; 44-20-7306-0055; npg.org. uk), head upstairs to the inviting top-floor restaurant, **Portrait** (44-20-7312-2490; $$$), for stunning chimney-

ABOVE Lunch at the National Portrait Gallery.

OPPOSITE Westminster Abbey, a repository of British traditions. To see it without tourist crowds, go at Evensong.

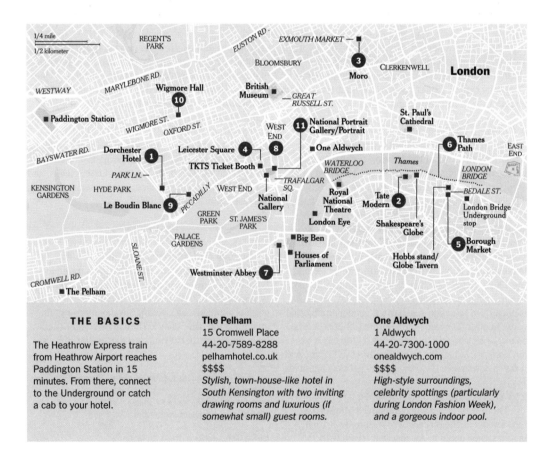

THE BASICS

The Heathrow Express train from Heathrow Airport reaches Paddington Station in 15 minutes. From there, connect to the Underground or catch a cab to your hotel.

The Pelham
15 Cromwell Place
44-20-7589-8288
pelhamhotel.co.uk
$$$$
Stylish, town-house-like hotel in South Kensington with two inviting drawing rooms and luxurious (if somewhat small) guest rooms.

One Aldwych
1 Aldwych
44-20-7300-1000
onealdwych.com
$$$$
High-style surroundings, celebrity spottings (particularly during London Fashion Week), and a gorgeous indoor pool.

East London

Known for its cutting-edge bars, funky galleries, and ethnic restaurants, East London is by far the city's trendiest area (celebrities such as Ralph Fiennes and Keira Knightley have called it home), packed with shoppers during the day and clubbers at night. Wear comfortable walking — and dancing — shoes to discover its neighborhoods: Shoreditch, Bethnal Green, Hackney Wick, and Dalston. You'll find some of London's best fashion, craft, and design businesses, mostly in renovated historic buildings and warehouses off leafy squares and winding streets. And though the current crop of creative merchants echo the area's 18th-century history as a center for silk weaving and furniture making, East London's artists today hail from anywhere but the past. — BY JENNIFER CONLIN

FRIDAY

1 *Gallery Adventure* 4 p.m.

Though some high-end galleries have decamped to Central London, an adventurous contemporary art scene remains. Dive into it at **Cell Project Space** (258 Cambridge Heath Road, 44-20-7241-3600; cellprojects.org), a nonprofit gallery founded in 2000. In a former warehouse, it mounts solo exhibitions by emerging and mid-career artists such as Ryan Mosley, Alistair Frost, and Ruth Ewan. Expect installations, video, paintings, photography, and sculpture. The gallery space isn't the whole picture; Cell also rents out studio space scattered around East and Southeast London at affordable rates to working artists.

2 *Cocktails With Art* 6 p.m.

The streets near Hoxton Square are chock-full of bars, clubs, and galleries, but the **Queen of Hoxton** (1 Curtain Road, Shoreditch; 44-20-7422-0958; queenofhoxton.com; $) is all three in one, with live bands and D.J.'s, art installations, photographic exhibitions, fringe theater, and even film screenings. Mellow out during happy hour over a cocktail in the games room or listen to a ukulele group jam on the rooftop terrace while watching the sun set. Later, if you feel like dancing off your dinner, return and hit the nightclub.

3 *Basement Foie Gras* 8 p.m.

Terence Conran, the designer and groundbreaking London restaurateur of the 1980s and '90s, moved east to Shoreditch in 2008 to convert a Victorian warehouse into a development called **Boundary** (2-4 Boundary Street; 44-20-7729-1051; theboundary.co.uk). On the ground floor is the British-themed **Albion** ($), which serves baked goods and breakfast in its bright cafe and sells Maldon salt in its food shop. There's a hotel on the higher floors and a bar on the roof. But the main event is the **Boundary Restaurant and Bar** ($$$), which manages an air of elegant French dining in the high-ceilinged, brick-arched former basement. One week's menu included suckling pig, breast of veal, and venison.

SATURDAY

4 *Ethnic Breakfast* 9 a.m.

Brick Lane, one of London's most famous immigrant streets, is also one of its most fragrant. The lingering smells of cumin, cardamom, and turmeric emanating from more than 50 Bangladeshi restaurants will no doubt wake you up, though it is the scent of baking bread and the sight of a long line that will direct you to the **Brick Lane Beigel Bake** (159 Brick Lane; 44-20-7729-0616). This one-room shop is one of the last holdovers from the Jewish immigrant community that thrived here in the 1800s. Try the famous salt beef bagel sandwich with mustard and gherkins, and wash it down with a cup of sweet mint tea from one of the nearby North African cafes.

OPPOSITE Hanging out in Hoxton Square.

BELOW Hats for sale at the Spitalfields Market.

5 *Shop Till You Drop* 10 a.m.

Not far from the top of Brick Lane is Cheshire Street, a charming little road filled with eclectic shops. Browse for vintage British clothing — schoolboy scarves, tweedy jackets, Barbour coats, and 1940s and 1950s workingmen's clothes — at **Levisons** (1 Cheshire Street; 44-20-3609-2224; levisons.co.uk). If you're looking for a '50s prom dress, try **Beyond Retro** (110-112 Cheshire Street; 44-20-7613-3636;

ABOVE The Columbia Road Flower Market.

BELOW Indian fare at a Brick Lane dining spot.

OPPOSITE Green Street on a Saturday afternoon.

beyondretro.com), where you also can pick through everything from military jackets to designer handbags. Look for reworked pieces bearing the shop's own label.

6 *French Accent* Noon

Be sure to reserve ahead at the bistro **Brawn** (49 Columbia Road; 44-20-7729-5692; brawn.co; $$$), a popular offshoot of a well-known London wine bar, Terroirs, and a hit with the neighborhood hipsters. The menu at this former charcuterie still includes prosciutto, terrine, and rillettes. Completed with a slice of Hackney wild sourdough and a glass of merlot, your lunch pays tribute to the French Huguenots who occupied this area in the 1700s. For vegetarians, there are dishes like the pumpkin and white bean soup, but really, you're here for the scene as much as the meal.

7 *Ye Olde House* 2 p.m.

Take some lessons in seriously retro home decorating at the **Geffrye Museum** (136 Kingsland Road; 44-20-7739-9893; geffrye-museum.org.uk). The building, a sprawling 18th-century almshouse, is an artifact in itself. Inside, period rooms are set up with authentic furniture and objects to show how middle-class Londoners — those with the funds to stay comfortable with a bit of style — lived from 1630 (no slouching in those chairs) to the present, represented by a sleek London loft. Part of the fun is in the details: real playing cards from the 18th century on a table in the 1790 room, overwrought Victoriana in 1890, a tiny-screened but mod-looking television set in 1960.

8 *Water Walk* 4 p.m.

Head north on Shoreditch High Street until you hit the 180-year-old **Regent's Canal**, once used to transport goods around the city. On the lively pedestrian and cycling path, walk under some arched low bridges and take in the varied architecture. You'll see scenic locks, new residential buildings, abandoned warehouses, and houseboats complete with floating gardens and outdoor fire pits. For a break, order a glass of wine at the bohemian **Towpath Café** (42 De Beauvoir Crescent; 44-20-7254-7606).

9 *National Tastes* 8 p.m.

Take a table at the **Rivington Grill** (28-30 Rivington Street; 44-20-7729-7053; rivingtonshoreditch.co.uk; $$$), where dishes often include ingredients like Yorkshire partridge, parsnip crisps, and turnips that the Scottish call "neeps." For the thirsty, the drinks list has more than a hundred gins. If you're going to hit the clubs, get some rest before heading out again after midnight. Though the hottest East London club is always a moving target, you're safe starting your explorations at Hoxton Square.

SUNDAY

10 *Good Morning, Poland* 9 a.m.

Famous for its perfectly swirled lattes and cappuccinos, **Leila's Shop** (17 Calvert Avenue; 44-20-7729-9789) serves Polish breakfast fare, such as baked eggs with sage, pumpernickel toast, and peppery sausages, at communal tables. It's also a grocery store for foodies, with baskets of root vegetables, wheels of cheese, and various British and Polish delicacies.

11 *Flowers and Fun* 11 a.m.

To truly catch the beauty of East London market day, head to the **Columbia Road Flower Market** (columbiaroad.info/flowermarket), a colorful spectacle of stalls with blooms and plants and even banana trees. Sixty shops include art galleries, pastry and antiques shops, and gardening stores. **Spitalfields** (spitalfields.co.uk), London's oldest market, is also out in force, with plenty of adornments for budget-conscious buyers. You may find prints and T-shirts from fledgling designers next to vintage bags and cheap dangly jewelry.

12 *Go Portuguese* 1 p.m.

Though the chef Nuno Mendes was born in Lisbon and trained mostly in the United States, it's his London restaurants that have gained attention. **Taberna do Mercado** (Old Spitalfields Market, 107b Commercial Street; 44-207-375-0649; tabernamercado. co.uk; $$$) looks like a sleek version of a Portuguese tavern and serves Portuguese-inspired fare. One menu included prawn turnovers—creamy shrimp croquettes cleanly fried—and meat and fish dishes like diced pork tartare and cod in a light broth.

ABOVE Gracious London living circa 1830 in one of the period rooms in the Geffrye Museum.

OPPOSITE Step around a corner to find quiet side streets near Hoxton Square.

THE BASICS

Get around East London on the Underground and by walking or bicycling.

Boundary
2-4 Boundary Street
44-20-7729-1051
theboundary.co.uk
$$$-$$$$
Twelve rooms and five suites, each inspired by a different designer or design movement, in Terence Conran's Boundary development.

Town Hall Hotel & Apartments
8 Patriot Square, Bethnal Green
44-20-7871-0460
townhallhotel.com
$$$
Individually decorated rooms in a renovated Edwardian Town Hall with an Art Deco addition.

East London

DALSTON · LONDON FIELDS PARK · MARE ST.

Towpath Café · WHITMORE RD. BRIDGE · KINGSLAND RD. · QUEENSBRIDGE RD. · Regent's Canal **8**

HAGGERSTON PARK · Cell Project Space **1** · Town Hall Hotel & Apartments · HACKNEY RD. · Columbia Road Flower Market · PATRIOT SQ.

Geffrye Museum **7** · Columbia Road Flower Market **11** · CAMBRIDGE HEATH RD.

SHOREDITCH · Brawn **6** · COLUMBIA RD. · BETHNAL GREEN

HOXTON SQ. · OLD ST. · **10** Leila's Shop · BETHNAL GREEN RD.

Rivington Grill **9** · BRICK LN. · Brick Lane Beigel Bake **4** · CHESHIRE ST.

Boundary/Albion/ Boundary Restaurant and Bar **3** · Beyond Retro

CURTAIN RD. · Levisons **5**

Queen of Hoxton **2** · Taberna do Mercado **12** · BISHOPSGATE

Spitalfields

ENGLAND · Area of detail · Thames · London · HEATHROW AIRPORT

1/4 mile · 1/2 kilometer · COMMERCIAL ST. · 10 miles · 15 kilometers

Literary London

There are many different Londons, and they appeal to people with many different passions: museum enthusiasts, theatergoers, opera buffs, devotees of royalty, students of history, people who like to walk in the rain. But richest of all, perhaps, is the London for book lovers. Because the city is the star and the backdrop of so much great literature, it is possible to believe you know it intimately — how it looks, how it feels — without ever leaving your home. But it is better to visit, if only for the joy of seeing the landscape of your imagination come to life. — BY SARAH LYALL

FRIDAY

1 *Wilde Scene* 2 p.m.

Walk along Sloane Street and take a look at No. 75, the **Cadogan Hotel**, where Oscar Wilde was arrested on April 6, 1895, on charges of "committing acts of gross indecency with other male persons" after dropping a libel suit involving his liaison with young Lord Alfred Douglas. Look for a place to sit as you read the poems "Arrest of Oscar Wilde at the Cadogan Hotel" by John Betjeman and the heartbreaking "Ballad of Reading Gaol" by Wilde himself.

2 *Acquisitions* 3 p.m.

Emerge for shopping: there is plenty of it in this part of London. For books, walk south to small stores like **John Sandoe Books** (10 Blacklands Terrace; 44-20-7589-9473; johnsandoe.com), the **Taschen** shop (12 Duke of York Square; 44-20-7881-0795; taschen.com), and the bookshop of the **Royal Court Theatre** (usually opens at 4 p.m. on Fridays; 50-51 Sloane Square; 44-20-7565-5024; royalcourttheatre.com). For a taste of the Victorian era, a rich period for British literature, go west into Kensington and pick out a period walking stick at **Michael German Antiques** (38B Kensington Church Street; 44-20-7937-2771; www.antiquecanes.com). You might find one with a handle shaped like a swooning swan or one that

doubles as a telescope. Back outside, imagine Peter Pan invading one of the nearby houses to lure away the Darling children, who lived at an unspecified address near Kensington Gardens.

3 *Vanity Fair* 8 p.m.

Treat yourself to dinner at the **Wolseley** (160 Piccadilly; 44-207-499-6996; thewolseley.com; $$$$), a glamorous restaurant near the Ritz Hotel beloved by the more social members of the London literati. Housed in a large, high-ceilinged space whose previous incarnations include a bank and car showroom, the restaurant has been meticulously refitted to evoke a sophisticated old-world Viennese cafe. The layout gives a feeling of tête-à-tête intimacy while also providing lots of people-watching opportunities. The menu is impeccable; leave room for the rich, beautiful desserts.

SATURDAY

4 *Where They Are Now* 9:30 a.m.

Arrive early at **Westminster Abbey** (westminster-abbey.org) to beat the crowds, and head straight for **Poets' Corner**. London so reveres its authors that it buried a number of the best ones in style, and here they are. The stars, with prominent spots marked on the floor, include Chaucer, Spenser, Samuel Johnson, Robert Browning, and Rudyard Kipling. Buried elsewhere but with memorials here are several more recent writers, like T. S. Eliot, W. H. Auden, and Dylan Thomas, and some belatedly recognized women, including George Eliot and Jane

OPPOSITE The Sherlock Holmes pub on Northumberland Street. Inside, patrons peek into a replica of Holmes's study as described in the stories by Arthur Conan Doyle.

RIGHT Canes at Michael German Antiques.

Austen. They're all in good company: Shakespeare also falls into the "memorials only" category.

5 *A Walk of One's Own* 10:30 a.m.

In London you can often spot blue plaques marking houses where writers lived. A good place to search — and to enjoy a stroll among graceful Georgian buildings and parklike squares — is Bloomsbury. Virginia Woolf lived in the neighborhood for most of her life, at one time in **Fitzroy Square**, which was also the home, at various times, of George Bernard Shaw, Roger Fry, Duncan Grant, and John Maynard Keynes. Ian McEwan lives there now, but you'll have to guess which is his house — there's no plaque. Have lunch in one of the ethnic restaurants on Charlotte Street, and then make your way to the **Charles Dickens Museum**, Dickens's onetime home at 48 Doughty Street (44-20-7405-2127; dickensmuseum.com), and go inside for a tour.

6 *Scribbles and Scrawls* 2 p.m.

Authors wailed and gnashed their teeth when the history-laden **British Library** was moved to a modern brick building (96 Euston Road NW1; 44-33-0333-1144; bl.uk). The library's famous **reading room**, used by generations of scholars and writers (Mohandas Gandhi, George Orwell, and Karl Marx, to name just three), remains in its old spot at the British Museum on Great Russell Street, and it is a pilgrimage site no book lover should miss. But the new library more than makes up for its lack of atmosphere with the Sir John Ritblat Gallery, displaying some of the greatest treasures of the written word. The collection includes much-scribbled-on first drafts of works by authors like James Joyce, treasures like a 600-or-so-years-old manuscript of *Sir Gawain and the Green Knight*, and John Lennon's first scrawled lyrics to "Help!"

7 *Lexicographer's Delight* 4 p.m.

Dr. Johnson's House (17 Gough Square EC4; 44-207-353-3745; drjohnsonshouse.org) is a little gem of a place tucked in a quiet spot near to, but worlds away from, the bustle of Fleet Street. Here Samuel Johnson worked in the mid-1700s on his famous English dictionary — an effort, he explained in his comma-heavy introduction, to regularize a language that had been "hitherto neglected, suffered to spread, under the direction of chance, into wild exuberance, resigned to the tyranny of time and fashion, and exposed to the corruptions of ignorance, and caprices of innovation." Easy-to-digest room-by-room exhibits culminate in the attic, where a team of clerks sorted through potential words for the dictionary.

8 *Tavern to Remember* 5:30 p.m.

The **George Inn** (77 Borough High Street; 44-207-407-2056; $$$), a 17th-century coaching inn, is now the only galleried pub — meaning that it has balconies — left in the city. The menu is modern; the ambience is noisy in the downstairs bar and quieter in the upstairs dining room. Dickens was a frequent patron of the George and mentions it in *Little Dorrit*.

9 *All the World's a Stage* 7 p.m.

If you're craving a Shakespeare performance (and of course you are), there's usually one to be found. One frequent venue is the Rose Theater, inside a modern building above the site of the original Rose, where Shakespeare plays were performed in his own day. The Royal National Theatre also often performs classical drama. But if you're visiting in the warmer months, the obvious venue is **Shakespeare's Globe** (22 New Globe Walk SE1; 44-207-902-1400; shakespearesglobe.com), a loving reconstruction of an Elizabethan theater, where Shakespearean plays are performed all season. The Globe also houses a permanent exhibition devoted to Shakespeare's life and times.

SUNDAY

10 *What They Looked Like* 10 a.m.

Yesterday you gazed respectfully at their graves; today you can see them in art. The **National Portrait Gallery** (St. Martin's Place; 44-20-7306-0055; npg.org.uk) has a wide representation of authors among the famous Britons depicted in its collection. The galleries are organized chronologically; you'll find, for example, Chaucer in Room 3,

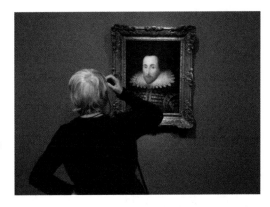

Shakespeare in Room 4, Austen in Room 14, Dickens in Room 24, and Dylan Thomas in Room 31. To focus on your special favorites, ask the staff to point you in the right direction.

11 *Elementary, Dear Holmes* Noon

The **Sherlock Holmes pub** (10-11 Northumberland Street; 44-207-930-2644; sherlockholmespub.com; $$) may be slightly kitschy, but it has an authentically musty-without-being-dingy ambience, enthusiastic service, and generous portions of traditional pub food. In an upstairs dining room decorated with pictures of the masterful fictional detective, enjoy dishes that his creator, Sir Arthur Conan Doyle, would have recognized, like beef with Yorkshire pudding or Toad in the Hole. The pièce de résistance is a meticulously reconstructed study decorated à la Holmes. If not for the stiff-looking mannequin in the corner, it might seem that Holmes had just stepped out for a second, laying down his cup of tea and his violin.

OPPOSITE The house where Samuel Johnson worked to tame the "wild exuberance" of the English language by corralling it in a dictionary.

ABOVE Shakespeare (here, at the National Portrait Gallery), still London's theatrical star.

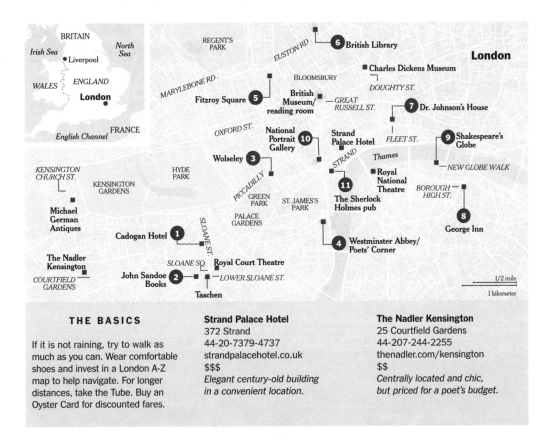

THE BASICS

If it is not raining, try to walk as much as you can. Wear comfortable shoes and invest in a London A-Z map to help navigate. For longer distances, take the Tube. Buy an Oyster Card for discounted fares.

Strand Palace Hotel
372 Strand
44-20-7379-4737
strandpalacehotel.co.uk
$$$
Elegant century-old building in a convenient location.

The Nadler Kensington
25 Courtfield Gardens
44-207-244-2255
thenadler.com/kensington
$$
Centrally located and chic, but priced for a poet's budget.

London With Children

London wows young visitors with its age. It's over 2,000 years old, an incredibly impressive number, perhaps even big enough to compete with the likes of Star Wars and Justin Bieber. The kids won't be able to throw a rock without running into something historical. From portions of the original Roman wall to Big Ben and the Houses of Parliament to the crypts of historical figures — the ones they are learning about in school — your children will have a weekend of living and breathing history, not to mention fun to be had in the city's parks and family-friendly neighborhoods. Really, what can be better for children than the city that gave birth to Oliver Twist, Peter Pan, and Paddington Bear? — BY SAMANTHA STOREY

FRIDAY

1 *Treasure Hunt* 1 p.m.

Head down to the **River Thames** at low tide to go mudlarking — scavenging the shores for treasure. Look for Elizabethan pipes — easy to spot as they are long and white — or broken bits of pottery from the last few centuries. Some lucky mudlarkers have even found roof tiles from the Roman era. It can get a bit swampy down there, so wear rubber boots. Bring along some wipes and a plastic bag to hold your finds. For low tide, check the Port of London Authority website (pla.co.uk). There are several points of entry along the river; try the steps next to the Millennium Bridge on the north bank. For a guided tour, London Walks hosts a "Thames Beachcombing" outing (walks.com).

2 *I Hear You!* 3 p.m.

St. Paul's Cathedral (St Paul's Churchyard; 44-20-7246-8350; stpauls.co.uk) is to London's skyline as the Empire State Building is to New York City's, and up close it's equally impressive. Step through the front entrance and stroll down the nave, a long and breathtakingly beautiful corridor that leads to Sir Christopher Wren's dome. Look up and marvel at his Baroque masterpiece. Climb the 257 steps to the Whispering Gallery — for kids, hands down the most popular spot in the cathedral — where an architectural quirk lets you whisper into the wall and be heard 100 feet away. Still not tired? Then keep climbing up to the Stone and Gold Galleries, where you'll be treated to views of the Thames, the Tate Modern, and Shakespeare's Globe theater.

3 *Beware of Death Eaters* 5 p.m.

Skip, run, sprint (as kids are wont to do on this pedestrian walkway) to the center of the nearly 1,100-foot **Millennium Bridge** with a copy of *Harry Potter and the Half Blood Prince*. Thumb to the scene where the Death Eaters destroy the Brockdale Bridge and read aloud (and read it loudly — it can be windy up there). In the 2009 movie adaptation, this is the suspension bridge that is used as the fictional Brockdale. You and your kids are now in a real-life location of Harry Potter's universe.

4 *Did Hamlet Like Brownies?* 6 p.m.

Now that you've dipped your toe into British literary waters, stroll over to **Shakespeare's Globe** for a full literary baptism and, most important, something to eat. The building, designed to be a rough replica of the original, opened in 1997 a few hundred yards from where the theater once stood in the early 17th century. Eat dinner at the **Swan** (21 New Globe Walk; 44-20-7928-9444; loveswan.co.uk; $$), where you can choose British fare like wild venison stew or battered haddock. The children's menu lists kid pleasers like fish and chips (French fries), not to mention the brownies and ice cream.

OPPOSITE Room to run in Hyde Park.

BELOW A sculpted angel at St. Paul's Cathedral.

SATURDAY

5 *Tales of the Tower* 9 a.m.

Treachery. Torture. Beheadings. **The Tower of London** (44-20-3166-6000; hrp.org.uk/TowerOfLondon) has all of that, not to mention a thousand years of royal history—from William the Conquerer, who built the iconic White Tower in the 11th century, to the execution

TOP Climb into a gondola and peer out at the city's landmarks from the London Eye.

ABOVE The Beefeater guides at the Tower of London tell thrilling (and true) stories of treachery, beheadings, and other perils of being royal.

site where three queens, Anne Boleyn, Lady Jane Grey, and Catherine Howard, were beheaded. Definitely join a tour with a Yeoman Warder (popularly known as a "Beefeater") for an overview. They are incredibly entertaining, especially to children, charming visitors with tales of imprisonment, infamy, and the usual bloody perils that accompany threats to the crown.

6 *Street Shows* 1 p.m.

Now it's time for some modern-day fun, albeit in another historical setting—they're hard to avoid in London—at **Covent Garden** (coventgardenlondonuk.com), a marketplace since the 17th century and a shopper's paradise. There are hundreds of stalls and boutiques. Toy hunting? Try **Benjamin Pollock's Toyshop** (Unit 44 The Market; 44-20-7379-7866; pollocks-coventgarden. co.uk), which has been in the business of selling traditional theater models and toys since the 1880s. Sweet tooth? Visit **Cybercandy** (3 Garrick Street; 44-84-5838-0958; cybercandy.co.uk), which specializes in candies based on computer games and comic book figures, like Angry Birds gummies and Marvel heroes Pez dispensers. Hungry for real food? Grab a sandwich from one of the cafes or food stalls and head over to either the West Piazza, outside St Paul's Church, or the North Hall of the Market Building. Picnic while you watch the street performers do bicycle stunts and juggling tricks.

7 *Park Central* 3 p.m.

Hyde Park (royalparks.org.uk/parks/hyde-park) is smack dab in the middle of the city, complete with playgrounds, a pretty little lake, and even a statue of the boy who never grew up, Peter Pan. In good weather, rent a pedal boat on the Serpentine, and take a dip in the Lido and Paddling Pool, an outdoor swimming hole for all ages. Don't miss the Princess Diana Memorial Fountain — so peaceful — and the playground next door with its life-size pirate ship where you can make the kids walk the plank. Nearby is Kensington Palace (hrp.org.uk/kensington-palace), a home of real-life princes and princesses.

8 *Supper Break* 5 p.m.

After all that fresh air and playing, refuel and rest a while. The **Lido Café** at the Serpentine (44-20-7706-7098; $$) is your best bet in the park. It sits on the south side of the lake and has plenty of outdoor seating. From beef rib eye to flatbread pizzas, there is something for everyone. Don't miss the café's own ice cream.

ABOVE A street performer at Covent Garden, where the available entertainment also includes shopping for Angry Birds gummies and Marvel heroes Pez dispensers.

RIGHT Touring at a home of modern-day princes and princesses, Kensington Palace, near Hyde Park.

9 *Higher and Higher* 7 p.m.

The **London Eye** (Westminster Bridge Road; 44-871-781-3000; londoneye.com), one of the largest Ferris wheels in the world, will bowl you over with its sheer magnitude and jaw-dropping views. On a clear day you can see Windsor Castle, about 25 miles away. Be sure to book your tickets in advance to avoid long lines. And pick up the "London Eye View 360" brochure from the gift shop on your way in. It will help you locate popular landmarks, as there is no commentary in the capsule. The ride takes 30 minutes. Play a game of I Spy, or who can spot, say, Buckingham Palace the fastest. The view is also great at night, when the landmarks are shimmering with light.

SUNDAY

10 *Where Days Begin* 10 a.m.

Catch the train to Greenwich to visit the **Royal Observatory** on Blackheath Avenue and the **National Maritime Museum** on Park Row (joint website: rmg.co.uk). At the observatory, stand astride the Prime Meridian — the line that designates Greenwich Mean Time, the official starting point for each new day — with one foot in the Eastern Hemisphere and the other in the Western. Wander through an exhibition on the history of clocks, see a film in the planetarium, and touch a 4.5 billion-year-old meteorite. At the maritime museum, get a sense of Britain's seafaring heritage. Then wrap up at the *Cutty Sark*, a 280-foot-long clipper ship launched in 1869. It's the real thing, with 32 sails, 11 miles of rigging, and a main mast 152 feet tall.

ABOVE Focusing in on a telescopic view from the Royal Observatory in Greenwich.

OPPOSITE The domed interior of St. Paul's Cathedral.

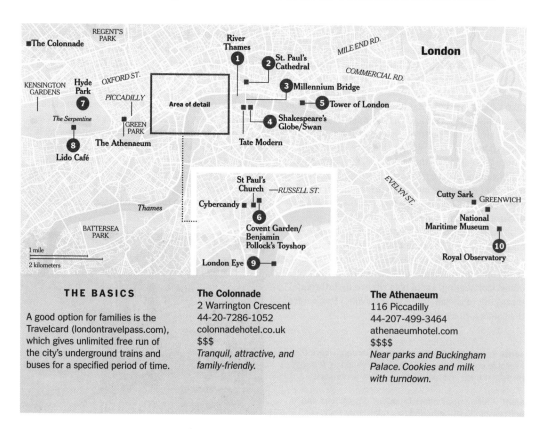

THE BASICS

A good option for families is the Travelcard (londontravelpass.com), which gives unlimited free run of the city's underground trains and buses for a specified period of time.

The Colonnade
2 Warrington Crescent
44-20-7286-1052
colonnadehotel.co.uk
$$$
Tranquil, attractive, and family-friendly.

The Athenaeum
116 Piccadilly
44-207-499-3464
athenaeumhotel.com
$$$$
Near parks and Buckingham Palace. Cookies and milk with turndown.

Hampstead

In Hampstead, London's worst-kept, high-altitude secret, the ghosts of Sigmund Freud, T. S. Eliot, and Robert Louis Stevenson mingle with Ricky Gervais, Ridley Scott, and more Madonna-accented American expats than you can shake a Land Rover key at. But all are equal when it comes to losing themselves in the charming lanes of Hampstead Village and the joyfully directionless expanse of the Heath, a metropolitan mini-wilderness that may be Europe's finest city park. Welcome to Hampstead, as serene, green, and lovely as ever. — BY MARK VANHOENACKER

FRIDAY

1 *Keeping It Local* 4 p.m.

Hampstead has seen some of Britain's fiercest attempts to preserve independent retailers and restaurateurs. The arrival of a McDonald's, for example, was preceded by a struggle that lasted more than a decade. Skip the Starbucks and join the bankers' wives at **Ginger & White** (4a-5a Perrins Court; 44-20-7431-9098; gingerandwhite.com). The employees are friendlier than the cafe's slogan ("We don't do grande") would suggest. Enjoy your caffeination while people-watching at the window. Or make a new friend at the shared table.

2 *Peter Pan's Precursors* 4:30 p.m.

On narrow Church Row, the history comes as tightly packed as the stately brick homes. H. G. Wells lived at No. 17; Oscar Wilde's lover at No. 26; George du Maurier, the cartoonist, and grandfather of the five boys who inspired the tales of Peter Pan, at No. 27. The prerecorded bells of the **Parish Church of St. John-at-Hampstead** (hampsteadparishchurch. org.uk) were extinguished after a 1960s choirboy hijacked the "electrical contrivance" with a "record of the latest popular music." Enjoy the silence as you wander through the churchyard, where some of London's most atmospheric benches lurk among the tombstones. Many of the grave markers are tilting, the inscriptions on their gray stone all but effaced by centuries of English weather. John Constable, the painter, is buried here, and so is John Harrison, whose legendary chronometers helped solve the ancient problem of determining longitude at sea. In the Additional Burial Ground across Church Row you'll find the graves of the boys who inspired Peter Pan, and of one Henry Kippin — "last of a long line of local chimney sweeps."

3 *The Gilded Screen* 6 p.m.

You're off to the movies. Peter Pan probably isn't showing, but it hardly matters at the **Everyman Hampstead** theater (5 Holly Bush Vale; everymancinema.com), where off-screen attractions include pillow-piled leather armchairs, a balcony of discreetly spaced love seats, waiter service at your seat, and a hopping lounge that is open to nonfilm-goers. No popcorn, sadly, but try the salt and pepper cashews. Does your seat have its own ice bucket? It does.

4 *Posh Pub Crawl* 9 p.m.

At the neighborly **Wells Tavern** (30 Well Walk; 44-20-7794-3785; thewellshampstead.co.uk; $$), embrace the local "champagne socialist" stereotype with a Jacuzzi — gin, schnapps, orange juice, and bubbly. Then it has to be the Cumberland pork sausages with mashed potatoes and onion gravy, followed by the sticky toffee pudding. The grande dame of Hampstead pubs is also nearby; it's the **Holly Bush** (44-20-7435-2892; hollybushhampstead.co.uk), in a reputedly haunted building at 22 Holly Mount that once belonged to George Romney, the 18th-century portraitist (and distant relation of Mitt Romney).

OPPOSITE A pond in Hampstead Heath.

BELOW Daunt Books, a literary haven.

SATURDAY

5 *A Special Relationship* 10 a.m.

A classic English breakfast (eggs, bacon, sausage, and toast), with a few healthful additions (mushrooms, beans, and roasted tomatoes), can be found all day at the **Coffee Cup** (74 Hampstead High Street; 44-20-7435-7565; villabiancagroup.

ABOVE Kenwood House, a museum with works by Rembrandt, Vermeer, and Turner.

BELOW Hampstead Butcher & Providore.

OPPOSITE A look at London from Parliament Hill.

co.uk/coffeecuph.html; $). This 1950s-era institution claims to be London's oldest coffee lounge. Whatever its pedigree, its survival into the 21st century has been a Hampstead cause célèbre. Elizabeth Taylor (born in nearby Hampstead Garden Suburb) was a regular; Paul McCartney and Sting have been spotted here, too. Required breakfast reading is the latest issue of Hampstead's revered satirical rag, *The Hampstead Village Voice*.

6 *It Takes a Village* 11 a.m.

Care for some shopping? Sample the independent retailers that line charming Flask Walk. Then stop at **Hampstead Antique & Craft Emporium** (12 Heath Street; 44-20-7794-3297; hampsteadantiqueemporium. com), where traders sell clothing, artwork, and vintage Hampstead photographs. Another round of distinctive shops is clustered in South End Green. The shelves of **Daunt Books** (51 South End Road; 44-20-7794-8206; dauntbooks.co.uk) interweave travel guides with a world of literature; the shop's cloth bags are de rigueur for London literary locavores. Staffers lead literary walks on the Heath.

7 *Picnic on the Heath* 1 p.m.

Grab a charcuterie picnic basket at **Hampstead Butcher & Providore** (56 Rosslyn Hill; 44-20-7794-9210; hampsteadbutcher.com) and take it with you to **Hampstead Heath**, a hilly, nearly Central

Park-size idyll of woodlands, meadows, and shimmering views over the metropolis. Enter the Heath via Well Walk (D. H. Lawrence lived at No. 32; Constable described the view from No. 40 as "unsurpassed in Europe"). Picnic spots include Parliament Hill, with its dazzling views, or the lawn beneath Kenwood House, a former home of earls and countesses that is now open as a museum. Or just spread out your meal under any of the trees on the meadow west of the Model Boating Pond.

8 *Art and Folly* 2 p.m.

Do some exploring on the Heath. Start in **Kenwood House** (Hampstead Lane; 44-20-8348-1286; www.english-heritage.org.uk/visit/places/kenwood), where the interior decoration is lavish and the renowned art collection includes paintings by Rembrandt, Vermeer, Gainsborough, and Turner. Outside, look for *Two Piece Reclining Figure No. 5*, a Henry Moore sculpture. And don't miss the **Pergola**, a folly

of gardens and elevated walkways built in the early 20th century, using fill from excavation for the Tube line that was just reaching Hampstead.

9 *Sashimi, Then Ale* 8 p.m.

Reservations are a must at **Jin Kichi** (73 Heath Street; 44-20-7794-6158; jinkichi.com; $$), and so is the gindara, grilled black cod marinated in white miso. For good reason, the sashimi tends to run out; order early. Stop off after dinner at the **Horseshoe** (28 Heath Street; 44-20-7431-7206; thehorseshoehampstead.com), a modern addition to Hampstead's pub scene, for a local Camden Town Brewery ale.

SUNDAY

10 *Royal Laundry* 10 a.m.

London Walks (44-20-7624-3978; walks.com) offers group walks in neighborhoods all over London,

led by knowledgeable and friendly guides. The two-hour saunter through Hampstead's centuries of architectural and cultural history could justly be called the jewel in its crown. You'll ponder the "fire marks" on old houses and the filled-in windows (think tax on windows, and the rumored origins of the phrase "daylight robbery") on gracious homes. You'll pass where Lord Tennyson's mother lived, learn where the Tudors sent their dirty laundry, and see where Charles de Gaulle, who Churchill unkindly called "the monster of Hampstead," came to pray during his London exile.

11 *History and Tea* Noon

Head to **Burgh House** (New End Square; 44-20-7431-0144; www.burghhouse.org.uk), built in 1704 during Hampstead's halcyon days as a spa. Rudyard Kipling's last-ever outing was here, visiting his daughter, who lived in the house in the 1930s. Start with Sunday lunch at the cafe, and then explore the excellent Hampstead Museum upstairs. Return to the verdant terrace for tea and cake. Here, in one of London's quietest corners, there's no better reason to linger.

ABOVE Swimming is one of the many attractions of the Heath, Hampstead's sprawling park.

OPPOSITE Church Row, a narrow street with connections to H. G. Wells and Peter Pan.

THE BASICS

Hampstead, in the northwest corner of London, is both walkable and well served by public transportation.

King's Boutique Hotel
77 Hampstead High Street
44-78-1601-3338
kingsboutiquehotel.co.uk
$$
Well-designed rooms in a 200-year-old pub near Hampstead Heath.

La Gaffe
107-111 Heath Street
44-20-7435-8965
lagaffe.co.uk
$$
Small family-style hotel with an Italian restaurant.

Langorf Hotel
20 Frognal
44-20-7794-4483
langorfhotel.com
$$
In a quiet residential area near a Tube stop.

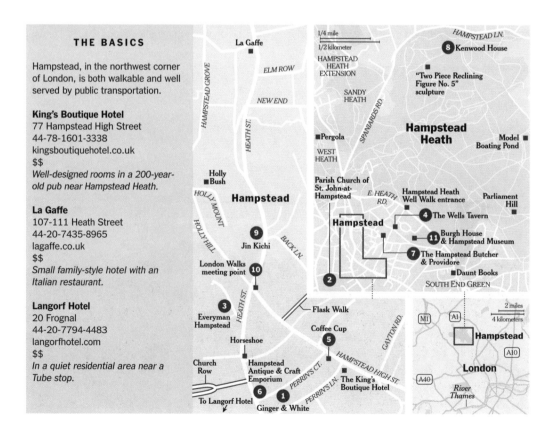

Brighton

Not long ago, the English port town of Brighton was considered louche and seedy, a has-been resort with crumbling piers and weathered hotels for so-called dirty weekends. But with London just an hour away, it was a matter of time before this funky town regained its color. Chic Londoners, including a substantial gay contingent, have rediscovered Brighton's lanes and Regency-style buildings. When Friday rolls around, weekenders check into boutique hotels and disappear into dance-till-dawn clubs. The scene is reminiscent of Miami Beach, except that it's the chilly English Channel at the end of the boardwalk.
— BY FINN-OLAF JONES

FRIDAY

1 *Pier-less Promenade* 5 p.m.

Join the crowd in what is practically a mandatory Brighton tradition: the sunset promenade. Stroll, drink, and play along the pebbled shores that have been keeping Londoners happy and cold for three centuries. The half mile between the wave-swept ruins of the old West Pier and the alive-and-kicking Brighton Pier is a much-celebrated walk in England.

2 *Pub Hop* 6 p.m.

The colorful labyrinth of alleys known as the Lanes District is an ideal spot for people-watching over a pint and a plate. The area around Brighton Place has three memorable pubs. The **Druids Head** (9 Brighton Place; 44-1273-325-490; taylor-walker. co.uk; $$) is in a cozy 16th-century building with enough dark wood to keep actual Druids happy. It serves hearty pub food, specializing in fish and chips. The **Sussex**, in a yellow Georgian house (33-34 East Street; 44-1273-327-591; taylor-walker.co.uk; $$), serves a hearty steak and ale pie. Wash that down with a pint of Old Speckled Hen ale. If you're hankering for fish and chips and skipped it at the Druids Head, walk to the **Market Inn** (1 Market Street; 44-1273-329-483; reallondonpubs.com; $$), where the outdoor tables are ideal for watching Brighton go by.

OPPOSITE The Royal Pavilion, Brighton's signature landmark, began its existence as a prince's private Xanadu.

RIGHT The Music Room in the Royal Pavilion.

3 *House of Abba* 8 p.m.

Pay tribute to rock legends at the **Brighton Dome** (29 New Road; 44-1273-700-747; brightondome.org), a former horse stable turned concert hall where Jimi Hendrix, Led Zeppelin, and Pink Floyd have performed, and where Abba was introduced to the world at the 1974 Eurovision Song Contest. If you're lucky enough to be here in May, the Dome hosts concerts and events in the innovative Brighton Festival of the arts (brightonfestival.org).

SATURDAY

4 *Royal Romp* 10 a.m.

Two centuries have not diminished the hedonism and extravagance of the **Royal Pavilion** (Pavilion Buildings; 44-1273-290-900; brighton-hove-rpml.org.uk), a gleaming multidomed Xanadu that was built by the Prince Regent in the early 19th century before he was crowned King George IV. This Indian-inspired palace features gilded palm trees, soaring minarets, and riotously painted chinoiserie. Pay attention to the fantastical dragon chandelier in the dining room, so lifelike that diners reportedly trembled, and the elaborate steam-powered kitchen, a modern marvel of its time. For a decadent Regency-era brunch, stop by the **Royal Pavilion Tearoom**, a serene rooftop cafe that serves classic English dishes like deviled kidneys and Welsh rarebit.

5 *Worshiping Art* 1 p.m.

For a more modern outlook, try **Fabrica** (40 Duke Street; 44-1273-778-646; fabrica.org.uk), a

Regency-era church converted into a contemporary art gallery. Exhibitions transform the vaulted interiors into often outlandish installation pieces. Past works have included a real meadow planted where the pews once stood and a dense tubular forest of compressed wood.

6 *Paging Miss Havisham* 3 p.m.

Looking for rare books, dueling pistols, or high-tech vibrators? You'll find them in the shops on the twisting alleyways that make up the districts of Lanes and North Laine. **Fidra Jewelers** (47 Meeting House Lane; 44-1273-328-348; fidra.com) is an Aladdin's cave of Victorian, Edwardian, and Art Deco baubles that is replenished often. The **Lanes Armoury** (26 Meeting House Lane; 44-1273-321-357; thelanesarmoury.co.uk) specializes in samurai swords and Napoleonic weaponry. And for those still spinning vinyl, the **Record Album** (8 Terminus Road; 44-1273-323-853; therecordalbum.com) has a trove of rare and quirky albums that on one visit included the Japanese version of the *Raiders of the Lost Ark* soundtrack.

7 *Remains of the Day* 5 p.m.

It may look like a kitschy tourist trap today, but the **Brighton Pier** (brightonpier.co.uk) endures as one of England's last great beach piers. Take a stroll along the seemingly endless boardwalk, a foam-topped feast of fish and chips, Victorian beer halls, and gut-churning thrill rides.

8 *Divine Wines* 8 p.m.

You won't find a lot of fish and chips at the **Hotel du Vin Bistro** (2 Ship Street; 44-1273-855-221; hotelduvin.com; $$$). On one visit, this congenial, clubby restaurant was packed with stylish Londoners in designer T-shirts and jeans, nibbling on modern Continental dishes like brioche topped with chicken liver and foie gras parfait.

9 *Dance the Night Away* 11 p.m.

A necklace of clubs dots the shoreline, and no one bats an eye when men in sequined dresses or women in business suits cuddle on the dance floor. One long-reigning hot spot is **Concorde 2** (2 Madeira Drive; 44-1273-673-311; concorde2. co.uk) an old Victorian tearoom where up-and-comers play. Don't be surprised if some joyful and hardy souls take a midnight swim in the sea, just 100 yards away. Other spots include the beachfront **Brighton Coalition** (171-181 Kings Road Arches; 44-1273-722-385; coalitionbrighton.com), where the Saturday night action continues until

ABOVE Brighton's seaside promenade, one of the most famous walks in England, curves along the city's pebbly beach and English Channel shore.

7 a.m. Sunday. If you like dancing until dawn, you're home.

SUNDAY

10 *Pressed for Success* Noon

Rejuvenate at the **Redroaster Coffee House** (1d St. James's Street; 44-1273-686-668; redroaster.co.uk), a Valhalla of caffeine where the croissants are fresh-baked and the coffee comes out of burlap sacks to be roasted and ground on the spot. Plop down on a sofa and order a pot of French-press.

11 *Coastal Rails* 1 p.m.

Chug down memory lane. **Volk's Electric Railway** (volkselectricrailway.co.uk) has been a going concern since 1883, making it one of the oldest continuously running trains in the world. It still operates from April to August. If the weather is good, grab an outside seat while this wooden Victorian contraption makes its way along Brighton beach past bohemian Kemp Town, the sculptural Peter Pan's playground, and a nudist stretch tucked behind a mound of pebbles. Does Brighton really have anything left to hide?

ABOVE Affluent Londoners, including a substantial gay contingent, have rediscovered Brighton's twisting lanes and Regency-style buildings.

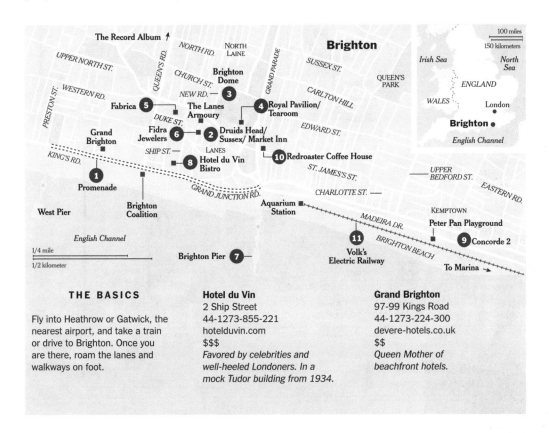

THE BASICS

Fly into Heathrow or Gatwick, the nearest airport, and take a train or drive to Brighton. Once you are there, roam the lanes and walkways on foot.

Hotel du Vin
2 Ship Street
44-1273-855-221
hotelduvin.com
$$$
Favored by celebrities and well-heeled Londoners. In a mock Tudor building from 1934.

Grand Brighton
97-99 Kings Road
44-1273-224-300
devere-hotels.co.uk
$$
Queen Mother of beachfront hotels.

Oxford

Three of the colleges that make up Oxford University were founded in the 1200s, and by the mid-16th century many of the eventual 38 had joined them. The result is a square-mile warren of buildings — in the Cotswold limestone that changes with the light from pale cream to an apricot glow — bristling with spires, pinnacles, and finials and abounding in quadrangles, passageways, chapels, halls, and alleys. Within this labyrinth are paintings by Botticelli, Uccello, and Frans Hals; a genuine dodo's beak; early astrolabes from the Arab world; and the room where England's first cup of coffee was drunk (in 1637 in Balliol College). Whether the university's thousands of students are in town or not, you can lose yourself and forget there ever was a century other than the 16th — except when you have to emerge briefly to get across the High Street, which with its "sublime curve" has been called the most beautiful street on earth. In late dusk, when the sky is luminous and the streets are already dark, the stone walls acquire the sumptuousness of a bowl of oranges in candlelight.
— BY HENRY SHUKMAN

FRIDAY

1 *Amid the Stones* 3 p.m.

One of Europe's great pleasures is to weave your way aimlessly through Oxford's cloisters and passages, letting the clock and the calendar recede. **Christ Church** (St. Aldate's Street; 44-1865-276-492; www.chch.ox.ac.uk), one of the largest and oldest of the colleges, is also one of the friendliest to visitors, scheduling regular hours and tours. Its Tom Tower, designed by Christopher Wren, holds a bell that rings 101 times every night; its Great Hall stood in for Hogwarts in the Harry Potter films. The oaks of Christ Church Meadow play their part in the profusion of trees that make Oxford look like a forest from the air and caused the French poet Mallarmé to complain of its "green sickness." If you prefer Alice to Harry, look for Wonderland souvenirs in the nearby shops. Alice was born at Christ Church,

OPPOSITE High Street in Oxford. The university's 38 colleges are packed inside a square-mile warren of buildings.

RIGHT Keble College, setting of this elegant dining hall, becomes a bed-and-breakfast when students are away.

where Charles Dodgson, who invented her under the pen name Lewis Carroll, studied and taught.

2 *Sartorial Sacrifice* 5 p.m.

The best English pubs are filled not only with the scent of yeast and hops, but also with banter and wit, and Oxford is thick with them. **The Bear Inn** (6 Alfred Street; 44-1865-728-164; bearoxford.co.uk), tucked down Blue Boar Lane at the back of Christ Church, has only two tiny wood rooms, but they date from 1242. They are covered, wall and ceiling, with picture frames containing short pieces of ties. Ties of clubs, regiments, schools — the Royal Gloucester Hussars, the Imperial Yeomanry, the Punjab Frontier Force, Lloyd's of London Croquet Club — telling of an older England. Croquet, beer, cricket, empire, and P. G. Wodehouse: a snip off your tie, and you'll get a free pint.

3 *Weaponry Not Required* 8 p.m.

Detour from essential England with dinner at **Pierre Victoire** (9 Little Clarendon Street; 44-1865-316-616; pierrevictoire.co.uk; $$), a popular bistro. The moules frites and bouillabaisse may not be traditional in this city, but the French penchant for wine definitely has Oxford echoes. One 20th-century student reputedly demanded a flagon of claret during his exams, having discovered an ancient rule in

the University Statute Book entitling him to it. The invigilator was able to annul the request because the student was improperly dressed: according to another statute, he should have been wearing a saber.

SATURDAY

4 *Tea and Pheasant* 9 a.m.

From the east, head up cobbled Brasenose Lane to the **Covered Market** (oxfordcity.co.uk/shops/market), Oxford's answer to the bazaar, fragrant with delicatessens, florists, coffee and tea merchants, and butchers that hang carcasses of venison, hare, pheasant, and woodcock outside their stalls. Oxford has been a market town since the ninth century; this incarnation dates to 1774. The crowds will tell you which are the counters for a breakfast bite. Exit onto Turl or Cornmarket and walk up for some browsing on Broad Street, which is lined with three colleges and rows of 18th-century shops, among them the labyrinthine **Blackwell's** bookstore (48-51 Broad Street; 44-1865-792-792; bookshop.blackwell.co.uk).

5 *Landmarks* 11 a.m.

You're now in the heart of Oxford, so wander a bit. There are treasures wherever you turn: the roseate stone tank of the quadrangle at the Bodleian Library; the stone Bridge of Sighs over Queen's Lane; the Radcliffe Camera (or "chamber"), a 90-foot-high rotunda that wouldn't be out of place in Renaissance Florence; All Souls College, home of the sinecure par excellence, where the only duties are to dine at college every so often and to converse brilliantly over the port. On Broad Street is Wren's **Sheldonian Theatre** (sheldon.ox.ac.uk), with its distinctive white cupola and 12 startled busts of Roman emperors. Check to see whether there's a performance you want to return for after dinner.

6 *In the Cloisters* Noon

Walk eastward on High Street to **Magdalen College** (www.magd.ox.ac.uk), which is renowned both for its architecture and for the influence of its former students, who have ranged from Oscar Wilde and Dudley Moore to aristocrats and cabinet ministers. Find the Grove, a park with a resident herd of deer, and the Meadow, which borders the Cherwell River and Addison's Walk, a tranquil footpath.

7 *On the Water* 2 p.m.

Have lunch at the cafe of the **Cherwell Boathouse** (52 Bardwell Road; 44-1865-552-746; cherwellboathouse.co.uk; $$) and watch the punters poling their way along the river. If you feel adventurous, rent one yourself and give it a try.

ABOVE Honey-colored stone is Oxford's backdrop.

8 *In the Galleries* 3 p.m.

The **Ashmolean Museum** (Beaumont Street at St. Giles; 44-1865-278-002; ashmolean.org) has reinvented itself with displays that emphasize the ultimate connection of art with varying geographic origins. Inspect the results, but don't miss the museum's Italian Renaissance treasures by Mantegna, Bellini, and especially Uccello: in his mystical *Hunt in the Forest*, hounds leap into the darkness of a seemingly endless wood.

9 *Inklings* 5 p.m.

As you make your way along the grand, short Beaumont Street, take a quick look at St. John Street:

ABOVE The Oxford Dodo at the Oxford University Museum of Natural History.

BELOW The bikes and backpacks are contemporary, but Oxford's colleges go back as far as the 1200s.

two simple rows of 18th-century houses clad in sandstone that has aged into rich tea-colored stains. J. R. R. Tolkien lived here, and used to meet his friend C. S. Lewis in the **Eagle and Child** pub round the corner (49 St. Giles; 44-1865-302-925; nicholsonspubs.co.uk). From the 1930s to the '60s they met with friends weekly, often in the pub, and called their gatherings the Inklings. Lewis recalled the "golden sessions" they enjoyed by the fire. It's still an oak-paneled hive rich with the aroma of yeast and hops, with the local Old Hooky on tap. Ale doesn't get hazelnuttier.

10 *Thai Flavors* 8 p.m.

Chiang Mai Kitchen (Kemp Hall Passage, 130a High Street; 44-1865-202-233; chiangmaikitchen.

co.uk; $$), another Oxford favorite, is known for Thai flavors and dishes strewn with fresh flowers. While away the evening over wine and dinner.

SUNDAY

11 *Curiouser and Curiouser* 11 a.m.

For a sense of the treasures that have made their way to Oxford, explore its cabinets of curiosities. The **Pitt Rivers Museum** (Parks Road; 44-1865-270-927; prm.ox.ac.uk) is a neo-Gothic brick hall crammed —crammed in a way no other museum is—with

tribal treasures from around the world. There are cases of shrunken heads, canoes of every design hanging from the ceiling, and unnumbered axes, plows, arrows, swords, pipes, staffs, tunics, paddles, shoes, and paraphernalia. The building heaves with the collective juju of the known world, gathered by Victorian travelers. The Pitt Rivers is entered through the adjoining **Oxford University Museum of Natural History** (oum.ox.ac.uk), where you can go eye to eye with the Oxford Dodo, a re-creation displayed along with the skull of a real dodo, one of the last relics of a species that went extinct in the 1600s.

ABOVE The Great Tower at Magdalen College.

OPPOSITE The Bodleian Library, where books from many centuries reside in Gothic grandeur.

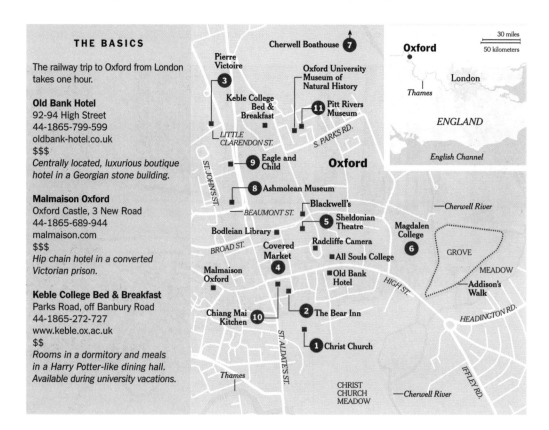

THE BASICS

The railway trip to Oxford from London takes one hour.

Old Bank Hotel
92-94 High Street
44-1865-799-599
oldbank-hotel.co.uk
$$$
Centrally located, luxurious boutique hotel in a Georgian stone building.

Malmaison Oxford
Oxford Castle, 3 New Road
44-1865-689-944
malmaison.com
$$$
Hip chain hotel in a converted Victorian prison.

Keble College Bed & Breakfast
Parks Road, off Banbury Road
44-1865-272-727
www.keble.ox.ac.uk
$$
Rooms in a dormitory and meals in a Harry Potter-like dining hall. Available during university vacations.

Cambridge

Cambridge, England, with its narrow medieval passageways and 800-year-old university, is more than just a college town. Students today are sticking around after graduation to run alternative art galleries and cafe collectives. The famous antiquities museum is proudly displaying contemporary works of art, and lively new restaurants and watering holes are rising to the standards of those down the road in London. Even the venerable university is throwing open its doors, admitting the common folk as hotel guests.
— BY RACHEL B. DOYLE

FRIDAY

1 *Abstract Lawn* 4 p.m.

It's where musty meets modern. With its antiquities and rare manuscripts, the **Fitzwilliam Museum** (Trumpington Street; 44-1223-332-900; fitzmuseum.cam.ac.uk) exemplifies old Cambridge. But the two-centuries-old institution got a fresh look in 2009, when the outdoor Sculpture Promenade was unveiled with nine abstract works cast in bronze, steel, fiberglass, and iron. City entrepreneurs have noted how museum attendance has spiked, especially among young people, offering a blueprint for other cultural attractions wishing to modernize.

2 *New England Fare* 7 p.m.

It used to be that Cambridge residents had to travel to London for fine dining. Not anymore. **Alimentum** (152-154 Hills Road; 44-1223-413-000; restaurantalimentum.co.uk; $$$) brings modern English fare to the old city, and has been voted among the top restaurants in Britain by the prestigious *Good Food Guide*. The Art Deco-style dining room draws a relaxed crowd of flannel-wearing professionals, who pair Rioja with seasonal English dishes like lamb sweetbreads or a grilled sirloin with oxtail, bone marrow, Madeira-mushroom puree, and bordelaise sauce.

3 *Sip Underground* 9:30 p.m.

For a sophisticated cocktail worlds away from the student bars, head to the subterranean watering hole at **Hotel Du Vin** (15-19 Trumpington Street; 44-1223-928-991; hotelduvin.com/hotels/Cambridge). This candlelit bar has a beverage list so lengthy it needs a two-page table of contents for the absinthe rinse cocktails, fig liqueur Champagne drinks, and Belgian beers. Against a brick and brown leather backdrop, fashionable patrons laugh and clink glasses.

4 *Star Search* 11 p.m.

Capture the energy of the incandescent young talents of Cambridge at a late-night theater performance. The 228-seat university playhouse **ADC Theatre** (Park Street; 44-1223-300-085; adctheatre.com), home of the celebrated student comedy troupe the Cambridge Footlights, is a good place to spot emerging talent — or glimpse visiting alumni like Sir Ian McKellen. There are regular shows at 7:45 p.m., but the experimental show at 11 p.m. offers a glimpse of the young dramatists in their natural nocturnal habitat, as entertaining as it is outré.

SATURDAY

5 *Icy Morning* 10 a.m.

Not everything is centuries old here. The sleek **Polar Museum** (Lensfield Road; 44-1223-336-540;

OPPOSITE Punting down the River Cam.

BELOW At night, stroll Cambridge's narrow medieval streets to find lively new restaurants, bars, and theater.

spri.cam.ac.uk) reopened in 2010 on the 100th anniversary of Robert Falcon Scott's last Antarctic expedition. Captivating displays include the personal letters and journals of polar explorers, and artifacts from their arduous journeys. After contemplating the poles, you might want to look at the rest of the planet at the **Sedgwick Museum of Earth Sciences** (Downing Street; 44-1223-333-456; sedgwickmuseum.org), the oldest of the university's museums. Occasional events like "dinosaur crafts" can make this a good stop if you have children in tow.

6 *Food for the Body* 12:30 p.m.

The **Michaelhouse Café,** tucked into the nave of a 14th-century church (St. Michael's Church; Trinity Street; 44-1223-309-147; michaelhousecafe.co.uk; $), gives new meaning to the word sanctuary. It's a bright, airy spot serving simple lunch fare, like bacon butties and sausage sandwiches with onion marmalade, in a quiet, congenial atmosphere. It's also a reminder of just how old Cambridge University really is: the church was the chapel for a college that had its heyday between 1323 and 1546.

7 *The Leather Scene* 2 p.m.

Has your wallet worn out from overuse? Replace it at **Cambridge Leather Bags** (1 Sussex Street; 44-1223-312-971), the sort of old-school shop — no website, no email — where an Agatha Christie character would be comfortable. Look for international brands as well as more locally made handbags, attaché cases, and luggage, in addition to wallets. There is also a repair service if you want to salvage that old wallet.

8 *On the Cam* 4:30 p.m.

Punting down the River Cam in a flat-bottom boat is the classic way to see Cambridge, but mastering the long wooden pole used to propel the boat takes practice. If you have a hankering to try it, book a 90-minute lesson with **Scudamore's Punting**

Company (Granta Place; Mill Lane; 44-1223-359-750; scudamores.com), which will assign a well-muscled tutor to punt you down the gorgeous stretch of river that runs behind the colleges. Halfway through, the pole will be handed to you, and you will be guided in managing the unwieldy craft. If you didn't come to Cambridge for aquatic tutoring, you can rent a kayak from Scudamore's and paddle on your own to the **Orchard Tea Garden** (45-47 Mill Way, Grantchester; 44-1223-551-125; orchard-grantchester.com), an outdoor tearoom where E. M. Forster, Virginia Woolf, and Bertrand Russell hung out a century ago.

9 *Jamie's Kitchen* 8 p.m.

The building is beautiful and the bar lively at **Jamie's Italian** (The Old Library; Wheeler Street; 44-1223-654-094; jamieoliver.com; $$), the hot spot run by the celebrity chef Jamie Oliver. Known for its freshly made pastas and modest prices, the restaurant is a destination for British foodies and operates inside a gorgeous former courthouse. A young, attractive crowd feasts on specials like porchetta with lentils in front of an open kitchen, where chefs sprinkle rosemary salt on polenta chips beneath stained-glass windows.

SUNDAY

10 *Sweet Start* 11 a.m.

Have breakfast at **Fitzbillies** (52 Trumpington Street; 44-1223-352-500; fitzbillies.com; $$), a Cambridge favorite briefly closed in 2011 before being

renovated and reopened under the ownership of Tim Hayward, a food writer for *The Guardian* and *The Financial Times*. The place has a full menu but is known for its syrupy Chelsea buns, made from a recipe that was kept secret for eight decades; the new owners acquired it with the restaurant. (The chocolate violet cakes have quite a following, too.) After breakfast, shop for silver jewelry and home-made soaps at the Sunday craft market at Market Square, where Martin Luther's works were once burned.

11 *Art Punks* 2 p.m.

Get a taste for the region's emerging contemporary art scene at **Wysing Arts Center** (Fox Road, near Bourn; 44-1954-718-881; wysingartscentre.org),

an enormous visual arts complex nine miles west of Cambridge. Performance art is big here, so don't be surprised if you stumble into a post-punk concert led by a Turner Prize winner. The 10-building campus has 24 resident artists splattering paint or shooting reels. Like the new students who arrive each year, the visiting artists provide steady infusions of creativity, helping to power the reinvention of a classic town for the next generation.

OPPOSITE ABOVE King's College Chapel, a Gothic masterpiece, took a century to complete after the young King Henry VI laid the cornerstone in 1441.

OPPOSITE BELOW A footbridge to King's College, where alumni include John Maynard Keynes and Salman Rushdie.

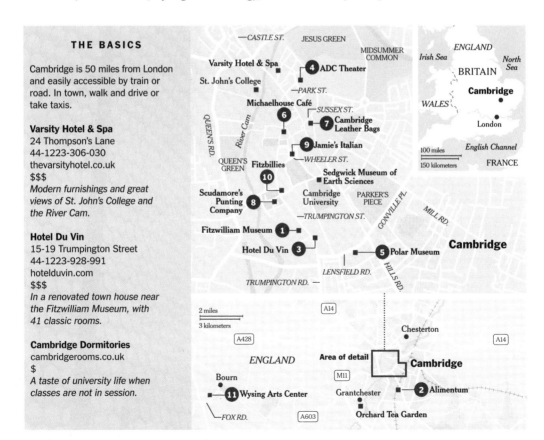

THE BASICS

Cambridge is 50 miles from London and easily accessible by train or road. In town, walk and drive or take taxis.

Varsity Hotel & Spa
24 Thompson's Lane
44-1223-306-030
thevarsityhotel.co.uk
$$$
Modern furnishings and great views of St. John's College and the River Cam.

Hotel Du Vin
15-19 Trumpington Street
44-1223-928-991
hotelduvin.com
$$$
In a renovated town house near the Fitzwilliam Museum, with 41 classic rooms.

Cambridge Dormitories
cambridgerooms.co.uk
$
A taste of university life when classes are not in session.

Birmingham

Birmingham, England's second-largest city, was a hotbed of the Industrial Revolution, a cityscape of soot and furnaces once described as "black by day and red by night." Today, with heavy industry gone from the city center, it has reinvented itself into an only-in-Britain tapestry of vividly multiethnic neighborhoods, postindustrial urbanity, bold new architecture, and a food scene that can't be ignored. Welcome to England's heartland metropolis: big-shouldered, friendly, and fun. — BY MARK VANHOENACKER

FRIDAY

1 *More Canals Than...* 4 p.m.

The miles of interlacing canals that carried the city's coal and helped make its fortunes have begun evolving into an attractive modern waterfront. (Birmingham is said to have more miles of canals than Venice, though further similarities are hard to spot.) Start your canalside explorations at the mixed-use **Cube** (196 Wharfside Street; thecube.co.uk), a Lego-like structure housing shops, a hotel, and apartments. From there walk along the canal northwest through the heart of the new Birmingham, turning right at the big canal intersection, past innumerable old locks and tollhouses. Feel your gentrification compass start to spin as postindustrial chic slowly gives way to just plain old postindustrial: the city's regeneration of its abandoned industrial byways is still a fascinating work in progress.

2 *Bill Was Here* 6 p.m.

For waterside drinks on a chilly evening, head to the **Malt House** (75 King Edwards Road; 44-121-633-4171; originalpubco.com), where President Bill Clinton downed a pint during a G8 summit.

3 *A Taste of Kashmir* 8 p.m.

Birmingham has more Michelin-starred restaurants than any other English city outside London, so haute cuisine — blessedly free of the hauteur — is often on the menu. But the city's most vigorous

kitchen tradition is the Balti, a Kashmiri curry imported and adapted by Birmingham's South Asian communities. Stroll Ladypool Road in the so-called Balti Triangle to find a spot amid the shops selling Korans and package tours to Mecca. **Al Frash** (186 Ladypool Road; 44-121-753-3120; alfrash.com; $) has many fans, though taxi drivers favor the chicken karahi at **Lahore Village** (202-208 Ladypool Road; 44-121-766-8477; $). **Adil's** (148-150 Stoney Lane; 44-121-449-0335), thought to be where the first Balti was served, in 1978, is still going strong. Few places in the Triangle sell alcohol; in its place, try a lassi.

SATURDAY

4 *Cafe Style* 10 a.m.

You can start your day at **Urban Coffee** (Warstone Lane; 44-121-233-1599; urbancoffee.co.uk), on the site of two former jewelers in the Big Peg building. A branch of a hugely successful operation on Church Street, it's an eclectically stylish cafe with spacious rooms, clean-lined décor, and beanbags. Try the delicious latte-like flat white, and order brunch if you're hungry.

5 *Birmingham Bling* 11 a.m.

From the windows of Urban Coffee you'll see several of the hundreds of jewelers that fill Birmingham's remarkable Jewellery Quarter. Jewelry factories are a centuries-old tradition here, and there are plenty of retail shops where you can find locally made pieces. Or follow the **Jewellery Quarter Heritage Trail** (jewelleryquarter.net) for a flavor of the area when the inventor James Watt lived in it and Washington Irving wrote *Rip Van Winkle* while visiting his sister here. Don't miss the guided tours at the Museum of the Jewellery Quarter (75-80 Vyse Street; 44-121-348-8140; birminghammuseums.org.uk/jewellery) in a factory that closed in 1981. The staff turned the key and walked away, leaving everything in place, including gold dust in the floorboards.

6 *Time for Tea* 1 p.m.

Before you leave the museum, stop by its **Tearoom** for lunch. Save room for the Victoria sponge cake — a raspberry jam, cream, and sponge creation that was a

favorite of Queen Victoria's. If the weather's good, you can eat in the charming courtyard.

7 *The Beautiful Game* 2 p.m.

Birmingham is just a scone's throw from Stratford-upon-Avon, Shakespeare's birthplace. If you have extra time, you can schedule a trip there. But today the subject is soccer, currently England's most popular contribution to humanity. Before you can take in the roaring, high-stakes exuberance of an afternoon match, though, you'll face the same Manichaean choice as every Birmingham native: **Aston Villa** (Villa Park, Trinity Road; 44-121-327-2299; avfc.co.uk), which counts Prince William and Tom Hanks among its fans, or **Birmingham City** (St. Andrew's Stadium; 44-844-557-1875; bcfc.com). Their rivalry, dating back to the 1870s, took on a hint of Shakespeare-caliber drama when Birmingham City's manager, Alex McLeish, defected to Villa. Check schedules; not all games are on Saturday.

8 *Sweet Victory* 5 p.m.

Toast your victory — or drown your sorrows —at the **Fighting Cocks** in the suburb of Moseley (1 St. Mary's Row, Moseley; 44-121-449-0811;

thefightingcocksmoseley.co.uk; $). With stained-glass windows scattering late-afternoon light over dark wood and some very busy bartenders, it's the quintessential British pub. Try the locally brewed Pure UBU ale. For top-notch modern pub food, don't budge from that barstool: the Fighting Cocks' Wensleydale pastry tart with fig, goat cheese, pecan, and roasted squash is as tasty as it sounds. For more formal fare, head to the stylish and contemporary **Adam's** (New Oxford House, 16 Waterloo Street; 44-121-643-3745; adamsrestaurant.co.uk; $$$$), but be sure you have made a reservation well in advance. This place has received so many accolades from critics, along with its Michelin star, that a stop there is on many a diner's to-do list.

9 *The Land of Ozzy* 9 p.m.

Birmingham is the birthplace of heavy metal: Ozzy Osbourne and company formed Black Sabbath here in the late 1960s. Judas Priest and Led Zeppelin's Robert Plant and John Bonham had roots here, too. More recently it's the city's world-class symphony, stewarded by Simon Rattle in the 1980s and '90s, that's lifted the city to a different genre of worldwide renown. To hear what's happening now in Birmingham, return to the Jewellery Quarter to take in the scene at **Actress & Bishop** (35 Ludgate Hill; 44-121-236-7426; theactressandbishop.co.uk), which often features local bands.

ABOVE Lighting at the Bloc Hotel, a cross between an upscale design hotel and a Japanese pod.

SUNDAY

10 *Sunday Best* 10 a.m.

Grab a coffee and a bench in quiet **St. Paul's Square**, a gorgeous quadrangle framed by red-brick structures and an 18th-century stone church. Watch as families, jewelers, and the occasional vicar amble past. It's urban England at its Sunday best.

11 *Sinuous Retail* 11 a.m.

Find a retail center as lively as any in Europe at the **Bull Ring** complex, where the crown jewel is **Selfridges** (44-113-369-8040; selfridges.com), part department store, part architectural representative for the new Birmingham. Its four fabulously fluid stories, overlaid with thousands of silvery disks,

will make you stop and stare. When you've finally torn your gaze away, head inside, where you'll find nearly every star in the galaxy of global couture. For lunch, head to nearby **Spiceal Street**, a collection of restaurants including the Birmingham branch of the chef Jamie Oliver's **Jamie's Italian** (Middle Mall, Bullring Shopping Center; 44-121-270-3610; jamieoliver.com/italian; $$).

ABOVE Sample Balti, a local curry tradition, at Adil's.

THE BASICS

Trains, motorways, and a busy international airport make Birmingham an easy city to reach. Once you are there and touring around, public transportation is convenient and inexpensive.

Staying Cool
Rotunda, 150 New Street
44-121-285-1290
stayingcool.com/birmingham
$$
Pie-slice-shaped rooms in a former office tower. Excellent views and '60s décor. Each room has an espresso machine, oranges, and a juicer.

The Bloc Hotel
St. Paul's, Caroline Street
44-121-212-1223
blochotels.com
$
An affordable cross between a seriously upscale design hotel and a Japanese pod.

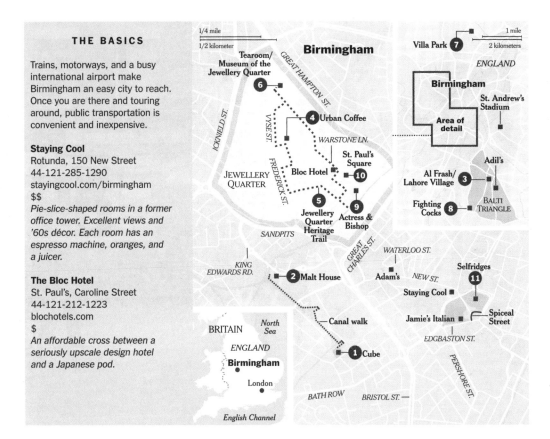

Liverpool

The name Liverpool invariably evokes two images: the Beatles and soccer. They're both revered here, but Liverpool, a revitalizing old port town in northwest England, has more. Avant-garde architecture and glassy museums share the skyline with red-brick warehouses and foggy quays. The city possesses its own roster of Turner Prize-winning artists. And the legendary music scene continues to put together new sounds. — BY BENJI LANYADO AND AMY ROSE DOBSON

FRIDAY

1 *Brews and Pool Cues* 5 p.m.

Pilgrims flock to the Cavern Quarter and the dingy reconstructed Cavern Club on Mathew Street, where the Beatles started out. Head in the same direction, but stop at the bright and airy **Hatch Bar** (entrance on Mathew Street though it's in the Euro Hostel Liverpool, 54 Stanley Street; 44-151-908-0098; eurohostels.co.uk/liverpool/the-hatch-bar), where multiple TV screens keep the focus on sports rather than rock 'n' roll nostalgia. The hostel upstairs ensures a touristy crowd, but Liverpudlians come in for the big selection of local brews and the pool table.

2 *Beery Batter* 7:30 p.m.

Hope Street in the Georgian Quarter is home to many of Liverpool's best restaurants. One of the most venerable, tucked into a Georgian town house, is **60 Hope Street** (60 Hope Street; 44-151-707-6060; 60hopestreet.com; $$$), which serves what are probably the finest fish and chips in the city. The thick, crunchy batter is laced with Cains Bitter, one of Liverpool's foremost brews. If you'd rather explore the menu a little more deeply, look for dishes like seared sea bream or roasted lamb.

3 *New Tunes* 10 p.m.

Liverpool's musical flame, which once burned in the Cavern Quarter, has relocated to the Ropewalks district, just south of the city center. The red-brick warehouses are now filled with dark pubs, cool clubs,

OPPOSITE The Cavern Quarter, where the Beatles started out.

RIGHT At Zanzibar, a home of breakthrough bands.

and feisty performance spaces. **Zanzibar** (43 Seel Street; 44-151-707-0633; thezanzibarclub.com), a musty club in the heart of the area, has been a teeth-cutter for breakthrough acts: the retro rock of the Coral, the soul-soaked Zutons, and the pop-punk trio known as the Wombats. The sound system is superb, the dance floor frantic, and the stage intimate, raised by barely a foot so fans are mere inches from the music.

4 *Rock Legacy* Midnight

Paul Du Noyer's book *Liverpool: Wondrous Place* offers an account of the city's music legacy. And at **The Attic Bar**, a dimly lit lounge also in the Ropewalks district (33-45 Parr Street; 44-151-708-6345; theatticliverpool.com), you're bound to find someone featured in the book's index. The bar is adjacent to the Parr Street Studios, whose clients have included Grace Jones, Bjork, Justin Bieber, and Coldplay, and it functions as something of a social club for music industry types. Echo & the Bunnymen might be relaxing after a recording session. Or the 1980s legends Ian McNabb and Pete Wylie might be sharing a laugh over a pint of Carlsberg.

SATURDAY

5 *On the Town* 10 a.m.

The waterfront **Museum of Liverpool** (Pier Head; 44-151-478-4545; liverpoolmuseums.org.uk/mol) opened in 2011, giving the city a large space to show off its history and tell the story of its people. An auditory exhibition takes you back to the early days

of the Beatles. A karaoke room has song choices originally sung by musicians from Liverpool. And a film chronicles the importance of soccer here. (If you want to see a game, head to Anfield Stadium and be prepared for the roar of 45,000 spirited fans.)

6 *Future Sound* Noon

Creativity is alive and well in the city. For a glimpse of the artistic future, check out the zinc-paneled **Foundation for Art and Creative Technology** or FACT (88 Wood Street; 44-151-707-4444; fact.co.uk). Three galleries display the work of visual artists like Mark Wallinger, Barbara Kruger, Tony Oursler, and Isaac Julien. Picturehouse, its cinema, shows international releases. Look around, and then stop in the cafe for lunch.

7 *Shop at the Docks* 2 p.m.

While away the afternoon at **Liverpool One** (5 Wall Street; 44-161-238-9400; liverpool-one.com), a 42-acre retail complex that is one of Europe's largest urban-regeneration projects. Its multitiered plazas were designed to complement existing architectural features in the area, including the original wall from Liverpool's first dock, said to be the oldest commercial dock in the world.

8 *Soul of Cuba* 6 p.m.

Hankering for something besides blood pudding and fish and chips? Make a reservation for **Alma de Cuba** (Seel Street; 44-151-702-7394; alma-de-cuba.com; $$), one of the city's most innovative restaurants, in terms of both food and design. It's housed in the former St. Peter's church, and the soaring nave and marble pillars serve as a dramatic, and sometimes outlandish, backdrop for a Caribbean-infused menu. Choices on one night's menu included a Gorgonzola and caramelized pear salad with pomegranate dressing and a jerk chicken dish with coconut rice and peas. The trendy and lively crowd looks beautiful in the candlelit space, which doubles some nights as a salsa club.

9 *On Stage* 7:30 p.m.

The **Everyman Playhouse** (Williamson Square; 44-151-709-4776; everymanplayhouse.com) is the

current incarnation of one of the oldest continuing repertory theaters in England, dating back to 1911. Actors who have played there include Michael Redgrave, Rachel Kempson, Anthony Hopkins, and Patrick Stewart. Buy tickets in advance.

SUNDAY

10 *Lyrical Beach* 11 a.m.

Liverpool is a coastal port town, once the epicenter of world trade routes, so enjoy a seaside stroll — one with a twist. Jump in a taxi and head to **Crosby Beach**, a length of Merseyside coastline now synonymous with the work of Antony Gormley, one of Britain's most lauded and divisive artists. A roughly two-mile stretch is home of Gormley's *Another Place,*

an installation that consists of 100 cast-iron men standing along the sand, staring toward the horizon. The eerie life-size sculptures encourage beachgoers to hang around and, perhaps, pen a few songs.

OPPOSITE ABOVE The Everyman Playhouse.

OPPOSITE BELOW One of the 100 cast-iron figures installed along two miles of Crosby Beach.

ABOVE The Museum of Liverpool, a repository of Beatles lore.

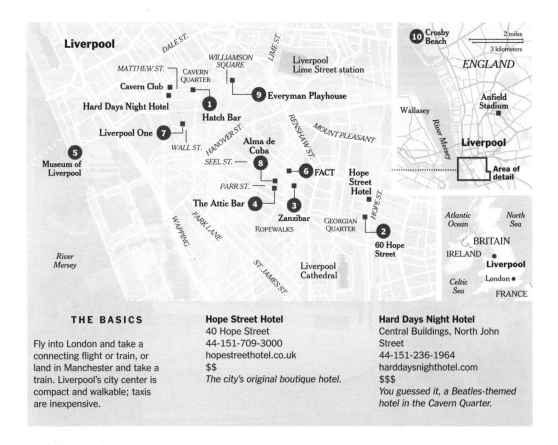

THE BASICS

Fly into London and take a connecting flight or train, or land in Manchester and take a train. Liverpool's city center is compact and walkable; taxis are inexpensive.

Hope Street Hotel
40 Hope Street
44-151-709-3000
hopestreethotel.co.uk
$$
The city's original boutique hotel.

Hard Days Night Hotel
Central Buildings, North John Street
44-151-236-1964
harddaysnighthotel.com
$$$
You guessed it, a Beatles-themed hotel in the Cavern Quarter.

South Wales

Wales, the land of mists at the edge of Britain, is a world of green hills, seaside castles, and a consonant-clogged language that persists in street signs and place names. In southern Wales, an easy reach from London, begin a weekend in Cardiff, where an old waterfront has been transformed from crumbling coal-era has-been to the gleaming and cool cultural capital of the Welsh. Then drive to the Black Mountains and Hay-on-Wye, the famous book town that has made words and authors its ticket to success. Each May, its population of 1,500 swells to a remarkable 80,000 for a festival that brings literary stars and book lovers from around the English-speaking world. For a quick visit, a better time is the off-season, when you can browse at your ease among Hay's dozens of bookstores without having to fight the crowds on the streets.
— BY SARAH LYALL AND PATRICK E. TYLER

FRIDAY

1 *Country Life* 2 p.m.

Restored villages don't all look alike, as the Welsh prove at the **St. Fagans: National History Museum** (four miles west of downtown Cardiff, just off the A4232 highway; 44-29-2057-3500; www.museumwales. ac.uk/en/stfagans). The look of the place, with its 40 buildings moved from all parts of Wales — and some reconstructed Celtic huts — reflects a culture that has always thought of itself as separate. The farm cottages and stone outbuildings, miners' houses, church, and mills are on the grounds of a manor house called St. Fagans Castle, and the walking tour is an intimate encounter with Welsh country life through the centuries.

2 *Castle Life* 4:30 p.m.

The wealthy few lived a bit better, of course, and some guarded their privileges at **Cardiff Castle** (Castle Street and High Street; 44-29-2087-8100; cardiffcastle.com), a collection of Roman foundations

OPPOSITE The scene in Hay-on-Wye, a small Welsh town with a high profile in the book world.

RIGHT Hay-on-Wye occupies only a few streets, but spread along them are three dozen bookstores. Its annual summer book festival draws 80,000 people.

and walls, a Norman keep that stands on a manmade hill ringed by a moat, and the wonderfully restored towers and halls conceived by the Third Marquis of Bute in collaboration with the Gothic Revival architect William Burges. Even if you have seen too many castles, the Winter Smoking Room in the Clock Tower and the green parrots of the Arab Room are worth the diversion.

3 *What a Barrage Can Do* 6 p.m.

The Cardiff waterfront used to be a sea of mud, ship channels, and cranes. Now it is a near-continuous crescent of hotels, apartments, and commercial buildings staggered among the concrete piers, ship basins, and boardwalks that overlook a 500-acre freshwater bay. The bay was created in the 1990s, when a low-slung dam, or barrage, was constructed to stop a 35-foot daily tidal swing from turning the whole estuary of the Taff River into mud flats twice a day. Now it looks a bit like Lake Geneva, without the fountain. As you walk alongside the bay, you won't be able to miss the eye-catching **Wales Millennium Center**, a boldly designed performing arts complex. "We wanted the building to have a confidence — not to be a timid structure," its architect, Jonathan Adams, said, and timid it is not. Over the theater, a sloping roof of bronze-colored steel is carved with the words of the poet Gwyneth Lewis, in Welsh, "Creating truth

like glass from inspiration's furnace," and alongside in English, "In these stones horizons sing."

4 *Bayside Levantine* 7 p.m.

Bosphorus (31 Mermaid Quay, Cardiff Bay; 44-29-2048-7477; bosphorus.co.uk; $$) sits on its own pier on the waterfront and serves Levantine feasts of meze, shish kebab, moussaka, and seafood. If the weather is good, take an outside table.

SATURDAY

5 *Turn the Page* 10 a.m.

Drive north through an undulating green landscape, over back roads crowded with ancient

farm vehicles, to Hay-on-Wye. The town is tiny, built around just a few main streets in the shadow of a large ruin of a castle that dates to the 13th century and has survived multiple sackings and multiple fires. For the festival, an elaborate city of tents rises, mushroomlike, out of the wet soil at one side of town. Literary lights and famous book lovers, from Dave Eggers and Kazuo Ishiguro to Alan Alda, have been on the program at this "Woodstock of the mind," as President Bill Clinton, a participant several years ago, put it. Writers are often taken with the charm of Hay, and you might see one or two wandering around in the off-season, too.

ABOVE Hills and meadows dominate the countryside near Cardiff and Hay-on-Wye.

BELOW The Wales Millennium Center, a performing arts center that opened in 2009 near Cardiff Bay. On the sloping steel roof, inscriptions appear in English and in Welsh.

6 *Pub Break* Noon

Have lunch, and maybe a libation, at a village pub. One popular choice is the **Three Tuns** on Broad Street (44-1497-821-855; three-tuns.com; $$-$$$), which returned to life a few years ago after a devastating fire. The bright reincarnated restaurant boasts home-baked breads, organic vegetables, and meat from local farms. At the **Blue Boar** (Castle Street; 44-1497-820-884; $$-$$$), you can choose hearty, traditional fare like lamb stew or scan the menu for something lighter, like ratatouille with goat cheese.

7 *The Book's the Thing* 2 p.m.

That Hay-on-Wye has an absurdly high concentration of used-book stores is due in large part to the efforts of Richard Booth, a zealous used-book seller who opened his first shop in 1961 and then actively encouraged others to follow. Which is the best store? Who knows? There's one devoted to mysteries and thrillers, one to poetry, another to rare children's books. There are huge ones, like the **Hay Cinema Bookshop** (Castle Street; 44-1497-820-071; haycinemabookshop. co.uk), and many smaller ones. Outside the castle is a 24-hour display of books that are sold on the "honesty" system—you make your selection and leave the correct cash. Take your time as you make your way through town, and beware. The bookshops call out to you in little siren voices as you pass by, begging you to browse, and even though you try to be strict, telling yourself that you have no more shelf space at home, that your suitcase is crammed full, that you already have a stack of unread books waiting by the bedside, you end up buying more.

8 *Literary Pampering* 8 p.m.

Llangoed Hall (Llyswen, Brecon; 44-1874-754-525; llangoedhall.co.uk; $$$$; dress code), about 15 minutes from Hay, is where the festival puts up its biggest-deal authors. Drive over for dinner in its restaurant. Featuring a manor house and acres of landscaped gardens, the property used to be a proper country estate and still has the look and feel of one. Menus are seasonal, and many ingredients are local. You might choose fresh-from-the-field lamb or wild-mushroom risotto, with orange and lemon tart or rhubarb mousse for dessert.

SUNDAY

9 *The Brecon Beacons* 10 a.m.

In Hay-on-Wye, you're already in the **Brecon Beacons National Park** (breconbeacons.org) a popular hiking destination of rivers, hills, and the

ABOVE Hay Castle, a ruin that dates back to the 13th century, has survived multiple sackings and multiple fires. It still dominates Hay-on-Wye.

Brecon Beacon peaks. It's a big park, covering 519 square miles, so get the lay of the land at the **Mountain Centre** (44-1874-623-366), a visitors' center where you can get maps, brochures, and directions—and, if you've made an early start, a Welsh breakfast of eggs, meat, beans, and mushrooms. The center is at a high elevation and has its own expansive view of Pen Y Fan, the highest mountain in South Wales. To get there, drive west to the town of Brecon, turn south onto Route A470, and turn right on the access road.

10 *Walk Your Way* 11 a.m.
Take a picnic lunch (obtained at the Mountain Centre or back in Hay-on-Wye) and set out to explore the Black Mountains. The hiking paths are well marked and cover a range—challenging treks to the peaks, riverside rambles, meadow jaunts. If you have another day, multiple trails can take you to waterfalls and caves. When it's time to head back to Cardiff, leave the park and drive south on Route A470.

ABOVE Hay bookstores are large and small, slick and simple. Many specialize in genres like crime, children's literature, or the supernatural.

OPPOSITE A cave in Brecon Beacons National Park, a favorite hiking spot near Cardiff.

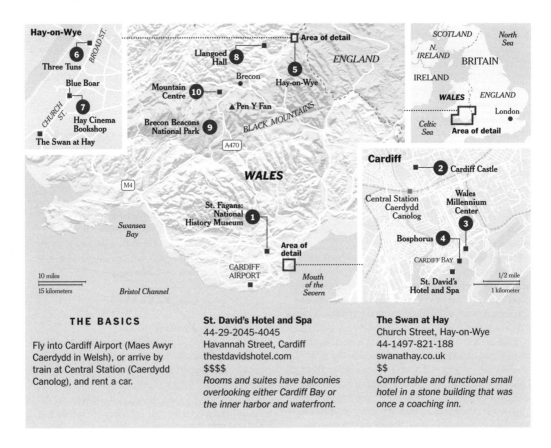

THE BASICS

Fly into Cardiff Airport (Maes Awyr Caerdydd in Welsh), or arrive by train at Central Station (Caerdydd Canolog), and rent a car.

St. David's Hotel and Spa
44-29-2045-4045
Havannah Street, Cardiff
thestdavidshotel.com
$$$$
Rooms and suites have balconies overlooking either Cardiff Bay or the inner harbor and waterfront.

The Swan at Hay
Church Street, Hay-on-Wye
44-1497-821-188
swanathay.co.uk
$$
Comfortable and functional small hotel in a stone building that was once a coaching inn.

Edinburgh

Every August, the global theatrical community — well, at least the part that is drawn to an all-male, musical version of Chekhov's Three Sisters *— heads to Edinburgh for a monthlong celebration of the dramatic arts. The main event is the Edinburgh International Festival, but for many people the real draw is the Fringe, a riotous collection of performances by hundreds of performance artists, comedians, memoirists, and monologuists. But Edinburgh exists apart from the Festival and the Fringe. In every season the city itself beckons, rich in history and cultural gifts as Scotland's traditional capital, dramatically sited amid rocky hills along an arm of the North Sea, and alive with contemporary creativity and verve.* — BY STUART EMMRICH

FRIDAY

1 *Higher Ground* 6 p.m.

Who's to argue with Robert Louis Stevenson? This native son of Edinburgh once wrote that the best views of the city could be found on **Calton Hill** — and he was right. The monument-studded hilltop, at the far east end of Princes Street and reachable by stairs from Waterloo Place, offers magnificent vistas of Edinburgh and the surrounding countryside, from the port town of Leith in one direction to Arthur's Seat and Salisbury Crags in another. When the skies are blue and the late-afternoon sun shimmers on the city below, it becomes clear why Edinburgh is considered among the most beautiful cities in the world.

2 *Starting the Weekend* 7 p.m.

Yes, there's also food, but cocktails are what it's really all about at the **Candy Kitchen and Bar** (113-115 George Street; 44-131-225-9179; candybaredinburgh.co.uk). Start the evening with one of its original concoctions, and survey the trendy crowd as you sip.

OPPOSITE A walk in the rain below Edinburgh Castle, traditional seat of Scottish kings. Visitors crowd into Edinburgh in summer for the Edinburgh Festival and Fringe, but the city beckons in any season.

RIGHT The Scottish Parliament Building, designed by Enric Miralles, opened in 2004.

3 *Catch of the Day* 8:30 p.m.

Rose Street, a long, narrow alley running between Princes and George Streets, is home to dozens of pubs, cozy cafes, and informal restaurants — one of the most popular being the **Mussel Inn** (61-65 Rose Street; 44-843-289-2481; mussel-inn.com; $). This bright and airy space, with wood floors and butcher-block tables, serves fresh, simply prepared seafood. As the name implies, mussels are the house specialty, served in a choice of different broths, from the traditional (white wine, garlic, shallots, and cream) to the unexpected (chilies, garlic, ginger, coriander, and cumin). All but the most ravenous of diners will find the half-kilo order plenty, particularly as it is accompanied by delicious freshly baked bread, perfect for soaking up juices.

4 *Before They Were Famous* 11 p.m.

There are dozens of excellent places around town to hear live music, from Bannermans, where you'll often find unsigned local bands looking for their big break, to Sandy Bell's, a place for devotees of traditional Scottish music. One of the best is **Whistlebinkies** (4-6 South Bridge; 44-131-557-5114; whistlebinkies.com), a sprawling basement bar that is often the first gig for start-up acts — from testosterone-fueled garage bands to soulful lesbian folk singers. The crowd ranges in ages and temperaments, and the talent runs from slickly polished to amusingly clueless. ("I know we have a song list here somewhere," a young rocker — surely not far

removed from high school — kept telling the small audience one night.) But nothing compares to the frenzy that grips the room when an unknown singer unleashes a powerful voice and sets the place on fire.

SATURDAY

5 *Old Masters* 10 a.m.

The **Scottish National Gallery** (off Princes Street; 44-131-624-6200; nationalgalleries.org) has an impressive collection of artists from van Dyck to van Gogh. But this inviting museum also offers a good introduction to Scottish art. Names

like Raeburn and McTaggart may not be so well known, but paintings by these Scottish artists compare well with those by their more famous contemporaries.

6 *Refreshed and Ready* 1 p.m.

Have a light bite at **Urban Angel** on Hanover Street (121 Hanover Street; 44-131-225-6215; urban-angel.co.uk; $) near Queen Street Gardens, where the cakes, muffins, and croissants pair nicely with a mug of fair-trade coffee or a cup of Earl Grey tea. Little plates and salads emphasize organic and seasonal greens, like polenta bites with rocket (arugula) and Parmesan. Or for a heartier but still health-conscious meal, go to **Henderson's** (94 Hanover Street; 44-131-225-2131; hendersonsofedinburgh.co.uk; $), an Edinburgh institution, first opened in 1962, that gives new meaning to the words "vegetarian restaurant." Look for dishes like apricot and lentil soup, broccoli and brie crumble, or offal-free haggis.

ABOVE The view from monument-studded Calton Hill, at the far east end of Princes Street, toward the Balmoral Hotel clock tower and the spires of churches and cathedrals.

LEFT Mute swans float on a loch below Arthur's Seat, a peak in Holyrood Park. Edinburgh commands a majestic setting amid hills, mountains, rivers, and the sea.

7 *Split Personality* 2:30 p.m.

Is there any major thoroughfare in the world more conflicted than Edinburgh's **Princes Street**? On one side is a cluster of stores catering to both tourists and Edinburghers (one, Jenners, first opened in 1838), sprinkled liberally with uninspiring fast-food joints and generic chain stores. But turn your gaze to the opposite side and you'll see elegantly landscaped gardens, inviting park benches, and massive trees framing a view of Edinburgh Castle off in the distance, looming over its former kingdom. It's a breathtaking sight, and one you should come back and experience again later in the evening, when the softly illuminated castle glows against the slowly darkening skies.

8 *Palms and Heather* 3 p.m.

If the weather is nice (it can shift quickly here) it's worth a visit to the 70-acre **Royal Botanic Garden** (20A Inverleith Row; 44-131-248-2909;

rbge.org.uk). You will see the usual palm trees and tropical plants, but also a Scottish Heath Garden featuring plants commonly found in the highlands. The garden's Terrace Cafe is a good place for an afternoon cup of tea. (To keep up

ABOVE The Palm House at the Royal Botanic Garden. Stroll the gardens to inspect all kinds of exotic plants as well as the flora native to Scotland itself.

BELOW The inviting Scottish National Gallery holds an impressive collection including continental European masters and Scottish artists like Raeburn and McTaggart.

with the Edinburghers, aim for several cups of tea every day.)

9 *Bistro Buzz* 8 p.m.

The minimalist décor at the **Outsider** (15 George IV Bridge; 44-131-226-3131; theoutsiderrestaurant. com; $$) contrasts with its stately views of Edinburgh Castle. Expect modern versions of Scottish mainstays like lamb, salmon, and venison.

SUNDAY

10 *Royal Promenade* 10 a.m.

You can't leave Edinburgh without doing the traditional tourist stroll along the **Royal Mile**, with Edinburgh Castle at one end and the Palace of Holyroodhouse and Parliament at the other. Predictable? Yes. Worth doing? Most definitely.

ABOVE Edinburgh Castle, high on the natural stronghold of volcanic Castle Rock.

OPPOSITE A cannoneer's vista from Calton Hill. Robert Louis Stevenson, a native of Edinburgh, wrote that the best views of the city could be had from here.

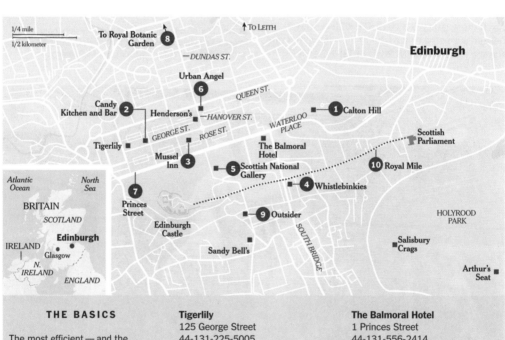

THE BASICS

The most efficient — and the cheapest — way to get into town from Edinburgh Airport is to take the airport bus; its several stops include one at the centrally located Waverley Station. The city center is compact and walkable.

Tigerlily
125 George Street
44-131-225-5005
tigerlilyedinburgh.co.uk
$$$
A popular address not just for visitors looking for a hip resting place, but also for the locals, who jam its bars and stylish lounge areas.

The Balmoral Hotel
1 Princes Street
44-131-556-2414
thebalmoralhotel.com
$$$$
If it's good enough for J. K. Rowling, then why not you? She holed up here while finishing the last chapter of the final Harry Potter book.

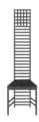

Glasgow

Glasgow has the classic second-city complex — locked in a never-ending comparison with its more popular and tourist-accessible sibling, Edinburgh, less than 50 miles away. But give Glasgow a little extra attention and you will find that, like the famously inscrutable dialect of its residents, this understatedly stylish Scottish city is worth deciphering. With its mix of modern and classic architecture, plentiful cultural and culinary options, shopping districts, and large green spaces, the city holds an appeal for travelers who find discovering a place is half the fun. — BY DAVID G. ALLAN

FRIDAY

1 *An Amble and a Dram* 4 p.m.

Decompress among the heather and orchids of the **Botanic Gardens** (730 Great Western Road; 44-141-276-1614; glasgow.gov.uk) in the hip West End. Join strolling couples — some with ecstatic children in tow — reveling in the 40-acre grounds, Victorian glass buildings, and, adjacent, the River Kelvin walkway. If that doesn't settle you, head across the street to **Oran Mor** (731 Great Western Road; 44-141-357-6200; oran-mor.co.uk), a converted church that houses an attractive whisky bar with more than 250 options, among them peaty Talisker, spicy Glenmorangie, and smooth and sweet Macallan. Ahhh, doesn't that feel better?

2 *Under One Roof* 7 p.m.

Oran Mor is more than a bar; it's a complex of multiple watering holes and restaurants, a beer garden, a nightclub, and a performance space that features "A Play, a Pie and a Pint," a popular lunch series. **Brasserie** (44-141-357-6226; $$), its primary dining spot, sports a dark oak décor and serves serious but thoughtful dishes: a light and flaky grilled halibut fillet might come with a bright romesco sauce, a baked ricotta and spinach roulade with a sweet potato puree. Dessert — maybe a pistachio and Bowmore whisky parfait or a warm apple and pear frangipane à la mode — is heavenly.

OPPOSITE The Kelvingrove Art Gallery and Museum.

RIGHT An interior at the Glasgow School of Art, designed by Charles Rennie Mackintosh.

3 *The King of Late Night* 10 p.m.

The compact **King Tut's Wah Wah Hut** (272a Vincent Street; 44-141-221-5279; kingtuts.co.uk), named for a defunct club in the East Village of New York, has been something of a divining rod for Glasgow's indie music scene for 25 years. Oasis was discovered there; Radiohead and Blur played the club before going big; Beck and the Strokes chose it as the site of their first Scottish gigs.

SATURDAY

4 *School's in Session* 10 a.m.

Start your Saturday with an early tour of the **Glasgow School of Art's** striking fin de siècle building (167 Renfrew Street; 44-141-353-4500; gsa.ac.uk) designed by Charles Rennie Mackintosh, Scotland's answer to Frank Lloyd Wright, whose genius lay in the kind of details you might miss on your own. Arrange your tour at the school's shop, in the Reid building (164 Renfrew Street). You'll see top-floor views of the city and the world's largest collection of Mackintosh-designed furniture. Continue the Mackintosh tour at the **Willow Tea Rooms** (217 Sauchiehall Street; 44-141-332-0521; willowtearooms.co.uk; $$$), which has maintained his 1904 design down to the waiters' uniforms. You can return later for afternoon tea with tiered sandwiches and sweets.

5 *Shop, Then Sip* Noon

Downtown Glasgow is dominated by the connected pedestrian shopping thoroughfares of Sauchiehall, Buchanan, and Argyle Streets. The area is a thriving hub of Victorian arcades, street performances, and stores that range from kitschy tourist shops to a glossy Apple Store. You can be fitted for a kilt at **Hector Russell** (110 Buchanan Street; 44-141-221-0217; hector-russell.com) or shop for more up-to-date apparel and anime-inspired toys at **Fat Buddha** (73 St. Vincent Street; 44-141-226-8972; fatbuddhastore.com). Then try one of the subterranean watering holes, like the youth-fueled **Republic Bier Halle** (9 Gordon Street; 44-141-204-0706; republicbierhalle.com). If you want to order like a

local, ask for a "heavy," referring to a category of light malty Scottish ales; a "wee heavy" is stronger in alcohol content and flavor.

6 *The Pipes Are Calling* 2 p.m.

The **Piper's Tryst** is a little-known culinary gem housed in the National Piping Centre (30-34 McPhater Street; 44-141-353-0220; thepipingcentre.co.uk; $), a tiny museum dedicated to the bagpipe. The traditional Scottish fare includes hearty sandwiches and a small plate of love-it-or-hate-it haggis, neeps (turnips), and tatties (potatoes) with a whisky-cream sauce.

7 *Gothic Views* 3:30 p.m.

Edinburgh has a castle. Glasgow has **Glasgow Cathedral**. This Gothic landmark (Castle Street; 44-141-552-8198; glasgowcathedral.org.uk), thought to have originated as a sixth-century chapel, is the oldest building in the city. Sharing its courtyard is the **St. Mungo Museum** (2 Castle Street; 44-141-276-1625;

ABOVE "Floating Heads," by Sophie Cave, is an unfailing eye-catcher among the eclectic works displayed at the Kelvingrove Art Gallery and Museum.

LEFT Among the 250 options at Oran Mor's attractive whisky bar are peaty Talisker, spicy Glenmorangie, and smooth and sweet Macallan.

glasgowmuseums.com), named after the city's patron saint, which offers displays and art illuminating the world's religions. Behind the cathedral is the hilltop Necropolis, a garden graveyard that serves as the resting place for tens of thousands of Glaswegians. It also offers terrific views of the city, including High Street, where the national hero Sir William Wallace (of *Braveheart* fame) and his men routed the English in 1297.

8 *Chip on the Old Block* 8 p.m.

Something of a Scottish Chez Panisse, **Ubiquitous Chip** (12 Ashton Lane; 44-141-334-5007; ubiquitouschip.co.uk; $$$$) started serving high-end organic local fare nearly 40 years ago, long before it was in vogue. The quiet plant-filled court-yard dining area, off a small cobblestone lane, is a retreat within a retreat. But it's the consistent high quality of the menu that keeps this place on the must-go list decade after decade. Try the prix fixe menu, which features fresh seafood like

organic Orkney salmon with lime and vanilla mash, followed by Caledonian oatmeal ice cream with fruit compote and its recommended whisky pairing, a 10-year-old Macallan.

9 *Swing Your Partner* 10 p.m.

Jump into traditional Scottish dancing, a ceilidh (pronounced KAY-lee) in particular, at **Avant Garde** (34-44 King Street; 44-141-552-7123; avantgardemusicbar.co.uk). Even if you can resist joining dancers of all ages in Strip the Willow or the Dashing White Sergeant, you can still enjoy a free concert featuring fiddle, accordion, and drums.

TOP Glasgow Cathedral, the city's oldest building, is thought to have originated as a sixth-century chapel. Behind it is the hilltop Necropolis, a garden graveyard that serves as the resting place for tens of thousands of Glaswegians.

ABOVE Glasgow loves statues. Many, like this one of the explorer David Livingstone, celebrate accomplished citizens.

SUNDAY

10 *Museum Makeover* 11 a.m.

The century-old **Kelvingrove Art Gallery** and Museum (Argyle Street; 44-141-276-9599; glasgowmuseums.com) offers an experience of Smithsonian proportions, with temporary exhibitions, a hands-on children's section, and an encyclopedic and eclectic collection of art, taxidermy, and historic innovations.

11 *Some Local Flavor* 12:30 p.m.

From the museum, stroll through the lovely Kelvingrove Park to the **Left Bank** (33-35 Gibson Street; 44-141-339-5969; theleftbank.co.uk; $$), a bright and airy restaurant that makes an art of breakfast. The focus is on local ingredients, with options like eggs mornay with a creamy Cheddar sauce and char-grilled bacon or housemade maple and walnut granola with dried cranberries and yogurt.

ABOVE A taxidermic gateway at the Kelvingrove.

OPPOSITE Meander along the outdoor pathways of the Botanic Gardens, with its 40-acre grounds, Victorian glass buildings, and adjacent River Kelvin walkway.

THE BASICS

Two airports serve Glasgow: Prestwick International where most international flights land, and Glasgow International, which is used mainly for domestic flights. The city has an extensive bus system and a subway loop (spt.co.uk) that connects downtown and the West End.

CitizenM
60 Renfrew Street
44-247-810-0917
citizenm.com
$$
Chic and affordable. The stylish bar can be noisy, so ask for a higher floor.

Malmaison Glasgow
278 West George Street
44-141-378-0384
malmaison.com
$$$
In a former Greek Orthodox church; exudes a stylish and stately feel.

Botanic Gardens
Brasserie
R. Kelvin
Oran Mor
GREAT WESTERN RD.
COWLAIRS PARK
1 mile
2 kilometers
Glasgow
Ubiquitous Chip
The Piper's Tryst/ National Piping Centre
SIGHTHILL PARK
Left Bank
KELVINGROVE PARK
Glasgow School of Art
MCPHATER ST.
Glasgow Cathedral
Kelvingrove Art Gallery and Museum
Area of detail
St. Mungo Museum
Necropolis
River Clyde
ARGYLE ST.
KING ST.
Avant Garde
Willow Tea Rooms
CitizenM
RENFREW ST.
SAUCHIEHALL ST.
PITT ST.
RENFIELD ST.
W. NILE ST.
Atlantic Ocean
North Sea
BRITAIN
SCOTLAND
Edinburgh
Malmaison Glasgow
HOPE ST.
BUCHANAN ST.
IRELAND
Glasgow
N. IRELAND
King Tut's Wah Wah Hut
VINCENT ST.
ENGLAND
DOUGLAS ST.
BOTHWELL ST.
Fat Buddha
GORDON ST.
WATERLOW ST.
Hector Russell
Republic Bier Halle

The Highlands & Isle of Skye

Do you like landscapes of coast and mountains, forests, castles, and arrestingly situated lakes? In the Scottish Highlands, draw a straight line from where you are to where you're going: that's the scenic route. Now draw a wavy line, or a figure eight: those routes are just as scenic. Offshore is an even more romantic vision: the Hebrides, a windswept archipelago where some residents still speak Gaelic. For a weekend driving trip with a taste of both the Highlands and the Hebrides, begin at Fort William, reached by driving north from Glasgow or south from Inverness, along the shore of Loch Ness. Then take the road west to the seacoast, allowing plenty of time to gaze out the window, and ride a car ferry to the Isle of Skye. Go in the late spring or early summer, and you should find the sun both piercingly clear and unusually gentle, a lulling bath of light that dies away well after 10:30 p.m. and moseys back again before 5:30 the next morning.

— BY FRANK BRUNI AND DAN SALTZSTEIN

FRIDAY

1 *Fort William* Noon

The trip from Fort William to the coast is best known as a scenic train route, and some travelers still experience it that way. The so-called **Road to the Isles** (Route A830) follows much the same path. Fort William itself is a pleasant town on Loch Linnhe, a long, narrow inlet of the sea. With about 10,000 people, it is the largest city in the western Highlands. Britain's highest mountain, Ben Nevis, hovers close by. Set out on A830 through a magical landscape of plunging mountains, lochs, and tiny towns.

2 *The Route to Hogwarts* 2 p.m.

A few miles after passing Loch Eil, stop at **Glenfinnan** and find the visitor center (44-1397-722-250; nts.org.uk/Property/Glenfinnan-Monument) near a stone tower facing Loch Shiel and the steep enfolding mountains. The tower was built 200 years ago to honor the patriotic Scots who fought

OPPOSITE Fans of the Harry Potter films know the Glenfinnan Viaduct as part of the route of the Hogwarts Express.

RIGHT Portraits of the Macdonald clan look down on diners at the Kinloch restaurant on the Isle of Skye.

the English in the doomed cause of Bonnie Prince Charlie. It's an interesting enough story, but there's a more contemporary landmark nearby. Take the path to a view of the **Glenfinnan Viaduct**, a massive, gracefully curving railroad bridge a quarter of a mile long and 100 feet high. Long considered an engineering marvel, it is familiar today as part of the route of the Hogwarts Express train in the Harry Potter films.

3 *Across the Strait* 4 p.m.

Get back on the road in plenty of time to make your ferry at **Mallaig** (44-800-066-5000 or calmac.co.uk for schedules and reservations). If you're early, look around in Mallaig, a pretty town on the Sound of Sleat. On the other side of the narrow strait, the Isle of Skye stretches out like a skeletal hand. Sheltered between its fingerlike peninsulas are sea lochs, source of a bounty of seafood that is one compelling reason to visit the island. On the other side of the strait, disembark in Armadale, in the island's far south.

4 *Dinner With the Macdonalds* 7 p.m.

Kinloch (Isleornsay, Sleat; 44-147-1833-333; kinloch-lodge.co.uk; $$$$), a holder of a Michelin star, is the grand lady of Skye dining. Claire Macdonald, who owns the spot with her husband, Godfrey, is a well-known British cookbook writer, and she also happens to be a real Lady. In the dining room, you'll be surrounded by portraits of Macdonalds past; theirs is one of two clans—the other being the MacLeods—that have dominated Skye for centuries. The menu here changes daily. One evening's four-course dinner began with a luscious amuse-bouche of

roasted tomato and olive soup; proceeded to a plate of scallops, lightly seared, with a warm crab mousse; then steamed organic salmon with avocado, beet, and red pepper sauces; and at last to the entree, hake in a garden of greens. This is the kind of meal to eat on Skye, if you can manage it. Stick with this super-fresh seafood while you have the opportunity.

SATURDAY

5 *Skye Perspective* 8 a.m.

Get out early with a good map, supplemented by directions from your hotel. Drive north to Sligachan and west toward the high Cuillin peaks, Skye's dominating mountains. Circle around to **Glenbrittle**, where a short hike will take you to the **Fairy Pools**, a series of clear aquamarine pools connected by the small waterfalls of a rushing stream (walkhighlands.co.uk/skye/fairypools). The trail continues toward the mountains, but leave that for another time and drive on. Everywhere off the main routes on Skye be prepared for single-lane roads with "passing places" — you end up playing a friendly little game with oncoming cars as to who will pull over. (Don't forget to wave as you pass by — it's considered rude not to.) And then there is the livestock. Sheep, it turns out, will move when you honk.

6 *Whisky Stop* 10:30 a.m.

You're in rural Scotland. It would be shame not to visit a whisky distillery. Stop at **Talisker Distillery** (Carbost; 44-1478-614-308; scotchwhisky.net/distilleries/talisker.htm). Spend an hour learning how the famous Scotch whisky is made; if you join a tour, you may be invited to sip a wee dram.

7 *Chowder and Tartan* 1 p.m.

Drive through Portree, Skye's main town, and out onto the Trotternish Peninsula. The coast here is occasionally broken by rock formations — one famous outcrop is called the Old Man of Storr. Your goal is the locavore restaurant at **Flodigarry Hotel** (Flodigarry, Trotternish; 44-147-0552-203; flodigarry.co.uk; $$$$). The stylish décor cleverly references the inn's original 1928 appearance with a lot of stone, wood, iron, and glass. Sample the satisfying seafood chowder (known in Scotland as cullen skink), with ingredients from local waters, like haddock, mussels, and langoustine, as you gaze at mountains on the Scottish mainland.

8 *Ancient Stonework* 3 p.m.

Skye has been inhabited since ancient times, and you may see ruins of stone dwellings, barns, and chapels. Even more intriguing are the standing stones, inevitably summoning thoughts of a small-scale Stonehenge, that date back thousands of years. Their builders and their purpose are lost to time. You'll find a good example at **Uig**, on the west coast of Trotternish.

9 *Drop In on the MacLeods* 5 p.m.

The chiefs of the MacLeods still live at **Dunvegan Castle** (44-1470-521-206; dunvegancastle.com), as they have since the year 1200 or so. It is also an active tourist site. Take the tour (which has a chilling moment when it reaches the dungeon), and stroll in the extensive gardens.

10 *Truly Regional* 7 p.m.

The **Three Chimneys** (Colbost, Dunvegan, Isle of Skye; 44-1470-511-258; threechimneys.co.uk; $$$$) is the French Laundry of Scotland, luring food-loving pilgrims from near and far, a destination in its own right. And it is a restaurant that can't be replicated outside Scotland. Within bare stone walls, under

a low, wood-beamed roof, you will find food that is emphatically regional: luscious Scottish salmon cured in Scottish malt whiskey; plump oysters from nearby beds; scallops with their mushy, enticingly funky roe; marvelous langoustines not pulled from their shells and obscured by other ingredients but left to their own sweet, delicate devices. The inn next door has a splendid view of an ocean inlet from its breakfast room. From there or from the lawn outside, take in the sea views and look for seals on the rocks.

(Armadale, Sleat; 44-147-1844-305; clandonald.com). Tales of the Macdonalds are not neglected, but there is also an informative summary of the wider history of the Highlands, from the days of the ancient Celts.

SUNDAY

11 *Last Stop: The Past* 11 a.m.

A good last stop before the ferry back to Mallaig is the **Museum of the Isles** at Armadale Castle

OPPOSITE Seen from the Highlands, the Cuillin peaks rise out of the mist on the Isle of Skye.

ABOVE The restaurant of the Three Chimneys inn lures food lovers from near and far to its stone-walled dining room on Skye. The fare is emphatically regional.

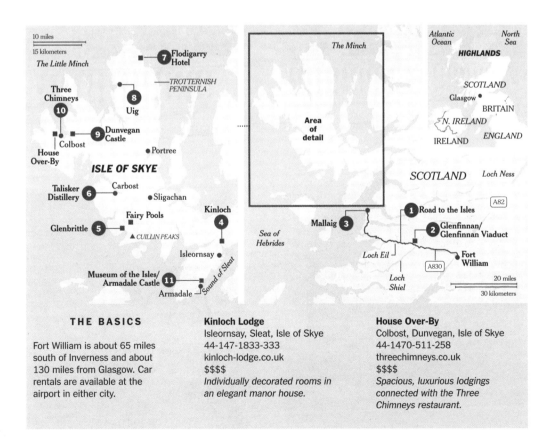

THE BASICS

Fort William is about 65 miles south of Inverness and about 130 miles from Glasgow. Car rentals are available at the airport in either city.

Kinloch Lodge
Isleornsay, Sleat, Isle of Skye
44-147-1833-333
kinloch-lodge.co.uk
$$$$
Individually decorated rooms in an elegant manor house.

House Over-By
Colbost, Dunvegan, Isle of Skye
44-1470-511-258
threechimneys.co.uk
$$$$
Spacious, luxurious lodgings connected with the Three Chimneys restaurant.

Dublin

Dublin has been through tumultuous change in the new millennium, from the Celtic Tiger years, when BMWs were de rigueur, to the post-crash depression, when the cacophony of incessant building suddenly went silent, to a chastened recovery. The city is finding a new way to exist — neither ostentatious with wealth nor bowed down under debt. A hugely popular bike share program has replaced the "beamers," craft beer is gaining precedence over elaborate cocktails, and Dublin restaurants are undergoing a creative renaissance that prioritizes imagination and Irish ingredients over heavily stylized and overpriced dishes. Throughout it all, from its centuries-old pubs to its Georgian architecture to the stately Trinity College at its center, the city has retained its glorious sense of history. — BY NELL MCSHANE WULFHART

FRIDAY

1 *Begin in the Bog* 3 p.m.

The **National Museum of Ireland-Archaeology** on (Kildare Street; 353-1-677-7444; museum.ie) is worth multiple visits and provides an excellent background for a visit to Ireland. Bronze Age gold jewelry dug up during turf cutting, Viking swords, and medieval farming tools are all on display in this handsomely decorated Palladian structure, which dates back to 1890. The stars of the show are the "bog people," preserved corpses of men who were killed and tossed into peat bogs during the Iron Age. The bodies are in remarkable condition — one of them still has nearly a full head of curly hair.

2 *Craft on Draft* 5:30 p.m.

The craft beer scene in Dublin has exploded in the last few years, with bottles of Irish-made lagers, ales, stouts, and ciders now standard issue at almost every city watering hole. For one of the biggest selections of craft brews, head to **Against the Grain** (11 Wexford Street; 353-1-470-5100; galwaybaybrewery.com), an unpretentious pub with hundreds of offerings, includ-

OPPOSITE An old port town on the River Liffey, Dublin reigns as Ireland's cultural and political capital.

RIGHT Graceful Georgian architecture, including these houses in Merrion Square, is part of the Dublin mix.

ing Irish-made bottles from O'Hara's, Eight Degrees Brewing, Mac Ivors, and the bar's owner, the Galway Bay Brewery.

3 *French-Irish Cuisine* 8 p.m.

The **Green Hen** (33 Exchequer Street; 353-1-670-7238; greenhen.ie; $$$) has won admiration with its French atmosphere and Franco-Irish dishes, like a pan-fried duck breast that came with a purée of parsnips and a celeriac mash. Be sure to order a side of bread, a moist, dark version of classic Irish wheaten bread, made with Guinness and black treacle. After dinner, tip a glass in the convivial wine cellar at **Fallon & Byrne** (11-17 Exchequer Street; 353-1-472-1010; fallonandbyrne.com).

SATURDAY

4 *Medieval Cathedral* 10:30 a.m.

Much of the Irish past can be read in **Christ Church Cathedral** (Christchurch Place; 353-1-677-8099; christchurchcathedral.ie), which dates back to circa 1030. William of Orange came here to give thanks after he ensured the Protestant ascendancy at the Battle of the Boyne, and Strongbow's tomb is here. The medieval crypt is full of treasures, including a mummified cat and rat discovered stuck in an organ pipe (James Joyce mentioned them in *Finnegans Wake*). The belfry tour provides a wide view and an up-close look at flying buttresses, as well as the chance to try bell-ringing. If you want to go even farther back in time, get the combination ticket that includes the Dublinia museum, where hokey but

entertaining exhibits impart information about Dublin's beginnings as a Viking settlement.

5 *Bikes by the Bridges* 1:30 p.m.

The enormous popularity of Dublin's bike share program has led to the creation of bicycle lanes and a cycling-friendly culture. Grab a bike from one of the many stations (locations are at dublinbikes.ie) and cycle along the Liffey River, which slices through the city, taking note of Dublin's famed bridges and their stories. The Ha'penny was the city's first pedestrian bridge; payment to cross was once a halfpenny. The O'Connell, a part of Dublin life since 1794, is said to be unique in Europe for being wider than it is long. The newest, the Rosie Hackett, is named for an activist who was involved in the 1916 Easter Rising.

6 *Go for a Guinness* 3 p.m.

A pint of "the black stuff" is required drinking on any trip to Dublin. The **Guinness Storehouse** museum (St. James's Gate; 353-1-408-4800; guinness-storehouse.com), amid the cobbled streets and

imposing buildings of the St. James's Gate brewery, explains how the stout is made and gives its history. Near the end of the tour, visitors learn how to pull a proper pint of Guinness — a procedure that involves holding the glass at a 45-degree angle and waiting 119.5 seconds before topping it off.

7 *A Fine Kettle of Fish* 8 p.m.

For Old World-style seafood, head to the **Lobster Pot** (9 Ballsbridge Terrace; 353-1-668-0025; thelobsterpot.ie; $$$), which displays its daily catch on a fish tray that is expertly explained by the staff. If they have them, order the crab claws, delicately seared with garlic butter, or the Dublin Bay prawns, which are pan-fried in garlic butter and sweetly melt in your mouth. Save room for crêpes suzette. It's worth the splurge.

8 *Beyond 'Trad' Music* 10 p.m.

Live music is in Dublin's blood, but just about the only Irish accents you would hear in a city-center pub advertising traditional music are either on the stage or behind the bar. Leave the renditions of "The Fields of Athenry" for the tourist trade, and head instead to the **Sugar Club** (8 Lower Leeson Street; 353-1-678-7188; thesugarclub.com), a central venue with an eclectic calendar of live music and a fun-loving vibe. Anything from indie-folk to soul to country music to hip-hop might be found most nights of the week, along with the occasional high-energy comedy, burlesque, or cabaret night.

ABOVE The Elephant & Castle in Temple Bar.

LEFT It's not all Guinness in Dublin's pubs.

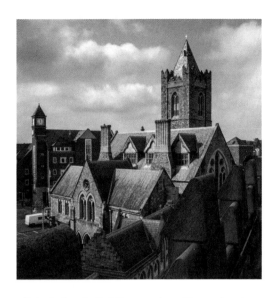

SUNDAY

9 *Brunch Strategy* 10:20 a.m.

Beat the breakfast stampede to the **Elephant & Castle** (18 Temple Bar; 353-1-679-3121; elephantandcastle.ie; $$), where much of Dublin seems to go for brunch. Try the French brioche toast or Irish pinhead oatmeal. The name comes from a London pub, Enfanta de Castile, whose Spanish moniker was too much for English tongues.

10 *Go North* Noon

The side of Dublin north of the Liffey, traditionally working class, offers scenes little different from those half a century ago. Stroll with the shoppers on Henry Street, and at O'Connell Street, check out the towering silver Spire of Dublin, nicknamed "the

stiletto in the ghetto." Re-energize with a pastry at the bright **Brother Hubbard** cafe (153 Capel Street; 353-1-441-1112; brotherhubbard.ie).

ABOVE The medieval Christ Church Cathedral.

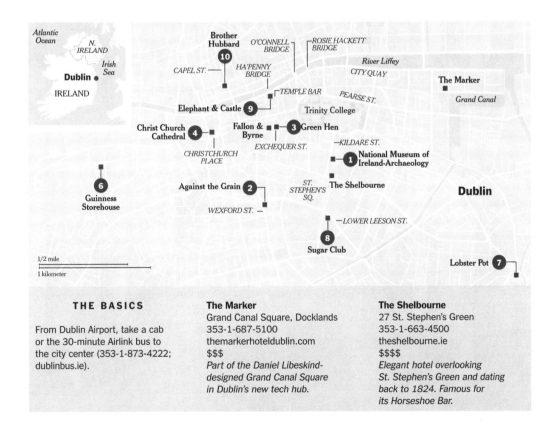

THE BASICS

From Dublin Airport, take a cab or the 30-minute Airlink bus to the city center (353-1-873-4222; dublinbus.ie).

The Marker
Grand Canal Square, Docklands
353-1-687-5100
themarkerhoteldublin.com
$$$
Part of the Daniel Libeskind-designed Grand Canal Square in Dublin's new tech hub.

The Shelbourne
27 St. Stephen's Green
353-1-663-4500
theshelbourne.ie
$$$$
Elegant hotel overlooking St. Stephen's Green and dating back to 1824. Famous for its Horseshoe Bar.

Dublin for Readers

Austere beauty and haunting ruins, dark humor and tragic lore — Ireland makes a good training ground for writers. With only 6 million people, this island has produced four winners of the Nobel Prize in Literature: George Bernard Shaw, William Butler Yeats, Samuel Beckett, and Seamus Heaney. Then there are the other Irish authors, like Jonathan Swift, Oscar Wilde, Brendan Behan, Bram Stoker, and C. S. Lewis. But when you're in Dublin, it's hard to miss the hero worship of one writer in particular. Though he may be the hardest of all to read, James Joyce sealed his place in Irish hearts by making his home city so central in his work that it is almost a character in its own right. The crowds who arrive here each June 16, Bloomsday, to celebrate Joyce's Ulysses *find themselves celebrating Dublin, too.*
— BY WENDY KNIGHT

FRIDAY

1 *Joyce's Tower* 2 p.m.

Take a 20-minute train ride to Dun Laoghaire, a harbor town with long piers, yachts, and, in adjacent Sandycove, a squat stone tower where Joyce set the opening scene of *Ulysses*. The tower was built during the Napoleonic wars, one of many on the Irish coast, and once held artillery to meet the feared French invasion. The walls are eight feet thick. Inside is the **James Joyce Museum** (DART train to Sandycove or Bus 59 from Dun Laoghaire; 353-1-280-9265; dun-laoghaire.com/profile/joyce_tower), which contains letters, books, manuscripts, photographs, and other memorabilia. Joyce lived briefly in the tower, by then converted into a house, in 1904. There's a good sea view from the gun ports, although you may see more than you care to at the nude beach below.

2 *Read the Menu* 6:30 p.m.

Arrive well before 7 p.m. at the **Winding Stair Restaurant & Bookshop** (40 Lower Ormond Quay; 353-1-872-7320; winding-stair.com; $$$) if you want time to buy something in the shop to read. If not, the food may be entertaining enough. Irish ingredients are prominent on the menu: John Stone's Irish beef, Knockanore cheese from County Waterford, Roaring Bay mussels from West Cork. Some tables overlook the River Liffey. (As those who have survived

attempts to read the book will remember, the Liffey plays a starring role in Joyce's notoriously difficult *Finnegans Wake*.)

3 *Inspiration* 10 p.m.

Leopold Bloom, the protagonist of *Ulysses*, mused that it would be a "good puzzle" to cross Dublin without passing a pub. Dublin has more than 1,000 of them, and many feature live Irish music. Skip the trendy Temple Bar area and wander north of the River Liffey to **Hughes Bar** (19-20 Chancery Street; 353-1-872-6540). Local musicians and sometimes international Irish-music stars, like the Cape Breton fiddler Paul Doyle, perform at the bar. The faded pumpkin-colored walls and old men wearing cardigan sweaters let you know you've found the real deal. For more merriment, head to **O'Donoghue's** (15 Merrion Row; 353-1-660-7194; odonoghues.ie), where musicians sip pints of Guinness and play their fiddles and tin whistles, just as the Dubliners, one of Ireland's best-known bands, did in the 1970s.

SATURDAY

4 *Illumination* 9:30 a.m.

Ireland has been a bookish place for a very long time. The **Old Library Building** at Trinity College (College Green, Nassau Street; 353-1-896-2308)

OPPOSITE In a city that venerates books, the Long Room at Trinity College holds 200,000 treasured volumes.

BELOW Fiddles, flutes, and traditional Irish music.

houses the renowned Book of Kells (tcd.ie/Library/ bookofkells). It is a richly illuminated manuscript of the Bible's four gospels thought to have been created around 800 in Scotland or Ireland and eventually taken to an Irish town called Kells to save it from Viking invaders. It serves as a reminder that Irish monasteries kept much of ancient literature alive during

ABOVE Wander north of the River Liffey to Hughes Bar. Step inside, and you'll know you have found the real deal, the kind of Irish pub that James Joyce knew.

BELOW Dun Laoghaire, a short train ride from town. A squat stone tower on its seafront was the setting for the opening scene of *Ulysses* and now holds the James Joyce Museum.

the Dark Ages. Two volumes are in a glass case, and the pages are turned regularly. Upstairs, the magnificent vaulted Long Room has 200,000 of the college's oldest books, stacked in neat floor-to-ceiling rows, including a rare first edition of Dante's *Divine Comedy*.

5 *Have a Scone* 11 a.m.

Breakfast is on the menu until noon at **Queen of Tarts** (Cows Lane, Dame Street; 353-1-633-4681; queenoftarts.ie; $), a darling confectionery in Dublin's quiet medieval area. Tuck into eggs, oatmeal, or fruit. But it's really all about the pastries here, and in the morning, that means the scones. The glass display cases overflow with more baked treats, like nectar-oozing plum tarts and chocolate ganache cake.

6 *A Different Page* 1 p.m.

You admired the sacred grandeur of the Book of Kells. Now turn your attention to *Dracula*. A first edition of Bram Stoker's novel is one of the literary artifacts at the **Dublin Writers Museum** (18 Parnell Square North; 353-1-872-2077; writersmuseum.com). There are also portraits, letters, personal items like Samuel Beckett's telephone and Mary Lavin's teddy

OPPOSITE Even the parks memorialize Irish writers. At St. Stephen's Green, there's a bust of James Joyce and a William Butler Yeats Garden.

bear, and George Bernard Shaw's signed refusal to a request for his autograph.

7 *Additional Editions* 3 p.m.

You can be forgiven if you want to do some nonliterary shopping. Anchoring Grafton Street, the city's most famous shopping strip, is **Brown Thomas** (88-95 Grafton Street; brownthomas.com), a grand department store. Stay in this area for clothing shops and Irish-themed souvenirs, some of which will not have been made in Ireland. But you are also in one of the best cities in the world for bookstores (even though, yes, electronic readers have invaded here, too), and it's a perfect time to choose a special edition of one of the Irish classics. There are big bookstores on Grafton Street; rare books around the corner on Duke Street; and a whole clutch of booksellers, general and specialist, on Dawson Street. For bargains, search at the open-air market in Temple Bar Square.

8 *Pre-Abbey* 5:30 p.m.

Close to the Abbey Theater, **101 Talbot** (100-102 Talbot Street; 353-1-874-5011; 101talbot.ie; $$) is used to catering to a pretheater crowd. Dishes are unpretentious, hearty, and seasonal: Irish chicken stuffed with goat cheese; pan-roasted venison with braised red cabbage, or maybe pan-fried salmon with crushed potatoes and pesto. The dining room is spare and pretty, with a hardwood floor and shining wood-topped tables.

9 *Irish Drama* 7:30 p.m.

The best of Irish drama, and some of the best anywhere, is still to be found at the historic **Abbey Theatre** (26 Lower Abbey Street; 353-1-878-7222; abbeytheatre.ie). Yeats and Lady Gregory, the Irish folklorist, were its principal founders in 1904, John Millington Synge was its star early playwright, and it established and has maintained a tradition of producing new Irish works. You might see a play in its first run (many have gone on to London's West End and Broadway); a revival of a classic that originated at the Abbey, like Sean O'Casey's *The Plough and the Stars*; or a work from abroad by an established playwright like Arthur Miller or Sam Shepard. The original Abbey was destroyed by fire and the replacement, built in 1966, was renovated a few years ago with interiors by the French designer Jean-Guy Lecat.

10 *Hops vs. Grapes* 10:30 p.m.

Leopold Bloom downed many pints of Guinness Stout on his odyssey around Dublin, but Joyce, his creator, spent most of his adult life on the Continent drinking wine. Follow his example by sampling from one of the hundreds of selections at the **Ely Wine Bar** (22 Ely Place; 353-1-676-8986; elywinebar.ie). It has an elegant dining room, cellar bars, and a romantic street-level lounge with an onyx bar and a stone fireplace.

Pavement plaques mark spots along the Bloomsday route. But the best Sunday stroll, even for literary types, may be in **St. Stephen's Green**, the 27-acre park just off Grafton Street. It's shady and restful, with gardens (including the William Butler Yeats Garden), fountains, a pond, and sculpture by Henry Moore. And, of course, a bust of Joyce.

SUNDAY

11 *Green Dublin* 11 a.m.

Take a walk and bring the camera along with you. A favorite photo op is a pose with the eight-foot bronze statue of Joyce, looking eccentric in his oversize hat and round eyeglasses, that stands at the corner of North Earl and O'Connell Streets. A languid multicolored Oscar Wilde sprawls on a granite stone in Merrion Square, begging to be snapped.

ABOVE In the morning, it's all about the scones at Queen of Tarts, on one of the city's quiet medieval streets. Later in the day, check out the chocolate ganache cake.

OPPOSITE James Joyce, the writer most venerated in the hometown he recreated in *Ulysses*, stepping out on North Earl Street.

THE BASICS

Traffic is heavy and cabs are expensive. When you have the opportunity, it's best to walk.

The Clarence
6-8 Wellington Quay
353-1-407-0800
theclarence.ie
$$$
An 1852 landmark facing the River Liffey. Handsome rooms and river views.

Number 31
31 Leeson Close
353-1-676-5011
number31.ie
$$
B&B in a Georgian town house feels more like a boutique hotel.

Camden Court Hotel
Camden Street
353-1-475-9666
camdencourthotel.com
$$
Business hotel in the non-touristy Portobello area, a 15-minute walk from the Temple Bar area.

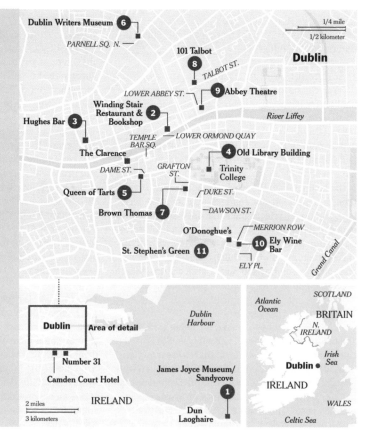

Cork

While Cork may officially be Ireland's second city, don't suggest that to one of its proud residents. The melodious reply — most likely delivered in a rich brogue sprinkled with gammin (Cork slang for Cork slang) — may contain playful swipes at that larger town over on the Irish Sea. But it's this spark and warmth of Cork, a remnant of the city's enduring rebel history, that captivate the visitor and — along with its picturesque setting along the River Lee and its dedication to the arts and good food and drink — make it a convincing rival to Dublin. On long summer days, Cork's compact size makes it a perfect city to tour on foot, providing you've packed walking shoes and a bit of ambition for a few hilly climbs.

— BY MICHAEL MCDERMOTT

FRIDAY

1 *Ring Bells on Arrival* 4:30 p.m.

For an introduction to the city, ascend the hill north of city center into the district of Shandon to the **Church of St. Anne**, built in 1722 of sandstone and limestone, a red and white color combination so popular among residents that they designed the city's flag to match. For the best view of the city, wind your way up the tower's stone stairs, alerting Cork to your arrival by ringing the eight bells you'll find along the way up. Handy music sheets demonstrate how to play appropriate classics such as "The Bells of Shandon," or more unlikely tunes like Meat Loaf's "Two Out of Three Ain't Bad."

2 *A Drink From the Well* 5:30 p.m.

Keeping with the sacred spirit, make your next stop the **Franciscan Well Brewery** (14b North Mall; 353-21-4393-434; franciscanwellbrewery.com), a microbrewery and pub built on the site of a Franciscan monastery where legend has it that the well water was a miraculous curative. These days, the water may come from the city pipes, but the beer pours freely and in lavish variety by Irish standards. The crisp, clean Friar Weisse wheat and the robust Rebel Red are excellent house choices. Or pick from a hand-

OPPOSITE Climb up for a view at the Church of St. Anne.

RIGHT A quiet day on the River Lee in Cork.

ful of other drafts and a range of import bottles, certainly plenty to get you langerated, magalorim, or mombolised (Corkonian ways to describe getting loaded).

3 *Tapas, Irish Style* 7 p.m.

Jacques (23 Oliver Plunkett Street; 353-21-427-7387; jacquesrestaurant.ie; $$), a small city-center place that is open for lunch and dinner, doubles in the evening as a tapas restaurant with seasonal menus offering dishes like house-smoked barbecued quail, fish cakes, monkfish stew, and barbecued ribs. Choose a few and sample some of the wines from small independent makers.

4 *Escape the Fiddles* 10 p.m.

Not everyone craves traditional Irish music. For a night out minus the plucking and pipes, head over to lively Oliver Plunkett Street and join the regulars at **An Brog** (72 & 73 Oliver Plunkett Street; 353-21-427-0074; anbrog.com), where a young and diverse crowd dances to indie, Irish rock, and alternative music, whether spun by D.J.'s or performed live (on the last Friday of each month). Later, keep the party going at one of the several other clubs along the street.

SATURDAY

5 *Rashers and Browsers* 9:30 a.m.

Fill a beer-worn belly with newly baked scones and traditional Irish breakfast ingredients like eggs, sausage, blood pudding, and rashers of bacon at the

Farmgate Café (English Market; 353-21-427-8134; farmgate.ie; $$). Ingredients are fresh from the surrounding English Market (City Center, entrances on Grand Parade, Princes Street, and Patrick Street), in operation for more than 400 years and clearly visible from your mezzanine perch in the cafe. Watch locals shop for fresh meats, fish, cheeses, and breads, or go out to browse the stalls yourself, satisfying your cravings for sheep's cheese or smoked meats at **On the Pig's Back** (353-21-427-0232; onthepigsback.ie) or reviewing various raw materials for the local specialty of tripe and drisheen (a blood sausage).

6 *Better Believe It's Butter* Noon

For a surprisingly engaging and multifaceted view of history, visit the **Cork Butter Museum** (O'Connell Square; 353-21-430-0600; corkbutter. museum). Subjects include everything from the medieval legacy of cattle raids and children's baptisms in milk to the economic growth of the dairy industry. When ready to trade savory for sweet, stop at nearby **Linehan's Handmade Sweets** (37A John Redmond Street; 353-21-450-7791), where the Linehans have been cooking up old-fashioned boiled candies like clove rocks, butter nuggets, and apple drops for four generations.

7 *Food and Art Unite* 2 p.m.

Feeling flahed out (wasted) from walking the hills? Stop in at the **Crawford Art Gallery and Café** (Emmet Place; 353-21-427-4415; crawfordartgallery. ie; $$). The airy former Custom House, built in 1724, defies the overpriced and govvy (snobby) reputation of museum restaurants. An ever-changing menu offers selections like a rich, creamy cucumber,

ABOVE At the English Market, in operation for more than 400 years, the fish is fresh and the raw materials are available for local delicacies like tripe and drisheen.

RIGHT Traditional music is alive and well at Sin E (pronounced shin-AY, Irish Gaelic for "That's It").

lettuce, and mint soup and a Spanish tortilla accompanied by a zinger of a country relish. Have a sconce (quick look) at the museum's collection of modern and classical works, and don't miss the designs on paper by the Irish stained-glass artist Harry Clarke.

8 *Retail Pilgrimage* 4 p.m.

Join the local shoppers along St. Patrick's Street and the surrounding neighborhood, where you might find buskers playing fiddle or tambourine alongside an odd mechanical troupe of doll performers. In this shopping hub are stores such as **Samui** (17 Drawbridge Street; 353-21-427-8080; samuifashions.com), which has international high-end women's threads as well as dresses and coats by the Irish designer Danielle Romeril.

9 *Worth the Climb* 7 p.m.

Find your way to a side door mounted with a winged bust of armor overhead and ascend to the **Ivory Tower** (35 Princes Street; 353-21-427-4665; ivorytower.ie; $$$$), a creation of Seamus O'Connell, an Arizona-born chef. Order individual items or choose one of the evening's several tasting menus. You'll find inventive dishes like tongue with ladyfingers and gentleman's relish, carpaccio of wood pigeon, and magret of duck with blackberry balsamic jus and braised endives.

10 *The Pipes Are Calling* 10 p.m.

Traditional music is alive and well at **Sin E** (pronounced shin-AY, Irish Gaelic for "That's It";

8 Coburg Street; 353-21-450-2266), a pub that could easily be a Lower Manhattan transplant if not for the occasional barber chair (formerly, one could get a trim and a pint simultaneously). A mishmash of rock concert posters, snapshots, and postcards dangles from the walls and ceiling, framing musical sessions where outsiders and regulars are equally welcome. A mix of young and old plays fiddles, banjos, and flutes into the night even when the house music is switched back on.

SUNDAY

11 *Take Ye to the River* 11 a.m.

While the River Lee may seem inescapable in the central city, its charms can be hidden in workaday guise. For more alluring views and a better chance to appreciate the water, head to **Fitzgerald's Park**, west of the city center along Mardyke Walk. Grab a scone at the **Riverview Café** (back of Cork Public Museum in the park; 353-21-427-9573) and stroll among the gnarly trees, splashing fountains, and well-manicured gardens where children's laughter and their parents' mellifluous replies merge with the lazy flow of the river.

ABOVE On a quiet Sunday morning, stroll along the river and among gnarly trees, splashing fountains, and well-manicured gardens in Fitzgerald's Park.

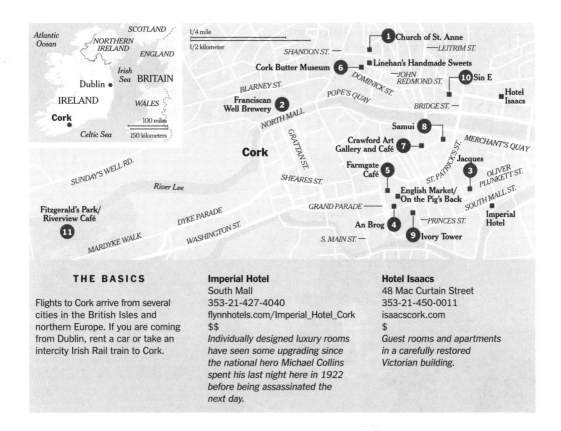

THE BASICS

Flights to Cork arrive from several cities in the British Isles and northern Europe. If you are coming from Dublin, rent a car or take an intercity Irish Rail train to Cork.

Imperial Hotel
South Mall
353-21-427-4040
flynnhotels.com/Imperial_Hotel_Cork
$$
Individually designed luxury rooms have seen some upgrading since the national hero Michael Collins spent his last night here in 1922 before being assassinated the next day.

Hotel Isaacs
48 Mac Curtain Street
353-21-450-0011
isaacscork.com
$
Guest rooms and apartments in a carefully restored Victorian building.

Brussels

As the seat of the European Union, Brussels gets its share of gray suits pouring off the Eurostar. Luckily, the neckties come off after work. Beneath the buttoned-down facade is a lively capital that follows its own sartorial trends, indulges in decadent flavors (especially involving beer and chocolate) and exhibits a witty, even wacky sense of humor. What other city would erect an entire museum to a single comic book series? Or to an artist famous for painting faceless men in gray suits? — BY ELAINE GLUSAC AND DAN BILEFSKY

FRIDAY

1 *Beer and Chocolate* 5 p.m.

Brave the hordes of tourists in the Grand Place, Brussels's signature square, to drink a Trappist beer (yes, the monks are Belgian) at **Le Roy d'Espagne** (Grand Place 1; 32-2-513-0807; roydespagne.be), an atmospheric bar in one of the grandest of the ornate guildhalls. Grab a seat on the outdoor terrace so you can look out at the Gothic, Flemish Renaissance, and Baroque architecture. Next, follow your cravings to **Elisabeth** (Boterstraat 43; 32-475-525-197; elisabeth. be). You can't go a block in the city's historic center without encountering a chocolate maker, but this boutique is also a vendor of artisanal Belgian sweets. Among the truffles, pralines, nougat, and meringues, you might also find orangettes, little sticks that sublimely combine orange and chocolate. If you miss the treats here, you might stumble upon them at one of Elisabeth's other shops nearby, each with a different specialty.

2 *Power Truffles* 8 p.m.

Kwint (Mont des Arts 1; 32-2-505-9595; kwintbrussels.com; $$$), a joint venture by two Parisian purveyors, Caviar Kaspia and La Maison de la Truffe, spotlights rich ingredients like a truffle-poached egg, a wild Baltic smoked salmon, and mussel casserole with truffle cream. The cathedral-like dining room is framed by handsome archways and a

OPPOSITE The Grand Place, with its stone paving and famous ornate guild houses.

RIGHT Artfully decorated chocolates, a Brussels specialty, in one of the city's many chocolate shops.

billowing metallic sculpture by the Belgian designer Arne Quinze, offering a dramatic backdrop for Eurocrat power diners and well-heeled foodies alike.

SATURDAY

3 *Bowler Hats Galore* 10 a.m.

Appearances can be deceiving in this town. Case in point: a 19th-century neo-Classical building housing an homage to absurdity. The **Magritte Museum** (Rue de la Regence 3; 32-2-508-3211; musee-magritte-museum.be) is a riot of bowler hats, strange birds, and other icons associated with René Magritte, the Belgian Surrealist who lived in Brussels for much of his life. Though many famous paintings are missing, this is a large Magritte collection with 250 works. There are also wacky artifacts, like a homemade film showing the artist and friends acting out *Alice in Wonderland*. Start at the basement level, where a clever 45-minute film introduces Magritte's life and artistic milestones.

4 *Moules Frites, Anyone?* Noon

For lunch, head to the **Aux Armes de Bruxelles** (Rue des Bouchers 13; 32-2-511-5550; auxarmesdebruxelles.com; $$$-$$$$), which has operated near the Grand Place since the 1920s, for some of the freshest buckets of mussels in town, complete with frites and mayonnaise. Real Bruxellois eat the first mussel with their fingers and use the empty shell as a utensil for scooping up the rest. Don't forget to mop up the mussel soup with a hunk of crusty bread. If you want a spot away from the tourists, moules

frites aficionados swear by **Au Vieux Bruxelles** (Rue St.-Boniface 35; 32-2-503-3111; auvieuxbruxelles.com; $$$) in the heart of a lively Congolese neighborhood.

5 *Wearables and Edibles* 1:30 p.m.

Though Brussels is well behind Antwerp when it comes to fashion, it has its own clutch of homegrown designers whose work can be found in shops along and near Rue Antoine Dansaert. One place to look is **Kure** (Rue Antoine Dansaert 48; 32-2-265-1217; kure-eshop.com), where the clothes are as stylish as the setting. For a more vintage men's and women's look, try **Gabriele** (Rue des Chartreux 27; 32-2-512-6743; gabrielevintage.com) where clothes from the 1920s mingle with outrageous '70s styles. More

interested in Belgium's taste temptations than in its couture? Stroll around and find one of the ubiquitous shops selling waffles topped with chocolate, berries, and whipped cream. You won't be alone as you stroll slowly, savoring every delicious bite. Belgium's waffles are world-famous for a reason.

6 *Break for Nouveau* 4 p.m.

If the institutional modernism of the European Union's sprawling offices leaves you cold, escape can be found in the city's Art Nouveau, the flowery architectural style popular at the beginning of the 20th century. One of the genre's finest practitioners, and a father of Belgian Art Nouveau, was Victor Horta. Visit his home and studio, the **Musée Horta** (Rue Américaine 25; 32-2-543-0490; hortamuseum.be). The exterior is typically Belgian: understated. Inside are astonishing details including a grand stairwell made of marble and wrought iron that undulates into the expressive shapes of an abstract painting. Natural light pours down from a stained-glass canopy onto floral mirrors, Tiffany lamps, mosaic floors, and the

ABOVE For a tour through the Belgian obsession with Tintin, the globe-trotting redheaded comic strip hero, travel out of town to the Musée Hergé, named for the strip's creator.

LEFT Waffle shops, selling one of the city's favorite specialties, are ubiquitous in the city center.

carved banister. The effect is dreamlike — until the crowds of tourists bring you back to earth.

7 *Sanctuary Cycling* 5:30 p.m.

Atone for your indulgences — and prepare for future rounds — by exploring the shady **Parc du Cinquantenaire** on two wheels. The 74-acre park, laid out in classical style, has hedge-bordered pathways for cycling free of cars. Hop on a yellow Villo bike (villo.be), part of a bike-sharing program with locations around town.

8 *Royal Feast* 8 p.m.

Over-the-top Belgian design and food meet in the aptly named **Belga Queen** (Rue Fossé aux Loups 32; 32-2-217-2187; belgaqueen.be; $$$). The owner, Antoine Pinto, runs a stylish string of successful restaurants. Belga Queen, his flagship, operates under the vaulted ceiling of a 19th-century bank and is favored by the see-and-be-seen set. The menu celebrates indulgence (loin of lamb, Chateaubriand, turbot with mousseline sauce). Between courses, you can pop into the basement, where the former bank vault now holds a cigar club.

9 *Swing Time* 10 p.m.

Ring the doorbell to get into **L'Archiduc** (Rue Antoine Dansaert 6; 32-2-512-0652; archiduc.net), a cozy lounge that feels like an Art Deco jewel box,

with a polished wood bar, patterned banquettes, and filigreed metal balcony. Live music mixes jazz with country and Creole. A bit closer to Grand Place, you're likely to find metal and rock and even "Turkish underground psych funk" at **Ancienne Belgique** (Anspachlaan 110; 32-2-548-2484; abconcerts.be), which has two performance spaces that draw young and enthusiastic crowds.

SUNDAY

10 *Vintage Everything* 10 a.m.

There are lots of antiques markets around town, but the most diverse may be the daily flea market at the **Place du Jeu de Balle**. The market swells on Sundays and is stocked with everything from refrigerators and wheelchairs to vintage clothing and cut glass. Before or after your browsing, have brunch at **Le Pain Quotidien** (Rue des Sablons 11; 32-2-513-5154; lepainquotidien.com; $$). You can find outlets of this bakery chain in many cities, but this store is the original. The wait can be irksome, but the pine tables are crammed with bread hot from the oven, jams, and chocolates.

ABOVE Mine the flea market at the Place du Jeu de Balle for timeworn treasures and collectibles, trash ready to be repurposed, and vintage everything.

11 *All About Tintin* Noon

Tintin, the fictional young reporter with a zany tuft of orange hair, is the star of the **Musée Hergé** (Rue du Labrador 26; 32-10-488-421; museeherge.com), a three-story museum named for his creator, Georges Prosper Remi, who used the pen name Hergé. The museum, about half an hour from the center of Brussels in the town of Louvain-la-Neuve, winds chronologically through his career, from advertising work to abundant success as the head of a small empire devoted to all things Tintin, from live-action films to souvenir key chains.

ABOVE Belgium hardly lacked for well-cooked food, but two Parisian gourmet specialists added their own restaurant vision, emphasizing seafood and truffles, with Kwint.

OPPOSITE A center of European commerce even before its 17th-century guildhalls were new, Brussels is now the headquarters of the European Union.

THE BASICS

Multiple airlines from around the world fly direct to Brussels. Take a train from the airport into the city.

Hotel Amigo
Rue de l'Amigo 1-3
32-2-547-4747
hotelamigo.com
$$$
Feels like a luxury pied-à-terre. Splashes of humor include Tintin prints on bathroom walls.

Welcome Hotel
Quai au Bois à Brûler 23
32-2-219-9546
hotelwelcome.com
$$
Models each of its 17 rooms after a country, from Congo to Vietnam.

Odette en Ville
25 rue du Châtelain
32-2-640-2626
chez-odette.com
$$$
Chic eight-room boutique hotel near the high-end shopping street Avenue Louise.

Antwerp

Antwerp's central railway station makes a grand first impression with its soaring glass ceiling, elegant hall, and ornate turn-of-the-century architecture. And it's a splendid entrance to this stylish city, the largest in the northern Belgian region of Flanders. Years ago, Antwerp established itself as a fashion hub following the international success of top designers like Dries Van Noten, Ann Demeulemeester, and fellow alumni from the local Royal Academy of Fine Arts, one of Europe's premier design schools. Today, the imagination and innovation that initially spurred the cerebral fashions for which the city became known is now blooming in diverse forms—from clothing to cuisine, and art to architecture.
— BY INGRID K. WILLIAMS

FRIDAY

1 *Rubens Revival* 2 p.m.

While the Royal Museum of Fine Arts is closed for renovations (scheduled to be completed at the end of 2018), a collection of its artworks is on display in another lofty location: the **Cathedral of Our Lady** (dekathedraal.be/en/bezoek.htm). This grand Gothic cathedral, notable for having just a single spire, also houses major paintings from the hometown artist Peter Paul Rubens. After touring the cathedral, visit Rubens's former home and studio, now called **Rubenshuis** (Wapperplein 9-11; 32-3-201-1555; rubenshuis.be), which today functions as a museum filled with many works from the artist and his pupils. Check the Royal Museum's website (kmska.be) for other exhibitions of its treasures around town during the renovation.

2 *Gables and Cobbles* 4 p.m.

Antwerp carefully maintains the medieval, Renaissance, and Baroque architecture of its intimate city center, and cars are banned on many streets, making it a great place to stroll. The two main squares are the **Grote Markt**, lined with elaborate 16th- and 17th-century guild houses, and the **Groenplaats**, dominated by the Gothic cathedral. To see the **Fashion Museum** (Nationalestraat 28; 32-3-470-2770; momu.be), turn your steps in its direction before 5:30 p.m., when the last ticket is sold.

3 *Intimate Brasserie* 8 p.m.

At **Invincible** (Haarstraat 9; 32-3-231-3207; invincible.be; $$$), a tiny brasserie, the emphasis is on the vin, as evidenced by windowsills lined with empty magnums. Pick an interesting bottle from the ever-changing assortment on display along one wall, and then retire to a seat at the long kitchen counter or in the nook of a dining room. Dinner is a three-course feast spanning traditional French fare, like a terrine starter, and pan-European dishes, like grilled gambas with black rice and chorizo.

4 *Musical Lairs* 9:30 p.m.

After dinner, soak up some jazz at **De Muze** (Melkmarkt 15; 32-3-226-0126; jazzcafedemuze.be), a bustling cafe with live nightly performances. If it's crowded around the bar, head to the upper levels still within earshot of the music. For dancing, the time-honored spot is **Café d'Anvers** (Verversrui 15; 32-3-226-3870; cafe-d-anvers.com), a club that put Antwerp on the European party map in 1989 and still draws crowds.

SATURDAY

5 *New Day on the River* 10 a.m.

The once-dreary district of docks and warehouses known as Het Eilandje has been transformed into an

OPPOSITE AND BELOW Antwerp, one of Europe's most fashion-forward cities, effortlessly mixes old and new, venerating its ornate Gothic cathedral and cobblestone alleys while nurturing young artists and designers.

attractive neighborhood with many small shops and cafes. At **Broer Bretel** (Nassaustraat 7; 32-48-415-8296; broerbretel.be), a coffee bar with a vintage vibe, scope out the new surroundings from the outdoor bench while sipping your favorite brew. Then continue to the **Museum aan de Stroom**, or **MAS** (Hanzestedenplaats 1; 32-3-338-4400; mas.be), an iconic piece of contemporary architecture formed of undulating glass and Lego-like sandstone blocks, designed by the Dutch firm Neutelings Riedijk. Inside is an ambitious, adventuresome museum with displays of contemporary art and exhibitions telling the story of this evolving city, as well as restaurants and an airy shop. Views from the rooftop observation deck take in a surrounding panorama of docks, locks, and city.

6 *Chocolate Garden* 1 p.m.

Belgium knows its chocolate, but that still doesn't fully explain the elaborate desserts that Roger van Damme concocts at the lunch-only restaurant **Het Gebaar** (Leopoldstraat 24; 32-3-232-3710; hetgebaar.be). In a brick cottage on the edge of the botanical gardens, a meal began with crisp fried sweetbreads before moving on to artistically styled creations like Botanique — an edible miniature "garden" punctuated by a chocolate river and a tiny milk-chocolate tree.

7 *Shop Hop* 2 p.m.

Whether your idea of shopping involves peering in windows or plunking down plastic, head to Kloosterstraat, a street packed with fashionable stores and antiques shops. Start in **Your** (Kloosterstraat 90; your-antwerp.com), an enormous two-story space where you'll find everything from headphones and ikat-print pants to a yellow 1975 Porsche 914. Then shop for a present with a past at **Arrangerie 13** (Muntstraat 13; 32-3-231-2161; arrangerie.be), a nearby shop where castoff furnishings are restored and reworked. Climb the steep wooden staircase to explore the treasures that are spread across three floors. **Marcy Michael** (Sint-

Jozefstraat 78; 32-47-622-8022; marcymichael.com) specializes in Pop Art-inspired collectible chairs.

8 *Futuristic Flemish* 7:30 p.m.

The elegant restaurant **De Godevaart** (Sint-Katelijnevest 23; 32-3-231-8994; degodevaart.be; $$$$) pushes Flemish cuisine far beyond basic dishes like mussels and fries. A traditional starter of gravlax, for example, was paired with parsley ice cream and a quail egg yolk "cooked" at minus 20 degrees Celsius. And a sweet-and-salty homemade candy bar was accompanied by a cool scoop of mojito ice cream. Even the restaurant's décor, with classical moldings, modern artworks, and glittering chandeliers, is refreshing.

9 *Beer With the Belgians* 9:30 p.m.

Entering the specialty beer pub **Kulminator** (Vleminckveld 32; 32-3-232-4538; facebook.com/Kulminator.friends) may require squeezing past crates bearing the name Westvleteren, a Trappist brewery whose beers are as renowned as they are rare. Inside this small pub with its eclectic beer-centric décor — a chandelier of corks, a wreath of caps — you'll find a menu with hundreds of beers, including many vintage and hard-to-find bottles. Make your last stop of the night **Frituur No. 1**

(Hoogstraat 1), a fantastic fry shop serving steaming piles of twice-fried Belgian fries topped with generous dabs of mayonnaise.

SUNDAY

10 *Art and Nature* 10 a.m.

Venture out to **Middelheimmuseum** (Middelheimlaan 61; 32-3-288-3360; middelheimmuseum.be), a 74-acre sculpture park south of the city center. Its more than 200 works range from bronze Rodins to a bubbling pond by the Flemish artist Philippe Van Snick. Stroll across open lawns, past a bridge by Ai Weiwei, and through an enclosed garden where temporary exhibitions are displayed inside Het Huis, a striking new outdoor pavilion. Then stretch out on the grass — perhaps beneath the swaying wires

strung between tall trees, a multisensory work by the Belgian artist Honoré d'O — and contemplate all the art and nature.

OPPOSITE ABOVE Seek out Belgian beer, a point of national pride, at one of Antwerp's pubs.

OPPOSITE BELOW The Cathedral of Our Lady.

ABOVE A grassy lawn for relaxing in one of Antwerp's public gardens. At Middelheimmuseum, a sculpture garden south of the city center, the greenery comes with a counterpoint of outdoor sculpture.

THE BASICS

Fly into the Brussels airport or take a train from Brussels or Paris. In the city center, get around on foot and by tram.

Hotel O Kathedral
Handschoenmarkt 3
32-3-500-8950
hotelokathedral.com
$$
Right across the square from the cathedral. Minimalist style.

Matelote Hotel
Haarstraat 11A
32-3-201-8800
hotel-matelote.be
$-$$
Well-priced small design hotel in a 16th-century building.

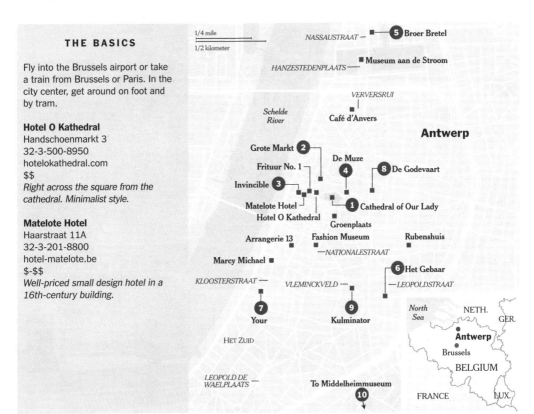

Bruges

Bruges, the capital of West Flanders in northwestern Belgium, owes its considerable charm to reverses of fortune. A wealthy commercial center 600 years ago, it became a backwater and slept for centuries, little changed by time. The result is a preserved medieval town with swans gliding on quiet canals, gabled houses on cobblestone lanes, and fine Flemish art. Now wide awake, Bruges prospers as a tourist favorite. Look beyond the usual cafes and souvenir stores to find ambitious restaurants run by talented young chefs and chocolate shops selling the confections of experimental chocolatiers. After dark, local pubs offer mind-boggling selections of rare Belgian beers from the region's celebrated breweries.
— BY INGRID K. WILLIAMS

FRIDAY

1 *Wonderland Wander* 3:30 p.m.

Much of the enchanting city center is truly reminiscent of a fairy tale, with stone footbridges spanning picturesque canals and cobblestone streets curving past turreted manor houses. To see the prettiest parts of this medieval wonderland, wander along the Dijver canal, which snakes through town, making sure to end your stroll at **Markt**, the main square, which is dominated by a 13th-century belfry. The energetic can spiral up the bell tower's 366 steps for a view over the city, but first exercise the panoramic capability on your camera at ground level, taking in the neo-Gothic courthouse, the belfry itself, and the quaint gabled buildings ringing the square.

2 *Chocolate Tasting* 5 p.m.

With the absurdly high concentration of chocolate shops in town, it may seem as if every other storefront is peddling piles of pralines and trays of truffles. Seek out the most innovative spots. Dominique Persoone's shop, the **Chocolate Line** (Simon Stevinplein 19; 32-50-341-090; thechocolateline.be),

OPPOSITE Reminiscent of a fairy tale, Bruges is a preserved medieval town with swans gliding on quiet canals, gabled houses on cobblestone lanes, and a 13th-century belfry.

RIGHT Beer connoisseurs find hundreds of choices at 't Brugs Beertje, a locally venerated pub.

is packed with creative confections and fanciful flavor combinations like bitter ganache with vodka, passion fruit, and lime. At **BbyB** (Sint-Amandsstraat 39; 32-50-705-760; bbyb.be), a sleek, all-white store, simple bars of fine Belgian chocolate are wrapped in Pantone-style numbered boxes; try No. 15 with milk chocolate, hazelnut, and babelutte (a regional caramel-like candy) or No. 50 with dark chocolate, tonka beans, and lemon.

3 *The Stars Are Shining* 8 p.m.

A few years ago, the elegant little **Hertog Jan** (Loppemsestraat 52; 32-50-673-446; hertog-jan.com; $$$$) became only the third restaurant in Belgium to earn a third Michelin star. If you can snag a table in the minimalist dining room, expect a parade of beautiful, pared-down plates from the chef Gert De Mangeleer, ranging from Limousin lamb served with candied turnips and lemon myrtle to sea scallops with veal marrow, thin slices of Jerusalem artichoke, and tiny dollops of herring eggs.

SATURDAY

4 *From Market to Market* 9 a.m.

Start the day as the locals do, at the street market on **'t Zand** square. Skip the bric-a-brac vendors and head to the northern end of the square to shop for Belgian cheeses, smoked herring, and freshly baked loaves of raisin-and-nut bread. Then buy a bag of fresh mini-boterwafels, sweet butter waffles, from the stand on nearby Hauwerstraat, and munch on them on the way to the **Beursplein** produce market.

Wijnants. Racks are packed with beautifully draped silk print dresses, asymmetric jackets, and voluminous wool capes: understated, cool pieces without a logo in sight.

5 *Potent Primitives* 10 a.m.

This early in the morning, crowds have yet to pack the museums, so take your time admiring paintings by the Flemish Primitives, a group of influential artists who flourished in the city in the 15th century. Start at the **Sint-Janshospitaal** museum in a centuries-old hospital (Mariastraat 38; 32-50-448-771; museabrugge.be), where six captivating works by Hans Memling adorn a small chapel. Then cross the canal to its sibling **Groeninge Museum** (Dijver 12; 32-50-448-751; museabrugge.be). Studying the stunning realism of Jan van Eyck's *Madonna With Canon Joris van der Paele* in person would be worth the price of admission even if there were no other works to see.

6 *Lunch With Locals* 1 p.m.

Avoid restaurants in the historic old town, where prices and quality reflect a reliance on tourists rather than repeat customers. Instead, head to **Tête Pressée** (Koningin Astridlaan 100; 32-470-212-627; tetepressee.be; $$$$), a stylish spot (with an adjacent deli selling takeout) in the residential neighborhood of Sint-Michiels. The menu is only in Dutch, but take a seat at the long counter framing the open kitchen anyway, because the friendly chef Pieter Lonneville will happily translate. But really, you can't go wrong with anything on the three-course prix fixe menu. One day it featured deconstructed pheasant stew with endive and grilled squash, followed by a wedge of pear clafoutis served warm with fresh figs.

7 *Flemish Fashion* 5 p.m.

Style mavens who can't make it to Antwerp, the capital of Belgium's avant-garde fashion scene, will be thrilled to discover the boutique **L'Héroïne** (Noordzandstraat 32; 32-50-335-657; lheroine.be). This unassuming shop stocks an outstanding collection of the country's most progressive designers, from established labels like Dries Van Noten and Ann Demeulemeester to young talents like Christian

8 *Fry Guy* 7 p.m.

After a filling lunch, dinnertime will very likely roll around before your stomach starts to rumble. (Chocolate nibbling might also be a culprit.) But that makes this a fitting time to indulge in another regional specialty: Belgian fries. Here, the twice-fried, thick-cut fries are practically unrecognizable as a relative of America's french fries, especially when topped with a generous dollop of mayonnaise or curry sauce. One fry shop, **Chez Vincent** (Sint-Salvatorskerkhof 1; 32-50-684-395; chezvincent.eu), delivers piping-hot fries with a fresh side salad and views of the neighboring Sint-Salvator Cathedral through the bay windows in the upstairs dining room. And yes, it also has ketchup.

9 *Make Mine a Tripel* 9 p.m.

There's no shortage of beer pubs in town, but there's also no reason your first and last stop for a beer should be anywhere but **'t Brugs Beertje** (Kemelstraat 5; 32-50-339-616; brugsbeertje.be). This venerated spot is undeniably gezellig, a Dutch word that perfectly encapsulates the cozy, homey feeling of the pub. Novices who can't tell a dubbel from a Duvel can rely on the knowledgeable staff to help select a brew from the hundreds of choices on the beer menu. Connoisseurs will delight in sifting through the fantastic options, which include St. Bernardus Tripel, La Rulles Estivale, and Orval Trappist ale.

SUNDAY

10 *For Whom the Bells Toll* 10 a.m.

Let your inner carillonneur ring at the **Sound Factory** ('t Zand 34; 32-702-23302; sound-factory.be), a new interactive museum inside the contemporary Concertgebouw (Concert Hall) building. Compose a symphony on the rooftop — inspired, perhaps, by the lovely views across town — with a touch-screen exhibit that puts control of (recorded) chimes from the city's various church bells at your fingertips. Then descend the staircase through an eerie

auditory installation to the fifth floor, where the highlight is the colorful artwork-cum-synthesizer titled OMNI.

11 *Ride With the Wind* Noon

When the streets start to swell with tourists, the best way to escape is on two wheels. Rent a bicycle at the train station, and pedal northeast along the wide canal that circles the city. A gentle, 30-minute ride meanders down a leafy bike path, through green parks, over a wooden footbridge, and past the city's four remaining windmills. On the return trip, take a short detour to **Begijnhof**, a quiet courtyard ringed with whitewashed cottages that were once home to Bruges's beguines, a religious order of single and widowed women that dates back to the 13th century.

Today Benedictine nuns live here, and a respectful order of silence is in place along the shady path, ensuring that these well-trodden cobblestones are among the most peaceful in Bruges.

OPPOSITE Art installation or music synthesizer? OMNI is both, and visitors can try it out at the Sound Factory, an interactive museum at a concert hall.

ABOVE Sightseers can spiral up 366 steps to the top of the belfry on the Markt, the main square.

THE BASICS

Pack shoes that work well on cobblestones. For swan's-eye views, ride a tour boat on the canals.

Grand Hotel Casselbergh
Hoogstraat 6
32-50-446-500
grandhotelcasselbergh.com
$$
Stylish rooms behind a modern silver-tiled facade that stands out among the quaint gables.

Hotel de Orangerie
Kartuizerinnenstraat 10
32-50-341-649
hotelorangerie.be
$$$
Elegant and romantic; wedged between a quiet cobblestone lane and the Dijver canal.

Die Swaene
Steenhouwersdijk 1
32-50-342-798
dieswaene.be
$$$$
Small, luxurious, and romantic. Located on the picturesque Groenerei canal in the city center.

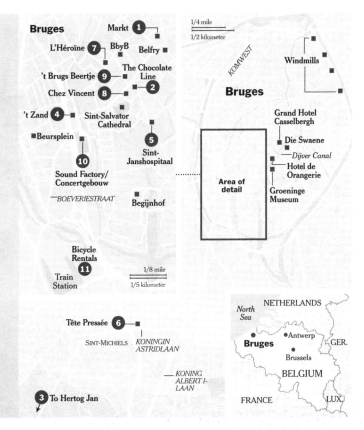

Amsterdam

Amsterdam will always woo travelers with the arched bridges, watery passageways, and crooked canal houses of its enchanting city center. But overlaying that 17th-century foundation is a cosmopolitan modern city with a lively spirit of innovation and the dynamic influences of residents from more than 150 countries. Rich in history and art yet quick to embrace the new, Amsterdam is the home of renowned museums full of masterpieces, cutting-edge galleries and studios, sophisticated cuisine, and intriguing shops full of avant-garde fashions and quirky home design. All along its harbor and in the South Axis area, futuristic buildings designed by architects like Renzo Piano and Rafael Viñoly have gone up—a modernist foil to the venerable canal houses. It's all within easy reach. To explore, just act like a local: hop on a bike and go.
— BY GISELA WILLIAMS

FRIDAY

1 *Find Some Wheels* 4 p.m.

First things first. Renting a bike is key in Amsterdam; you can avoid expensive taxi rides and feel like a local from the start. Don't be nervous. Two-wheelers rule the roads, it's difficult to get lost, and there are bike paths everywhere. One of many places to rent a bicycle is **Amsterdam City Tours** (Spuistraat 30; 31-29-941-1111; amsterdamcitytours. com). Keep the sturdy three-speed bike for three hours or three days. It's best to reserve a day or two in advance.

2 *Get Your Bearings* 5 p.m.

The tower at **Westerkerk** (Prinsengracht 281; westerkerk.nl), nearly 280 feet tall, is the highest church tower in Amsterdam and, on a clear day, affords stunning views of the entire city, including the glittering modern towers of the South Axis neighborhood and the old Prinsengracht Canal area where Anne Frank and her family hid from the Nazis. (It's not too late in the day for a visit there: **Anne Frank House**,

OPPOSITE A time-honored way to see Amsterdam: by boat on the city's 17th-century canals.

RIGHT Cycling over the Prinsengracht, one of the largest links in Amsterdam's 65-mile canal network.

Prinsengracht 267; 31-20-556-7100; annefrank.org) Westerkerk is also where Rembrandt was buried and where Queen Beatrix and Prince Claus were married.

3 *Eat Your Vegetables* 7 p.m.

Take a cozy storefront with an open kitchen in the up-and-coming Westerpark neighborhood, mix in food trends like farm-to-table and supper club dinners, and you get **Culinaire Werkplaats** (Fannius Scholtenstraat 10; 31-65-464-6576; deculinairewerkplaats.nl; $$$$). Part restaurant and part atelier, it was opened a few years ago by Marjolein Wintjes and Eric Meursing, a former designer and chef. Every few weeks they create a theme that inspires the cooking, like Light or Flowers, and then serve a five-course meal that focuses on seasonal vegetables, fruits, and grains. One menu included Jerusalem artichoke prepared three ways (roasted, whipped, and fried), croquettes of black quinoa with ras al hanout, and a "deconstructed" apple pie: apple soup with frozen Champagne cubes and a stick of sugared crust.

4 *Music in the Night* 10 p.m.

Nearby, the Westergasfabriek, a former factory complex full of artists' studios and cultural venues, is home to the **North Sea Jazz Club** (Pazzanistraat 1; 31-20-722-0980; northseajazzclub.com), which on weekends serves up American R&B, blues, soul, and a variety of jazz from around the world. You're likely to find an even livelier scene at the music temple **Paradiso Amsterdam** (Weteringschans 6-8; 31-20-626-4521; paradiso.nl), where dancers almost brush up against

the performers. You'll have to buy an inexpensive monthly membership in addition to the evening's ticket to enter this former church.

SATURDAY

5 *Rembrandt in the Morning* 9 a.m.

Every city seems to have art museums. But few can equal Amsterdam's. There's the **Van Gogh Museum** (vangoghmuseum.nl), with the world's largest collection of work by perhaps its most popular painter; the newly renovated **Stedelijk** (stedelijk.nl) for modern art; and the **Hermitage Amsterdam** (hermitage.nl), showing traveling treasures from the Hermitage in St. Petersburg. But Amsterdam belongs most profoundly to Rembrandt, and the

place to see his masterpieces — along with the rest of one of the world's greatest collections of art — is the **Rijksmuseum** (Jan Luijkenstraat 1; 31-20-674-7000; rijksmuseum.nl). Even if you've been there before, brave the crowds and go back.

6 *Go North* Noon

North Amsterdam has become an edgy cultural center populated by the young. It attracted MTV's offices, and a skate park and a hive of artists' studios moved into the same warehouse complex. The Eye Film Institute's spaceship of a building (eyefilm.nl) is on the Amstel River waterfront. Right off the NDSM ferry stop is the cheerful **IJ-Kantine** (Mt. Ondinaweg 15-17; 31-20-633-7162; ijkantine.nl), where parents tank up on caffeine while their children tackle one another in the play corner of the soaring light-filled dining room. A five-minute walk away is the **Noorderlicht** (NDSM wharf, T.T. Neveritaweg 33; 31-20-492-2770; noorderlichtcafe.nl), a sort of trans-

ABOVE Westergasfabriek, a former coal gas plant, has been reborn as a space for galleries, restaurants, and studios.

LEFT Gartine, a favorite spot for the much honored custom of taking afternoon tea on a weekend day.

OPPOSITE Upscale houseboats line up in a floating neighborhood on the Prinsengracht Canal.

parent hangar, where a cafe shelters an arty crowd who sit on mismatched chairs at driftwood tables. In summer, everyone sits outside, turning the industrial lots into partylike spaces.

7 *Afternoon Tea* 3 p.m.

The Dutch, even the younger generation, still like to take time out on weekend afternoons to practice the high art of tea. One favorite is the spread at **Gartine** (Taksteeg 7; 31-20-320-4132; gartine.nl; $$), a cozy cafe in the historic center. Another good option is the Amsterdam South branch of **De Bakkerswinkel** (Roelof Hartstraat 68; 31-20-662-3594; debakkerswinkel.nl; $$), a chain of bakeries with a homey atmosphere. At this outpost, manicured locals curl up on chairs and savor scones served with clotted cream.

8 *Dressed to the Nines* 4 p.m.

For some serious consuming, head to the renowned shopping zone known as the **Nine Streets**

(theninestreets.com), which is loaded with independent stores. Explore the boutiques and galleries for avant-garde or glamorous clothing, designer denim, and decorative objects. An essential stop close by is **Frozen Fountain** (Prinsengracht 645; 31-20-622-9375; frozenfountain.nl), stocked with contemporary furniture and practical yet often wacky home accessories. For 30 years, fans of Dutch design have shopped here for their Piet Hein Eek tables and Hella Jongerius vases.

9 *In the Red Light District* 8 p.m.

In 2010, the ambitious chef Rogier van Dam and his sommelier girlfriend, Elise Moeskops, opened the very respectable **Restaurant Lastage** (Geldersekade 29; 31-20-737-0811; restaurantlastage. nl; $$$$) in the midst of sex shops. Van Dam attempts to surprise his guests not only with the location but also with his elegant twist to Dutch cuisine.

SUNDAY

10 *Flat Food* 10 a.m.

The Dutch love their pancakes. Pancakes with cheese, pancakes with butter, and even pancake sushi. You name it, stick it in a pancake and they'll eat it. You'll find all these options and much more (how about endive, ham, Camembert cheese, and raspberry sauce?) at the often packed **Pancakes!** (Berenstraat 38; 31-20-528-9797; pancakesamsterdam.com; $$).

11 *Indoor Tropics* 1 p.m.

Even if you don't have the slightest interest in Holland's former colonies, which include Indonesia and Suriname, the **Tropical Museum** (Linnaeusstraat 2; 31-88-004-2800; tropenmuseum.nl) is worth a visit. The architecture — a towering and grand early-20th-century building that wraps around an entire city block — is impressive. And the gilded interiors, especially the library, hide many romantic nooks where you can read up on your next exotic adventure.

ABOVE Young painters at work in the Van Gogh Museum.

OPPOSITE Souvenir magnets at a street market.

THE BASICS

Take a train from Schiphol Airport into Amsterdam. In the city, there are trams and a subway, but the Dutch way to get around is on a bicycle.

Hotel De L'Europe
Nieuwe Dolenstraat 2-14
31-20-531-1777
leurope.nl
$$$$
Recently renovated 19th-century grand hotel on the Amstel River and Muntplein square. One wing of suites is inspired by Dutch master painters.

Conservatorium
Van Baerlestraat 27
31-20-570-0000
conservatoriumhotel.com
$$$$
Contemporary grand hotel in a smartly repurposed landmark 19th-century building.

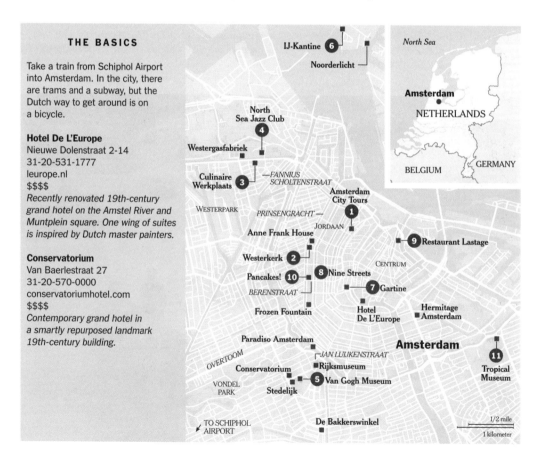

Haarlem

It could be argued that one of the best introductions to Amsterdam lies 20 minutes outside of its borders, in the tiny jewel of a city called Haarlem. There, you'll find bustling restaurants, smooth-as-glass canals, ornate 17th-century architecture, a thriving bike culture, and museums rich with both art and Nazi-resistance history. And just a short bus ride away, there's even a beach and a national park.
— BY BETH GREENFIELD

FRIDAY

1 *Old Master* 3 p.m.

Haarlem is fiercely proud of Frans Hals, and rightly so. A pre-eminent painter of the 17th-century Dutch Golden Age, he lived nearly all of his life in Haarlem, painting his fellow citizens with a style and mastery that was recognized in his own day and admired by the Impressionists 200 years later. The **Frans Hals Museum** (Groot Heiligland 62; 31-23-511-5775; franshalsmuseum.nl) is small, but it has the world's largest collection of Hals paintings, including dramatic, larger-than-life portraits and genre paintings that belie their intimate surroundings, plus militia-company portraits. Work of his contemporaries is on display as well, along with furniture and decorative objects. The tile-roofed brick building is a 17th-century former old men's home, and there's a peaceful, leafy courtyard with greenery and flowers.

2 *Line Up for Frites* 5 p.m.

Leaving the museum, wind your way through quiet brick lanes and buzzing main thoroughfares lined with cafes and boutiques and jammed with walkers and bicyclists. Soon you will find yourself in the center of Haarlem's action: the stunning main square, **Grote Markt**. It's a dramatically sweeping space, hemmed in by beautiful brick gabled buildings and the alfresco tables of high-ceilinged brasseries, where people cram in to enjoy glasses of beer or wine at the end of balmy workdays. Vendors hawk little

paper plates of fresh raw herring with chopped onion. Join the line at the tiny **De Haerlemsche Vlaamse** (Spekstraat 3; 31-23-532-5991) and buy a paper cone of perfect frites with a dozen toppings to choose from.

3 *As You Like It* 8 p.m.

Stempels (Klokhuisplein 9; 31-23-512-3910; stempelsinhaarlem.nl; $$$), a hip hotel-restaurant-brasserie-lounge complex, occupies the building that used to house the Enschedé printing company, which printed Dutch currency and stamps there. The pub is in the former printer's office, and the restaurant has something for everyone on a menu that changes frequently. One constant: a nice stiff martini.

SATURDAY

4 *Under the Spire* 10 a.m.

Return to the Grote Markt to see it in its Saturday guise, as a large, busy farmers' market with bundles of white asparagus, hunks of Gouda and Edam cheese, and baked goods. There's much more to buy, from designer wear to handmade toys, in the multitude of shops on nearby streets. The action is all dwarfed, though, by the square's star attraction: the Gothic **St. Bavo Church** (31-23-553-2040; bavo.nl), whose elaborately ornamented spire juts 249 feet into the sky, visible from just about any spot in town.

OPPOSITE In spring, rent a bike in Haarlem and head out toward Lisse for a technicolor display of tulip fields.

RIGHT Teylers Museum, one collector's quirky version of a natural history museum.

The church's light-filled interior soars with towering white transepts and a gigantic crimson and silver Müller pipe organ that was played by a young Mozart in the 18th century; organists now frequently give free concerts. The grand floor is made up of nearly 1,500 worn ebony gravestones marking tombs below, including that of Frans Hals. To attend a service, return at 10 tomorrow morning.

5 *Lunch on the Square* Noon

Grand Café Brinkmann (Grote Markt 13; 31-23-532-3111; grandcafebrinkmann.nl; $$), in business since the 19th century, is a sprawling brasserie with outdoor seating on Grote Markt, and a good place for lunch with a view of the human parade. It serves pastas, meats, salads, and sandwiches. And though the massive, high-ceilinged interior manages also to pull off a cozy feel behind its floor-to-ceiling windows, most folks prefer to join the nonstop conviviality in the square by grabbing a coveted outside table.

6 *Wartime Haven* 1 p.m.

Perhaps the most fervently beloved place in Haarlem is the **Corrie ten Boom Museum** (Barteljoris-straat 19; 31-23-531-0823; corrietenboom.com), which is tucked down a narrow lane and draws admirers from all over the world. It is the house that the Ten Boom family, deeply religious Christians, ran as a safe haven for Jews hiding from the Nazis during World War II. The family was eventually caught and sent to concentration camps. But Corrie ten Boom survived, wrote 22 books about her experiences, and died in 1983 on her 91st birthday. "Throughout this house, 800 Jewish lives were saved," the guide said on one tour, before allowing everyone to take a turn

ABOVE The beach at Bloemendaal, on the North Sea, is a short bus ride out of town.

RIGHT The Dutch art at the Frans Hals Museum includes the world's largest collection of paintings by Hals, who lived and worked in Haarlem.

shimmying into the tight space in the bedroom wall that had served as a hiding place.

7 *Off to the Sea* 3 p.m.

Make the rest of the day a wind-in-your-hair experience by hopping the No. 81 bus to the beautiful beach of **Bloemendaal aan Zee**. This short jaunt takes you to another world — a sweeping, sandy beach along the North Sea, a resort with a lineup of sleek beachfront restaurants, and the rolling dunes of a nature reserve, **Zuid-Kennemerland National Park** (np-zuidkennemerland.nl). It's an easygoing, come-one-come-all kind of place: kids bounce gleefully on a series of huge public trampolines lined up in the sand while their hipster parents clink beer glasses in the nearby cafes. Come nighttime, D.J.'s take over the clubs and a well-dressed crowd turns out to party.

8 *Salad and Sand* 7 p.m.

At **Beachclub San Blas** (31-23-573-2172; sanblas.nl; $$), kick back barefoot for pastas, salads, seafood, and cocktails, right at the edge of the sand. The vibe is festive, the food is tasty, and you can watch the sunset from a sea-facing counter.

SUNDAY

9 *What a Cyclist Sees* 9 a.m.

You've been seeing bikes roll over the streets since you arrived, so join them for a few hours. Find wheels and advice on the best routes at **Rent a Bike Haarlem** (Parklaan 47; 31-23-542-1195; rentabikehaarlem.nl). Spend some time tooling through the heart of town,

before streets get too crowded, to gain a locals' perspective. Then explore the quieter outskirts, passing picturesque canals and quiet residential streets. If you're really up for a pedal adventure, this is the place to be. Follow N200 back out toward the beach, exploring the small communities en route, or head in the general direction of Lisse, a route that in springtime will take you past Technicolor tulip fields. And those are sights not to be missed.

10 *One Man's Fancy* Noon

Not far from the Grote Markt, right on the calm Spaarne River, is the **Teylers Museum** (Spaarne 16; 31-23-516-0960; teylersmuseum.nl), the Netherlands' oldest museum. The pieces laid out through this

building, built through the benefits of the will of a merchant and philanthropist, Pieter Teyler van der Hulst, range from the quirky to the urbane. There are fossils, skeletons, tusks, crystals, and antique, mad-scientist inventions, many displayed in the stunning, sun-drenched Oval Room, plus salon-style paintings from the Dutch and French schools.

ABOVE Gothic-style St. Bavo Church towers above Grote Markt, Haarlem's main square.

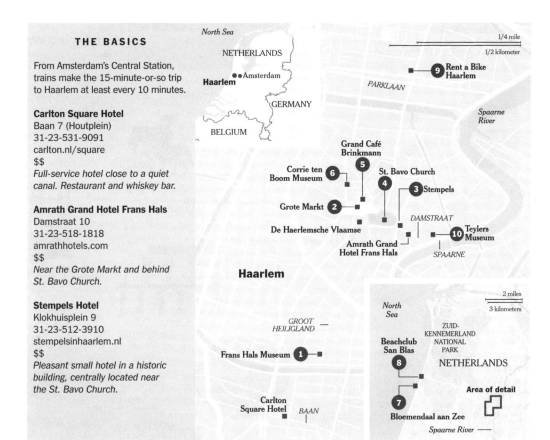

THE BASICS

From Amsterdam's Central Station, trains make the 15-minute-or-so trip to Haarlem at least every 10 minutes.

Carlton Square Hotel
Baan 7 (Houtplein)
31-23-531-9091
carlton.nl/square
$$
Full-service hotel close to a quiet canal. Restaurant and whiskey bar.

Amrath Grand Hotel Frans Hals
Damstraat 10
31-23-518-1818
amrathhotels.com
$$
Near the Grote Markt and behind St. Bavo Church.

Stempels Hotel
Klokhuisplein 9
31-23-512-3910
stempelsinhaarlem.nl
$$
Pleasant small hotel in a historic building, centrally located near the St. Bavo Church.

Madeira 286

CORSICA 192

SOUTH WEST

Honfleur & Deauville 1

Santiago de Compostela 222

Biarritz 154

San Sebastián 210

Porto 282

Pamplona & Bilbao 216

MADRID 204

BARCELONA 250

Tarragona 244

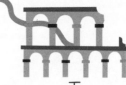

LISBON 272

Évora 278

Seville 226

Valencia 232

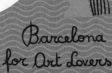

Barcelona for Art Lovers 256

Paris

"You'd have a ball! You'd go to a party every night, drink nothing but Champagne, swim in perfume, and have a new love affair every hour on the hour!" These lines were spoken by Fred Astaire to Audrey Hepburn in the film Funny Face *in 1957, but the vision of Paris that it caricatures stays with us today. And Paris never disappoints. Far smaller than London, Madrid, Berlin, or Rome, it is an embraceable city that can be walked from one end to the other in hours. Within its artfully contrived spaces, it operates on many levels. There is a constant interplay between the permanence and grandeur of monumental Paris and the serendipity and surprise of intimate Paris. There is a perpetual anticipation when you turn a corner that something wonderful is waiting to be discovered. It may be true love. It may be a marble sculpture. Or it may just be the perfect espresso.*
— BY ELAINE SCIOLINO

FRIDAY

1 *Two Wheels Along the Seine* 2 p.m.

Rent a Vélib' bike (velib.fr) and get an overview of Paris in a ride along the Seine. Locations for these publicly owned bicycles dot the city, but pick yours up at **Notre-Dame de Paris**, near the medallion in the pavement that marks the origin of all the roads of France. Turn in the direction of the Île St.-Louis and take bike path No. 10 (paris.fr/velo), past monuments including the National Assembly and Les Invalides, where Napoleon is buried. Drop your bike at the foot of the Pont de l'Alma bridge and stop by the Quai Branly museum, one of the city's newest (37 quai Branly; 33-1-56-61-70-00; quaibranly.fr), which is devoted to African, Asian, Oceanic, and pre-Columbian art. Then it's a short walk to the Eiffel Tower.

2 *Picture Perfect* 5 p.m.

Across the Iéna Bridge at the Place du Trocadéro is **La Cité de l'Architecture et du Patrimoine** museum

OPPOSITE Lounging by the Seine, Paris's charismatic river, within sight of Notre-Dame cathedral.

RIGHT Care to tour by bicycle? Borrow a city-owned Vélib' bike at one of the docking locations and pedal away.

(1 place du Trocadéro et du 11 novembre; 33-1-58-51-52-00; citechaillot.fr), a shrine to 12 centuries of French architecture. Nearby streets and pocket parks offer some of the best views of Paris. Put yourself in one: a selfie with the Eiffel Tower behind you.

3 *Bistro Best* 8:30 p.m.

If you go to only one Paris bistro in your life, go to **Paul Bert** (18 rue Paul Bert; 33-1-43-72-24-01; $$$). Its owner, Bertrand Auboyneau, will warmly welcome you in this former horsemeat butcher shop, with its zinc-topped bar, wooden tables, and red, yellow, and blue tiled floors. The food is traditional, perfectly prepared, seasonal French bistro cuisine, delivered with exceptional service. It's the favorite Paris bistro of Jean-Claude Ribaut, a food critic for *Le Monde*.

SATURDAY

4 *Early to the Orsay* 9:15 a.m.

No matter how many times you have been to the **Musée d'Orsay** (62 rue de Lille; 33-1-40-49-48-14; musee-orsay.fr), the repository of the world's greatest collection of Impressionist works, it remains a must destination, especially if you haven't seen it since it reopened in 2011 after extensive renovation. Space within its well loved building, a Beaux-Arts former

railway station, was reorganized to add new galleries, and white walls were replaced by backdrops in deep gray, midnight blue, vermilion, violet, and green. It's always crowded — nearly three million visitors a year — so get there before it opens at 9:30. Even better, reserve tickets online.

ABOVE A sculpture by Auguste Rodin at the Musée Rodin. Admission to the garden, where many of the artist's works are displayed, costs only a few euros.

BELOW The Quai Branly museum, one of the city's newest, shows African, Asian, Oceanic, and pre-Columbian art.

OPPOSITE A favorite photo op: the Eiffel Tower from across the Seine at the Place du Trocadéro.

5 *Rodin for a Euro* 11:30 a.m.

Museums in Paris are expensive. Multiday museum passes make them less pricey, but only if you have time to cram in a lot of museums. At the **Musée Rodin** (19 boulevard des Invalides; 33-1-44-18-61-10; musee-rodin.fr), admission to the garden, which displays some of Auguste Rodin's most famous sculptures, is inexpensive, and the garden cafe offers a respectable and quick lunch.

6 *Bargains for Back Home* 2 p.m.

To pick up useful gifts that say "Paris," head to one of the city's five **La Vaissellerie** porcelain and crystal shops. The website (lavaissellerie.fr) gives the addresses. What's offered at the shops ranges from plastic trays with Paris scenes to white Limoges porcelain plates and bowls for half what they would cost elsewhere. The best bargains fill bins outside. Worried about breakage on the trip back home? Wrap your purchases in bistro-style cotton

dishtowels and napkins from Toto (toto.fr), a textiles shop that also has several locations.

7 *Meal of a Lifetime* 8:30 p.m.

You've saved money on shopping and are staying in a reasonably priced hotel. So this once in your life, don't you deserve to experience the cuisine of an iconic Paris master chef? If the answer is yes, turn yourself over to **Guy Savoy** at his three-star namesake restaurant (11 quai de Conti; 33-1-43-80-40-61 guysavoy.com; $$$$). Savoy mingles with the crowd and poses for pictures. The tasting menus are hallucinating-expensive: hundreds of euros, without wine. (Weekday lunch is considerably less.) Savoy's signature dish, artichoke soup with black truffles, is a favorite of Nicolas Sarkozy. In addition to his main restaurant, Savoy has six lower-priced alternative restaurants in Paris.

8 *Street de Jazz* 11 p.m.

Paris went wild for jazz in the 1920s and has nurtured it ever since. One of Paris's more durable spots for jazz is **Le Duc des Lombards** (42 rue des Lombards; 33-1-42-33-22-88; ducdeslombards.com). To "promote, celebrate, and democratize" all jazz forms, it has formed an association with two other clubs on the same street, **Le Sunset/Le Sunside** at No. 60 (33-1-40-26-46-60; sunset-sunside.com) and **Le Baiser Salé** at No. 58 (33-1-42-33-37-71; lebaisersale.com).

9 *Shopping Martyrs* 10 a.m.

Cars are banned on Sundays until 1 p.m. on the **Rue des Martyrs**, a half-mile-long, mostly uphill street in Montmartre, making its specialty food shops, boutiques, and restaurants easy to navigate. The lower end of the street has been gentrified by upwardly mobile families moving in on the heels of artists, filmmakers, and writers. The upper part, with cabarets and clubs and proximity to the still somewhat seedy Pigalle, retains a distinctly bohemian feel. All along are delightful visual detours: a glimpse of a private gated courtyard at Cité Malesherbes; tranquil, tree-lined Place Charles Dullin; a steep staircase at the end of the Rue Chappe. Floor-to-ceiling bookcases at the **Librairie des Abbesses** bookstore (30 rue Yvonne le Tac; 33-1-46-06-84-30; librairiedesabbesses.blogspot.com) are trimmed in red and gold. At **Chine Machine** (100 rue des Martyrs; 33-1-80-50-27-66), which opens at noon, you might find a Loewe handbag for 35 euros or suede Escada pumps for 7.

10 *Lunch With Love* 1 p.m.

For lunch, head to one of the restaurants or bars at the lively **Place des Abbesses**, with its Belle Époque Hector Guimard Métro station that was made famous in the 2001 film *Amélie*. One choice for

your meal is **Le Progrès** (7 rue des Trois Frères; 33-1-42-64-07-37; $$), a comfortable bar and brasserie where customers park their baby strollers at the entrance. There's beer on tap, a menu that revolves around various duck dishes, and upscale drinks like caipirinhas and black Russians. Nearby, you can take a photo in front of the wall tiled with 311 declarations of love in the park at the Square Jehan-Rictus. Another lunch option is to walk back down to **Terra Corsa** (42 rue des Martyrs; 33-1-48-78-20-70)

for a glass of its red wine and a platter of its Corsican charcuterie and cheese, by far the best in Paris.

ABOVE Much smaller than London, Berlin, or many other European capitals, Paris is an embraceable size, walkable from one end to the other in hours.

OPPOSITE Notre-Dame-de-Lorette with Sacré-Coeur in the background. Shop nearby on the Rue des Martyrs.

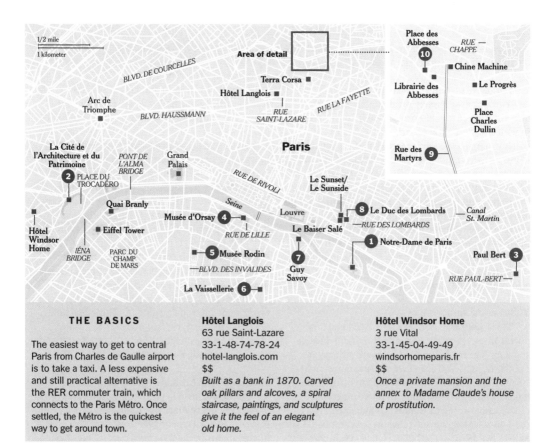

THE BASICS

The easiest way to get to central Paris from Charles de Gaulle airport is to take a taxi. A less expensive and still practical alternative is the RER commuter train, which connects to the Paris Métro. Once settled, the Métro is the quickest way to get around town.

Hôtel Langlois
63 rue Saint-Lazare
33-1-48-74-78-24
hotel-langlois.com
$$
Built as a bank in 1870. Carved oak pillars and alcoves, a spiral staircase, paintings, and sculptures give it the feel of an elegant old home.

Hôtel Windsor Home
3 rue Vital
33-1-45-04-49-49
windsorhomeparis.fr
$$
Once a private mansion and the annex to Madame Claude's house of prostitution.

Paris
at Night

Late-night Paris belongs to the stroller, the idle walker with no purpose except to roam. There is always beauty to be discovered, and perhaps even adventure and love. By day, Paris streets are clogged with too many people in a hurry. Traffic snarls the intersections and circles. Shoppers lead with their elbows at the bargain stalls in front of the Galeries Lafayette and Printemps department stores. Bicyclists compete with motorcyclists to frustrate even the most determined pedestrians. At night, though, the streets empty, the pace slows. Inhibitions evaporate. Restaurants empty as nightclubs fill. The later the hour, the fewer the people, the more closely Paris enfolds you.
— BY ELAINE SCIOLINO

FRIDAY–SATURDAY

1 *Bridge to Discovery* 7 p.m.

By day the **Pont Royal** is an unremarkable stone bridge streaming with motorists making their way from the Left to the Right Bank. At night, as artfully lighted monuments emerge from their darkened surroundings, it is transformed into a platform of visual seduction. Stroll north across the Seine, with the imposing facade of the Louvre dominating the foreground. To the right, the towers of Notre-Dame and the dome of the Institut de France appear through the trees. Farther on, the illuminated curves of the Grand Palais's glass roofs beckon. From behind, the twin clocks of the Musée d'Orsay burn bright; the tip of the Eiffel Tower peeks through. Look up as you approach the end of the bridge for a glimpse of Jean-Baptiste Carpeaux's small sculpture on the Flore Pavilion of the Louvre, with its laughing, naked nymph. It is a moment of magic. You look around — no one else seems to notice. The city is yours.

2 *Forget Mona Lisa* 7:30 p.m.

On Friday evening, when it is open until 9:45 p.m., seek out the secrets of the **Louvre** (33-1-40-20-50-50; louvre.fr), its hidden, little-noticed treasures. Who knew that the right hand of *Winged Victory* sits

in a protective glass case to the statue's left? And what about Michelangelo's two marble nude slaves, meant to adorn the tomb of a pope and not quite finished? The 14th-century portrait of Jean II le Bon in profile, the oldest French portrait painting of a single individual and perhaps the oldest in Western Europe, sits alone on the second floor of the Richelieu wing. Look for the Degas pastel *La Sortie du Bain*; Charles V's gold scepter, carried by the kings at their coronations; vestiges of Khorsabad Palace in what is now Iraq. And there is the unsettling sculpture *Hermaphrodite Asleep*, a second-century Roman copy probably inspired by a Greek original. From behind, the figure is a sensuous female nude; the other side reveals male genitalia.

3 *Perfect Square* 9:30 p.m.

Outside again, find the perfectly proportioned 16th- and 17th-century square courtyard at the Louvre's east corner known as the **Cour Carrée**. Peeking out through each of its four archways, you can see the Louvre's brightly illuminated Pyramid on the west, the St.-Germain l'Auxerrois Church on the east, the Rue de Rivoli on the north and the Institut de France on the south. Sit on a bench and watch the play of light.

4 *Nighttime Palace* 10 p.m.

There is nothing particularly Japanese about the **Palais de Tokyo** (13 avenue du Président-Wilson; 33-1-47-23-54-01; palaisdetokyo.com). But this contemporary art space has emerged as a place to browse, eat, and meet until midnight. In a city

OPPOSITE Stroll around Paris after dark and discover its beauty in a new dimension.

RIGHT The bar scene as the Paris night plays out.

where fusion food tends to be either overpriced or just not good, **Tokyo Eat** ($$$), the restaurant on the main floor, serves well-prepared, well-priced dishes: assorted steamed and stir-fried vegetables, paper-thin raw tuna in sesame oil and eggplant caviar, beef sate with thick French fries and arugula salad. The exhibitions (ranging from courageously avant-garde to just plain dreadful) are mounted in vast, warehouselike spaces. The kitschy Black Block gift shop sells funk — books, but also sex toys and action figures. Leave in time for a quick walk to the Trocadéro to view the midnight show across the river at the Eiffel Tower: every hour on the hour from dusk until midnight, the tower lights up with twinkly lights that sparkle like the whitest diamonds.

5 *Play Until Dawn* 12:30 a.m.

Looking for a poker game? The **Cercle Clichy Montmartre** (84 rue de Clichy; 33-1-48-78-32-85; pokerccm.com) is calling. A gentleman gamblers' haunt in the 19th century, renovated as a working-class restaurant in 1901, the Cercle was used by the Nazis as a horse stable and barracks. Reopened in 1947, it dazzles with 30-foot ceilings, carved moldings, and grand mirrors. Worn bentwood chairs and bar stools, patched tile floors, and tawny, nicotine-stained walls give it just enough Zolaesque grit. In addition to poker games, there is multicolore, a bizarre combination of roulette and English billiards that's usually found in social clubs, not casinos. The only disincentive is the fee for an annual membership (about 30 euros), required because there are games of chance. Women get in free. Once inside, you can hold 'em and fold 'em until 5:45 a.m.

SATURDAY–SUNDAY

6 *Literary Warmup* 5 p.m.

Have a drink and a light snack at **Les Éditeurs** (4 carrefour de l'Odéon; 33-1-43-26-67-76; lesediteurs. fr; $$$) in St.-Germain, a cafe frequented by a literary

ABOVE A nighttime view from the Arc de Triomphe.

LEFT A late-night picnic on the bank of the Seine.

set. Settle in on a red banquette, order steak tartare or a cheeseburger, and pull one of the books off the well-filled shelves. Reading them is encouraged. Don't read French? Never mind. It's the ambience that counts.

7 *Above It All* 7 p.m.

Climb to the top of the **Arc de Triomphe** (33-1-55-37-73-77; arc-de-triomphe.monuments-nationaux.fr). It's a less popular overview of Paris than the one from the top of the Eiffel Tower, but less stressful to get to, much more accessible, and closer to the city's heart. Look down at the flow of lights as traffic streams toward you and away from you on the Champs-Élysées.

8 *Let the Show Go On* 8 p.m.

Visitors tend to shy away from live performances in Paris. But there's plenty to choose from. Top of the list is the gilded Belle Époque **Opéra Garnier**

BELOW The Louvre and its illuminated Pyramid.

(Place de l'Opéra; 33-1-71-25-24-23; operadeparis.fr), with its colonnades and statues, where you sit in red velvet seats under a vaulted ceiling painted by Marc Chagall; if nothing's on, try the colder but acoustically superior Opéra Bastille or Salle Pleyel, or the Théâtre du Châtelet. *Time Out*'s music and night life site can guide you to concert or opera tickets (timeout.fr/paris/en/music-nightlife).

9 *Night-Owl Dining* 10:30 p.m.

No matter how late the performance ends, find old-fashioned gastronomic excellence—until 5 a.m.—near Les Halles at **La Tour Montlhéry—Chez Denise** (5 rue des Prouvaires; 33-1-42-36-21-82; $$$$). Try leeks vinaigrette and calf's liver with some of the best frites in Paris.

10 *Lights Out* 1 a.m.

The city turns off the lights on most public structures at about 1 a.m. It is a Cinderella moment

in which suddenly, they seem to disappear. The jazz clubs and most bars shut down at 2 a.m. So better to linger on the bridges and banks of the Seine, still lighted by streetlamps, which take on a muted, more distant look.

11 *Gold Illusion* 2 a.m.

Silencio (142 rue de Montmartre; silencio-club. com/en), which is named after the creepy theater in David Lynch's 2001 *Mulholland Drive*, is an architectural execution of Lynch's cinematic passion for shapes, textures, light, and illusion. As you enter,

the darkness of the black staircase opens into a series of golden spaces, with soft gold leaf on arches and walls constructed from small blocks of raw oak. Walls are covered with natural materials like decomposed marble. Ceilings are lined with strips of golden metal that function as distortion mirrors. There is a 24-seat movie theater and a loungelike library and a stage with a translucent and reflective dance floor. Early in the night the club is members-only, but from midnight until 6 a.m., the doors open to all.

ABOVE Stop in mid-river on a bridge across the Seine to see the play of light and water after dark.

OPPOSITE At the top of the list for seeing a live performance is the gilded Belle Époque Opéra Garnier.

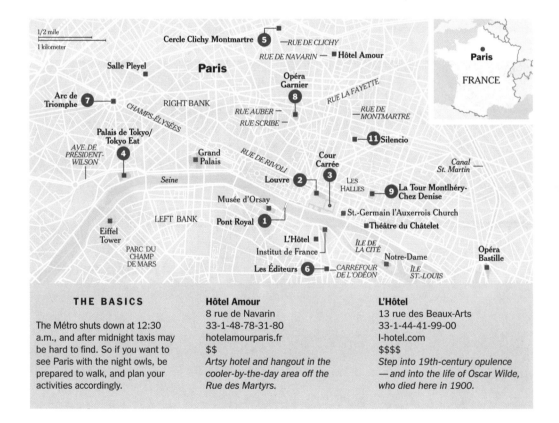

THE BASICS

The Métro shuts down at 12:30 a.m., and after midnight taxis may be hard to find. So if you want to see Paris with the night owls, be prepared to walk, and plan your activities accordingly.

Hôtel Amour
8 rue de Navarin
33-1-48-78-31-80
hotelamourparis.fr
$$
Artsy hotel and hangout in the cooler-by-the-day area off the Rue des Martyrs.

L'Hôtel
13 rue des Beaux-Arts
33-1-44-41-99-00
l-hotel.com
$$$$
Step into 19th-century opulence —and into the life of Oscar Wilde, who died here in 1900.

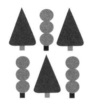

Paris Gardens

Famous for its monuments, Paris is also rich in green spaces, with more than 400 gardens and parks, woods and squares. The grandest are the famous parks: the Bois de Vincennes and Bois de Boulogne at the city's edges, the Tuileries and the Luxembourg Gardens in its heart. But tucked away unnoticed by most travelers is more, much of it the legacy of former President Jacques Chirac, who in 18 years as mayor of Paris put his personal stamp on his city by painting its hidden corners green. Lightly trafficked and often quirky, the small gardens of Paris can be ideal places to explore, relax, play sports, dine well. — BY ELAINE SCIOLINO

FRIDAY

1 *Artifice as Beauty* 3 p.m.

Just off the Champs-Élysées, next to the Palais de la Découverte and to the right of a sculpture of a poet daydreaming about his lovers, a path leads down into a stage set called **Jardin de la Nouvelle France**. Built in the late 19th century, the garden remains a lovely illusion where nothing is quite what it appears at first sight. The rocks that form the pond and waterfall are sculptured from cement; so is the "wooden" footbridge. But here in one of the most urban swaths of Paris are 1.7 acres of semi-tamed wilderness. Sit on a bench and let yourself be enveloped by evergreens, maples, bamboo, lilacs, and ivy. There are lemon trees; a Mexican orange; a bush called a wavyleaf silktassel, with drooping flowers, that belongs in an Art Nouveau painting; and another whose leaves smell of caramel in the fall.

2 *Banana Tree Break* 4:30 p.m.

Have a hot chocolate or a glass of wine at the cafe garden of the **Petit Palais** museum (Avenue Winston Churchill; 33-1-53-43-40-00; petitpalais.paris.fr) with its palm and banana trees and sculptures and mosaic floors lighted from below. Marble tables with metal chairs offer the ideal setting to watch the museum's

stone walls change from buff to tawny yellow as the sun moves. Inside is a portrait of Jean-Charles Adolphe Alphand, who designed the Jardin de la Nouvelle France (formerly called the Jardin de la Vallée Suisse) as well as more famous parks like the Bois de Boulogne and the Parc Monceau. He is in a top hat, his pince-nez hanging from his black overcoat.

3 *Island Dining* 8 p.m.

Picture dinner in an island garden in the middle of a huge park, only a few miles from the center of Paris. Then experience it at **Le Chalet des Îles** (Lac inférieur du Bois de Boulogne, 16th Arrondissement; 33-1-42-88-04-69; lechaletdesiles.net; $$$$). This rustic pink-and-green Second Empire chalet with outdoor terraces is surrounded by a lake and reachable by a minute-long boat ride.

SATURDAY

4 *Parisian High* 9 a.m.

Start the day with a walk or a jog along the **Promenade Plantée** (promenade-plantee.org), a strip park that follows the defunct Vincennes freight railway line. Climb the staircase above the red-brick-arched, boutique-and-gallery-filled Viaduc des Arts near the Bastille Métro and head east. You will pass through the Jardin de Reuilly, with planted terraces and statues, and into a landscape of rock waterfalls, railroad tunnels, rose bushes, and wisteria. Near the path are a police headquarters decorated with 12 reproductions of Michelangelo's *The Dying Slave* and an immigration museum (histoire-immigration.fr)

OPPOSITE Off the avenues and away from the buzz, Paris tells another story in its parks and hidden patches of green.

RIGHT The Fountain of the Medicis, in the Luxembourg Garden, was built for Marie de Medicis, the grandmother of Louis XIV.

in a little-heralded Arts and Crafts masterpiece. The Promenade was an inspiration for New York's High Line park.

5 *You Are George Sand* 11 a.m.

At the end of a narrow path at 16 rue Chaptal in the Ninth Arrondissement is the **Musée de la Vie Romantique** (33-1-55-31-95-67; vie-romantique.paris. fr), once the home of the 19th-century artist Ary Scheffer. Its garden offers a country setting and a view of mid-19th-century Paris. Sit among the poppies and foxglove, sip tea (a cafe opens in the summer), and pretend to be George Sand, whose personal effects (and even a lock of her hair) have been assembled in a reconstructed drawing room inside.

6 *Montmartre Living Room* 2 p.m.

At **Sacré-Cœur Basilica**, the white church at the city's highest point, light a candle and take in the view. Then find the adjacent **Parc de la Turlure** (Rue de la Bonne or Rue du Chevalier de la Barre), a series of discrete spaces that form a sort of garden apartment — a living room of grass, a corridor with a linden arcade, a bedroom that seems to belong to oiled women in bikinis, and a rec room for boules-playing. Around the corner at 12 rue Cortot, the 17th-century abbey that is now the **Musée de Montmartre** (museedemontmartre.fr) documents this district's 2,000-year history and has a tree- and bird-filled garden that was painted by Renoir in *The Garden in the Rue Cortot, Montmartre*. From an upper-floor window, look down into a working vineyard no bigger than a basketball court (Clos Montmartre, 14-18 rue des Saules). Its grapes are said to make the most expensive bad wine in the city.

7 *Medici Hideaway* 5 p.m.

The vast **Luxembourg Garden** can overwhelm with too many joggers, sunbathers, musicians,

ABOVE The Luxembourg Garden is used daily by Parisians for jogging, play, and quiet moments under the trees.

LEFT To those who are not in the know, a secluded Parisian garden is a rare find, even with a sign to point the way.

newspaper readers, pony riders, chess players, and tulip admirers. But it was loved for the beauty of its layout and its statuary by Baudelaire, Victor Hugo, Balzac, Hemingway, and Sartre. Find the shaded, quiet 17th-century Fountain of the Medicis (senat.fr/visite/jardin/fontaine_medicis.html) named after Marie de Medicis (Louis XIV's grandmother) and built on her instructions.

8 *French Classics* 8 p.m.

La Maison de l'Amérique Latine (217 boulevard St.-Germain; 33-1-49-54-75-10; mal217.org/restaurant-bar; $$$$) serves classic French cuisine in an elegant "jardin à la Française" tucked behind two 18th-century

ABOVE A sculpture of a poet dreaming of love stands at the entrance to the Jardin de la Nouvelle France, just off the Champs-Élyseés.

BELOW A Luxembourg Garden fence serves as display space.

mansions. Thirty tables under white parasols overlook two acres of manicured lawn.

SUNDAY

9 *Refuge for a Rendezvous* 11 a.m.

Jardin des Plantes (best entrance, 36 rue Geoffroy-Saint-Hilaire; 33-1-40-79-56-01; mnhn.fr) with its greenhouses and odd species and identifying labels, can seem too much like work. But there are gardens within the garden, including a spiraling stone walkway up to a pergola of iron, copper, bronze, lead, and gold that is France's oldest metal decorative construction. Find the concrete tunnel beneath the main garden that leads to the craggy, flowering

Jardin Alpin. Deep inside is a space secluded enough to have become a trysting place—a valley with a stream and a leafy canopy that only the strongest beams of light can penetrate. If your companion is the right one, share a kiss.

10 *Feel Close to the Seine* 1 p.m.

For quiet magic, join Paris insiders passing the time on the lawn and benches of the **Square du Vert-Galant** (equipement.paris.fr/square-du-vert-

galant-2825), a spit of land at the westernmost tip of the Île de la Cité that resembles the prow of a ship. Bring a picnic lunch and enjoy it with the Louvre on the right, the dome of the Institut de France on the left, and the river on both sides and straight ahead. To get there, walk down two flights of stairs at the equestrian statue of Henri IV on the Pont Neuf. It is here, in the 1991 film *Les Amants du Pont Neuf*, released in the United States as *The Lovers on the Bridge*, that Juliette Binoche, as a homeless artist who is going blind, struggles to paint her companion's portrait.

ABOVE The secluded Jardin Alpin in the Jardin des Plantes.

OPPOSITE The cafe garden of the Petit Palais.

THE BASICS

Find guidance to parks and gardens at paris.fr or paris-walking-tours.com, or in *Paris: 100 Jardins Insolites* by Martine Dumond. Or you can simply wander on foot, confident that around the next corner there will be something new.

Hotel Lancaster
7 rue de Berri
33-1-40-76-40-76
hotel-lancaster.fr
$$$$
Not far from the Arc de Triomphe. Ask for a room overlooking the cork oaks and jasmine.

Hotel des Grandes Écoles
75 rue du Cardinal Lemoine
33-1-43-26-79-23
hotel-grandes-ecoles.com
$$
In three houses surrounding a beautiful flower garden in the Latin Quarter.

Honfleur & Deauville

On France's northern coast, in Normandy, the stretch of craggy, windswept shore known as the Côte Fleurie attracts weekenders from Paris, British tourists from across the English Channel, Sunday sailors, and artists drawn by the same play of light and color that caught the eye of the Impressionists. The visitors cluster in seaside villages, especially Honfleur, the old port at the mouth of the Seine, and Deauville, a beach town known for its September film festival. They walk the cobbled lanes and the beach promenades, dance and gamble in bars and all-night casinos, sample seafood-laden local cuisine, and quaff Calvados, the apple liqueur made in Normandy's famous orchards. Although the Rothschilds, Gérard Depardieu, and Yves Saint Laurent are among current and former homeowners on the Côte Fleurie, a casual ambience prevails and mega-yachts with helipads are rare.

— BY SETH SHERWOOD

FRIDAY

1 *Ravished by Honfleur* 3 p.m.

Explore the byways and shops of Honfleur, an old maritime town whose 17th-century buildings escaped the destruction of World War II. Victor Hugo, who called Honfleur "a ravishing port full of masts and sails, crowned with green hills and surrounded by narrow houses," would still find it familiar. French tourists fill the spider web of cobbled streets, ambling past town houses — some in red brick, some in gray stone, some with shingled facades — that sport copper lanterns or wooden signs advertising candle and soap stores. Almost every lane seems to turn up some romantic hideaway or hole-in-the-wall. Just as abundant are galleries and exhibition spaces — no surprise in a town that begs to be painted. Find the **Église Ste.-Catherine**, whose exterior of wooden boards and shingles was transferred to canvas by Raoul Dufy. Now it adorns postcards that fill souvenir shops. Inside, the church rises to a curved wooden ceiling that looks like the upside-down hull of a boat.

OPPOSITE Bars and cafes line the old Port at Honfleur.

RIGHT Movie stars' names painted along the boardwalk in Deauville. The town's annual festival of American film has attracted stars like Meryl Streep and Clint Eastwood.

2 *The Minimalist* 5 p.m.

Stop at **Maisons Satie** (67 boulevard Charles V; 33-2-31-89-11-11; ot-honfleur.fr/decouvrir-honfleur/les-lieux-de-visite/les-maisons-satie), a high-tech, borderline-surrealistic museum devoted to the minimalist music and eccentricities of the composer and writer Erik Satie. Satie spent part of his childhood in Honfleur before moving to Paris, where he became part of an artistic avant-garde that also included Ravel and Picasso. Then wander to the old harbor, which was painted by Georges Seurat, the founder of Neo-Impressionism, and today is surrounded by tiny bars and expansive terrace cafes serving Belgian beers and croque-monsieurs. Settle in for a drink under a cafe umbrella, and watch the boats.

3 *Asian Tinge* 8 p.m.

At Place Hamelin, two excellent restaurants have sprouted — you can take your choice. Under the wooden beams of **Entre Terre et Mer** (12-14 place Hamelin; 33-2-31-89-70-60; entreterreetmer-honfleur.com; $$$) fish are prepared with occasional Asian ingredients. Opposite, in the spare black-and-white dining room of the Michelin-starred **Sa.Qua.Na** (22 place Hamelin; 33-2-31-89-40-80; alexandre-bourdas.com; $$$$), dishes also have an Eastern flair, courtesy of Alexandre Bourdas, a French chef who used to live in Japan.

SATURDAY

4 *Boudin and Friends* 10 a.m.

The biggest artistic splash on the Côte Fleurie was made by the Impressionists and pre-

Impressionists, who began coming out from Paris in the 1860s after a new railroad line made the trip fast and easy. The **Musée Eugène Boudin** (Place Erik Satie; 33-2-31-89-54-00; musees-honfleur.fr) is filled with works by its namesake painter and other Impressionist masters. A self-taught artist, Boudin wasn't beholden to the orthodoxies of the French Academy and became a pioneer in the unmooring of painting from strict rules and realistic storytelling styles. He had particular influence on Claude Monet, who soon was coming often to Honfleur, capturing scenes that are still played out along the Côte Fleurie: weekenders filling the sands of the beach, sailboats buffeting along the whitecaps outside Deauville harbor, people ambling along cobbled streets. The fashions may have changed — the beachgoing ladies have swapped their long white dresses and chairs for bikinis and beach towels — but the seaside rituals endure.

5 *Deauville Vibe* Noon

The vibe morphs from the artistic to the aristocratic as you make the 20-minute drive or bus ride along snaking, tree-lined roads from Honfleur to Deauville. After crossing the Touques River, you emerge in an impeccable town of Norman mansions: elegant Old World half-timbered houses with wooden balconies, Queen Anne-style protrusions, steep A-frame roofs, and witches' hat turrets. It could easily be some storybook village if it weren't for the Louis Vuitton shop and the Lancel boutique with its pricey Adjani handbags. Coco Chanel opened her first shop in Deauville, which morphed from fishing village to luxury resort under the guidance of the Duke of Morny, a half-brother to Emperor Napoleon III. Europe's crème de la

crème flocked in: King Alphonso XIII of Spain, King Farouk of Egypt, Queen Elizabeth II, the Aga Khan.

6 *Sea Bar* 1 p.m.

Lunch with a trendy crowd at the outdoor **Bar de la Mer** restaurant (Les Planches; 33-2-31-88-27-51) on the beach at Les Planches, Deauville's celebrated boardwalk. Inside is an Art Deco restaurant with a fair-sized dining room, but most of the seating is on the beach. This is a spot for fresh oysters, langoustines, and people-watching.

7 *Beach Stars* 2 p.m.

Join the human sprawl under the forest of colorful umbrellas that are permanent fixtures along **Les Planches**. If you're a hardy type, take a dip in the Channel. You'll see the names of American movie stars — Samuel L. Jackson, Clint Eastwood, Robert Duvall, Kim Novak — on the dressing cabins that line the boardwalk, a sign of Deauville's obsession with film, and American films in particular. Every September the town hosts the Deauville American Film Festival, an event that has drawn the likes of Harrison Ford and Meryl Streep.

8 *Upper Crust* 8 p.m.

Deauville is mainly a getaway for Parisians—a Gallic answer to New York's seaside retreat at East Hampton—where deep-pocketed visitors arrive in Range Rovers and BMWs. Find these weekenders drinking Bordeaux among the celebrity photos at the **Chez Miocque** brasserie (81 rue Eugène-Colas; 33-2-31-88-09-52; chez-miocque.fr/contact.htm; $$$-$$$$). Take a sidewalk table and order a steak or some oysters.

9 *Night Games* 10 p.m.

The lights are on all night at Deauville's sumptuous **Casino** (2 rue Edmond Blanc; 33-2-31-14-31-14), a 1912 construction that still crowns the town. It had a heyday of well-publicized celebrity traffic in the 1920s and is thought to have been the inspiration for the gambling hall in *Casino Royale*, Ian Fleming's first James Bond novel. If gambling holds no charm, no need to turn in early. You can dance until dawn in the casino's basement, at **Brummel Club**, a haven of retro 1970s kitsch.

SUNDAY

10 *Equestrian Dawn* 8 a.m.

Deauville's other obsession, besides film, is horses. France's main horse-breeding region is in this part of Normandy, and there are several stud farms nearby. In town, you can practically chart the seasons by the attire of the riders or handlers. Colored silks and whips? It's racing season, primarily July and August. Long mallets and impossibly tight white trousers? Get ready for the August polo championships, with international teams. Suits and ties? The October yearling sales have arrived. If there are no events while you're in town, get up early and watch the morning activity at the **Hippodrome de la Touques** (45 avenue Hocquart de Turtot). Visitors are allowed in to watch the trainers and horses limber up.

OPPOSITE Les Planches, Deauville's celebrated boardwalk. Affluent Parisians crowd into town for its beach and for the equestrian events at its Hippodrome.

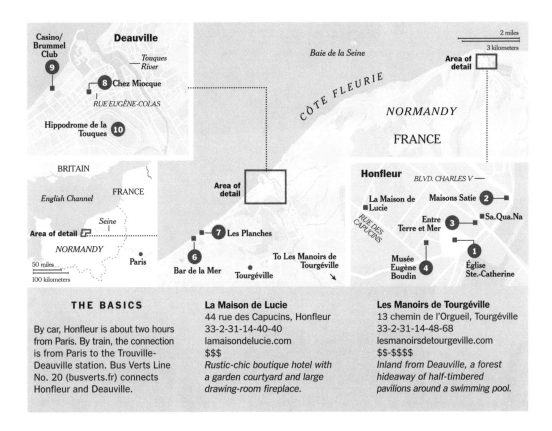

THE BASICS

By car, Honfleur is about two hours from Paris. By train, the connection is from Paris to the Trouville-Deauville station. Bus Verts Line No. 20 (busverts.fr) connects Honfleur and Deauville.

La Maison de Lucie
44 rue des Capucins, Honfleur
33-2-31-14-40-40
lamaisondelucie.com
$$$
Rustic-chic boutique hotel with a garden courtyard and large drawing-room fireplace.

Les Manoirs de Tourgéville
13 chemin de l'Orgueil, Tourgéville
33-2-31-14-48-68
lesmanoirsdetourgeville.com
$$-$$$$
Inland from Deauville, a forest hideaway of half-timbered pavilions around a swimming pool.

Lyon

"I know of only one thing that you can do well in Lyon, and that's eat," the French novelist Stendhal remarked. Two centuries later, the image of France's third-largest metropolis is still buried under a heap of food. No surprise. The celebrated chef Paul Bocuse saw his first kitchen in Lyon, and the city's bouchons — homey restaurants serving throwback cuisine — are famous countrywide. But once you shovel off the tons of blood sausage and Saint-Marcellin cheese, you find updated dining and much more. Lyon, the gateway to the Alps and birthplace of cinema, holds Roman ruins, Renaissance-era architecture, abundant art spaces, talented young designers, newly renovated riverfronts, and a neighborhood of futuristic architecture. — BY SETH SHERWOOD

FRIDAY

1 *Up River* 2 p.m.

Lyon's Rhône and Saône riverbanks are being transformed in a long-term project, and exhibit A is the promenade along the Rhône on the Rive Gauche, a favorite of walkers, runners, cyclists, and loafers. For lovely views, start at the reflecting pools along Quai Claude Bernard and head north. Along Quai Victor Augagneur, check the posters outside floating nightclubs to see the weekend's agenda. Beyond Pont Wilson, the boat-cafe called **La Passagère** (Quai Victor Augagneur; 33-4-72-73-36-98) is a cozy spot for some hot chocolate or Kronenbourg beer. From there, walk or take the 171 bus up to **Parc de la Tête d'Or**, a lovely green space with ponds, gardens, and forested trails.

2 *Trash and Treasures* 5 p.m.

Oversized outdoor refuse welcomes you to the **Musée d'Art Contemporain** (Cité Internationale, 81 quai Charles de Gaulle; 33-4-72-69-17-17; mac-lyon. com), which abuts Parc de la Tête d'Or. Wang Du's *World Markets* is a massive silvery interpretation of a crumpled financial newspaper, while Olivier Mosset has taken old stone slabs — thought to be remnants of Paris's Bastille — and piled them flat like discards

OPPOSITE The postmodernist Pavillon des Salins at La Confluence, a former docklands renewed by development.

awaiting the junk heap. Inside the museum building, an Art Deco edifice modified by the architect Renzo Piano, top-notch contemporary shows come and go.

3 *Park Yourself Here* 8 p.m.

Enjoy France's culinary capital in summer with a light dinner in a parking space. At **La Bouteillerie** (9 rue de la Martinière; 33-4-78-08-62-48; $$) you are at one of a handful of tables on a wooden platform occupying what should be a parking spot in front of the cafe—though it's not really a cafe. It's more like a wine shop with a kitchen and an owner who cooks and serves as the waiter. In colder months your table is indoors. Choose several small plates or the plat du jour and let the owner select a glass of wine for you — he will ask you to guess what it is.

4 *Lyonnaise Libations* 11 p.m.

Food claims the spotlight in Lyon, but drinks are doing their own diva act. James Brown and Frank Sinatra haunt **Soda** (7 rue de la Martinière; soda-bar.fr).Their jailhouse mug shots and others decorate this dark plush den, where cocktails include choices like a spicy Slumdog Millionaire (Bombay gin, cherry jam, lemon juice, red vermouth, cardamom) or smooth Globetrotter (pisco, elderflower liqueur, lemon juice, and Aperol). Nearby, the strains of old American jazz fill **L'Antiquaire** (20 rue Hippolyte Flandrin; 33-6-34-21-54-65), where bowtied bartenders serve up seasonal cocktails.

SATURDAY

5 *Celluloid Heroes* 10 a.m.

The street name says it all: Rue du Premier Film. There, on March 19, 1895, Louis Lumière activated the "Cinématographe" that he had designed with his brother, Auguste, and recorded a 50-second film of employees leaving their family's photo-plate factory. And so cinema was born. The early history of moviemaking is paid homage at **Institut Lumière** (25 rue du Premier Film; 33-4-78-78-18-95; institut-lumiere.org). The brothers' Art Nouveau mansion is now a museum that shows original Lumière films and displays the famous Cinématographe and other early filmmaking devices, including a boxy wooden Edison Kinetoscope.

6 *Frapanese Food* 12:30 p.m.

Like a love-hotel bedroom, **Au 14 Février** (6 rue Mourguet; 33-4-78-92-91-39; au14fevrier.com; $$$$), a tiny jewel-box restaurant, has mirrors lining its ceiling. And as in a love hotel, those mirrors reflect ecstatic reactions from the delighted clients below. The stimulation is provided by chef Tsuyoshi Arai, a Tokyo transplant who landed a Michelin star for what he calls "la cuisine Française made in Japan." The menu changes daily but has included blood pudding sheathed in dark chocolate tubes, pumpkin soup with spice bread croûtons, warm foie gras with strawberry vinegar and cooked figs, and roasted pheasant with colorful vegetables cut to resemble gumdrops.

7 *Gargoyles and Lard* 3 p.m.

A Renaissance-era balade digestive — digestive walk — awaits in the cobbled alleys of Vieux (Old) Lyon. Built when the city was a rich silk-making center, the neighborhood is known for the **Cathedral of Saint John the Baptist** (8 place Saint Jean; 33-4-78-38-05-18; cathedrale-lyon.cef.fr). The facade is decorated with 25 gargoyles, 36 prophets and patriarchs, 36 martyrs and saints, and 72 angels — but who's counting? — while the interior contains a towering 16th-century astronomical clock topped by automatons of humans and angels. (It goes into motion at 12, 2, 3, and 4 p.m.) If your stroll makes you hungry again, sample the artisanal ice creams at **Terre Adélice** (1 place de la Baleine; 33-4-78-03-51-84; terre-adelice.eu), which come in unexpected flavors. A scoop of smoked lard, anyone?

8 *Time to Get Creative* 5 p.m.

With its steep staircase streets and Bohemian vibe, the La Croix-Rousse neighborhood recalls Montmartre. Its creative heart is the **Village des Créateurs** (Passage Thiaffait, 19 rue René Leynaud; 33-4-78-27-37-21; villagedescreateurs.com), an alley of independent local design boutiques. Look for intriguing earrings, bracelets, and necklaces in a variety of metals and other materials. Menswear ranges from faux-gritty street clothes to châteaux-appropriate attire, while women will find whimsical prêt-à-porter outfits. The younger set goes to the **Blue Mustach Shop** (Passage Thiaffait, 20 rue René Leynaud; bluemustach.fr) for athletic-inspired not-so-casual wear.

9 *Pick Nic* 8 p.m.

Take Tramway line T1 to "Hôtel de Région – Montrochet," walk west on Rue Paul Montrochet, and head toward the postmodernist building resembling a block of orange cheese. You are at **La Confluence**, a formerly downbeat docklands that has sprouted futuristic new structures. Stop in at the wine bar before moving on to dinner at **Le Selcius** (upstairs at 43 quai Rambaud; 33-4-78-92-87-87; selcius.fr; $$$), where, with your cardiologist nowhere in sight, you can dine handsomely on terrine of duck liver and rabbit, beef carpaccio, and plates of charcuterie and cheese. It's not all French — there are pastas and risottos that nod toward Italy, and Argentine-style grilled beef. The cocktail list has all the usual concoctions and tosses in a Lillet rosé spritz for the more sophisticated guests.

10 *Tie Up to the Dock* 10 p.m.

Follow the scent of aftershave and D&G perfume to **Docks 40** (40 quai Rambaud; 33-4-78-40-40-40; docks40.com), another warehouse-like space. An industrial chic restaurant-lounge, it is a sea of bar stools, dinner tables, and rushing servers until mid-

night. Then the furniture is cleared, the dancing starts, and the D.J.-spun music — soul, disco, and house — explodes. If a thousand-euro magnum of Cristal Roederer is too steep, a glass of Taittinger bubbly at a hundredth of that price also gets the party started.

SUNDAY

11 *Play the Markets* 10 a.m.

The aromas turn fresh at the lively and crowded riverside outdoor market called the **Marché Saint-Antoine** (Quai Saint-Antoine and Quai Célestins). You will catch pungent whiffs of ripe cheese, baked bread, fresh fish, soil-coated carrots and potatoes, steaming roasted chickens, briny oysters. **Jouvray**

(33-4-74-01-16-85) can furnish hockey pucks of Saint-Marcellin cheese and local dry salami, while **Côté Desserts** (33-4-78-45-19-45) does excellent quince tarts. After tending to your appetite, feed your mind among les bouquinistes — outdoor book dealers — along the adjacent Quai de la Pêcherie. You'll find hometown authors like Racine and Antoine de Saint-Exupéry as well as vintage maps, postcards, and vinyl records. You might even chance across works by Stendhal. In Lyon, he's never likely to be far from the food.

OPPOSITE ABOVE The courtyards and cobbled alleys of Vieux Lyon (Old Lyon) invite an afternoon stroll.

OPPOSITE BELOW The wine bar at Le Selcius.

THE BASICS

Walk, use the métro system, or rent a Vélo'v bicycle.

Ibis Styles Lyon Part Dieu
54 Rue de la Villette
33-4-72-68-25-40
ibis-styles-lyon.com
$$
Near Lyon's main train station, 99 non-smoking rooms in a chain hotel.

DockOuest
39 Rue des Docks
33-4-78-22-34-34
dockouest.com
$
Design hotel with Ligne Roset furnishings.

Cour des Loges
2-8 Rue du Boeuf
33-4-72-77-44-44
courdesloges.com
$$$$
Luxurious hotel occupying four mansions dating from the 14th to 17th centuries.

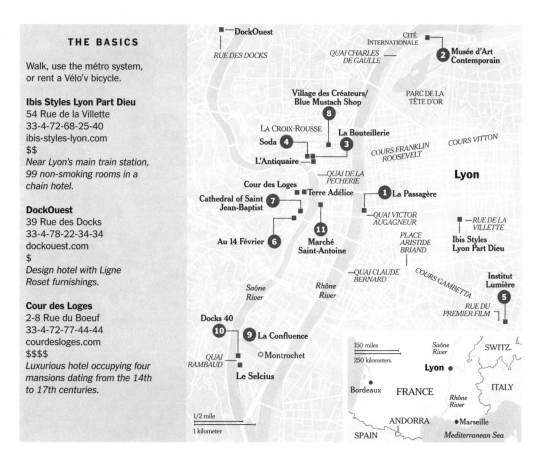

149

Bordeaux

Tasting notes for Bordeaux — the stony French city, not its famous wine — might have read something like this at the turn of the 21st century: lifeless and bland; aromas of dirt and dust; a once majestic city well past its prime. But today's Bordeaux is smooth and elegant, thanks to a beautification effort that has both restored its old polish and updated its mien. Centuries of soot have been removed from the ornate medieval churches, Baroque-era facades, and Art Nouveau town houses that make it one of the world's largest Unesco heritage sites. Inviting cafes and upscale night spots have made a destination of the once seedy dock-lands. And a new liveliness is evident at avant-garde art spaces and new restaurants. But don't fear — those blue-black grapes are still ripening in the celebrated vineyards just outside of town. — BY SETH SHERWOOD

FRIDAY

1 *Exhibit A, Harborside* 4 p.m.

Start your exploration by riding the futuristic tram system to the Bassins à Flot, a once seedy harbor that has been cleaned up and is now home to innovative galleries. **Fonds Régional d'Art Contemporain** (Hangar G2, Bassin à flot No. 1, quai Armand Lalande; 33-5-56-24-71-36; frac-aquitaine. net) is run by the regional governmental body that collects works by contemporary artists in France and beyond. In the same building is **Arrêt sur l'Image** (33-5-56-69-16-48; arretsurlimage.com), specializing in works on paper and photography. And **Le Garage Moderne** (1 rue des Étrangers, 33-5-56-50-91-33; legaragemoderne.org) is a junk-filled hangar with an auto-repair shop, a snack bar, and a raw contemporary art gallery under the same roof.

2 *Water Mirror* 6 p.m.

The left bank of the Garonne River is another 21st-century urban-planning success story. An ultra-thin miroir d'eau (mirror of water), shallow enough to walk on and refreshed several times a day by jets that send out fine spray, reflects the palace-like

buildings of the grand 18th-century **Place de la Bourse**. Old warehouses are home to outlet stores (Quai des Marques), and cafes dot the waterfront. For a drink, order a pastis at **L'Ibaïa Café** (Quai des Chartrons; 33-6-31-90-41-58; Facebook: ibaia.cafe), where you can see the sunset and watch the river flow past amid pulsing house music.

3 *The Real Stuff* 8 p.m.

Bordeaux is not known for leafy salads and other light fare, so go for the traditional and very French food at **L'encoche** (11 rue de la Devise; 33-5-57-34-47-01; $$$). Candles light the limestone walls and arches that give the dining room the feel of a cave. Diners feast on foie gras, whatever fish looked best at the market that day, veal chops with a mushroom cream sauce, roasted lamb, and even simple steak-frites. The owner is often on hand to explain the dishes and help you choose a wine. This is the sort of dining experience that you're likely to ache for when you return home. However, if the cave-like interior is not what you want on a warm summer evening, you can try one of the many inviting sidewalk cafes in this lively neighborhood, Quartier Saint-Pierre.

4 *Do-It-Yourself Drinking* 11 p.m.

You don't have to be a wine tourist to enjoy **Aux Quatre Coins du Vin** (8 rue de la Devise; 33-5-57-34-37-29; aux4coinsduvin.com), just across the street from L'encoche. This is not the first or the last of its type of wine bar, but it takes some explaining: When you go in, you get a credit card-like card. You tell the bartender what euro limit you want on the card. You

OPPOSITE An expert assessment of the grapes at Château Lascombe, a Bordeaux winery.

RIGHT Wines lined up in a futuristic vending machine.

then insert the card into one of several futuristic-looking contraptions that dispense wine. You choose from more than 30 wines; you choose whether you want a sip, something more than a sip, or a regular glass of wine. When you're ready to leave, take the card to the bartender and pay your bill. Technology in the service of pleasure.

SATURDAY

5 *Updated Decoratives* 11 a.m.

The **Musée des Arts Décoratifs et du Design** (39 rue Bouffard; 33-5-56-10-14-00; bordeaux.fr/p63910) was once a predictable dollhouse of period rooms filled with harpsichords, antique vases, and other relics of Bordeaux's past. Then a new wing devoted to 20th- and 21st-century design opened, offering yet another symbol of the city's playful rejuvenation. Some of the highlights, many from French designers, include a 1980s Baroque-Dadaist aluminum and wood chair from Philippe Starck; a fuzzy, Chia Pet-like dresser by Christian Astuguevieille; and a disjointed checkerboard mirror by Andrée Putman.

6 *Wine Forest* 1 p.m.

A gold medal for Bordeaux wine bars easily goes to **L'Autre Petit Bois** (12 place du Parlement; 33-5-56-48-02-93; $$), whose kitsch-cool design and unstuffy attitude breathe new life into a Bordeaux institution. Under the shade of leafy (and artificial) indoor trees, diners tuck into tomatoes with mozzarella, goat cheese salads, and toasted bread tartines. Just as surprising is the wine list, which includes wines from — gasp! — English-speaking nations like the United States and Australia.

7 *Gothic to Avant-garde* 3 p.m.

Lose yourself amid the narrow streets, centuries-old squares, and medieval churches in the city center. To find the **St.-André Cathedral**, follow its Gothic spires, which resemble sharpened pencils studded with clove-like nubs. The majestic 18th-century

Hôtel de Ville is nearby. Also worth photographing is the **St.-Seurin Basilica**, which sits atop one of Bordeaux's most venerable attractions, a sixth-century Gallo-Roman crypt. The crypt, open from June through September, holds sarcophagi, amphorae, and other relics of a long-vanished Bordeaux. For interesting shopping, escape the swarms at the Rue Ste.-Catherine, anchored by Galeries Lafayette, and explore the avant-garde boutiques and designer furnishing stores on the Rue du Pas St.-Georges or the concept stores around Place Fernand Lafargue.

8 *A Place to Taste* 6 p.m.

The **Max Bordeaux Wine Gallery and Cellar** (14 cours de l'Intendance; 33-5-57-29-23-81; maxbordeaux.com) is one wine shop where you don't have to buy blind. Almost everything can be tasted, thanks to dispensers like those at Aux Quatre Coins du Vin. Choose from the products of eight Bordeaux wineries, put your glass under the spout, press the button, and out comes a top vintage, kept at ideal temperature and free from over-oxygenation. After the sample, of course, you're invited to buy a bottle.

9 *Waterfront Star* 8 p.m.

The chef François Adamski has the Midas touch. He's been awarded two of France's top culinary prizes, the Bocuse d'Or and Meilleur Ouvrier de France — one of only two people to achieve both — and his very white, very elegant restaurant **Le Gabriel** (10 place de la Bourse; 33-5-56-30-00-80; bordeaux-gabriel.fr; $$$$), grabbed its first Michelin star after barely a year of existence. Credit the fine-tuned French menu enhanced and enlivened with international accents. Mediterranean France and southwestern Basque country meet in dishes like squid stuffed with risotto, candied tomatoes, and peppers. Lamb, meanwhile, sometimes is served three ways simultaneously (a succulent gigot, a roasted crispy-salty rack, and a proletarian sausage) with a purée of dates, nuts, and cumin.

10 *Bordeaux Beats* 11 p.m.

Stevie Wonder, Isaac Hayes, and the Meters all haunt **L'Apollo Bar** (19 place Fernand Lafargue; 33-5-56-01-25-05), at least in musical form. Young women in thrift-store finery and scruffy young men shoot pool, hobnob, and drink pints of Paulaner at this retro-trendy bar. The music is live at **Le Comptoir du Jazz** (58-59 quai de Paludate; 33-5-56-49-15-55) and it's often blues and funk as well as jazz, in an intimate, almost stylish cavern-like space.

SUNDAY

11 *See the Wine* 8:30 a.m.

Sampling Bordeaux's wine region — a quarter-million acres that produce 800 million bottles a year — is a Herculean labor. (Not to mention a

Dionysian one.) Fortunately, the **Bordeaux Tourism Office** (12 cours du 30 Juillet; 33-5-56-00-66-00; bordeaux-tourisme.com) offers suggested driving routes or will connect you to a bus tour — choose the half-day, and you should be back in the city by 1 p.m. The nearby wine appellations (districts) are famous indeed, with names like St.-Émilion, Médoc, and Margaux.

OPPOSITE The water mirror at Place de la Bourse.

ABOVE The mechanically inclined Garage Moderne.

THE BASICS

The tram is handy for getting around the city center. To see the vineyards, rent a car or join a bus tour.

L'Avant-Scène
36 rue Borie
33-5-57-29-25-39
lavantscene.fr
$$
Stylish nine-room hotel in an 18th-century stone town house just off the waterfront.

Grand Hotel de Bordeaux & Spa
2-5 place de la Comédie
33-5-57-30-44-44
ghbordeaux.com
$$$$
Presides grandly over Bordeaux's most famous square.

Seeko'o Hotel
54 quai de Bacalan
33-5-56-39-07-07
seekoo-hotel.com
$$$
Jagged white exterior, high-design décor, and electronic gadgetry.

Paris

GER.

FRANCE

•Bordeaux   ITALY

SPAIN   Med. Sea

Bordeaux

Le Garage Moderne

RUE DES ÉTRANGERS

Fonds Régional d'Art Contemporain 1

Arrêt sur L'Image

Seeko'o Hotel

RUE NOTRE-DAME

QUAI DE BACALAN

L'Avant-Scène   Garonne River

QUAI DES QUEYRIES

L'Ibaïa Café

QUAI DES CHARTRONS

Bordeaux Tourism Office

11

St.-Seurin Basilica

Musée des Arts Décoratifs et du Design   5

Hôtel de Ville

St.-André Cathedral   7

Area of detail

8 Max Bordeaux Wine Gallery and Cellar

Grand Hotel de Bordeaux & Spa

Le Gabriel 9

Galeries Lafayette

L'Autre Petit Bois   6

2 Place de la Bourse

3 L'encoche

4 Aux Quatre Coins du Vin

10 L'Apollo Bar

RUE STE.-CATHERINE

PL. FERNAND LAFARGUE

To Le Comptoir du Jazz

1/2 mile
1 kilometer

Biarritz

Long ago the reigning vacation spot for Europe's noble and gentry classes and then dethroned by the Riviera, Biarritz, in southwestern France on the Bay of Biscay, is now enjoying a renaissance. New sun seekers have discovered its surf and sandy beaches, and while it retains an aristocratic air, these days its golden shores are shared by everyone from bronze beauties in designer sandals to dropout surfers in frayed flip-flops. Biarritz is a place where worlds collide and expectations are upended. Even the languages are mixed up. Walk into any of the town's creaky old bars, and the patrons might strike up a conversation by saying a few words in rapid-fire French, Spanish, English, or even Basque, the local language that, like Biarritz, is in a class by itself. — BY KABIR CHIBBER

FRIDAY

1 *The Beautiful People* 5 p.m.

Biarritz is a tale of two beaches, so start by getting acquainted with the **Grande Plage**, a curved stretch of golden sand dotted with brightly colored parasols. Buy a gelato and watch the impossibly pretty young things in oversize Christian Dior shades flirt for hours in the blazing sun. Farther down the beach, the crowd splits between chic-looking families frolicking in the water and wealthy 50-year-olds enjoying their early retirement.

2 *Duck!* 9 p.m.

Linguists have long been stumped by Basque, a language that bears no relation to Latin or any other European tongue. Hear it shouted at a pelote match, played in a fronton — a court with a wall and lines. Pelote, similar to handball, is reputed to be the fastest sport in the world and is played in almost every Basque village (jai alai, common in Latin America, is a variant). Watch a competitive match, sometimes using a curved wooden glove called a xistera, at the **Fronton Couvert Plaza Berri** (42 avenue du Maréchal Foch; 33-5-47-64-53-41). For information

OPPOSITE The beach at Biarritz in France's far southwest, an oceanside resort since the 19th century.

RIGHT Take a surfing lesson, bask on the sand, or follow the locals to find a spot for diving.

and a schedule, stop in at the Biarritz tourism office on Square d'Ixelles (33-5-59-22-37-00) or ask at your hotel.

3 *La Côte Basque* 10:30 p.m.

Avoid the tourist-trap fish restaurants and head straight for **Chez Ospi** (6 rue Jean Bart; 33-5-59-24-64-98; chezospi.com), an easy walk from the crowds in the center of town. Most places in Biarritz specialize in fish, but here you'll find Basque lamb and beef dishes in addition to seafood like crab ravioli and stuffed baby squid. Wash it down with Basque wine, and you'll be smiling when you leave.

SATURDAY

4 *Cake Walk* 10 a.m.

Pick up a gâteau Basque, a small cake filled with a delicious eggy custard, from the posh pâtisserie **Loubère** (11 rue Larralde; 33-5-59-24-01-82). Then head down to the **Côte des Basques**, a plain beach with rowdy waves where Peter Viertel, a Hollywood screenwriter, introduced surfing to the stunned French more than 50 years ago. Expect to find rows of beat-up vans with makeshift clotheslines parked along the road leading to the sea. There are no changing rooms, so be prepared to shed your modesty or practice changing beneath a towel.

5 *École du Surf* 11 a.m.

If you'd like a surfing lesson, call in advance to set one up with **Hastea** (7 perspective Côte des

Basques; 33-6-81-93-98-66; hastea.com), a professional surfing school. Expect a 90-minute lesson with a gruff-but-friendly instructor in a group session. And don't worry about all the small jellyfish in the water. They don't sting…much.

6 *Recharge* 1 p.m.

Walk straight up from the shore to **Le Surfing** (9 boulevard du Prince de Galles; 33-5-59-24-78-72; lesurfing.fr; $$$), a cozy bar on this undeveloped stretch of coast. It may be the most casual place in Biarritz, with groovy boards, black-and-white surf posters, and friendly employees who don't mind if you're dripping water everywhere. Order the brandade de morue, a sort of purée of salt cod, or the hefty rib-eye steak.

7 *Fashion Victim* 4 p.m.

As the day progresses, the unspoken dress code goes from beach bum to Diddy and Donatella. Pay a visit to **64** (16 rue Gambetta; 33-5-59-26-82-45; 64.eu), a fashion label that has several stylish stores on Biarritz's most fashionable street, including a beachwear shop and one for children, and was set up by local designers. Named for the area code of this département of France, 64 is famous for making T-shirts with the eponymous number in every color. Devotees of the brand collect them all.

8 *Food as Art* 8 p.m.

With an air of cockiness, the Ducasse-trained chef Philippe Lafargue may come across as a pretentious rock star. But his restaurant, **Restaurant Philippe** (30 avenue du Lac Marion; 33-5-59-23-13-12; restaurant-biarritz.com; $$$$), serves some of the most exciting nouveau Basque cuisine in the region. Start with an aperitif of txakoli, a lightly effervescent wine from the Spanish Basque country, and then sample the degustation menu, which features delights like roasted pork loin and sea bass with herbs from the restaurant's own garden.

9 *Beer-itz* 10 p.m.

People in Biarritz don't booze, but they certainly know how to unwind. For a drink and another look at local culture, find a spot at the **Red Café** (9 avenue du Maréchal Foch; 33-5-59-24-21-02), one of the Biarritz bars for the rugby-obsessed. Red is the team color for Biarritz Olympique Pays Basque, the local squad, and the bar's theme is a reminder of how proud (and borderline fanatical) everyone here is about Biarritz's solidly competitive standing in European rugby. Strike up a conversation or just take in the scene.

10 *Up Until Dawn* Midnight

European nobility always enjoyed disposing of its money at gambling tables, and its elegant old

city casino, now **Casino Barrière Biarritz** (1 avenue Edouard VII; 33-5-59-22-77-77; lucienbarriere.com), still offers the opportunity, though the clientele may have undergone a few changes since the place first opened in the 1920s. After your turn to play (or gawk), if you're still not ready to call it a night, check out the dance clubs along the beach. Or just cross the road and sit on the Grande Plage with the other diehards until the sun rises.

SUNDAY

11 *One-Stop Shop* 11 a.m.

Pick up goodies at the **Halles,** a large covered market just off the Rue Gambetta, where getting elbowed by a local who jumps the line is part of the fun. Overwhelmed? Pick up a few slices of the

famed Bayonne ham from the **Didier Carrère** stall (33-5-59-22-13-01; halles-biarritz.fr). Then, walk down the road to **Mille et Un Fromages** (8 avenue Victor Hugo; 33-5-59-24-67-88), where you can expect to find the finest in Basque cheeses and wines. Try a patxaran, a bright-red Pyrenees liquor made from sloe berries.

OPPOSITE Biarritz retains its air of elegance.

ABOVE Restaurant Philippe specializes in nouveau Basque cuisine, reflecting Biarritz's Basque culture and heritage.

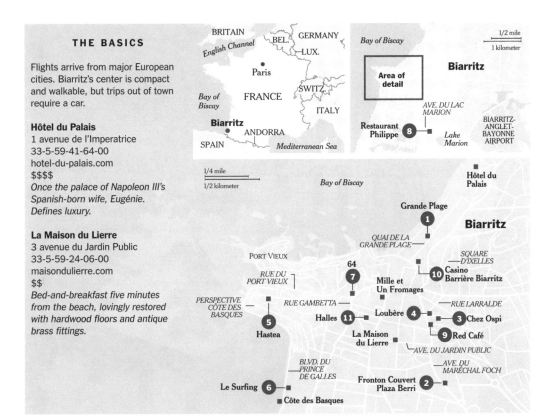

THE BASICS

Flights arrive from major European cities. Biarritz's center is compact and walkable, but trips out of town require a car.

Hôtel du Palais
1 avenue de l'Imperatrice
33-5-59-41-64-00
hotel-du-palais.com
$$$$
Once the palace of Napoleon III's Spanish-born wife, Eugénie. Defines luxury.

La Maison du Lierre
3 avenue du Jardin Public
33-5-59-24-06-00
maisondulierre.com
$$
Bed-and-breakfast five minutes from the beach, lovingly restored with hardwood floors and antique brass fittings.

Toulouse

Paris is the capital of France, but Toulouse is the nation's campus. With three major universities and a thriving high-tech center, including the headquarters of Airbus, France's fourth-largest city hums with inventiveness and creativity. Under its medieval church spires, the spiderweb of cobblestone lanes brims with art museums, theaters, upstart fashion boutiques, all-hours night life, and an expanding bevy of fine restaurants serving everything from haute cuisine to hearty cassoulet. And thanks to its location in France's sunny southwest — closer to Barcelona than to Paris — Toulouse is suffused with a laid-back Latin vibe. No wonder "La Ville Rose," so called for the dusty rose-hued bricks in many of its old edifices, is France's fastest-growing city. — BY SETH SHERWOOD

FRIDAY

1 *Channel Surfing* 5:30 p.m.

A cruise along the Garonne River and its offshoot canals offers the perfect vantage point to get the lay of the land and glimpse Old World monuments. The Croisière Été Canal (Summer Channel Cruise) offered by **Les Bateaux Toulousains** (Quai de la Daurade; 33-5-61-80-22-26; bateaux-toulousains.com) passes through the lock of St. Pierre, beneath the venerable Pont Neuf bridge, and past classic edifices like the 19th-century Château d'Eau, a brick water tower transformed into a photography museum. The commentary is in French, but an English text translation is provided. Cruises run about 75 minutes and operate from July through October.

2 *Your Goose Is Cooked* 8 p.m.

Thick with white beans, pork, pork fat, red sausage, white sausage, and abundant goose confit, the classic cassoulet served at **Le Colombier** (14 rue Bayard; 33-5-61-62-40-05; restaurant-lecolombier. com; $$$) won't win the endorsement of any cardiologists. But the hearty slow-cooked stew is an essential

experience in southwestern France, and this simple stone and brick dining room is among the best places in town to appreciate it. Finish with some strawberry soup with lime sorbet, a blast of tart-sweet acidity to cut the heaviness of the meaty maelstrom.

3 *Bedtime With Bacchus* 9:30 p.m.

You half expect to run into factory workers and fishwives from a Zola novel at **Au Père Louis** (45 rue des Tourneurs; 33-5-61-21-33-45), a wine bar with oak barrels and dusty bottles dating back to 1889. These days, wine is still its universal solvent, washing away the distinctions between the different social types — students, well-heeled couples, young professionals, rock-and-rollers — who sip glasses of Fronton, Côtes du Rhône, and other appellations under the antique chandelier. Squeeze in before the 11 p.m. closing time.

SATURDAY

4 *Couture Club* 11 a.m.

Rue Cujas, an easy-to-miss lane in central Toulouse, might better be called Style Street. The spirits of the film directors Russ Meyer and Ed Wood haunt **Brock n' Roll** (16 rue Cujas; 33-5-62-27-08-21), which sells B-movie-chic clothing and furniture. Look for military-style women's clothing from 0-105 Zero Cent Cinq, or eco-friendly Piola sneakers made with wild rubber from the rainforests of Peru. Nearby is **La Gabardine** (12 rue Cujas; 33-5-61-12-11-70), which specializes in clothes from young designers.

OPPOSITE St.-Sernin Basilica, built in the 11th and 12th centuries, is Toulouse's medieval heart. Its distinctive octagonal tower is the city's landmark.

RIGHT Artwork at Les Abattoirs, the city's premier modern and contemporary art museum.

5 *Bean Town* 1 p.m.

If you didn't get to have cassoulet at Colombier, relax. And even if you did, you can have another version of this Languedoc classic at **Restaurant Emile** (13 place St. Georges; 33-5-61-21-05-56; restaurant-emile.com; $$$), which also has a full and tempting menu of other dishes. Nevertheless, get the cassoulet, which Toulouse claims to have invented and which is named for the earthenware *cassole* dish that it's cooked in. Cassoulet is to baked beans what a French crêpe is to a plebeian pancake.

6 *Pablo's Puzzle* 3 p.m.

You can't help but wonder: Where did the dead Minotaur score that nifty harlequin suit? And where on earth is that eagle-headed strongman carrying him? Alas, Picasso isn't around to decode the theater curtain he painted in 1936 for the play *Le 14 Juillet* by Romain Rolland. But that doesn't stop the masses from admiring the staggering work (not always on display; check with the museum) at **Les Abattoirs** (76 allées Charles-de-Fitte; 33-5-62-48-58-00; lesabattoirs.org), the city's premier modern and contemporary art museum. Examine it yourself, and then see the museum's many other holdings.

7 *Church and State* 5 p.m.

The city's medieval heart is the **St.-Sernin Basilica** (13 place St.-Sernin; 33-5-61-21-80-45), which claims to be the largest Romanesque church in the world. The basilica was built during the 11th and 12th centuries and still inspires wonder with its octagonal tower and soaring barrel-vaulted interior. After your visit there, stroll to the Old World

ABOVE Outside Les Abattoirs. Inside is the museum's best known piece, a theater curtain painted by Picasso in 1936 for the play *Le 14 Juillet*.

RIGHT A rooftop view from the Fondation Bemberg.

OPPOSITE Brock n' Roll on rue Cujas.

brasserie **Le Bibent** (5 place du Capitole; 33-5-34-30-18-37) for a kir aperitif on the terrace. The dusk glow enhances the 18th-century municipal buildings along the Place du Capitole.

8 *From Gotham to Gaul* 8 p.m.

After training in kitchens as far away as Japan and the United States—including Daniel Boulud's restaurants in New York—the young chef Romain Brard returned to his native France and opened **Le Genty Magre** (3 rue Genty Magre; 33-5-61-21-38-60; legentymagre.com; $$$$). The living-room-like restaurant draws stylish professionals with its jazzy Franco-international cuisine. On one evening's menu, crispy grilled jumbo shrimp went Asian, courtesy of sprouts and a subtle peanut and vinaigrette sauce. Beef cheek, meanwhile, was elevated to four stars, thanks to a truffle crust that locked in the juices and mashed potatoes larded with truffles and bacon. Pop a Lipitor and finish your night with a tempting dessert.

9 *Alcohol and Acronyms* 10:30 p.m.

For a digestif, the brick-lined interior of **Le St.-Jérôme** cocktail bar (21 rue Saint-Antoine-du-T; 33-5-61-22-90-66; lesaintjerome.com) brims with B.C.B.G. (French lingo for *"bon chic bon genre"* or good style, good breeding) and effervescent music. A Cuba libre makes for a fine nightcap.

SUNDAY

10 *Tales of the City* 9:30 a.m.

You've seen a lot just by being in Toulouse, enough to make you curious about some of the buildings and districts. Sign up online with **Toulouse Walking Tours** (33-6-77-28-39-60; toulousewalkingtours.com) for a two-hour outing that usually begins near the Place Capitôle Metro Station. Join one of the group tours or arrange a private one. All involve stories about Toulouse.

11 *Wear Sunglasses* Noon

Don't be fooled by the 16th-century exterior of the **Fondation Bemberg** (Hôtel d'Assézat, Place d'Assézat; 33-5-61-12-06-89; www.fondation-bemberg.fr). Yes, this museum in a mansion has plenty of antiques: Chinese porcelain, Renaissance-era Swiss clocks, and more gilded gewgaws than you can shake your cane at. But the works here were collected by Georges Bemberg, a local art lover whose interests also extended to the modern era, and the best treats are the galleries of modern French painting. Protect your retinas and step into the Pointillist Room for eye-popping, pixilated canvases like Paul Signac's *Le Clocher de Saint-Tropez* before taking in the bold, color-soaked visions of Raoul Dufy, Georges Braque, and Henri Matisse in the Fauve Room. In the Pierre Bonnard room, don't miss the haunted nocturnal painting *Le Moulin Rouge*.

THE BASICS

Most international flights to Toulouse come through Paris. High-speed trains take about five hours from Paris's Gare Montparnasse.

Les Bains-Douches
4 and 4 bis rue du Pont Guilheméry
33-5-62-72-52-52
hotel-bainsdouches.com
$$
A self-consciously sleek boutique hotel with a chic cocktail lounge.

Hotel Albert 1er
8 rue Rivals
33-5-61-21-17-91
hotel-albert1.com
$
Cozy, clean, central, friendly, and an excellent value.

Hotel Ambassadeurs
68 rue Bayard
33-5-61-62-65-84
hoteldesambassadeurs.com
$
Good spot for frugal travelers.

Roman France

Traces of Roman civilization are scattered all over France. Paris has ancient baths at the Cluny museum; ruins in Lyon date from its days as Lugdunum, the capital of Gaul. But for the best modern look at Roman France, head south. The Romans annexed the parts of France closest to the Mediterranean first, in about 125 B.C., and the civilization that evolved there was ancient Rome with a French twist, a synergistic blend of two cultures and lifestyles that left a permanent imprint on both of them. Set aside for a moment images of Provence's lavender fields, the Riviera's beaches, and Marseille's bouillabaisse. The south-eastern swath of France seems almost as crammed with ancient Rome as Rome itself: temples, theaters, amphitheaters, aqueducts, roads, arches, monuments, mosaics, and every sort of object from daily life.
— BY ELAINE SCIOLINO

FRIDAY

1 *Over the River* 2 p.m.

With its three tiers of receding arches, the first-century **Pont du Gard** (400 route du Pont du Gard in Vers-Pont-du-Gard; 33-4-66-37-50-99; pontdugard.fr), the supreme artifact of Roman France, is the highest Roman bridge-aqueduct in the world, about as tall as a 16-story building. It is also as worthy as the Eiffel Tower for consideration as the national symbol of France. Once you have gone through the visitors' center, find a perch on the bank of the river Gardon to take in the grace of the aqueduct's architecture and the genius of its engineering. Its blocks of limestone were cut from a local quarry and were pieced together largely without mortar. Using gravity, the aqueduct carried water from Uzès to Nîmes 30 miles away. A path will take you to ruins of the watercourse in an expanse of fields and sparse forests with laurel, oak, and juniper trees.

2 *Caesar's Town* 8 p.m.

The epicenter of Roman Gaul is **Nîmes** (ot-nimes.fr), once one of the largest cities of the empire and now a town of 150,000. The Emperor Augustus founded the city, rewarding his retired legionaries with land there. Today it flaunts a rich collection of unusually well-preserved Roman ruins, surviving in various places around the city and upstaging not only the modern city, but a much newer "old town" of cobblestones and squares. Leave the exploring for tomorrow and relax over dinner at **Aux Plaisirs des Halles** (4 rue Littré, Nîmes; 33-4-66-36-01-02; auxplaisirsdeshalles.com; $$$). This elegant bistro has a lavish regional menu and features local wines. Try the signature bouillabaisse, and savor it on the patio.

SATURDAY

3 *Temple to Tower* 9 a.m.

Hit a few Nîmes landmarks in a whirlwind tour. Prominent in the city center, where it has stood for 2,000 years, is the **Maison Carrée** (maisoncarree.eu), an almost perfectly preserved Hellenistic-style temple. The recently cleaned limestone shines so brightly in the afternoon sun that some residents complain that it looks too new. Across the courtyard — once the forum — is a clever complement, a contemporary art museum designed by Norman Foster with references to the temple. Other intriguing stops include Roman gates, the so-called Temple of Diana tucked in gardens built around ruins of the Roman baths, and the Tour Magne, a brooding tower with a commanding view that was part of ancient fortifications.

OPPOSITE The towering Pont du Gard, the highest Roman bridge aqueduct in the world, was built in the first century A.D. to carry water to the nearby city of Nîmes.

BELOW A frieze at the Arles archaeological museum. Many of the museum's artifacts were found by Rhône River divers.

4 *Picture the Gladiators* 11 a.m.

Leave plenty of time for the main event, the unusually shaped elliptical **Arena of Nîmes** (arenes-nimes.com), which although partly restored, is well preserved and suffered much less degradation than the considerably larger Colosseum in Rome. (It's also a lot less crowded.) The amphitheater survived for centuries with other buildings on top of it before being dug out and returned to daylight in the days of Napoleon. Gladiators once did battle here; now crowds come to watch modern-day re-enactments, bullfights, and concerts. Take the tour, which explains which doors were for the wild beasts and how a gigantic awning was unfurled to keep the sun off the crowd.

5 *Arena View* 1 p.m.

Chez Hubert (2 boulevard des Arènes, Nîmes; 33-4-66-67-68-69; la-grande-bourse.com; $$) is more than the brasserie across the street from the arena. A well-positioned sidewalk table becomes the perfect perch to absorb the grandeur of the site. Along with the visual exploration, have a salad or a three-course meal for lunch.

6 *Augustan Wall* 3 p.m.

Drive about 40 minutes to Orange, another town founded by the legionaries, and tour its amazing first-century theater, the **Théâtre Antique d'Orange** (theatre-antique.com). It is remarkable because of its theatrical wall, one of the greatest works of Roman architecture and engineering to have survived the cruelty of the centuries. Despite its scarred and stained stones, the wall stands defiantly, still deserving of the description: "the finest wall in my kingdom," bestowed by Louis XIV. A statue of Caesar Augustus occupies a prominent niche. Arrayed in front are the tiers of seats, now restored, that were carved out of a hillside. The acoustics are still excellent.

ABOVE 21st-century life, here in the form of a practice with fans, plays out at an ancient temple in Nîmes.

LEFT The Roman amphitheater in Nîmes, where gladiators once fought, is now used for performances and bullfights.

7 *One of the Crowd* 7 p.m.

Practice being a Gallo-Roman by seeing a live performance in one of the ancient venues. In the theater at Orange, concerts and operas take place in a three-week summer festival (choregies.fr). At one performance of *Carmen*, the audience was transfixed as singers' shadows rose 100 feet and danced across that original stage wall. The theater also hosts festivals featuring fake gladiators, processions, and demonstrations of ancient Olympic games. There is another opportunity at the August theatrical festival in Arles (festival-arelate.com), which also uses Roman sites. Or check the season's schedule at the arena in Nîmes.

SUNDAY

8 *Before Vincent* 9 a.m.

Start the day with a walk around the city of **Arles** (www.arlestourisme.com). Best known as the place where Vincent van Gogh did some of his most ambitious painting, it is also home to an ancient amphitheater (arenes-arles.com), a Roman theater that is missing its top layer of stones, and an underground vaulted gallery that supported the esplanade around its forum.

9 *Treasures From the Mud* 11 a.m.

The **Musée Départemental Arles Antique** (Presqu'île du Cirque Romain, Arles; 33-4-13-31-51-03;

www.arles-antique.cg13.fr), an airy modern building on the banks of the Rhône River, contains a collection of Roman artifacts, including jewelry, mosaics, and art. Some of the objects were recovered by modern divers probing the mud bottom of the Rhône.

10 *Sunday Lunch* 1 p.m.

For an inventive Sunday lunch, try **La Chassagnette** (Le Sambuc, Arles; 33-4-90-97-26-96; chassagnette.fr; $$$$), where you might find aioli hake served with vegetables from the chef's organic

TOP Posing at ruined columns of the theater in Arles.

ABOVE A cafe in front of the amphitheater in Nîmes.

garden. Or stop in for artichokes stuffed with meat at **Le Galoubet** (18 rue du Docteur Fanton, Arles; 33-4-90-93-18-11; $$$), a bistro renowned as a place once frequented by van Gogh.

11 *Motion in Stone* 3 p.m.

Drive about 15 miles east of Arles to **St.-Rémy-de-Provence**. Outside of town are a 60-foot mausoleum — one of the best preserved of the Roman world — and a triumphal arch (saintremy-de-

provence.com/sites-and-museums). A stone relief carved into the base of the arch is a tribute to movement: a horse rearing up on its hind legs looks as if it's dancing; a fallen warrior is so alive that you can feel his struggle to get up. Nearby are the ruins of the Roman town of Glanum, where you can picnic under olive trees and walk along the paths of imagined streets, strolling among the ruins of fountains, shops, baths, and houses.

ABOVE The amphitheater in Nîmes is the most prominent of the city's abundant Roman ruins.

OPPOSITE The Roman town of Glanum, where paths trace the streets and ruins outline fountains, shops, baths, and houses.

THE BASICS

Take the high-speed train from Paris to Nîmes and rent a car to get around.

Hôtel Marquis de la Baume
21 rue Nationale, Nîmes
33-4-66-76-28-42
bookinnfrance.com/fr/
hotel-marquis-de-la-baume-nimes
$$
*Former mansion with courtyard,
17th-century staircase, and vaulted
breakfast room.*

Les Cabanes Oxyzen
Impasse du Couchant, Nimes
33-4-66-84-99-80
chambres-hotes-nimes.com
$$
*A cool hideaway with three cabins
and a pool a short drive from the
Maison Carrée.*

Hôtel Jules César
9 boulevard des Lices, Arles
33-4-90-52-52-52
hotel-julescesar.fr
$$
*In a 17th-century convent. Book a
room facing the quiet cloister.*

Paris • FRANCE • Lyon • Area of detail • Marseille

Les Cabanes Oxyzen ■

Théâtre Antique d'Orange **6** • Orange

ROMAN FRANCE

Uzès •
Vers-Pont-du-Gard •
Avignon •

1

Pont du Gard

11 St.-Rémy-de-Provence

2
Nîmes

*Rhône
River*

Glanum

LANGUEDOC

8
Arles

PROVENCE

La Chassagnette **10** ■

10 miles
15 kilometers

Tour Magne
Temple of
Diana ■

*RUE
NATIONALE*

Aux Plaisirs
des Halles ■

Hôtel Marquis
de la Baume ■

3 Maison Carrée

Chez Hubert **5**

Nîmes

*BLVD.
DES ARÈNES*

4
Arena of
Nîmes

*Rhône
River*

Le Galoubet ■

Hôtel Jules César ■

Musée Départemental
Arles Antique ■

9

Arles

Aix-en-Provence

When you're brushing up your French, here's one word you won't need to know in Aix-en-Provence: vitesse. It means speed, and you won't find much of it in the sun-drenched and easygoing hometown of Paul Cézanne and Émile Zola. In a portrait of laid-back leisure, museumgoers and market shoppers amble through lanes where venerable fountains cast their lazy spray. Locals in soft white robes relax in the town's celebrated spas, which are fed by natural hot springs first exploited by the Romans. And come dusk, everyone fills the cafe terraces to sip pastis or a local rosé before heading off to enjoy three-hour dinners of slow-cooked daube de boeuf Provençale. Better, then, to add the word lenteur, or slowness, to your vocabulary. — BY SETH SHERWOOD

FRIDAY

1 *Local Merchandise* 5 p.m.

Leaving behind the crowds of the broad Cours Mirabeau and strolling among Aix's small shops in the Old Town acquaints you with the city's layout while simultaneously furnishing your home in southern French style. Within the minimalist-cool confines of **La Compagnie de Provence** (63 rue des Cordeliers; 33-4-42-27-37-41; compagniedeprovence. com), you'll find regional produce transformed into high-end beauty products, including olive oil shaving cream, cherry hand cream, and fig liquid soap. And neighboring shops will delight any Francophile with everything needed to fulfill a Peter Mayle retirement fantasy: wood-framed prints of lavender plants, fancy cheese knives, rustic serving trays, and more. If you're here in a rented car, mark your parking spot on your tourist map lest tracking down the car makes you late for dinner.

2 *A Feast for the Ears* 8:30 p.m.

Bossa nova with your beef? Duck with a side of jazz? Live music on Friday nights makes **Ô Zen Le Passage** (10 rue Villars; 33-4-42-37-09-00; le-passage.

OPPOSITE Aix-en-Provence, a sunny city of hot springs, shaded squares, and Cézanne.

RIGHT Les Deux Garçons cafe, opened in 1792 and familiar to Picasso, Édith Piaf, Jean Cocteau, and Jean-Paul Sartre.

fr; $$) one of the most appealing spots in Aix. Opened in 2004, the former factory incorporates elements both neo-industrial (exposed girders, exposed ducts) and cozy (candlelight, plush banquettes), as a backdrop for modern French-Mediterranean cooking. A pan-fried strip of foie gras gets nice crunch from spice-bread crumbs, sweetness from stewed strawberries, and zing from balsamic vinegar. A hefty veal chop was served with a piping-hot potato gratin topped with molten, stringy Beaufort cheese.

3 *A Beer in Provence* 10 p.m.

Édith Piaf, Jean Cocteau, Pablo Picasso, Jean-Paul Sartre: the coolest out-of-towners have indulged in the pleasures of Aix's beloved outdoor cafe **Les Deux Garçons** (53 cours Mirabeau; 33-4-42-26-00-51; lesdeuxgarcons.fr), which dates back to 1792. And no wonder. Shaded by tall plane trees and situated on the stately boulevard of Cours Mirabeau, it's the perfect spot to enjoy a late-evening bottle of Paulaner beer or a glass of chilled Bandol rosé while gazing at the impressive old town houses and the slow-flowing nocturnal crowds.

SATURDAY

4 *Water, Water Everywhere* 11 a.m.

Some two millenniums after the Romans built their stony thermal baths at Aix, self-styled Caesars are still luxuriating in the therapeutic waters shot up from underground springs. These days the pampering unfolds at **Thermes Sextius** (55 avenue des Thermes; 33-4-42-23-81-82; thermes-sextius.com),

a vast modern spa built atop the old baths (still visible through glass panels in the lobby). Treatments vary from hot stone therapy to warm mud wraps, but the hydrotherapy cabins and tubs are the real draw. A luxurious treatment might direct five jets to spray on your back as you receive an almond oil massage. The enveloping warm water adds a dimension of relaxation, like swimming in amniotic fluid. Book in advance.

5 *Chez Grandma* 1 p.m.

If you don't have a Gallic grandmother, you at least have **Chez Féraud** (8 rue du Puits Juif; 33-4-42-63-07-27; $$$$). Within the rustic dining room of this ivy-draped restaurant, bourgeois couples and business partners devour pistou soup, daube de boeuf, and other southern French favorites that evoke a classic farmhouse kitchen. You might finish off with a purely Provençal sundae: warm stewed figs served with cold caramel ice cream.

6 *Paint by Hexagon* 3 p.m.

Wear sunglasses and get clearance from your psychiatrist before wading into the interlocking, honeycomblike galleries of the **Fondation Vasarely** (1 avenue Marcel Pagnol; 33-4-42-20-01-09; fondationvasarely.fr). Opened in the 1970s by Victor Vasarely, the Hungarian-born mastermind of the Op Art movement, this retro-futuristic museum is packed with soaring, kaleidoscopic, and mind-bending geometric art that will blow out your retinas and sizzle your brain—think M. C. Escher abstractions on a cathedral scale.

7 *Mirabeau Repast* 8 p.m.

Hidden in plain sight among the tourist-filled cafes and restaurants that line one side of Cours Mirabeau is a local favorite, **Côté Cour** (19 cours Mirabeau; 33-4-42-93-12-51; restaurantcotecour.fr), tucked into the courtyard of a grand old town house. Some tables are open-air and some are in a glass pavilion. The chef, Ronan Kernen, who made his name on the French version of *Top Chef*, keeps regu-

lars coming back with dishes like guinea fowl with a pine nut crust served with mushroom shortbread. He also offers what he calls "my grandmother's platters"—truffle ravioli and beef filet with seared duck livers. He comes from a food-minded family: an uncle was a horse butcher.

8 *Aix Rated* Midnight

Ladies, paint your toenails, don your most stylish open-toed shoes, and strut to the oval bar at **La Rotonde** (2A place Jeanne d'Arc; 33-4-42-91-61-70; larotonde-aix.com). Sultry and seductive, Aix's premier pre-clubbing spot is where the guys in suit jackets and dolled-up women gather to rub elbows—and occasionally more—over a mojito or cosmopolitan. Then it's down the steps into the bunker-chic confines of **Le Mistral** (3 rue Frédéric Mistral; 33-6-74-63-04-92; mistralclub.fr). It may not be a real fallout shelter, but there are nonetheless plenty of people getting bombed—on Champagne—and the thumping bass is nothing short of explosive.

SUNDAY

9 *Roving Feast* 10 a.m.

Dieters, sleep in. With its mountains of eggplants, ranks of honey jars, and fields of fresh goat cheese, the morning market at **Place Richelme** is sure to doom even the most fervent intentions of slimming down. The south side of the square is a Provençal cornucopia. Olive oil, tapenade, anchovies, octopus salad, and sun-dried tomatoes are among the bounty found at small épiceries that could pass for high-end

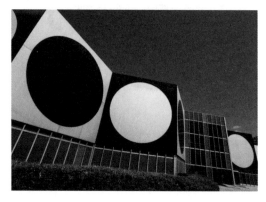

gourmet shops. A more-than-passable brunch is a baguette, dried sausage, and mustard. The vendor who sells the sausage can probably also sell you a handy knife for cutting it and the bread. For very good calissons—small, almond-shaped pastries that are an Aix specialty—head to **Calissoun** (9 avenue du Dr. Bertrand; 33-4-42-63-11-51; calissoun.com), which crafts them in lavender and other flavors.

10 *Searching for Cézanne* Noon

"He was like a father to us all," Picasso once said of Cézanne. Picasso bought a chateau in nearby Vauvenargues, but it is Cézanne who came back again and again to Aix, finally reaching the end of his life not far from where he grew up. The **Musée Granet** (Place St.-Jean-de-Malte; 33-4-42-52-88-32; museegranet-aixenprovence.fr) proudly displays

Cézannes, along with works by Rembrandt, Rubens, Klee, and Giacometti. To see more of Cézanne and his close connection to the local landscapes, arrange through the Tourist Information Office (300 Avenue Giuseppe Verdi; 33-4-42-16-11-61; aixenprovencetourism.com) to visit **Les Lauves**, his studio (9 avenue Paul Cézanne; atelier-cezanne.com) and the **Jas de Bouffan**, his family home (17 route de Galice). Or get directions and take a hike in the **Bibémus Quarry** to share the master's views of Mont Sainte-Victoire, the massif hulking over Aix that appears in many of his paintings.

OPPOSITE ABOVE Foods of Provence at the market in Aix.

OPPOSITE BELOW Fondation Vasarely will sizzle your brain with geometric works from the Op Art movement.

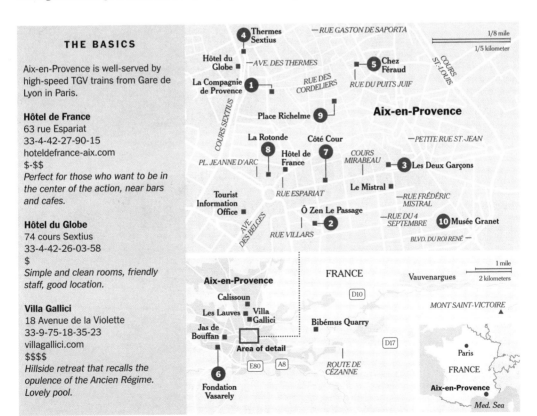

THE BASICS

Aix-en-Provence is well-served by high-speed TGV trains from Gare de Lyon in Paris.

Hôtel de France
63 rue Espariat
33-4-42-27-90-15
hoteldefrance-aix.com
$-$$
Perfect for those who want to be in the center of the action, near bars and cafes.

Hôtel du Globe
74 cours Sextius
33-4-42-26-03-58
$
Simple and clean rooms, friendly staff, good location.

Villa Gallici
18 Avenue de la Violette
33-9-75-18-35-23
villagallici.com
$$$$
Hillside retreat that recalls the opulence of the Ancien Régime. Lovely pool.

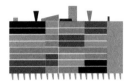

Marseille

First the bad news: Marseille is not Paris. Unlike its culture-rich rival, France's second-largest city has no must-see monuments, or internationally renowned chefs. Now the good news: Marseille is not Paris. Kissed by the Mediterranean, Marseille can claim an un-Parisian combination of near-constant sun, miles of beaches, and an ethnic mix—French, North African, Italian, Corsican, Armenian—that lends a flavor unmatched anywhere else in the country. No wonder the rest of France calls it Planète Mars. And the news gets better. Already known for groundbreaking architecture by Le Corbusier, in the past few years Marseille has remade the face it presents to the world, transforming its waterfront with inviting pedestrian plazas and bold new museums and other buildings by top-tier contemporary architects.

— BY SETH SHERWOOD

FRIDAY

1 *The New Old Port* 2 p.m.

Marseille has been a maritime center since the Greeks first settled here, and you'll find its new incarnation in its ancient heart, its Mediterranean port. The designation of the city as a European Capital of Culture for 2013 prompted an investment of public and private money that has replaced ramshackle wharves and dilapidated buildings with gleaming new structures. Walk around the new plazas and esplanades. The shimmering sheet of reflective steel supported by eight slender poles is a pavilion and sun shade designed by Foster & Partners, Norman Foster's firm. The two dazzling new buildings dominating the once-abandoned J4 Pier are the **Museum of European and Mediterranean Civilizations**, or MuCEM, a filigreed gray cube designed by Rudy Ricciotti, and the white **Villa Méditerranée**, a conference center and exhibition space cantilevered over a reflecting pool designed by Stefano Boeri. Both offer breathtaking, panoramic views of the city and the sea.

OPPOSITE The Museum of European and Mediterranean Civilizations, or MuCEM, one of the landmarks of contemporary architecture on Marseille's newly vibrant waterfront.

RIGHT Diving into the Mediterranean from a city beach.

2 *Treasures in a Cube* 3 p.m.

The **MuCEM** (7 promenade Robert Laffont; 33-4-84-35-13-13; mucem.org/en) doesn't just look good—although it certainly does that, with its facade of concrete lace, an aquamarine Mediterranean backdrop, and a suspended footbridge linking it to the neighboring 12th-century Fort Saint-Jean. It is also remarkable on the inside: the first French national museum outside Paris, with a collection that documents the history of cultures across the Mediterranean and Europe through everything from ethnographic drawings to costumes to jewelry. Explore its three floors of art and artifacts, and don't miss the rooftop terrace.

3 *Ride the Waves* 5 p.m.

Contemplate the sea and rocky coast from the water, on a one-hour boat ride operated by **Croisières Marseille Calanques** (Vieux Port; 33-4-91-58-50-58; croisieres-marseille-calanques.com). You'll glide between the 17th-century forts that flank the port, St.-Jean and St.-Nicolas, then past the neo-Byzantine Cathédrale de la Major, and then around the Île d'If and its fortress, the Château d'If, which is best known as the prison in *The Count of Monte Cristo*.

4 *Super Soup* 8 p.m.

Although Marseille is known for bouillabaisse, relatively few restaurants serve it. However, Quai du Port, on the north side of the Vieux Port, is lined with bouillabaisse restaurants, and one of the best is **Restaurant Miramar** (12 quai du Port; 33-4-91-91-10-40; bouillabaisse.com; $$$$). It's foolish to order

a starter course if you're having bouillabaisse here; it is an all-evening two-course affair, starting with a large bowl of piquant seafood bisque. After you've eaten as much as you want, the server will take it away, add wonderful shellfish, other seafood, and more broth, and return it to you.

SATURDAY

5 *Beach Buffet* 10 a.m.

Marseille's coast serves up a smorgasbord of beaches. The golden sands of Plage des Catalans and the soft gravel of Plage du Prado tend to be overrun, but a peaceful spot is hidden between them on the rocky outcropping below **Le Petit-Nice Passédat** restaurant. Catch the No. 83 bus in the Vieux Port, get off at Anse de la Fausse Monnaie, take the passageway from the road to the boat harbor, and go to the right around the point. The large rocks are a tranquil spot for listening to the waves and gazing out at nearby islands.

6 *Déjeuner, Italian-Style* Noon

You would have to go to Italy to find an Italian restaurant as authentic and consistently excellent as **La Cantinetta** (24 cours Julien; 33-4-91-48-10-48; restaurantlacantinetta.fr; $$$$). Prosciutto hangs overhead in fatty joints and is sliced on a hand-cranked machine from Parma, while the ultra-creamy mozzarella is a special cow's milk variety from Puglia. Reserve—preferably for the lovely garden. After lunch, hit the rue Sainte for some shopping. The misleadingly named **American Vintage** (10 rue

Sainte; 33-4-91-33-02-26; american-vintage-store.com) is a Marseille-based brand selling new threads. Colors and design get adventurous at **Sessun** (6 rue Sainte; 33-4-91-52-33-61; sessun.com), and **Kothai** (53 rue Sainte; 33-4-91-33-55-26), is noted for leather bags embossed with photo images of skylines, Vespas, and James Brown.

7 *César's Palace* 4 p.m.

The emperor of Marseille's art scene was certainly the late César Baldaccini—known simply as César—and his temple is the **Musée d'Art Contemporain** (69 avenue de la Haïfa; 33-4-91-25-01-07; culture.marseille.fr/musees/musee-dart-contemporain-mac), which is filled with his playful neo-realist sculptures, from crushed automobiles to gooey quicksand-like puddles. The other artists represented—including Jean-Michel Basquiat and Dieter Roth—are no slouches, either.

8 *Designer Dinner* 8 p.m.

At **Le Ventre de l'Architecte** (280 boulevard Michelet; 33-4-91-16-78-23; hotellecorbusier.com; $$$$), chefs come to cook in the spotlight for several years and then move on with their careers elsewhere. The restaurant, in a hotel that occupies a Le Corbusier-designed building, is appropriately sleek and modern, and diners are treated to a lovely view of the Mediterranean. The creative menu changes daily.

9 *The Liquor Lobby* 10:30 p.m.

Swanky. Style-conscious. Sophisticated. Marseille's night-life scene is none of these things. But the **Victor Café** in the lobby of the Newhotel of Marseille (71 boulevard Charles Livon; 33-4-88-00-46-00; victorcafemarseille.com) and **Le Carré** bar in the lobby of the Sofitel Vieux Port (36 boulevard Charles Livon; 33-4-91-15-59-00; sofitel.com) are trying to add a jigger of luxe. With its pink-illuminated interior and green-glowing outdoor pool, Victor

LEFT Sightseers on a tour boat in the ancient harbor of Marseille. The city has been a maritime center since the ancient Greeks settled here.

OPPOSITE Frozen confections at Le Glacier.

Café serves up a colorful environment to match its glass of anise-flavored Ricard, a Marseille specialty. Across the street, sink into a couch, order a Margarita Especial (tequila, Cointreau, agave honey, lemonade), and listen to lounge singers as you gaze at the Vieux Port.

and stop for gelato at **Le Glacier du Roi** (4 place de Lenche; 33-4-91-91-01-16; leglacierduroi.com).

SUNDAY

10 *Mummies and Ice Cream* 11 a.m.

The hillside Le Panier neighborhood is one of the most atmospheric places to stroll. Once a refuge of sailors, the cobbled streets, shady squares, and pastel-hued town houses began welcoming immigrants — Italian, Corsican, Algerian — in the 20th century and are now filling with young professionals and arty types. Meander along its narrow streets,

11 *Some Like It Hot* 1 p.m.

Tucked in an alley along the Vieux Port, the **Zein Oriental Spa** (16 quai Rive Neuve; 33-4-91-59-11-11; marseille.zeinorientalspa.fr), is an upscale hammam (the classic Turkish bath, with heat and cold water splashes) and modern spa. It is very *1,001 Nights* with its keyhole doorways, Moorish tilework, spice-scented air, and soft Arabo-electro music. Check the spa menu, and prepare to be pampered.

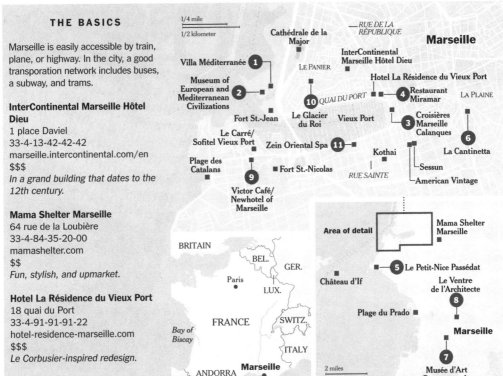

THE BASICS

Marseille is easily accessible by train, plane, or highway. In the city, a good transporation network includes buses, a subway, and trams.

InterContinental Marseille Hôtel Dieu
1 place Daviel
33-4-13-42-42-42
marseille.intercontinental.com/en
$$$
In a grand building that dates to the 12th century.

Mama Shelter Marseille
64 rue de la Loubière
33-4-84-35-20-00
mamashelter.com
$$
Fun, stylish, and upmarket.

Hotel La Résidence du Vieux Port
18 quai du Port
33-4-91-91-91-22
hotel-residence-marseille.com
$$$
Le Corbusier-inspired redesign.

St.-Tropez

France's most famous summer playground can be captured in one word: indulgence. Once the sun starts to heat its bougainvillea-draped lanes and Mediterranean beaches, mega-yachts pack into the harbor, Maseratis and Bentleys prowl the cobbled streets, gazillionaires arrive by helicopter at music-pounding beach clubs, and Middle East royals and Asian industrialists shell out tens of thousands of dollars on Champagne in celebrity-packed nightclubs. Still, not all indulgences are reserved for the seven-figure set. Whatever your income bracket, St.-Tropez has a place for you to play in. — BY SETH SHERWOOD

FRIDAY

1 *St.-Tropez 101* 5:30 p.m.

Where does Paris Hilton crash when she's in town? How much does it cost to rent a multideck yacht for a week? How many cats and dogs has Brigitte Bardot crammed into her seaside house? For a crash course in the St.-Tropez lifestyle and lovely views of its coastal mansions, book a one-hour cruise on **Brigantin II** (Vieux Port, in front of Café de Paris; 33-6-07-09-21-27; lebrigantin.com) and let the captain regale you (in English and French) with anecdotes.

2 *An Indian Interlude* 8 p.m.

The sunset apéro — short for apéritif — is a St.-Tropez ritual. Like bulls to a matador's cape, tourists charge for the red terrace of the Sénéquier cafe. Instead, seek out the **Pan Dei Palais** hotel (52 rue Gambetta; 33-4-94-17-71-71; pandei.com), whose carved wooden screens and statues of Hindu gods feel right out of Rajasthan. Surrounded by chaise longues and four-poster beds, the colonial-chic pool bar is a rarefied spot to sip a Red One (Monkey Shoulder Scotch, amaretto, lemon, strawberry juice, fig syrup) while nibbling curried nuts and nuggets of Emmental.

3 *Star-Studded Supper* 9 p.m.

Stars are everywhere at **Colette**, at the **Hôtel Sezz** (151 route des Salins; 33-4-94-55-31-55; saint-tropez. hotelsezz.com; $$$$). They're overhead, glimmering down on the minimalist patio. They're on the clever neo-Mediterranean menu, which was dreamed up by the Michelin-starred chef Pierre Gagnaire. And

at the Sezz, one of the town's poshest crash pads, there might be some stars of screen or boardroom lurking. On one season's menu, sea bream was given finesse via a carpaccio-thin preparation, cubes of red pepper gelatin, and Mideast spices. For a coda, lush black-currant mousse was topped with pear sorbet and spiked with caramelized sugar.

4 *The Caves or the Quay?* Midnight

The stars also fill **Les Caves du Roy** (Hotel Byblos, Avenue Paul Signac; 33-4-94-56-68-00; www.lescavesduroy.com). Like a 1970s Las Vegas casino, this den of celebrities, princes, and corporate titans is outfitted with pile carpet and electric palm trees. And like a casino, it's a place where you can lose your fortune in 20 minutes — courtesy of expensive Champagne. Far more wallet-friendly high jinks await at **Le Quai** (22 quai Jean Jaurès; 33-4-94-97-04-07; lequaisaint-tropez.com), with its black carpet, black banquettes, black glass tables, and dolled-up crowd sipping mojitos while dancing to funk, soul, and R&B legends.

SATURDAY

5 *One-Stop Shopping* 10 a.m.

If your shopping list includes horse-meat sausages, camouflage bikinis, and Iranian carpets, the Saturday-morning market in the central **Place**

OPPOSITE Saturday-morning shopping in St.-Tropez.

BELOW The colonial-chic pool bar at Pan Dei Palais.

des Lices is a must. Everyone from Ferrari-driving hotshots to aged local housewives converges there, snapping up paella, soap blocks, and linen clothing. Olive hounds should seek La Kemia (33-6-63-46-79-61), which sells regional olive oil and jars of olive tapenade. Sweet tooths will prefer the biscuits flavored with anise, lemon, and orange-flower water at Chez Cathy (33-6-14-30-39-19).

6 *Afternoon à la Plage* 2 p.m.

Choosing a beach club here is as much a philosophical issue as a practical one. Club 55 is for the self-styled elite, Aqua is popular with gays, and so on. Bikini tops are optional at Nikki Beach (Plage de Pampelonne, Route de l'Epi; 33-4-94-79-82-04; nikkibeach.com/sttropez). So are sobriety, frugality, and timidity—all of which are in ever shorter supply as the afternoon advances, the house music booms louder, and the bottles of Champagne flow more freely. Stylish but more chilled-out, New Coco Beach (Plage de Pampelonne, Route de l'Epi; 33-4-94-79-83-25; newcoco.fr) is almost next door. Equipped with a restaurant and bar, it provides music whose volume won't rattle your fillings and purple chaises that fill with a more bourgeois crowd.

7 *Le Shopping* 5 p.m.

You can scarcely hurl a diamond in St.-Tropez without hitting an international luxury boutique. If that's your shopping nirvana, this is a place to indulge, or at least window-shop. For something a little more earthbound, browse among the storefronts for the

ABOVE Yachts at rest in the St.-Tropez port.

OPPOSITE The pool and patio at the Hôtel Sezz.

independent shops that come and go, sometimes as summer pop-ups. The Rue Gambetta is a good place to start.

8 *An Italian Evening* 8 p.m.

You know you're entering Italian territory when you spot breadsticks and hear the staff members rolling their r's: "T-r-r-r-r-r-è-s bien, monsieur-r-r-r!" Cristina Saulini (13 rue des Feniers; 33-4-94-97-46-10; cristinasaulini.com; $$$$), in a tiny passageway, has become one of the town's hottest tables. Here, you'll find eggplant sliced thin and topped with zippy tomato sauce and hot Parmesan. Plump as dinner rolls, the tortelli are sunk in Bolognese sauce and spill out a jackpot of molten cheese. For the strong, the house-made cannoli beckon from the finish line.

9 *Only Stars Above You* 10 p.m.

The roof bar at Kube hotel (Route de St.-Tropez, Gassin; 33-4-94-97-20-00; kubehotel-saint-tropez.com) offers you the starry sky as a ceiling and a view of the dark sea as you sip a Salzburg ice tea (vodka, rum, tequila, Cointreau, sour, and Red Bull) or perhaps sangria made with Champagne. Or you can keep your feet firmly planted on the ground and savor your Kube Royal (strawberry, vodka, and Champagne) at the restaurant's poolside lounge, which has white couches that highlight the clientele's tans.

SUNDAY

10 *Village of Yore* 10 a.m.

It's easy to forget that there's a charming fishing village hidden underneath the tides of Porsches and tourist throngs. Climb the hill to the 17th-century citadel (33-4-94-97-59-43; sainttropez.fr) and gaze

down at the blue Mediterranean, the green hills across the bay, the orange roofs of the village, and the sunflower-yellow dome of Notre-Dame de l'Assomption church. Then hit the **Musée de l'Annonciade** (Place Grammont; 33-4-94-17-84-10), a 16th-century church turned museum with exhibitions dedicated to the painters—from Matisse to André Derain—who found inspiration along the Côte d'Azur.

11 *Lunch on the Sand* Noon

Media types, BMW-driving lawyers, hipster parents with their children, and others congregate at **La Cabane Bambou** (Plage de Pampelonne, Route de Bonne Terrasse; 33-4-94-79-84-13; cabanebambouplage.com), a laid-back beach club, for Sunday lunch. The menu offers seafood and Gallic sweets like a crackly crème brûlée. Afterward, collapse on a beach mattress or into the massage cabin for a final indulgence.

THE BASICS

Fly into Nice or Toulon, or take a train to St.-Raphaël, and board a bus to St.-Tropez. A car can be an impediment; roads to St.-Tropez are often jammed in summer, and parking is difficult.

Hôtel Ermitage
14 avenue Paul Signac
33-4-94-81-08-10
ermitagehotel.fr
$$$
Effortlessly cool, with impeccably sourced retro furniture and a panoramic terrace restaurant.

B. Lodge
12 rue de l'Aioli
33-4-94-97-06-57
hotel-b-lodge.com
$$
Decorated in modern gray and white tones. Pleasant bar and restaurant.

Pan Dei Palais
52 rue Gambetta,
33-4-94-17-71-71
pandei.com
$$$$
Carved wooden screens and statues of gods feel right out of Rajasthan.

Cannes

With its marinas full of white megayachts and water-front streets abuzz with Ferraris and Mercedeses, the glittery French Riviera resort of Cannes at first gives off the rarefied vibe of a town where huffing around on foot must surely offend local mores and offer glaring proof of D-List status. But footwear gets plenty of use in Cannes, and not only by the stars who traipse down the red carpet during the annual Cannes International Film Festival in May. Whether you're strolling along the celebrated seaside promenade known as La Croisette, ambling up the twisting streets of the city's historical Le Suquet neighborhood, hiking the trails on one of the nearby islands, or sashaying across a dance floor, you'll need at least a few pairs of shoes. Luckily, you can find abundant specimens while strutting down the fashionable Rue d'Antibes, yet another essential Cannes walk. — BY SETH SHERWOOD

FRIDAY

1 *Walk of Fame* 5 p.m.

You'll run into the likes of Quentin Tarantino, Angelina Jolie, and Catherine Deneuve—or at least their handprints and signatures in the pavement—as you walk along the western part of La Croisette, around the **Palais des Festivals et des Congrès**, the site of the film festival's main red carpet, and the Esplanade Georges Pompidou. Heading east along the Mediterranean, you'll find yourself alongside Chanel-clad women walking tiny dogs and other Cannes types as the golden sands and music-pounding beach restaurants drift past. Across the palm-lined street, note the grandiose Belle Époque and Art Deco hotels. For culture, **La Malmaison** (cannes.com/fr/culture/centre-d-art-la-malmaison.html) hosts rotating exhibitions of major artists from the Riviera.

2 *A Perfect Perch* 7:30 p.m.

Even if your chopper is in the shop, you can get helicopter views of the city from **Le 360** bar (2

OPPOSITE The Carlton Hotel, overlooking the Mediterranean. Some suites are named for movie stars who came to town for the Cannes International Film Festival.

RIGHT Shopping for sweets at Intuitions, a patisserie and tearoom in the Five Seas Hotel & Spa.

boulevard Jean Hibert; 33-4-92-99-73-10; radissonblu.com/hotel-cannes) atop the Radisson Blu hotel. The tiny indoor lounge is perfect for an intimate twilight tryst over Chablis or a cocktail, while the large outdoor deck offers a livelier atmosphere and vistas of the nighttime city and sea.

3 *Chef's Surprise* 9 p.m.

Have trouble making decisions? Let the chef Bruno Gensdarme, a veteran of the celebrated Guy Savoy restaurant in Paris, choose dinner for you. There's no menu at **La Table du Chef** (5 rue Jean Daumas; 33-4-93-68-27-40; $$$$), his tiny, friendly restaurant, which draws cologne-scented professionals, patrician couples, and other local cognoscenti. Instead, Monsieur Gensdarme roves the daily produce markets and decides on a nightly four-course menu accordingly. His concoctions have included seared tuna with sweet potato purée, rare filet de boeuf with foie gras gravy, and chocolate terrine with strawberry-raspberry foam.

4 *Local Libations* 11 p.m.

Avoid the tourist-trap La Croisette bars and direct your feet instead to the old quarter of Le Suquet, where Cannes natives party. For a laid-back glass of wine amid candlelight and orchids, slip into **L'Endroit** (10 rue du Suquet; 33-4-93-99-09-23). Then cross the street to **Charly's Bar** (5 rue Suquet; 33-4-97-06-54-78), a lively stone cave of a spot where everyone from gilded youth to overtanned divor-cées packs in to grind to '60s soul, '80s remixes, and French pop.

5 *Cannes-o-Copia* 10 a.m.

Marché Forville (cannes-tourism.com/en/ cannes-open-markets.html), a three-block-long covered market, is a riot of produce and meats. The northwest corner is the spot to stock up on gifts that transport well, like dry sausage made from pork, duck, or boar; jams in flavors like plum-prune and fig; and olive oil and olive tapenade.

6 *Castle in the Air* Noon

Village life emerges as you climb the streets of Le Suquet. Ascending cobbled lanes and zigzagging stairways, you pass town houses with peach and lime facades, decked with lanterns. On the hilltop, the fortress houses the **Musée de la Castre** (33-4-93-38-55-26; www.culture.gouv.fr/culture/nllefce/fr/mu_06400). Its collection of ethnographic art — Indonesian shadow puppets, stone Etruscan sarcophagi, Tibetan Buddhist tablets — is impressive, but the museum's marquee attraction is the 12th-century tower, which offers a commanding view.

7 *Culinary Curiosities* 2 p.m.

Go back down to the seafront at Plages du Midi and lunch at **Le Cabanon** (Boulevard du Midi; 33-6-21-56-26-09; lecabanoncannes.com; $$$), where your meal can be as light as a seafood salad

or as hearty as a lamb tagine with lemon confit. For a more involved lunch experience, consider **Les Apprentis Gourmets** (6 rue Tesseire; 33-4-93-38-78-76; lesapprentisgourmets.com; $$$), a cooking school. One offering is a single-dish, 30-minute class, after which the student eats the lesson.

8 *The Retail Trail* 4 p.m.

A Saturday stroll along the boutique-packed Rue d'Antibes is what the French call "un must," but look for shops selling indie design and fashion among the Zara-Camper-Swarovski-Mont Blanc mafia. **Bathroom Graffiti** (52 rue d'Antibes; 33-4-93-39-02-32; bathroomgraffiti.com), a vast emporium, sells T-shirts, funky throw pillows, and night lights shaped like gummy bears. Closet-size **Augustin Latour** (8 rue Chabaud; 33-4-93-99-08-94) has home décor like garlands of small paper lanterns by Paris-based Tsé & Tsé Associées. Fashion and design go global at ethno-chic **Ahimsa** (148 rue d'Antibes; 33-4-93-43-78-24; ahimsacannes.com). Those red ceramic lamps from Morocco would look lovely hanging over that goat-hair carpet from Turkey, non?

ABOVE Even on a cool day, it's worth visiting Le 360, a rooftop deck atop the Radisson Blu hotel, for a panoramic view of sea and sky at sunset.

9 *Discreet Dinner* 8 p.m.

Illicit lovers, camera-shy celebrities, and vampires avoiding daylight will appreciate **L'Affable** (5 rue Lafontaine; 33-4-93-68-02-09; restaurant-laffable.fr; $$$$). The discreet dining room, an elegant padded space in neutral beige, has no windows, ensuring that no prying paparazzi or jealous spouses can peer inside. Light and color come from the prix fixe menu of attractively presented Mediterranean dishes and French classics. Past menus have included a velvety yellow squash soup with foie gras and splashes of green pistou; veal with mustard sauce and crunchy carrot; and a bright orange soufflé spiked with Grand Marnier.

10 *Flames and Stars* 10 p.m.

Women in black dresses and guys with untucked dress shirts ring the rectangular bar of **B. Pub** (22 rue Macé; 33-4-93-38-17-30), an ersatz neo-Classical-style nightclub that brims with gilt-painted columns and moldings. Sometimes flames ring the bar, such as when the bartenders douse it with lighter fluid and toss matches, or when someone orders a bottle of Champagne, which arrives in a glowing ice bucket shooting off sparks. Afterward, hit up the uberflashy nightclub **Le Bâoli** (Port Canto Boulevard; 33-4-93-43-03-43; lebaoli.com), where Jude Law, Beyoncé,

ABOVE Saturday night at B. Pub, a nightclub devoted to gilt and glow. Bartenders here have been known to douse the bar with lighter fluid and then toss matches.

BELOW The Île St.-Honorat, a 20-minute ferry ride from Cannes. Take a walk along the island's craggy coast and visit its landmark, the Abbey of Lérins.

Snoop Dogg, and Prince Albert of Monaco have all been sighted.

SUNDAY

11 *Offshore Chilling* 10 a.m.

A restorative nature walk awaits on **Île St.-Honorat** (cannes-ilesdelerins.com), the smaller of the two Îles de Lérins, which lie just off the coast. A ferry from the tip of the marina of the Vieux Port, past Quai Laubeuf, drops you 20 minutes later on the craggy coast of the island, whose inhabitants are monks of the Abbaye de Lérins. Strolling the

island's perimeter requires two to three hours and takes you past rocky coves, promontories, wildflowers, vineyards, and the ruins of centuries-old stone chapels. The highlight is the abandoned medieval abbey, an eerie Gothic edifice out of a ghost story. In the current abbey, next door, a gift shop sells monk-made wines. Near the island's ferry landing, the Mediterranean's bounty awaits at **La Tonnelle** (33-4-92-99-54-08; tonnelle-abbayedelerins.fr; $$$), an upscale open-air seafood restaurant.

ABOVE A prawn brochette ready for consumption at La Tonnelle, an upscale restaurant on the Île St. Honorat that specializes in Mediterranean seafood.

OPPOSITE The medieval walls and arches of an abandoned fortified monastery building on the Île St. Honorat. Monks still populate the island.

THE BASICS

From Nice, take the SNCF train for a half-hour trip to Cannes with seaside views.

Five Seas Hotel & Spa
1 rue Notre-Dame
33-4-63-36-05-05
five-seas-hotel-cannes.com
$$$$
Spa, rooftop pool, restaurant, tearoom created by a pastry chef, and an 88-foot yacht.

Hôtel Pruly
32 boulevard d'Alsace
33-4-93-38-41-28
hotel-pruly.com
$
A white town house with a garden and 14 colorful rooms.

Carlton Cannes
58 boulevard de la Croisette
33-4-93-06-40-06
intercontinental-carlton-cannes.com
$$$$
Century-old grand old hotel with white cake-frosting facade.

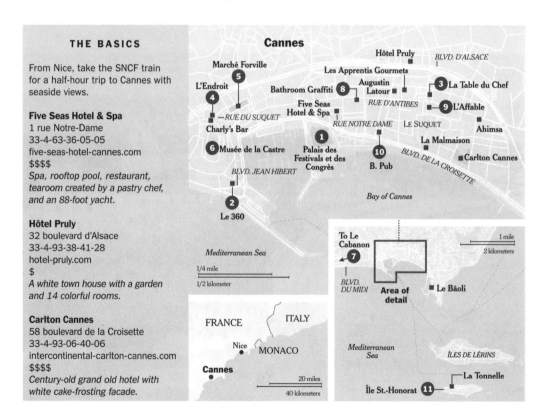

Nice & the Côte d'Azur

Nice, the unofficial capital of the French Riviera, is a place of palm-lined boulevards, pastel terra cotta buildings, and the blue waters of the Baie des Anges, the Bay of Angels. The fifth-largest city in France, it is also more urban and more complicated than other towns on the Côte d'Azur. When Czarist aristocrats and British royals began arriving to take the sun in the 1800s, Nice was politically linked to Italy (Garibaldi, the Italian nationalist, was born there), and Italian influences remain in food, architecture, and local culture. After a Belle Époque heyday as a resort, the city declined in the 20th century, but it has now been rediscovered by a new generation of sun seekers, hoteliers, chefs, fashionistas, and backpackers. Given the beauty of its setting and the appeal of its Old Port and Old Town, that rejuvenation was probably inevitable. — BY SETH SHERWOOD

FRIDAY

1 *Pebble Beach* 2 p.m.

Get acquainted with Nice by taking a stroll on the **Promenade des Anglais**, the waterfront walkway where aristocrats once sedately took the sea air. Now it's the playground of everyone in Nice, busy with joggers, bicyclists, skateboarders, and baby strollers. To lounge in the sun or dip a toe in the water, trot down to one of the public beaches along the promenade. They're pebbly, not sandy, but that doesn't seem to hurt their popularity.

2 *Choose Your Painter* 4 p.m.

Hit one (or both) of Nice's brand-name art collections. The **Musée Matisse** (164 avenue des Arènes; 33-4-93-81-08-08; musee-matisse-nice. org), in a 17th-century Genoese villa, has a sizable cache of Henri Matisse's work: gorgeously abstract stained glass, paper cutouts, and paintings. Matisse moved to Nice in 1917 and spent most of his life here. Nearby is the **Musée National Marc Chagall** (Avenue du Docteur Ménard; 33-4-93-53-87-20; musee-chagall.fr), famous for a series of Chagall's biblical paintings.

3 *Go Niçois* 8 p.m.

You're in Nice, so look for real Niçoise cuisine, which you are most likely to find at small, unpreten-

tious restaurants. At **L'Escalinada** (22 rue Pairolière; 33-4-93-62-11-71; escalinada.fr; $$), grab an outdoor table and take in neighborhood views while you dine. (La Table Alziari, next door, is an equally good choice.) This is your chance to try starters like pissaladière—the local, tomato-less, onion-laden version of pizza—or stuffed encornets (squid bodies, filled with chard and rice). Entrees include secca d'Entrevaux, dried beef in the style of a nearby mountain town, sprinkled with oil and raw garlic. After dinner, sip a digestif in the **Cours Saleya**, a long plaza in the old town. Flower sellers reign here during the day, but it becomes an outdoor cafe scene at night.

SATURDAY

4 *Local Color* 10 a.m.

Lose yourself in Nice's postcard-perfect Old Town. Within this spider web of narrow paved passageways, a myriad of olive-oil dealers, soap sellers, spice merchants, sidewalk cafes, and Baroque churches burst from among richly colored buildings—peach, sunflower yellow, pistachio green—that seem to have absorbed all the colors of the Riviera's bounty. Be sure to stop for tastes like tomatoes, avocados, and beer, all in ice-cream form, at the creative ice-cream parlor **Fenocchio** (2 place Rossetti; 33-4-93-80-72-52; fenocchio.fr).

OPPOSITE Dinner high over the Mediterranean in Éze.

BELOW L'Escalinada, in Vieux Nice, serves traditional dishes of authentic Niçoise cuisine.

5 *Socca to You* Noon

Don't let the tourists keep you away from **Chez Theresa** (Cours Saleya; 33-4-93-85-00-04; $), a walk-up stand that is likely to have a line. You're here for socca — hot, peppery flatbread that is a Niçois staple. It's made of chickpea flour, water, olive oil, and the occasional onion, and it's authentic and local, a Nice must-try.

6 *Food and Clothing* 1 p.m.

Get your clubwear at **Espace Harroch** (7 rue Paradis; 33-4-93-82-50-23; espace-harroch.com), a four-level concept store stocking top labels for women and men, as well as home décor. Then stroll into the Provençal food shops on Rue St.-François

de Paule. **Terre de Truffes** (11 rue St.-François de Paule; 33-4-93-62-07-68; terresdetruffes.com), is a trove of puréed Provençal truffles, black truffles from Périgord, and similar delicacies. The venerable olive oil specialist **Boutique Nicolas Alziari** (14 rue St.-François de Paule; 33-4-93-62-94-03; alziari.com.fr) stocks fresh olives, olive oil soaps, and, of course, extra virgin olive oil.

7 *Iconoclasts* 3 p.m.

To prove to yourself once again that art can be fun, check out the **Musée d'Art Moderne et d'Art Contemporain** (Place Yves Klein; 33-4-97-13-42-01; mamac-nice.org), an institution stocked with iconoclasts, outlaw artists, and avant-garde figures. Ellsworth Kelly, Frank Stella, James Rosenquist, Andy Warhol, Robert Indiana, and Keith Haring are major names in the American-heavy collection.

8 *Back in the Water* 4:30 p.m.

The best beaches tend to be private, but accessible for a reasonable fee. If you crave more beach

ABOVE Éze, built on a cliff 1,400 feet over the sea, preserves its fairy tale appearance. Automobiles and visible power lines do not intrude to spoil the medieval illusion.

LEFT The Palais de la Mediterranée, renovated for today's guests, once hosted Jazz Age stars like Josephine Baker.

time, try **Lido Beach**, across from the Palais de la Méditerranée, where you can rent a cushioned chaise longue.

9 *Go All Out* 8 p.m.

Splurge once on the taxi ride into the hills overlooking the city and again at **Parcours Live** (1 Place Marcel Eusebi, Falicon; 33-4-93-84-94-57; restaurant-parcours.com; $$$$), in Falicon. The restaurant offers a sublime view and an ever-changing menu focused on local produce. One standout dinner included risotto with summer truffles and Mediterranean tuna crusted with sesame seeds on a soy-soaked potato purée. The globe-spanning wine card represents France, Slovenia, Thailand, and beyond.

SUNDAY

10 *Along the Coast* 10 a.m.

To see another face of the Côte d'Azur, drive or take a bus to **Villefranche-sur-Mer**, a few miles closer to Italy. Villefranche has the same radiant sun, warm waters, and succulent Provençal cuisine that's found in Nice, Cannes, and Monaco, but last year's fashions can be sported with impunity, and almost no one arrives by mega-yacht. Walk the cobbled streets, look over the bric-a-brac at the weekly Sunday flea market, and have lunch at one of the restaurants at the ancient port. Jean Cocteau lived here, and

entertained friends like Picasso, Stravinsky, and Isadora Duncan. Much later, the Rolling Stones arrived, escaping fame and British taxes; rented space; and recorded an album, *Exile on Main Street*.

11 *Above It All* 1 p.m.

Take the steep road up to **Éze**, a medieval town perched on a cliff 1,400 feet over the Mediterranean. Éze has kept many trappings of modernity at bay.

TOP Villefranche-sur-Mer is the Côte d'Azur without the yachting crowd and designer boutiques.

ABOVE A statue of Jean Cocteau in Villefranche. At his home there, he entertained friends like Picasso and Stravinsky.

Automobiles, electric signs, and visible power lines don't penetrate this fairy tale setting of tapering spires and ivy-draped Gothic stone structures. Make the spiraling ascent to the ruined chateau at the village pinnacle. You will pass studded wooden doors and iron-barred windows, iron caldrons overflowing with fiery red flowers, and the 14th-century Chapelle de la Ste.-Croix. All the scene lacks is a group of chanting Gregorian monks. At the top, the castle ruins have been reborn as a "jardin exotique."

Plants brought from far away — yucca, aloe, agaves, cactuses — grow amid the collapsed battlements and crumbled stones.

ABOVE A regatta off the shore of Nice in the blue Baie des Anges—the Bay of Angels.

OPPOSITE St. Nicholas Orthodox Cathedral in Nice, a relic of the days when Russian counts and princes arrived for long, lazy stays by the Mediterranean.

THE BASICS

Downtown Nice and the adjacent Old Town are easily walkable. The bus system is useful; taxis are expensive.

Palais de la Méditerranée
13-15 promenade des Anglais
33-4-93-27-12-34
lepalaisdelamediterranee.com
$$$$
Art Deco palace frequented by Jazz Age stars like Josephine Baker; now renovated with contemporary style.

Hi Hotel
3 avenue des Fleurs
33-4-97-07-26-26
hi-hotel.net
$$$$
A spot for seekers of the future of hotel design to park their spaceships. Couches with stereo speakers, beds that become tables.

Hôtel Beau Rivage
24 rue St.-François de Paule
33-4-92-47-82-82
nicebeaurivage.com
$$$
Updated Belle Époque-era hotel with a private beach.

Corsica

The ancient Greeks sailed into Corsica's dazzling turquoise bays and declared the island Kalliste: the Most Beautiful. Henri Matisse strode down a gangplank and found a "marvelous land," where "all is color, all is light." Blessed with seaside cliffs and grottoes, jagged mountains, sublime gorges, and sun-baked white beaches, the island bursts with landscapes that could melt a photographer's lens. Part of France but still harboring a fierce sense of independence, Corsica has sometimes seemed isolated. But these days, rising tides of European vacationers and the jet-setters that the French call "Les Beautiful People" are washing up in the medieval harbor towns and modern beach bars. Train travel is scenic — the journey from coastal Ajaccio, Corsica's largest city, to Corte in its rugged center inspires universal awe — but in a short trip, it's most practical to rent a car and brave the vertiginous roads. — BY SETH SHERWOOD

FRIDAY

1 *Mediterranean Odyssey* 2 p.m.

It's said that Ulysses and his men took shelter in the cliff-lined port of **Bonifacio**, at Corsica's southern tip. Today, you can take in the scenes of its centuries-old citadel, dramatic harbor, and restaurant-filled quays. To view the spectacular cliffs and grottoes nearby, buy tickets at one of the kiosks here and spend an hour on a tour boat, perhaps the *Gina* (33-4-95-10-97-50; ginacroisiere.com) or the *Corsaire* (33-6-23-25-14-60; vedetteslecorsaire.com). Immense chalk-white cliffs, horizontally grooved like a geological mille-feuille, will dwarf the boat as it cuts through water the color of Curaçao liqueur. At sea level, enormous grottoes open darkly in the cliff walls and wind-eroded rock formations sprout mysteriously from the sea. Afterward, drive north up the coast to stop in at the Tahitiesque beaches of **Santa Giulia** and **Palombaggia**, where leisurely travelers go to be bronzed.

2 *Kisses in the Air* 8 p.m.

The nexus of V.I.P. action is **Porto-Vecchio**, a picturesque old port built in the days when Corsica was ruled by Genoa, and long rhapsodized over for its rustic 16th-century buildings. Now summer evenings transform the town into Corsica's night-life mecca. On cafe terraces, glasses fill with rosé from the nearby Domaine de Torraccia vineyard or Corsican Pietra beer, flavored with chestnut. Air kisses flutter like fireflies — "Ciao!" "Bonsoir!" "Hola!" If you can get a reservation, have dinner at the cozy and traditional **Bistro la Table de Nathalie** (4 rue Jean Jaurès; 33-4-95-71-65-25; $$$$), where Nathalie is likely to chat with you, and then follow the beat to one of the pre-club bars where outdoor D.J.'s spin.

3 *Club Goliath* Midnight

But this is all a mere preamble for **La Via Notte** (just south of Porto-Vecchio; 33-4-95-72-02-12; vianotte.com) the island's nocturnal temple. The scale is enormous, bombastic, as if Napoleon himself had ordered it. Five bars and a restaurant spread over multiple levels and pavilions. Inside the D.J. booth, three men operate long flashing control panels as if trying to pilot a rock and funk and fusion hip-hop spaceship. Go-go dancers grind on platforms as streaks of laser light shoot past. The club is a favorite of French soccer stars and film personalities, and to woo them, it flies in big names from the international D.J. circuit.

OPPOSITE Clear Mediterranean waters near Bonifacio.

BELOW The citadel above Corte, an inland town where some still yearn for independence from France.

4 *Mountain Redoubt* 10 a.m.

Drive inland to **Corte**, where shop windows beckon with traditional delicacies — sausage, cheese, honey, wine — and more than a few walls drip with graffiti shouting slogans for Corsican independence. In the cafes, old men chat in the native Corsican language. Corte was the island's capital during its lone flicker of independence, from 1755 to 1769. Its leader then, Pascal Paoli, is a local deity. His name adorns

TOP The island's interior mountains, seen from Corte.

ABOVE A train from Ajaccio, Napoleon's home, to Corte.

the university, the main street, and even the sweet shop on the main square — as well as the square itself. In its center he lives on in statue form, a well-dressed Enlightenment gentleman with an intense gaze.

5 *Corsican Fare* 1 p.m.

Classic Corsican wines and foods are on sale at **La Vieille Cave** (2 ruelle de la Fontaine; 33-4-95-46-33-79; villedecorte.fr/cave_vin.php), but take your meal for today at the terrace restaurant **U San Teofalu** (3 place Paoli; 33-4-95-38-15-71; villedecorte. fr/resto; $$). One day's three-course Corsican menu included a charcuterie and cheese plate, grilled trout, and dessert.

6 *An Island's Song* 2 p.m.

For a crash course in the history and cultural traditions of Corsica, visit the **Musée de la Corse** (Citadel; 33-4-95-45-25-45; musee-corse.com) on the high point above town occupied by the city's old citadel. The museum, in a modern building, tells the story of Corsica's unique culture — its folk traditions, crafts, and history. A row of soundproof booths allows visitors to listen to the unusual native music, group singing in an Old World polyphonic style. The songs, in the Corsican language, sound somewhere between Gregorian chant and folk ballads, with sprightly reels and sea-chantey-like rounds. Behind the museum, a viewing platform looks out over a mountain valley.

7 *Fortress and Festivals* 6 p.m.

Back in the car, drive about 50 miles on a good highway to the city of **Calvi** on the northwest coast, where a medieval hilltop citadel shoots up from the sea and old streets are a warren of cobbled lanes. Take a walk before dark and get a sense of the multifaceted beauty of the setting. The town sits on a high point at the end of a curving bay, the Gulf of Calvi. Pleasure boats are anchored in its marina, and a long sand beach hugs the translucent turquoise sea. Just a dozen miles inland, snow-capped mountains rise against the sky. The town has become a music destination, sponsoring inter-national festivals celebrating "Calvi on the Rocks" electronic music in July, and polyphonic vocal music in September.

8 *Mussels in Muscat* 8 p.m.

For fashionable beachside dining, the white villa-like **Octopussy** restaurant (Pinede Plage; 33-4-95-65-23-16; plage-octopussy.com; $$) does jazzy riffs on Corsican ingredients, like melon with Corsican ham and baked cod with artichokes. It's attached to the Octopussy beach club, where sunbathers bask and D.J.'s sometimes spin.

ABOVE Bonifacio clings to a coastal cliff.

RIGHT The port of Calvi, in the northwest.

SUNDAY

9 *Lurking History* 10 a.m.

Explore Calvi's streets, where exiles, explorers, and renegades seem to lurk around every bend. One old house on the Rue de Fil, now a ruin, is thought by some to be the real birthplace of Christopher Columbus (in his day, Calvi was part of the Republic of Genoa). Tucked away nearby, near the Church of St. John the Baptist, is Maison Pacciola, a small build-ing where Napoleon hid from Corsican nationalists during the French Revolution. A third small street, Rue St.-Antoine, reveals **Chez Tao** (33-4-95-65-00-73; cheztao.com), a nightclub founded in 1935 by a former Russian military officer named Tao Kerefoff. He

escaped the Russian Revolution and fled to New York, where he was persuaded by Prince Felix Yusupov, one of the conspirators against Rasputin, to go to Calvi. His club still fills nightly with stylish seasonal refugees from Paris, London, and other capitals.

10 *Join the Foreign Legion* Noon
 A cavern in the citadel hillside reveals the **Musée de la Légion Étrangère** (33-4-42-18-12-41; samle.legion-etrangere.com), dedicated to the French

Foreign Legion, which maintains a base outside of Calvi. Amid mannequins in paratrooper outfits, exhibitions detail the history of this shadowy branch of the French military, once known for accepting recruits of any background from any country, no questions asked. If you bought all of the curious souvenirs on sale here, you could lie on a Foreign Legion beach towel, read a book of Foreign Legion Christmas tales, and fill your Foreign Legion mug with Foreign Legion Esprit de Corps rosé, whose label depicts violently charging troops firing weapons.

ABOVE Clubbing at La Via Notte, near Porto-Vecchio.

OPPOSITE Immersed in the sea near Bonifacio.

THE BASICS

Airports in the towns of Ajaccio, Bastia, Calvi, and Figari all have Air France service and rental car agencies. A scenic rail route to Corte and Calvi originates in Ajaccio, the coastal city where Napoleon was born. Many hotels and other businesses catering to tourists close from November through March.

Casa del Mar
Route de Palombaggia,
Porto-Vecchio
33-4-95-72-34-34
casadelmar.fr
$$$$
Arrive by helicopter, yacht, or car at this white and airy hotel with lush grounds, a Carita spa, and a Michelin-starred restaurant.

Hotel Saint Christophe
Place Bel'Ombra, Calvi
33-4-95-65-05-74
saintchristophecalvi.com
$$
In Calvi's town center, a stone's throw from both the citadel and the bustling port.

Map labels

Church of St. John the Baptist
Hotel Saint Christophe
9 Chez Tao
Calvi Gulf of Calvi
Octopussy **8**

10 miles
15 kilometers

Bastia
5 La Vieille Cave
10 Musée de la Légion Étrangère
7
Calvi

Mediterranean Sea

Corte **4**
U San Teofalu
6
Musée de la Corse

CORSICA
Ajaccio FRANCE
Tyrrhenian Sea

ITALY
Genoa
FRANCE
Marseille Ligurian Sea

Area of detail

Mediterranean Sea

ITALY
SARDINIA

Tyrrhenian Sea

100 miles
150 kilometers

Bistro la Table de Nathalie/ Porto-Vecchio
2
La Via Notte **3**
Casa del Mar
Figari
Palombaggia
Santa Giulia
Bonifacio **1**

Monaco

Monaco, a constitutional monarchy on the Riviera measuring less than a square mile, evokes high-stakes gambling, multimillion-dollar yachts, Russian oligarchs, race-car drivers, James Bond films, spotless sidewalks, and no public debt. Hotel suites with a view of the Mediterranean during the annual spring Grand Prix can cost thousands, even tens of thousands of euros. A starter of soup at a top restaurant can cost as much as a meal for two at a more modest place. Monaco is a place where high-priced female "escorts" with long legs and exotic accents decorate the nightclubs and hotel lobbies. Visitors can drop their dogs off at free kennels, and car owners feel safe enough to leave their keys in the ignition. Prince Albert II is pushing to make Monaco a family-friendly, environmentally correct vacation spot. Look hard enough, and you will discover a world of art, natural beauty, and good food and lodging at affordable prices.
— BY ELAINE SCIOLINO

FRIDAY

1 *An American Princess* 3 p.m.

The story of Grace Kelly — the Oscar-winning American actress who married a prince, became a princess and died tragically — is woven into the fabric of Monaco's history. An avenue, a rose garden, a foundation, even a polka-dotted fish have been named after her. Her body is buried alongside that of her husband, Prince Rainier III, in the Roman-Byzantine-style Monaco Cathedral. You can get close to her spirit in a second-story suite known as the **Princess Grace Irish Library** (9 rue Princesse Marie-de-Lorraine; 377-9350-1225; pgil.mc). Her personal Irish book collection is here, as are her sheet music, a scrapbook of news clippings about her, floral napkins she designed for Springmaid, the chairs from the dining room of her apartment in Paris, and her mother's sewing box.

2 *Northern Italian* 6:30 p.m.

Head up to the Jardin Exotique district and stop at **La Chaumière** (60 boulevard du Jardin Exotique; 377-9770-0492; la-chaumiere.mc) for a cocktail and a postcard-perfect view of Monaco. It is just about the only public spot where you can see the palace from above. Then make your way to **La Piazza** (9 rue du Portier; 377-9350-4700; lapiazza-monaco.com; $$$$), where the chef and owner Giovanni Orsolini prepares excellent Northern Italian food. The restaurant specializes in seafood and features such signature dishes as stuffed zucchini flowers with ricotta and tomato and the lightest cannelloni filled with pumpkin or veal. A mural of the main square in Orsolini's hometown of Ascoli Piceno fills one of the peach-colored walls.

3 *Not for Gamblers Only* 10:30 p.m.

The **Casino de Monte-Carlo** (Place du Casino; casinomontecarlo.com), besides being the world's most famous casino, is an architectural delight. Inaugurated in 1863, reconstructed in 1878 by Charles Garnier, it has an atrium paved in marble and surrounded by 28 Ionic columns in onyx. On one side, the Opera Hall, with red and gold décor, bas-reliefs, and sculptures, is an ode to Garnier's other architectural masterpiece, the Paris Opéra. On the other is the Casino itself (which you can visit without having to play). It leads into the **Salle Blanche**, which opens to the sea and is the most elegant place in town to have a cocktail and hear live music.

OPPOSITE The Casino de Monte-Carlo, the world's most famous casino and the symbol of Monaco, was designed by Charles Garnier, architect of the Opéra in Paris.

BELOW Bags at Le Dressing, a shop that sells designer fashion items lightly used by wealthy former owners.

4 *What's Under the Waves* 10 a.m.

Prince Albert I, a scientist and an oceanographer as well as a sovereign, built the **Musée Océanographique** (Avenue St-Martin; 377-9315-3600; oceano.mc) in 1910 as a temple of the sea combining art and science. The building pays homage to the Mediterranean: the facade is decorated with crabs, shrimp, scorpion fish, jelly fish, calamari eggs, and other oddities from the deep; the mosaic floors evoke the sea. Albert's whaling ship and Jacques Cousteau's diving bell are here. The aquarium features a world-class collection, including sharks, octopuses, and tortoises.

5 *Classy Fast Food* 12:30 p.m.

Every morning, the **Place d'Armes** esplanade in the heart of Monaco pitches red and yellow shade umbrellas and becomes an open-air food and flower market, the **Marché de la Condamine** (mairie.mc/poles/pratique/les-marches). Some of the vendors come from their farms in Italy 100 miles away, bringing with them homemade olive oil and jars of preserved vegetables. Indoors are cafeteria-style operations serving sandwiches, vegetarian specialties, and fresh dishes like a mountain of fried squid.

6 *Secondhand Luxury* 2 p.m.

Even if you can't afford the black crocodile Birkin bag at **Le Dressing** (2 rue des Orangers; 1 rue Princesse Florestine; 377-9325-8226; ledressingmonaco.com) for 28,000 euros, you might fall in love with a Stephen Sprouse leather jacket with a painted image of Marilyn Monroe on the back for 1,590 euros, or red patent leather Yves Saint Laurent pumps at 195 euros. Most of the inventory is like new. "Women in Monaco can't wear the same dress twice," said Helen Rimsberg, the owner. "Otherwise people would think your husband had money problems."

TOP The Musée Océanographique pays homage to the sea, its creatures, its sailors, and Jacques Cousteau.

ABOVE Pouring a Cocktail Grace at the Hôtel Columbus.

7 *Hit the Beach* 3:30 p.m.

The picture-postcard beaches in the eastern **Larvotto** district are a mix of public and private. Ask your hotel for detailed directions. The weather can be too hot for some people in July and August, but June and September are reliably good times to enjoy both the sun and the warm water. Don't expect movie stars — most beach-goers will be mere tourists like yourself — and keep your flip-flops on as a defense against the abrasive sand.

8 *Trip to the Palace* 4:30 p.m.

Tour the "Grands Appartements" of the royal palace, the **Palais Princier de Monaco** (377-9325-1831; palais.mc) — not Versailles but still impressive. While you're there, take a look at Prince Rainier III's private collection of antique cars, including Rolls-Royces, Cadillacs, and Maseratis.

9 *On the French Side* 6 p.m.

It is hard to find markers indicating that you've left Monaco and crossed into France. On one side of the Avenue du Port is the Fontvieille district of Monaco, on the other (French) side, the Riviera

ABOVE Yachts at rest in the Fontvieille harbor.

RIGHT The Palais Princier de Monaco, home and stronghold of the ruling Grimaldi family.

Marriott hotel. To the left of the Marriott is a walkway that borders the water. Expect to see beach volleyball players, Belle Époque villas, catamarans, joggers, and fishing boats. Stone steps lead down to sheltered coves where you can skip stones and be alone. Turn back anywhere along the way, or go to the end (three hours round trip) at **Cap d'Ail**'s Plage Mala, a beautiful hidden cove.

10 *Dinner by the Sea* 8:30 p.m.

Back in Cap d'Ail, near the Marriott, is **A'Trego** (Port de Cap d'Ail; 33-4-9328-5822; byatrego.com), a futuristic complex that juts out into the sea and offers three dining spaces. **La Cantine** ($$$$), designed by Philippe Starck, is the liveliest. Try the tasting menu:

three starters, three entrees, and three desserts. After dinner take the free shuttle bus back to your hotel—or the free shuttle boat to your yacht.

SUNDAY

11 *Exotic Garden* 10 a.m.

More than 1,000 varieties of cactuses and other succulents grow between the rocks and on the steep crags in the **Jardin Exotique** (62 boulevard du Jardin Exotique; 377-9315-2980; jardin-exotique.mc). Park

benches offer views of the water, and the charming footbridges appear to be carved wood although they are actually made of concrete. Below is a prehistoric cave complete with stalagmites and stalactites. At the nearby **Nouveau Musée National de Monaco** (Villa Paloma, 56 boulevard du Jardin Exotique; 377-9898-4860; nmnm.mc), which emphasizes modern and contemporary art, architecture, and design, exhibitions can include paintings, sculpture, photographs, videos, films, costumes, and relics of Monégasque history.

ABOVE A bust of Princess Grace at the Princess Grace Irish Library, which houses her collection of Irish books.

OPPOSITE The view from the Jardin Exotique, a garden with more than 1,000 varieties of plants in a craggy landscape.

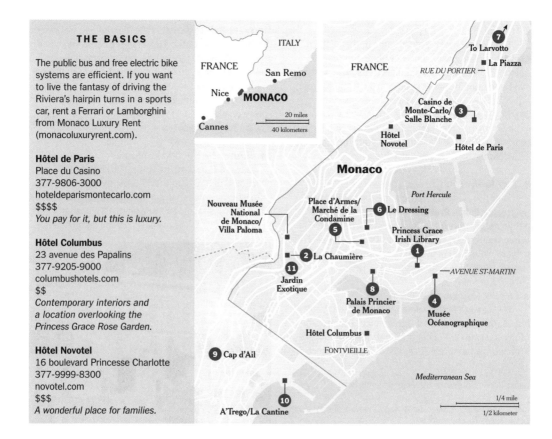

THE BASICS

The public bus and free electric bike systems are efficient. If you want to live the fantasy of driving the Riviera's hairpin turns in a sports car, rent a Ferrari or Lamborghini from Monaco Luxury Rent (monacoluxuryrent.com).

Hôtel de Paris
Place du Casino
377-9806-3000
hoteldeparismontecarlo.com
$$$$
You pay for it, but this is luxury.

Hôtel Columbus
23 avenue des Papalins
377-9205-9000
columbushotels.com
$$
Contemporary interiors and a location overlooking the Princess Grace Rose Garden.

Hôtel Novotel
16 boulevard Princesse Charlotte
377-9999-8300
novotel.com
$$$
A wonderful place for families.

ITALY

FRANCE

San Remo

Nice **MONACO**

20 miles

Cannes

40 kilometers

FRANCE

RUE DU PORTIER —

To Larvotto ⑦

■ La Piazza

Casino de Monte-Carlo/ ③
Salle Blanche ■

Hôtel Novotel ■

Hôtel de Paris ■

Monaco

Port Hercule

Nouveau Musée National de Monaco/ Villa Paloma ■

Place d'Armes/ Marché de la Condamine ⑤

⑥ Le Dressing

Princess Grace Irish Library ①

■ ② La Chaumière

⑪

Jardin Exotique

—AVENUE ST-MARTIN

⑧

Palais Princier de Monaco

④

Musée Océanographique

Hôtel Columbus ■

FONTVIEILLE

⑨ Cap d'Ail

Mediterranean Sea

1/4 mile

⑩

A'Trego/La Cantine

1/2 kilometer

Madrid

Once again, Madrid has become a city for walkers. For years, a massive urban renovation project turned much of the Spanish capital into a massive construction site. Sidewalks and roads were dug up; parts of the ring road on the city's outskirts were buried underground. Now the city is seeing the benefits. The six-mile-long park called Madrid Río has brought swaths of the city closer in spirit to the Manzanares River, replacing intrusive roadways with new bridges and green spaces. There are new paths, fountains, trees, and play areas, and the population was quick to get out and enjoy them. Faster metro lines take suburbanites more quickly to the city center for work or play. Some plans had to be scaled back after boom times became slim times, but that may be just as well. What Madrid has gained is all at human scale. — BY ELAINE SCIOLINO

FRIDAY

1 *The Centerpiece* 4:30 p.m.

With its arches, balconies, and painted facades, the **Plaza Mayor**, the 17th-century square where bullfights, trials, and executions were once held, is the most splendid place to encounter Madrid. Ignore the arcades full of flamenco-dancer refrigerator magnets and knee socks that say "Madrid," and walk to the **Plaza de la Paja**. Peek into the Jardín del Príncipe de Anglona, whose brick-and-concrete walls hide the small garden with brick paths and pomegranate and almond trees. Then stop for an herbal tea served in a Moroccan mug at the **Delic** cafe and bar (Costanilla de San Andrés 14; 34-91-364-54-50). A few steps away, see the two colored ancient Roman mosaics at the **Museo de los Orígenes**, Casa de San Isidro (Plaza de San Andrés 2; 34-91-366-74-15; madrid.es/museosanisidro).

2 *Art for the Soul* 6 p.m.

Dash into the magnificently tiled **San Francisco el Grande Basilica** nearby (Plaza de San Francisco; 34-91-365-38-00). The dome is bigger than that of St. Paul's Cathedral in London. But the real attraction is

the painting of San Bernardino de Siena, one of the earliest of Goya's Madrid paintings. Goya painted himself into its right side. Also often overlooked are the paintings by Zurbarán and Velázquez.

3 *Updated Classics* 9 p.m.

La Gastroteca de Santiago (Plazuela de Santiago 1; 34-91-548-07-07; lagastrotecadesantiago.es; $$$$) is a simple and modern red-walled, white-tiled space, with glass doors offering a peek into the kitchen where Juan Carlos Ramos, the chef and owner, makes magic. The first courses are large enough to split. The menu changes often, with such offerings as grilled marinated octopus salad with anticucho sauce or chocolate ingot stuffed with vanilla and coffee cream.

4 *Night Music* Midnight

The music is good and the atmosphere is even better at the **Café Central** (Plaza del Ángel 10; 34-91-369-41-43; cafecentralmadrid.com). With its high ceilings, mirrored pillars, marble-topped tables, and Art Deco touches, it attracts the city's true blues and jazz lovers, who encourage the performers with loud applause and shouts of "Bravo!"

SATURDAY

5 *Serendipity* 10:30 a.m.

Almirante 23 (Calle Almirante 23; 34-91-308-12-02; almirante23.net) attracts serious postcard collectors, who patiently sift through the thousands of offerings —from Italian postcards of Brigitte Bardot in the 1950s to a half-century-old postcard of Niagara Falls

OPPOSITE To feel the spirit of Madrid, explore on foot.

RIGHT The Madrid Río park follows the Manzanares River.

in pastel colors. There is more, much more: old movie posters, music boxes, oil paintings, toys, perfume bottles, cameras, thimbles, opera glasses, rosaries, cosmetic compacts, calendars, tins, all from another era. Plan on taking time to browse.

6 *Originals* 1 p.m.

The corner of Almirante and Conde de Xiquena is the starting point for an adventure in and out of small boutiques. **Laura Caicoya** sells her fashion designs in

a shop with her name (General Arrando 5; 12; 34-91-319-80-99; lauracaicoya.blogspot.com.es). Her whole family seems to have been involved in assembling this shop: feather-topped hats sewn and crocheted by her mother, collarlike raffia necklaces made by her grandmother, and paintings on the walls by her sister. A few blocks away at **Castañer** (Claudio Coello 51, 24; 34-91-578-18-90; castaner.com), you'll find the shoes to match that new Laura Caicoya dress.

7 *Cultural South* 3 p.m.

Matadero Madrid (Plaza de Legazpi 8; 34-91-722-04-00; mataderomadrid.org), an alternative art space, was created by Madrid's City Council from a century-old municipal slaughterhouse complex. The vast space is part of Madrid's effort to stretch its cultural reach into the southern part of the city, and it has become more popular since the Madrid Río made it more easily reachable. Lectures, films, concerts, art exhibitions — all are free.

8 *Classy Cocktails* 7 p.m.

For a change from the small draft lagers, or cañas, served in the dozens of bars that line the

ABOVE The Plaza Mayor, where it all happened in Madrid.

LEFT Matadero Madrid, a space for alternative art.

streets of Madrid, head up a short flight of stairs to **Del Diego**, a small cocktail bar (Calle de la Reina 12; 34-91-523-31-06). The bar, started by Fernando del Diego, a former barman from the 85-year-old Museo Chicote round the corner, mixes some of the best cocktails in Madrid. Try the signature Diego (vodka, apricot brandy, Bols advocaat, and a splash of lime).

9 *Braving the Crowds* 10 p.m.

Don't head to **El Mollete** (Calle de la Bola 4; 34-91-547-78-20; $$) without a reservation. Set in an old charcoal cellar, this restaurant is always full. Put yourself in the hands of the owner, Tomás Blanco, and hope he will serve you mollete (fried bread in oil), Gorgonzola croquettes, artichokes and scallops, and, of course, huevos rotos.

10 *Unadorned Flamenco* Midnight

There is nothing fancy about the small flamenco club called **Cardamomo** (Echegaray 15; 34-91-805-10-

38; cardamomo.es). The dancing here is raw, sweaty, and fun; the costumes, working class; the crowd,

ABOVE Running for six miles along the river, the Madrid Río park combines walkways, green spaces, fountains, gardens, and areas for play and fitness training.

BELOW The Arganzuela footbridge, designed by Dominique Perrault, in the Madrid Río park.

younger and cooler than at the other clubs in town. Reservations a must.

SUNDAY

11 *Seeing the Prado* 10 a.m.

So you think you know the **Prado** (Paseo del Prado; 34-902-10-70-77; museodelprado.es), Spain's most famous museum? You've seen the El Grecos, the Velázquezes, the Goyas, and the Bosches. But

there are still surprises. The cafe on the ground floor is the perfect place to sip a cortado, an espresso topped with milk. The new wing that opened in 2007 is worth a look, but its statues are much less impressive than the Greek and Roman sculptures on the first floor. Look for the Caravaggio with the beautiful arm and Antonello da Messina's *The Dead Christ Supported by an Angel* (perhaps his most beautiful work). Discover the blues of Joachim Patinir, the 16th-century Flemish painter considered the father of landscape painting.

ABOVE Flamenco practice at a dance school in Madrid.

OPPOSITE One of the Twin Bridges in Madrid Río.

THE BASICS

The metro from the airport into town takes a bit less time than a taxi, for a tenth of the price.

AC Palacio del Retiro
Calle Alfonso XII 14
34-91-523-74-60
achotels.marriott.com
$$$-$$$$
Modern design in an early-20th-century mansion.

Room Mate Óscar
Plaza de Pedro Zerolo 12
34-91-701-11-73
oscar.room-matehotels.com
$$-$$$
Part of the Room Mate chain. Its hotels look a bit like nightclubs with bedrooms.

Posada del León de Oro
Cava Baja 12
34-91-119-14-94
posadadelleondeoro.com
$$-$$$
A 19th-century posada, or inn, that was shuttered for a decade and has been reborn with a modern face-lift.

Madrid

1/4 mile
1/2 kilometer

Almirante 23 — **5**
CALLE ALMIRANTE

El Mollete — **9**
CALLE DE LA BOLA

PLAZA DE PEDRO ZEROLO
Room Mate Óscar
CALLE DE LA REINA
Del Diego — **8**

La Gastroteca de Santiago — **3**
Plaza Mayor — **1**
PLAZUELA DE SANTIAGO

Cardamomo — **10**
AC Palacio del Retiro
CALLE ALFONSO XII

CALLE ECHEGARAY

Posada del León de Oro
Plaza de la Paja
CALLE CAVA BAJA
Delic — Museo de los Orígenes/ Casa de San Isidro
PLAZA DE SAN ANDRÉS

Café Central — **4**
PLAZA DEL ÁNGEL

PASEO DEL PRADO
Prado — **11**

San Francisco el Grande Basílica — **2**
PLAZA DE SAN FRANCISCO

Manzanares River
CASA DE CAMPO

Laura Caicoya — **6**
Castañer

Area of detail

Madrid

MADRID RÍO
PLAZA DE LEGAZPI
Matadero Madrid — **7**

1 mile
2 kilometers

Bay of Biscay
FRANCE
ANDORRA
PORTUGAL
Barcelona
Madrid
SPAIN
Mediterranean Sea

San Sebastián

To visit San Sebastián, on Spain's northern coast, is to fall in love. The first sight of the shimmering scallop-shaped bay, replete with crescents of golden sand and turquoise waves, will sweep you off your feet. Pairing this natural beauty with the unrivaled local cuisine — from decadent Michelin-starred feasts to delectable bite-sized pinchos (Basque-style tapas) — may leave your head spinning. A spruced-up seaside promenade, a renovated museum, and a culinary school all add to the city's allure. But this love affair doesn't have to be a fling. The city's cultural investments have been widely recognized and ensure that it will put its best foot forward for years to come.
— BY INGRID K. WILLIAMS

FRIDAY

1 *Phantom Beach* 4 p.m.

Start with a stroll along the four-mile oceanfront promenade that hugs the city's three sandy beaches. The loveliest segment cradles La Concha beach and the bay. Or, for a new perspective of this gorgeous shore scene, take the 10-minute boat ride offered by **Motoras de la Isla** (Plaza la Lasta; 34-943-00-04-50; motorasdelaisla.com) from the port to Isla Santa Clara in the middle of the bay. Depending on the tides, the uninhabited islet might reveal its own slip of sand — San Sebastián's phantom fourth beach.

2 *Museo Paseo* 6:30 p.m.

Take the scenic route to the **San Telmo Museoa** (Plaza Zuloaga 1; 34-943-48-15-80; santelmomuseoa.com), in the Parte Vieja (Old Town), by following the promenade from the port around **Mount Urgull**, the wooded peak crowned with a statue of Jesus on the eastern edge of the bay. The museum's new facade — a stark gray wall pocked with holes through which greenery sprouts — mimics the natural rocky surroundings but sharply contrasts with the adjoining building, a refurbished 16th-century former Dominican convent where the permanent collection of Basque art and historical artifacts is displayed.

OPPOSITE The fastest way to be seduced by San Sebastián is to begin at the beach and the oceanfront promenade.

RIGHT A modern twist on boat traffic at the port.

3 *Dramatic Dining* 9 p.m.

Ni Neu (Avenida de Zurriola Iribidea 1; 34-943-00-31-62; restaurantenineu.com; $$$-$$$$), which means "I Myself" in Basque, is the restaurant at the **Kursaal**, the auditorium and convention center occupying a pair of glowing modernist cubes beside Zurriola beach. The restaurant's slick black walls and spotlighted tables are the stage upon which the stylish set gathers to dine on tuna tartare with green lemon cream, or roast lamb with flourishes of coffee and cardamom. If you prefer less drama with dinner, consider **Narru** (Zubieta Kalea 56; 34-943-42-33-49; narru.es; $$$$), beneath the Hotel Niza, a popular subterranean restaurant that serves pared-down, unpretentious fare like a meltingly tender secreto Ibérico with Basque apples.

4 *The Laid-Back Option* 11:30 p.m.

Avoid the cheesy beachfront discos and seek out the laid-back bar **Ondarra** (Avenida de Zurriola 16; 34-943-32-60-33) in Gros, the neighborhood that flanks the surfing beach Zurriola. Early in the evening, the tables that spill onto the sidewalk are the ideal spot for a round of gin and tonics with new friends. Later, the downstairs club, Club 16 Bis, plugs in.

SATURDAY

5 *Eat Your Homework* 9:30 a.m.

Don't sleep through this class. A multi-Michelin-starred chef might be at the head of the classroom at the **Basque Culinary Center** (Paseo Juan Avelino Barriola 101; 34-943-53-51-03; grado.bculinary.com),

a culinary school and research institute with an international consultancy board headed by the nonpareil chef Ferran Adrià. The center has a four-year degree program as well as continuing-education courses for professional chefs and half-day classes for "gastronomic enthusiasts" (the rest of us) — you might be able to join an introduction to avant-garde sweets or a summer grilling lesson.

6 *Stellar Cellar* 2:30 p.m.

Hidden among the pincho bars of the Parte Vieja is a simple staircase that descends to the sunny-walled restaurant **Bodegón Alejandro** (Fermín Calbetón 4; 34-943-42-71-58; bodegonalejandro.com; $$$$), a longtime bastion of stellar Basque cuisine.

The colorful tile and sturdy wooden tables feel traditional, but the six-course tasting menu is a modern riff on regional classics. One version included "lasagna" of anchovies and ratatouille atop gazpacho cream, and a rich risotto infused with cuttlefish oil and Idiazábal cheese.

7 *T-Shirt Time* 5 p.m.

At **Kukuxumusu** (Mayor Kalea 15; 34-943-42-11-84; kukuxumusu.com), goofy cartoons are slapped on everything from T-shirts to flasks. This storefront in the Parte Vieja was this design company's first, but the kooky brand has since expanded all over Spain. If you find yourself needing a jacket that will make your friends envious, step into

ABOVE Ondarra, a laid-back bar where tables spill onto the sidewalk and a downstairs club opens late.

BELOW The retro amusement park at Mount Igueldo.

Six Store (Avenida Zurriola 1; 34-943-32-19-43), which has brands like Rains, Igor, and Paez. The Bohemian Shop (Iñigo 1; 34-943-42-45-73) has cool vintage clothing for men and women.

8 *For Hipsters and Kids* 6:30 p.m.

The sublime mingles with the absurd atop **Mount Igueldo** (34-943-21-05-64; www.monteigueldo.es) on the western edge of the bay. Ride the rumbling funicular to the summit, where the **Mount Igueldo Tower** claims to offer "the best view in the world" (it is indeed grand). Then revisit childhood at the ancient amusement park, where the rickety rides and classic carnival games are all so ridiculously — though unintentionally — retro that they transcend tackiness and become hilariously fun for small children and hipsters alike.

9 *Chikiteo Cheat Sheet* 9:30 p.m.

Tailor a chikiteo — the Basque term for a pincho-bar hop — around the bars in the Parte Vieja where traditional pinchos are being elevated to haute cuisine in miniature. Start at the long wooden counter of **Astelena** (Euskal Herria 3; 34-943-42-58-67) with croquetas coated in crunchy pistachios, or crispy crepes stuffed with salmon and cheese. Then squeeze into the narrow **La Cuchara de San Telmo** (31 de Agosto Kalea 28; no phone; lacucharadesantelmo. com) for sumptuous seared foie gras with apple compote, or tangy orzo and goat cheese risotto. Round

out the tour at the black-and-red bar **A Fuego Negro** (Calle 31 de Agosto 31; 34-650-13-53-73; afuegonegro. com), the pinnacle of pincho prowess. Order the Makcobe, a mini wagyu burger on a ketchup-infused bun with fried banana "chips," but don't miss the three icy scoops of spider crab, avocado, and licorice (a strangely delicious trio), or strawberry and chocolate zombie.

SUNDAY

10 *Breadcrumb Trail* 9 a.m.

The 800th anniversary of the consecration of the cathedral in Santiago de Compostela, the final destination of the pilgrimage trail known as the Camino de Santiago, was observed in 2011. One major route of the Camino passes through San Sebastián, so for a taste of the celebrated trek, hike up **Zemoriya Kalea** in Gros and follow the yellow trail markings (in reverse), weaving through lush forests and past postcard-perfect panoramas of cliffs sinking into the sea. Before you set off, carbo-load with a moist, chewy brioche or a crusty baguette from **Galparsoro** (Mayor Kalea 6; 34-943-42-10-74), a phenomenal little bakery that supplies the area's top restaurants.

ABOVE Called Donostia in Basque, San Sebastián has evolved from a quaint fishing village and port into a world-class seaside resort.

11 *Two If by Land . . .* 1:30 p.m.

At **Mugaritz** (Aldura Aldea 20, Errenteria; 34-943-52-24-55; mugaritz.com; $$$$), a two-Michelin-star restaurant in an understated country house nestled in the hills outside town, the chef Andoni Luis Aduriz puzzles and delights diners — often simultaneously — with ingenious dishes like an aromatic mortar soup (which requires diners to pestle-pound spices and seeds before servers add finishing touches of herbs and fish broth) and crispy shredded beef tongue

(presented as "mystery meat"). Curious to find out what clinches that elusive third star? Book a table with a view overlooking the sea at **Akelarre** (Padre Orcolaga 56; 34-943-31-12-09; akelarre.net; $$$$), the three-Michelin-star gastronomic temple where Pedro Subijana has been feeding foodies for over 30 years, with concoctions that range from edible paper and foie gras with sugar to ethereal mousses.

ABOVE The black-and-red bar A Fuego Negro is the pinnacle of prowess in creation of the pincho, the exuberant Basque version of tapas.

OPPOSITE Alluring when its waters shimmer in the sun, the town takes on a softer aspect by the light of the full moon.

THE BASICS

Connecting flights from Madrid arrive in San Sebastián. The town is eminently walkable, and cycling is also a great way to get around.

Hotel Gran Bahía Bernardo
Trueba Kalea 1
34-943-29-80-49
hotelgranbahiabernardo.com
$-$$
A few blocks from Zurriola beach, 10 simple rooms with hardwood floors, cool photography on the walls, and free Wi-Fi.

Hotel Astoria 7
Familia Santua Kalea 1
34-943-44-50-00
astoria7hotelsansebastian.com
$-$$
Pays homage to the cinema stars of San Sebastián's annual film festival with rooms dedicated to directors and actors.

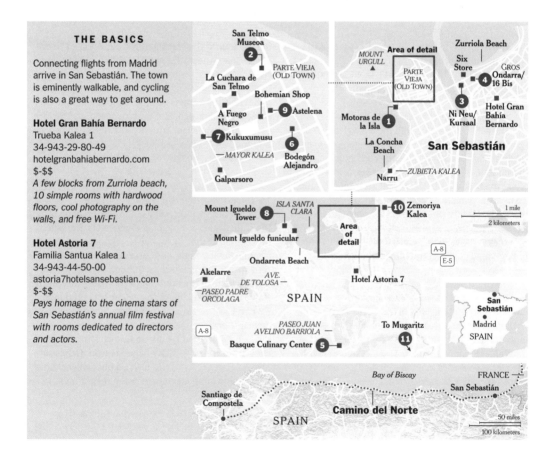

Pamplona & Bilbao

Many people around the world know Pamplona for little but the testosterone-fueled running of the bulls through its ancient stone streets during the San Fermín Festival every July. Within Spain, Pamplona is often dismissed as a cultural backwater, a brief stop for Camino de Santiago pilgrims or day-trippers from San Sebastián and Barcelona. But visit outside of festival time, without the rowdy San Fermín crowd, and you will find a city worth knowing for itself: filled with cultural and culinary high points, teeming with chatty night owls and sophisticated wine aficionados, and framed by the pointy foothills of the French Pyrenees to the north and wide plains to the south. And while you're in Basque country, you may as well go on to Bilbao, to see (or see again) the famous Frank Gehry-designed Guggenheim Museum. — BY LIONEL BEEHNER

FRIDAY

1 *Pompey's Maze* 2 p.m.

Pamplona is the historic capital of Navarre—now with 200,000 residents—and a walk around the **Old Quarter** will take you through sun-kissed plazas, past parks scattered with contemporary sculptures and medieval fortresses, and over crumbling ramparts constructed by Pompey, the Roman general who was a rival of Julius Caesar's and is Pamplona's namesake. You could spend hours getting happily lost in the Old Quarter's maze of narrow canyonlike alleyways, hopping from bar to bar for the tangy red liqueur called pacharán and colorful small-plate combinations called pinchos. Quaint boutiques lining the labyrinthine streets will call out, too.

2 *Hemingway Haunt* 5 p.m.

Snag a seat in the daily ritual of musical chairs at the **Café Iruña** (Plaza del Castillo 44; 34-948-22-20-64; cafeiruna.com), a Parisian-style spot once frequented by Ernest Hemingway. The Iruña sits on the Plaza del Castillo, Pamplona's buzzing nucleus, and the facades ringing the square look as if they haven't

changed since Hemingway set part of *The Sun Also Rises* there in the 1920s. Settle in for a drink and some of the best people-watching in Spain: children playing around the gazebo, older men in berets chain-smoking, backpackers wandering and gawking, and clusters of hipsters huddling over their cellphones.

3 *Pinchos, Dressed for Dinner* 8 p.m.

Pamplona's culinary traditions do not disappoint. One old standby restaurant, **Café Bar Gaucho** (Calle Espoz y Mina 7; 34-948-22-50-73; cafebargaucho.com; $$) serves up extravagant spreads of pinchos in combinations like salmon with asparagus carpaccio, borage flower and cabbage cream or pickled quail tart, mushrooms, cream, and Pedro Ximénez reduction.

4 *Doodles and Discos* 11 p.m.

Night life is more relaxed and family-friendly in Pamplona than in Barcelona or San Sebastián. It is not uncommon to see bars crammed with baby strollers or kids doodling on coloring books while their parents sip wine. You could join the lines of svelte model-types and university students that snake down the street outside **Marengo** (Avenida de Bayona 2; 34-948-26-55-42), perhaps the busiest disco in town. Or continue on Avenida de Bayona to the more subdued and less touristy district of **San Juan**, a 10-minute walk from the Old Quarter. It's speckled with underground cinemas,

OPPOSITE Dwarfed by Frank Gehry's titanium curves at the Guggenheim Museum in Bilbao.

RIGHT The Cathedral of Santa María la Real in Pamplona, a stop for pilgrims on the Way of St. James.

gay-friendly bars, and even a Japanese-style park inspired by Pamplona's Japanese sister city, Yamaguchi.

SATURDAY

5 *Camino Stop* 10 a.m.

Tucked within the old town is an impressive collection of medieval churches and Roman monuments. The Gothic interior of the main cathedral, **Cathedral of Santa María la Real** (Calle Curia; 34-948-21-25-94; catedraldepamplona.com), contains the alabaster tomb of Charles III, ruler of Navarre in the 1400s. The cathedral is a standard stop for pilgrims walking from France to Santiago de Compostela along the ancient Camino de Santiago,

or Way of St. James, and you may see some inside, with heads bowed.

6 *If the Bulls Were Here…* 11 a.m.

A less spiritual route to follow is the path of the bulls that are harried through Pamplona's streets in the San Fermín Festival. As you stand in the center of the small square called **Plaza Consistorial**, marveling at the ochre-colored edifice of Pamplona's Baroque town hall, picture the bulls corralled here — along with bull-runners wearing red-and-white neckerchiefs. Walk on to Estafeta Street, the final section of the route where the bulls run. It's now an area of quirky bars and balconies that calls to mind Bourbon Street in New Orleans.

7 *Pinchos, Casual for Lunch* Noon

Duck into **Bodegón Sarria** bar (Estafeta 50-52; 34-948-22-77-13; bodegonsarria.com; $$), where large slabs of cured hams dangle above a bar strewn with every kind of colorful pinchos imaginable (anchovies with tomato, stuffed peppers, pig's trotters). Try a plate of patatas bravas, crispy potatoes smothered in spicy sauce, with a kalimocho, a cocktail of cola and wine.

ABOVE Gehry's Guggenheim has so raised the profile of Bilbao that urban planners now speak of "the Bilbao effect."

LEFT A statue of Ernest Hemingway in Pamplona.

8 *Indoor, Outdoor* 1 p.m.

The **Museo de Navarra** (Calle de Santo Domingo 47; 34-848-42-64-92) can easily consume an afternoon with its assortment of Goyas, mosaics, and murals. If it's the kind of day when you just have to be outdoors, relax on the patio at El Caballo Blanco, a cafe with live music tucked behind the cathedral, or walk into the large park called Taconera Gardens, admire the work of its landscapers, and gaze at its exotic wildlife, including white peacocks.

9 *Dinner in Bilbao* 8 p.m.

Make your way to Bilbao in time for dinner at **Mina** (Muelle Marzana; 34-944-79-59-38; restaurantemina. es; $$$$), an innovative home of Basque cooking on the Nervión River. The tasting menus are based on what is available in the market across the river. One night's selections included shrimp tartare with sherry-infused chunks of melon and a sauce of green apple gelée with tapioca pearls. A "risotto" contained not a grain of rice, but was made from the squid called begi haundi. Álvaro Garrido and his wife, Lara Martín, the chefs behind Mina, met while they

were working for Paco Torreblanca, Spain's premier pastry chef, and their desserts are especially good.

SUNDAY

10 *Architectural Who's Who* 9 a.m.

Frank Gehry may have been the most notable pioneer, but other internationally known architects had already been lured to work in Bilbao, and more followed. It adds up to a cluster of new structures worthy of an architectural tour. Santiago Calatrava designed a footbridge and an airport terminal, César Pelli contributed an office tower, Norman Foster designed the subway system, and Philippe Starck converted an ornately designed early 20th-century

TOP Best known for its running of the bulls every July, Pamplona is also worth visiting in quieter seasons.

ABOVE Sample the colorful Basque small plates called pinchos, and pair them with pacharán, a tangy red liqueur.

warehouse into a culture center. A shopping mall is by Robert A. M. Stern, and the Sheraton hotel is by the Mexican architect Ricardo Legorreta. The city, once an industrial center blighted with decline, did its part by replacing old shipyards with parks and cafes. And it built on good bones: boulevards lined with neo-Baroque facades.

11 *On the Map* 10 a.m.

Frank Gehry's spectacular **Guggenheim Bilbao Museum** (Abandoibarra 2; 34-944-35-90-80; guggenheim-bilbao.es) has raised the profile of Bilbao so profoundly and positively that urban planners now speak of the Bilbao effect: extravagant improvement

in a city's image because of creative new architecture. The art inside the museum, spanning the mid-20th century to the present, is excellent and absorbing; Willem de Kooning, Robert Motherwell, Anselm Kiefer, and Richard Serra are among the more famous of the boldface names whose work is on display. But the million or so visitors a year flood here mostly to see the building, an intricate jumble of shiny titanium curves with wings of Spanish limestone, set grandly on the riverbank. Plan on several hours for seeing it all. To stay for lunch, make reservations in advance for one of the Guggenheim's restaurants.

ABOVE During the running of the bulls, it is the spectators, not the livestock, who are behind the fences.

OPPOSITE The Plaza del Castillo in Pamplona. A cafe here was a hangout for Ernest Hemingway.

THE BASICS

Flights to Pamplona usually arrive from San Sebastián or Barcelona; Bilbao flights may come through Paris or Madrid. In both cities, plan to walk, although Bilbao also has a metro system that is an attraction in itself.

Gran Hotel La Perla
Plaza del Castillo 1, Pamplona
34-948-22-30-00
granhotellaperla.com
$$-$$$$
Luxurious rooms. A suite where Hemingway once wrote has been left largely intact.

Gran Hotel Domine Bilbao
Mazarredo Zumarkalea 61
34-944-25-33-00
hoteldominebilbao.com
$$-$$$$
Across the street from the Guggenheim; rooftop terrace with museum views.

Pamplona

Plaza Consistorial

CALLE DE SANTO DOMINGO

Cathedral of Santa María la Real

Museo de Navarra **8**

6

5

1 Old Quarter

Café Iruña **2**

Gran Hotel La Perla

Marengo

4

AVE. DE BAYONA

PLAZA DEL CASTILLO

Café Bar Gaucho **3**

7 Bodegón Sarria

AVE. DEL EJÉRCITO

SAN JUAN

AVE. DE BAJA NAVARRA

Ciudadela

11 Guggenheim Bilbao Museum

Gran Hotel Domine Bilbao

MAZARREDO ZUMARKALEA

Bilbao

Nervión River

MUELLE MARZANA

9 Mina

Bay of Biscay

FRANCE

San Sebastián

10

Bilbao

Pamplona

NAVARRE

SPAIN

50 miles

100 kilometers

Santiago de Compostela

For a thousand years, pilgrims have trekked dozens and sometimes hundreds of miles to the cathedral city of Santiago de Compostela in Galicia, a sparsely populated region in Spain's northwest. Their ancient routes, converging from around Europe, are collectively known as the Camino de Santiago, or Way of St. James, named for the belief that the cathedral houses the remains of the apostle St. James. While many of today's walkers are motivated by piety, a growing number (attracted perhaps by the route's epic appeal) are making the journey as a rigorous secular hike or multiday bike ride. Whatever their motives, all are arriving in a place eager to expand its appeal beyond the devoutly religious, with new or updated restaurants and hotels, and most notably, a spectacular (and controversial) complex of buildings called the City of Culture of Galicia. — BY INGRID K. WILLIAMS

FRIDAY

1 *End of the Trail* 1 p.m.

Find a vantage point on the paving stones of the plaza in front of the ornate granite **Cathedral of Santiago de Compostela** (Praza do Obradoiro; catedraldesantiago.es), and take in the scene. A crowd should be emerging about now from the midday Pilgrim's Mass, and the plaza will be heaving with tourists, many toting walking sticks and bulging backpacks. Some hike just a few days to get here, after picking up the end of a pilgrimage route in a nearby town. Others acquire scarred feet and blackened toenails in months on the camino. The cathedral, constructed starting in 1078, is Romanesque with a 17th-century Baroque face-lift. Go inside and find the 12th-century arch called the Portal of Glory, where the custom is to place your fingers in the well-worn indentations made by the touch of those who came before you. Pilgrims also hug the bejeweled statue of St. James.

2 *Street Scenes* 3 p.m.

Take a walk near the cathedral. Off to the side on the main square is the **Parador Hostal Dos Reis Católicos,** built to accommodate pilgrims by King Ferdinand and Queen Isabella in 1499, a few years after they bankrolled Christopher Columbus's adventures in the New World. Now it's a luxurious hotel. On the streets behind the cathedral and to the south, like the Rúa do Villar, cafes and shops have moved into centuries-old buildings. You're also close to the university. Santiago's 30,000 students, mingling with the pilgrims dangling scallop-shell symbols of St. James, help make this town anything but somber. **Alameda Park**, between Rúa do Pombal and Avenida Xoan Carlos I, is a good spot for perspective on the cathedral. Amid the oak trees are girls in school uniforms, strolling older couples, and small children eating ice cream.

3 *Avant-Garde Menu* 9 p.m.

A block from the cathedral, in the cozy, stone-walled dining room at **Casa Marcelo** (Rúa das Hortas 1; 34-981-55-85-80; casamarcelo.net; $$$$), the first sign of an innovative approach arrives with the menu, presented on a glowing iPad. Marcelo Tejedor, the chef, trained with the Basque chef Juan Mari Arzak, a pioneer of modernist, avant-garde cooking, and the ever-changing set menu reflects that influence. One day's fare included a warm "cappuccino"

OPPOSITE The Cathedral of Santiago de Compostela, goal of pilgrims on the Camino de Santiago, or the Way of St. James, for the past thousand years.

BELOW The Hostal Dos Reis Católicos, built for pilgrims by Spain's Ferdinand and Isabella, is an elegant hotel today.

of beet soup topped with beet foam, savory quail legs paired with sweet strawberries, an airy pea purée with chunks of yuzu and tart lemon sorbet, and fresh sardines rolled like sushi with ribbons of tempura-fried asparagus.

SATURDAY

4 *What's for Lunch?* 10 a.m.

Foodies and people watchers are in their element at the bustling **Mercado de Abastos** (Rúa das Ameas; 34-981-58-34-38; mercadodeabastosdesantiago.com), a traditional street market where the locals come for fresh food from oranges and figs to sardines and prawns. Whole octopuses simmer in caldrons, and wheels of homemade cheese top linen-covered benches. Stroll around and plan your next dinner party.

5 *How About Barnacles?* Noon

Nestled into a stone wall beside the market is **Abastos 2.0** (Rúa das Ameas 13-18; 34-981-57-61-45; abastosdouspuntocero.es), a creative tapas joint that relies on the market's daily specialties. "We have no fixed menu because we have no refrigerators," said one of its owners, Iago Pazos, "though we always say we have the world's largest fridge, the market behind us." A computer screen takes the place of a chalkboard menu, continually updating with offerings like alien-like percebes (goose barnacles) and flaky Galician-style empanadas.

6 *Creative Chocolate* 2 p.m.

For an unusual dessert, walk a few blocks to the minimalist, white-walled **Casal Cotón Chocolat** (Rúa do Franco 53; 34-981-88-82-46; casalcotonchocolat.com),

ABOVE At O Dezaseis, a restaurant widely known as 16, the octopus, or pulpo, is cooked until tender and then tossed on a super-hot grill. The empanadas are tasty, too.

RIGHT An afternoon stroll in the City of Culture of Galicia.

set among the traditional tapas bars that line Rúa do Franco. This tiny chocolate shop offers sweets like orange-flavored white chocolate discs studded with pistachios, as well as its own velvety caramel liqueur.

7 *City on a Hill* 3 p.m.

The sprawling new **City of Culture of Galicia** (Monte Gaiás; 34-881-99-75-65; cidadedacultura.gal), on a hill overlooking the old city less than a mile away, was designed by the American architect Peter Eisenman and opened in 2011 even though most of its buildings were not yet complete after a decade of construction. The ambitious project includes a performance center (Bjork was one of the first acts to be booked), museum, historical archive, library, and offices. Some praise it as a 21st-century beacon of culture in a city that since the Middle Ages has relied on its renown as a religious destination. Critics have decried it as a white elephant. Come to your own conclusions. The granite buildings nestle together to form giant rolling waves of stone and glass, conscious references to the old city and the terrain. Take the long view, and then go inside to experience the colorful curved and angled spaces.

8 *Pulpo and Pimentón* 8 p.m.

O Dezaseis (Rua do San Pedro 16; 34-981-56-48-80; dezaseis.com; $$$) — or 16, as it's widely known,

feels at first like many European tourist traps: sub-terranean, a little cavelike, an intentionally charming converted stable of brick and stone and wood, proba-bly 300 years old, with wooden tables and chairs, and with farm and cooking implements hanging from walls and ceilings. But any fears you may be enter-taining of having entered the domain of an inferior cook will fall away when you dip your fork into your food. You are in Galicia, the home of empanadas, so sample some, perhaps with tuna and pimentón (Spanish paprika). Galicia is also a world capital of pulpo — octopus. At 16, it's cooked until tender, then tossed on the plancha (a super-hot griddle) and sprinkled with smoked pimentón. In a region where every town has several pulperías — restaurants spe-cializing in pulpo — 16's pulpo is exceptional.

SUNDAY

9 *Walk the Walk* 10 a.m.

Get into the original spirit of Santiago de Compostela by walking the last, climactic small section of the Camino de Santiago yourself. To join the pilgrims, take a taxi out toward San Marcos, east of the city, and look for the steady, if ragged, procession of backpackers heading toward the great cathedral. Get out and join them for a couple of miles. You may meet college students, retirees, teenagers on a school outing, veterans of the pilgrimage who have walked the long route more than once. Almost certainly, you will find people of many nationalities. And you will be with them in the exhilarating moments when at last they reach their goal.

THE BASICS

Fly into the city's airport and take a taxi or bus to town, or drive to the city on major auto routes.

Parador Hostal Dos Reis Católicos
Rúa de San Francisco 1
34-981-58-22-00
paradores-spain.com/spain/
pscompostela.html
$$-$$$
*Opulent hotel in a travelers'
lodge built at the end of
the 15th century.*

Hotel Pazo de Altamira
Rúa Altamira 18
34-981-55-85-42
pazodealtamira.com
$-$$
Bright, modern rooms.

Los Abetos
San Lázaro
34-981-55-70-26
granhotellosabetos.com
$-$$
*A favorite of business travelers,
with comfortable rooms, pool,
and fitness center.*

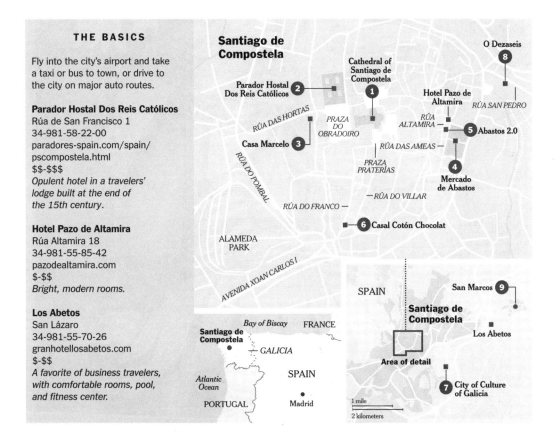

Santiago de Compostela

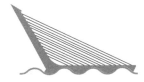

Seville

Seville is easily Spain's most flamboyant city. A former Moorish capital, it is awash in a sultry jumble of Christian-Muslim architecture, with many grand buildings in need of a fresh coat of paint. And unlike much of Spain, Seville has largely resisted the urge to make its tiled courtyards and medieval sidewalks, some as narrow as a bicycle tire, sleek and trendy. Flamenco dancers, gypsy street performers, and Andalusian cowboys in wide-brimmed boleros still strut in 2,000-year-old plazas shaded by orange trees and palms. On balmy nights, parties can erupt spontaneously over bottles of red wine. It's a contagious street theater in which everyone can join.
— BY JULIA CHAPLIN

FRIDAY

1 *Dress Up (for Him)* 5 p.m.

To fast-forward into Seville's soap operatic mood, get into costume. Don't waste time on the chintz (hand fans, plastic roses) sold at street stands around the Cathedral of Seville. The quality Andalusian outfitters are headquartered in the winding streets around the Plaza de la Alfalfa. (Beware: stores are typically closed between 2 and 4:30 p.m.) Men should bypass the cliché matador look, with those embarrassing tight pants, and go for the stately equestrian style of the local horsemen. **Antonio García** (Alcaicería de la Loza 25; 34-95-422-23-20; sombrerosgarcia.com), a traditional shop that specializes in high-end riding paraphernalia, has tasseled leather calf guards and hard-brimmed Córdoba panama hats that cast a mysterious-stranger shadow over the eyes.

2 *Dress Up (for Her)* 6 p.m.

Imitate the look of the gypsy heroine Carmen. Splurge on an authentic flamenco dress at **Taller de Diseño** (Calle de Luchana 6; 34-95-422-71-86;

angelayadela.wordpress.com). A favorite of local flamenco starlets, the upscale boutique carries fetching gowns in polka dots, stripes, and bright florals by the designer team Angela and Adela. The heavier and more elaborate the ruffles, the more expensive they are. If the price tag seems ungypsy-like, look for a tiara-esque beaded hair comb made of tortoise shell or an embroidered silk shawl with tassels.

3 *Fish and Kitsch* 8:30 p.m.

Not many tapas bars can claim to be more than 340 years old. **El Rinconcillo** (Gerona 40; 34-95-422-31-83; elrinconcillo.es; $$$-$$$$) is a classic hole-in-the-wall that looks like a kitschy Spanish galleon, with stained glass windows, dusty bottles of Fundador brandy, and a long wooden bar where the curt waiters scrawl out orders in chalk. Likely menu choices include fritos (tiny fried fish), taza de caldo (pork soup), and a half-portion of jamón serrano, which is worth ordering just to see the waiter pull the pig leg down from a hook in the vaulted ceiling.

4 *The Late Show* 10 p.m.

Seville is chock-full of touristy flamenco shows, but **La Carbonería** (Calle Levies 18; 34-95-456-37-49) pleases aficionados. Housed in a former coal storage warehouse, the rambling, makeshift space has communal picnic tables and a small stage where ponytailed flamenco guitarists and dancers give impromptu performances late into the night. The crowd of university students and flamencophiles streams in and out between shows, puffing on cigarettes in the leafy garden.

OPPOSITE Intricately designed ceramic tiles blanket a good portion of Seville. In the ceramic shops of the Triana district, shoppers find tiles to buy and take home.

RIGHT El Rinconcillo, a classic hole-in-the-wall tapas bar, is more than 340 years old. Order the Serrano ham to see the waiter pull the pig leg down from a hook in the ceiling.

SATURDAY

5 *Moorish Tiles* 11 a.m.

If you're wondering where to pocket some of the intricately designed ceramic tiles that blanket a good portion of the city, head to Triana, the old Gypsy enclave on the left side of the Guadalquivir river. Its streets are lined with ceramics shops, often with their wares displayed flamboyantly on their storefronts. Most of Triana's kilns have closed, but

ABOVE At La Carbonería, a club known to flamenco aficionados, guitarists and dancers perform late into the night.

BELOW Casa de Pilatos, a 16th-century palace open for tours.

for a look at the techniques and traditions of the tile craft, drop in at the **Centro Cerámica Triana** (Calle Antillano Campos 14; 34-95-434-27-37; andalucia.com/cities/sevilla/ceramiccentre), a museum in the former Cerámica Santa Ana factory.

6 *River Tapas* 2 p.m.

Stay on this side of the Guadalquivir and have lunch a few blocks away at **Café Bar Altozano** (Calle San Jacinto 4; 34-655-88-69-25). If it's not too hot (it often is) and not too cold (it often is), sit outside and enjoy a plate of Bosqueño sheep's milk cheese or shrimp. Other tapas might include pork cheeks, cod fritters, grilled squid, or rabo de toro (bull tail stew). It's a great spot for people-watching as Triana residents go about their midday errands.

7 *Flamenco 101* 4:30 p.m.

Follow the flamenco acolytes with their slicked-back hair buns and clicking castanets to the 18th-century mansion that's the **Museo del Baile Flamenco** (Calle de Manuel Rojas Marcos 3; 34-95-434-03-11; museodelbaileflamenco.com). Run by the renowned dancer Cristina Hoyos, the museum is an obsessive homage to the art form, with high-tech exhibits, archival photos, and costume displays. Best of all, you can sit in the patio to spy on the dance classes and pick up some moves.

8 *Tapas Crawl* 9:30 p.m.

In Seville, dinner is rarely a single-setting affair; a meal can stretch all the way across town and well past midnight. Begin an evening of dining at **Casa Morales** (Garcia de Vinuesa 11; 34-95-422-12-42; $$), a dusky, time-honored tapas joint in business since 1850, with a dish of salchicha al vino blanco, sausage cooked in white wine to juicy perfection. Immense haunches of serrano ham hang from the ceiling here; and sardonic, battle-scarred barmen siphon wine from wooden barrels built into the wall. Next, head for **Bodeguita Romero** (Harinas 10; 34-95-422-95-56; bodeguita-romero.com; $$) for a succulent pringá montadito, a toasted mini baguette sandwich of slow-cooked beef, chicken, and sausage. Finish at atmospheric **Las Columnas** (Alameda de Hércules 19; 34-95-438-81-06; Facebook: Bar Restaurante Las Columnas; $$), where your order is scrawled in chalk on the bar in front of you. Under the columns that are the restaurant's namesake, mingle with a convivial mix of tourists and Sevillanos washing down pinchito kebabs and manchego cheese with cold glasses of Cruzcampo beer.

SUNDAY

9 *Uncrowded House* Noon

Seville's main tourist attractions include the Seville Cathedral, a massive gothic masterpiece where Christopher Columbus is said to be buried, and the Alcázar, the royal palace and a shining example of Mudéjar, an architectural hybrid of Moorish and Christian styles popular between the 12th and 16th centuries. For a less-trafficked alternative, go to the **Casa de Pilatos** (Plaza de Pilatos; 34-95-422-52-98; fundacionmedinaceli.org/monumentos/pilatos). The building, a 16th-century palace also in Mudéjar style, is delightfully dilapidated with swirling tiled walls,

TOP Casa de Pilatos, an example of the hybrid Christian-Moorish Mudéjar style, has swirling tiled walls and elaborate domed ceilings with inlaid wood.

ABOVE Flamenco style that can't be missed at the Museo del Baile Flamenco, a homage to Seville's favorite dance.

elaborate domed ceilings with inlaid wood, and overgrown gardens that are perfect for a siesta or for glimpsing the palace's current residents, the Dukes of Medinaceli.

10 *Future Walk* 2 p.m.

Seville is not all ancient history. The city has recently commissioned a stable of celebrity architects like Zaha Hadid and Norman Foster, and the requisite bridge by Santiago Calatrava, to add a dash

of modernism. For a frontline glimpse, stroll around the **Metropol Parasol** (Plaza de la Encarnación), designed by the Berlin architect Jürgen Hermann Mayer. It's a giant, wafflelike grid above an old market and ruins, providing not only shade, but a unique, visual experience.

ABOVE Triana, the city's old Gypsy quarter.

OPPOSITE A palace courtyard in the Mudéjar style.

THE BASICS

Instead of renting a car, it's easier to flag down taxis, which are plentiful and inexpensive. Walking is the best way to see the city center.

Hospes Las Casas del Rey de Baeza
Plaza Jesús de la Redención 2
34-95-456-14-96
hospes.com
$$
Andalusian-modern boutique hotel in a converted 18th-century monastery.

Casa Sacristía Santa Ana Hotel
Alameda de Hércules 22
34-95-491-57-22
hotelsacristia.com
$-$$
Country-chic modern establishment popular with the bohemian set.

EME Catedral Hotel
Alemanes 27
34-95-456-00-00
emecatedralhotel.com
$$-$$$
A cluster of fourteen 18th- and 19th-century houses ingeniously cobbled together into a chic 70-room hotel.

SPAIN

25 miles
50 kilometers

Córdoba

Seville Guadalquivir River

SEVILLE PROVINCE

Seville

1/8 mile
1/5 kilometer

CALLE SAN LUIS BUSTOS TAVERA

Casa Sacristía Santa Ana Hotel

CALLE SANTA ANA

ALAMEDA DE HÉRCULES

Las Columnas

CALLE PASCUAL DE GAYANGOS

El Rinconcillo **3**

CALLE GERONA

Metropol Parasol **10**

PLAZA PONCE DE LEON

Guadalquivir River

CALLE DE ALFONSO XII

PLAZA DE LA ENCARNACIÓN

CALLE SANTIAGO

Hospes Las Casas del Rey de Baeza

CALLE MARQUÉS DE PARADAS

CALLE ARJONA

C. SAN ELOY

Antonio García **1**

Plaza de la Alfalfa

9

Taller de Diseño **2**

7

Casa de Pilatos

PLAZA NUEVA

Museo del Baile Flamenco

Centro Cerámica Triana **5**

Bodeguita Romero

EME Catedral Hotel

Casa Morales **8**

Cathedral of Seville

La Carbonería **4**

PASEO DE COLÓN

TRIANA

Café Bar Altozano **6**

CALLE DEL BETIS

Alcázar

JARDINES REALES ALCÁZAR

CALLE SAN JACINTO

Valencia

Valencia, best known as the birthplace of paella, has made its way higher onto the radar of savvy travelers since work was completed on Santiago Calatrava's futuristic museum complex, the City of Arts and Sciences. In the meantime, its Moorish-accented neighborhoods have been filling up with playful boutiques, innovative restaurants, and booming night spots. These days this seaside town, Spain's third-largest city, is cooking up a lot more than rice.
— BY CHARLY WILDER

FRIDAY

1 *Shop the Carmen* 4 p.m.

In hilly Barrio del Carmen, the oldest part of the city and its creative center, bearded students and elegant urbanites trek over graffitied passageways where cafes and galleries spill onto medieval squares. The sprawling **Mercado Central** (mercadocentralvalencia.es) has gone upscale, hosting parties for companies like Prada and Aston Martin. Stylish boutiques are tucked behind the 15th-century late Gothic Lonja de la Seda (silk exchange). Two of the best, **Bugalú** (Carrer de la Llotja 6; 34-963-91-84-49) and **Madame Bugalú y Su Caniche Asesino** (Carrer de les Dances 3; 34-963-15-44-76; madamebugalu.es), carry clothing and accessories by Spanish, French, and Swiss designers as well as international labels like Paul Frank.

2 *Valencian Original* 6 p.m.

Valencia is the birthplace of horchata, a drink made from the juice of chufas, or tiger nuts, and said to date from the city's Islamic period in the eighth to 13th centuries. You can sample it at the **Horchatería Santa Catalina** (Plaça de Santa Caterina 6, 34-963-91-23-79; www.horchateriasantacatalina.com) in El Carmen. Pair a glass with a café cortado and another Valencian original: the farton, a fluffy pastry finger dusted in powdered sugar.

3 *Carmen at Night* 9 p.m.

Carosel (Carrer de la Taula de Canvis 6; 34-961-13-28-73; $$), a chic but unpretentious restaurant in the Carmen, serves up delectable twists on traditional cuisine, like a mini cuttlefish stew with artichokes and almonds. The prix fixe menu changes weekly. After dinner, stroll out into the night. Late-night action converges on the Plaça del Tossal. Locals avoid the splashy tourist traps and pour into the Stone Age-themed **Bar los Picapiedra** (Carrer dels Cavallers 25), where students, bohemians, and miscellaneous walk-ins guzzle cider out of large, spouted glass porrones, which look vaguely like watering cans, and listen to Spanish alt-rock.

SATURDAY

4 *Future City* 10 a.m.

Valenbisi (valenbisi.es) is Valencia's bargain public bicycle rental system. Pick up a bike near the **Torres de Serranos**, one of the gates to the city, and cycle under a series of bridges through the palm-filled Jardín del Turia to the **City of Arts and Sciences** (Avenida Professor López Piñero 7; 34-902-10-00-31; cac.es). The buildings' curved, billowing facades resemble everything from the skeleton of a whale to the upper half of a giant eye completed by its mirror image in a reflecting pool. At the Oceanogràfic marine

OPPOSITE The curved, billowing facades of the City of Arts and Sciences resemble images from the skeleton of a whale to the upper half of a giant eye.

BELOW A belly view of a shark from a tunnel at the Oceanogràfic marine complex.

complex, you can wander through underground tunnels as sharks float overhead.

5 *An Alternative Hub* 2 p.m.

Built largely in the 1920s, the neighborhood of Russafa became a center for the city's Muslim immigrant community in the second half of the 20th century. This influence still dominates, with Middle Eastern and East Asian markets and cafes dotting the streets. But as the Carmen has become increasingly touristy, Russafa has also become an alternative hub for artists and students. A combination bookshop, bar, performance space, publishing house, and gallery, **Slaughterhouse Books** (Carrer de Denia 22; 34-963-28-77-55; slaughterhouse.es) used to be a butchery and still has the meat hooks to prove it. **Gnomo** (Carrer de Denia 12; 34-963-73-72-67; elblogdegnomo.blogspot.com), a design boutique, carries things like ceiling lamps made from recycled cola bottles and oil and vinegar pourers shaped like beakers. For midday tapas, try the tiny **Maipi** (Carrer del Mestre Josep Serrano 1; 34-963-735-709; $$$), which serves plates like fresh artichoke and morcilla sausage wrapped in a thin dough.

6 *Ruins Under Glass* 5 p.m.

One of the best spots for exploring Valencia's history is at the museum **L'Almoina** (Plaça de Dezim Juni Brut; 34-962-08-41-73; valencia-cityguide.com/tourist-attractions/museums/la-almoina.html), on the site in the Carmen where Valencia was founded by the Romans in 138 B.C. It's open into the evening,

ABOVE Balansiya, an out-of-the-way restaurant that re-creates the cuisine of medieval Moorish Valencia. The décor, matching the theme, is Arab-Andalusian.

LEFT Café Negrito, a good spot for an after-dinner drink in the hours before club life begins at 1 a.m.

and visitors can walk over glass floors, looking down at a stunning assemblage of ruins excavated in the area. The exhibition includes Roman baths, Visigoth tombs, and a medieval Moorish ward for plague victims.

7 *Moorish Courses* 9 p.m.

The city's Islamic past is the focus of **Balansiya** (Passeig de las Facultades 3; 34-963-89-08-24; balansiya.com; $$), an out-of-the-way restaurant that authentically re-creates the culinary experience of medieval Moorish Valencia. The décor is exquisite Arab-Andalusian, and the prix fixe dinner menus include tabbouleh, tagine, and couscous plus lesser-known Moorish specialties, like assaffa (Andalusian pasta with chicken, cinnamon, and nuts), waraka inab (grape leaves stuffed with cereal in an almond-mint vinaigrette), and xarab Andalusi (a drink made of fruits, flowers, spices, and herbs).

8 *Party Under the Museum* Midnight

Club life doesn't kick off until after 1 a.m., so hit **Café Negrito** (Plaça del Negret 1; 34-963-91-42-23) for an after-dinner drink. Later, witness Valencian late-night decadence at **MYA** (Avenida del Saler 5, City of Arts and Sciences; 34-661-68-00-68; umbracleterraza.com), a domed club underneath

ABOVE L'Estimat, one of the restaurants that serve paella, an originally Valencian dish.

BELOW The Ayuntamiento, Valencia's City Hall. An ornate architectural extravaganza, it was built in the 18th century and dominates the city's main square.

a landscaped walkway leading to the Príncipe Felipe Science Museum. It's Studio 54 meets imperial Spain meets *Jersey Shore*.

SUNDAY

9 *Shop the Lot* 11 a.m.

Every Sunday, Valencia's antiques and junk shop owners convene at the **Plaça de Luis Casanova**, a giant lot tucked behind the 55,000-

OPPOSITE At the sprawling Mercado Central, Valencia's main market, nearly 1,000 vendors sell everything from jamón serrano and bomba rice for paella to Marcona almonds and saffron.

seat Camp de Mestalla stadium, the home field of Valencia Club de Fútbol, to sell their goods at huge markdowns to a fantastically eclectic cross section of locals.

10 *Paella en La Playa* 1 p.m.

The shore is lined with large restaurants that have made paella their specialty. **La Pepica** (Passeig Neptuno 6; 34-963-71-03-66; lapepica.com; $$$) is the best known, for good reason, but a few doors down is an another good choice, **L'Estimat** (Passeig Neptuno 16; 34-963-71-00-18; $$$). On Sunday afternoons, the place fills up with the after-church crowd chowing down on paella Valenciana, made with chicken and rabbit.

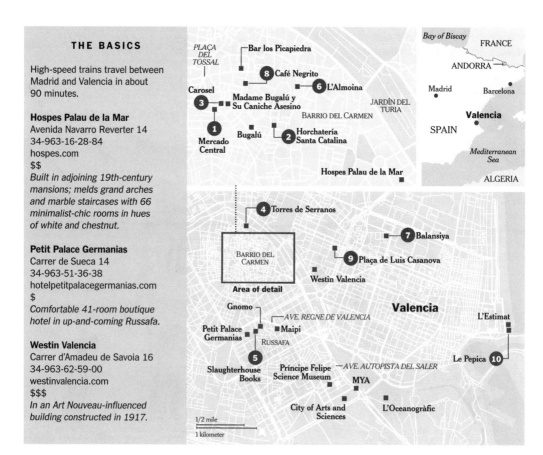

THE BASICS

High-speed trains travel between Madrid and Valencia in about 90 minutes.

Hospes Palau de la Mar
Avenida Navarro Reverter 14
34-963-16-28-84
hospes.com
$$
Built in adjoining 19th-century mansions; melds grand arches and marble staircases with 66 minimalist-chic rooms in hues of white and chestnut.

Petit Palace Germanias
Carrer de Sueca 14
34-963-51-36-38
hotelpetitpalacegermanias.com
$
Comfortable 41-room boutique hotel in up-and-coming Russafa.

Westin Valencia
Carrer d'Amadeu de Savoia 16
34-963-62-59-00
westinvalencia.com
$$$
In an Art Nouveau-influenced building constructed in 1917.

PLAÇA DEL TOSSAL
Bar los Picapiedra
8 Café Negrito
6 L'Almoina
Carosel
3 Madame Bugalú y Su Caniche Asesino
JARDÍN DEL TURIA
BARRIO DEL CARMEN
1 Bugalú
2 Horchatería Santa Catalina
Mercado Central
Hospes Palau de la Mar

4 Torres de Serranos
7 Balansiya
BARRIO DEL CARMEN
9 Plaça de Luis Casanova
Westin Valencia
Area of detail

Gnomo
AVE. REGNE DE VALENCIA
Petit Palace Germanias
Maipi
RUSSAFA
5
Slaughterhouse Books
Príncipe Felipe Science Museum
AVE. AUTOPISTA DEL SALER
MYA
Le Pepica **10**
L'Estimat
Valencia
City of Arts and Sciences
L'Oceanogràfic

1/2 mile
1 kilometer

Bay of Biscay
FRANCE
ANDORRA
Madrid
Barcelona
Valencia
SPAIN
Mediterranean Sea
ALGERIA

Ibiza

As a nucleus of the electronic music scene, Ibiza, in Spain's Balearic Islands, attracts party people of every age and demographic, from London fashionistas and Goa-style ravers to French bobos and Spanish government ministers. After October 1, when the club season comes to a euphoric finale, the island eases back into a Mediterranean groove. Whether it's hibernating in yoga retreats, trekking through Unesco World Heritage sites, or lounging by turquoise blue water and white-sand beaches, Ibiza offers plenty of laid-back after-party spots. Plus, there are phenomenal seafood and glamorous hippies. For a different kind of escape, take the ferry to the neighboring island of Formentera, a largely undeveloped spot where you can escape the party scene, though perhaps not all of the crowd that inhabits it. — BY ANN MARIE GARDNER

FRIDAY

1 *Beach Spotting* 4 p.m.

Get into the groove at the **Jockey Club** (Playa Salinas; 34-971-39-57-88; jockeyclubibiza.com), a trendy but casual restaurant along the powdery white sands of Salinas Beach, a beautiful stretch with the beautiful people. It's a great place to grab a late-afternoon drink and watch sunbathers while D.J.'s spin their Balearic beat.

2 *Get the Party Started* 8 p.m.

For decades, during high season the beachside bar **Café Mambo** in Sant Antoni village (Vara del Rey 3; 34-971-34-66-38; cafemamboibiza.com) has been the place to watch the late-evening sunset. It still is, and now you can also shop for Mambo-branded T-shirts and hoodies.

3 *Late Late Dinner* 11 p.m.

It's dinnertime in Ibiza — so head to the foodie village of Sant Rafel. On the beautiful Plaça de la Iglesia, across from the cathedral, sit under the trees at **El Clodenis** (Plaça de la Iglesia; 34-971-19-85-45; elclodenis.com). The food is French, and you can

drink lovely Spanish and French wines. After dinner, go to **Restaurant L'Elephant** (Plaça de la Iglesia; 34-871-23-81-78; elephant-ibiza.com), a minimalist-white restaurant with a happening roof bar that offers wonderful views of historic old Ibiza Town. Then, as the night wears on, it's time for clubbing. The center of Ibiza night life is **Pacha** (Avenida 8 d'Agost; 34-971-31-36-12; pachaibiza.com), and it has been for 40 years. After 2 a.m., it turns into a sea of people dancing with their arms in the air.

SATURDAY

4 *Shopping Fix* 11 a.m.

Don't miss the outdoor hippie market **Las Dalias**, near the tiny village of Sant Carles on the island's northeastern tip (Carretera Eivissa-Sant Carles, Kilometer 12; 34-971-32-68-25; lasdalias.es). This is not a cheap flea market but a kind of year-round trunk show where vacationing fashion designers and editors come to forage for one-of-a-kind jewelry, amazing dresses from India and Bali, and handmade leather sandals. Afterward, duck into **Ganesha** in Ibiza Town (Montgri 14), a vintage shop run by Vicente Hernández and filled with treasures from his trips to South America. He is an institution — Jade Jagger, Elle, and all the Ibiza girls have been known to shop here.

OPPOSITE A beach on craggy, pristine Formentera.

RIGHT Mud bath technique: slather, dry, jump in the sea.

5 *Out to Sea* 1 p.m.

Take a boat to **Ses Illetes**, the famous white-sand beach with turquoise water on Formentera. Hike to the natural mud baths on the island's northernmost tip, dunk yourself in mud — it will dry and crack as you walk under the hot sun — and then plunge into the sea to rinse it off. Ferries depart hourly from Ibiza Town and Sant Antoni (balearia.com). If you prefer to charter a boat, a

ABOVE The lighthouse on Formentera. The island is not too remote to have an elegant restaurant.

BELOW If you lack a yacht to anchor off Formentera, you can always charter a boat. Or just arrive by ferry from Ibiza.

concierge service called **Deliciously Sorted** (Carrer Venda de Llatzer 25, Santa Gertrudis; 34-971-19-78-67; deliciouslysortedibiza.com) can locate Rivas, sailboats, Sunseekers, and Turkish schooners.

6 *Pageantry of Boats* 3 p.m.

In Formentera, you can feast on calamari and drink sangria under giant white umbrellas at **Juan y Andrea** (Playa de Illetes; 34-971-18-71-30; juanyandrea.com; $$$$), an elegant and expensive restaurant tucked in the sand dunes overlooking a clear blue harbor filled with yachts. It is a favorite hangout for the beautiful people, who come to nibble paella and baked fish and argue over who has the biggest boat at the beach — the Saudi prince or the Russian millionaire?

7 *Cultural Break* 7 p.m.

Ibiza Town was a fortress before its cobblestone streets were filled with quaint restaurants

and endlessly cute clothing and crafts shops, many of them built into the stone ramparts. The oldest part, **Dalt Vila**, is a Unesco World Heritage site and within it is a tiny modern art museum, **Museu d'Art Contemporani** (Ronda Narcís Putget; 34-971-30-27-23) that is worth seeing. After your visit, climb to the top of the **Our Lady of the Snows** cathedral for panoramic views of Ibiza and the sea.

8 *Happy Waiters* 10 p.m.

Grab a cheap predinner drink at the gay hangout **Café Tomate & Company**, with tables right on the market square (Mercado Viejo; 34-871-57-68-68). Then walk up the hill to **La Brasa** (Carrer Pere Sala 3; 34-971-30-12-02; labrasaibiza.com; $$$$), a cozy seafood restaurant inside the town's old stone walls where the good-natured waiters set the mood for your next party. The kitchen serves traditional Ibizan seafood like mussels with almond sauce and chicken with lobster. This is the real Ibiza — in this neighborhood, laundry hangs to dry and kids play in the doorways while parades of neighbors and tourists pass.

9 *Jazz Interlude* Midnight

For a break from the usual Ibiza scene, trot down to **Teatro Pereyra** (Conde de Rosselló 3; 34-971-30-44-32; teatropereyra.com) for some live jazz. Or stop by **Km5** (Carretera Eivissa-Sant Josep Kilometer 5; 34-971-39-63-49; km5-lounge.com), a restaurant and bar that goes until 4 a.m. and bills itself as an escape from the "pounding club culture."

ABOVE Ibiza Town was a fortress before its cobblestone streets were filled with quaint restaurants and endlessly cute clothing and crafts shops, many built into the ramparts.

BELOW Even on Ibiza, known internationally as a party island, there are pockets of tranquility to be found.

SUNDAY

10 *Downtime* 11 a.m.

Have a coffee and croissant from **Croissant Show** (Plaça de la Constitució 2; 34-971-31-76-65) in Ibiza Town's market square. Then hit the beach clubs on **Playa Es Jondal** in San José, the perfect antidote to the island's kinetic scene. **Tropicana Beach Club** (Cala Jondal; 34-971-18-75-20; tropicanaibiza.com) is popular with families, while **Blue Marlin** draws

Speedo- and thong-wearing singles (Passeig Joan Carles I; 34-971-19-37-06; bluemarlinibiza.com). Both offer lounge chairs, umbrellas, chill music, waiter service, and surfside massages along the sheltered cove. After a beachfront lunch and some rosé, the decision is clear: extend the trip and leave mañana.

ABOVE A view at dawn from the old town of Ibiza.

OPPOSITE Ganesha, a vintage clothing shop in Ibiza Town.

THE BASICS

Rent a car to get around the island.

Cas Gasi
Camino Viejo de Sant Mateu
34-971-19-77-00
casgasi.com
$$$$
Large farmhouse converted into a beautiful agritourism hotel. Guests have included Robert De Niro and Kate Moss.

El Hotel Pachá
Passeig Marítim
34-971-31-59-63
elhotelpacha.com
$$
Glitzy party hotel across the street from the famous Pacha nightclub.

Atzaró
Carretera Sant Joan Km. 15
34-971-33-88-38
atzaro.com
$$-$$$
Gym, holistic spa, boutique, and patio restaurant.

Balearic Sea

Sant Carles
4 Las Dalias

IBIZA

Cas Gasi
Café **2** Mambo
Sant Antoni
Deliciously Sorted

Mediterranean Sea

El Clodenis/ **3** Restaurant L'Elephant
Sant Rafel

Playa Es Jondal/ Tropicana Beach Club/ Blue Marlin
Km5
Ibiza
Atzaró

Ibiza
Pacha
El Hotel Pachá

Jockey Club **1**
Salinas Beach

Teatro Pereyra
Ganesha
Café Tomate & **8** Company
9
10 Croissant Show

La Brasa
Museu d'Art Contemporani

7
Dalt Vila
Our Lady of the Snows

Ses Illetes
5

6 Juan y Andrea

FRANCE
Barcelona

SPAIN
MINORCA
MAJORCA

IBIZA
BALEARIC ISLANDS

FORMENTERA

4 miles
5 kilometers

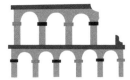

Tarragona

What draws travelers to the northeast of Spain? Cutting-edge food, of course. To Barcelona? Modernist architecture, perhaps. Along the coast, the beaches. And to Tarragona, a laid-back city about 60 miles south of Barcelona, the ancient ruins. Despite the occasional aqueduct, vestiges of ancient Rome are rarely the primary attractions for visitors to Spain, which makes the wealth of ruins in Tarragona so exceptional. Although it was one of the most important Roman cities in Spain, founded by Gnaeus Scipio in 218 B.C. and named a colony by Julius Caesar, relatively few tourists seem to know about it. But this is a secret that is meant to be shared.
— BY FLORENCE FABRICANT

FRIDAY

1 *Business, Pleasure* 3 p.m.

Do your homework first. Pick up excellent maps and orientation at the municipal **Tourist Office** (Carrer Major 39; 34-977-25-07-95; tarragonaturisme. cat). Expect to be on foot in town; the rich array of sights within the city are all within about 15 minutes' walk of one another, and signs labeled "Tárraco" — one of Tarragona's ancient Roman names — point the way, with explanatory text in several languages. Spend about 15 euros for a Tarragona card, good for 48 hours and offering admission to the Roman sites and to guided tours, as well as discounts for taxis, restaurants, and shops. Next, reward yourself for your careful preparation by heading down the broad promenade of the Rambla Nova, the city's main artery, and stopping for a drink at one of the outdoor cafes.

2 *Layered Ellipse* 5 p.m.

The boulevard ends at a palm-fringed terrace overlooking the beach and the sea beyond. Just below is the second-century **Roman Amphitheater**, which once held up to 15,000 spectators for games and grim spectacles. Descend the staircase and go inside. Minimally restored, the amphitheater is

OPPOSITE Two millenniums ago, Tarragona was one of the most important cities of the Roman world.

RIGHT Marked trails take hikers close to the Aqueduct de les Ferreres, a marvel of Roman engineering.

an elliptical arena with banks of seats built into a sloping hillside. By the third century, Christians were martyred here, and later a commemorative basilica was built. The basilica, in turn, became a church — Holy Mary of the Miracle — and then a convent and a prison. It's a vivid reminder of the richly layered history of Tarragona, most of which is situated above the amphitheater, within the Old City's ancient walls. Below the arena, walk out onto the rocky Mediterranean shore.

3 *Sorry, No Chariots* 6 p.m.

Where the Rambla segues into the historic district, stop at the **Roman Circus**, a stunning praetorium and racetrack complex built by the Emperor Domitian for chariot races. It was once a part of the immense main forum of the city. The circus is said to have been the largest in the Roman Empire and is considered one of the best preserved in Europe. (Even with a good map, though, navigating its confusing network of tunnels and walkways is a challenge.) Within the circus is a massive tower from the first century B.C. that was turned into a Gothic-style palace during the Middle Ages. Throughout the complex are interpretive signs in several languages.

4 *Early Bird* 9 p.m.

Vestiges of ancient walls are part of the setting at **Degvsta** (Carrer dels Cavallers 6; 34-977-25-24-28; degvsta.com; $$), a somewhat formal restaurant in the Old City. A 9 p.m. reservation may make you an early bird here, but take the risk. The food is creative and satisfying. A five-course menu might

include crispy cuttlefish, gratin of turbot with leeks, roast lamb, and carrot cake. In general, Tarragona's restaurants are varied, emphasize seafood, and are reasonably priced, with a wealth of wines from nearby regions — Priorat, Penedes, Terra Alta, and Tarragona itself — on their lists.

SATURDAY

5 *Roman Capital* 10 a.m.

Return to your tour of the ruins, beginning at a gate in the ancient walls. There, at the **Plaça del Pallol**, there's a model of the city in its Roman heyday, starting in 218 B.C. It was then, during the Punic Wars against Carthage, that the Romans began building

the walls and paving the forums to create a major provincial capital and their base of operations for conquering the Iberian Peninsula. Around the first century A.D., Tarragona may have had a population many times greater than its current 140,000. Between conquests, emperors like Caesar Augustus and Hadrian lingered here. The city fell into decline in the fifth century. Today, fortified walls run along the perimeter of about a third of the historic district, with a park-like promenade on top.

6 *Life Among the Ruins* 11 a.m.

Tarragona is the kind of living museum where you might come across ruins almost anywhere. Vestiges of the forum and the theater can even be found among the office buildings and apartment houses that line the avenues. Some in the city would like to see some of the development stripped away to spotlight the ancient city better, but many locals seem oblivious to the familiar shards of buildings from the days of the Caesars. At the **Tarragona National Archaeological Museum** (Plaça del Rei 5; 34-977-23-62-09; mnat.cat), in an elegant building

ABOVE Street soccer against the backdrop of ancient Roman walls in the Plaça del Forum.

LEFT Cafes and restaurants in the newer Tarragona built over and amid the Roman ruins.

that incorporates the first-century Praetorium, examine marble and bronze sculptures, a number of stunning mosaics, and other artifacts.

7 *On the Square or at the Sea* 1 p.m.

In the Old City, on a square filled with restaurants, **Sentits** (Plaça de la Font 25; 34-977-22-26-26; $$) is one of the best choices for tapas. There are tables inside and out. The menu features classics like anchovies on tomato bread, baby eels with garlic, and seared green pimientos del padrón. If you prefer a seaside lunch, the fishing port, El Serrallo, is dotted with restaurants specializing in seafood, the most desirable of them on Trafalgar, with shaded tables spilling onto the street closest to the docks.

8 *The Devil's Hike* 3 p.m.

Drive about five miles outside the city to the **Aqueduct de les Ferreres** (N-240 toward Lleida), nicknamed the Pont del Diable, or Devil's Bridge, and you'll quickly forget that you just passed the entrance to the autoroute that leads to the city.

TOP A cobbled street in Tarragona. Many locals seem oblivious to their legacies from the days of the Caesars.

ABOVE A sarcophagus in a Tarragona museum. The city may have had a population many times greater than its current 140,000 before falling into decline in the fifth century.

The aqueduct is a knockout. This marvel of Roman engineering once stretched for 25 miles. Really doing it justice means spending a few hours hiking along the nearby marked trails.

9 *Salsa Romesco* 9 p.m.

Back in the Old City, not far from the Roman Amphitheater and Forum, is **Barquet** (Carrer del Gasometre 16; 34-977-24-00-23; restaurantbarquet. com; $$$), where the chef and owner, David Solé, interprets the local specialty, romesco sauce (made with nuts, tomatoes, chilies, and olive oil), in various dishes, even whisking it into fish stews. Try one of the set menus for about 30 to 50 euros, or order from the à la carte menu.

Escipiones, Scipio's Tower, a first-century family funeral monument nearly 20 feet high, with two carved figures about halfway up. Another nine or so miles farther along on this road, which was once the Via Augusta, is the Barà Arch, a triumphal arch from the first century that was dedicated to Augustus. Had enough ruins? Follow signs to the Playa Larga, a popular and beautiful public beach, and jump into the Mediterranean blue. Or head back down the coast just a bit to the resort town of Cambrils, where a couple of Michelin-starred restaurants attract the Tarragonese.

SUNDAY

10 *Arch to Beach* 10 a.m.

Drive back toward Barcelona along the coast for evidence of the Romans' rather grandiose views of themselves. Just off the autoroute N-340, about four miles from the city limits, is the **Torre de los**

ABOVE Rambla Nova, the city's main boulevard, ends near the second-century Roman Amphitheater, which once held up to 15,000 spectators for games and grim spectacles.

OPPOSITE The Praetorium, a Roman tower that served in the Middle Ages as a palace for the kings of Aragón.

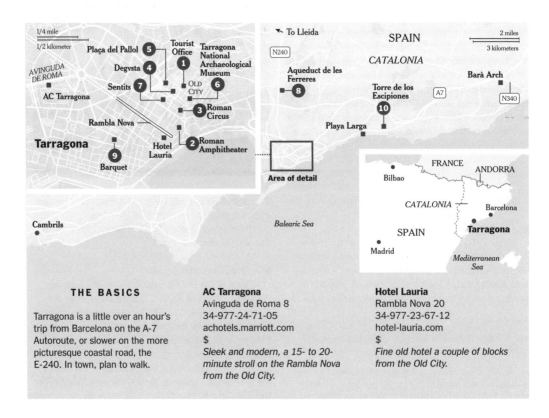

THE BASICS

Tarragona is a little over an hour's trip from Barcelona on the A-7 Autoroute, or slower on the more picturesque coastal road, the E-240. In town, plan to walk.

AC Tarragona
Avinguda de Roma 8
34-977-24-71-05
achotels.marriott.com
$
Sleek and modern, a 15- to 20-minute stroll on the Rambla Nova from the Old City.

Hotel Lauria
Rambla Nova 20
34-977-23-67-12
hotel-lauria.com
$
Fine old hotel a couple of blocks from the Old City.

Barcelona

The once-gritty neighborhoods of Born, El Raval, and Barceloneta have established themselves as the new face of Barcelona — home to some of its best restaurants, bars, and designer shops. You will want to venture beyond the borders of these vibrant areas, of course, but spending most of a weekend amid their narrow streets and shadowy alleyways will provide you with a crash course in what's going on in Barcelona today. — BY STUART EMMRICH

FRIDAY

1 *Rambling Along* 5 p.m.

First things first. Whether it's your first visit to Barcelona or your 10th, you must hit **La Rambla**. Dive into the sensory overload that is this city's most famous avenue, with its bird markets, flower stalls, street musicians, mimes, overpriced tapas bars, and hundreds upon hundreds of people — locals and tourists alike — out for an afternoon stroll. When you have had enough of the crowds (it won't take long), duck into the lovely, palm-tree-dotted Plaça Reial for a restorative break and perhaps an icy caña (draft beer) at one of the cervecerías that line this historic square.

2 *The Perfect Sandwich?* 7 p.m.

Mark Bittman of *The New York Times* once called the flauta d'ibéric d.o. jabugo at the **Café Viena** (Rambla dels Estudis 115; 34-933-17-14-92; $$) the best sandwich he had ever eaten — it's a simple, salty masterpiece of crispy bread and lightly cured ham. The lines of diners who crowd this tiny restaurant — sometimes two or three deep at the counter — surely agree. The flauta (accompanied by a caña poured from the porcelain and brass tap) is a perfect snack to tide you over until you can have dinner in about four hours.

3 *High Art, Low Cost* 9 p.m.

World-class musical performances in stunning architectural settings can be found at the renowned Gran Teatre Del Liceu — more than 150 years old and

the survivor of three major fires and one bombing by anarchists — and the Palau de la Música Catalana concert hall. But more affordable classical music concerts — in an equally beautiful setting — are at the **Basílica de Santa Maria del Mar** (Plaça de Santa Maria 1; 34-933-10-23-90), a lovely and elegant church in Born that dates from the mid-14th century. After the music, walk across the courtyard to join the stylish crowd gathered at **La Vinya del Senyor** (Plaça de Santa Maria 5; 34-933-10-33-79) for tapas and one of its many excellent wines featured by the glass.

4 *Heating Up, Icing Down* 12:30 a.m.

South Beach, Miami meets Barcelona at the strip of open-air nightclubs along Passeig Marítim de la Barceloneta. With its elegantly appointed space and its inviting daybeds where couples lounge as they drink the night away, the **Carpe Diem Lounge Club** (No. 32; 34-932-24-04-70; cdlcbarcelona.com) has perhaps the highest profile of these beachside boîtes. But **Shôko** (No. 36; 34-932-25-92-00; shoko.biz) seems to have the edge in youth and energy, while the neighboring **icebarcelona** (Ramon Trias Fargas 2; 34-932-24-16-25; icebarcelona.com), with its premises cooled as low as minus 8 Celsius (that's 17.6 Fahrenheit; average stay 45 minutes) has the quirkiest appeal.

SATURDAY

5 *Market Research* 10 a.m.

Join what feels like the city's entire population on a morning shopping expedition at the sprawling **Boqueria** (La Rambla 91), which has been around, in

OPPOSITE Taking a break in the Plaça Reial.

RIGHT The modern art museum Macba (Museu d'Art Contemporani de Barcelona).

one form or another, since the early 18th century. If a trip among the hundreds of stalls becomes a dizzying experience, grab a counter seat at the hugely popular tapas spot **Bar Pinotxo** (La Rambla 89; 34-933-17-17-31; pinotxobar.com) for a brief rest and a late morning bite. (Try the salt cod croquettes.)

6 *The Art of the Everyday* 11:30 a.m.

There are some superb examples of present-day Catalan art at **Museu d'Art Contemporani de Barcelona** (Plaça dels Àngels 1; 34-934-12-08-10; macba.cat), plus another show in the adjoining plaza, a lively scene of young families on weekend outings, couples, street vendors, and whizzing skateboarders practicing their moves.

7 *El Raval Afternoon* 2 p.m.

The museum also provides an excellent jumping-off point for exploring the nearby neighborhood of **El Raval**. One of the city's oldest areas, it has been rescued from seediness (it was once a red-light district) and is gentrifying, but still has a diverse population and a feeling of the authentic, non-touristy city. Wander the streets, where you will find some of Barcelona's most interesting shops and fashion outlets, as well as an ever-changing selection of cafes. Then, before heading back to your hotel for a rest, stop by the ever-crowded **BarcelonaReykjavik** bakery (Carrer del Doctor Dou 12; barcelonareykjavik.com) for its organic treats, like a delicious leek and olive oil bread.

8 *Using Your Senses* 9 p.m.

The eight-course Sensations menu at the elegant **Cinc Sentits** (Carrer d'Aribau 162; 34-933-23-94-90; cincsentits.com; $$$$) can be counted on to surprise. One evening it began with a bracing shot

ABOVE The beach and waterfront at Barceloneta, where much of Barcelona seems to head for a Sunday stroll, or for a sunbath and a swim.

LEFT A flower shop along La Rambla, an avenue of shops, entertainers, restaurants, and weekend crowds that is an integral element of Barcelona.

glass of maple syrup, chilled cream, cava sabayon, and a layer of rock salt; wound its way through Mediterranean tuna in smoked tomato water and Iberian suckling pig cooked sous-vide; and finally ended up with olive oil ice cream and shattered bread. The price is not for the fainthearted, but you can expect a superb progression of dishes — each accompanied with a well-chosen wine — and a memorable meal that will leave you sated but not stuffed. If you're not ready to call it a night (and few locals are at this hour), head to **Dry Martini** (Carrer d'Aribau 162; 34-932-17-50-72; drymartiniorg.com) for its signature drinks and its laid-back crowd.

SUNDAY

9 *Gather Round* Noon

Every Sunday, the **Plaça de la Seu**, which fronts Barcelona's imposing Gothic cathedral in the city's historic center, becomes a stage for aficionados of the sardana. The dancers — mostly women, elegantly dressed in full makeup and jewelry — toss their purses and jackets into the middle of a circle and then join hands as they master the intricate

ABOVE Flowers and balconies in the Barcelona sun.

BELOW Skateboarders congregate at the plaza in front of Macba to practice their moves.

steps (and tiny hops) of this traditional Catalan dance. You'll probably be asked to donate a euro or two, as part of a collection for the band members playing on the cathedral steps.

10 *A Seaside Feast* 1 p.m.

Much of Barcelona seems to head to the seaside neighborhood of Barceloneta for a Sunday stroll along the waterfront. Watch the passing parade from an outdoor table at **La Mar Salada** (Passeig Joan de Borbó 59; 34-932-21-10-15; lamarsalada.cat; $$$), one of the less touristy restaurants along this busy strip, and have a lunch of excellently prepared calamari, followed by the house specialty, seafood paella, all accompanied by a crisp white Spanish wine.

ABOVE Shop in the hundreds of stalls at the sprawling Boqueria market on La Rambla.

OPPOSITE Variety and abundance at La Boqueria. The market dates back to the early 18th century.

THE BASICS

Rent a car at the airport. For getting around the city, you can't beat the efficient and easy-to-navigate Metro system.

Omm
Carrer del Rosselló 265
34-934-45-40-00
hotelomm.es
$$$

Home to both an acclaimed restaurant and a happening late-night bar.

Market Hotel
Carrer del Comte Borrell 68
34-933-25-12-05
markethotel.com.es
$
Budget hotels don't get more stylish. Well designed and comfortable.

Hotel Arts
Carrer de la Marina 19-21
34-932-21-10-00
hotelartsbarcelona.com
$$$$
A Ritz-Carlton with a luxe spa and a huge steel-lattice fish sculpture by Frank Gehry.

Barcelona for Art Lovers

Conventional thinking holds that Barcelona is Spain's gateway to European culture. Insofar as culture means innovative architecture and modern art, smart urban planning that prizes pedestrian-friendly boulevards, and an arm's-length attitude toward some deep Spanish traditions, like bullfighting, such thinking is right on the money. It was in Barcelona in the 1890s that Picasso found the artistic vanguard that propelled him to Paris and world renown. Joan Miró grew up here and left the city some flamboyant public art. And this is where Antoni Gaudí spun Art Nouveau into his own quirky architectural idiom. For travelers interested in art and architecture, there is plenty here, along with ample distractions if museum fatigue sets in. — BY ANDREW FERREN

FRIDAY

1 *Picasso, the Early Years* 6 p.m.

Spain's greatest 20th-century export is the subject at the **Picasso Museum** (Carrer de Montcada 15-23; 34-932-56-30-00; www.museupicasso.bcn.cat), which has a rich collection of the artist's early works — Blue Period, Rose Period, Cubism — from the years before he permanently settled in Paris. Set in a complex of 12th- and 13th-century Catalan palaces, the museum manages to show how the young Picasso arrived in Barcelona as a teenager in 1896 and literally found the world. One can almost hear the buildings' giant stone blocks bending to his artistic will.

2 *Be Well Fed* 10 p.m.

Cal Pep (calpep.com) may be an iconic place to eat in Barcelona, but its sibling, **Restaurant Passadís del Pep** (Plaça del Palau 2; 34-933-10-10-21; passadis.com; $$$$), remains an under-the-radar favorite precisely because it is so hard to find: down an unmarked narrow passage (*passadís* in Catalan), with a brooding figure standing in its arched portal. Tell the brooding figure you have a reservation, which

you should make well in advance, and he will wave you in. Once inside, you don't even have to order (and you can't, since there's no menu). Just say sí when the waiter offers a glass of cava and a plate of something succulent, perhaps jamón serrano. The rest — delectable ingredients of a long, relaxing dinner — just starts showing up.

SATURDAY

3 *Getting to Know Miró* 9 a.m.

Another of the artists that Barcelona launched to world renown was Joan Miró, who identified strongly with his Catalan heritage. Take the metro to the **Parc de Joan Miró** for a look at his *Dona i Ocell*, a lovable if suggestive 70-foot-high phallic sculpture commissioned by the city not long before the artist's death. Then make your way to the leafy slope of Montjuïc (there's a funicular from the Paral-lel metro stop), overlooking Barcelona and the Mediterranean, and the **Fundació Joan Miró** (Parc de Montjuïc s/n; 34-934-43-94-70; bcn.fjmiro.es). The gallery holds a comprehensive collection of Miró's colorful, surrealistic work and also hosts traveling exhibitions.

4 *Pre-Picasso* 11 a.m.

The **Museu Nacional d'Art de Catalunya**, better known as MNAC (Parc de Montjuïc; 34-936-22-03-60;

OPPOSITE The Sagrada Família, under construction since the 1880s and long a beloved symbol of Barcelona.

RIGHT Inside the Sagrada Família, the eccentric masterwork of the architect Antoni Gaudí.

www.museunacional.cat/en), appears as a vast palace crowning the Montjuïc park. Not to be missed are the Romanesque paintings—many exhibited in artfully made concave frames to simulate the church apses they came from. They are sculptural master-pieces in their own right. Also worthwhile are the late 19th- and early 20th-century paintings by Rusiñol, Casas, and others who had a profound impact on the young Picasso and, thus, the course of Modernism. Back down the hill are Mies van der Rohe's 1929 **Barcelona Pavilion** (Av. Francesc Ferrer i Guàrdia 7; 34-934-23-40-16; miesbcn.com) and **CaixaForum** (Av. Francesc Ferrer i Guàrdia 6-8; 34-934-76-86-00), a converted textile factory that houses temporary exhibitions.

5 *Casual Tapas* 2 p.m.

Bar Mut (Carrer de Pau Claris 192; 34-932-17-43-38; $$$$) is a bustling joint where local people go to feast on a casual lunch of cañas (small beers) and

no-fuss tapas like herb-infused steamed mussels; fried egg carpaccio with prawns; or eggs with liver, potatoes, and sausage). The easygoing servers never seem to be fazed no matter how many times you call them back to order something else.

6 *Meeting Gaudí* 3 p.m.

Barcelona's most famous monument, the extra-ordinary, many-towered **Sagrada Família** (Carrer de Mallorca 401; 34-932-08-04-14; sagradafamilia. org), was consecrated as a basilica by Pope Benedict XVI in 2010 even though it is still far from complete. The church, under construction since the 1880s, is the best known work of the eccentric architect Antoni Gaudí, whose singular vision has become part of the city's identity. Take some time

BELOW A room inside MNAC, the palace-like National Museum of Catalonian Art.

absorbing the complex, strictly one-of-a-kind design, inside and out, and then check out Gaudí's equally eye-catching **Casa Milà**, also known as **La Pedrera**, (Provença 261-265; 34-902-20-21-38; lapedrera.com) and **Casa Batlló** (Passeig de Gràcia 43; 34-932-16-03-06; casabatllo.es).

7 *Make a Splash* 5 p.m.

Overwhelmed by too much art and artistry? Take the water cure. In Barcelona's balmy Mediterranean climate, the beach is an option much of the year. Among the liveliest city beaches is **Platja de Sant Sebastià** at the end of la Barceloneta, a wedge of land jutting into the Mediterranean near the Port Vell (Old Harbor). You can moisten your insides as well with the cheap beers at the very chilled-out **Chiringuito del Mar**, a beach shack where the pavement of Plaça del Mar meets the sand of Sant Sebastià.

8 *Modernisme Over Dinner* 10 p.m.

If Gaudí's structural theatrics strike you as over the top, go see some work by Lluís Domènech i Montaner, an under-sung hero of Catalan modernism. The best way is to catch a concert at Domènech's 1908 **Palau de la Música Catalana**, a stunning classical music hall with an interior adorned on every surface with color, texture, relief, and, because the walls and ceiling are made almost entirely of stained glass,

colored light. Failing that, have dinner at **La Fonda España** in the Hotel España (Carrer Sant Pau 9-11; 34-935-50-00-10; hotelespanya.com; $$$$). The hotel hired Domènech to renovate this restaurant a century ago and now, recently spruced up, it shines anew with his strappy wood and ceramic wainscoting, murals by Ramon Casas, and a sculptural fireplace by Eusebi Arnau. The food is respectable enough, and the dining room is spectacular.

ABOVE The Palau de la Música Catalana, a stunning classical music hall by Lluís Domènech i Montaner.

BELOW The lobby at Room Mate Emma, a boutique hotel with interiors by the the Madrid designer Tomás Alía.

SUNDAY

9 *Overpay for the O.J.* 11 a.m.

It's touristy, it's overpriced, and it gets away with it because everyone in town meets at **Café Zurich** (Plaça de Catalunya 1; 34-933-17-91-53), which occupies the busiest corner on the busiest square in the city. Angle for a table outside for people-watching or the quieter mezzanine for a tête-à-tête. The coffee is excellent, the beers are Wagnerian in scale, and the sandwiches, or bocadillos, are just so-so — unless you ask for a side of tomatoes and olive oil, which makes all the difference.

10 *Above the Fray* 1 p.m.

Head to the northern edge of the city and **Parc Güell**, Gaudí's bulbous and mosaic-carpeted gardens on a hill near Mont Tibidabo. The terraces and promontories offer exquisite views of the city, with the Sagrada Família looming in the center. If you're really game, go even higher on the Ferris wheel or the Aeroplane at the **Tibidabo Amusement Park** (Plaça del Tibidabo 3-4; 34-932-11-79-42; tibidabo.cat), two old-school rides that still soar above Spain's most mod city.

ABOVE Barcelona may be the soul of young and trendy, but some of the best views of the city are from the old-school rides at the Tibidabo Amusement Park.

OPPOSITE Casa Batlló, another manifestation of Gaudí's singular architectural vision.

THE BASICS

The Articket Barcelona (bcnshop. barcelonaturisme.com) covers admission at seven museums and will allow you to skip long ticket lines.

Hotel Casa Fuster
Passeig de Gràcia 132
34-932-55-30-00
hotelescenter.es/hotel-casa-fuster
$$$
Stylish lodgings in a modernist building.

Mandarin Oriental
Passeig de Gràcia 38-40
34-931-51-88-88
mandarinoriental.es/barcelona
$$$$
In a mid-20th-century structure.

Room Mate Emma
Carrer de Rosselló 205
34-932-38-56-06
emma.room-matehotels.com/en
$
Interiors by Tomás Alía, known for flashy discos.

The Costa Brava

Along the Costa Brava, Spain's northeastern "wild coast" in the autonomous region of Catalonia, fishing villages still feel like fishing villages, medieval mountain towns are still hushed at siesta, and artists still paint on quiet streets. Tourists can mingle with residents both in the high season, when a cacophony of European languages fills the air, and in the late spring and early fall, when visitors are fewer and Catalan, the local language, fully asserts itself. A refreshing resistance to change — and preservation efforts that have helped to control development — keep this stretch of the Mediterranean radically different from the more congested, frenetic southern coasts. For a weekend tour, drive north from Barcelona toward dusty medieval hamlets and equally ancient churches and farmhouses, set against a backdrop that falls away suddenly, breathtakingly, into the sea.
— BY SARAH WILDMAN

FRIDAY

1 *First Stop: Begur* 2 p.m.

About an hour and 40 minutes from the Barcelona airport, drive into **Begur**, a medieval town built on a hill. On foot, explore its maze of lanes dotted with excellent fish restaurants, ancient towers, and cozy bars. Flowers spill out from window boxes, and overhead is a dominating fortress where women and children ran for safety from 17th-century pirates. Orient yourself with the help of the local experts. Most Costa Brava villages have tourist information centers to direct wanderers, and the one in Begur (Avenida Onze de Setembre 5; 34-972-62-45-20; visitbegur.com) is especially good, with a spirited multilingual staff.

2 *Beach Time* 3 p.m.

Within a 10-minute drive from Begur, there are eight official beaches (and many more unmarked coves), paved and unpaved walking routes to reach them, and shorelines of rock, pebbles, and sand. Put

OPPOSITE The beach in Calella de Palafrugell, a town on the Costa Brava in far northeastern Spain.

RIGHT Sant Martí d'Empúries, one of the whirlwind stops on a weekend Costa Brava road trip.

on a bathing suit and spend a few hours swimming and meandering. **Calella de Palafrugell**, a smaller beach town, is a short drive south from the center of Begur; closer are the volcanic black, almost Hawaiian-like sands of **Fonda** and, linked to it by a footpath, the larger harbor of **Aiguablava**, where a clutch of fishing families still live year-round and little has changed in 100 years.

3 *Fresh From the Sea* 8 p.m.

Back in the center of town, while away the evening over dinner at **Restaurant Rostei** (Carrer Concepció Pi 8, Begur; 34-972-62-42-15; www.rostei.com; $$$), on a narrow, quiet street. Choose from a variety of seafood, including grilled fresh fish. Try to reserve seats in the garden.

SATURDAY

4 *Village Hop* 9 a.m.

Give yourself an early start for a day of venturing deeper into the Costa Brava and its sunny, terra-cotta-colored villages. Start by veering slightly inland. In tiny, touristy **Pals**, narrow cobbled streets lead to clusters of stone buildings: a castle, a Gothic church, aged houses with doorways that open into restaurants or shops selling kitschy souvenirs and the occasional treasure. **Peratallada** has a well-preserved central

square filled with cafes, making it feel livelier than some sleepier neighboring towns. Around them, on the plain of L'Empordà, is a rich landscape of wheat and sunflowers, olive groves and almond trees.

5 *Ruins With a View* Noon

Drive up the coast to **Sant Martí d'Empúries** for a quick look at the ruins left by the ancient Greeks from their days as the dominant Mediterranean power. Toppled and truncated columns and remains

ABOVE A sunflower field on the plain of L'Empordà.

BELOW The beaches and towns are easy to enjoy along this relatively untrammeled stretch of coast.

of villas with mosaic floors look out over the lustrous aquamarine of the Mediterranean. The town's name dates back to its earliest days; the Greeks built their settlement here as an emporium—a trading post—in the sixth century B.C. Back in the car, drive on past **Roses**, long famous as the location of the restaurant El Bulli, which had an internationally renowned run before shutting its doors in 2011. Beyond that, the road passes the **Cap de Creus** nature preserve, a moonscape of scrub brush and hardy trees clinging to a mountain.

6 *Your Hello to Dalí* 1 p.m.

In Cadaqués, bright whitewashed buildings recall a Greek party island, but this town is best known for art. Picasso spent time here, as did Max Ernst, Matisse, Magritte, and Man Ray. The favorite son, however, is Salvador Dalí, who lived part-time in the village as a child and eventually settled nearby. Have lunch under the bougainvillea vines at Lebanese-

influenced **El Barroco** (Carrer des Pla d'en Retalla 2, Cadaqués; 34-972-25-86-32; $$$$), and then walk about half an hour to Port Lligat. The **Salvador Dalí House** there (34-972-25-10-15; salvador-dali.org; reserve in advance) is the home Dalí shared with his wife, Gala. (If you crave more Surrealism, detour to Figueres, about 20 miles west, which has a larger Dalí museum.)

7 *Art in Cadaqués* 4 p.m.

You could spend days in Cadaqués, winding around the old city's narrow corners, down the uneven cobblestone alleyways. Galleries offer an opportunity to see the work of contemporary Costa Brava artists. Try **Taller Galeria Fort** (Horta d'en Sanés 9; 34-972-25-85-49), which hosts an annual "Mini Print International" exhibition every summer. Another good bet is **Galeria Marges-U** (Carrer Unió 12; 34-972-25-85-43; galeriamarges-u.com), a space run by the artists Gustavo Carbó Berthold and his wife, Nobuko Kihira.

Interesting independent shops are also scattered among the storefronts, selling carefully curated and artisanal textiles, jewelry, and ceramics.

8 *Tucking It Away* 8 p.m.

Tucked into a corner of Cadaqués near the frequently painted hilltop Santa Maria cathedral, **La Sirena** (Carrer d'Es Call; 34-972-25-89-74) is a quiet place for a leisurely dinner. The grilled fish "à la Basque" is one excellent choice.

ABOVE The Salvador Dalí House in Port Lligat.

BELOW Tiny, touristy Pals, a town of cobblestone alleyways and stone buildings that hold restaurants and shops.

SUNDAY

9 *The Road to France* 10 a.m.

Leave Cadaqués and drive north on the narrow **N-260**, keeping bathing suits at the ready. The coves will be ever less populated and more tempting as you near the French border. A crazy, breathtaking zigzag road pulls you through the mountains and hugs the coast.

10 *Farewell Tortilla* Noon

In Llançà, a tiny dot on the map that is one of the last towns before the Costa Brava melts almost seamlessly into coastal France, find **Platja Grifeu**, a

glorious beach with clear tropical-looking water to swim in. Savor an alfresco lunch—your own picnic or food from a nearby vendor—as you face the sea, watching the local families sunning themselves and children splashing in the water. Worldwide, beach shacks aren't known for their cuisine, but on one visit to Platja Grifeu, an informal beachside kitchen here yielded a perfect version of the tortilla española, the ubiquitous potato omelet of Spain.

ABOVE A quiet scene in Peratallada, which also has a well-preserved central square filled with cafes.

OPPOSITE The old stone buildings and walkways of Pals.

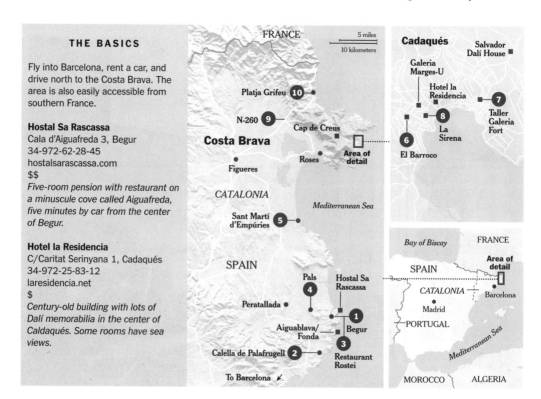

THE BASICS

Fly into Barcelona, rent a car, and drive north to the Costa Brava. The area is also easily accessible from southern France.

Hostal Sa Rascassa
Cala d'Aiguafreda 3, Begur
34-972-62-28-45
hostalsarascassa.com
$$
Five-room pension with restaurant on a minuscule cove called Aiguafreda, five minutes by car from the center of Begur.

Hotel la Residencia
C/Caritat Serinyana 1, Cadaqués
34-972-25-83-12
laresidencia.net
$
Century-old building with lots of Dalí memorabilia in the center of Caldaqués. Some rooms have sea views.

FRANCE

5 miles
10 kilometers

Platja Grifeu 10

N-260 9
Cap de Creus

Costa Brava

Roses · **Area of detail**

Figueres

CATALONIA

Mediterranean Sea

Sant Martí
d'Empúries 5

SPAIN

Pals
4 · Hostal Sa Rascassa

Peratallada ·

Aiguablava/
Fonda · Begur 1

3

Calella de Palafrugell 2 · Restaurant Rostei

To Barcelona ↙

Cadaqués · Salvador Dalí House ■

Galeria
Marges-U

Hotel la
Residencia

8 · 7 · Taller
Galeria
Fort

6 · La
Sirena

El Barroco

Bay of Biscay · FRANCE

SPAIN · **Area of detail**

CATALONIA · Barcelona

Madrid

PORTUGAL

Mediterranean Sea

MOROCCO · ALGERIA

Majorca

Majorcan summers are infamous for the swells they attract: the billionaires on their mega-yachts, the movie stars at their mountain estates. Then there's that other summer crowd, the European lads who flood the developments that spread out from lovely, medieval Palma and make the beach scenes there cautionary tales of the evils of alcohol. During the off-season, which runs from fall to early summer, however, this mountainous, gnarled island, one of Spain's outposts in the Mediterranean, is largely yours. Set yourself up with a rental car (there's a lot of driving to be done) and prepare to be hypnotized by the ancient terraced landscapes with twisted olive trees, the tiny medieval villages, and the extraordinary food and wine. — BY PENELOPE GREEN

FRIDAY

1 *Church and Cappuccino* 2:30 p.m.

Start exploring Palma at its striking many-spired 800-year-old cathedral, **La Seu** (Plaça de la Seu; 34-902-02-24-45); in the depths of the off-season, if you want to go inside you need to be there before it closes in midafternoon. As you enter, its massive and empty volume hits you like a freight train. A few blocks away, stop for fortification at the **Cappuccino Palau March** (Carrer del Conquistador 13; 34-971-71-72-72; grupocappuccino.com). Part of an island-wide chain, it has a kind of swanky blankness, and a killer view; have a cup of the cappuccino alongside the well-heeled Germans you'll find sitting on the outdoor patio.

2 *Shopping for Specialties* 4 p.m.

Palma's medieval and mostly car-free streets have plenty of charm on their own but also are home to little pleasures in the form of shops offering local specialties. Head north up Passeig des Born and make a left onto Carrer de Sant Feliú for a visit to **Rialto Living Palma** (Carrer de Sant Feliú 3; 34-971-71-33-31; rialtoliving.com), a kaleidoscopic store selling home furnishings and clothing augmented by an art gallery and a cafe, all set in a converted theater. On a nearby sunken side street is a grocery store, **Colmado Colom** (Carrer de Santo Domingo 1; 34-971-71-11-59), which carries a required Majorcan souvenir: the Balearides flor de sal sampler, a

selection of five flavored sea salts, from hibiscus to olive. Back home, you will sprinkle them on everything you eat.

3 *Quaffing With the Natives* 8 p.m.

You can drink wine by the centimeter, or order an Estrella Galicia, a Barcelona-made pale lager, at **Bar Dia** (Carrer dels Apuntadors 18; 34-971-71-62-64), which draws a local crowd for its tapas, its hierbas (anise-based liquors not unlike ouzo), and its crispy quarter chicken.

4 *By the Barrels* 9 p.m.

At **La Bodeguilla** (Carrer de Sant Jaume 3; 34-971-71-82-74; grupoamida.com/la-bodeguilla; $$$$), there are hundreds of wines on the wine list. The restaurant is quiet, with an appealing red and black décor. You can eat on glass-topped wine barrels or farther in, by the extensive cellar. (Locals call it the Barrel Bar.) On the tapas menu, look for dishes like grilled lobster with lemon thyme oil and fresh vegetables or Sóller prawns croquettes. Sheep

OPPOSITE The harbor and the 800-year-old La Seu cathedral in Palma, Majorca's main town.

BELOW Deià, a village on the northwest corner of Majorca, dates to the island's Moorish era.

are as much a part of the Majorcan landscape as its olive trees, so it's no surprise that the baby lamb is predictably delicious, as is a local wine, a smooth red, Bodegues Ribas Sió.

SATURDAY

5 *A Fragrant Jaunt* 11 a.m.

On the northwest corner of the island, the village of Deià, butter-colored and antique (it dates to the Moorish era), is a hub for the walking trails and mule tracks that lace the Serra de Tramuntana, the mountains that surround it. It's also the home of **Hotel la Residencia** (Son Canals s/n; 34-971-63-60-11; belmond.com/es/la-residencia-mallorca), a celebrity magnet with stunning views. Follow the little trail just opposite the hotel's parking area for a sweet half-hour walk over stiles and along stone terraces lush with almond, lemon, and orange trees and wild lavender. You might even see wild asparagus.

6 *Cafe With a View* 1:30 p.m.

Cafeteria Sa Fon Fresca (Carrer Arxiduc Lluís Salvador 36; 34-971-63-94-41; $$$) is a small cafe

ABOVE From the cliffs, the views are vertiginous as waves crash against the rocks below.

RIGHT Hotel la Residencia, in the island's northwest.

that overlooks a stream and many backyards. There are no culinary fireworks, but the terrace is a lovely spot (or head inside for a televised soccer game). Have a bocadillo de jamón and a cold beer.

7 *Going the Distance* 3 p.m.

Head southeast on the vertiginous coastal road called MA-10 to the town of Banyalbufar; the trip may be the loveliest and the most terrifying drive you'll ever undertake. Lookout points are strategically placed. At the **Mirador Torre del Verger**, you can climb the little tower and have a Kim Novak moment gazing at the surf crashing at the cliffs below. Follow the coast until the road veers left toward Andratx, and keep going till you hit the sea

again, at Port d'Andratx, a picturesque fishing village and resort town.

8 *Coffee by the Sea* 5 p.m.

There's a Grupo Cappuccino outlet in the middle of **Port d'Andratx** (Avinguda de Mateo Bosch 31; 34-971-67-22-14), and it's situated perfectly for watching the fishing boats come in. Have a coffee before you visit the fish market here, which is a particularly satisfying one, with a vast array of often unidentifiable local sea critters.

9 *Dinner on a Grand Scale* 8:30 p.m.

Cavernous with a haute-medieval theme, **Oleum** (Carrer Castillo de Son Net s/n; 34-971-14-70-00; sonnet.es/oleum-restaurant; $$$$), in the nearby village of **Puigpunyent**, is in a 17th-century estate's olive pressing room; the huge press is still here, and it sets the scale for everything else. Dinner is elaborate, and draws heavily from local sources. Cordero

de la Tramuntana on one menu was lamb flavored with rosemary and Mahones, a creamy cheese. For an accompaniment, try the Oleum's own label, a blend from a Majorcan winery, Macià Batle.

SUNDAY

10 *Fusion Power* Noon

At the top of a high-walled street in the village of Orient, about a 40-minute drive from Palma, is **Mandala** (Carrer Nueva 1; 34-971-61-52-85; $$$$), a Spanish-French-Asian fusion restaurant nestled onto the side of a hill. Bright rows of arugula and herbs glow green in the garden out back, under a bleached-out Tibetan prayer flag. With its Gauguin-like island-themed portraits and medieval hangings, Mandala's cozy rooms are where you want to settle in for a nice long (say, two- or three-hour) meal of something like chicken breast curry or lamb fillets with apples in a saffron red wine sauce.

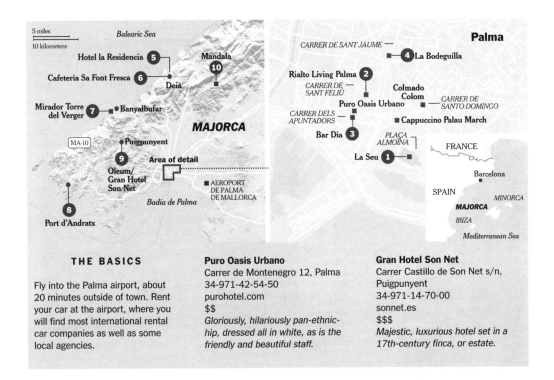

THE BASICS

Fly into the Palma airport, about 20 minutes outside of town. Rent your car at the airport, where you will find most international rental car companies as well as some local agencies.

Puro Oasis Urbano
Carrer de Montenegro 12, Palma
34-971-42-54-50
purohotel.com
$$
Gloriously, hilariously pan-ethnic-hip, dressed all in white, as is the friendly and beautiful staff.

Gran Hotel Son Net
Carrer Castillo de Son Net s/n,
Puigpunyent
34-971-14-70-00
sonnet.es
$$$
Majestic, luxurious hotel set in a 17th-century finca, or estate.

Lisbon

Cheap. That's the label usually slapped across the forehead of Portugal's capital. Around the Continent, Lisbon is mostly seen as the charmingly faded seat of a centuries-gone trade empire where you can plunk down some coins to ride an old yellow cable car, visit Baroque churches and squares, fill up on cut-rate seafood meals, sip two-euro glasses of Portuguese red, and retire to your budget hotel. But Lisbon is getting fancier. By day, ambitious upstart museums and renovated industrial districts offer an infusion of contemporary art and design. By night, a fledgling wave of neo-Portuguese restaurants, stylish night spots, and innovatively designed hotels provide happening places to play. The best part? The city remains a terrific bargain. — BY SETH SHERWOOD

FRIDAY

1 *Industrial Chic* 5 p.m.

Lisbon's metamorphosis comes vividly to life at **LX Factory** (Rua Rodrigues de Faria 103; 351-21-314-3399; lxfactory.com), a disused manufacturing complex housing young architecture firms, Internet start-ups, boutiques, and cozy cafes. Housed in a hangarlike space that's filled with enormous old printing machines, **Ler** (351-21-325-9992; lerdevagar.com) is packed from floor to soaring ceiling with new and used books (many in English) on everything from Madeira architecture to Jack the Ripper. The shelves of **Organii** (351-91-293-2221; organii.pt) display organic cosmetics by Myeko, a specialty Portuguese brand, and other international cult labels. For a snack, hit **Landeau** (351-91-727-8939; landeau.pt), which produces only one thing — devilishly good chocolate cake.

2 *Portuguese Stories* 8 p.m.

A mix of neo-Classical-style and ultra-modern chairs, bits of architectural salvage, antique mirrors and loads of knick-knacks set the stage for authentic but refined Portuguese cuisine at **Casa da Comida** (Travessa das Amoreiras 1; 351-21-388-5376; casadacomida.com). Chef Miguel Carvalho has updated the vision of Jorge Vale, who founded the restaurant in the 1970s and won Portugal's first Michelin star, presenting a seasonal menu full of "Portuguese stories," some in the form of petiscos

or snacks. Four of the most intriguing dishes are partridge in vinegar sauce with a salad of watercress and orange; foie gras with red grape jelly and frozen white grapes; monkfish with baby squid; and roasted potatoes wrapped in hog jowls. The eclectic décor complements the innovative food.

3 *On the Waterfront* 10 p.m.

For most of its life, the waterfront Cais do Sodré district was a mire of sailors, sirens, and sleaze. These days, innovative night-life spots are popping up amid the seedy old dives. **Sol e Pesca** (Rua Nova do Carvalho 44; 351-21-346-7203) pays homage to the city's maritime history with fishing tackle covering the walls, and hundreds of small tins of sardines, tuna, anchovies, and other fish — all for sale — piled like Pop Art soup cans in lighted display cases. All pair well with a glass of Super Bock beer. Farther inland, **Buedalouco Pharmacia di Cultura** (Rua do Norte 60; 351-93-347-9161) is a funky bar with sporadic poetry readings and a hostess who sometimes breaks out in song.

SATURDAY

4 *Stylish Fantasies* 11 a.m.

Ever dreamed of strutting about in a Jean Paul Gaultier crocodile-skin gown while pouring chai from

OPPOSITE The charm of Lisbon's past, as the seat of a vanished empire, now coexists with a lively present.

BELOW A shop in the Intendente district.

an Andrea Branzi silver teapot with a white birch-log handle? Sartorial and furniture fantasies come to life at **Mude** (Rua Augusta 24; 351-21-888-6117; mude.pt), a former bank converted into a fashion and design museum. The underground vault and second-floor gallery host rotating shows, while the ground floor showcases a permanent collection of iconic and experimental clothing, housewares, furnishings, album covers — even a Vespa.

5 *Organic Pizza* 1:30 p.m.

Like bees to flowers, Lisbon's cool kids and creative set have been buzzing in swarms to the fast-rising Principe Real neighborhood, which has become a haven of cafes and design shops. One attraction is **In Bocca al Lupo** (Rua Manuel Bernardes 5; 351-21-390-0582; inboccaallupo.pt) where diners chose from menu of organic and even vegan pizzas and a long list of cocktails, beer, and wine.

6 *Made in Lisboa* 3 p.m.

Nothing works off a hearty brunch like vigorous window-browsing and credit-card swiping around the upstart boutiques of Principe Real and its environs. A former bakery, **Kolovrat 79** (Rua Dom Pedro V 79;

351-21-387-4536; www.lidijakolovrat.org) now sells delicate weblike silver necklaces, scarves printed with tiny images of long-ago Portuguese royalty, and more from the designer Lidija Kolovrat. An even more diverse selection awaits at **Loja do Chiado** (Rua da Misericórdia 102; 351-21-347-2293), which offers three Portuguese indie brands: elegant leather footwear by Catarina Martins, richly embroidered Asian-inspired fashions from TMCollection, and cowskin handbags and accessories by Muu.

7 *Hit the Tagus* 6 p.m.

Most Lisbon visitors neglect its greatest natural resource: the Tagus River. For sublime sunset views, head to the Cais do Sodré ferry terminal (351-808-203-050; transtejo.pt/pt/homepage/index.html) and catch one of the regular boats across the river to Cacilhas. After debarking, walk to the right for about 10 minutes along the thin waterside path to arrive at **Atira-te ao Rio** (Cais do Ginjal 69-70; 351-21-275-1380; atirateaorio.pt). This rustic whitewashed riverfront restaurant is the perfect spot to sip a glass of white port while watching the sun cast its final rays on the 25 de Abril bridge and the venerable hilly cityscape of Lisbon.

8 *Top Chef, Low Cost* 9 p.m.

For a celebrity-chef meal at a common man's prices, you can't do better than **Tasca da Esquina**

(Rua Domingos Sequeira 41C; 351-21-099-3939; tascadaesquina.com; $$), opened in 2009 by the Portuguese food guru Vitor Sobral. Featuring cheerful décor—red concrete floor, unadorned white walls, big windows—and friendly young servers, the restaurant fills mostly with middle-aged business folks and couples who tuck into a menu of small and medium-size plates intended for sharing. You'll find everything from pig tails in coriander to sautéed quail legs (in a buttery and lemony garlic sauce) to ultra thin slices of warm black pork on toast. Abbot Priscos, a lush pudding made with a dash of port wine, provides a fine finale.

9 *The Glass Palace* 11 p.m.

The name of this bar is French for "the cat," but the elegant and softly glowing glass-box architecture of **Le Chat** (Jardim 9 de Abril; 351-21-396-3668; lechatlisboa.com) instead suggests a long rectangular aquarium in which boozefish swim on tides of Porto Flip cocktails (ruby port wine, brandy, egg yolk, nutmeg) and D.J.-spun house music. The space, with hillside views over the Tagus, is a striking

ABOVE Mude hosts rotating shows and displays iconic clothing, furnishings, and everyday objects.

BELOW Ler is a shop packed with books (many in English) on everything from Madeira architecture to Jack the Ripper.

contrast to the impressive stone **Museu Nacional de Arte Antiga** (351-21-391-2800; museudearteantiga.pt) next door.

SUNDAY

10 *An Artful Excursion* 11 a.m.

Cross the Surrealist with the grotesque, toss in some Freud and Jung, add huge dollops of folklore and mythology, and you begin to have a recipe for the wild oeuvre of Paula Rego, perhaps the most important living Portuguese artist. And now there's a fittingly unusual structure to exhibit her works

and those of her late husband, the British painter Victor Willing. Known as **Casa das Histórias** (Avenida da República 300, Cascais; 351-21-482-6970; casadashistorias.com), or House of Stories, the red fortress-like museum is situated in the upscale oceanside suburb of Cascais, a 45-minute train ride from the Cais do Sodré station (www.cp.pt). Their canvases are by turns psychedelic, naughty, and downright strange, but always thought-provoking. Better still, like much in Lisbon, admission at this museum is a fantastic deal: it's free.

ABOVE Artfully placed paving stones create the distinctive mosaic patterns that are a signature of Lisbon.

OPPOSITE Lisbon's trolleys suggest a faded charm, but they flourish in the here and now. The tramway system is a vital network on the narrow streets and steep hills.

THE BASICS

Lisbon is a user-friendly city for tourists to navigate. Getting around on foot is easy, and taxis are plentiful and cheap.

Inspira Santa Marta Hotel
Rua de Santa Marta 48
351-21-044-0900
inspirasantamartahotel.com
$$
Scandinavian-cool design rooms in four color themes: earth, fire, metal, and tree.

LX Boutique Hotel
Rua do Alecrim 12
351-21-347-4394
lxboutiquehotel.pt
$$
Sushi in the restaurant and wall-size Lisbon-themed photo murals in the guestrooms.

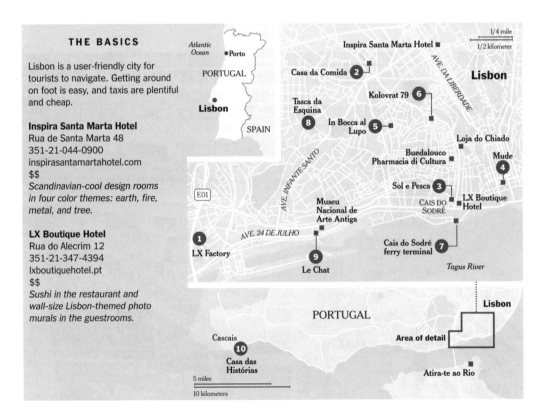

Évora

The old city walls of Évora, the storied Portuguese city less than two hours by car from Lisbon, enclose a stunning combination of Roman, Gothic, and Baroque architecture. An important Roman mercantile city and later a fortified Moorish bastion, Évora became the center of the Portuguese court in the Avis dynasty (1385-1580), when many of its grandest buildings were constructed. Equally relevant to its appeal today is its location in the Alentejo region, a prime gastronomic and oenological destination, and a relatively inexpensive and unfussy one at that. Évora's charms come in varied and delectable bites, much like the petiscos, or appetizers, that start off most meals here. The city is a bit like its churches—seemingly staid and whitewashed until you step inside to discover sumptuous interiors adorned with gleaming gold leaf and thousands of dazzling tiles.
— BY ANDREW FERREN

FRIDAY

1 *Crowded Hilltop* 2 p.m.

At the city's highest point, a brooding medieval cathedral sits next to a museum full of precious art, which in turn rubs shoulders with a 15th-century convent, which faces a palace, which overlooks a Roman temple. It adds up to about 2,000 years of history in 20 paces. Begin in the **Cathedral of Évora**, which dates in part to the 12th century and is visible from all over town. Take a look at its narrow nave and Baroque additions, and if you have time and interest, peek into its museum and find the reliquary studded with more than 1,400 jewels. Next door, the city's major art and archaeology museum, the **Museum of Évora** (Largo Conde de Vila Flor; 351-266-730-480; museudevora.pt) grew from the collection of an 18th-century archbishop. Wander up to the Roman temple, which dates to the first century A.D., when this area was the city's forum.

2 *Fine Tiles* 4 p.m.

The **Church of St. John the Evangelist** (Igreja São João Evangelista; 351-967-979-763; palaciocadaval.com) is dwarfed by the cathedral but a treasure house inside, with a golden altar and walls covered by the hand-painted blue-and-white tiles called azulejos, mounted together to form large images or patterns. This is the private church of the noble Cadaval family and shares a courtyard with their palace. The Cadavals have opened the palace as a quirky house museum where you'll find grand family portraits and royal decrees from the family's glory years in the 17th century as well as some Louis Vuitton luggage from the 20th century's golden age of travel. Back outside, find the pretty little park near the church, with ice-cream vendors and views of Évora's red tile rooftops and 16th-century aqueduct.

3 *The Food* 8 p.m.

Among the city's most cherished culinary experiences is dining at **Tasquinha do Oliveira** (Rua Cândido dos Reis 45-A; 351-266-744-841; $$$) a tiny place with an oversize array of petiscos like stewed artichokes with ham, breaded baby lamb chops, salads of fava beans and chorizo, mushrooms with fresh mint, or bacalhau with white beans and cilantro. All are beautifully presented and waiting at the table when guests arrive. As diners make their way through the dishes, new ones arrive. Simply put, Alentejan food is zestier than most Portuguese fare, with a bolder use of herbs like coriander in a surprising array of dishes. Most of the country's excellent ham (presunto in Portuguese) and other pork products come from here. As does most of the world's cork; the region's famous

OPPOSITE Évora, an old city less than two hours from Lisbon, was once the home of Portuguese kings.

BELOW A walk at what was once the Roman forum will take you through centuries of architecture, from Roman to medieval and Baroque, in a few steps.

black-footed pigs fatten themselves up on acorns that drop from the cork and holm oaks looming over the Alentejo's gently rolling hills.

SATURDAY

4 *The Wine* 10 a.m.

Like spokes of a wheel, the busiest streets lead into the shaded shopping arcades of Évora's main square, the **Praça do Giraldo** in the center of the old city. Here you'll find the tourist office and major banks as well as several large emporia of colorful linens and ceramics. Not too far away is the place to get some background on the local wine, at the tasting room and information center of **Alentejo Wine Route** (Praça Joaquim António de Aguiar 20-21; 351-266-746-498; vinhosdoalentejo.pt). Évora justly takes pride in the region's crisp, light whites that take the edge off the summer heat and hearty, full-bodied reds that pair perfectly with savory stews and game in cooler months. Pick up maps and advice here for a winery tour later.

5 *The Cork* 11 a.m.

Just north of the plaza, seek out **Mont'Sobro** (Rua 5 de Outubro 66; 351-266-704-609) for an almost impossibly extensive range of products — from fruit bowls and floor tiles to suitcases and umbrellas — all made out of cork. (Even its business cards are printed on paper-thin cork.) Buy your cork souvenir and then spend a little time exploring Évora's dense tangle of

narrow streets. One of the most unusual sights is the **Capela dos Ossos**, or Chapel of Bones, at the Church of São Francisco (Praça 1 de Maio) at the southern edge of the old town. Here the bones and skulls of more than 5,000 monks have been put to striking decorative effect as wall treatment. On the surrounding streets are more than a few unusual shops selling updated and traditional local handicrafts. As lunchtime approaches, shops close and Évora slows down. You should, too. This area offers lots of small cafes and taverns where time can be killed most pleasantly.

6 *Falcon's Nest* 3 p.m.

It's worth going a bit out of the way to find **O Arco** (Rua dos Penedos 15; 351-917-349-690). Here a lifelong Évora resident, Francisco Piteira, has painstakingly restored a 15th-century aviary that once housed falcons for a princely family and made it into a gallery for antiques. Look for treasures among the classic, curvy-legged Portuguese commodes and cabinets, or the paintings and sculpture by contemporary Portuguese artists.

7 *Long Before the Romans* 4 p.m.

Drive a few miles into the country to see Portugal's Stonehenge, which was created 2,000 years before England's. **Almendres Cromlech** is a megalithic formation made of 96 stones in the shape of crude

ABOVE The Capela dos Ossos, or Chapel of Bones, at the Church of São Francisco.

BELOW The Praça do Giraldo in the center of Évora's old city.

pillars, arranged in a mysterious pattern and planted in the ground about 7,000 years ago. It is among humanity's oldest known monuments.

8 *Authentically Updated* 8 p.m.

Back in town, have dinner at the popular **Dom Joaquim** (Rua dos Penedos 6; 351-266-731-105; $$$). The chef, Joaquim Almeida, advises diners to try just one or two petiscos before sampling his elegant riffs on rustic Alentejan fare. You may find dishes like the Almofada—a hearty pork pie that serves two.

SUNDAY

9 *Walk the Watercourse* 9 a.m.

Start before the heat of the day for a walk beginning at the 16th-century **Agua da Prata** (Silver Water) aqueduct. It may not be of Roman vintage, but it is suitably impressive. Find the green path that allows 21st-century hikers to follow the structure out into the Alentejan countryside. Hike as much of the five-mile trail as you like, and then return.

10 *Vineyard Drive* Noon

Take out the itinerary you mapped out yesterday in town and start your Alentejo winery tour. There are vineyards galore near Évora, like **Herdade de Coelheiros**, whose labels for its Tapada de Coelheiros wines are inspired by the famous needle-work rugs of the nearby town of Arraiolos. Even closer to Évora is **Adega da Cartuxa**. Since Alentejo is not as well-known a wine region as the Douro, the actual visits are informal, but advance bookings are a good idea.

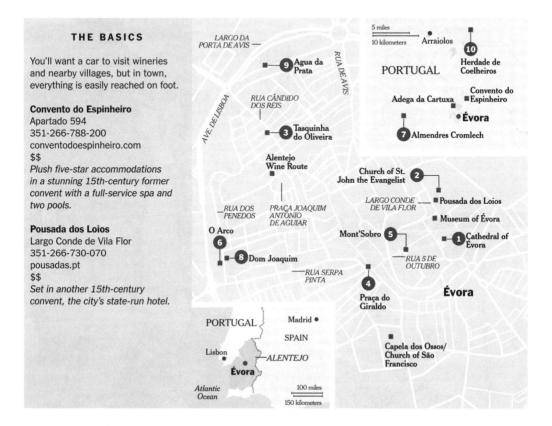

THE BASICS

You'll want a car to visit wineries and nearby villages, but in town, everything is easily reached on foot.

Convento do Espinheiro
Apartado 594
351-266-788-200
conventodoespinheiro.com
$$
Plush five-star accommodations in a stunning 15th-century former convent with a full-service spa and two pools.

Pousada dos Loios
Largo Conde de Vila Flor
351-266-730-070
pousadas.pt
$$
Set in another 15th-century convent, the city's state-run hotel.

Porto

For years, Porto's motto was, in essence, "You've tried the wine; now try the city!" But these days Portugal's second-largest metropolis — an attractively faded hillside city of venerable town houses and Baroque churches — no longer needs to coast on the reputation of its famous digestif. A jam-packed new night-life district is taking shape, and a blossoming creative scene features everything from an upstart design center to the avant-garde Rem Koolhaas-designed Casa da Música, a stunning concert space. And there's great news for oenophiles as well. With the Douro region's emergence as a hotbed of prize-winning red wines — not just port — Porto (also known as Oporto) can now intoxicate you with myriad vintages, new ambitious restaurants, and even wine-themed hotels.

— BY SETH SHERWOOD

FRIDAY

1 *Go West* 6 p.m.

A cheap tour of Porto awaits on tram line No. 1, which starts near **Praça do Infante** square and heads west to the Atlantic coast. Outfitted with old leather seats and wood paneling, the half-hourly tram cars clatter up and down hills alongside the Douro River, past city squares, churches, and port wine houses. The 20-minute journey drops you in the seaside district of Foz do Douro, where you can easily stop for a drink and perhaps a sushi snack at **Shis** (Praia do Ourigo; Esplanada do Castelo; 351-22-618-9593; shisrestaurante. com), a stylish beachfront restaurant-bar.

2 *Not for Dieters* 9 p.m.

The Francesinha is a cardiologist-unapproved local sandwich of ham, beef, sausage, and cheese with a warm tomato-beer sauce. At **Restaurante DOP** (Palácio das Artes; Largo de São Domingos 18; 351-22-201-4313; ruipaula.com; $$$$), a crisp minimalist space opened by the celebrity chef Rui Paula, the working man's snack is elevated to an epicure's ambrosia, with ingredients like tenderloin beef,

artisanal sausage, mozzarella, and a bit of lobster in the meat gravy. The extensive wine list features vintages from the Douro region.

3 *A Market Reborn* 11 p.m.

Nearby, the venerable Beaux-Arts-style covered market known as Mercado Ferreira Borges has been reborn as **Hard Club** (Praça do Infante D. Henrique 95; 351-70-710-0021; hard-club.com). The renovated glass-and-steel structure houses a bookstore, an art exhibition area, a restaurant, a patio, bars, and concert halls. The hardest thing about Hard Club is simply deciding among all the events, from indie rock concerts to craft fairs. For weekend club nights, crowds arrive after 2 a.m. and don't leave before sunrise.

SATURDAY

4 *Some Like It Old* 10 a.m.

Unlike Mercado Ferreira Borges, the still-functioning **Mercado do Bolhão** (corner of Rua Formosa and Rua de Sá da Bandeira) seems untouched since it was opened in 1914. Majestic and dilapidated, the huge indoor-outdoor space recalls a classic European rail station thanks to acres of wrought iron, grand staircases, white tile walls, and pointed domes. Inside, the aging vendors gossip amid chestnuts, octopus, sardines, dangling pigs' hooves,

OPPOSITE You no longer have to drink port wine in order to enjoy a visit to Porto. But have a glass anyway.

RIGHT Barrels on the Douro River. The region's reputation for winemaking has expanded to include many vintages.

sounds — bird chirps, percussion — as you step on it. But the highlight is the main hall, decorated with gold tiger-stripe designs. Be sure to check the roster of concerts and D.J. parties.

and live roosters. Upstairs, in the northeast corner, a stall called Manteigaria do Bolhão stocks enough cured meat to feed a corporate picnic (or spark a PETA protest): chouriço, presunto, salpicão sausage, and much more.

5 *Beef, Buns, and Beyond* 12:30 p.m.

To the many paintings, sculptures, and installations displayed in the galleries along Rua Miguel Bombarda, add two more types of creative endeavors: beef and fish preparations. In the airy confines of **Bugo Art Burgers** (Rua Miguel Bombarda 598; 351-22-606-2179; bugo.com.pt; $$), the burgers are culinary collages of local materials. The Porto e Serra Burger is beef soaked in port and topped with Serra da Estrela cheese. The Cod Burger transforms bacalhau into a patty served with classic açorda (bread purée and coriander).

6 *Saturday at the Mall* 2 p.m.

Hip and innovative aren't words that normally describe shopping malls. But **Centro Comercial Bombarda** (Rua Miguel Bombarda 283-285; ccbombarda.blogspot.com) is an exception. You can browse the creations of fashion designer Eugenia Cunha, collections of exotic teas, and Portuguese handicrafts and other products including chic leather handbags. Cinema and comic book buffs should plan to spend some time at Vertigo Store, which stocks hundreds of reproduction posters (and toys) from movies and comics.

7 *Whorls and Angles* 4:30 p.m.

Resembling a jagged white meteorite, the futuristic **Casa da Música** (Avenida da Boavista 604-610; 351-22-012-0220) is both Porto's architectural masterpiece and its music mecca. Tours in English take visitors through the whorls of the angular 17-sided building, designed by the Dutch star architect Rem Koolhaas. Treats include the VIP Room, an angled salon covered with blue ceramic tiles, and the so-called Orange Room, whose floor gives off wild

8 *Feed Between the Lines* 8 p.m.

Books abound — holding the menus, lining the walls — at **Book** (Rua de Aviz 10; 351-91-795-3387; restaurantebook.pt; $$$), a cozy, candlelit, and self-consciously literary restaurant. Thanks to nouveau Portuguese cuisine that burnishes prosaic ingredients into poetic dishes (pork cheeks with tripe, on one menu, or veal steak in Torres wine sauce), Book has become a best seller. The smooth house wine, a Terras do Grifo red, is additional proof that Porto can do more than just port.

9 *Join the Congregation* 10 p.m.

Formerly a haven of dowdy fabric shops, the neighborhood of Clérigos (Clergymen) now bursts with bars and a Mardi Gras-like crush of partiers — college kids, young professionals, 50-something socialites — who pack the streets by night. **Galeria de Paris** (Rua Galeria de Paris 56) is filled to its soaring rafters with vintage radios, old sewing machines, and other retro finds. Even the pump that pours the Sagres beer is Jules Verne-ish. More contemporary is the low-lighted **Baixa** bar (Rua Cândido dos Reis

ABOVE Skateboarders near the Casa da Música.

BELOW For an overview, tour through Porto's streetscape, with its old buildings and wine houses, on one of the city's trams.

52; Facebook: baixabar), where a boulder-size disco ball hangs over the dance floor and cocktails like the Cosmo Porto (Cointreau, port wine, red fruit) are featured on the menu.

SUNDAY

10 *A Solid Foundation* 10 a.m.

Art is everywhere at the **Fundação Serralves** (Rua Dom João de Castro 210; 351-22-615-6500; serralves.pt): in the gardens, where oversize outdoor works like Claes Oldenburg's trowel sculpture loom, and in the exceptional bookshop, lined with volumes covering topics from Art Nouveau jewelry to modern photography. And it's abundant in the foundation's museum, which holds contemporary art exhibitions.

11 *Enter Sandeman* Noon

Why do most port wines—Graham's, Cockburn, Taylor—have British names? What's the difference between a white, a tawny, and a ruby port? The answers come pouring out during guided tours of the cellars of **Sandeman** (Largo Miguel Bombarda 3, Vila Nova de Gaia; 351-22-374-0534; sandeman.eu). If a bottle of 40-year-old tawny is out of your price range, take home a box of chocolates made with port.

ABOVE Wheels down at Galeria de Paris.

THE BASICS

Fly into Porto's Francisco Sá Carneiro Airport or come through Lisbon, a three- to four-hour drive or train ride away. Public transportation in Porto includes buses, trams, and a hillside funicular.

The Yeatman
Rua do Choupelo, Vila Nova de Gaia
351-22-013-3100
the-yeatman-hotel.com
$$$
Billed as a "luxury wine hotel." Wine cellar, wine bar, wine restaurant, special wine dinners, and even a wine spa.

Palácio do Freixo
Estrada Nacional 108
351-22-531-1000
pestanacollection.com
$$$
Spacious contemporary rooms on an 18th-century estate, one of Portugal's pousada hotels in converted historical buildings.

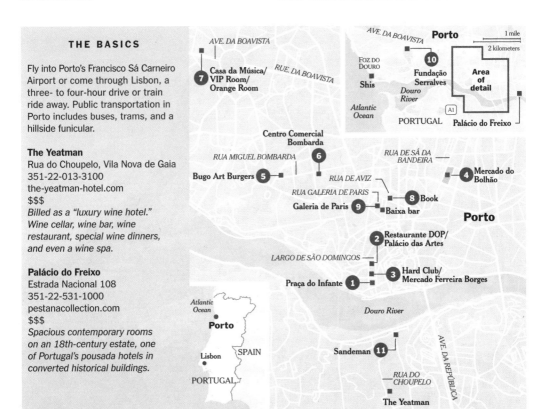

Madeira

The subtropical Portuguese island of Madeira has historically been a retreat for the British, especially the unhealthy and the elderly, who drank the famous wine and luxuriated in the year-round springlike weather. Photographs found on a bookshelf in the island's grande-dame hotel, Reid's Palace, showed a white-bearded George Bernard Shaw getting a tango lesson in 1924 and Winston Churchill painting watercolors in 1950. Now a younger breed of traveler is increasingly drawn here as new boutique hotels and night life make a beguiling addition to old assets: spectacular scenery in the form of dramatic sea cliffs and hundreds of miles of levadas, or irrigation channels, that make for terrific hiking. — BY HENRY ALFORD

FRIDAY

1 *Downhill Slide* 2 p.m.

One way to get a first view of the local streets and habitations is on a mile-long slide downhill. Madeira's famed **Monte toboggan ride** (351-291-783-919) starts near the waterfront in Funchal, the island's major town. You take the cable car called the teleférico (telefericojardimbotanico.com) for 15 minutes up to the village of Monte at 1,804 feet. There you sit in a go-kart-like wicker basket whose wooden runners are greased with lard. Two drivers, whose boots' soles are made of rubber tires, run alongside the sled as it coasts down the steep hill; when the sled starts to spin, they hop on it for counterbalance. The sled ride, though not the cable car, dates back to the mid-1800s, and Ernest Hemingway is said to have described it as exhilarating. It may be less so if Monte is crowded with too many other tourists, so avoid going when a cruise ship is in the harbor.

2 *Drink With Jefferson* 5 p.m.

Back in Funchal, take a tour of the old **Blandy's Wine Lodge** (Avenida Arriaga 28, Funchal; 351-291-228-978; blandyswinelodge.com) and learn all about the island's namesake beverage. Madeira, still made from grapes grown in small plots all over the island, was the fortified wine with which Thomas Jefferson and other United States Founding Fathers toasted the signing of the American Declaration of Independence. The half-hour tour winds through storage areas and a memorabilia room and ends in the tasting room.

3 *Atlantic Dinner* 7 p.m.

Restaurante Gavião Novo (Rua de Santa Maria 131, Funchal; 351-291-229-238; $) is one of the many small, charming restaurants in the old part of Funchal that serve Madeiran specialties. Freshly caught fish are displayed at the entrance; you may find squid, tuna, swordfish, or a local fish called espada, or scabbard, which is like a less flaky cod. The restaurant also serves espetada—beef seasoned with garlic, olive oil, and bay leaves and then grilled over open fire. The limpets, served sizzling in butter and garlic, are calling for you.

4 *Bar Scene* 9 p.m.

Because Madeirans haven't cottoned to the glamour of rooftop bars, you may find yourself all alone if you go for a drink at the 360° Sky Bar at the trendy **Vine Hotel** (Rua dos Aranhas 27, Funchal; 351-291-009-000; hotelthevine.com), but the view—think twinkly lights and hills, with a spectrally glowing pool as foreground—is stunning. When you tire of it, make your way down to the **Mini Eco Bar** (Rua da Alfândega 3; 351-934-835-868; fresh-citrus.com) a trendy, ecologically friendly cafe by day that turns into an indoor-outdoor stand-up bar scene after 9 p.m.

OPPOSITE The settlements of Madeira, far out to sea off Morocco, spill down dramatic cliffs toward the Atlantic.

RIGHT In the old town of Funchal, menus may include limpets or the beef dish called espetada.

Many of the cleverly designed furnishings have been rescued from the dump: a TV set is now a fish tank; truck tires are now the base of a couch.

SATURDAY

5 *Walk the Levadas* 9 a.m.

The levadas of Madeira are irrigation channels that take water all over the island, passing through terrain from terraced fields to rainforest. The main channels, a couple of feet across, have paths alongside, and joining an organized walk on the levada paths is a great way to grasp the island's surprising diversity. On one walk, the itinerary wound through so many microclimates that it felt as though a slide projector had jumbled together pictures from several vacations: a lush scrum of ferns, a hushed meeting of pines, a spray of birds of paradise, a bougainvillea-dappled high meadow. If your hotel doesn't organize levada walks, get in touch with one of the local companies offering them, like **Madeira Explorers** (351-291-763-701; madeira-explorers.com) or **Madeira Seekers** (351-918-375-661; madeira-seekers.com).

6 *Life Is an Artwork* 2 p.m.

Drive to the town of Calheta to see **Casa das Mudas** (Estrada Simão Gonçalves da Câmara 37; 351-291-820-900), an art museum that has staged exhibitions that later traveled to major art destinations including Paris and New York. A huge, bunkerlike series of galleries is built into a cliff at the ocean's edge. Windows in the cavernous, uncrowded galleries overlook the sea, inviting existential questions. To stand and stare at art while, just over your left shoulder, there's an implied opportunity to plunge several hundred feet to a pile of rocks and the sea

below is to distill life's bigger questions down to the essential dyad: beauty or death? Choose the former.

7 *Swimming Holes* 4 p.m.

Serious ocean swimmers take a two-and-a-half-hour ferry to the neighboring island of Porto Santo, whose sand beach is said to cure rheumatism, but Madeira's own shores can also be inviting. There is no natural sand beach, but a drive on the coast road, besides yielding beautiful vistas, can take you to hidden swimming holes. (Ask around in the towns; Calheta also has a nice artificial beach.) One day's exploration in the charming village of **Ponta do Sol** led to a rock beach with a small patch of black sand and water that was balmy and delightful, though walking in it was not comfortable for bare feet. Nearby, a 40-foot waterfall poured over a sheer cliff wall.

8 *Updated Classics* 8 p.m.

Back in the old area of Funchal, near the docksides, make your way to **Armazém do Sal** (Rua da Alfândega 135; 351-291-241-285; armazemdosal.com; $$$), a restaurant housed in a 200-year-old former salt warehouse. It's a handsome, somber spot, all stone and wooden beams, and offers a modern take on Madeiran classics. Try tuna carpaccio or fresh anchovies in an herbed crust.

9 *Clubs With Character* Midnight

No one may come to Madeira solely for the clubbing, but it's here to round out a vacation if you like lively night life. **Marginal, Jam,** and **Vespas** (Avenida Sá Carneiro 7, Funchal; discotecavespas.com), the holy trinity of Madeiran clubgoing, are all located under one slanted roof, giving you the impression of being inside a giant airplane wing. The party usually

starts at midnight, and each place has its own style. Marginal: shaved heads, hipster hauteur, music you've never heard of. Jam: oldies, girls in tank tops, laughter. Vespas: somebody hands you a tambourine.

SUNDAY

10 *Swim With the Dolphins* 10 a.m.

You're way out to sea here, 360 miles west of the Moroccan coast, so you may as well see some of what's in the water. A number of companies, including **Rota dos Cetáceos** (Avenida Arriaga 75, Funchal; 351-291-280-600; rota-dos-cetaceos.pt) offer dolphin and whale watching on small boats, including catamarans or small Zodiacs from which one can swim. Depending on the time of year, boats go either two or three times daily for trips lasting about two and a half hours. You're likely to experience several charmed sightings of dolphins, and the view back to the island is another inducement for getting on the boat. It will give you perspective on Madeira's dramatic topography of mountains, beaches, cliffs, and grottoes.

OPPOSITE Looking down from Casa das Mudas, a modern art museum built on a cliff high over the water.

ABOVE Schedule a guided levada walk, a jaunt on the pathways next to Madeira's ubiquitous irrigation canals, or levadas. The microclimates are surprisingly numerous and diverse.

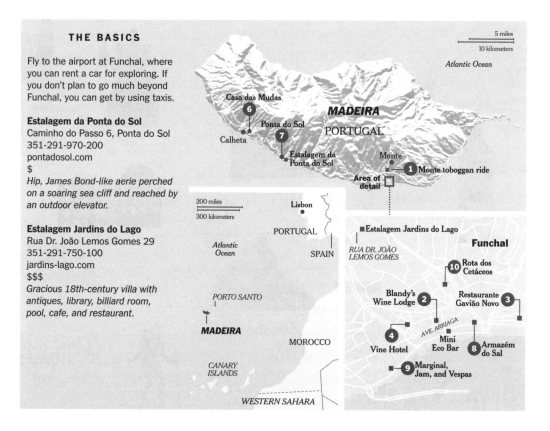

THE BASICS

Fly to the airport at Funchal, where you can rent a car for exploring. If you don't plan to go much beyond Funchal, you can get by using taxis.

Estalagem da Ponta do Sol
Caminho do Passo 6, Ponta do Sol
351-291-970-200
pontadosol.com
$
Hip, James Bond-like aerie perched on a soaring sea cliff and reached by an outdoor elevator.

Estalagem Jardins do Lago
Rua Dr. João Lemos Gomes 29
351-291-750-100
jardins-lago.com
$$$
Gracious 18th-century villa with antiques, library, billiard room, pool, cafe, and restaurant.

5 miles
10 kilometers

Atlantic Ocean

Casa das Mudas
6

MADEIRA
Ponta do Sol
PORTUGAL

Calheta

Estalagem da
Ponta do Sol
7

Monte

1 Monte toboggan ride

Area of
detail

200 miles
300 kilometers

Lisbon

PORTUGAL

Atlantic
Ocean

SPAIN

PORTO SANTO

MADEIRA

MOROCCO

CANARY
ISLANDS

WESTERN SAHARA

■ Estalagem Jardins do Lago

Funchal

RUA DR. JOÃO
LEMOS GOMES

10 Rota dos
Cetáceos

Blandy's
Wine Lodge **2**

Restaurante
Gavião Novo **3**

4
Vine Hotel

AVE. ARRIAGA

Mini
Eco Bar

8 Armazém
do Sal

9 Marginal,
Jam, and Vespas

Lübeck
306

Hamburg
302

BERLI

Leipzig 314

COLOGNE 324

Dresden

Pilsen
392

Frankfurt 330

Munich

Basel
344

ZURICH 340

Bern 350

Innsbruck
382

Lake
Geneva
360

Zermatt
366

St. Moritz
370

GENEVA
356

CENTRAL

Hiddensee 310

Gdansk & Sopot 426

East Berlin 298

WARSAW 418

Lviv 414

KraKow 422

PRAGUE 386

Moravia 396

VIENNA 374

Bratislava 402

BUDAPEST 406

Kiev 410

Berlin

The word has been out for years about Berlin's cheap rents and youthful appeal as the old neighborhoods of the former East Berlin come into their own. Prices have gone up and the central, artist-friendly Mitte, in particular, has gentrified. But the air here still crackles with a creativity that comes only from a city in transition. A quarter of a century after the Berlin Wall tumbled down, the city's two sides are still locked in a kind of cultural dialectic as the center of gravity shifts from west to east. Bullet-scarred buildings are still metamorphosing from squatters' homes to artists' studios and then to retail showrooms. Gray Communist alleys are laboratories for trendy bars, restaurants, and galleries. And, like the city itself, Berliners continue to reinvent themselves as a cultural vanguard, pushing the boundaries of art, fashion, and design. With so much to explore and create, the city never sleeps. — BY DENNY LEE

FRIDAY

1 *Reichstag Airlift* 3 p.m.

No building is more symbolic of Berlin than the **Reichstag** — built under the kaiser, burned in a 1933 fire that ushered Hitler into power, hollowed out in World War II, and in 1999 restored as the house of Germany's parliament under a glass dome designed by Norman Foster. That dome is also a good place to get your bearings with views over Berlin. Skip the long line by making reservations (at least 24 hours in advance) for afternoon tea at the **Dachgartenrestaurant**, or roof garden restaurant (49-30-226-2990; feinkost-kaefer.de). Afterward, you're free to loop around the glass igloo.

2 *It All Happened Here* 5 p.m.

Sightseeing mainstays are within an easy stroll of the Reichstag, and you can hit several of them in a couple of hours. Start at the **Brandenburg Gate**,

OPPOSITE The glass dome, designed by Norman Foster, atop the historic Reichstag. Loop around inside, and get your bearings with intimate views over Berlin.

RIGHT The Reichstag from the park outside. Sightseeing mainstays of the city are within an easy stroll of this spot, and you can hit several of them in a couple of hours.

where victorious armies from Germany's own to Napoleon's horde and Stalin's Russians have marched through, and where the Berlin Wall decisively tottered in 1989. Take some time at the sobering **Memorial to the Murdered Jews of Europe** (holocaust-mahnmal.de). Scan the skyscrapers in the crystalline **Potsdamer Platz** (potsdamer-platz.net). For an unblinking look at Nazi horror, walk on to the **Topography of Terror** (Niederkirchnerstrasse 8; 49-30-2545-0950; topographie.de).

3 *Nothing Wurst* 9 p.m.

Forget bratwurst. For lighter versions of Teutonic cuisine, try **Schneeweiss** (Simplonstrasse 16; 49-30-2904-9704; schneeweiss-berlin.de; $$-$$$), a nouvelle German restaurant in the up-and-coming Friedrichshain district. Seasonal dishes like pumpkin-lemongrass soup and duck breast with a quince-apple chutney are served in a spare candlelit room that draws young couples and trend-conscious diners.

4 *Cafe to Club* 11 p.m.

Stay in Friedrichshain, where affordable beer flows. The cafes around **Simon-Dach-Strasse** are full of young Berliners priced out of the Mitte district. Later, cross the Spree River into the borough of Kreuzberg, the former punk quarter and Turkish enclave that has experienced a revival. The bars and clubs along **Oranienstrasse** offer something for everyone. The night is still young, so pick up a copy of *Zitty* (zitty.de), a biweekly arts magazine, or *Exberliner* (exberliner.com), an English-language monthly, for the club of the moment.

SATURDAY

5 *Mitte Art Mile* Noon

O.K., you're still asleep. But when you do wake up, you'll need to take in some fuel before hitting the much-hyped art scene in the Mitte district. Do both at **Monsieur Vuong** (Alte Schönhauser Strasse 46; 49-30-2016-9543; monsieurvuong.de), a Vietnamese restaurant that serves as a kind of high school cafe-

ABOVE The lobby of the Hotel de Rome, where the décor has Art Deco touches.

BELOW Try a bowl of glass noodles with chicken at Monsieur Vuong, a Vietnamese restaurant in the Mitte district.

teria for the neighborhood's galleries. Try a spicy bowl of glass noodles with chicken. Then hop over to August-strasse, Mitte's Art Mile, where the buzz originated at places like **Galerie Eigen+Art** (No. 26; 49-30-280-6605; eigen-art.com) and **Kunst-Werke Berlin** (No. 69; 49-30-243-4590; kw-berlin.de). The galleries, which have spread out over nearby streets and into new territory like Potsdamerstrasse, can afford to be refreshingly uneven and irreverent. For a handy gallery map, pick up the free *Index* (indexberlin.de).

6 *Postmodern Shopping* 3 p.m.

While global brands like American Apparel and Diesel have colonized Mitte, concept stores, micro-boutiques, and streetwear designers are still around, blurring the line between gallery and galleria. Male and female fashion victims are drawn to the coolness of **Kauf Dich Glücklich** (Rosenthaler Strasse 17; 49-30-2887-8817; kaufdichgluecklich-shop. de). **The Apartment** (Memhardstrasse 8; 49-30-2804-2251; apartmentberlin.de) looks like an empty white box until you descend into the dark cellar crammed with fashion labels like Bernhard Willhelm and Kaviar Gauche. Find more possibilities on Rosenthaler Strasse and in Rosenthaler Platz.

7 *A Floating Pool* 7 p.m.

Berliners have rediscovered the Spree, for pocket-park lounging, sun bathing, promenading,

and even beach bars, which have washed up along the river with outdoor tables, pools, and pavilions. A favorite is **Badeschiff**, a summer swimming pool on a barge just east of gritty Kreuzberg (Eichenstrasse 4; 49-30-533-2030; arena.berlin/veranstaltungsort/badeschiff).

8 *What's 'Bistro' in Deutsch?* 9 p.m.

In another sign of Berlin's ascension, the city now has a full roster of Michelin-starred restaurants, several of them in the former German Democratic Republic. But as in Paris and Hong Kong, good food is not confined to white-tablecloth establishments. Take **Altes Europa**, a tavern in Mitte (Gipsstrasse 11; 49-30-2809-3840; alteseuropa.com; $$). Without parting with all of your euros, you get Old World ambience, a smart-looking crowd, and bistro-quality fare like plump green salads, velvety soups, and tender steaks. A neighborhood gem, to be sure, and one that isn't rare.

9 *Hedonist Heaven* Midnight

Maybe it's the hypnotic techno, hedonistic frisson, or illicit party favors, but globe-trotting clubbers rave about **Berghain**, a huge disco in a weedy stretch behind the Ostbahnhof station in Friedrichshain (berghain.de). The crowds may still be lining up at 4 a.m. Usually described with words

ABOVE Biking along the promenade that follows the Spree River in the city.

BELOW The stark, unevenly honeycombed Memorial to the Murdered Jews of Europe covers five acres near the Reichstag and Brandenburg Gate. As visitors walk deeper inside, tall pillars seem to enclose and disorient them.

like "hedonistic," "decadent," and "licentious," it keeps a night's party going well into the next day.

SUNDAY

10 *Birds and Beers* 1 p.m.

The huge and green **Tiergarten** — Berlin's central park — is an urban oasis popular with joggers, bird-watchers, and nude sunbathers alike. Take a long stroll through this swampy expanse, a former hunting ground of German princes. Wander among the planned landscapes and scattered statuary—one group of several sculptures shows

those aristocratic hunters triumphant over their prey. Drop in on the pandas and penguins at the **Zoological Garden and Aquarium** (Hardenbergplatz 8; 49-30-254-010; zoo-berlin.de). Or grab an outdoor seat at **Café am Neuen See** (Lichtensteinallee 2; 49-30-254-4930; cafeamneuensee.de), a calming beer garden and restaurant that sits on the edge of a lake. It is your quiet time in Berlin.

ABOVE The Brandenburg Gate, designed in the 1700s as a monument to peace, is symbolic today for its connection to the 1989 breaching of the Berlin Wall, which once stood just behind it.

OPPOSITE The Hauptbahnhof, Berlin's glass and steel central train station. In the morning, as trains arrive from far-flung cities and commuters crowd in, it's a place to watch daily life unfold.

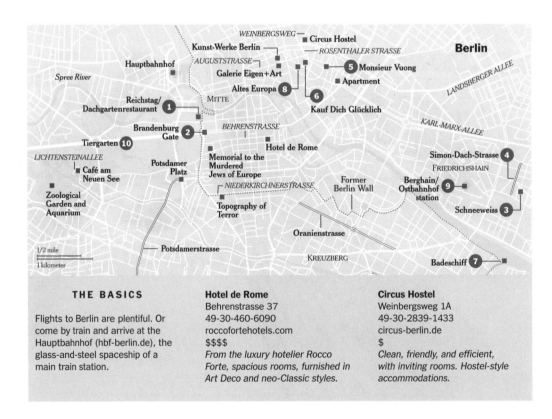

THE BASICS

Flights to Berlin are plentiful. Or come by train and arrive at the Hauptbahnhof (hbf-berlin.de), the glass-and-steel spaceship of a main train station.

Hotel de Rome
Behrenstrasse 37
49-30-460-6090
roccofortehotels.com
$$$$
From the luxury hotelier Rocco Forte, spacious rooms, furnished in Art Deco and neo-Classic styles.

Circus Hostel
Weinbergsweg 1A
49-30-2839-1433
circus-berlin.de
$
Clean, friendly, and efficient, with inviting rooms. Hostel-style accommodations.

East Berlin

Berlin has melded back into one city, now reunited more than half as long as it was divided. But travelers who want to see what the old East Berlin was all about can still find traces of it, sometimes locally beloved as part of the lingering nostalgia called Ostalgie, sometimes deliberately cultivated to lure outsiders fascinated by the history of a city that was torn apart and survived. A rare Trabant may still belch its exhaust along Karl-Marx-Allee. Black-red-and-yellow East German flags flutter from storefronts. Retro-chic bars resemble cold war bomb shelters. From stylish hotels that resemble 1970s Soviet housing to boutiques that elevate kitschy East German goods to high design, Berlin is still divided — on whether the Iron Curtain was cool. — BY DENNY LEE

FRIDAY

1 *A Little Bit of Wall* 5 p.m.

Most of the Berlin Wall has been reused as gravel or chipped apart to sell to souvenir hunters. But a few chunks remain. The **East Side Gallery** (Mühlenstrasse; 49-30-251-7159; eastsidegallery.com) is a stretch eight-tenths of a mile long, covered with fading murals painted by 118 international artists in 1990 and showing what an emphatic barrier this 10-foot-high construction was. The **Berlin Wall Memorial Site** (Bernauer Strasse 111 and 119; 49-30-467-986-666; berliner-mauer-gedenkstaette.de) has a section of wall and a museum that puts it in context. You can even walk the course of the old wall on the **Berlin Wall Trail** (berlin.de/mauer/mauerweg/index/index.en.php), an unassuming biking and walking path. Don't expect to tackle the whole thing. This was a serious barrier — the trail is about 100 miles long.

2 *TV Dinner* 7 p.m.

The Sputnik-inspired **Television Tower** (Panorama-strasse 1A at Alexanderplatz; 49-30-247-5750; tv-turm.de) was erected in the 1960s by East Germany to demonstrate its technical superiority. At 1,207 feet, it remains Berlin's tallest structure, as well as one of its most touristy. Skip the line by dining at its space-saucer-style restaurant, **Sphere** ($$-$$$), which offers revolving views of all of Berlin — a sprawling city that's eight times the area of Paris. The tower is every bit as cheesy and memorable as it sounds. Not much seems to have changed since Erich Honecker was the leader of East Germany: dishes like veal roulade with potato dumplings are served by wait-resses with big perms. Reserve online and early (at least six weeks ahead) for the sunset seating. After dinner, stroll Alexanderplatz.

SATURDAY

3 *Hello, Lenin!* 10:30 a.m.

Berlin has more than 100 museums, but one is dedicated to examining how East Berliners lived their daily lives under Communist rule. The small, privately financed **DDR Museum** (Karl-Liebknecht-Strasse 1; 49-30-847-123-731; ddr-museum.de) offers a playful trip behind the Iron Curtain with authentic artifacts and archival film. For a darker look at that era, pay a visit to the **Stasi Museum** (Ruschestrasse 103; 49-30-553-6854; stasimuseum.de), housed in the former offices of the Stasi, East Germany's sinister secret police.

4 *Embassy Sweets* Noon

If the weather is nice, head north to the leafy district of **Pankow**, where the East German elite lived. Along the way, stop by Stavanger Strasse, the old embassy row where the Cuban flag still flies, before heading to Majakowskiring, a road lined

OPPOSITE The Sputnik-inspired Television Tower.

RIGHT A Trabant, the Communist-era car, at Checkpoint Charlie, once a famous crossing point in the Berlin Wall.

with stately villas including No. 29 — the former home of Wilhelm Pieck, the first president of East Germany. Take in the **Schönhausen Palace** (Tschaikowskistrasse 1; spsg.de), which once served as the seat of the East German president, before heading south for lunch. Try **Gugelhof** (Knaackstrasse 37; 49-30-442-9229; gugelhof.de), which offers a selection of traditional and updated Alsatian dishes along with pleasant sidewalk tables.

5 *Neue Galleries* 3 p.m.

Karl-Marx-Allee, the monumental boulevard of Stalinist architecture, has welcomed a steady parade of art dealers. Galleries like the **Capitain Petzel** (No. 45; 49-30-2408-8130; capitainpetzel.de) and **Galerie Jette Rudolph** (Strausberger Platz 4; 49-30-6130-3887; jette-rudolph.de) have planted flags along the concourse, and private collectors have taken over palatial spaces. Take a five-minute subway ride to reach **Sammlung Haubrok** (Herzbergstrasse 40-43; 49-172-210-9525; haubrok.com), which showcases contemporary artists like Jonathan Monk and Martin Boyce.

6 *Cuddly Cars* 5:30 p.m.

Berlin was a huge city even when it was divided. To cover more ground, see old East Berlin behind the wheel of a Trabant, the plastic car that was a symbol, for better or worse, of the Communist regime. **Trabi-Safari** (Zimmerstrasse 97; 49-30-3020-1030;

ABOVE An irreverent work at the East Side Gallery, a stretch of the old Berlin Wall now covered with art.

RIGHT Browse for antiques and memorabilia of the old East Germany at VEBorange in Prenzlauer Berg.

trabi-safari.de) has a cuddly fleet that chortles past landmarks like Checkpoint Charlie and the East Side Gallery.

7 *Western Boeuf* 9 p.m.

See how the other side lived. While East Berliners were scouring markets for fresh fruits and vegetables, Iggy Pop and others were drinking absinthe and ordering entrecôte at the **Paris Bar** (Kantstrasse 152; 49-30-313-8052; parisbar.de; $$$$), in the upscale Charlottenburg district of what was West Berlin. The storied bistro still wears its affluence on its sleeve. One Saturday, there were white-shoe bankers popping Champagne bottles, an artsy couple with electric-blue hair, and two elegantly dressed women squeezed into a wine-red leather banquette under a large photograph of Yves Saint Laurent.

8 *Party Spree* Midnight

During the cold war, Berlin turned its back to the Spree River, which was itself divided. Now the

riverfront has some of the city's coolest night life. Find some at the **Watergate Club** (Falckensteinstrasse 49; 49-30-6128-0394; water-gate.de), where the lines are perpetually long.

SUNDAY

9 *People-Owned Goods* 11 a.m.

Plastic blue egg cups. Interflug luggage tags. Vintage drink carts. For groovy East German goods at moderate prices, take your tote bag to **Arkonaplatz**, a little park at the edge of Mitte that becomes a retro-trendy flea market on Sundays (troedelmarkt-arkonaplatz.de). Cute cafes ring the park. Still looking for those retro sunglasses? Walk

along Bernauer Strasse to the sprawling flea market at **Mauerpark**, or Wall Park (flohmarktimmauerpark. de). There may be some hidden treasures among the pirated DVDs.

10 *Ostalgie Treasure Hunt* Noon

Continue your capitalist spending spree in **Prenzlauer Berg**. Retail highlights include **VEBorange** (Oderberger Strasse 29; 49-30-9788-6886; veborange. de), a cluttered antiques shop that has a huge assortment of funky lamps and ostalgie memorabilia, and **Da Capo** (Kastanienallee 96; 49-30-448-1771; da-capo-vinyl.de), a music shop that carries artists like the Puhdys, who once recorded for the state-run Amiga label.

THE BASICS

In East Berlin, trams supplement the U-bahn subway and other public transit.

Ostel
Wriezener Karree 5
49-30-2576-8660
ostel.eu
$
A "Communist retro" hostel with East German interiors.

Arcotel John F
Werderscher Markt 11
49-30-405-0460
arcotel.com
$$
Cosmopolitan hotel in the former East Berlin, centrally located and a good value.

Alexander Plaza
Rosenstrasse 1
49-30-240-010
hotel-alexander-plaza.de
$$
In a renovated 1897 office building a short walk from Alexanderplatz.

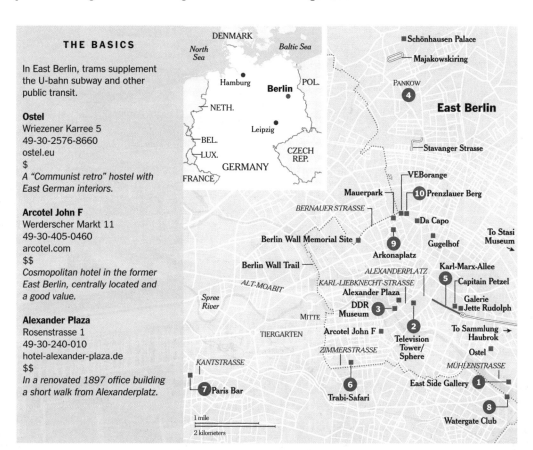

Hamburg

No one tells you how pretty Hamburg is. That's because so few people mention Hamburg in the first place. American tourists and businesspeople gravitate toward other German cities: Berlin, Munich, Frankfurt. And so Hamburg, bigger than all but Berlin, remains a bit of a mystery, poised to become a thrilling discovery. Did you know about the lake? It's smack dab in the city center and skirted by regal buildings, a postcard-ready tableau if there ever was one. And the canals? They lattice the part of the city nearest the Elbe River, allowing Hamburg to joust with Stockholm, Amsterdam, and Bruges for informal rights to call itself the Venice of northern Europe. Warm-weather visitors can get out onto the water on lake ferries and Elbe cruises. In winter, activity moves indoors, but even blustery weather isn't an obstacle to appreciating Hamburg's formidable charms. — BY FRANK BRUNI

FRIDAY

1 *Sights and Shops* 4:30 p.m.

Plant yourself in front of the **Rathaus**, Hamburg's stunning architectural centerpiece and, fittingly, city hall. A neo-Renaissance-style sandstone structure, it sprawls and swirls across an entire city block, offering a first hint of Hamburg's longstanding vanity and ambition. Hamburg is not only a major port but also the capital of Germany's news media and one of its wealthiest cities, with more gilt than grit. You'll appreciate this as you walk north from the Rathaus to Jungfernstieg, a majestic thoroughfare that faces the central lake, Binnenalster. From there zigzag among the narrower streets to the south and west, sizing up the luxury shops and well-heeled shoppers around Neuer Wall, in particular. Pause along Alsterarkaden, a Venetian-style arcade of shops and cafes along a broad canal.

2 *Dinner Aboard Ship* 7:30 p.m.

Hamburg is Europe's second-busiest port and its canals and the Elbe River are populated by a variety of boats, from houseboats to pleasure craft to freighters. One of the more unusual is **Das Feuerschiff** (City Sporthafen, Vorsetzen 1; 49-40-362-553; das-feuerschiff.de; $$-$$$), a former English Channel lightship converted into a bar and restaurant and tied up on the riverfront. You can have a pre-dinner drink on deck or down in the old engine room, which has

been transformed into a pub-style bar. Dinner, naturally featuring a number of seafood dishes, is served in a small but comfortable dining room on the main deck. Afterward, stroll along the water and look back at the red boat, the only lightship that has ever fed you.

3 *After-Hours Lair* 10 p.m.

If Das Feuerschiff connects you with the river, **Le Lion** (Rathausstrasse 3; 49-40-334-753-780; lelion. net) tugs you inland. Just a quick taxi ride away, it's a stylish, cozy lounge with all the tropes of contemporary cocktail culture: boutique spirits, classic glassware, ambiguously marked entrance. Press a tiny doorbell in the mouth of a lion's head, and only if there's space — or if you've made a reservation — are you allowed inside a plush room with felt wallpaper, dim lighting, and superb drinks, served past 3 a.m. if the demand warrants it.

SATURDAY

4 *Stroll Across Borders* 10 a.m.

A counterpoint to the upscale shopping district near the Rathaus is the scruffier, cheekier, more

OPPOSITE Hamburg, old and new, on a winter day.

BELOW The Baroque St. Michaelis Church.

ethnically diverse craft stores, galleries, and cafes along Lange Reihe, in the St. George neighborhood. Here you'll find Chinese, Portuguese, and Italian restaurants; terrific German bread; Tibetan art; and bulky Himalayan woolens. Start by fueling yourself at a marble table in the shag-carpeted back room at **Cafe Gnosa** (Lange Reihe 93; 49-40-243-034; gnosa.de; $$), an amusing place for breakfast, coffee, and desserts—try the ethereal cheesecake. As you cover the five or so blocks from Gnosa back toward Binnenalster lake, note the inadvertently hilarious New Age redoubt **Kräuterhaus** (Koppel 34-36; 49-40-240-000; kraeuterhaus.net). It sells spices and teas along with illuminated Himalayan salt crystals, which, an employee told us, "clear the air of ionic smog."

5 *A Lilliputian World* Noon

The humdrum entrance to the **Miniatur Wunderland** (Kehrwieder 2-4; 49-40-300-6800; miniatur-wunderland.com) and the drab rooms that house it don't prepare you for this eccentric museum's singular collection of model train scenes. Lilliputian locomotives move through mountains, forests, seacoasts, and cities that replicate parts of Germany, Scandinavia, and even America. Watch miniature figures flick on miniature lighters as they stand before a miniature concert stage with miniature portable toilets nearby.

6 *Glorious Glass* 1:30 p.m.

Head south a few blocks and over several canals into **HafenCity**, an urban construction project of dazzling heft and quality. It came into being when Hamburg decided to repurpose nearly 400 acres of docklands on the Elbe as a commercial, residential, and recreational district that would increase the city center's size by 40 percent and showcase mesmerizing glass towers. In a watery area of about 15 square blocks are stunning examples of contemporary architecture, including apartment buildings with jagged, terraced exteriors; the shiplike Unilever building (Strandkai 1); and the Elbphilharmonie, or philharmonic, at the western point of Am Kaiserkai,

a deliberately lopsided, wavy, spectacular monument of what looks like frosted glass.

7 *Tea Time* 3 p.m.

Break up your amble through HafenCity with a stop at **Messmer Momentum** (Am Kaiserkai 10; 040-7367-9000; messmer.de/messmer-momentum), a teahouse and tea museum that honors Hamburg's role as the port through which much of Europe's tea has flowed. There are hundreds of teas for sampling or sale, an enchanting gift shop with tea paraphernalia and exotically flavored candies to be dissolved in tea, and a sleek cafe with a wall of windows and wood deck overlooking a canal.

8 *Altitude and Attitude* 7 p.m.

A fashionable place for cocktails is **20Up**, on the 20th floor of the Empire Riverside Hotel (Bernhard-Nocht-Strasse 97; 49-40-311-190; empire-riverside. de), but drinks aren't its real glory. The view is. The bar, with walls of glass, overlooks the Elbe, and as you survey the ships and docks and cranes, you get a sense of Hamburg's maritime might. Walk to the northeast corner and you can see the pulsing neon of the **Reeperbahn**, the city's famous red-light district.

9 *Not for Vegans* 9 p.m.

For a festive atmosphere, handsome crowd, and superior beef, pork, and more, **Bullerei** (Lagerstrasse 34b; 49-40-3344-2110; bullerei.com; $$$$) hits the bull's-eye. Apart from a wine bar, the restaurant is one enormous industrial-chic room with walls of concrete and exposed brick. Fleshy atmospheric

motifs include a display window of hanging beef and a thick piece of transparent plastic over each menu that evokes the vertical strips in the doorway of a meat locker. There's fish here, too, and salads.

SUNDAY

10 *Prayer and Cardio* 10 a.m.

Whether you're in need of God or exercise, **St. Michaelis Church** (Englische Planke 1; 49-40-376-780; st-michaelis.de) can oblige you. It's a Baroque gem that's also a monument to resilience, having rebounded from, and been rebuilt after, lightning, fire, and World War II bombing. And its white-and-gold interior makes you feel as if you're inside a royal wedding cake. (Check its website for the current schedule of regular concerts held there.) You can come for the 10 a.m. service or wait until it's over to explore the church;

either way, visit the viewing platform in its tower. There's a tiny elevator, but the staircase—twisting, narrow, endless—is the way to go, a calorie burner that gives you a sense of having earned the 360-degree panorama.

OPPOSITE ABOVE Hamburg is a city of boats and bridges, with canals threading through the area closest to the Elbe River.

OPPOSITE BELOW Neuer Wall, a district of narrow streets and luxury stores favored by well-heeled shoppers.

ABOVE A landscape at Miniatur Wunderland.

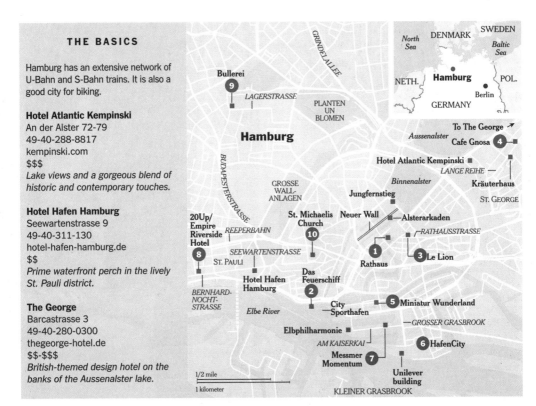

THE BASICS

Hamburg has an extensive network of U-Bahn and S-Bahn trains. It is also a good city for biking.

Hotel Atlantic Kempinski
An der Alster 72-79
49-40-288-8817
kempinski.com
$$$
Lake views and a gorgeous blend of historic and contemporary touches.

Hotel Hafen Hamburg
Seewartenstrasse 9
49-40-311-130
hotel-hafen-hamburg.de
$$
Prime waterfront perch in the lively St. Pauli district.

The George
Barcastrasse 3
49-40-280-0300
thegeorge-hotel.de
$$-$$$
British-themed design hotel on the banks of the Aussenalster lake.

Map labels:
GRINDELALLEE
North Sea
DENMARK
SWEDEN
Baltic Sea
NETH.
Hamburg
Berlin
POL.
GERMANY
Bullerei **9**
LAGERSTRASSE
PLANTEN UN BLOMEN
Hamburg
To The George
Aussenalster
Cafe Gnosa **4**
Hotel Atlantic Kempinski
LANGE REIHE
Binnenalster
Kräuterhaus
BUDAPESTERSTRASSE
GROSSE WALL-ANLAGEN
Jungfernstieg
ST. GEORGE
20Up/ Empire Riverside Hotel
REEPERBAHN
St. Michaelis Church **10**
Neuer Wall
Alsterarkaden
RATHAUSSTRASSE
8
ST. PAULI
SEEWARTENSTRASSE
1
Rathaus
3 Le Lion
BERNHARD-NOCHT-STRASSE
Hotel Hafen Hamburg
Das Feuerschiff **2**
City Sporthafen
5 Miniatur Wunderland
Elbe River
GROSSER GRASBROOK
Elbphilharmonie
AM KAISERKAI
6 HafenCity
Messmer Momentum **7**
Unilever building
1/2 mile
1 kilometer
KLEINER GRASBROOK

305

Lübeck

An hour from Hamburg by rail or car, Lübeck, a city of 214,000, offers a chance to revel in a dreamlike panoply of architectural history. Some 1,300 buildings — Gothic, Baroque, Renaissance, and Classical — are situated within the city's compact center on an island that is surrounded by the Trave River and a canal that leads to the Elbe River. Barely a mile long, the island can be traversed on foot in less than an hour. But don't rush, because there is much to explore — from quiet side streets and busy thoroughfares to historic squares and medieval churches. Amid the soaring spires, ubiquitous crow-step gables, and dozens of courtyards lined with centuries-old houses, it's easy to see why Unesco placed a large swath of Lübeck on its list of World Heritage Sites. — BY OMAR SACIRBEY

FRIDAY

1 *Grand Entrance* 3 p.m.

A good place to start in Lübeck is the 15th-century Holstentor, or **Holsten Gate** (49-451-122-4129; luebeck-tourism.de), which sits across the Trave and once guarded Lübeck's western entryway. For centuries Lübeck was a free city-state governed not by royalty but by wealthy merchants who were part of a powerful cartel, the Hanseatic League, that kept tight control over shipping on the Baltic Sea. Today the gate is the city's symbol, with its arched entrance, stout walls, and two towers overlooking a wide green lawn. Inside is the Holsten Gate Museum with interactive exhibits as well as swords and armor. Climb one of the spiral staircases and peer out the tiny windows for a view of ships and the town.

2 *Theater Figures* 4 p.m.

Walk back into the city and stop off at the **Puppet Museum** (TheaterFigurenMuseum, Kolk 14; 49-451-786-26; theaterfigurenmuseum.de), where a United Nations of puppets collected from countries as diverse as Iran, Japan, and Tunisia proves that puppetry is not just a European tradition. The neighboring theater's busy schedule of shows has included puppet *Rigoletto*. Here on the west side of the town, the curvy streets are too narrow for cars and emanate a fairy tale feel. Some of Lübeck's most enchanting buildings are found serendipitously, by exploring the city's myriad alleys and courtyards.

3 *Courtyard Dinner* 8 p.m.

Reserve well before your trip to get a table at **Restaurant Wullenwever** (Beckergrube 71; 49-451-704-333; wullenwever.de; $$$$). The chef and owner, Roy Petermann, serves imaginative dishes in a 16th-century house and, during the summer, in its lovely courtyard. Seafood is a specialty.

4 *Multilingual Party* 10 p.m.

For a drink and a chance to mingle with partying Lübeckers, check out the constellation of bars on the east side, especially along Hüxstrasse and Fleischhauerstrasse. You'll hear revelers speaking a mix of German, Turkish, and English. Before you head back to your hotel, allow yourself time for an aimless stroll through the streets illuminated by gas lamps. It's yet another way to lose yourself in the time warp that is Lübeck.

SATURDAY

5 *Spires and History* 10 a.m.

Lübeck is known as the City of Seven Spires for the Gothic churches that punctuate its skyline. Best known are the **Church of St. Mary**, one of Germany's largest churches (Marienkirchhof 1; st-marien-luebeck.de), and the **Lübeck Cathedral** (Mühlendamm 2-6; domzuluebeck.de), with its nearly 400-foot spires.

OPPOSITE The Gothic Church of St. Mary, one of the churches that gave Lübeck the nickname "City of Seven Spires."

BELOW Have a home-brewed ale at Im Alten Zolln.

Their size is impressive, but it is the details that are most captivating. At St. Mary's, skeletons carved in stone lurk on the walls and columns, while two bells lie broken on the ground where they fell in 1942 after an Allied attack. At the cathedral are iron gates donated by riverboat captains hoping to improve their odds of salvation. The acoustics are remarkable in both buildings. Lübeck's churches host frequent organ recitals and choral concerts. The cathedral is a venue for the summer Schleswig-Holstein Music Festival.

6 *River Traffic* 1 p.m.

Near the cathedral, a stroll down **Hartengrube** street leads to medieval homes and, at the end of the street on a grassy bank, a bench with a romantic view of the Trave River. Have lunch at one of the waterfront cafes while taking in the intriguing juxtaposition of ancient architecture, cargo ships, and tour boats. You will see a swirl of people, too: laborers, businesspeople, women wearing colorful head scarves, student types decked out in leather. For all its pride in its history, there is nothing stuffy about Lübeck. Its independent air and egalitarian sensibility are abetted by three universities and a vibrant community of immigrants.

ABOVE The Holsten Gate was part of Lübeck's defenses in its days as a city-state run by wealthy merchants.

OPPOSITE A devil figure at the Church of St. Mary.

7 *Virtuoso Marzipan* 3 p.m.

Café Niederegger (Breitestrasse 89; 49-451-530-1127; niederegger.de), across the street from the 13th-century Rathaus city hall, is the flagship store of the famed producer of Lübeck marzipan, which, like Gouda cheese, enjoys European Union protection as a geographic indication of origin. The shop sells marzipan in a dizzying array of shapes—eels, onions, carrots, rabbits—as well as marzipan liquor and marzipan coffee. In the adjoining cafe, in a room with tall windows that overlook the always-busy Breitestrasse, you can savor rich cakes (the Prince Heinrich, packed with marzipan, is the classic). Upstairs, a small museum is dedicated to marzipan.

8 *Try the Zander* 8 p.m.

Schiffergesellschaft, or the Seamen's Society (Breitestrasse 2; 49-451-767-76; schiffergesellschaft.com; $$), in a crow-step gable building from 1535, is quintessential Lübeck. In operation since 1868, the restaurant, with its original banquet tables and 200-year-old model ships dangling from the ceiling, features regional specialties like baked zander—a game fish found only in Europe—and medallions of roasted lamb, beef, and pork served atop ratatouille and fried potatoes. After dinner, stop at **Im Alten Zolln** (Mühlenstrasse 93-95; 49-451-723-95; www.alter-zolln.de), in a 16th-century customs house at the southern tip of the city. Its beer

selection includes a delicious dark ale the owners brew themselves.

SUNDAY

9 *The Red-Tile Sea* 10 a.m.

Get an overview of the city seven floors up the steeple at **St. Peter's Church** (Am Petrikirchhof 1; st-petri-luebeck.de). From there, you can look across the sea of red-tiled rooftops and out to the flatlands, marvel at the giant wind holes in the upper walls of the Rathaus, and gaze at the flying buttresses atop St. Mary's.

10 *Literary Giants* 11 a.m.

Across the street from St. Mary's, you'll find a courtly white house that once belonged to the

grandparents of Thomas Mann, one of Lübeck's two Nobel Prize-winning novelists. Today the **Buddenbrookhaus** (Mengstrasse 4; 49-451-122-4190; buddenbrookhaus.de), which recalls the name of Mann's masterpiece, is a museum dedicated to the novelist and his writer brother Heinrich. A short walk away the **Günter Grass Haus** (Glockengiesserstrasse 21; 49-451-122-4230; grass-haus.de) focuses on the other Nobel novelist. It is devoted primarily to Grass's nonliterary pursuits —sculpturing, painting, and drawing—but includes literary artifacts like his first typewriter.

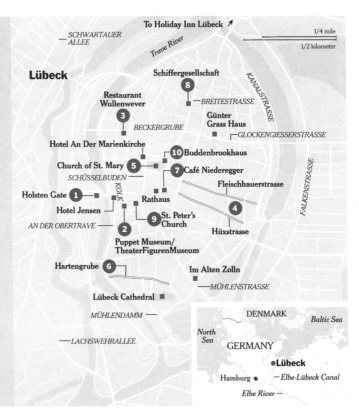

THE BASICS

Trains from Hamburg depart several times a day for the 40-minute trip to Lübeck. In town, walk.

Hotel An Der Marienkirche
Schüsselbuden 4
49-451-799-410
hotel-an-der-marienkirche.de
$
Scandinavian décor in the heart of the city next to St. Mary's Church.

Hotel Jensen
An der Obertrave 4-5
49-451-702-490
hotel-jensen-luebeck.de
$
In a 14th-century building on the riverfront facing the Holsten Gate.

Holiday Inn Lübeck
Travemünder Allee 3
49-451-370-60
ihg.com
$$
A short walk to the historic Burgtor, the north entrance to the city.

Hiddensee

In the 1920s, when Berlin roared with decadence, revolution, and cabaret, the quiet, sandy German resort island of Hiddensee off the Baltic Sea coast drew fame as a sun-drenched bohemian retreat. Today, families and sock-and-sandal-clad retirees have replaced the bold young artists and literati who once inhabited the century-old thatched-roof vacation houses, but Hiddensee still feels a world away from contemporary urban life. It has become a kind of German Nantucket, a popular escape for city dwellers, though largely undiscovered by foreign tourists. The vibe is distinctly mellow. Private cars are forbidden, so the only sounds of traffic are the heavy clomping of horses' hooves and the occasional screech from children bicycling wildly around the lovely heaths, moors, and salt marshes. — BY CHARLY WILDER

FRIDAY

1 *Find Your Way* 1 p.m.

In Vitte, the island's main town, get your bearings near the ferry harbor at the **Hiddensee Information Center** (Achtern Diek 18a; 49-383-006-08685; seebad-hiddensee.de). Most of the island is protected as part of the West Pomerania Lagoon National Park (nationalpark-vorpommersche-boddenlandschaft. de), and **Nationalparkhaus** (Norderende 2; 49-383-006-8041), the park information center in Vitte, is another good stop for orientation, with information on the island's animals, plants, and trails.

2 *Two Wheels Only* 1:30 p.m.

Visitors can travel among Hiddensee's four villages — Vitte (the largest, with fewer than 500 people), Grieben, Kloster, and Neuendorf — on cartoonishly slow horse-drawn covered wagons or on one vaguely sad-looking bus that traverses the island on weekdays. You're better off getting around on one of the comfortable bicycles that can be rented for less than $10 a day. Options include **Fuhrmannshof & Fahrradverleih** (Süderende 4; 49-383-006-8015; pferdundfahrrad.de) in Vitte and **Fahrradverleih Pehl** (Hafenweg 4;

OPPOSITE Hiddensee island, a quiet retreat of meadows and beaches off Germany's Baltic Sea coast.

RIGHT The vibe is mellow and cars are banned.

49-383-00437; hiddensee-pension.de) in Kloster. Bike paths are extensive and easy to use.

3 *View to Denmark* 3 p.m.

Hiddensee's white sand beaches, heady profusion of wildflowers, and hilly northern landscapes still attract an array of artists, whose locally inspired works appear often in exhibitions around the island. You may see painters out with their easels as you set out to see the island's northern end. Go first to the 19th-century **Leuchtturm Dornbusch**, or Burning Bush Lighthouse, so that you can arrive early enough to climb it before the closing at 4 p.m. It looks exactly as a lighthouse should: a tapering 90-foot white tower, with five stories of narrow windows above the first level and a red cap on top. It offers a panoramic view of the sea, mainland Germany, and even Denmark.

4 *Super Berry* 4 p.m.

Take a walk through the nature trails webbing Hiddensee's northern tip, amid sandy hills and thorny cliffs. Look for bushes thick with tiny orange berries called sea buckthorn — Sanddorn in German. Each mineral-rich berry has 15 times as much vitamin C as an orange, and although sea buckthorn is too tart to eat raw, it's a staple of Hiddensee kitchens. The berries, which taste something like a cross between sour apricot and sandalwood, are pressed into fruit juices and added to honey, cakes, and preserves; products ranging from buckthorn face cream to buckthorn whiskey can be found at any souvenir shop on the island. Find your way to **Grieben**, the island's tiniest village, for a quick look around.

5 *Sunset Repast* 8 p.m.

Tucked away in a converted country house near the cliffs is the low-lit **Zum kleinen Inselblick** (Birkenweg 2; 49-383-006-8001; $$), where you can sample the day's catch, fresh pasta dishes, or modern twists on regional favorites. The atmosphere is jovial and salon-like, and the restaurant is covered floor-to-ceiling in a wild miscellany of concert posters (particularly the Rolling Stones), old maps of the East German Communist republic, transistor radios, and random antiquarian kitsch. Everything you see is for sale, including the furniture. Sit on the lively patio to watch the sun set over the rolling hills and sip rosebud punch until midnight. Then cycle back to your hotel past flowered fields swept with salt winds as the pulse of city life fades further into the Baltic hush.

<h3 style="text-align:center">SATURDAY</h3>

6 *Thinking Man's Vacation* 10 a.m.

Drawn by its dramatic landscape and liberal atmosphere, visitors like Einstein, Freud, Billy Wilder, and Thomas Mann came to Hiddensee at the beginning of the 20th century. Their likenesses adorn many hotels and restaurants. The **Gerhart-Hauptmann-Haus** (Kirchweg 13, Kloster; 49-383-003-97; hauptmannhaus. de), the sumptuous summer house of Gerhart Hauptmann, the Nobel Prize-winning German author and pacifist, offers a peek into Hiddensee's literary past and is one of the island's most popular attractions. For those unfamiliar with his work, the modest **Heimatmuseum** (Kirchweg 1, Kloster; 49-383-003-63; heimatmuseum-hiddensee.de) may prove more interesting. Its exhibits, most of which are translated into English, cover the cultural, natural, and political history of the island.

7 *Along the Dunes* 11 a.m.

Hiddensee is 10 miles long and narrow, the perfect size for exploring by bike. You've already seen its northern end. Now cycle along the gentle dune heaths in the south and then up through the center. Stop for picnic supplies at the market in Vitte. Or ask around for a good restaurant or cafe when you're ready for lunch; Hiddensee is dotted with nautical-themed restaurants similar to each other and serving adequate, if not inspiring, food. Along the way, cycle into **Neuendorf**, the southernmost village.

8 *Wet All Over* 2 p.m.

Swim as you go. The best beaches are around Vitte. The waves can be treacherous, so pay attention to the signal flags. A century ago, Hiddensee's beaches were popular with the German nudist movement, or Freikörperkultur, which translates to "Free Body Culture." The practice was banned repeatedly, usually with little success, until the Nazis managed to end it completely; they also dismantled the artists' colony and barred Jews from the beaches. Later Hiddensee became a popular vacation spot for Communist government officials and well-connected civilians. The beaches once again became clothing-optional. Today bathing suits seem more the exception than the rule.

9 *Freshly Smoked* 7 p.m.

Räucherkutter (Hafen Kloster; 49-383-005-9996; $), built directly into an old wooden fishing boat at the Kloster harbor, serves thick, juicy cuts of fish smoked on-site, served on warm crusty rolls. From the small seating area on the roof, you can watch the boats pull lazily into the harbor.

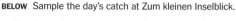

ABOVE To sample the beaches, bike from one to the next.

BELOW Sample the day's catch at Zum kleinen Inselblick.

SUNDAY

10 *Amber Quest* 10 a.m.

When the wind comes out of the East, beachgoers on Hiddensee keep their eyes out for bright flashes among the waves. The coastline is rich with amber, the fossilized ancient tree resin known here as Bernstein. Around 80 percent of the world's accessible amber is at the bottom of the Baltic Sea. Strong winds tear it from the sea floor, and it is brought up by "amber fishers" who comb the shore with large nets. Some pieces escape and are found by beachcombers. If you find one, you can take it to one of Hiddensee's two amber workshops to have it polished or made into jewelry. Owned by rival brothers who grew up on the island,

the shops sell amber jewelry and are worth a visit even if you haven't won the amber lottery yourself. **Engels & Corrigan Bernstein Werkstatt Hiddensee** (Mühlberg 17; 49-383-006-0494; bernstein-werkstatt-hiddensee.de) is in Kloster. Its counterpart in Vitte is **Bernsteinwerkstatt Vitte** (Norderende 142; 49-383-006-0730; bernsteinwerkstatt-vitte.de).

ABOVE Don't look for speed on the horse-drawn wagons.

THE BASICS

The trip from Berlin to Hiddensee takes about five hours, including the last leg, which is by boat. Take a Deutsche Bahn train (bahn.de) or drive to a passenger ferry (reederei-hiddensee.de) in either Schaprode or Stralsund. No private cars are allowed on the island, but once there it is easy to get around by bicycle and walking, or on horse-drawn wagons.

Hotel Hitthim
Hafenweg 8, Kloster
49-383-006-660
hitthim.de
$
Renovated century-old hotel in the village of Kloster with marina views.

Godewind
Süderende 53
49-383-006-600
hotelgodewind.de
$$
Near the beach in Vitte. Rustic charm and a restaurant offering typical local specialties.

Zum kleinen Inselblick **5**
Engels & Corrigan **10** Bernstein Werkstatt Hiddensee
Baltic Sea
Leuchtturm **3** Dornbusch
4 Grieben
Fahrradverleih Pehl
Kloster
Heimatmuseum
KIRCHWEG
—HAFENWEG
Hotel Hitthim
Nationalparkhaus
6
Gerhart-Hauptmann-Haus
9 Räucherkutter
8 Vitte
Vitte Bodden
Bernsteinwerkstatt Vitte
Hiddensee
NORDERENDE —
— ACHTERN DIEK
Fuhrmannshof & Fahrradverleih **2**
1
Hiddensee Information Center
7 Neuendorf
Godewind
—SÜDERENDE

DENMARK
SWEDEN
Baltic Sea
Schaproder Bodden
North Sea
Area of detail
Lübeck
Hamburg
GERMANY
Berlin
GERMANY

50 miles
100 kilometers
1 mile
2 kilometers

Leipzig

Leipzig's story goes back to its founding in the 1100s and proceeds to mercantile success, Johann Sebastian Bach, and anti-Communist revolt. Yet for all its proud history, a few decades ago this city of half a million people was a place to be avoided: a polluted, down-on-its-luck Eastern Bloc town known mostly for its book publishing industry and the trade fairs that have been held there since the Middle Ages. Since then, it has made a spectacular rebound. The charming city center, with Baroque, modernist, and Stalinist-era buildings coexisting in an odd harmony, is alive with bustling shops, restaurants, coffee bars, and clubs. Its abandoned factory buildings have become an asset, attracting creative entrepreneurs, artists, and musicians who have reclaimed the old spaces. The canals that once served industry now flow past cafes, and parks lace the city with green.

— BY GISELA WILLIAMS AND JAMIE TRECKER

FRIDAY

1 *Contemporary Spin* 3 p.m.

Find Leipzig's up-to-the-minute art scene at the **Spinnerei** (Spinnereistrasse 7; 49-341-498-00; spinnerei.de), a cultural complex in a former cotton mill. The sprawling collection of brick buildings is now home to a cafe, a quirky pension called the Meisterzimmer, artists' studios, and about a dozen galleries. One of them, owned by Gerd Harry Lybke, is **Eigen + Art,** one of the most influential galleries in Germany, with locations in Leipzig and Berlin. Lybke is often credited with placing Leipzig on the global art scene by promoting the now much-hyped New Leipzig School. Neo Rauch, the "father" of this group of neo-realistic painters, is considered one of Germany's greatest living artists. Take in the Spinnerei's variety of contemporary art along with Leipzig's palpable sense of creative possibility, which is traceable in part to the city's dirt-cheap rents.

OPPOSITE Auerbach's Cellar, where Mephistopheles entertains his victim in *Faust,* is still a good place for a Saxon meal. Goethe, the author, knew the place himself.

RIGHT Face to face with Johann Sebastian Bach at the Bach Museum. Nearby is the church where Bach was organist and choirmaster.

2 *The Greens* 5 p.m.

Despite Leipzig's industrial history, about a third of the city's landscape is parks and gardens, the largest of them being the Auenwald, about 22 square miles of fields and flood-plain forest. Find some greenery closer to the city center in the more manageable **Clara Zetkin Park** (Käthe-Kollwitz-Strasse; leipzig.de/de/buerger/freizeit/leipzig/parks), where musicians often hang out and young Leipzigers gather.

3 *Saxon Supper* 7 p.m.

In Goethe's *Faust*, Mephistopheles takes Faust to **Auerbach's Cellar** (Mädler Passage, Grimmaische Strasse 2-4; 49-341-216-100; auerbachs-keller-leipzig.de; $$), and the place is still a good spot for a traditional Saxon dinner. Bronze statues outside show Mephistopheles at his devilish work, and an actor dressed as Mephistopheles has been known to leap about the tables, but the food is good enough without the show. Entrees emphasize meat, from wild boar to saddle of lamb.

4 *Indie Crowd* 10 p.m.

The streets buzz after dark in Connewitz, an emerging neighborhood of artists and students with a critical mass of music venues. (Perhaps, if he were living in Leipzig today, Bach would be composing experimental electronic dance music.) **Werk II** (Kochstrasse 132; 49-341-308-0140; werk-2.de), once a large factory that produced industrial testing devices, is a popular multicultural event complex that has hosted indie rock bands from as far away as Canada. **UT Connewitz** (Wolfgang-Heinze-Strasse 12A;

49-341-462-6776; utconnewitz.de), one of the oldest cinemas in Germany, now hosts alternative film and music events. And at **Conne Island** (49-341-301-3028; Koburger Strasse 3; conne-island.de), student types crowd in to hear mostly alternative hardcore, punk, ska, and hip-hop bands.

SATURDAY

5 *Toccatas and Fugues* 10 a.m.

You can listen to all 175 hours of Johann Sebastian Bach's lifelong work or rearrange the instrumentals for one of his compositions at the **Bach Museum** (Thomaskirchhof 15/16; 49-341-913-7202; bachmuseumleipzig.de), which emphasizes interactive exhibits, and sells tickets for the annual Bachfest. It's close to **St. Thomas Church** (Thomaskirchhof 18; 49-341-222-240; thomaskirche.org), where Bach played the organ and directed the boys' choir (which still exists) from 1723 to 1750. The congregation got more than it bargained for as its choirmaster filled the church with his own extraordinary music. The building is striking, with a large white turret and capacity for 1,700 worshipers. It hosts frequent Bach performances.

6 *Caffeine for Composers* Noon

Take a break at **Coffe Baum** (Kleine Fleischergasse 4; 49-341-961-0060; coffe-baum.de), which has been open since 1696 and has a small coffee museum upstairs. Bach may have missed out, but Coffe Baum served its pastries to Wagner, Schumann, and Liszt — as well as, according to legend, the Emperor Napoleon. Leipzig doesn't call itself the City of Music for nothing. Mendelssohn founded Germany's first conservatory here, Robert and Clara Schumann's house is a local museum, and music

ABOVE Surveillance photos, relics of the old East German Communist regime, at the Museum of the Stasi.

OPPOSITE The Leipzig Museum of Fine Arts.

is performed virtually every night year round, with top-caliber productions held at the **Leipzig Opera House** (oper-leipzig.de) and **Gewandhaus** concert hall (gewandhausorchester.de), both on Augustusplatz square, and in St. Nicholas Church.

7 *Medieval to Modern* 1 p.m.

Spend some time in the dense city center, the Zentrum, where medieval buildings crowd next to stark modernist boxes and gorgeous Baroque complexes. The **Old City Hall** (Markt 1; 49-341-965-1320; stadtgeschichtliches-museum-leipzig.de) dates back to 1557 and has a history museum inside. The cobblestone plaza at **St. Nicholas Church** (just north of Grimmaische and Ritterstrasse; nikolaikirche-leipzig.de) was the scene of demonstrations in 1989, involving tens of thousands of people, that were instrumental in bringing about German reunification. Today, you're more likely to find book collectors than protesters. Stores selling used and rare books cluster on streets radiating out from the plaza. The selection at the enormous, marble-columned **Leipziger Antiquariat** (Ritterstrasse 16; 49-341-211-8188; leipziger-antiquariat.de) runs from sheet music to elegantly bound books of maps.

8 *New School, Old School* 4 p.m.

Neo Rauch is a force behind the Spinnerei and has a studio there, but to view some of his neo-realistic works — which look something like Stalinist art tripping into the surreal — in a museum setting, walk over to the **Leipzig Museum of Fine Arts** (Katharinenstrasse 10; 49-341-216-990; mdbk.de), a modern glass cube with minimalist galleries. The museum's collection reaches far back before the New Leipzig School, emphasizing Dutch 17th-century masters and German art back to the Middle Ages.

9 *Legendary Brew* 8 p.m.

Leipzig was traditionally famous for a completely different art form, the brewing of its own signature beer, called Gose. It's a deep orange brew flavored with salt and coriander, said to date to the 10th century. Gose production stopped during the Communist era, but now it is back, and with it the specialty bars and restaurants that are devoted to serving it. At **Bayerischer Bahnhof** (Bayrischer Platz 1; 49-341-124-5760;

bayerischer-bahnhof.de; $$), in the city's magnificent old train station, sample Gose with traditional foods like sausages or pork knuckle with sauerkraut.

SUNDAY

10 *Going Süd* 10 a.m.

Start the day in the Süd district, along Karl-Liebknecht-Strasse in the south (süd) side of the city. The vibe here is youthful and contemporary, with cafes and boutiques lining the retail strip. Find your way to **Hotel Seeblick,** (Karl-Liebknecht-Strasse 125; 49-341-225-3952; $$), which, despite its name, is a restaurant. Intimate and retro-styled, this is a popular hangout with the music crowd. It serves a hearty brunch and great burgers.

11 *Stasi Secrets* Noon

The linchpin of Communist rule in East Germany was the hated Stasi, or secret police, who spied on millions of citizens — and one another. For a glimpse of life during this period, visit the **Museum of the Stasi**, in the former Stasi headquarters in the Runde-Ecke building (Dittrichring 24; 49-341-961-2443; runde-ecke-leipzig.de).The permanent exhibit, titled "STASI—Power and Banality," is in German, but an English audioguide and English-language tours are available.

THE BASICS

Leipzig is just over an hour from Berlin by train (bahn.de). An excellent tram system reaches just about everywhere in the city.

Westin Leipzig
Gerberstrasse 15
49-341-9880
westin-leipzig.de
$$
Impressive views of the historic center and an excellent restaurant, the two-Michelin-star Falco, on the 27th floor.

Abito Suites
Grimmaische Strasse 16
49-341-985-2788
abito.de
$
Stylish modern hotel in Leipzig's center.

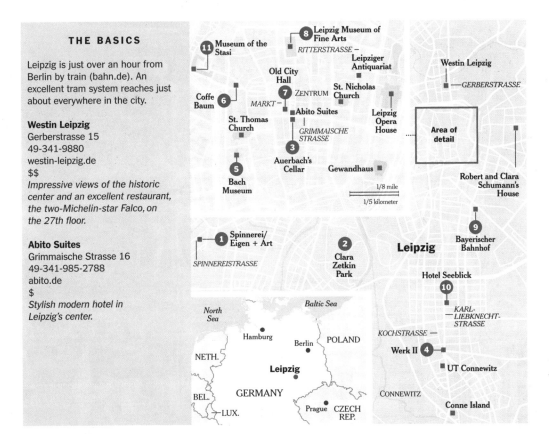

Dresden

For a city whose very name evokes scenes of destruction, Dresden, Germany, is looking much like its prewar self. Midway between Berlin and Prague, Dresden was on travelers' routes for more than 700 years, accumulating wealth and landmarks, before the devastating bombing raids of World War II. Now it has largely restored its major architectural treasures — the Zwinger palace, the Frauenkirche church, and the Semperoper opera house — to what they were before the war. But while the Altstadt, or old town, was turning the clock back, the Neustadt (new town) across the Elbe River was continuing to look forward. The student quarter there is filled with shops and bars catering to a young generation that doesn't remember the days under communism, much less the war. Old and new come together in the military museum reconceived by Daniel Libeskind, a stark, contemporary rethinking of the past. — BY RACHEL B. DOYLE

FRIDAY

1 *Baroque to Modern* 4 p.m.

Although much of the Altstadt has been modernized, the striking panorama of Baroque buildings along the Elbe provides evidence of why the prewar city was often compared to Florence. The postcard views can be found along the **Brühlsche Terrasse**, an elevated riverside promenade. After a stroll there, head behind the esplanade to the **Albertinum** (Georg-Treu-Platz 2; 49-351-4914-9731; skd.museum), an art museum that reopened in 2010 after a 51 million-euro renovation. Since its beginnings in the late 19th century, this has always been a "modern" art gallery, and its collection spans the two centuries separating the works of Caspar David Friedrich, a Romantic painter, and those of the contemporary artist Gerhard Richter. Both artists spent much of their lives in Dresden.

2 *Grand Opera* 7 p.m.

Return to a time when ladies wore fur and feathered hats at the grand **Semperoper** (Theaterplatz 2;

49-351-491-1705; semperoper.de), where both Richard Strauss and Richard Wagner premiered many of their works. A revered hall for ballet and concerts as well as opera, the Semperoper was inaugurated in 1841, destroyed in 1945, reopened by the East German regime in 1985, and then painstakingly restored in 2002. It has superb acoustics, red velvet seats, elaborate friezes, and loyal patrons who dress to the nines for premieres and traditional yet brilliant stagings of operas like *La Bohème* and Dvorak's *Rusalka*.

3 *Swimming Entrees* 9:30 p.m.

A modern seafood restaurant inside a rebuilt rococo palace, **Kastenmeiers im Kurländer Palais** (Tzschirnerplatz 3-5; 49-351-4848-4801; kastenmeiers. de; $$$) is an elegant dinner option in the city center. The first sight for diners entering the restaurant is an open kitchen beneath a long glass tank filled with fish and lobsters. These creatures later show up in the exposed brick dining room as delicious dishes like sturgeon with salmon caviar sauce or lobster risotto.

SATURDAY

4 *War Stories* 10 a.m.

Dresden's **Military History Museum** (Olbrichtplatz 2; 49-351-823-2803; mhmbw.de), one of the largest and gutsiest museums in Germany, has been

OPPOSITE The Frauenkirche, reconstructed after its destruction in World War II firebombing.

RIGHT Fine dining in a Volkswagen factory.

transformed in steel and glass by Daniel Libeskind. The exhibition space offers two experiences. One is a chronological history of German war, with an emphasis on the 20th century. The second, housed in the five-story trapezoid inserted by Libeskind into the original 1870s building, explores the social effects of war.

5 Beer on the Elbe 1 p.m.

Have a hearty Saxon lunch at **Ball- & Brauhaus Watzke** (Kötzschenbroder Strasse 1; 49-351-852-920; watzke.de; $), a waterfront restaurant, ballroom, and brewery that has been in business since the 1890s. Alongside a very local crowd, enjoy house brews and seasonal regional specialties like pork neck in beer sauce with mushroom goulash. The walls are decorated with old photographs of Dresden, and the green leather booths are filled with laughter. In summer, Watzke has a lively beer garden on the banks of the Elbe.

6 Old Masters 2:30 p.m.

Starting in the 17th century, the rulers of Saxony, whose capital was in Dresden, began collecting European art in earnest. It was a propitious time to do so, and most of the major works housed in the **Gemäldegalerie Alte Meister** (Theaterplatz 1; 49-351-4914-6679; skd.museum) were assembled within a 50-year period (and safely stored away three centuries later, during World War II). Most famous is Raphael's *Sistine Madonna*, with its iconic pair of cherubs, but equally impressive are Albrecht Dürer's melancholic *Dresden Altar* and the world's largest collection of paintings by the two Lucas Cranachs, Older and Younger.

7 Cows and Angels 4:45 p.m.

Explore the Äussere Neustadt neighborhood, with its 19th-century architecture (this area was hardly damaged by the bombing) and many trendy bars, cafes, and independent shops. Duck into the **Spot**, a unisex boutique (Alaunstrasse 29; 49-351-312-6591; wearethespot.com), and **Pfunds Molkerei** (Bautzner Strasse 79; 49-351-808-080; pfunds.de), a gorgeous dairy shop dating back to 1880 and covered floor to ceiling with Neo-Renaissance hand-painted tiles of cows and angels ferrying milking tools.

8 Dinner in a Jar 7 p.m.

Feast on German tapas served in glass preserves jars at **lila Sosse** (Alaunstrasse 70; 49-351-803-6723; lilasosse.de; $$), a stylishly dim, dark wood restaurant in an artist-decorated courtyard complex. The tapas are elevated versions of traditional fare like cheese spätzle with fried onions and herring tartar with beetroot. A Russian chocolate cheesecake with pears is baked in its jar, but in a case of German practicality winning over cuteness, a terrific spinach

and goat cheese salad with lavender dressing comes on a plate.

9 *Eastern Rock* 9:30 p.m.

For drinks and music in an uncanny atmosphere of the Communist German Democratic Republic, head to **Ost-Pol** (Königsbrücker Strasse 47; no phone; ost-pol.de), where the year is 1968, the color scheme is yellow and orange, and the beers listed above an ancient Robotron computer all come from the former Communist bloc. Intimate rock concerts

are often presented in a room next to retro arcade games and a green coal oven. Continue the night at nearby **Altes Wettbüro** (Antonstrasse 8; 49-351-658-8983; altes-wettbuero.de), a one-time betting parlor, with dancing to the soul or electro records of local D. J.'s.

SUNDAY

10 *Assembly Line* 11 a.m.

Brunch in a car factory at **Lesage** (Lennestrasse 1; 49-351-420-4250; lesage.de; $$$; reservations recommended), a gourmet restaurant in the Volkswagen production plant called the Transparent Factory. The Sunday brunch package consists of an extensive

OPPOSITE Stop off for a stroll at the Grosser Garten, a 147-acre park, after touring the nearby Transparent Factory, a hospitable Volkswagen production plant.

ABOVE Table tennis at Ost-Pol, a bar that playfully evokes the days of the Communist bloc.

BELOW The Semperoper, reconstructed after World War II.

hot and cold buffet, live piano music, and a tour through the soaring glass building (49-18-420-4411; glaesernemanufaktur.de) where Phaeton sedans are assembled. Afterward, stroll around the pond and fountains of the **Grosser Garten**, a 147-acre landscaped park just outside.

11 *All That Sparkles* 2 p.m.

In G.D.R. times, citizens could trade bottles of **Schloss Wackerbarth** sparkling wine, or sekt, for car parts or kitchen appliances. Now, every Sunday, the winery where it originates (Wackerbarthstrasse 1, Radebeul; 49-351-895-50; schloss-wackerbarth.de), first established in 1727 as a getaway for the court of Augustus the Strong, opens its Baroque castle and gardens to the public. After your tour, settle in for a long lunch at the vineyard's amazing Saxon-meets-Mediterranean restaurant ($$$), with a glass of the house Riesling.

ABOVE Ball- & Brauhaus Watzke, a restaurant and brewery on the Elbe that first opened in the 1890s.

OPPOSITE A tram cruising through Theaterplatz, the square that is the home of the grand Semperoper.

THE BASICS

Dresden is two hours from Berlin and easily accessible by car or Deutsche Bahn train (bahn.de).

Innside by Meliá Dresden
Salzgasse 4
49-351-795-150
innside.com
$$
In the Altstadt, with well-designed rooms, a stylish wellness center, and VEN, one of Dresden's top restaurants.

Maritim Hotel Dresden
Devrientstrasse 10-12
49-351-2160
maritim.com
$$
Fashioned from a nearly century-old riverside warehouse, an architectural monument.

Rothenburger Hof
Rothenburger Strasse 15-17
49-351-812-60
dresden-hotel.de
$$
Comfortable family-run hotel in the happening Äussere Neustadt.

5 Ball- & Brauhaus Watzke

OLBRICHTPLATZ

KÖTZSCHENBRODER STRASSE

HANSASTRASSE

KÖNIGSBRÜCKER STRASSE

4 Military History Museum

11 To Schloss Wackerbarth

Dresden

Ost-Pol 9

8 lila Sosse
ALAUNSTRASSE

Altes Wettbüro

7 Spot Pfunds Molkerei

ANTONSTRASSE

Rothenburger Hof

BAUTZNER STRASSE

NEUSTADT ROTHENBURGER STRASSE

GERMANY

POL.

Berlin

Elbe River

Elbe River

Maritim Hotel Dresden

DEVRIENTSTRASSE

Dresden

Prague

CZECH REP.

Area of detail

1 Albertinum

3 Kastenmeiers im Kurländer Palais

Innside by Meliá Dresden

Semperoper
2

THEATERPLATZ

Lesage 10

STÜBELALLEE

Brühlsche Terrasse

ALTSTADT

6

Gemäldegalerie Alte Meister

Frauenkirche

GROSSER GARTEN

1/4 mile

1/2 kilometer

Cologne

One of the oldest cities in Germany, Cologne has been drawing visitors since at least the year 50 A.D., when it was officially founded as a Roman out-post, or colonia, on the Rhine River. Today the big attractions are the city's ancient (and gargantuan) cathedral, vibrant night life, sophisticated shopping, a great native beer called Kölsch, and eau de cologne, invented here in 1709. Winding through it all is the ever-present Rhine. — BY EVAN RAIL

FRIDAY

1 *Main Attraction* 3 p.m.

Too big and dominating to miss, the **Cologne Cathedral** (koelner-dom.de) draws attention by its contrast to its modern surroundings as well as with its powerful statement as one of Europe's largest Gothic cathedrals. Most of old Cologne was flattened by World War II bombing and replaced by 20th-century buildings; the cathedral, which was constructed beginning in 1248, was damaged but survived. Inside are stained glass windows from the medieval era as well as a recent one designed by Gerhard Richter. Take a deep breath if you want to climb the bell tower; the stairway has more than 500 steps. Close by, the **Museum Ludwig** (Heinrich-Böll-Platz; 49-221-2212-6165; museum-ludwig.de) displays art from the 20th and 21st centuries, including a large collection of American Pop Art featuring Andy Warhol, Roy Lichtenstein, and other familiar artists.

2 *Something Special* 7:30 p.m.

Given its location on a quiet, residential lane and a name that echoes the Spanish word for "nothing," the loungelike restaurant **Nada** (Clever Strasse 32; 49-221-8889-9944; nada-koeln.de; $$$) might be accused of setting low expectations, only to demolish them once the inventive, playful cooking — one evening's menu included a porcini soup disguised as a cappuccino, and slow-cooked roast beef and root vegetables in a gingery Barolo glaze — hits the table. Considering the culinary pyrotechnics and stellar service, the prices seem (almost) understated.

OPPOSITE Cologne Cathedral, a landmark since the 1200s.

RIGHT Along the Rhine, near the Hohenzollern Bridge.

3 *Late at Heart* 11:30 p.m.

Originally opened as an exhibition space for a group of young visual artists, **Gewölbe**, or Vault (Hans-Böckler-Platz 2; 49-171-379-5511; gewoelbe.net) has evolved into a serious music venue for techno and electronic acts, turning a section of the city's Westbahnhof (West Train Station) into one of the best clubs in town. You can't be sure of exactly what you'll find here without checking the schedule, but this much is certain: the doors won't open until 11 p.m., and the dancing and partying will keep going until very late.

SATURDAY

4 *A Snail's Pace* 10 a.m.

Given the stylish appearance of most residents, you can imagine how much of their time and energy is spent shopping. To fuel up in the heart of the Ehrenstrasse, a street that overflows with new clothing stores, local shoppers grab snacks from the **Zimmermann** bakery (Ehrenstrasse 75; 49-221-255-632; baeckereizimmermann.de), founded in 1875, where a sublime frosted schnecke (or "snail," meaning a raisin Danish) will keep you going at least as far as the next boutique.

5 *Chic Belgique* 11 a.m.

The Belgisches Viertel (Belgian Quarter) has become the neighborhood of choice for many art and media types, who have brought dozens of cool cafes, shops, and restaurants in their wake. Browse through women's clothing from young German designers at **Simon und Renoldi** (Maastrichter Strasse 17;

49-221-9458-7031; simonundrenoldi.com) and then move along to the men's jeans and rustic workwear at **Monsieur Courbet** (Maastrichter Strasse 49; 49-221-1791-5425), which also houses the excellent **Groove Attack** record store (49-221-522-037; grooveattackrecordstore.com), a specialist in obscure hip-hop and rap, in the basement. At the area's main square, Brüsseler Platz, the charming **Bob 10.5.10** (Brüsseler Platz 6; 49-221-1686-9348; bob10510.de) sells urbane, club-friendly men's wear from cult brands like Hannibal, Stephan Schneider,

ABOVE Traffic in the Breite Strasse shopping area.

BELOW The Groove Attack record store.

and Rick Owens. The three or four streets surrounding the square have enough to keep your credit card busy for several hours. Afterward, you can unwind with a millionaire's shortbread and an espresso at **Madame Miammiam** (Antwerpener Strasse 39; 49-221-271-9242; madamemiammiam.de), a beloved bakery and cafe.

6 *Lucky Hans* 1 p.m.

There are tons of places for a quick lunch on the Ring, the bustling boulevard that encircles the city center — and then there is **Hans im Glück** (Hohenzollernring 38-40; 49-221-2989-2163; hansimglueckburgergrill.de; $). Named after a Brothers Grimm fairy tale, "Hans in Luck," this outpost of a Munich restaurant serves what must be the best hamburgers in town — if not the Continent — including a delicious house special topped with Parma ham, Parmesan cheese, arugula, and a teriyaki-like balsamic vinegar sauce. Though it's perfect for lunch, the killer cocktails and cool atmosphere make this also a good choice for a late-night snack.

7 *Vertigo* 3 p.m.

It's hard to say what makes more impact at the **Kolumba** museum (Kolumbastrasse 4; 49-221-933-1930; kolumba.de): its vertiginous mix of ancient religious and modern secular artworks or its astounding, vintage-2007 building by the Pritzker-winning

Swiss architect Peter Zumthor. Shift your gaze from an oversize late-12th-century carved ivory crucifix to installations and art in changing exhibitions, and then take in the spires of the cathedral, artfully framed in a floor-to-ceiling window.

8 *Wines of the Rhine* 7:30 p.m.

Yes, Cologne loves its native Kölsch beer, but the Rhine, which runs through the city, is also the geographic focal point of some of Europe's favorite wine regions. Sample the wares at **Wein am Rhein** (Johannisstrasse 64; 49-221-9124-8885; weinamrhein. eu; $$$$), where more than 20 great vintages from the Rheingau, Rheinhessen, Mosel, and other terroirs are all available by the glass. Hardly upstaged by the bottles, the kitchen has been regularly called one of Cologne's best since its opening in early 2009.

BELOW Old and new: the cathedral and the Ludwig Museum.

Indulge yourself with the multi-course weinschmecker (wine taster) menu.

9 *The Living Room* 9:30 p.m.

Older breweries and classic Kölsch pubs may be more famous, but none is as welcoming and playfully genre-bending as the charming **Braustelle** (Christianstrasse 2, at Venloer Strasse; 49-221-285-6932; braustelle.com), a tiny brewpub that functions as the up-and-coming Ehrenfeld district's main meeting point and de facto public living room. Try a Helios, the house take on the city's own style, albeit unfiltered, and then sample something few other Cologne brewers would even consider: an Alt, the traditional brewing specialty of the city's longstanding rival, Düsseldorf.

10 *Bunker Down* Midnight

With its mix of immigrants and working-class residents, the Ehrenfeld district has turned into a favorite address for musicians, students, and artists,

which makes for great evenings out. One spot for late-night fun is **E-Feld** (Venloer Strasse 601; 49-221-9465-7063; e-feld.com), a cavernous, bunker-like cellar where acts like Swedish minimalist techno D.J. Pär Grindvik rival those a few blocks away at the classic **Underground** (Vogelsanger Strasse 200; 49-221-542-326; underground-cologne.de).

ABOVE The Vault, a venue for techno and electronic music.

OPPOSITE Cologne Cathedral's Gothic interior.

SUNDAY

11 *Please Touch* 11 a.m.

Unlike most museums and galleries, with their buttoned-down attitude, **Rautenstrauch-Joest-Museum** (Cäcilienstrasse 29-33; 49-221-2212-3620; museenkoeln.de/rautenstrauch-joest-museum) asks visitors to touch and interact with some of its displays. They focus on the world's great diversity of cultures, best symbolized by the sailboat-size, ornately decorated rice storage vessel from Sulawesi taking up most of the museum lobby. The building, dating from late 2010, is in stark contrast with the attached Schnütgen Museum, which shows its vast collection of medieval and Gothic Christian art in the renovated Romanesque St. Cäcilien church.

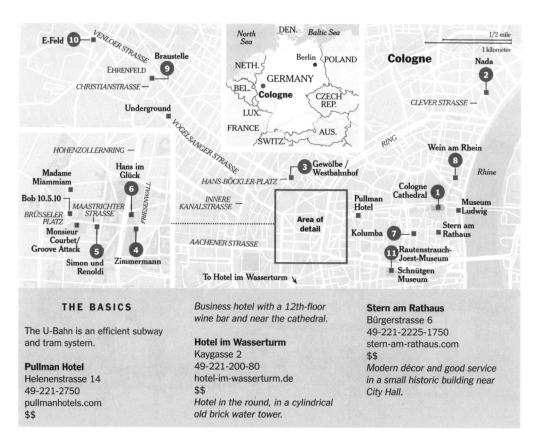

THE BASICS

The U-Bahn is an efficient subway and tram system.

Pullman Hotel
Helenenstrasse 14
49-221-2750
pullmanhotels.com
$$

Business hotel with a 12th-floor wine bar and near the cathedral.

Hotel im Wasserturm
Kaygasse 2
49-221-200-80
hotel-im-wasserturm.de
$$
Hotel in the round, in a cylindrical old brick water tower.

Stern am Rathaus
Bürgerstrasse 6
49-221-2225-1750
stern-am-rathaus.com
$$
Modern décor and good service in a small historic building near City Hall.

Frankfurt

The glittering skyscrapers along the Main River in Frankfurt have inspired a cartoonish nickname, Mainhattan. Frankfurt's role as Germany's financial center reinforces the image, and even after global economic setbacks, there are still plenty of Porsches and bankers in chalk-stripe suits to be seen on the streets near the stock exchange and big bank headquarters. But beneath its master-of-the-universe pretensions, Frankfurt is a user-friendly Hessian town with big-city accouterments. Its museums are the best in Germany, after Berlin's, and its opera and ballet are top notch. Its population is international, with dozens of nationalities, including a large Turkish contingent. Whether you're there to make a deal or see the sights, with an alert eye you can find Frankfurt's essential charm. — BY MARK LANDLER

FRIDAY

1 *Rebuilt Charm* 2 p.m.

Get in the Old World mood with a stroll through Römerberg, the heart of what used to be the largest medieval quarter in Germany. The half-timbered houses are picture-perfect, and well they might be, since they were meticulously rebuilt after being flattened in World War II. There are several starkly modern galleries and museums nearby; the effect is deliberately jarring. Stop for a cold one at **Haus Wertheym** (Fahrtor 1; 49-69-281-432; haus-wertheym. de), a quintessentially German joint with brusque service and steins hanging from the ceiling.

2 *Museum Kilometer* 4 p.m.

Seven of Frankfurt's museums are strung conveniently along the south bank of the Main, a graceful tree-lined promenade that can be reached from the north bank over a pair of pedestrian bridges. If your interests run to Mies van der Rohe or Stanley Kubrick, stop at the **Deutsches Architekturmuseum** (Schaumainkai 43; 49-69-2123-8844; dam-online.de) or the **Deutsches Filmmuseum** (Schaumainkai 41;

OPPOSITE Medieval houses and bright office towers are both integral to the identity of Frankfurt.

RIGHT Haus Wertheym dispenses its beer in Römerberg, Frankfurt's reconstructed medieval quarter.

49-69-961-220-220; deutsches-filminstitut.de). But save the most time for the **Städel Museum** (Schaumainkai 63; 49-69-6050-9800; staedelmuseum.de), one of Germany's finest galleries, with works by Botticelli, Dürer, and Holbein.

3 *Masterpiece Dining* 6:30 p.m.

Frankfurt is synonymous with link sausage, but when Frankfurters go out, they crave anything but German food. Trattorias, tandoori places, and Thai cuisine are all well represented. One lovely option is **Holbein's**, in the Städel courtyard (access, Holbeinstrasse 1; 49-69-6605-6666; meyer-frankfurt. de; $$$$). With its soaring glass walls and stylish décor, it is a contemporary jewel box amid the old-master paintings. Begin in the bar and then proceed to a hearty dinner: this is the place for entrees like Argentine filet mignon and grilled Canadian lobster.

4 *Nights of Sachsenhausen* 10 p.m.

Frankfurt's left bank, Sachsenhausen, is its most beguiling quarter. Its warren of cobblestone streets is lined with cider taverns that serve an apple wine, sometimes called Ebbelwoi. To say it is an acquired taste doesn't quite do it justice. Few other cities in Germany would want to claim this tangy brew, which is made with fermented apple juice and served in glazed jugs known as Bembel. **Adolf Wagner** (Schweizer

Strasse 71; 49-69-612-565; apfelwein-wagner.com), a cheerfully raucous tavern, is the best place try it.

SATURDAY

5 *Cruising the Main* 10 a.m.

Few European cities are as defined by their skylines as Frankfurt. Get an ant's view from the deck of the *Goethe* or one of its sister vessels of the **Primus-Linie** (Mainkai 36; 49-69-133-8370; primus-linie.de). The sightseeing boats leave every hour from the north bank most months of the year, offering excursions of about an hour or two. Two tall towers, Helmut Jahn's pyramid-topped Messeturm and Norman Foster's jagged Commerzbank, anchor an urban forest that overlooks the nearby Kaiserdom, the Gothic church where Holy Roman emperors were once crowned. The boat also sails past the headquarters for the European Central Bank, which rises on land that was once the Grossmarkthalle, a wholesale market.

6 *From Gross to Klein* Noon

The **Kleinmarkthalle** (Hasengasse 5-7; kleinmarkthalle.de), the centrally located little brother of the wholesale market, teems with life on Saturdays. Locals converge on this two-story covered market for fresh fish, cheese, bread, olive oil, and, yes, an artery-clogging assortment of sausages. From there, it's a short hop to the retail district, which features a full complement of designer boutiques on Goethestrasse, among them the Mercedes-Benz of eyeglass shops, **Rainer Brenner** (Goethestrasse 24; rainerbrenner.de). If the shopping makes you peckish, head for the neighboring Fressgasse (literally, feeding street), where the first stop is **Zarges** (Kalbächer Gasse 10; 49-69-299-030; zarges-frankfurt.com), a pricey but out-of-this-world delicatessen. Order a Windbeutel, a lighter-than-air cream-filled pastry with strawberries. You'll also find other worthwhile snacking opportunities in the neighborhood.

7 *Urban Jungle* 3 p.m.

Though known for steel and concrete, Frankfurt has a sublime botanical garden. The **Palmengarten** (Siesmayerstrasse 61; 49-69-2123-3391; palmengarten. de) is in the middle of the fashionable Westend and has 50 acres of tropical and subtropical trees, orchids, and ferns. Many are tended in greenhouses, like the Tropicarium, which has a mini-rainforest. A children's train wends its way past the park's lake and gardens. Grown-ups flock to jazz concerts here in August, and the **Caféhaus Siesmayer** (49-69-9002-9200; palmengarten-gastronomie.de; $$) serves meals and cakes on the edge of the greenery.

8 *Bookish Pursuits* 5 p.m.

The Frankfurt Book Fair, the world's largest gathering of publishers and literary agents, is in early October. But literature has a gracious year-round home at the **Literaturhaus** (Schöne Aussicht 2; 49-69-756-1840; literaturhaus-frankfurt.de), a club in a refurbished 19th-century library on the north bank. There is a full calendar of book signings, readings, and lectures — mostly in German — by writers like Joseph Brodsky and Rafik Schami. Have a coffee or a glass of wine at the club's cafe.

9 *The Chef's Place* 8 p.m.

The Austrian chef Mario Lohninger shook up the food scene with the long-closed Silk, where diners reclined on white leather daybeds. Now fans find him at the more sedate **Restaurant Lohninger** (Schweizer Strasse 1; 49-69-247-557-860; lohninger.de; $$$$) on the River Main. Lohninger, who has cooked at Guy Savoy in Paris and Danube in New York, offers a cuisine-spanning menu that includes Austrian specialties like Wiener Schnitzel and the dessert pancakes called Kaiserschmarrn.

10 *Jazz International* 10 p.m.

Frankfurt's reputation as a jazz town rests in no small part on the **Jazzkeller** (Kleine Bockenheimer Strasse 18A; 49-69-288-537), where, since the 1950s, international stars from Dizzy Gillespie to Lenny Popkin have played in a basement grotto. Now you might hear jazz artists from the United States, Europe, or Latin America. Check the schedule at jazzkeller.com.

11 *A Last Blast of Culture* 11 a.m.

Like so much else, the original **Goethe House** was destroyed in World War II. Still, the 1950s reconstruction (Grosser Hirschgraben 23-25; 49-69-138-800; goethehaus-frankfurt.de) that stands today provides an evocative feeling for the early life of Johann Wolfgang von Goethe, who was born into a wealthy Frankfurt family, although he later forsook his hometown. A few blocks east of the Goethe House is the **Museum of Modern Art** (Domstrasse 10; 49-69-2123-0447; mmk-frankfurt.de) in a wedge-shaped building known popularly as "the piece of cake," and its neighbor, the **Schirn Kunsthalle**

(Römerberg, 49-69-299-8820; schirn.de), an internationally respected exhibition space. Intimate and rarely crowded, it feels like a secret find in a city full of such unexpected discoveries.

OPPOSITE Frankfurt's skyscrapers are its trophies as Germany's center of finance and commerce.

ABOVE The Museum of Modern Art, part of Frankfurt's trove of museums and galleries.

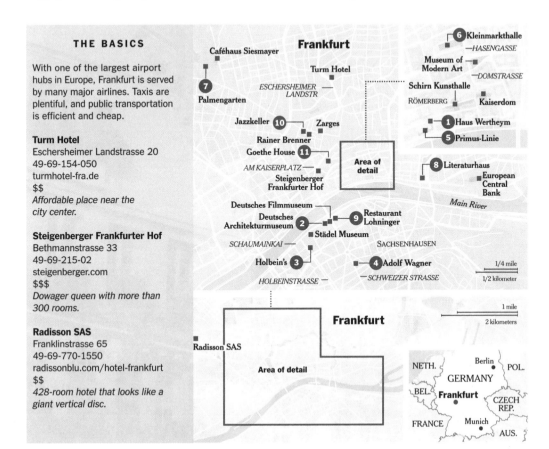

THE BASICS

With one of the largest airport hubs in Europe, Frankfurt is served by many major airlines. Taxis are plentiful, and public transportation is efficient and cheap.

Turm Hotel
Eschersheimer Landstrasse 20
49-69-154-050
turmhotel-fra.de
$$
Affordable place near the city center.

Steigenberger Frankfurter Hof
Bethmannstrasse 33
49-69-215-02
steigenberger.com
$$$
Dowager queen with more than 300 rooms.

Radisson SAS
Franklinstrasse 65
49-69-770-1550
radissonblu.com/hotel-frankfurt
$$
428-room hotel that looks like a giant vertical disc.

Map labels:

Caféhaus Siesmayer
Frankfurt
Turm Hotel
7 ESCHERSHEIMER LANDSTR
Palmengarten
Jazzkeller **10** — Zarges
Rainer Brenner
Goethe House **11**
AM KAISERPLATZ
Steigenberger Frankfurter Hof
Deutsches Filmmuseum
Deutsches Architekturmuseum **2**
SCHAUMAINKAI
Holbein's **3**
HOLBEINSTRASSE
Area of detail
6 Kleinmarkthalle
—HASENGASSE
Museum of Modern Art
—DOMSTRASSE
Schirn Kunsthalle
RÖMERBERG | Kaiserdom
1 Haus Wertheym
5 Primus-Linie
8 Literaturhaus
European Central Bank
Main River
Restaurant Lohninger **9**
Städel Museum
SACHSENHAUSEN
4 Adolf Wagner
—SCHWEIZER STRASSE

1/4 mile
1/2 kilometer

Radisson SAS
Area of detail
Frankfurt

1 mile
2 kilometers

NETH. Berlin POL.
GERMANY
BEL. **Frankfurt**
CZECH REP.
FRANCE Munich
AUS.

Munich

Munich has long been a major destination for history buffs, music fans, and lovers of the Oktoberfest, but in the past several years this southern German city, capital of Bavaria, has developed a new reputation as a place to eat and stroll and enjoy life. It is known for its livability, and Monocle magazine praised its "general feeling of Gemütlichkeit." Its public transportation was deemed Europe's best by a leading automobile club. Public art has sprung up on its streets. Even if you don't want to move in, a place with these comfortable virtues demands a visit. And that's without even mentioning the beer. — BY EVAN RAIL

FRIDAY

1 *West Enders* 4 p.m.

Take the pulse of the Schwanthalerhöhe, a.k.a. the West End, a mixed-use neighborhood with an attractive blend of artists' studios, cafes, and immigrant communities. Scan the English-language titles at **Kunst & Textwerk** (Ligsalzstrasse 13; 49-89-4410-9849; kutv.de), a bookstore and cafe with comfortable couches and chairs for browsers. Explore the other shops, and stop by the atelier of **Stefanie Duckstein** (Parkstrasse 7; 49-89-3610-5392; stefanie-duckstein.de), a quirky artist. For a pick-me-up, the **Marais** (Parkstrasse 2; 49-89-5009-4552; cafe-marais.de) is a cafe cum antiques store where you can shop for glass pitchers while sipping your milchkaffee.

2 *Teutonic Plates* 7:30 p.m.

For more than a century, the luxury **Bayerischer Hof** (Promenadeplatz 2-6; 49-89-212-0993; bayerischerhof.de; $$$$) has been one of the city's best addresses. The hotel's see-and-be-seen Garden restaurant's cool décor is a blend of modern, open, and airy that feels like a cross between an Apple Store and a greenhouse. The menu offers refined Mediterranean and German cuisine that looks south for inspiration. You might find a black-rice risotto

with braised cherry tomatoes and leeks, a hearty oxtail ravioli, or a praline panna cotta.

3 *Room to Dance* 10 p.m.

Yes, the crowd might be young, but the tracks of hard techno and trance played at **Neuraum** (Arnulfstrasse 17; 49-89-381-538-999; neuraum.net), a monstrous dance club, can actually be surprisingly cool and sophisticated. Set in a bomb-shelter-like space under the main bus station, the club claims to have room for more than 2,000 revelers, spread over various rooms and floors. The décor is dark, sparse and minimalist, leaving plenty of space for the enthusiastic student crowd to dance, drink, and check one another out.

SATURDAY

4 *Victuals Aplenty* 10 a.m.

The heart of Munich is an eminently pleasant place to stroll, in no small part because of **Viktualienmarkt** (Viktualienmarkt Square; muenchen.de/int/en/shopping/markets/viktualienmarkt), one of Europe's most delightful outdoor markets. Its bounty of produce, sausages, fish, cheese, baked goods, and snacks spills from more than 100 stalls. Adjacent is the Schrannenhalle, an indoor food hall on the site of a former grain market.

OPPOSITE Known for its beer and gemütlichkeit, Munich holds tight to its Bavarian spirit.

RIGHT Décor in the Maria Café, a favorite local breakfast spot in Glockenbachviertel, a gay-friendly neighborhood.

5 *Rustic Restaurant* 12:30 p.m.

The Glockenbachviertel, a family-friendly, gay-friendly neighborhood with lots of shops and cafes could make you consider a much longer stay. Have a homestyle brunch with the regulars at **Maria Café** (Klenzestrasse 97; 49-89-2023-2745; $$), a rustic restaurant at one end of Klenzestrasse, the area's main drag. There's no rush, as the breakfast menu is served until 6 p.m., overlapping both the regular lunch menu and daily specials like a big green salad

ABOVE The view down into the Munich city center from high up in the St. Peter Church.

BELOW The Zentrum Neue Technologien in the Deutsches Museum.

with grilled goat cheese, or schnitzel with potato and cucumber salad.

6 *Science, New and Old* 2 p.m.

The **Deutsches Museum** (Museumsinsel 1; 49-89-217-91; deutsches-museum.de), in the old city center, was already one of the world's largest technology and science museums before adding a new wing, the Zentrum Neue Technologien, devoted to pioneering nano- and biotechnology. Learn with touch screens and hands-on demonstrations, and then have fun gawking at the Messerschmitts and Fieseler flying bombs in the vast aviation room.

7 *Bavarian Comfort* 7 p.m.

When a restaurant is down an alley and up two flights of stairs, it's no surprise that the clientele skews young and in-the-know. But the main reason to seek out **Spezlwirtschaft** (Ledererstrasse 3; 49-89-2323-2973; spezlwirtschaft.me; $$) is for its modern twists on German comfort food, such as lightly breaded schnitzel complemented by tart lingonberries and a sprout salad, or pumpkin knödel dumplings with seared chard.

8 *More Variety* 9:30 p.m.

Touching on the traditions of Weimar-era cabaret and earlier forms of Continental vaudeville, a new breed of varietés mixes song, dance, juggling, acrobatics, trapeze, and physical comedy, creating

a performance that often transcends language — if any words are spoken at all. The **GOP Varieté-Theater** (Maximilianstrasse 47; 49-89-210-288-444; variete.de) has great shows Tuesday through Saturday.

SUNDAY

9 *Modern Masters* 10 a.m.

The history of the Kunstareal, or Art District, dates to the 16th century, when Duke Wilhelm IV commissioned a series of history paintings for the royal palace. Now the **Museum Brandhorst** (Türkenstrasse 19; 49-89-238-052-286; museum-brandhorst.de) displays a collection of 20th- and 21st-century art, and the **Lenbachhaus** (Luisen-strasse 33; 49-89-2333-2000; lenbachhaus.de) houses works by Wassily Kandinsky, Franz Marc, Paul Klee, and other artists from the Blue Rider, a group founded in Munich in the early 20th century.

10 *Forest and Garden* Noon

You could take a walk or bike ride in the Englischer Garten, a favorite park near the royal palace. But for quiet and introspection, head for the **Perlacher Forst**, a large forest in the city's southeast with hiking and cycling trails. Pay your respects at the Friedhof am Perlacher Forst cemetery (Stadelheimer Strasse 24), where Sophie Scholl and other members of the White Rose anti-Nazi

ABOVE Warmth and sunshine attracts a basking crowd to the Englischer Garten.

BELOW Station Münchner Freiheit, part of the city's extensive and efficient subway and rail system.

resistance movement are buried, before partaking in Munich's traditional liquid refreshments. For a memorable brew, try the tiny beer garden at the **Forschungsbrauerei** (Unterhachinger Strasse 78; 49-89-670-1169; forschungsbrauerei.de), a former research brewery that functions as a brewpub.

ABOVE Cool and modern, the Museum Brandhorst shows works of Andy Warhol, Cy Twombly, and Damien Hirst. It also has an inviting cafe.

OPPOSITE In the Munich Airport Center, travelers passing through can find architecture worth at least a brief pause. The mall's supermarket is open from dawn to midnight.

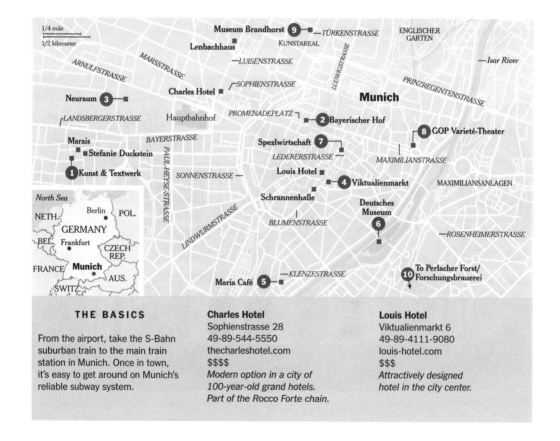

THE BASICS

From the airport, take the S-Bahn suburban train to the main train station in Munich. Once in town, it's easy to get around on Munich's reliable subway system.

Charles Hotel
Sophienstrasse 28
49-89-544-5550
thecharleshotel.com
$$$$
Modern option in a city of 100-year-old grand hotels. Part of the Rocco Forte chain.

Louis Hotel
Viktualienmarkt 6
49-89-4111-9080
louis-hotel.com
$$$
Attractively designed hotel in the city center.

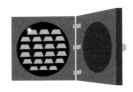

Zurich

Zurich, Switzerland's largest city, is divided into 12 districts, or kreise. The center of town, Kreis 1, is the Zurich the world knows, a global financial capital where the gears of capitalism move with Swiss precision against the backdrop of a cobblestoned Old Town. But Zurich is more than a city of plutocrats and financial courtiers. Kreis 2, which hugs the west side of Lake Zurich, offers entertainment, youth hostels, and handsome beaches. The industrial district of Kreis 5 is filled with big-name contemporary art. And for youthful chaos and culture, take the tram to Kreis 4, where the red-light district is gentrifying and has come alive with bohemian design, food, and night life. — BY ROBERT GOFF

FRIDAY

1 *Water Views* 2 p.m.

The heart of Zurich may seem blemish-free and a little too perfect, but the rigorously preserved medieval and 20th-century architecture is a sight to behold. The setting, on the Limmat and Sihl Rivers and Lake Zurich, is ravishing, too. For the best vantage point, walk south along the western bank of the Limmat and hike up to the **Lindenhof**, once the site of a Roman customs house. (Nearest tram stop is Renneweg.) It's at the highest point of the Old Town and overlooks the city, with views of the nearby hills. For a closer view, get out onto the water. Tour boats leaving from docks at the end of Bahnhofstrasse, the main street, take sightseers on the Limmat, beneath arched bridges and past cityscapes. Or take a commuter boat out onto the lake (zuerich.com/en/visit/getting-around-in-zurich).

2 *Window Shopping* 4 p.m.

Names like Dior and Prada dominate on the storefronts of Bahnhofstrasse, joined by the local label **Akris** (in the Greider department store, Bahnhofstrasse 30; akris.ch) and other well-appointed stores. For less expensive indulgence, stop in at **Sprüngli** (Bahnhofstrasse 21; spruengli. ch), Zurich's favorite chocolatier, which dates to

1836. Next, stroll to **Grossmünster** (Zwingliplatz; 41-44-252-5949; grossmuenster.ch), a church founded by Charlemagne, to see the German artist Sigmar Polke's stained glass windows, installed in 2009. Some are unevenly and lustrously kaleidoscopic; some are a modern take on biblical themes. Other windows in Grossmünster are by **Augusto Giacometti** (uncle of Alberto). The Fraumünster church, just across the river, has Chagall windows.

3 *The Big Giacometti* 6 p.m.

The **Kunsthaus** (Heimplatz 1; 41-44-253-8484; kunsthaus.ch), the city's main art museum, has a collection of 19th-century and early 20th-century European work and is also a notable place to see sculptures by that more famous Giacometti — Alberto, the surrealist known worldwide for his elongated and emaciated figures. The Kunsthaus is easy to navigate in a quick visit, and it's open on Fridays until 8 p.m.

4 *Crossover Fare* 9 p.m.

Step out of the gilded cocoon of the Altstadt and into Kreis 4, where the **Helvetia** (Stauffacherquai 1; 41-44-297-9999; hotel-helvetia.ch; $$$$), a restaurant and boutique hotel just over the Sihl River, divides picture-postcard Zurich and the grittier city you will wish you had more time to explore. In the 1930s, the Helvetia was a meeting place for Communists and other agitators. Today, it draws well-heeled diners seeking modern Swiss cuisine with a seasonal flair. After dinner, have a nightcap at the dark-wood-paneled bar downstairs or on the terrace overlooking the river.

OPPOSITE Flussbad Oberer Letten, a well-loved urban park.

RIGHT Trams connect the Kreise, Zurich's neighborhoods.

SATURDAY

5 *Edgy, Not Naughty* 10 a.m.

At night, the narrow streets of Kreis 4 are populated by sex workers. But by day, it's the young hustlers of fashion and style who rule. Design fetishes are satisfied at **Bord** (Badenerstrasse 123a; 41-43-243-6911; bord.ch), a stripped-down former garage that sells midcentury modern furniture by stalwarts like Jean Prouvé alongside that of up-and-coming designers. For Swiss urban wear, pop into **Street-Files Studio** (Badenerstrasse 156; 41-43-322-0323). Zurich's best young galleries are scattered along these streets, too. And when you're ready for a pick-me-up, choose from the selection of bright, newly minted cafes.

6 *Art to Ogle* 2 p.m.

With so much money sloshing around, it's no surprise that Zurich contains some of the world's fanciest galleries, many of them in a converted Löwenbräu brewery called the **Löwenbräu Areal** (Limmatstrasse 270), in Kreis 5, just northwest of the city center. The complex is also home to the **Kunsthalle Zürich** (kunsthallezurich.ch), a contemporary art museum, and the **Migros Museum** (migrosmuseum.ch), which features its own collection as well as temporary exhibitions of contemporary art. While you're in the area, don't miss the flagship shop of **Freitag** (Geroldstrasse 17; 41-43-366-9520; freitag.ch), a popular maker of stylish bags from recycled materials. The building is made of 17 rusted shipping containers in a pile 85 feet high.

7 *Exalted Company* 5 p.m.

To rub elbows with the captains of capitalism, sidle up at the **Kronenhalle Bar** (Rämistrasse 4; 41-44-262-9900; kronenhalle.com; $$$$), inside one of the city's most venerable restaurants. Dark mahogany paneling, green leather walls, and marble tables with legs designed by yet another Giacometti (Diego, Alberto's brother) exude the Zurich of old money, discretion, and fat Swiss bank accounts. Peek into the restaurant for a look at its renowned art collection, including the likes of Picasso, Miró, and Klee.

8 *Opera Jewel* 7 p.m.

The **Zurich Opera House** (Falkenstrasse 1; 41-44-268-6666; opernhaus.ch) maintains a crowded schedule of high-quality opera and ballet, with world-class singers, conductors, and dancers. This is culture in an elegant setting: the theater is a classic beauty, gilded and ornate, worth an evening for its own sake. Zurich has opera in summer, too, at its arts festival, the Zürcher Festspiele.

9 *Fish Choice* 10 p.m.

It's a quick walk from the opera to the **Opéra Restaurant** in the hotel **Ambassador à l'Opéra** (Falkenstrasse 6; 41-44-258-9898; ambassadorhotel.ch/restaurant; $$$) for a leisurely late dinner in a quiet, stylish dining room. Standard meat dishes like Wienerschnitzel and pork breast are available, but the real specialty is fish. You might find whitefish from Lake Zurich or sea bass with pasta and white beans, but the most interesting option is to choose a fish from the display, specify the way you want it cooked, and sip wine as you wait for it to be served.

ABOVE Boating through Zurich, with its spires and graceful old buildings, on the Limmat River.

BELOW Shop for sweets on Bahnhofstrasse at Sprüngli, Zurich's favorite chocolatier. It traces its history back to 1836.

SUNDAY

10 *Veggie Buffet* 10 a.m.

Please your doctor with brunch at **Hiltl** (Sihlstrasse 28; 41-44-227-7000; hiltl.ch; $$), a huge vegetarian restaurant with an outdoor patio in the Altstadt. Founded in 1898, it has a spectacularly diverse menu—everything from Swiss staples like spaetzle to surprisingly authentic Thai and Indian curries. The casual atmosphere balances out the traditional chandelier-and-linen décor. Go for the buffet, which is all-you-can-eat or priced by weight.

11 *Bathing and Beauty* Noon

In warm-weather months, the **Flussbad Oberer Letten** (Lennsteg 10; badi-info.ch/oberer_letten.html), in the middle of Zurich, is a laid-back, all-welcoming,

antiurban riverfront oasis. Bohemians and bankers, athletes and young mothers go there to unwind, swim, and play volleyball. A patchwork of wooden terraces and squares of grass encrusts the banks, with room to stretch out for a nap or picnic with friends. Cafes and small beer gardens abound, offering a perfect place to return to after exploring the larger city.

ABOVE The flagship store of Freitag, a popular maker of stylish bags from recycled materials. The store itself is made from 17 shipping containers.

THE BASICS

An inexpensive train from the airport reaches the city center in 10 minutes. Use a transit pass to hop on and off trams, buses, and ferries.

Greulich Hotel
Herman-Greulich-Strasse 56
41-43-243-4243
greulich.ch
$$$
A full-service 28-room boutique hotel with clean, stylish décor and a tree-shaded courtyard.

Limmatblick Hotel
Limmatquai 136
41-44-254-6000
limmatblick.ch
$$
Honors Dada, a Zurich invention, with Dadist-inspired artistic touches and room names. Bar may be noisy.

Basel

When it comes to contemporary art and architecture, Basel, Switzerland, seems an unlikely hotbed. Hugging a bend of the Rhine River where Switzerland, France, and Germany meet, this picturesque enclave of fewer than 200,000 residents has the quaintness of a small town. But every June, tens of thousands of artists, collectors, and dealers from around the world descend for Art Basel, the mother ship of contemporary art fairs. One need not rub so many shoulders, however, to enjoy the city's cultural offerings. Flush with pharmaceutical money (Novartis and Roche have headquarters there), Basel is home to an astounding array of museums and important art collections that are accessible year-round. It is also a showcase for new architecture, best exemplified by the cache of buildings by the hometown firm of Herzog & de Meuron. Basel may be small in size, but its creative pulse and overheated arts scene are more befitting of a teeming metropolis. — BY ARIC CHEN AND STEVEN ERLANGER

FRIDAY

1 *Basel Builders* 2 p.m.

This capital of cutting-edge architecture has simply too many distinguished buildings to see in one trip: among them, buildings by Richard Meier, Mario Botta, Diener & Diener, and, of course, Herzog & de Meuron. Pick up an architecture brochure at the **Basel Tourism** office on Barfüsserplatz (Steinenberg 14; 41-61-268-6868; www.basel.com/en). As you make your way around town, you will find yourself referring to its map and key.

2 *First, the Holbeins* 2:30 p.m.

It's nearly impossible to look up in Basel without seeing a museum, whether it's of fine arts, dolls, cartoons, or even paper. You will be in special danger of overdosing on modern and contemporary art, so start with the traditional at the **Kunstmuseum Basel** (St. Alban-Graben 16; 41-61-206-6262; kunstmuseumbasel.ch), which has the world's largest collection of Hans Holbein paint-

ings. Hold on to your ticket in case you find time later to get to the other museum it also covers, the **Museum of Contemporary Art**, or Gegenwartskunst, a few blocks away (St. Alban-Rheinweg 60; 41-61-206-6262). It specializes in post-1960s artists like Joseph Beuys, Robert Gober, and Matthew Barney.

3 *Rhineland* 6 p.m.

Earlier architects arrived sometime in the 14th century to build a still-dominant downtown landmark, the Gothic cathedral, or **Münster** (Rittergasse 3; baslermuenster.ch). Its two red sandstone spires are unmissable, and the cathedral square makes a good orienting point amid the cobblestone streets nearby, which are worth a wander. The old city on this side of the river is Altstadt Grossbasel, or Big Basel; look across to the small winding streets of Kleinbasel (Little Basel), which occupies part of a curious municipal salient that's actually surrounded by Germany. To cross the Rhine, you could go by tram or on foot using one of the six bridges, but a more atmospheric way is to take one of Basel's unusual wooden ferryboats. Propelled solely by the current, they are attached to cables and steered by oar. You can catch one near the Münster.

4 *Pasta Serra* 8 p.m.

For dinner where the art crowd gathers, go to **Chez Donati** (St. Johanns-Vorstadt 48; 41-61-322-0919; lestroisrois.com; $$$-$$$$). Wood-paneled and traditional, it has a kind of Mediterranean warmth fitting for its Piedmontese theme. There's an outdoor balcony with a pretty riverside view, and the elegant

OPPOSITE Basel is a center of contemporary architecture. This fire station by Zaha Hadid is on the Vitra Furniture campus.

RIGHT The headquarters building of Art Basel.

interior is outfitted with works on paper by Willem de Kooning, Richard Serra, and others.

SATURDAY

5 *Dealer's Display* 10 a.m.

There's much more on the must-see museum circuit, and some of it comes with must-see architecture. Take the No. 6 tram to the **Fondation Beyeler** (Baselstrasse 101; 41-61-645-9700; fondationbeyeler.ch),

ABOVE Outside the Fondation Beyeler gallery.

BELOW A work at the annual Art Basel, the premier international fair of contemporary art.

a Renzo Piano-designed gallery that houses an extraordinary collection of Picassos, Cézannes, Rothkos, and Légers, and mounts special exhibitions. Ernst Beyeler, the dealer who made a fortune selling modern art, established this exquisite museum.

6 *Contemporary Spin* 1 p.m.

Back in Grossbasel, head to the **Kunsthalle Basel** (Steinenberg 7; 41-61-206-9900; kunsthallebasel.ch) for art that's strictly of the moment, as well as an outdoor restaurant that's another favorite of the Art Basel crowd. Take time for a walk to the nearby Theaterplatz to see the **Tinguely Brunnen**, a fountain by the kinetic sculptor Jean Tinguely. It's an odd-looking collection of squirters, spinners, and ungainly-looking shapes that spray in whimsical harmony.

7 *Art on the Move* 3 p.m.

See more of Tinguely's playful productions at the **Museum Tinguely** (Paul Sacher-Anlage 1;

41-61-681-9320; tinguely.ch), in a building designed by Mario Botta. Kids especially will love the work, which combines wit, high art, and a Rube Goldberg kind of gearing. They can stamp a button on the floor to get the sculptures to move, and even clamber over some of them. Don't miss the amazing *Grosse Méta Maxi-Maxi Utopia* of 1987 or the paralyzing and hypnotic ode to death *Mengele Totentanz*, a set of 14 machine sculptures constructed from the charred remains of a farmhouse and stable.

8 *Search for Adornment* 5 p.m.

If you find yourself underdressed in this well-heeled city, head to Freie Strasse, the main shopping street, for all your St. Laurent and Jil Sander emergencies. The Swiss fashion temple **Trois Pommes** has

BELOW At the Hotel Der Teufelhof, each guest room is conceived by a different designer. This one, Room No. 9, is the work of the Swiss designer Lea Achermann.

a store at No. 74 (41-61-272-9255; troispommes.ch). For more offbeat, but equally fashionable wares, including antiques and jewelry, explore the area around Schneidergasse and Spalenberg Streets. Find clever accessories and totes at **Seven Sisters** (Spalenberg 38; 41-61-262-0980; sevensisters.ch) and a tightly edited trove of well-designed clothing and objects at **Hand Made** (Nadelberg 47; 41-61-261-3161; h-made.ch).

9 *Deer and Apricot* 8 p.m.

One of the best and most imaginative meals you will have in Basel is south of the city center at **Stucki** (Bruderholzallee 42; 41-61-361-8222; stuckibasel.ch; $$$$), a house with a long lawn and garden. The owner and chef, Tanja Grandits, combines local products with touches of Asia and offers a superb wine list. She has combined saddle of deer with ginger pimento tea, roasted pumpkin, and apricot paste, and has served codfish steamed with green tea, tarragon taboule, and sesame leek.

10 *Bar Scene* 10:30 p.m.

During the art fair, virtually everyone ends up at the **Campari Bar** at the Kunsthalle Basel. Many gravitate to its leafy outdoor garden (Steinenberg 7; 41-61-272-8383). This is the kind of spot where minor aristocrats and other heirs and heiresses have been known to steadily lose composure as the night unfolds. For a place to unwind from on high, ride the elevator to the mellower **Bar Rouge** (Messeplatz 10; 41-61-361-3031; barrouge.ch), a red-swathed lounge with 31st-floor views.

SUNDAY

11 *Viva Vitra* 11 a.m.

Save that last bit of energy for the Vitra campus, 20 minutes away by bus in Weil am Rhein, Germany. Vitra, the famous furniture maker, has turned its assembly plant into an architectural wonderland with buildings by Zaha Hadid, Tadao Ando, Jean Prouvé, and others. The **Vitra Design Museum** (Charles-Eames-Strasse 2; 49-7621-702-3200; design-museum. de), by Frank Gehry, takes center stage.

ABOVE Dining with a Rhine River view at Chez Donati.

OPPOSITE Inside the Vitra Design Museum, by Frank Gehry, at the Vitra furniture complex in Weil am Rhein.

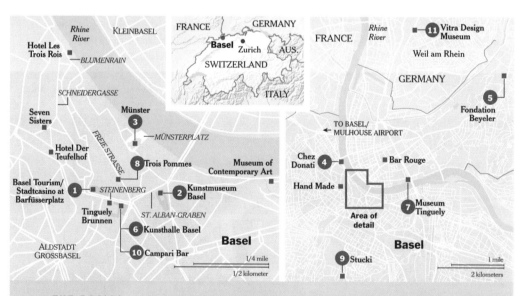

THE BASICS

Fly to Basel/Mulhouse, shared by Basel and neighboring cities in France and Germany, or land in Zurich and take a train to Basel. Within moments of arrival at Basel hotels, all guests are given their first taste of the city's hospitality: a free pass to the city's trams and buses for a stay of up to 30 days.

Hotel Les Trois Rois
Blumenrain 8
41-61-260-5050
lestroisrois.com
$$$$
Famed luxury hotel on the Rhine.

Hotel Der Teufelhof
Leonhardsgraben 49
41-61-261-1010
teufelhof.com
$$$
Small hotel with a strong focus on art and design.

Bern

Ask a Swiss to describe Bern and you may hear a joke about how the people move so slowly that their souls take centuries to reach heaven. While it is true that this city of about 140,000 people in western Switzerland must be counted among the most relaxed of Europe's capitals, Bern is also one of the most beautiful, a pocket-size Prague of arcades and whimsical fountains, all framed by leafy hills and the glacial-green currents of the Aare River. The urban and rural mingle closely here. Forests of ash and oak push up against a clutch of embassies off a city square. You can dance till dawn or rise early and take a walk under the gaze of the Alps and be back in time for lunch. Why rush through that? — BY TIM NEVILLE

FRIDAY

1 *Mountain Views* 5 p.m.

The terrace bar of the **Bellevue Palace** (Kochergasse 3-5; 41-31-320-4545; bellevue-palace. ch), a luxurious Art Nouveau hotel whose guests have included Nelson Mandela and Winston Churchill, offers sweeping views of the Alps to the south and is one of the few places in the city that sells stiff (though pricey) cocktails. Try the Fancy Hendrick's, with cucumber syrup and lemon juice, or a tumbler of Swiss Highland single malt, aged in an ice cave on the Jungfrau, a 13,000-foot mountain you can see from the deck.

2 *Above the River* 7 p.m.

Few restaurants can offer riverside dining like the **Schwellenmätteli** (Dalmaziquai 11; 41-31-350-5001; schwellenmaetteli.ch; $$), where swift currents course beneath a deck cantilevered over the Aare. The terrace menu tips toward Mediterranean with dishes like tilapia and polenta; go inside for Italian cuisine like tagliatelle with scallops and saffron. For dessert, walk up the hill to **Restaurant Luce** (Zeughausgasse 28; 41-31-310-9999; ristoranteluce. ch) for a creamy tiramisu big enough for two.

OPPOSITE Bern, a city of laid-back charm, rewards those who are willing to slow to its pace.

RIGHT Vintage style at Glanz & Gloria. Bern's arcades offer miles of covered shopping promenades.

3 *No Yodeling* 11 p.m.

In 1987 anarchists and leftist groups commandeered a defunct horse-riding school near the main train station. Since then the **Reitschule**, a graffiti-covered complex, has evolved into one of Bern's most colorful performance and entertainment centers. On Friday nights white-collar professionals sit next to purple-haired punks over bottles of Einsiedler beer inside the **Sous le Pont** restaurant, while bands from all over the world rock late into the night in the **Dachstock** venue upstairs. In the heart of the compound you'll find the **Frauenraum**, one of the city's few lesbian-centric hangouts (Neubrückstrasse 8; 41-31-306-6969; www.reitschule.ch).

SATURDAY

4 *Market Meal* 9 a.m.

Every Saturday and Tuesday morning, artisan butchers and cheesemakers converge on **Parliament Square** (the Bundesplatz) to sell smoked meats, cheese, and pastries. For breakfast, head to the northwest corner of the square and look across the street, Schauplatzgasse, where you'll see Bernese lined up for bulbous loaves of zopf, a traditional bread, and warm raisin pastries called schnägge, or snails, named for their spiral shape. Grab a coffee from the **Beck Glatz Confiseur** a few blocks east at

Marktgass-Passage 1 (41-31-300-2020; glatz-bern.ch) and fuel up for the walk ahead.

5 *City Stroll* 10 a.m.

At more than 800 years old, Bern has had plenty of time to develop architectural quirks. Most visitors never notice; don't be one of them. Head to the **Bern Tourism Office** in the main railway station (Bahnhofplatz 10a; 41-31-328-1212; bern.com) and rent an iPod preloaded with a multimedia guide (complete with local music and photos) that complements a self-guided walking tour of the oldest parts of the city. You'll wander by a section of the former city wall and see the house at Mattenenge 2 that bears a cannonball mark made by Bernese rebels who fired on the city during an uprising in 1802.

6 *Of Bears and Brews* Noon

Visit **BärenPark**, a 64,500-square-foot grassy enclosure that houses the city's mascots, brown bears named Björk, Finn, and Ursina (Grosser Muristalden 6; 41-31-357-1525; baerenpark-bern.ch). The **Altes Tramdepot** (Grosser Muristalden 6; 41-31-368-1415; altestramdepot.ch; $$) next to the park brews the best Hefeweizen in town and serves a decent bacon and onion spaetzle. Climb the steep cobblestone path across the street, Alter Aargauerstalden, for views of the city from the **Rosengarten** (Alter Aargauerstalden 31b; 41-31-331-3206; rosengarten.be), a park with 220 types of roses and a restaurant that serves a fine lunch. Look for items like pork saltimbocca and saffron risotto ($$).

7 *Undercover* 2 p.m.

With more than 3.5 miles of arcades, Bern offers some of the longest covered shopping promenades in Europe. Madeleine Lüthi stocks her shop, **Glanz & Gloria** (Brunngasse 48; 41-31-311-1950), with vintage women's clothing. The Tschirren family has been making chocolate in Bern since 1919, and you

can taste their Champagne truffles and pralines at their shop, **Confiserie Tschirren**, on Kramgasse 73 (41-31-311-1717; www.swiss-chocolate.ch). **Heimatwerk** (Kramgasse 61; 41-31-311-3000; heimatwerk.ch) carries high-end fondue pots, edelweiss neckties, and Mondaine clocks designed to look like those used at Swiss train stations.

8 *Snack Time* 4 p.m.

So many Swiss Germans stop what they're doing at 4 p.m. for a snack break that the tradition even has a name: z'vieri, not to be confused with z'nüni, the 9 a.m. version. Swing by **Adriano's** (Theaterplatz 2; 41-31-318-8831; adrianos.ch; $$), a lively cafe where hip baristas pull espresso shots through ground beans roasted no more than 72 hours ago. One sandwich in particular, with bûche de chèvre cheese, dried figs, arugula, and acacia honey on whole-grain bread, is a fine way to ruin your dinner.

9 *Cheese Melt* 7 p.m.

Few self-respecting Swiss would eat a meal of melted cheese before it's cold outside, but tourists

OPPOSITE The outdoor terrace at the Sous le Pont.

ABOVE Salad of the day at Zehendermätteli.

RIGHT Berries at the market on Parliament Square.

can get away with it anytime. **Le Mazot** (Bärenplatz 5; 41-31-311-7088; mazot-bern.ch; $$-$$$) remains popular for its numerous fondues, but if you're willing to trade the cozy wood-wall ambience for contemporary décor, head to **Lötschberg** (Zeughaus-gasse 16; 41-31-311-3455; loetschberg-aoc.ch; $$), where the fondues themselves are more traditional — true Gruyère-vacherin mixes with garlic and fendant, a Swiss white wine. Call ahead to reserve a table in a gondola car parked outside.

10 *Jazz Time* 9 p.m.

While Montreux, on Lake Geneva, might host the best-known jazz festival, Bern is home to a jazz school, its own festival and **Mahogany Hall**, a club started in 1968 on the riverbank, where

Swiss musicians like Philipp Fankhauser and Stephan Eicher once played. Today's Mahogany Hall (Klösterlistutz 18; 41-31-331-6000; mahogany.ch), next to the BärenPark, has room for 180 people, and the music ranges from Dixie jazz to funk and soul.

SUNDAY

11 *Bern Rolls* 10 a.m.

Sundays are slow in Bern, with most shops closed: a good day for a bike ride. Four rental stations offer free bicycles for up to four hours, after you've provided a small deposit. The main pickup point, on Milchgässli at the southwest corner of Bern's main train station (41-79-277-2857 on-call service; bernrollt.ch), also rents electric bikes. Ride out of town through the woodsy Enge peninsula, where Roman roads lead past the ruins of an ancient bath, toward a drift ferry that shuttles hikers across the Aare. Take a left before reaching the ruins and stop at the **Zehendermätteli** (Reichenbachstrasse 161; 41-31-301-5447; zehendermaetteli.ch; $$$), a restaurant at a working farm. The cheese selection is enormous, and it comes with the brunch trimmings you'd expect.

ABOVE Vintage accessories at Glanz & Gloria.

OPPOSITE Summer at Zehendermätteli.

THE BASICS

Bern is about 75 miles from Zurich. Arrive by train and take trams and buses in town, or walk. In the compact city center, with few places to park, a rental car is impractical.

Hotel Schweizerhof
Bahnhofplatz 11
41-31-326-8080
schweizerhof-bern.ch
$$$$
Guests like Grace Kelly and Albert Schweitzer precede you at this 150-year-old hotel. It's been renovated, but your room may still have a chandelier.

Hotel Landhaus
Altenbergstrasse 4-6
41-31-348-0305
landhausbern.ch
$$
Basic but comfortable rooms at the edge of the old city.

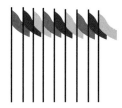

Geneva

Geneva, tucked in a corner of Switzerland that just misses being France, is a cosmopolitan hub. Skiers on their way to the Alps, diplomats negotiating treaties, business types making contacts, and shoppers with an eye for the most elegant of watches and chocolates all pass through. The sweeping vistas are over Lake Geneva, the river spilling out of it is the Rhône, and on clear days you might see snow-capped Mont Blanc floating in the horizon. Inside its medieval ramparts, Geneva long served as a cultural haven for the world's exiles and freethinkers, and Switzerland's famous neutrality still makes it a comfortable city for a community of expatriate polyglots, many of whom work for international agencies like the Red Cross and the United Nations. — BY FINN-OLAF JONES

FRIDAY

1 *Date With a Fountain* 4:30 p.m.

Walk or bicycle along the glamorous lakefront, starting at the immaculate **Jardin Anglais**, with its famous 15-foot flower clock, one of Geneva's signature sights. Then glide over to the Jetée des Eaux-Vives, a breakwater that leads out to the **Jet d'Eau**, one of the world's largest fountains. From afar, the fountain might not seem remarkable. But from under the 459-foot-tall column of misting water, it's an awesome spectacle, especially when it's illuminated at night. (Find wheels at **Rent a Bike** — 41-41-925-1170, rent-a-bike.ch — at the Gare Cornavin, the main train station.)

2 *Fondue Rendezvous* 8 p.m.

Every visitor to Switzerland should sample at least one bubbling cauldron of cheesy stuff, and **Restaurant les Armures**, inside the Hôtel les Armures (1 rue Puits-St-Pierre; 41-22-310-3442; hotel-les-armures.ch; $$$), is a fondue institution. It's at the top of Old Town, which winds around a hill on the Left Bank of the lake and river, and inside there are wooden beams on the ceiling and muskets on the wall. If you're famished, order the cheese fondue with mushrooms.

OPPOSITE Geneva, Lake Geneva, and the Jet d'Eau.

RIGHT Fondue at Restaurant les Armures.

3 *Crossroads for Cocktails* 10 p.m.

Walk dinner off with a stroll through the narrow medieval streets and head toward one of the city's favorite meeting places, the leafy **Place du Bourg-de-Four**, the former medieval marketplace in the heart of Old Town. A dozen restaurants and cafes surround a tiny 18th-century marble fountain in the cobblestone square. **La Clémence** (20 place du Bourg-de-Four; 41-22-312-2498; laclemence.ch) is a popular morning spot for café au lait and a croissant, and at night its drinks list draws a lively mix of students, businesspeople, and politicians.

SATURDAY

4 *Christian Contrast* 10 a.m.

Though the walls of the tiny Old Town are covered in graffiti, the cobblestones and stone facades look much as they did during the Reformation, when John Calvin and John Knox found refuge there and created a "Protestant Rome." Signs of the Reformation are evident at **Cathédrale St.-Pierre** (cours St.-Pierre; 41-22-311-7575; saintpierre-geneve.ch) with its green-copper spire crowning the hill. A side chapel with 15th-century angel frescoes is a riotous contrast to the austerity of the cathedral's nave, which was stripped of its decorations by 16th-century Protestant reformers. Climb to the top of the north tower for an expansive view over the city and the lake.

5 *Discover the Swiss* 1:30 p.m.

The airy **Musée d'Art et d'Histoire** (2 rue Charles-Galland; 41-22-418-2600; ville-ge.ch/mah)

displays an admirable cross section of European art, including exceptional works by Monet, Renoir, van Gogh, Cézanne, and Picasso. Head to the second-floor galleries and get lost in the Genevoise landscapes of the Swiss painters François Diday and his student Alexandre Calame.

6 *Villa Voltaire* 3 p.m.

Anyone who says there's no money in philosophy should visit Voltaire's former home, now the **Institut et Musée Voltaire** (25 rue des Délices; 41-22-418-9560; ville-ge.ch/imv). Voltaire was a shrewd businessman, and his writings on liberty and his sharp wit won him rich and powerful patrons, including Catherine the Great and Frederick the Great. From his Palladian villa set in an immaculate garden, Voltaire in the 18th century set forth the ideas that would help spark the French Revolution. You can read them, along with his personal letters and manuscripts, in the philosopher's sumptuous salons.

7 *Do You Have the Time?* 5 p.m.

If there's any doubt that you're in the world capital of watches, wander down Rue du Rhône with its diamond-encrusted and gold-plated shops. Check out **Bucherer** (No. 45; 41-22-319-6266; bucherer.com), which has been selling high-end timepieces since 1888 and has what is thought to be the world's largest selection of Rolexes. If you're looking for something in the $50,000

range, this is the place to stop. Not unusual enough? Go up the street to **Marconi** (No. 53; 41-22-311-3630; marconigeneve.com), a boutique watchmaker that makes only small-run editions. Its jewel-encrusted, over-the-top productions look like something Willy Wonka would wear if he could afford them.

8 *Alpine Arabia* 8 p.m.

Geneva has a growing Middle Eastern community, as evidenced by Arabic script on some storefronts, banks, and offices. For a cultural taste, follow your nose to Rue de Berne, where Libyan bakeries, small teahouses, and Middle Eastern restaurants stand side-by-side with the city's small and surprisingly tidy red-light district. **La Caravane Passe** (11 rue du Dr. Alfred-Vincent; 41-22-731-3431; lacaravanepasse. ch; $$) is a casual family-run restaurant. Order one of its traditional meze dishes or anything with lamb and wash it down with pots of foaming mint tea.

9 *Technocrats* 11 p.m.

Geneva tends to shut down early, but there are a few spots where you can party. The music can be funk, soul, rock or even, gasp, Euro-pop at **Zoé Live Bar** (23 rue Ferdinand Hodler; 41-22-777-1515; zoelivebar.com) where the doors don't even open on Saturdays until 11 p.m. The crowd dances to bands from across Europe and to D.J.'s when the bands stop, the lively scene sometimes almost

overheated by moving and flashing lights. The only drawback: you have to leave by 5 a.m.

SUNDAY

10 *The League* 11 a.m.

When you hear news reports of "negotiations taking place in Geneva," they invariably refer to the **Palais des Nations** (14 avenue de la Paix; 41-22-917-4896; unog.ch), home to the second-largest United Nations office, after the center in New York. Sprawled along Geneva's Right Bank, this complex of grand offices was built from 1929 to 1936 to serve as the headquarters of the League of Nations. When the United Nations was formed after World War II, the League buildings became its European headquarters, housing an alphabet soup of organizations like Unicef and WHO. The hourlong tours — in any of the organization's six official languages — take you through the enormous Assembly Hall and the commemorative galleries. Later, stroll the surrounding 87.5-acre **Parc de L'Ariana**. Avoid being nipped by the peacocks that roam wild. In a city as safe as Geneva, this might be the greatest danger you'll face.

OPPOSITE Walk out on the breakwater for a close-up view of the Jet d'Eau, a 459-foot-tall column of misting water.

ABOVE At the Musée d'Art et d'Histoire, climb to the second floor to see Genevoise landscapes by Swiss painters.

THE BASICS

Arrive by train or plane. From Cointrin International Airport, take the six-minute train ride to the central rail station, Gare Cornavin. In the city, plan to walk or use taxis.

Hôtel de la Cigogne
17 place Longemalle
41-22-818-4040
cigogne.ch
$$$$
Elegant lodging on a quiet square between the lake and Old Town.

Hotel Admiral
8 rue Pellegrino Rossi
41-22-906-9700
hoteladmiral.ch
$$
Simple and comfortable rooms near the train station.

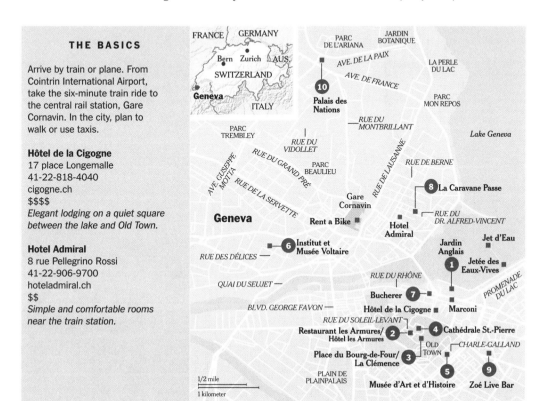

Lake Geneva

Croissant-shaped Lake Geneva, 45 miles long, is the largest, deepest, and bluest of Swiss lakes, and its beauty is only heightened by its surroundings — thriving vineyards, historic architecture, and, in the distance, peaks dipped in snow all year round. The winters are mild and the summers hot and dry, earning its shores the title "Swiss Riviera." There are even palm trees at the eastern end, and the water is warm enough for swimming from pebble beaches from June to September. A parade of notable tourists and expatriates have passed through since at least as far back as 1816, when Lord Byron, Percy Bysshe Shelley, and Mary Wollstonecraft Godwin (soon to be Mary Shelley) arrived for a summer that turned out to provide far more Gothic inspiration than anyone had expected.
— BY TONY PERROTTET

FRIDAY

1 *Ripples of Inspiration* 1 p.m.

The trains are efficient, but take a leisurely trip from Geneva to Lausanne at least partway on an antique paddle steamer (41-84-881-1848; cgn.ch). Mary Shelley raved in her letters about the near-tropical color of the lake, "blue as the heavens which it reflects," and you may feel called to do the same. A distant volcanic eruption turned Europe's weather freakish in 1816, while the poets and their friends were staying near Geneva, and Mary wrote then of "an almost perpetual rain." Terrific thunderstorms rippled back and forth across the lake. One night, perhaps assisted by an evening of wine and laudanum, Mary experienced the famous nightmare that gave her the plot for *Frankenstein*. She soon set about writing it, using Lake Geneva as one of the settings. Lord Byron picked up the mood and had an idea for a vampire tale; another member of the party, John Polidori, wrote it up as a sinister short story, "The Vampyre," that later influenced Bram Stoker's *Dracula*.

2 *Soirée Story* 3 p.m.

Stop at Coppet to see perhaps the most evocative relic from 1816: the **Château de Coppet** (swisscastles.ch/vaud/coppet), mansion of Madame de Staël, whose salon was the only one in Switzerland that Byron would deign to attend. She was famous for her best-selling novels, her collection of famous lovers, and

her soirées attracting the greatest minds of Europe. The count who now lives in the chateau opens many of its rooms to the public. Walk through to see the original furnishings, including Madame de Staël's personal bathtub and pianoforte.

3 *Captain's Table* 6:30 p.m.

The most distinctive gastronomic experience at Lake Geneva (called Lac Léman by the French, who claim part of the shore) is a meal on one of the Belle Époque ferries of the CGN line (cgn.ch). Dine in aristocratic style, in a mint-condition dining room of walnut paneling and linen, as you gaze at terraced vineyards and sip Swiss sauvignon blanc.

4 *Go Vertical* 8 p.m.

Lausanne, the most spectacular and vibrant city on Lake Geneva, extends from its harbor up steep hills crowned by a Gothic cathedral. High-tech funiculars let you easily explore vertically as well as horizontally, and the view from the hills out over the lake, backed by the Savoy Alps, is spectacular. Find the Place St.-François, a lively square that is the hub of town. For a vaguely bohemian vibe, head to **Le Bleu Lézard** (Rue Enning 10, Lausanne; 41-21-321-3830; bleu-lezard.ch), which has a cafe-restaurant upstairs and a nightclub below.

OPPOSITE Lake Geneva fired Lord Byron's romantic imagination and put Mary Shelley in the mood to create *Frankenstein*.

BELOW The medieval Château de Chillon, already a tourist attraction when Byron and Shelley visited in 1816.

SATURDAY

5 *Olympic Event* 10 a.m.

When the rain finally eased back in 1816, Shelley and Byron set sail for the eastern end of the lake. In Lausanne, they stayed in Ouchy, the port area below town. Their inn has been expanded into the glamorous lakeside Hotel d'Angleterre, with blood-red velvet armchairs and contemporary art on every wall. Some of its guests may be on business of the International Olympic Committee, which has its headquarters nearby and runs the **Olympic Museum** (Quai d'Ouchy 1, Lausanne; 41-21-621-6511; olympic.org/museum), a must-stop if you're an Olympics fan. Video walls and interactive consoles bring back all of the great

moments, from Johnny Weissmuller's victorious swim in Amsterdam in 1928 to ski events of the 21st century. Other exhibits include displays of artifacts from the original Olympics in ancient Greece.

6 *Outsider Art* 11 a.m.

Art Brut is the unschooled, often enigmatic artwork of people who have lived isolated from larger artistic influences and gone off on creative tangents all their own: shut-ins, loners, eccentrics, mental patients, prisoners. Some 10,000 such items were assembled by the painter Jean Dubuffet over three decades and in 1975 donated to the city of Lausanne. See them and others at **Collection de l'Art Brut** (Avenue des Bergières 11, Lausanne; 41-21-315-2570; artbrut.ch), a fascinating trip into byways of the artistic impulse and the human mind.

7 *Next Stop: Vevey* 1 p.m.

Nestled between terraced vineyards, the lake, and Alpine peaks, Vevey, the hometown and head-quarters of Nestlé, has long attracted authors and

ABOVE A hiking path in Lauterbrunnen, high in the Alps.

LEFT Byron's name carved at the Château de Chillon. He was moved by the story of a prisoner once held in the dungeon.

OPPOSITE Peaks of the Alps over Lake Geneva.

artists. Henry James set the first half of *Daisy Miller* at the Hotel des Trois Couronnes, still a luxury hostelry. The **Vevey Tourist Office** (Grande-Place 29, Vevey; 41-84-886-8484; montreux-vevey.com) on the main square of the picturesque Old Town, will be happy to point you to the spots once frequented by Dostoyevsky, Hemingway, Courbet, Le Corbusier, and other icons of high culture, not to mention the bronze statue of Charlie Chaplin on the Quai Perdonnet. In 1730, Jean-Jacques Rousseau stayed nearby. Have a lunch of grilled lake fish at the **Café La Clef** (rue du Théâtre 1; 41-21-921-2245; $$).

8 *Pillar Talk* 3:30 p.m.

Take a brief walk on the waterfront promenade in the fashionable town of Montreux. Lined with gardens, it is normally a quiet spot, although less placid during the Montreux Jazz Festival each July. Then stroll two miles along the lakefront (or take a ferry) to the **Château de Chillon** (Avenue de Chillon 21, Veytaux; 41-21-966-8910; chillon.ch), a medieval fortress whose turrets rise dreamlike from the waters. Stairs inside lead up through endless chambers, many with traces of medieval frescoes, into the highest keep, where every arrow slit offers a stunning lake view. The dungeon is still a major attraction, as is the pillar where Byron's name is carved — though perhaps not by Byron himself. Byron and Shelley did visit here, and were moved by the macabre story of a 16th-century political prisoner who was chained to a pillar in the dungeon for six years. In their hotel in Ouchy, Byron stayed up late into the night writing *The Prisoner of Chillon*, a chilling work and one of his most popular poems.

9 *Dinner by the Tracks* 8 p.m.

A train station restaurant is seldom the obvious choice for dinner, but **Buffet de la Gare de Clarens** (rue du Collège 5, Clarens; 41-21-964-5050; buffetdelagare-clarens.ch; $$$) may be the smart choice. The service is warm and friendly, and the

wood-paneled room is pleasant, with the occasional train reminding you where you are. In warm weather, outdoor tables are available. The international wine list includes bottles from Montreux. Dinner can be adventurous, perhaps filet of horse, or less so, maybe rack of lamb or asparagus risotto. Incidentally, Clarens is where Rousseau composed and set a favorite novel of his era, *Julie, or the New Heloise.*

SUNDAY

10 *Peak Train* 7:45 a.m.

Get up early for the stunning train ride from Montreux to **Interlaken**, a Victorian resort town once favored by Mendelssohn, Mark Twain, and Queen Victoria herself. (Golden Pass Line; 41-84-024-5245; goldenpass.ch). The panoramic carriages offer sweeping views over the whole of Lake Geneva, then delve through tunnels and switchbacks into the heart of the Alps, where the three signature peaks of the Jungfrau, Eiger, and Mönch loom like a Lindt chocolate box cover. Byron and his party made grueling excursions by horse and mule to see these vistas; you'll make the trip to Interlaken and back in a few hours. If you can take the time, make an extra stop in the village of **Lauterbrunnen**, stunningly set in a deep gorge. Byron described one of its waterfalls as "the tail of a white horse streaming in the wind."

ABOVE Madame de Stäel's home, where great minds met.

OPPOSITE A rainy Saturday evening in Montreux, a lakeside town long favored by the rich and fashionable.

THE BASICS

Trains from Geneva and its airport run to Lausanne, Vevey, and Montreux. Ferries crisscross the entire lake.

Angleterre & Residence
Place du Port 11, Lausanne
41-21-613-3434
angleterre-residence.ch
$$$
Where Byron and Shelley stayed in the summer of 1816.

Fairmont le Montreux Palace
Avenue Claude Nobs 2, Montreux
41-21-962-1212
fairmont.com/montreux
$$$$
Belle Époque luxury. Vladimir Nabokov's residence for 16 years.

Map labels:

6 Collection de l'Art Brut
4 Le Bleu Lézard
Lausanne
2 miles
3 kilometers
SWITZERLAND
E72
5 Olympic Museum
E62
Angleterre & Residence
Café La Clef
Buffet de la Gare de Clarens
Lake Geneva
9
Vevey
Vevey Tourist Office 7
Clarens **Montreux**
FRANCE GERMANY
Fairmont le Montreux Palace
•Zurich
SWITZERLAND AUS.
Area of detail
ITALY
Thunersee Brienzersee
Interlaken 10
Area of detail
Lauterbrunnen
Lake Geneva
Veytaux
SWITZERLAND
Coppet
2 Château de Coppet
8 Château de Chillon
1 Geneva
20 miles
FRANCE
30 kilometers

Zermatt

Zermatt is defined by altitude, by the principle of the vertical, where the highest peaks in Switzerland tower overhead on all sides. To glide among the pale blue glaciers, breathing the hard, clean wind on nearly 200 miles of marked trails, is the essence of skiing. The town is rich in history, dating back to the famously fatal climbing accident that ended the first successful ascent of the Matterhorn and cemented the town's legend. Glitz and glamour may be the allure, but class and understatement are still the rule, with a mum discretion among the town's famous guests that would not be out of place in Zurich's private banks.
— BY NICHOLAS KULISH

FRIDAY

1 *Watch Out* 4 p.m.

Ski trips usually begin with the realization of an absence, the taunting solitary glove or partnerless wool sock. Zermatt's main commercial street, Bahnhofstrasse, can fill most worldly wants, as well as orient you to the town itself. Start at the train station and pop into the bakery **Biner** (Bahnhofplatz 1; 41-27-967-7007; biner.ch) for mini baumnusstörtli, a Swiss walnut treat, to nibble as you walk the cobblestone lane. For luxury watches, visit **Haute Horlogerie Schindler** (Bahnhofstrasse 5; 41-27-967-1118; schindler-zermatt.ch), which carries timepieces by Cartier, Blancpain, and Vacheron Constantin. Duck into one of the kitschy cuckoo clock stores down the block to catch your breath from the five-figure price tags. It may be the first — but not the last — sticker shock you'll encounter in Zermatt.

2 *Mountain Icon* 6 p.m.

The stark, jagged silhouette of the Matterhorn is the symbol of Zermatt, as well as a local obsession, featured on every photograph and logo as if required by law. To understand why, visit the subterranean **Matterhorn Museum** (Kirchplatz 11; 41-27-967-4100; zermatt.ch). Enter through the 3-D glass rendering of

OPPOSITE The village of Zermatt, high in the Alps, and its signature peak, the Matterhorn.

RIGHT The forbidding Matterhorn challenges climbers and is a landmark to skiers on some of the world's best slopes.

the mountain jutting upward in the town's Kirchplatz. Follow the stairs down to discover a village being excavated by archaeologists. Exhibitions range from a Neolithic stone ax to the very rope that snapped and sent four of the first climbers to reach the Matterhorn's summit to their deaths. The museum is a good primer, but nothing resonates like the rough tombstones at the nearby church, where the climbers are buried.

3 *The Lilt of the Lamb* 8 p.m.

There are more than a few mediocre, yet overpriced, restaurants in Zermatt specializing in uninspired lamb dishes. The taxidermy- and glitter-filled funhouse **Chez Heini** (Wiestistrasse 45; 41-27-967-1630; dandaniell.ch; $$$$) is the happy exception, a cult favorite in town for its food and madcap décor. The chef, Dan Daniell, tends to the succulent lamb on an open wood fire in one corner of the restaurant. When the lights dim, this chef-cum-recording star grabs a microphone and serenades diners with his own brand of Switzo-pop, under a giant screen showing videos of his choice. An example: helicopters swooping around the Matterhorn like a karaoke fusion of *The Swiss Family Robinson* and *Apocalypse Now.*

SATURDAY

4 *Over the Borderline* 8:30 a.m.

There are few attainable real-life experiences that make one feel like James Bond, and fewer still that don't involve tuxedos and roulette. Crossing a border on skis is one of them. Take three gondolas up over

12,500 feet on the Klein Matterhorn. Blaze through the fresh snow on Theodul glacier, so high you can ski it year-round. When you're ready to switch nationality, glide over the Plateau Rosa into Italy. There's no border post, but your cellphone might trill and vibrate as you carve down the Italian slope, pledging its allegiance to a new national carrier. To complete your mission, have a cappuccino at picnic tables on the wooden terrace at **Bontadini** (Piste 6 on the Italian side of the Theodul Pass; 39-335-250-312).

5 *Ski-Up Dining* 1 p.m.

Before exploring Rothorn and Sunnegga, on the other side of Zermatt, make your way to the quaint village of Findeln for lunch. **Findlerhof bei Franz und Heidi** (41-27-967-2588; findlerhof.ch; $$$) offers unbeatable views and Swiss classics (reservations strongly recommended). One day's quiche with leeks, onion, and cheese set a new standard, worth every penny. A rösti, a kind of potato pancake, could fuel a full afternoon of skiing. After lunch, experts should make a beeline for the famous moguls at the Triftji glacier, the traditional home of the annual

Bump Bash, a half-party, half-competition held in Zermatt every March. Beginners beware!

6 *Boots Off* 4:30 p.m.

You won't find a more festive après-ski scene than at **Papperla Pub** (Steinmattstrasse 36; 41-27-966-7600; papperlapub.ch), where live bands hammer out classic rock tunes and the revelers dress up as everything from gorillas to Teletubbies.

7 *Dinner at a Movie* 8 p.m.

Between a full day on the slopes and a few pints worth of après-ski, a little rest is needed. Instead of a nap, head over to the Swiss Army knife of night life, the **Backstage Hotel** (Hofmattstrasse 4;

ABOVE With nearly nearly 200 miles of marked trails, Zermatt accommodates skiers at all levels of skill.

RIGHT Vernissage, a cozy bar in the Backstage Hotel, which also has a movie theater that serves dinner.

41-27-966-6970; backstagehotel.ch; $$$), which offers the stylish bar Vernissage, the restaurant After Seven, and the rather unusual Cinedinner, in which you enjoy drinks before a movie and are served your dinner at intermission. Built by the local artist and architect Heinz Julen, the space is a technical and aesthetic marvel. Glass panes seal off the cinema from the hubbub of the bar upstairs.

8 *A Touch of Tartan* 10 p.m.

For a pick-me-up, stop by **Edward's Bar Café** in the rustic but elegant Hotel Monte Rosa (Bahnhof-strasse 80; 41-27-966-0333; seiler-hotels.ch), the city's oldest hotel. Watch the bartender lovingly prepare your Irish coffee, lighting the whiskey on fire and swirling it in the glass to melt the sugar.

9 *Not Quite Disney* Midnight

The D.J.'s spin into the morning at **Schneewittli** (German for "Snow White") **Nightclub**, adjoining

the Papperla Pub. Schneewittli is the spot for theme parties and costume nights. The **Unique Hotel Post** (Bahnhofstrasse 41; 41-27-967-1931; hotelpost.ch) has five bars and clubs, featuring live music, laid-back lounges, and the notorious Broken Bar Disco, where you can dance on a wine barrel into the morning.

SUNDAY

10 *Slideways* 10 a.m.

Don't let the innocent-looking wooden toboggan fool you. This is not taking your Flexible Flyer to the neighborhood hill. The **Gornergrat** toboggan course (41-27-921-4711; zermatt.ch) is steep and curving, and for a few francs an hour you can let gravity take its course. Acceleration is rapid, and there are no brakes, except for your feet. So make like Fred Flintstone and plow down the speedy, combed turns, and expect a hard wipeout or two. The adrenaline thrill will have you back up the hill in no time.

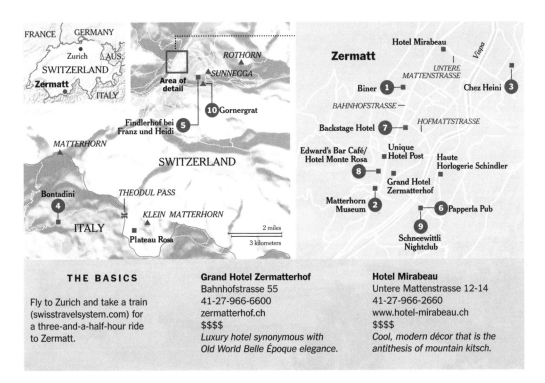

THE BASICS

Fly to Zurich and take a train (swisstravelsystem.com) for a three-and-a-half-hour ride to Zermatt.

Grand Hotel Zermatterhof
Bahnhofstrasse 55
41-27-966-6600
zermatterhof.ch
$$$$
Luxury hotel synonymous with Old World Belle Époque elegance.

Hotel Mirabeau
Untere Mattenstrasse 12-14
41-27-966-2660
www.hotel-mirabeau.ch
$$$$
Cool, modern décor that is the antithesis of mountain kitsch.

St. Moritz

St. Moritz, the 150-year-old synonym for excess with a side of skiing, boasts that it gets 322 days of sun a year. The reason is a peculiar mix of altitude and mountain alignment. But it's easy to wonder if those who frequent this rarefied strip of property in Switzerland haven't simply ordered up the sun, like a piece of perfectly seared tuna at one of the high-franc mid-mountain restaurants. Perhaps this will occur to you when you stroll down Via Serlas — past Chanel, Gucci, Bulgari, Chopard, and Pucci — watching would-be shoppers descend from picturesque horse-drawn carriages and peel bills from rolls the size of baseballs to tip groomsmen. Or when you hit the clubs at night, descending into the gloom of neon-lit, booming dance halls. Whenever the moment, soon you will realize: St. Moritz is an opportunity for pure cultural anthropology, a safari to a land of 300-Swiss-franc lunches and free-flowing Cristal.
— BY SARAH WILDMAN AND GABRIEL SHERMAN

FRIDAY

1 *Fur, Not Fleece* 3 p.m.

The international flotsam of aristocrats, financiers, and socialites that began arriving in the mid-19th century is still leaving its mark. In **St. Moritz-Dorf**, as the main village is known, Bentleys jockey with S.U.V.'s for parking, and fur — not fleece — is the winter attire of choice. A collection of Alpine chalets is tucked between luxury hotels. Explore the winding streets and browse in designer boutiques, souvenir outlets selling Swiss wood carvings, and ski shops eager to outfit you for forays on the 200 miles of local ski runs. At the family-run **Hotel Hauser** (Via Traunter Plazzas 7; 41-81-837-5050; hotelhauser.ch), choose something sweet at the pastry shop, which is famous for house-made chocolate and Engadine Nusstorte, a nut and caramel cake. The hotel's Roo bar is a popular après-ski hangout.

2 *Blend In* 5 p.m.

Even travelers on a budget can sample a bit of the high life by dressing up (ties and jackets for gentlemen) and starting the night with an aperitif in the Renaissance Bar at **Badrutt's Palace Hotel** (Via Serlas 27; 41-81-837-1000; badruttspalace.com), named for the hotelier who first brought winter vacationers to St. Moritz. Ease into a plush armchair with a Bellini and take in the expansive view of the frozen Lake St. Moritz stretching out below. The indoor view isn't bad, either — tycoons, supermodels, and princesses, their furs strewn haphazardly across the backs of velvet divans or nestled like pets beside their owners. Despite the scent of exclusivity, in St. Moritz, perhaps more than in any other spot frequented by the rich and the very rich, you are free to mingle.

3 *Grand and Less Grand* 8 p.m.

The **Kempinski Grand Hotel des Bains** (Via Mezdi 27; kempinski.com/en/stmoritz) offers three reliable, if pricey, restaurants to choose from (reservations, 41-81-838-3081), from the most formal, the **Cà d'Oro**, to **Les Saisons**, which presents itself as family-friendly. In the middle is **Enoteca**, the most daring and most interesting. The tasting menu changes regularly with seasons and availability of ingredients.

4 *Midnight on the Mountain* 11 p.m.

Watch shadows falling on the snow and lights glowing in the valley as you go night skiing at **Piz Corvatsch** (41-81-838-7373; corvatsch.ch), kept lighted every Friday night in ski season until 1 or 2 a.m.

OPPOSITE Sun and snow have brought the wealthy to St. Moritz for 150 years. Chanel and Gucci have followed.

BELOW Gondolas carry skiers up to the peaks and drop less ambitious passengers off for lunch at La Marmite.

Corvatsch, known for its bowl skiing, boasts that it has the "longest floodlit piste in Switzerland." In addition, there is a mountain restaurant, the Alpetta, which stays open for dinner, as well as the Hossa Bar, where a D.J. entertains crowds.

SATURDAY

5 *Early Downhill* 9 a.m.

Get back on the skis. A sizeable proportion of the mink-clad crowd here seems content to stick to the casino, the spas, and the shopping — a village press representative once estimated that nonskiers make up "55 to 60 percent" of winter visitors. But as you zoom downhill in the early sunshine, you will be reminded that these mountains are as well worth navigating on fiberglass skis as by private jet. Cheeks reddened from whipping down the nearly empty runs, skiers and snowboarders quickly realize that there is a benefit to hitting the slopes early in a town that encourages nonskiing. No lift lines.

6 *Melting Pot* 1 p.m.

You can still meet the no-ski crowd at the most exclusive restaurant on the mountain. Above the tree line and easily accessible via funicular trains is a two-part restaurant invention: the indoor **La**

Marmite and its outdoor counterpart the **Terrazza** (mid-mountain Corviglia; 41-81-833-6355; mathisfood. ch; $$$$), where you are invited to drop hundreds of francs on truffles and caviar. Those who take the funicular in ski clothing, breathing heavily from heaving a pair of skis and shuffling along in multi-buckled Nordica boots, may find themselves in the minority. There are invariably women on the train wearing delicate boots barely meant for winter, let alone the pistes, who are headed only for a meal and a great view. To keep the bill within range, order from the à la carte menu. Stick around for the afternoon and sip Prosecco.

7 *Alpine Fusion* 7 p.m.

You needn't be staying at Hotel Salastrains to try the **Restaurant Salastrains** (Corviglia; 41-81-830-0707; salastrains.ch; $$$), where hearty Swiss fare is woven seamlessly with Northern Italian favorites (like tissue-thin tuna carpaccio) in an invitingly warm dining room. The combination is an appropriate nod to the nearby international border — Italy is just a few Alps away.

8 *The In Crowd* 11 p.m.

Claudia Schiffer, Liz Hurley, Kate Moss, and Robert De Niro have all been regulars at the **King's Club** (Via Serlas 27; 41-81-837-1000), a celebrity hangout owned by Badrutt's Palace. Outside of Christmas week and New Year's Eve, when the club is hit by boldface names in droves, keeping lesser-known visitors on the other side of the heavy oak doors, mortals can descend into the depths of the sunken dance floor illuminated by a massive '70s-style disco ball. This is your opportunity to imbibe expensive beverages and rub shoulders with those who own nearby holiday apartments. To mix with a different crowd, try the **Cava Bar** (Sonnenplatz; 41-81-836-9696; steffani.ch), in the basement of the Hotel Steffani, where a young clientele sips pints of beer and tumblers of Red Bull and vodka cocktails.

LEFT Clicquot Champagne, the daily elixir of St. Moritz.

OPPOSITE Badrutt's Palace Hotel, named for the founder of winter vacationing in St. Moritz.

SUNDAY

9 *Light or Hearty* 10 a.m.

Have a cup of coffee and a pastry at **Hanselmann** (Via Maistra 8; 41-81-833-3864; hanselmann.ch), in the town square, and linger in the tearoom. Or prepare for another outdoor day with something heartier —tuck into sennenrösti, a concoction of potatoes, bacon, onions, leeks, and cheese, at Hotel Hauser.

10 *Snow and Ice* 11 a.m.

For a change of scene, trade downhill for cross-country skiing. From St. Moritz, skiers glide over more than 100 miles of groomed trails fanning into the Upper Engadine Valley. Detailed maps of the trails are available at most hotels in town. Or quicken the pace exponentially at **Olympia Bob Run** (Plazza Gunter Sachs; 41-81-830-0200; olympia-bobrun.ch).

St. Moritz has the world's oldest bobsled track, a milelong channel slicing 19 turns down the mountainside. Riding with professional drivers, audacious thrill-seekers can race down at speeds topping 80 miles an hour on the 101-year-old track, the last of the world's courses made from natural ice.

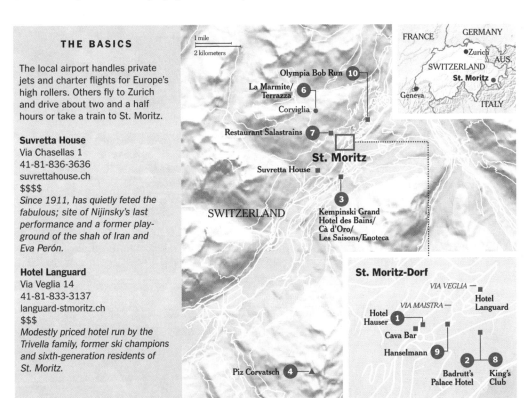

THE BASICS

The local airport handles private jets and charter flights for Europe's high rollers. Others fly to Zurich and drive about two and a half hours or take a train to St. Moritz.

Suvretta House
Via Chasellas 1
41-81-836-3636
suvrettahouse.ch
$$$$
Since 1911, has quietly feted the fabulous; site of Nijinsky's last performance and a former playground of the shah of Iran and Eva Perón.

Hotel Languard
Via Veglia 14
41-81-833-3137
languard-stmoritz.ch
$$$
Modestly priced hotel run by the Trivella family, former ski champions and sixth-generation residents of St. Moritz.

Vienna

For years, Vienna lingered in the fading glory of the fin de siècle era, understandably satisfied with the grandeur of its Hapsburg-era architecture and parks. Now a new wind is blowing through this imperial city, bringing dazzling hotels, new and renovated museums, and reinvention of the gasthaus, that ubiquitous pub where Viennese artists and philosophers, workers, and shopkeepers tarry over schnitzel and beer well into the night. — BY SARAH WILDMAN

FRIDAY

1 *The Quartier* 2 p.m.

The **MuseumsQuartier**, the former Hapsburg stables turned culture plaza, brings together museums, opulent architecture, performances, and restaurants. Wander the galleries at **Mumok** (Museumsplatz 1; 43-1-525-00-0; mumok.at), the museum of contemporary art housed in a basalt lava cube on the plaza. Then stop at **Café Halle** (Museumsplatz 1; 43-1-523-7001; www.diehalle.at) for a mini-obstkuchen, a fresh fruit tart. This romantic yet modern restaurant, its walls hung with billowing sheer curtains, is tucked into the former private quarters of the emperor. Downstairs, photography exhibitions in the **Kunsthalle Wien** (Museumsplatz 1; 43-1-5218-9211; kunsthallewien.at) draw crowds.

2 *Café-Kultur* 5 p.m.

Café Sperl (Gumpendorferstrasse 11; 43-1-586-41-58; cafesperl.at) is among the most iconic of the city's legendary turn-of-the-century coffeehouses, with velvet banquettes where you can have a small brauner (espresso). Cross the street to **Phil** (Gumpendorfer-strasse 10-12; 43-1-581-0489; phil.info), a Berlin-style bookstore/music shop/coffeehouse with mismatched furniture, D.J.'s, and a late-night bar ripe for experiencing the newer side of Vienna's cafe culture.

3 *Traditional, or Not* 8 p.m.

For classic Viennese cuisine at an old-is-new-again gasthaus, head for **Schilling** (Burggasse 103; 43-1-524-1775; schilling-wirt.at; $$), distinct for its 1950s fixtures and traditional dishes like Kalbbutterschnitzel (veal butter schnitzel) and böhmische palatschinken (a dessert pancake with plum sauce). Some Viennese swear the future

is places like **Skopik & Lohn** (Leopoldsgasse 17; 43-1-219-8977; skopikundlohn.at; $$), which kicks Austrian food up a notch with dishes like Arctic char over creamed yellow beets. It's in a wildly artistic space, with walls covered in black scribbles. You won't have trouble finding an after-dinner drink, maybe an absinthe at **Grande** (Josefstadter Strasse 56; 43-676-499-8177; grande.at/josefstadt).

4 *Decisions, Decisions* 10 p.m.

Fluc (Praterstern 5; fluc.at) is a club built in a former pedestrian passageway at the Prater metro stop. It has large beer steins, D.J.'s, and a stage for live music. Or, to experience the new underground scene, go to **Brut** (Karlsplatz 5; 43-1-587-8774; brut-wien.at), a center for "international, experimental, and innovative performance art" (i.e., general mayhem) held in a wing of the Wiener Konzerthaus. Looking for calm? Have a drink at **Motto am Fluss** (Franz Josefs Kai 2; 43-1-252-5511; motto.at/mottoamfluss), a bar on the Danube Canal.

SATURDAY

5 *Mile-Long Market* 9 a.m.

Order an espresso and breakfast at one of the dozens of restaurants that line the edge of the century-old **Naschmarkt**. The open-air market

OPPOSITE A performance at the Musikverein concert hall, a temple of classic Viennese culture.

BELOW Visit the Bruegels at the Kunsthistorisches Museum.

is a mile long, stretching between the Karlsplatz and Kettenbrückengasse U-bahn stations. Filled with stalls stocked with produce, baked goods, flowers, and spices, it is easily one of the best in Europe. On Saturdays, hawkers selling antiques and bric-a-brac branch out for another mile.

6 *Royal Affair* 11 a.m.

If you've seen one royal boudoir, you've seen them all, so skip the Imperial Apartments and head to the magnificent **State Hall of the Austrian National Library** (Josefsplatz 1; 43-1-5341-0444; onb.ac.at), tucked inside the Hapsburg palace complex in the First District. It was built by Emperor Charles VI in the late 17th century, with a soaring frescoed ceiling, 200,000 books dating from 1500, and antique globes scattered about. You'll feel as if you'd stepped inside a storybook. Then stop at **Café Bräunerhof**, (Stallburggasse 2; 43-1-512-3893), the late novelist Thomas Bernhard's favorite cafe. Some think it caters too much to tourists, but with classical musicians playing, it's not a bad place to while away an afternoon.

7 *Shop Around* 3 p.m.

In the Seventh District many stores carry maps showing all the locally made and European-sourced clothing shops. Try **Camille Boyer** (Lindengasse 25; camilleboyer.at) for buttery soft, dove-gray hobo bags from Lumi. Or **Buntwäsche** (Kaiserstrasse 52; 43-699-1944-0789; buntwaesche.at) for super-soft cotton children's clothing in adorable prints. **Wabisabi** (Lindengasse 20; 43-664-545-1280; alle-tragen-wabi-sabi.at/) sells Japanese-style geometric-cut women's clothing, entirely in black and white. Across the street at **Werkprunk** (Kirchengasse 7/11, enter at Lindengasse 25; 43-680-403-5537; werkprunk.com), sisters Jasmin and Silvia König make jewelry out of sterling silver and precious stones.

8 *Return to the Classics* 7:30 p.m.

Classical music is everywhere in this city, from the Musikverein to the Wiener Konzerthaus to the Volksoper and beyond. Not to be overlooked is the **Wiener Staatsballett** (the Vienna State Ballet) at the **Staatsoper**. A former star of the Paris Opera Ballet, Manuel Legris, is the director; a seat in his house is a treat.

9 *Kitchen Confidential* 9:30 p.m.

Down a winding First District street is **Gasthaus Pöschl** (Weihburggasse 17; 43-1-513-5288; $$), with simple wood tables, whitewashed walls, and a menu that is consistently excellent. Try Austrian favorites like roasted calf's liver or gnocchi with a sauce of spinach and sheep cheese. Too heavy? Duck into **Kleines Café** (Franziskanerplatz 3) and try an inexpensive open-faced tartine. Later, have a drink at **Rote Bar**, at the magnificent Volkstheater (Neustiftgasse 1; 43-699-1501-5013; rotebar.at), opened in 1889. It is a Belle Époque marvel, with a chandelier and frescoes of revelers from the 1880s, dressed (and lighted) entirely in red.

SUNDAY

10 *Amuse Yourself* 10 a.m.

In the mid-18th century, the **Prater**, once a royal hunting ground, morphed into what it is today: a European Coney Island. The iconic red Riesenrad — the Ferris wheel of *Third Man* fame — still dominates.

A recent addition is the stomach-dropping Prater Turm, a swing that takes you nearly 400 feet in the air and whips you around at 38 m.p.h. The 360-degree view of the city, if you can open your eyes, is spectacular. When winter sets in, ice skating rinks open across the city. One to try, if you're there at the right time, is the enormous **Wiener Eislaufverein** (Lothringerstrasse 22; 43-1-713-6353; wev.or.at), near the InterContinental Hotel.

11 *The Home of Klimt* 1 p.m.

Newest isn't always best. The Bruegels at the **Kunsthistorisches Museum** (Maria Theresien Platz; 43-1-525-24-0; www.khm.at) were part of the Hapsburgs' personal collection; the building

itself is an astounding mix of murals, marble, and royal excess. But even more crowd-pleasing is the **Schloss Belvedere** (Oberes, Prinz-Eugen-Strasse 27/ Unteres, Rennweg 6; 43-1-7955-7134; belvedere.at), two facing Baroque palaces surrounded by gardens. The collections are superb, but before straying far, join the crowds homing in on the Klimts (yes, Gustav Klimt lived most of his life in Vienna) in search of the hands-down international favorite: *The Kiss*.

OPPOSITE ABOVE The national opera house, the Staatsoper, another of the opulent remnants of Vienna's Hapsburg glory.

OPPOSITE BELOW The lines of stalls of the Naschmarkt, a century-old outdoor food market, stretch out for a mile.

THE BASICS

The City Airport Train takes 15 minutes to get to the city center. Once there, use the extensive U-Bahn and tram system.

25 Hours
Lerchenfelder Strasse 1-3
43-1-521-510
25hours-hotels.com
$$
Stylish outpost of a small hotel chain from Germany. The rooftop bar offers fantastic views of downtown.

Fleming's Deluxe Hotel Wien City
Josefstädter Strasse 10-12
43-1-205-990
flemings-hotels.com
$$
Gorgeous wood-paneled rooms; "city view" rooms offer great vistas.

Sofitel Vienna Stephansdom
Praterstrasse 1
43-1-906-160
sofitel-vienna-stephansdom.com
$$$-$$$$
A sleek Jean Nouvel hotel with a view of old Vienna and a hopping upstairs bar.

Salzburg

With its medieval citadel, Baroque palaces, and yodel-ready Alpine vistas, Salzburg, Austria, has never had trouble luring visitors. The city abounds with tourists, most searching for the sound of music, whether Mozart or the von Trapps. Yet some of its best offerings are not at all historic: contemporary galleries, fair-trade coffeehouses, and the futuristic Hangar-7 complex. In summer, its river, the Salzach, glitters against a backdrop of green hills, and classical-music superstars from around the world perform at its music festival, Europe's largest. In winter, the city is at its most hospitable, as squares transform into bustling Christmas markets and candlelit taverns fill with skiers refueling on Teutonic comfort food. Salzburg is not frozen in the past, but its appeal is timeless. — BY CHARLY WILDER

FRIDAY

1 *Baroque and Blue-Chip* 4 p.m.

There's hardly a more potent introduction to Salzburg than the Baroque **Mirabell Palace** and Gardens, the setting for many of Mozart's early performances, several scenes in *The Sound of Music*, concerts year-round, and Christmas markets in December. Originally constructed in 1606, Mirabell is a picture of Renaissance overachievement, with its grand Papagena fountain, the Orangerie housing paintings by Rubens and Bernini, and balustrades topped with 17th-century statues of Roman gods. For more updated artfulness, the **Galerie Thaddaeus Ropac** (Mirabellplatz 2; 43-662-881-390; ropac.net), headquarters of Austria's perhaps most important gallerist, is in the Villa Kast overlooking the gardens. European and American contemporary art stars like Jules de Balincourt and Robert Longo are on the roster.

2 *Rustic Repast* 6 p.m.

Steer clear of the tourist-trap restaurants cluttering the Altstadt (Old City) and head to the Steingasse, a cobbled alleyway just up from the Salzach riverside. The **Andreas Hofer Weinstube** tavern (Steingasse 65; 43-662-872-769; dieweinstube.at; $) serves up no-frills

OPPOSITE Cathedral Square in holiday dress.

RIGHT The Salzach River and the lights of Salzburg.

regional cuisine, like Knödelgeheimnis (bread dumplings cooked with sauerkraut and fried egg). Come dinnertime, a student-heavy local crowd packs in under candle-illuminated arched ceilings.

3 *Amadeus Town* 8 p.m.

Classical dominates the musical landscape, so take in a concert or performance at the **International Mozarteum Foundation** (Schwarzstrasse 26; 43-662-889-400; mozarteum.at). The foundation runs a world-class orchestral and operatic program and seems to have its hands in nearly everything in town devoted to Salzburg's best-loved son. Coinciding with the composer's birthday, January 27, the foundation's annual Mozart Week draws many of the world's best orchestras, singers, and conductors.

4 *Local Grapes* 9 p.m.

Austrian wines are not nearly as well known internationally as wines from neighboring Italy and Germany, but that's not because they can't compete. Find this out for yourself at **Enoteca Settemila a.C.** (Bergstrasse 9; 43-662-873-257; enotecasettemila.at), which focuses on organic wines. Try a dry Grüner Veltliner or a Riesling. Or go red with a peppery Blaufränkisch, a fruity Zweigelt, or a pinot noir-like St. Laurent. End the night with a sweet ice wine.

SATURDAY

5 *Austrian Joe* 10 a.m.

Follow your caffeine compass to the Altstadt, full of coffeehouses in the high-Austrian style. In

business since 1700, **Café Tomaselli** (Alter Markt 9; 43-662-844-4880; tomaselli.at) is of the "if it ain't broke" school: waiters in bow ties zigzag through the two-level Biedermeier-style salon brandishing trays of cream-topped, brandy-laced coffee drinks in porcelain. A cheaper cup is down the street at **220 Grad** (Chiemseegasse 5; 43-662-827-881; 220grad. com), an ultramodern fair-trade cafe. Fortified, take in the Altstadt, especially Cathedral Square. Salzburg Cathedral, with tall towers, elaborate frescoes, and a huge pipe organ, fronts the square; so do the Residenz Palace and St. Peter's Abbey. In December, this area is transformed as mitten-clad children ice skate around the Mozart statue, choirs perform, and vendors in wooden stalls sell mulled wine and cartoonish nativity figures.

6 *Emerging Art* Noon

Contrary to its less-than-cosmopolitan reputation (the writer Thomas Bernhard once called it a "cretinous provincial dump"), Salzburg has long supported its artists. When it opened in 1844, the **Salzburger Kunstverein** (Hellbrunner Strasse 3; 43-662-842-2940; salzburger-kunstverein.at) was one of the first Austrian associations to focus on the sale and exhibition of contemporary art. Today it includes exhibition space, a cafe, and 24 ateliers for working artists. Across the river, **Periscope** (Sterneckstrasse 10; 43-676-704-2566; periscope.at) is an artist-run gallery and project space that opened in 2006 in Neustadt (New City).

7 *Medieval Altitude* 3 p.m.

Take the 19th-century funicular 322 feet up the Festungsberg mountain to the **Hohensalzburg Fortress** (Mönchsberg 34; 43-662-8424-3011; festung-salzburg.at), one of Europe's best-preserved medieval castles. Though many of the furnishings were nicked by Napoleon, the rooms themselves have held up remarkably. The ornate royal apartments of the Palace Museum are a highlight, but so is the view of the city and the Alps from the courtyard.

8 *Modern Mountain* 5 p.m.

From the fortress, hike to the **Museum der Moderne** (Mönchsberg 32; 43-662-842-220-403; museumdermoderne.at), a rectangular glass-and-white-marble structure that juts from a 19th-century water tower atop the Mönchsberg mountain. Glazed stairways open onto four floors of rooms housing 20th- and 21st-century works. Watch the sun set through the open roof of the American artist James Turrell's 2005 *Sky Space* installation before sitting down under a light fixture made of 390 antlers in the Matteo Thun-designed dining room of the restaurant **m32** (43-662-841-000; m32.at; $$$-$$$$), where you can feast on Mediterranean-inflected Austrian cuisine by Sepp Schellhorn.

9 *Belgian Pints* 9 p.m.

By night, Salzburg's student population hangs out at the bars skirting the base of the Kapuzinerberg mountain in Neustadt. **Alchimiste Belge** (Bergstrasse 10; 43-660-646-94-0; alchimiste-belge.at), a Belgian beer bar popular with chain-smoking musicians from the Mozarteum conservatory, serves more than 50 varieties like Kriek and Westmalle Tripel.

SUNDAY

10 *Imperial Breakfast* 9 a.m.

The **Café Bazar** (Schwarzstrasse 3; 43-662-874-278; cafe-bazar.at; $$), on the right bank of the Salzach, is a century-old Viennese-style coffeehouse with crystal chandeliers, wood paneling, and marble tabletops. The view of the river and Old City is as gratifying as the fare: perfectly poached eggs, paper-thin slices

of honey-crusted ham, fresh-baked pastries, and phenomenal coffee. No surprise that the guest book, kept since 1927, includes the names Thomas Mann, Marlene Dietrich, and Arthur Miller.

11 *Energy Rush* 11 a.m.

Head to the glass-domed **Hangar-7** (Salzburg Airport, Wilhelm-Spazier-Strasse 7A; 43-662-2197; hangar-7.com), owned by Red Bull mogul Dietrich Mateschitz and built to showcase his vintage aircraft (the "Flying Bulls"). Glass walkways snake around Red Bull-emblazoned planes, motorcycles, and muscle cars, while a glass-floored bar suspended from the roof hangs above a contemporary art exhibition and space for live musical performances. There's also an upscale restaurant that features a different guest chef (and

menu) every month, as well as two bars, a cafe, and an outdoor lounge. A bit over the top? Sure, but then, so was Mozart.

OPPOSITE ABOVE The International Mozarteum Foundation. Classical music, always in the Salzburg air, permeates in the winter Mozart Week and the summer Salzburg Festival.

OPPOSITE BELOW An exhibit at the Museum der Moderne.

ABOVE Vintage airplanes at Hangar-7.

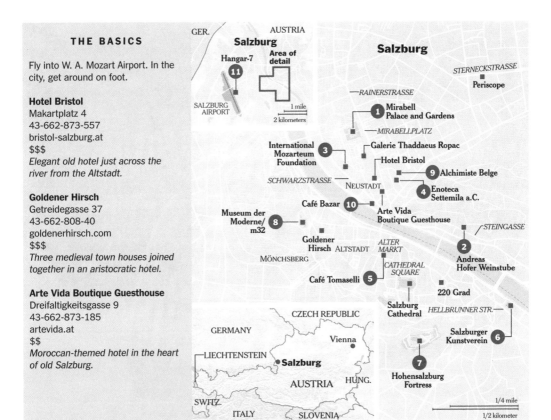

THE BASICS

Fly into W. A. Mozart Airport. In the city, get around on foot.

Hotel Bristol
Makartplatz 4
43-662-873-557
bristol-salzburg.at
$$$
Elegant old hotel just across the river from the Altstadt.

Goldener Hirsch
Getreidegasse 37
43-662-808-40
goldenerhirsch.com
$$$
Three medieval town houses joined together in an aristocratic hotel.

Arte Vida Boutique Guesthouse
Dreifaltigkeitsgasse 9
43-662-873-185
artevida.at
$$
Moroccan-themed hotel in the heart of old Salzburg.

Innsbruck

The Alps might be for skiing, but the self-styled "capital" of the Austrian Alps, Innsbruck, lives for just about everything après — eating, drinking, shopping and partying. Despite its founding as the capital of the Tyrol in the Middle Ages, the city on the Inn River maintains a consistently youthful attitude, thanks in part to 30,000 university students in a population of just 125,000 residents, while a new interest in world-class modern architecture by the likes of David Chipperfield, Dominique Perrault, and Zaha Hadid is starting to compete for attention with the Renaissance-era buildings and labyrinthine lanes of Old Town. By all means, enjoy the nearby slopes, like those at the Stubai Glacier. But don't be surprised if the lifts you enjoy most are the ones that take you to the city's many rooftop bars, upscale restaurants, and dance clubs that go all night. — BY EVAN RAIL

FRIDAY

1 *Kaffeeklatsch Contest* 4 p.m.

Locals love to argue over which is Innsbruck's best konditorei, or pastry cafe, with many picking the more-modern **Valier** (Maximilianstrasse 27; 43-512-586-180; www.konditorei-innsbruck.at), just south of the city center, while hard-liners swear by the storied **Munding** (Kiebachgasse 16, at Mundingplatz; 43-512-584-118; munding.at) in Old Town, which claims to have served its pie-like apple strudels and sugary stollen since 1803. Pick either one, grab a table and enjoy the afternoon kaffeeklatsch hour like a regular. Then move on to the other and order a second round of cake and coffee, just to make sure.

2 *Local Brews* 5 p.m.

With its crisp gruner veltliners, fruity gelber muskatellers and steely rieslings, Austria's enviable wine culture steals much of the attention that might otherwise go to the country's growing — but largely overlooked — craft beer scene. In Innsbruck, one of the top-rated bars is **Cafe Sowieso** (Kapuzinergasse 8; 43-650-553-0506), a gritty, romper-room-like student pub with four to six unusual brews on draft

and about 40 bottles, including rarities like Gerhard Forstner's hoppy amber Styrian Ale. No, your beer-loving friends back home have never heard of it.

3 *Meal With a View* 8 p.m.

Though the centrally situated, glass-covered **Rathausgalerien** seems to be nothing more than a flashy shopping mall, in-the-know epicures come for the top-level restaurant, **Lichtblick** (Maria-Theresien-Strasse 18; 43-512-566-550; restaurant-lichtblick.at; $$$$): an open, light-filled space with commanding views of the city from atop the seventh floor of a tower on Maria-Theresien-Strasse. Can you see all the way to the Alto Adige, just across the border? The cooking certainly seems to leap from Austria to Italy: earthy parsnips in a foam soup paired with fresh tuna fillets, or tender salt-marsh lamb accompanied by hearty polenta in tomato sauce with rich goat cheese.

4 *After-Dinner Stops* 10:40 p.m.

Just how lazy are you? For an easy finish to the night, walk 20 feet from Lichtblick's door to **360°** (Maria-Theresien-Strasse 18; 43-664-840-6570; 360-grad.at), a stylish, circular glass salon overlooking the entire city. Finish up with a local wine, like the house white cuvée, produced for the bar by the Hiedler winery in Kamptal. Then set out for the city's best cocktails around the corner at the **5th Floor**, another rooftop bar, this time inside the Penz hotel (Adolf-Pichler-Platz 3; 43-512-575-6570; the-penz. com). Sample one of the 100 rare whiskeys (like Talisker, from the only distillery on the Isle of Skye) or try a picker-upper with a twist, like the all-German

OPPOSITE AND RIGHT Innsbruck takes skiers up the mountain with cable cars, a funicular railway, and cable car stations with glass canopies, designed by Zaha Hadid.

gin and tonic, made with Monkey 47 gin from the Black Forest and Thomas Henry tonic from Berlin.

SATURDAY

5 *Pottery's High Point* 10 a.m.

Austria's influence on the global studio ceramics movement includes both the Wiener Werkstatte and the great Vienna-trained (but London-based) potter Lucie Rie. The high point for quality earthenware in Innsbruck is the 20-year-old **Töpferstudio Kathrein** (Viaduktbogen 1; 43-512-573-218); toepferstudio.at), nestled in the arch of a railway viaduct on Viaduktbogen, where Hansjörg Kathrein makes and sells stylish but very functional hand-thrown cups, bowls, plates, and pitchers.

6 *Sweet Empire* 1 p.m.

The imperial-era home of the Sacher torte now boasts a small empire of its own: beyond the original Hotel Sacher in Vienna, there are related branches in Graz, Salzburg, and here in the Old Town, the **Café Sacher** (Rennweg 1; 43-512-565-626; sacher.com/en-cafe-innsbruck; $$$). Though most visitors come here for the cake, the kitchen's savory fare — from classic tafelspitz to contemporary cuisine — is not to be missed. Ornate fin-de-siècle-style décor and princely service create an Old World setting that complements the classical Austrian cuisine, dishes like its award-winning beuschel, calf's heart and lung in a creamy sauce.

7 *Multifaceted* 3 p.m.

Pretend to contemplate the art while shopping for shiny baubles at the **Swarovski** (Herzog-Friedrich-Strasse 39; 43-512-573-100; innsbruck.swarovski.com) crystal shop. Produced just a half-hour outside town, the crystals decorate the ground floor's exhibition of stiletto heels from eight different designers, as well as changing exhibitions by different designers using Swarovski crystals. The shopping-cum-gawking continues upstairs, where crystals light up with synchronized music in a darkened wunderkammer, or chamber of wonders, and you can brace yourself with sparkling wine at the stylish bar.

8 *Tyrolean Style* 4 p.m.

Half-Austrian, half-Italian, the Tyrol is a strange region for outsiders to understand. You can get a few visual cues at the **Museum of Tyrolean Folk Art** (Universitätsstrasse 12; 32-512-5948-9111; www.tiroler-landesmuseen.at), which charts the history of the region using handicrafts like combs and carved spoons, traditional costumes and even complete living rooms, filled with the carved wood and quirky design. Next, check out the connected **Hofkirche**, or Court Church, where the ornate cenotaph of Holy Roman Emperor Maximilian I is watched over by Renaissance-era statues of kings, queens, ladies, knights, and courtiers.

9 *Sit Still (and Eat Well)* 8 p.m.

Housed in a former primary school on Gilmstrasse, **Sitzwohl** (Gilmstrasse 4; 43-512-562-888; restaurantsitzwohl.at; $$$$) includes its own ground-floor deli and cocktail bar; in the second-floor restaurant, onyx light boxes create intimate nooks where diners sample updated local recipes, like the unexpected take on head cheese, served with tiny corn fritters, or a main course of tender, prosciutto-wrapped pheasant breast accompanied by spicy, cinnamon-scented red cabbage and crunchy-on-the-outside, fluffy-on-the-inside potato dumplings. If only every school served meals like this.

10 *Out All Night* 11 p.m.

Innsbruck's substantial student population means that night life here often doesn't end until dawn. At clubs like the mod-themed **Weekender** (Tschamler-strasse 3; 43-512-570-570; weekender.at), a young crowd dances to a variety of tunes, depending on the night, from live metal and punk bands to techno and house D.J.'s. Right along the banks of the Inn River, the **Aftershave** club (Herzog-Otto-Strasse 8; 43-660-121-2241; club-aftershave.at) is often fairly empty until around 1 a.m., when the crowd begins to arrive for the after-hours hip-hop and dance hall tracks.

SUNDAY

11 *Into Thin Air* 9 a.m.

It's hard to say which is more photogenic: the above-the-clouds views across the valley from the **Hungerburgbahn** funicular railway and its nifty self-leveling cars — or the swooping, spaceshiplike railway stations themselves. Designed by Zaha Hadid, who also created the Bergisel ski jump nearby, the four strangely beautiful stops start at **Congress** station, just outside Old Town, and top out halfway up the mountain at **Hungerburg** with an elevation of 860 meters, or about 2,820 feet. Take a snapshot of the view. Then one of the station. Repeat as needed.

OPPOSITE A skier atop Seegrube mountain.

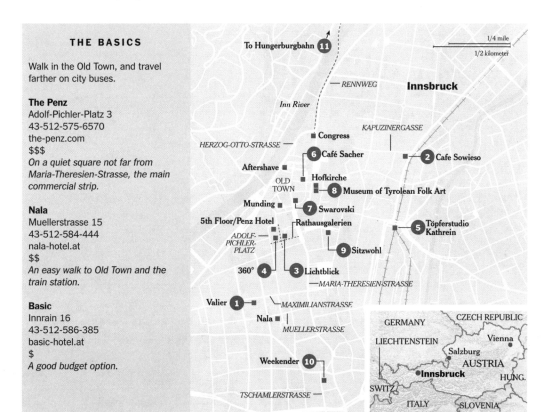

THE BASICS

Walk in the Old Town, and travel farther on city buses.

The Penz
Adolf-Pichler-Platz 3
43-512-575-6570
the-penz.com
$$$
On a quiet square not far from Maria-Theresien-Strasse, the main commercial strip.

Nala
Muellerstrasse 15
43-512-584-444
nala-hotel.at
$$
An easy walk to Old Town and the train station.

Basic
Innrain 16
43-512-586-385
basic-hotel.at
$
A good budget option.

To Hungerburgbahn 11

1/4 mile
1/2 kilometer

RENNWEG · **Innsbruck**

Inn River

KAPUZINERGASSE

■ Congress

HERZOG-OTTO-STRASSE —

6 Café Sacher

Aftershave ■

■ — 2 Cafe Sowieso

OLD TOWN

Hofkirche

8 Museum of Tyrolean Folk Art

Munding ■

7 Swarovski

5th Floor/Penz Hotel

Rathausgalerien

5 Töpferstudio Kathrein

ADOLF-PICHLER-PLATZ

9 Sitzwohl

360° 4

3 Lichtblick

— MARIA-THERESIEN-STRASSE

Valier 1 ■

MAXIMILIANSTRASSE

Nala ■

MUELLERSTRASSE

GERMANY

CZECH REPUBLIC

LIECHTENSTEIN

Vienna

Salzburg

Weekender 10

AUSTRIA

•Innsbruck

HUNG.

SWITZ.

TSCHAMLERSTRASSE —

ITALY

SLOVENIA

Prague

Midway between Old and New Europe, Prague is the most Western, literally and figuratively, of the post-Communist capitals (with the complicated exception of Berlin), and it has been in the lead as they have emerged into the modern era. Cosmopolitan and extremely livable, the Czech capital is now home to excellent new restaurants, to innovative artists and designers, and to a well-educated, tech-savvy population. Fortunately, the Gothic spires, cobblestone lanes, graceful bridges, and supermodel-stylish locals are all still gorgeous. — BY EVAN RAIL

FRIDAY

1 *Great Glass* 3 p.m.

The soaring stained-glass windows of St. Vitus Cathedral have inspired generations of the faithful and visitors alike. For an up-close glimpse of original windows and the master craftsmen who made them, visit the overlooked **Umelecke Sklenarstvi Jiricka-Coufal** (U Milosrdnych 14; 420-737-666-851; vitraz.cz) in the Old Town. It's an "artisanal glassworks" where some of the cathedral's windows were produced and are now restored. Replicas of historical windows are available for purchase. One example: a reproduction of a medieval window depicting Charlemagne, resplendent in knight's armor and wielding a sword, for about $1,500.

2 *Dining House* 7 p.m.

One of Prague's most prominent modern constructions is the **Dancing House**, a curvy riverfront building designed by Frank Gehry and Vlado Milunic, resembling a couple — often called Fred and Ginger — in midstep. Ascend to the top floor for dinner at **Ginger & Fred** (Jiraskovo namesti 6; 420-221-984-160; ginger-fred-restaurant.cz; $$), where the dining room offers views of the Vltava River and Prague Castle. Served alongside the panoramic scene are intriguing creations like venison with red cabbage, roasted apples, and puff pastry.

OPPOSITE The Charles Bridge and the hilltop Prague Castle, Prague's unforgettable landmarks.

RIGHT Windows of St. Vitus Cathedral have been made and restored by artisans at Umelecke Sklenarstvi Jiricka-Coufal.

3 *Sky High* 10 p.m.

Most hotel bars in Prague are forgettable, but not so **Cloud 9** (Pobrezni 1; 420-224-842-999; cloud9.cz), a sky-high lounge in the Hilton Prague. (Be aware that the Hilton Prague and the similarly named Hilton Prague Old Town are not the same.) Long and spacious, the bar has many intimate nooks and corners, along with spectacular views of the river and city rooftops. Though house cocktails are excellent, the nonalcoholic "mocktails," like the Baby Zombie, made with ingredients like guava juice and ginger syrup, are even more refreshing.

SATURDAY

4 *Prague Essentials* 7:30 a.m.

Even this early, you won't be the first tourist of the day on the **Charles Bridge**, the 14th-century arched span over the Vltava that is lined with Baroque statues. But you will be early enough to avoid the worst of the tourist hordes and late enough to miss the partying mobs that can rob Prague's most famous and beautiful sights of all their power to enchant. Walk to the Prague Castle and past the Romanesque Basilica of St. George and the wedding-cake-like Archbishop's Palace. Nearby, the tiny photogenic lane known as Novy Svet will be quiet enough for you to see its antique streetlamps and broad doorways unobscured.

5 *Coffee, Cubed* 10 a.m.

No other Prague cafe is quite like the restored **Grand Café Orient** (Ovocny trh 19; 420-224-224-240; grandcafeorient.cz; $) in the Black Madonna House, a century-old Cubist structure that is now home of the **Museum of Czech Cubism** (420-778-543-901; czkubismus.cz/en). Have breakfast; then proceed to the displays of Cubist paintings, furniture, and architecture. Though the Gothic is far more obvious, Cubism remains one of the city's fundamental styles. Sometimes the two collide spectacularly, as in the Jungmannovo namesti, a square in New Town where a 1912 Cubist street lamp stands next to the Church of Our Lady of the Snows from 1347. Some of the city's most important buildings have a Cubist touch: a later variant, Rondo-Cubism, was adopted as the so-called National Style in Prague's golden age between 1918 and 1938, during the still-revered First Republic of Czechoslovakia.

6 *Adornments* 1 p.m.

Around the corner is the **Artel Design Shop** (Celetna 29, entrance on Rybna; 420-224-815-085; artelglass.com), where you can see today's interpretations of Bohemian glass. Artel updates traditional crystal designs with modern colors and shapes. For a look at Czech fashion design, walk a few blocks to the Josef quarter to see graceful knitwear at **Boheme** (Dusni 8; boheme.cz), comfortably chic designs at **Timoure et Group** (V Kolkovne 6; timoure.cz), sophisticated stylings of **Hana Havelkova** (Dusni 10; havelkova.com), and trendy dresses at **Boutique Tatiana** (Dusni 1; tatiana.cz).

7 *A Little Bread* 3 p.m.

Not to be missed are a number of the city's delicatessens, pastry shops, and cafeterias that have been serving lunch and treats since early in the 20th century. **Jan Paukert** (Rohanske nabrezi 671/15;

TOP The towering spires of the medieval St. Vitus Cathedral at the Prague Castle.

ABOVE A table with a view at a restaurant in the Dancing House.

420-774-534-355; Facebook: JanPaukertLahudkarstvi), a deli that's been in business for a nearly a century, claims to have invented the chlebicek, or "little bread," a popular open-faced sandwich. Closer to the river, the **Mysak** pastry shop (Vodickova 31; 420-222-513-713; gallerymysak.cz), which was founded in 1911, will be happy to serve you the house special, karamelovy pohar, a bowl of ice cream topped with caramel, chocolate, and walnuts. To keep in mind for later: **Erhartova Cukrarna** (Milady Horakove 56; 420-233-312-148; erhartcafe.cz), a tempting 1937-vintage confectionery on the other side of the river.

8 *End of the Line* 7 p.m.

Though the Czech Republic is home to more than 100 breweries, it is challenging to find anything beyond a few international mega-brands in the city center. For a full night of rare brews, take the No. 11 tram out to Namesti bratri Synku, where you will find **Zly Casy** (Cestmirova 5; 420-723-339-995; zlycasy.eu; $), a pub with a rotating selection of microbrews and hearty Czech pork-with-more-pork fare. About five minutes away, the brewpub **Pivovar Basta** (Taborska 389/49; 420-724-582-721; ubansethu.cz) serves one of the city's richest and most full-bodied amber lagers,

as well as seasonal specials and pickled sausages. To finish up the night, get back on the No. 11 tram and continue out to its terminus at Sporilov, where you'll find the **Prvni Pivni Tramway**, or the "first beer tram" (Na Chodovci 1a; 420-272-765-683; prvnipivnitramway. cz), a theme pub decorated with old tram seats. Be sure to cover your ears: the bar staff rings an old tram bell whenever a guest leaves.

SUNDAY

9 *Uphill Romance* 10 a.m.

Burn off last night's excess with a hike up **Petrin Hill**, which overlooks the tile rooftops of Old Town and has been a romantic spot since before Casanova was cruising there. If you're feeling more adventurous,

ABOVE Saints and souvenirs on the Charles Bridge.

RIGHT Café Savoy recalls the era between the world wars.

climb to the top of the hill, go through the **Hunger Wall** at the south end, and continue upward to the massive sandstone boulder that has enough overhangs, handholds, cracks, and footholds to give even seasoned climbers a workout. Don't worry if you forgot your climbing shoes. Prague climbers have

ABOVE Strolling in front of the Museum of Czech Cubism, where displays document an essential Prague style.

OPPOSITE The Dancing House, designed by Frank Gehry and Vlado Milunic and fondly nicknamed Fred and Ginger.

been spotted on this rock wearing everything from combat boots to dress oxfords.

10 *Golden Age* Noon

Old-timers threw a fit when their beloved **Café Savoy** (Vitezna 5; 420-257-311-562; cafesavoy.ambi. cz; $) was cleaned up not once but twice in the 2000s, wiping away the tobacco stains, spilled beer, and dusty Stalinist décor of the earlier incarnation, and restoring Art Nouveau touches. Is this the new Prague or the old one? The prices for the hearty, meal-size soups and the ham-Gruyère-egg sandwiches almost recall the bargain-filled first post-Communist days. But the efficient, waistcoated staff brings to mind an entirely different time: the glorious First Republic, when Prague boasted one of the highest standards of living on the Continent.

THE BASICS

A taxi from Vaclav Havel Airport takes about 40 minutes to the city center.

Sheraton Prague Charles Square
Zitna 8
420-225-999-999
sheraton.com/prague
$$$
Splashy hotel in renovated group of 19th-century buildings.

Hotel Yasmin
Politickych veznu 913/12
420-234-100-100
hotel-yasmin.cz
$-$$
Stylish rooms decorated by the local designer Barbora Skorpilova.

Aria Hotel
Trziste 9
420-225-334-111
ariahotel.net
$$$
Italian modernist décor and a music theme.

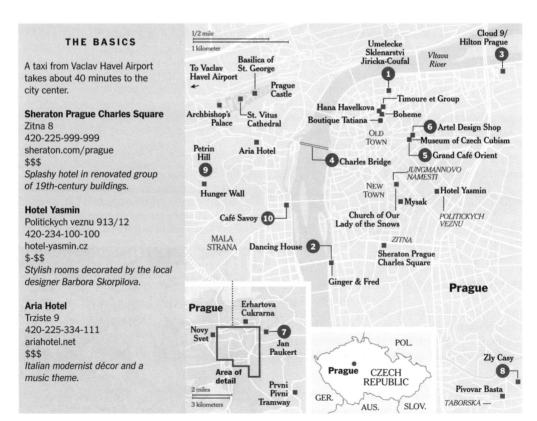

Pilsen

For years, travelers went to the Czech city of Pilsen, about an hour and 40 minutes from Prague by train, mostly to see the Pilsner Urquell brewery, the first and still a dominant maker of the city's most famous export: Pilsner beer. When they arrived, they found a city at the confluence of two rivers, the Mze and the Radbuza, with an appealing old town, some elegant religious architecture, and a grim overlay of Soviet-style buildings from the Communist era. But now Pilsen (Plzen to the Czechs) has cleaned itself up, brushed off the cobwebs, and opened several new attractions, both beer related and not. The result is a worthwhile destination for visitors — the city was designated as one of two European Capitals of Culture for 2015. — BY EVAN RAIL

FRIDAY

1 *Sacred Places* 3 p.m.

Pilsen's historic core, like those of many Czech cities, is organized around a storied main square. Here it's Namesti Republiky, dominated by the enormous **Cathedral of St. Bartholomew** (temporaliabona.unas.cz), a Gothic construction built between the 13th and 16th centuries. Step inside to see the 14th-century statue in the Czech "beautiful Madonna" style and find the 301 steps to the top of the tower. A few blocks away is the **Great Synagogue** (Sady Petatricatniku; pilsen.eu/tourist/visit/top-tourist-destinations), the world's third-largest synagogue, built in the Moorish style in 1893. It survived World War II (although its congregation did not), when the Nazis found its massive spaces useful for storage, and it has now been restored.

2 *World on a String* 4 p.m.

Across from the cathedral, the **Muzeum Loutek** (Namesti Republiky 23; 420-378-370-801; muzeumloutek.cz), or Puppet Museum, celebrates a longtime Czech art form. The beautifully restored late Gothic town house is filled with automated

puppet performances and historic puppets and marionettes, including original versions of local favorites Spejbl and Hurvinek, a puppet comedy duo invented in Pilsen in the 1920s. The combination of interactive displays and a gorgeous Old World atmosphere makes for a loving tribute, even for the uninitiated.

3 *New Brews* 8 p.m.

Building on the tradition of Pilsner Urquell, excellent smaller breweries have cropped up. The best would have to be the **Purkmistr** brewery (Pivovar Purkmistr, Selska naves 2; 420-377-994-311; purkmistr.cz; $) on the city's south side, home to a September festival featuring beers from about 40 indie breweries. Have dinner in the spacious main beer hall, where you may find yourself sharing a table with another group. Expect a feast of excellent Bohemian pub fare: meaty yet juicy bucek or pork belly; skvarkova pomazanka, a creamy spread of lard and cracklings; and rounds of hoppy pale lagers, chocolatey dark lagers, fruity bock beers, and lemony, crisp Hefeweizens.

SATURDAY

4 *Art in Transit* 10 a.m.

Several blocks south of the main square, the **Moving Station** (Nemejcova 1; johancentrum.cz; sometimes closed in winter) is an alternative culture center in part of a functioning commuter railroad station. Wander the halls of the building to see the current exhibitions. Though the artwork may sometimes be of questionable merit, it is an interesting

OPPOSITE Coasters at the Small Breweries Club, a spot for unusual beers in a city long identified with its Pilsner.

RIGHT Pivovar Groll, a small brewery named after the Bavarian brewmaster at a much larger one, Pilsner Urquell.

contrast to the soaring ceilings, arabesque balustrades, and intricate plasterwork hiding behind the building's dim facade of chipped paint and boarded-over windows.

5 *Patton Was Here* 11 a.m.

Less than 50 miles from the German border, Pilsen was one of the rare Czech cities to have been liberated by American troops during World War II, and remarkably, a pro-United States vibe remains to this day. During the city's annual Liberation Festival in May, local re-enactors in period uniforms drive around in restored United States Army jeeps. Surviving veterans leave their signatures on the walls of the **Patton Memorial Pilsen** (Pobrezni 10; 420-378-037-954; patton-memorial.cz), a museum dedicated to the city's occupation and liberation.

6 *Classic Pilsner* 2 p.m.

Take a tour at the **Pilsner Urquell** brewery (U Prazdroje 7; 420-377-062-888; prazdroj.cz), which has been making its beer since 1842. These days, the company takes its tour business seriously, too, offering an entertaining spin on the basic information

ABOVE The St. Bartholomew Cathedral in the city center.

OPPOSITE Fantastic faces at Muzeum Loutek, which celebrates and practices puppetry, a favorite Czech tradition.

about Pilsner and Urquell. You'll see a bottling plant, a film, and brewing facilities new and old, including part of an extensive system of cavelike underground storage vaults. (Take along a jacket or sweater.)

7 *A Bit of Vienna* 5 p.m.

Take a break from beer with cake and coffee, or even a glass of wine, in the richly decorated Viennese-style cafe at **Mestanska Beseda** (Kopeckého sady 13; 420-378-037-922; mestanska-beseda.cz). The larger spaces in this restored Art Nouveau building are used for performances and exhibitions.

8 *Czech Specials* 8 p.m.

Try the restaurant at **Pivovar Groll** (Truhlarska 10; 420-602-596-161; pivovargroll.cz; $), a small brewery named after the Bavarian brewmaster who first fired the kettles at Pilsner Urquell. Keeping to the Pilsen theme, the menu is traditionally Czech, replete with items like pork roast and sauerkraut, sausage, red cabbage, dumplings, and mushrooms. One visit also turned up a couple of very crisp and hoppy lagers. The outdoor terrace has a play area for children, perfect for imbibing parents.

9 *Bar Options* 10 p.m.

In a sign that even the big brewers are getting dressed up for Pilsen's new era, Gambrinus, an enormous brewery owned by the same people

behind Pilsner Urquell, now has a stylish pub, **Sedmy Nebe** (Bezrucova 4; 420-378-609-696; moravkaplzen.cz), downtown. It's a good stop if you're yearning for the ambience of a sports bar. An alternative is the Klub Malych Pivovaru, or **Small Breweries Club** (Nadrazni 16; 420-774-790-979; klubmalychpivovaru.cz), a youthful, easygoing spot where eight unusual beers from regional Czech and Bavarian producers are usually on tap. You might find live music, too.

SUNDAY

10 *Your Inner Techie* 10 a.m.

Find your inner child — or inner techie — at **Techmania** (Areál SKODA nározi ulic Borská a Brenkova; 420-737-247-585; techmania.cz), a science center focused on the technology that keeps the modern world going. The staff offers live presentations on electricity and magnetics, and curious visitors are given hands-on access to working Van de Graaff generators, luggage scanners, turbines, and train engines. Accompanying explanations of the technology behind the devices are in Czech, English, and German. Techmania is on the sprawling grounds of the Areál SKODA, an interesting place in itself. It's a 150-year-old factory complex that turns out train cars, locomotives, and charismatic trams for cities including Portland, Oregon.

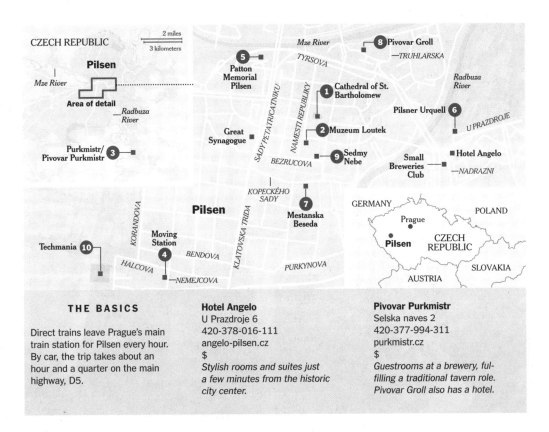

THE BASICS

Direct trains leave Prague's main train station for Pilsen every hour. By car, the trip takes about an hour and a quarter on the main highway, D5.

Hotel Angelo
U Prazdroje 6
420-378-016-111
angelo-pilsen.cz
$
Stylish rooms and suites just a few minutes from the historic city center.

Pivovar Purkmistr
Selska naves 2
420-377-994-311
purkmistr.cz
$
Guestrooms at a brewery, fulfilling a traditional tavern role. Pivovar Groll also has a hotel.

Moravia

Just across the border from Austria's Weinviertel, the South Moravian region of the Czech Republic has long been known as the home of cheap (but increasingly high-quality) local wines, as well as an almost inappropriate number of castles, mansions, and aristocratic residences originally built for the Austrian noble families who once called the area home. Despite easy connections from Vienna and Prague, the region lies in a pronounced travel shadow, helping to keep both costs and crowds low. While public transportation is cheap and efficient, this is a perfect area to explore in a weekend car trip. Start out in the hilltop wine-making town of Mikulov and move on to the twin castle towns of Valtice and Lednice, about 20 minutes away, before checking out the Archbishop's Palace and priceless collection of Dutch masters in the garden city of Kromeriz. — BY EVAN RAIL

FRIDAY

1 *Historic Enclave* 3 p.m.

In contrast to the immense castle at the summit of the hilltop town of Mikulov, the old houses of the **Mikulov Jewish Quarter** are tiny and intimate. The once-vibrant community here included Rabbi Judah Loew ben Bezalel, who according to legend created a powerful giant called the Prague Golem sometime in the 1500s. At the southwestern base of the hill, a well-marked trail will lead you through the quarter, stopping at Rabbi Loew's home and noting several examples of remarkable Renaissance-era Jewish architecture, finishing not far from the recently restored mikveh, or ceremonial bath. The Jewish cemetery is set on the scenic hillside just to the north of the town.

2 *Eating as Art* 7 p.m.

The culinary revolution sweeping through Prague hasn't yet reached most of rural Moravia. That said, **Eat Art Gallery** (Kapucinska 1, Mikulov; 420-724-900-204; eatartgallery.eu; $) serves

OPPOSITE The Lednice Castle in Moravia, a region of vine-yards and palaces good for a weekend of motorized exploring.

RIGHT Falconry for show at the Lednice Castle. Austrian nobles scattered their chateaux over Moravia's countryside.

surprisingly cosmopolitan fare, like stewed chicken and veggies with couscous, as well as traditional Czech recipes. The atmosphere suggests an English tearoom somehow transported to a small Moravian village.

SATURDAY

3 *Napoleon Woke Up Here* 10 a.m.

With its superjacent setting at the top of the hill, **Mikulov Castle** (Zámek 1, Mikulov; 420-519-309-019; rmm.cz) is just about impossible to overlook, even once catching the attention of Napoleon, who bunked here the night before he won the Battle of the Three Emperors in 1805. Today, guests are welcomed on castle tours showing off the former living quarters of the Dietrichstein noble family, as well as their extensive Baroque library, filled with 20,000 ancient volumes and a collection of priceless historical globes and maps. A third tour focuses on the area's viticultural traditions, finishing at the castle's Renaissance-era wine barrel, a massive vessel with a capacity of about 27,000 gallons.

4 *Wine at Lunch?* Noon

The long and narrow main square in Mikulov is filled with Baroque and Renaissance architecture. After gawking at the beautiful buildings, make your way to **Sojka & spol.** (Namesti 10; 420-518-327-862; sojkaaspol.cz; $), which is an organic grocery selling products from local farmers, an "eco-drugstore," and, finally, an organic restaurant, a rarity in the Czech Republic. In warm weather there are a few sidewalk

tables; otherwise, try to grab a table upstairs by a window with views of the square. On the menu, expect traditional dishes like duck or a mushroom risotto, along with more adventurous fare, like Asian-inspired soups, all artfully presented. Locally produced wines are featured on a surprisingly long list. Try a veltlinske zelene, a flinty dry white wine that you might know by its German name: Grüner Veltliner.

5 *Self-Serve Sampling* 1:30 p.m.

Just 20 minutes down the road from Mikulov by car, sprawling and curlicued **Valtice Castle** was once home to the Liechtenstein aristocratic family. Today, it serves a far more noble purpose, housing the Czech Republic's **National Wine Center** (Zámek 1, Valtice; 420-519-352-072; salonvin.cz), including an expansive cellar exhibition and tasting room dedicated to the country's 100 best wines, many of which have recently picked up international awards. Everything you try in the cellar is available for purchase, with even more bottles stocked in an additional wine shop located on the castle's ground floor.

6 *In Praise of Follies* 3 p.m.

The landscape between Valtice and Lednice — twinned castle towns about five miles apart — is positively littered with follies: faux Greek and Roman ruins, Gothic fortresses, and Asian imports created by the Liechtensteins, mostly in the 19th century, for

hosting parties and entertaining guests. All of them, as well as both castles, are part of the **Lednice-Valtice Cultural Landscape** (lednicko-valticky-areal.cz), and information on how to find them is available at the **Valtice Tourist Information Center** (Namesti Svobody 4, Valtice; 420-519-352-978). About a mile southwest of Valtice, visit the **Rajsna**, a fake Classical colonnade perched on the hill overlooking the castle. Then drive another mile or two to the **Rendezvous**, also known as the Temple of Diana, a Roman-style arch constructed around 1810 in the middle of a forest. Once in Lednice, wander the vast expanse of sculptured gardens at the wedding-cake **Lednice Castle** until you find the ersatz minaret whose three observation platforms provide vertiginous panoramas over the park, including views of the **Januv Hrad**, a would-be crumbling castle ruin.

7 *Between Places* 7 p.m.

The South Moravian region thrived in a strange niche between two cultures. Nowhere is that more

ABOVE Traditional Czech costumes make an appearance at a Moravian wine festival.

OPPOSITE ABOVE The wines of South Moravia remain inexpensive but are of increasingly high quality.

OPPOSITE BELOW Vineyards near the Januv Hrad.

apparent than at the **Hranicni Zamecek** (Hlohovec 16; 420-519-354-354; hranicnizamecek.cz; $), or Border Chateau, a Classicist palace built directly on top of what was the actual border between Austria and Moravia until the frontier was renegotiated in 1920. Today, this former Liechtenstein chateau houses a better-than-decent restaurant and hotel. From the terrace overlooking a lake, you can sample more South Moravian white wines from the chateau cellars, along with traditional schnitzels, goulash, and trout fillets. Above, the motto high up on the building's back wall makes clear exactly where you are: "Zwischen Österreich und Mähren," or "Between Austria and Moravia."

SUNDAY

8 *Flower Power* 9:30 a.m.

An hour and a half to the northeast, the beautiful Baroque buildings in the town of Kromeriz would be enough reason to visit. But just a 10-minute walk from the scenic main square, the **Kromeriz Flower Garden** (Generála Svobody, Kromeriz; 420-573-502-01; zamek-kromeriz.cz) ranks as one of the greatest sculptured landscapes in Europe. Designed by the imperial architect Giovanni Pietro Tencalla around 1665, the garden blends Italian Renaissance landscaping with Versailles-style French Classicism, offering hedge mazes, historic greenhouses, a central rotunda, and hundreds of original flower and sculptural decorations.

9 *Picture Perfect* 11 a.m.

You wouldn't expect a small town in Moravia to house one of Europe's greatest collections of Dutch

works by Lucas Cranach the Elder and Titian, whose immense *Flaying of Marsyas* has pride of place in the picture gallery's main viewing room. After your viewing, cool off in another celebrated sculpted garden, just outside the castle.

and Italian masters, but a 17th-century archbishop, Karl II von Liechtenstein-Kastelkorn, assembled an entire museum's worth of great oils and housed them all in the **Archbishop's Palace** (zamek-kromeriz. cz). Now the property of the Czech state, most of the collection is open to the public, including numerous

ABOVE Liechtenstein aristocrats built Valtice Castle. Inside today is the Czech Republic's National Wine Center, featuring the country's top 100 wines.

OPPOSITE Mikulov's Church of St. Wenceslas and the commanding hilltop Mikulov Castle.

10 *Midday Brew* Noon

Moravia might be the Czech Republic's wine region, but the country's best-loved beverage is still pivo, or beer. Sample the wares at the outstanding **Cerny Orel** brewpub (Velke Namesti 24, Kromeriz; 420-573-332-769; cerny-orel.eu; $), which turns out classic Czech lagers, spot-on German-style Hefeweizens, and occasional innovations including Belgian-style sours. The kitchen operates at the same high standard as the brewery, turning out excellent classics like beef in cream sauce as well as pan-fried chicken cutlets, crisp salads, and other updated dishes.

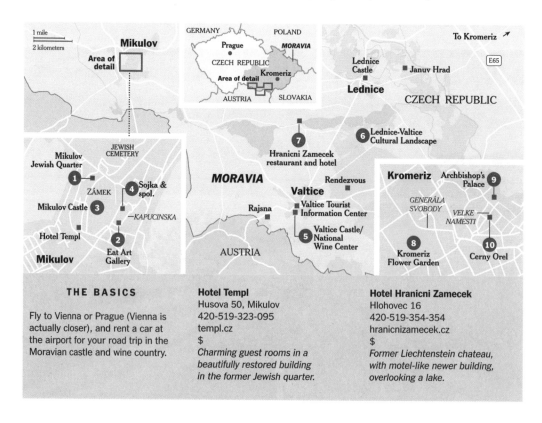

THE BASICS

Fly to Vienna or Prague (Vienna is actually closer), and rent a car at the airport for your road trip in the Moravian castle and wine country.

Hotel Templ
Husova 50, Mikulov
420-519-323-095
templ.cz
$
Charming guest rooms in a beautifully restored building in the former Jewish quarter.

Hotel Hranicni Zamecek
Hlohovec 16
420-519-354-354
hranicnizamecek.cz
$
Former Liechtenstein chateau, with motel-like newer building, overlooking a lake.

Bratislava

Bratislava, the capital of independent Slovakia since 1993, could teach a master class in European relations. Sitting at a historically strategic crossroads between Vienna, Prague, and Budapest — Vienna is just up the Danube, a 45-minute drive away — the city was a pawn in Central Europe's power struggles for a thousand years. Some Viennese still call it Pressburg, its name under the Austro-Hungarian Empire. Now, against a backdrop of Baroque buildings, Viennese cafes, and East Bloc concrete boxes, its cafes, bars, shops, and restaurants cater to laid-back locals, a large student population, and international travelers. With its combination of well-worn cobblestones by day and well-mixed cocktails after dark, Bratislava has become a popular weekend destination for a free-spirited crowd from across Europe and beyond.
— BY ANDREW FERREN

FRIDAY

1 *Shades of Baroque* 3 p.m.

Explore Bratislava's compact Old Town, starting at the medieval **St. Michael's Gate**. The major streets, like Michalska and Panska, are lined with giddy Baroque palaces in shades of marigold and lavender. Onion-domed turrets and spires rise above churches. Sidewalk cafes and fin de siècle coffee houses fill up in late afternoon — stop in for a glass of wine or a beer. Less trafficked lanes look like 19th-century paintings. One of them, Kapitulska, ends with the soaring verticality of **St. Martin's Cathedral**, a Gothic church consecrated in 1452 that has tremendous historic importance. (Now, thanks to a project from the Communist days, it's hemmed in by a major highway.) Eleven monarchs were crowned here, including the Hapsburg Empress Maria Theresa, whose partiality for Bratislava is reflected in the jewel-box look of the Old Town.

2 *White Castle* 5 p.m.

You won't have any trouble finding **Bratislava Castle** (421-2-2048-3110; bratislava-hrad.sk). Built

on a high cliff, it towers over the city, a stately white-and-red palace that seems almost austere compared to ornate castles elsewhere. It has a long history, but in its current form it dates to the 1950s, when it was finally rebuilt after being mostly destroyed in a fire in 1811. Climb up and look down. If you ignore the concrete apartment buildings from the Communist era, this is a great place to imagine the view in the days when Maria Theresa frequently held court here.

3 *Top Tower* 8 p.m.

The **Novy Most**, or New Bridge, built in 1972 by the Soviet-backed government, is easily Bratislava's most visible structure, surpassing even the castle. For many, the enormous asymmetrical bridge is an eyesore that destroyed the scale and perspective of the riverfront along with some historically important neighborhoods, like the ancient Jewish quarter. But for anyone with a taste for chunky modernism and architectural audacity, the bridge holds some appeal. That appeal became easier to savor when the discus-shaped observation deck atop its tower was converted from a kitsch coffee shop to a swanky cocktail lounge and restaurant called **UFO** (421-2-6252-0300; u-f-o.sk). Reserve a table for dinner to avoid the admission charge.

SATURDAY

4 *Hit the High Spots* 9:30 a.m.

Start a morning landmarks tour at the **Blue Church** (Bezrucova 2; open daily), an Art Nouveau

OPPOSITE   St. Michael's Gate, entry to old Bratislava.

RIGHT   The Novy Most bridge over the Danube River. Atop the tower is a swanky cocktail lounge.

confection that really is very blue, down to blue pews inside. At the art gallery in the **Primate's Palace** (Primacialne nam. 1; 421-2-5935-6435; bratislava.sk), speed through the Hall of Mirrors where Napoleon and Austrian Emperor Franz I signed a treaty and make a beeline for the 17th-century English tapestries. Next, hit the City Art Gallery in the stunning **Palffy Palace** (Panska 19; 421-2-5443-3627; gmb.sk). Look for *Passage*, an installation by the Slovakian artist Matej Kren that uses mirrors to expand stacks of books into an infinite library, and other works by 20th-century Slovakian artists. Beyond the City Art Gallery, Bratislava also has the **Slovak National Gallery** (Razusovo Nabrezie 2; 421-2-2047-6237; sng.sk), which betrays the Austro-Hungarian predilection for Dutch painters.

5 *Take It Home* Noon

Time for some souvenir hunting. From the courtyards of the city's glorious buildings, multiple doors and passageways wind through former palaces, leading to art galleries, shops, beer gardens, and other enterprises. Look for etched glassware, wines from the nearby vineyards, ceramics, and embroidery. The Slovakian fashion designer **Dana Kleinert** (421-2-903-459-833; kleinert.sk) has a tempting showroom at Zelena 10.

6 *New Town* 2 p.m.

See a newer Bratislava at **Eurovea** (eurovea. com), a 57-acre complex at the edge of the Danube that opened in 2010 and is often compared to Canary Wharf in London. It includes restaurants and bars, stores, a hotel, a movie theater, apartments, and offices. Check out the scene in the shopping center,

which announces itself with eye-catching curved glass, and do some people-watching outside at the park and promenade. The city has other shopping centers, but this one has made a splash.

7 *D.J. Dinner* 8 p.m.

Primi (Michalská 21; 421-2-5464-7344; medusagroup.sk; $$) follows the vogue for pasta and carpaccio, but with fantastic D.J.'s. The place is a favorite of the local young and rich, so have dinner and stay a while to join in. If you'd prefer higher culture, have an earlier dinner and catch a concert or performance. **The Slovak Philharmonic** (filharm.sk) plays in an elegant hall, the **National Theater** (snd.sk) stages opera that draws music lovers from neighboring Austria, and the **Nova Scena Theater** (nova-scena.sk) is a venue for plays and musicals. In summer, a cultural festival brings performances all season long.

8 *Techno Fallout* 10 p.m.

Not for nothing does Bratislava have a reputation as a party destination. An active club scene includes places like **Subclub** (Nabrezie armadneho generala L. Svobodu; 421-903-776-633; subclub.sk), a former nuclear fallout shelter where narrow tunnels lead to a large vaulted chamber in which the D.J. and dance floor take the place of whatever accommodation the Communist government had in mind for itself in case of nuclear Armageddon.

ABOVE The Old Town reflects Bratislava's prominence and prosperity in the Austro-Hungarian Empire.

OPPOSITE The narrow passageway under the imposing medieval tower of St. Michael's Gate.

SUNDAY

9 *Viennese Breakfast* 10 a.m.

Have some bacon and eggs or spinach pie at **Kaffee Mayer** (Hlavne namestie 4; 421-2-5441-1741; kaffeemayer.sk; $), but keep in mind that what this place is really all about is the pastries. Save room. A century-old Viennese-style coffeehouse, patisserie, and restaurant, it's a comfortable place in the heart of the Old Town.

10 *Lost World* 11 a.m.

Using artifacts and photos, the **Museum of Jewish Culture** (Zidovska 17; 421-2-5934-9142; snm.sk), a branch of the Slovak National Museum, chronicles the thriving Jewish community that existed in Bratislava before the Holocaust. Nearly all of the city's Jews emigrated or were murdered between 1939 and 1945; the Communist government bulldozed what was left of their neighborhood as part of its building projects. The museum is part of a national effort to recognize the place of ethnic minorities in Slovakia's history and culture.

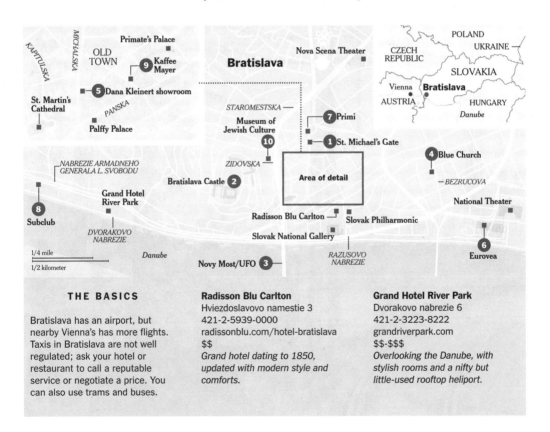

THE BASICS

Bratislava has an airport, but nearby Vienna's has more flights. Taxis in Bratislava are not well regulated; ask your hotel or restaurant to call a reputable service or negotiate a price. You can also use trams and buses.

Radisson Blu Carlton
Hviezdoslavovo namestie 3
421-2-5939-0000
radissonblu.com/hotel-bratislava
$$
Grand hotel dating to 1850, updated with modern style and comforts.

Grand Hotel River Park
Dvorakovo nabrezie 6
421-2-3223-8222
grandriverpark.com
$$-$$$
Overlooking the Danube, with stylish rooms and a nifty but little-used rooftop heliport.

Budapest

Like much of post-Communist Europe, Budapest has replaced the image of the impoverished East with symbols of international luxury, like a Four Seasons hotel and a new branch of Nobu, the high-end Japanese restaurant. But the brightest spots in Hungary's capital city are often native-born, rather than imports. From stately Buda in the west to Pest's shabby-chic streets east of the Danube, new attractions show off the achievements of local artists, producers, vintners, and chefs. None of this means that the city's rich cultural heritage has been displaced. You'll still find Old World grandeur, stunning architecture, ornate public bathhouses (Budapest was known for its hot springs as far back as Roman times), and beautiful museums that don't cost a cent. A weekend here provides a glimpse of the city's justifiable pride, as well as an authentic sense of place. — BY EVAN RAIL

FRIDAY

1 *Get Your Kicks* 5 p.m.

Buda has steep hills, while Pest's long boulevards are seemingly without end, and the time-honored way to get from one to the other is by walking across the **Chain Bridge**. Get ready for legwork with new sneakers from **Tisza Cipo** (Karoly korut 1; 36-1-266-3055; tiszacipo.hu), the flagship store of a once-reviled Communist-era brand that was revived as a modern line of streetwear in 2003. Though the flashy colors, plush material, and quality construction of today's Klasszik models are unlike just about anything from the former regime, no one exposed to their distinctively Eastern Bloc retro vibe will mistake them for a pair of Nikes. Your favorite souvenirs? You're wearing them.

2 *Wine Kitchen* 7:30 p.m.

Home to the oldest classified wine regions in Europe, Hungary is also a fount of excellent Old World cooking. The two combine splendidly at **Borkonyha** (Sas utca 3; 36-1-266-0835; borkonyha.hu;

$), or "wine kitchen," an airy, modern bistro with a list of about 200 outstanding domestic bottles, many of which are available by the glass. Hungarian fare with international accents, like venison from the western village of Oreglak prepared with dried fruit and celery thyme, pairs gloriously with unusual local varietals like Zoltan Gunzer's kadarka, an elegant dry red whose rich black currant and blackberry notes compare with those of a great zinfandel.

3 *Garden Bar* 10 p.m.

In warm weather, vacant lots around the city are transformed into kert (garden) bars: grungy outdoor dives occupying a middle ground between beer gardens and anarchist squats, generally with a down-market vibe. But one manifestation of the trend, **Otkert** (Zrinyi utca 4; 36-70-330-8652; otkert.hu), takes the idea upscale, creating what one Budapest cultural blogger called a "posh kert." Find a quiet corner nook and chill out over a shot of pear or apricot palinka, the local take on schnapps. Then join the crowd, and it is a crowd, of beautiful people for a spin on the open-air dance floor.

SATURDAY

4 *Your Style* 11 a.m.

Although cultured travelers have long had many reasons to visit Budapest — outstanding wine, glorious music, hip night life — it is probably safe to say the local sense of fashion and style was not among them until recently. Head down to the area between the Dohany Street Synagogue, the Hungarian

OPPOSITE The Hungarian Parliament building in Pest, seen from across the Danube River in Buda.

RIGHT Garden bars, or kerts, were traditionally grungy, but the crowd and surroundings are upscale at Otkert.

National Museum, and the Danube, where numerous small boutiques like **Black Box** (Iranyi utca 18; 36-30-414-8979; Facebook: Black Box Concept Store) offer everything from club wear to haute couture confections, all by local designers, often at very affordable prices. Treat yourself to something new to wear when you hit the clubs later.

5 *Cold War Memories* 1 p.m.

Grab an extra layer for your trip to the oddball cold war museum **Sziklakorhaz** (Lovas ut 4/c; 36-70-7010-101; sziklakorhaz.hu), a former secret hospital and nuclear bunker hidden deep inside the mountain under Buda Castle. No matter how hot it is outside, it will be cold underground. Take the hourlong tour in Hungarian or English, buy a Marka soda, and browse such bunker-worthy tchotchkes as Communist-era military helmets and gas masks.

6 *Off the Liszt* 3 p.m.

Expect to hear a lot about the local hero Franz Liszt — even the airport is called Liszt Ferenc. You may find a concert or other event around town in his honor. The **Liszt Museum** (Vorosmarty utca 35; 36-1-322-9804; lisztmuseum.hu) re-creates Liszt's final Budapest apartment with tons of his personal belongings, instruments, and furniture, including an original writing desk with its own three-octave piano keyboard.

7 *Over the Top* 7:30 p.m.

Budapesters groaned when Prague became the first post-Communist capital with a Michelin-starred restaurant in 2008. But the Hungarians soon got into

ABOVE Sziklakorhaz, a Cold War museum, occupies a former secret hospital and nuclear bunker below Buda Castle.

RIGHT The Liszt Museum. Budapest is so proud of Liszt, its homegrown music superstar, that its airport is named for him.

OPPOSITE Tisza shoes, a revived East Bloc brand.

the race. **Onyx** (Vorosmarty ter 7-8; 36-30-508-0622; onyxrestaurant.hu; $$$) is the second Budapest restaurant to earn a Michelin star, after the stylish Costes. Jaded diners might find the gold-on-black walls, heavy armchairs, and oh-so-formal table service somewhat over the top, but dishes like goose liver torte with strawberry jelly and kolache, and confit of beef shoulder with creamy carrot purée come across as remarkably accomplished, effortlessly bridging the traditional flavors of the country with contemporary international culinary techniques. For cheap dates, the Tuesday-through-Friday lunch menu features much of the same excellent cooking at much lower rates.

8 *For Music Lovers* 9:30 p.m.

Jazz has become an international music, free from its American roots. At **Budapest Jazz Club** (Hollan Erno utca 7; 36-70-413-9837; bjc.hu), sit back and marvel as energetic Hungarian and international musicians venture far beyond the John Coltrane and Miles Davis repertoire. Reserve to snare one of the small tables in front of the stage. A less intense and much more romantic place to enjoy music and cocktails is the cozy and dark **Suttogo Piano Bar** (Hajos utca 27; 36-20-455-7329; suttogopianobar.hu).

9 *Up All Night* 11:30 p.m.

Some of the best new bright spots here echo the glories of the city's interwar period. A legendary fashion center when it first appeared in 1926, the giant Corvin department store is now better known as **Corvinteto** (Blaha Lujza ter 1-2, enter from

Somogyi Bela utca; 36-20-772-2983; corvinteto.hu), a club and after-hours lounge that has taken over the building's top levels. Inside, concerts of dub, drum 'n' bass, and electroclash run year-round, but if it's going to be a really late night, the enormous rooftop bar—open from spring to autumn—might just be the best spot to watch a sunrise over the city skyline.

SUNDAY

10 *Taste to Go* Noon

On Sundays, trendy locals and expats go to the second Pest branch of **Culinaris** (Balassi Balint utca 7; 36-1-373-0028; culinaris.hu; $), a lunch counter with a separate specialty-foods shop. It's near the Hungarian Parliament building (that's the unmissable mess of spires with a huge dome that looks like one very creepy church, or perhaps the corporate headquarters of Vampires Inc.). First grab a loosely wrapped burrito or Cobb salad at the cool and bright Culinaris counter. Then head around the corner to the shop, which has a collection of cheeses, cookies, crackers, pastas, wines, and beers so extensive it could be a costly mistake to gawk on an empty stomach. Before you leave, think of a typical airport meal. Then order a to-go ham and cheese, custom-built on a fluffy, house-made black-olive loaf for a final taste that will stay with you at least as far as the departure gate.

THE BASICS

Airlines from around the world fly into Budapest's airport. The city's subway anchors an extensive public transit system, and the Danube, dividing Buda and Pest, makes orientation easy.

Palazzo Zichy
Lorinc pap ter 2
36-1-235-4000
hotel-palazzo-zichy.hu
$
Neo-Baroque stairwells and modern minimalist décor blend stylishly in a converted 19th-century mansion.

La Prima
Piarista utca 6
36-1-799-0088
laprimahotelbudapest.com
$$
Closer to the action in Pest, just off touristy Vaci utca.

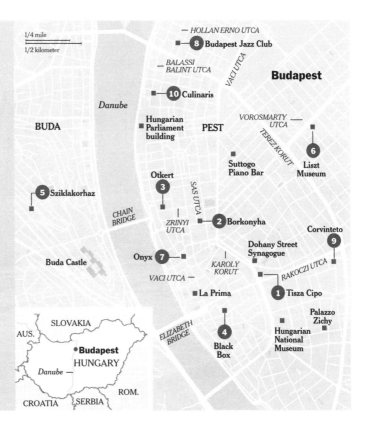

Kiev

Kiev, the capital of Ukraine, is a vibrant 21st-century metropolis, but its thriving art scene, contemporary cuisine, and dance-till-dawn night life are only the latest layer on an ancient city. A repository of Slavic tradition, Kiev has centuries-old catacombs, churches, and monasteries. It looks as if it had been painted like a Ukrainian Easter egg, with brightly colored buildings and gold domes glittering on the hills above the Dnieper River. Heirs of a tumultuous and often tragic history featuring frequent conquests, seven decades of Soviet rule, and destruction in World War II, Kievans have been tested anew by national conflicts with Russia over territory to the south and east. But their resilience is on display in the seemingly boundless hunger for fun that keeps their cafes bustling, their beaches thronged, and their bars open all night. — BY FINN-OLAF JONES

FRIDAY

1 *Stadium Seat to History* 2 p.m.

A glance around stadium-shaped **Independence Square**, the city's traditional nerve center, encapsulates much of Kiev's history. Czarist, Beaux-Arts, and Stalinist buildings represent the old, and the glass-enclosed Globus luxury mall and McDonald's assert the new. The Slavic goddess Berehynia stands atop a towering column that replaced a Lenin monument. Grab a mug of the local brew, Obolon, at one of the sidewalk cafes, and soak in the atmosphere. Street performers, students, vendors, and political demonstrators all gravitate here.

2 *New Constantinople* 3 p.m.

The bulbous green and gold domes of **Saint Sophia** (24 Vladimirskaya Street; 380-44-278-6262), on the high ground of the old town, dominate Kiev's skyline. Constructed beginning in the 11th century, the church was built to rival Hagia Sophia in Constantinople and echoes its name. Inside, it

feels like a medieval man cave, with incense hanging thickly in the air, dramatic rays of light coming in through tiny windows, and monks, priests, and novices scurrying back and forth in black frocks. Stick around long enough and you may hear prayer accompanied by the a cappella choral music for which the Ukrainians are renowned.

3 *Feed Your Inner Peasant* 8 p.m.

Though the fake chickens, straw roof, and wandering singers might seem over the top, the delicious Slavic dishes at **Tsarske Selo** (Ivana Mazepy St 42/1; 380-44-288-9775; tsarske.kiev.ua; $$$) are the real deal — as evidenced by the crowds of locals here for a fancy night out. The restaurant is a celebration of hearty Ukrainian fare including pickled almost-anythings, borscht, the traditional grilled meats called shashlyk, and yes, if your cardiologist will let you, chicken Kiev. There's also an extraordinary assortment of gorilka — Ukrainian vodka.

4 *Ukrave* 11 p.m.

Kiev's nightclubs attract jet setters from Europe and Russia for weekend bacchanals. At the vast entertainment complex **Arena** (2A Basseynaya Street; 380-44-492-0000; arena-kiev.com), an outdoor hookah bar, a cabaret, and sports and karaoke bars all attract a variety of eager patrons. Rich Russians mingle with local celebrities and trendsetters whose cheekbones are as high as the drinks prices. At **Privilege** (2 Parkovaya Doroga; 380-44-451-6790; privilege.kiev.ua), an ongoing summer rave in the open-air Green Theater, the hordes dance until sunrise.

OPPOSITE The Museum of the Great Patriotic War 1941-1945. The displays inside detail World War II's epic toll on the Ukrainian people.

RIGHT Cooling off at a fountain in Independence Square, the traditional city center of Kiev.

his unique museum and to describe how he crafted these micron-sized projects "between heartbeats."

7 *The War at Home* 1 p.m.

Take a 10-minute stroll on a park path, from the monastery and through a grotto decorated with World War II fighters, to the base of the 203-foot-tall stainless steel statue *Motherland*. Designed by Yevgeny Vuchetich, it towers above the **National Museum of the Great Patriotic War 1941-1945** (44 Lavrska Street; 380-44-285-9452; warmuseum.kiev.ua). The museum dates to the Soviet era (Leonid Brezhnev came for the opening), but the story it tells transcends tension between Ukrainians and Russians. The galleries circle the statue's base, displaying gruesome and heroic relics — gloves and soap made from concentration camp victims, captured weapons and banners — and detailing the epic toll that World War II took on Ukraine. Recent additions include a Christian cross made from gun parts dramatically juxtaposed against the giant dome decorated with Communist motifs.

8 *Food Shrine* 2 p.m.

The Ukrainians are the Italians of Eastern Europe when it comes to the love of good food and passion for the national cuisine. The venerable central food market **Besarabsky Rynok** (2 Besarabs'ka Ploscha) is the source of ingredients for some of Kiev's best dishes. The market, built in 1912, resembles a cavernous Victorian train station engulfing a plethora of stands bursting with local cheeses, red and black caviar, pickles, wild boar and other game, borscht, vodka, and other local treats. Vendors offer enough samples to make a stroll through the market akin to a pass through an all-you-can-eat buffet.

9 *Night in the Museum* 7 p.m.

The **PinchukArtCentre** (38 Velyka Vasylkivska; 380-44-590-0858; pinchukartcentre.org), a world-class center for contemporary art created by the Ukrainian steel billionaire Victor Pinchuk, stays open until 9 p.m. The collection of art by local and international superstars is astounding, but perhaps the most provocative installation is the fifth-floor bathroom, a neon-lit funhouse with mirrors and windows providing sly

SATURDAY

5 *Them Bones* 10 a.m.

Dress respectfully and start early to beat the weekend crowds to the **Kievo-Percherskaya Lavra** (25 Lavrska Street; 380-44-280-3071; kplavra.kiev.ua), a Unesco World Heritage Site. Pilgrims approach this sprawling monastery wearing icons and pictures of saints around their necks. Buy candles at the entrances to the upper and lower catacombs, and follow the twisty subterranean tunnels past ancient glass-encased tombs of monks, many of them Orthodox saints, whose hands and feet occasionally stick out from their richly textured burial clothes. All is dramatically lighted by colorful hanging lanterns. After re-emerging into daylight, check out the richly gilded 11th-century Dormition Cathedral, reconstructed after its destruction in World War II.

6 *It's a Small World* Noon

A full chessboard on the head of a pin, a sand-grain-sized working mechanical engine, a flea wearing golden shoes — these are some of the small miracles created by Mykola Syadristy, a self-taught master famed throughout the old Soviet Union. His miniatures are exhibited under microscopes at the **Museum of Microminiatures** (9 Lavrska Street, Building 5; 380-44-280-8137; microart.kiev.ua) on the monastery grounds next to the cathedral. The dapper Syadristy is often at hand himself to give tours of glances between the men's and women's rooms. Grab supper at the sixth-floor **One Love Coffee** ($), a high-style cafe where you can browse art books while having a sandwich or a full dinner. Wine is served along with Seattle-worthy coffees. If it's warm, enjoy the view of the city from the terrace.

SUNDAY

10 *Slavic-Cuban Brunch* 11 a.m.

If you've over-indulged this weekend, **Arbequina** (4 Grinchenko Street; 380-44-223-9618; $), a pierogi's throw from Independence Square, is the antidote. Its Cuban and Ukrainian chefs put a light touch to

OPPOSITE The domes of Saint Sophia. Listen inside for traditional Ukrainian a cappella choral music.

Slavic brunch with homemade pastries, a variety of pancakes, a mélange of imaginatively mixed fresh juices, and, for an effective head-clearer, a miraculous concoction of fresh mint tea laced with lemon and honey. Take a seat on the terrace if the weather is good.

11 *Rio on the Dnieper* 12:30 p.m.

About halfway across the scenic Parkovy pedestrian bridge from downtown to **Trukhanov Island**, you should begin to pick up the seductive aromas from dozens of barbecues. With its lovely beach and stunning views of the city, the island is a favorite Kiev weekend spot. Swimming in the Dnieper has its hazards, given fluctuating levels of pollution. But the verdant island looks like a spot on the Mississippi, and the glamorously tiny swimwear on some of the well-conditioned locals brings to mind Rio or Miami.

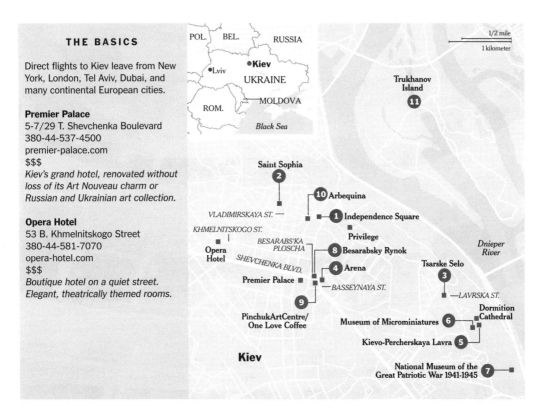

THE BASICS

Direct flights to Kiev leave from New York, London, Tel Aviv, Dubai, and many continental European cities.

Premier Palace
5-7/29 T. Shevchenka Boulevard
380-44-537-4500
premier-palace.com
$$$
Kiev's grand hotel, renovated without loss of its Art Nouveau charm or Russian and Ukrainian art collection.

Opera Hotel
53 B. Khmelnitskogo Street
380-44-581-7070
opera-hotel.com
$$$
Boutique hotel on a quiet street. Elegant, theatrically themed rooms.

POL. BEL. RUSSIA
•Lviv •**Kiev**
UKRAINE
MOLDOVA
ROM.
Black Sea

1/2 mile
1 kilometer

Trukhanov Island
11

Saint Sophia
2

VLADIMIRSKAYA ST.
KHMELNITSKOGO ST.
BESARABS'KA PLOSCHA
Opera Hotel
SHEVCHENKA BLVD.
Premier Palace ■
10 Arbequina
1 Independence Square
Privilege
8 Besarabsky Rynok
4 Arena
BASSEYNAYA ST.
9

PinchukArtCentre/
One Love Coffee

Dnieper River

Tsarske Selo
3
LAVRSKA ST.

Dormition Cathedral
Museum of Microminiatures **6**
Kievo-Percherskaya Lavra **5**

National Museum of the **7**
Great Patriotic War 1941-1945

Kiev

Lviv

Roughly 45 miles from the Polish border, Lviv, the unofficial capital of western Ukraine, is an architectural gem of a city with a polyglot past. In the 20th century alone it changed hands between Austria-Hungary, Poland, and the Soviet Union (as well as being occupied by Nazi Germany), and was called Lemberg, Lwow, and Lvov depending upon who was in charge—all this before Ukrainian independence in 1991. With its ornately handsome buildings and its gala Viennese ball, Lviv still bears vestiges of its days as part of the Austro-Hungarian Empire. But behind the Old Europe vibe is a city that has reclaimed its Ukrainian heritage and still retains a substantial Russian influence in its population of 830,000. An influx of money for tourism development, tied to its role as a host of an international soccer tournament in 2012, has allowed Lviv to revamp its airport and add hotels and restaurants to complement its venerable beauty. — BY JEFF SCHLEGEL

FRIDAY

1 *Survivor Cityscape* 4 p.m.

Although meandering along cobblestone streets lined with shoulder-to-shoulder buildings and centuries-old churches of various faiths is a pleasant way to meet the city's people and its history, Lviv's medieval layout can be a warren of confusion. Start in **Plosha Rynok**, or Market Square, the heart of the old city. If you're feeling up to it, climb up to the observation deck in the 210-foot-tall **Town Hall** at the center of the square and look out over the rich trove of architecture that makes the city a Unesco heritage site. In contrast to Kiev, whose old structures were devastated by both the Nazis and the Soviets, Lviv survived World War II with its historic buildings intact. Back on the ground, admire the fountains with statues of Greek gods and goddesses at the square's four corners, and take a close look at some of the 44 townhouses ringing the square. Dating to the 16th century, they were refurbished over the centuries in Baroque, Gothic, and Renaissance styles. Find a spot at one of the outdoor cafes and order Lvivske Premium Lager, a potent local brew.

OPPOSITE The Austro-Hungarian-era Opera House.

RIGHT Ukrainian heritage is resurgent in Lviv.

2 *Viennese Ukrainian* 7 p.m.

Videnska Kavyarnya, or the Viennese Coffeehouse (Wien Hotel, 12 Prospekt Svobody; 380-322-235-8721; wienhotel.com.ua; $) the oldest cafe in Lviv, dates back to the Austro-Hungarian Empire and still feels Viennese, but it's a good spot for Ukrainian cuisine. Ask whether there are any variations on the menu of the traditionally humble specialties like sausages and the dumplings known as varenyky, filled with potatoes or cabbage, sweet cheese, or cherries. Sit outside on one of the patios if it's warm.

3 *On the Avenue* 8:30 p.m.

Stroll along the wide, chestnut-lined esplanade of **Prospekt Svobody**, or Freedom Avenue, the main thoroughfare. During the day and early evening in good weather, the promenade is usually crowded with strollers and lined with packed benches; frequent chess matches attract spectators. Nearby, the plaza in front of the **Lviv Opera and Ballet House**, a majestic 1900 building with a richly decorated, neo-Renaissance facade, is a daytime playground of horseback rides and kiddie go-karts. At night, people cram the restaurants and outdoor cafes along the avenue and Eurobeat dance music is everywhere.

SATURDAY

4 *Don't Skip the Chocolate* 10 a.m.

Shop the open-air markets scattered through the city center. Some are fresh food bazaars where old women in scarves sell flowers and vegetables from the countryside. For crafts and souvenirs, look for

treasures at the **Art Market** (Lesi Ukrayinky) near Market Square, where you might find traditional Ukrainian costumes like those still worn for festivals, along with flea market wares. For souvenirs and handicrafts, including intricately embroidered textiles, try the **Vernisazh Market** near the Opera House, in front of Zankovetska theater. The shops are fun, too. The bookstore **Dom Knigi** (8 Adam Mickiewitz Square) is a good bet if you're looking for a map in English. And for handmade chocolates that will make you wish you could come to Lviv every week (or at least every Valentine's Day), sample the goods at the **Lviv Chocolate Workshop** (3 Serbska; 380-50-430-6033; chocolate.lviv.ua).

5 *Spires of Their Own* Noon

Lviv's particular brand of Old World charm is the work of many groups who settled here. Its winding streets reflect the overlapping cultures — most obviously in the variety of eye-catching cathedrals. One of the oldest and most elegant, with graceful arches and beautiful frescoes inside, is the **Armenian Cathedral** (7 Virmenska Street). The **Latin Cathedral** (Katedralna Square), which is both Gothic and Baroque in style, is Roman Catholic; the **Dominican**, east of Market Square, has a landmark Baroque dome and now serves as a Ukrainian Greek Catholic Church. The **Church of the Assumption** (5 Ruska) is Ukrainian Orthodox. On your travels, don't miss **Halytska Square**, dominated by a bronze statue of Danylo, a 13th-century Galician prince who founded the city and named it for his son, Lev.

6 *Harsh History* 1 p.m.

Lviv's buildings survived, but not all of its people were so fortunate. Many citizens were tortured or killed by the Gestapo or in the Stalinist era at a forbidding prison on **Lonsky Street**, away from the city center. In 2009 it became the location of a **National Museum and Memorial to the Victims of Occupation** (1 Stepan Bandera Street, entrance on Bryullova Street; 380-322-474-220). Check at the tourist center on Market Square for opening hours and more information. The city's Jewish population of more than 100,000 was annihilated by the Nazis, along with about 100,000 Jewish refugees who were in the city when it fell to the German army in 1941; a memorial stands on **Chornovola Street**, and plaques mark the locations of destroyed synagogues. For centuries, Jews had thrived in Lviv; Sholem Aleichem, whose tales are the basis for *Fiddler on the Roof*, wrote some of his stories here.

7 *Lift a Mug* 2 p.m.

Time for conviviality. Head to **Kumpel** (6 Volodymyra Vynnychenka Street; 380-322-421-780; $), a popular brewpub, open day and night, with open-air and indoor seating. The hearty food is pub-appropriate: sausages, goulash, and meat platters. The beer comes in dark, light, and red, and it has a coterie of fans.

8 *In Search of Bohemia* 4 p.m.

The **Dzyga Cultural Center** (35 Virmenska Street; 380-322-975-612; dzyga.com), a contemporary art space with a music hall and bar, is the nexus of bohemian life in Lviv. Wander through the gallery to see what the city's contemporary artists are doing; rotating exhibits feature paintings, sculpture, and

ABOVE Halytska Street, one of the cobblestoned streets near the city's central square, Plosha Rynok.

BELOW Lviv's collection of cathedrals — Armenian, Roman Catholic, Ukrainian Greek Catholic, Ukrainian Orthodox — reflects a complex past of many worshipers and many rulers.

RIGHT Town Hall in Plosha Rynok. In daylight, climb the tower for views out over the city.

graphic art by local and international artists. Sip coffee in the indoor cafe or under an umbrella on the patio. Dzyga (the names means "spinning top") is run by an association that puts together music and ballet performances and art events across the city, and this cultural center is housed in a former Dominican monastery.

9 *Savory and Sweet* 8 p.m.

Have dinner at **Café Veronika** (21 Shevchenka Street; 380-322-986-028; $$), a justly popular restaurant attached to a pastry shop known for its luscious desserts. Dine outdoors, or sit inside in a dark, cozy brick grotto lighted only by Tiffany-style lamps.

Save room for the sweets. Veronika is also a tempting place in the morning, with good breakfast food including fabulous pastries.

SUNDAY

10 *Look Down, Look Back* 10 a.m.

It's a long climb, but brave the 220 spiral metal steps of **Castle Hill**, northeast of the city center. At the summit are the ruins of a 14th-century castle that is supposedly on the site where Danylo founded Lviv. It's a favorite spot for the people of Lviv, and the best place to look back at their city.

THE BASICS

Many flights to Lviv require connections in Kiev. By train, the trip from Kiev to Lviv takes eight hours.

Chopin Hotel
7 Malaniuka Square
380-322-611-020
chopinhotel.com.ua
$
Boutique hotel with a romantic theme.

Leopolis
16 Teatralna Street
380-322-959-500
leopolishotel.com
$$$
Polished, individually designed rooms and marble baths in an 18th-century building.

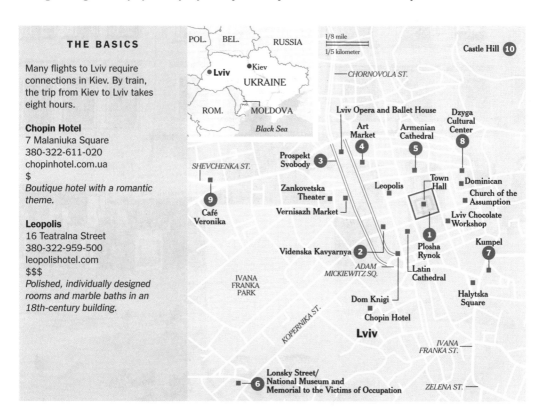

Warsaw

Determined to reclaim their capital, Poles reconstructed much of Warsaw brick by brick after the damage of World War II — no easy task since much of it had been pulverized. Using everything from oil paintings to postcards, news photos, and old family albums, architects and engineers painstakingly rebuilt the medieval Old Town Market Square and the adjacent 15th-century New Town, from scratch. Virtually everything a visitor sees there today is a re-creation, as are most of the city's palaces, cathedrals, and landmarks (a postwar reality that this Old Town has in common with large chunks of several others in Europe). While it can feel a bit Disneyesque, the reconstructions represent the Poles' determination to rebuild their lives on their own terms, after both the war and the Communist era. Drab Soviet-style buildings remain in Warsaw amid its new skyscrapers, but the Poles are far from finished with constructing their future. — BY DENNY LEE AND STEVE DOUGHERTY

FRIDAY

1 *The City's Heart* 4 p.m.

Start in Stare Miasto, or Old Town, with its castles and pastel-colored burgher houses. Stroll around and look closely. This square was originally laid out sometime around 1300. The postwar reconstruction of the buildings used some of the original bricks, and surviving decorative elements found in the rubble were put back in place. Don't miss having an ice cream at **Lody** (Ulica Nowomiejska 7/9; 48-22-635-7346; lody-warszawa.pl), a popular ice cream parlor. If you're a music lover, walk a few blocks south to the **Chopin Museum** (Ulica Okólnik 1; 48-22-441-6251; chopin.museum/en), dedicated to Poland's most famous composer, for a look at his handwritten musical scores and his last piano. Nearby is an illustration of the national fondness for this favorite son. In the Church of the Holy Cross, Chopin's heart is buried in a pillar. (The rest of him is in Paris, where he died in 1849.)

OPPOSITE The Stare Miasto, Warsaw's Old Town, is part history, part postwar labor of love.

RIGHT For a workout that doubles as sightseeing, swim at the RiverView Wellness Center in the InterContinental Hotel.

2 *Upscale Peasantry* 8 p.m.

U Fukiera (Old Town Square 27; 48-22-831-1013; ufukiera.pl; $$), is an eccentric grotto filled with flickering candlelight, brothel-red lamp shades, and the odd birdcage and parakeet. It caters unabashedly to foreign tourists. The owner, Magda Gessler, sees herself as something of an ambassador for traditional Polish peasant cuisine. Dishes include herring lathered in creamy sauce, chopped onions, and capers, and veal dumplings sprinkled with pig cracklings.

3 *Bright Lights* Midnight

Look for Warsaw night life in the Champagne-fueled bars of the city center. Clubs come and go, but one with a track record is **Platinium** (Ulica Fredry 6; 48-22-596-4666; platiniumclub.pl), which keeps the crowds coming with a full calendar of live music and D.J.'s.

SATURDAY

4 *Factory Fashion* 10:30 a.m.

Warsaw's bohemian heart has shifted across the Vistula River, to the old working-class district of **Praga**, where buildings survived the war and some still bear bullet scars. Now it's a haven for galleries, designers, and alternative performance spaces, and increasingly for chic cafes and restaurants. Much of

the new artistic activity is in former factories — the old Koneser vodka factory, which straddles Ulica Zabkowska and was a location for scenes in *Schindler's List*, has now been declared a center of cultural excellence by the city. Start your exploration on Zabkowska and wander back toward the river.

5 *Cheap Nostalgia* 1 p.m.

Most milk bars — the no-frills, Communist-era canteens that serve Polish staples like pirogies and borscht — have disappeared, converted into bars or restaurants. But the few that remain are cherished institutions, not only out of nostalgia, but for the low prices. **Bar Zabkowski** (Ulica Zabkowska 2; 48-22-619-1388; $) is an orange-and-beige time capsule favored by senior citizens and students who line up along a narrow window for their cabbage soup. The babushka-like cashier even keeps an English menu under the cash register.

6 *Remembrance* 2 p.m.

The brutal destruction of Warsaw, with special attention to its historic buildings and monuments, was ordered by Nazi overlords in their fury over the Warsaw Uprising of 1944. The underground Polish Home Army had battled German troops to a standstill before being crushed, while Soviet troops nearby failed to offer expected support. That story, along with what happened in Poland after the war, is well told through artifacts, eyewitness accounts, film, and hands-on exhibits in the **Museum of the Warsaw Uprising** (Ulica Grzybowska 79; 48-22-539-7905; 1944.pl). For a memorial to the predecessor of that event, the 1943 uprising in the Warsaw Ghetto, find the **Ghetto Heroes Monument** at the corner of Ulica Anielewicza and Ulica Zamenhofa. It stands in the center of the ghetto where the city's Jews were penned by the Nazis before being sent to death camps.

ABOVE A fragment of the wall of the Warsaw Ghetto.

RIGHT Praga, an old industrial district turned chic.

7 *Skyline Plunge* 6:30 p.m.

For a pre-dinner workout that doubles as sight-seeing, swim a few laps at the **RiverView Wellness Center** in the InterContinental Hotel (Ulica Emilii Plater 49; 48-22-328-8640; riverview.com.pl). Floating 43 stories high, the aquatic aerie affords terrific views of the **Palace of Culture and Science** (pkin.pl), a controversial gift from Stalin that towers over Warsaw like a pretentious insult. Despite that reminder, Poland's post-Communist move to economic recovery has been one of the most solid in the East Bloc. It built a foundation that kept it out of recession when the rest of Europe plunged into financial trouble at the end of the first decade of the new millennium.

8 *Kitchen Stadium* 8 p.m.

One place that caters to dedicated carnivores is **U Kucharzy** (Ulica Dluga 52; 48-22-826-7936; gessler.pl; $$$), where Polish cooking is turned into a spectator sport: a camera in the kitchen live-streams to the restaurant's website. The chefs in their toques, the rustic wooden tables, the sizzling

pans, and the flaming grills create a real-life reality cooking show. Meanwhile, in the dining room, patrons dine on stuffed beef, "roasted young bulls" stewed in Bordeaux wine; veal brains on toast and other slaughterhouse produce. In a nod to the diverse nature of the world, there are also vegetarian items.

SUNDAY

9 *Found Objects* 9 a.m.

Take your leftover zlotys to **Bazar na Kole** (Ulica Obozowa 99), an outdoor flea market on the east side of Warsaw that sells oddities like rusty World War II helmets, Prussian lamps, and various reminders of a recent Soviet past. Get there early or miss the boat.

10 *Art in a Castle* Noon

Stroll the stately grounds of the **Center for Contemporary Art** (Ulica Jazdów 2; 48-22-628-1271; csw.art.pl). Housed in the reconstructed Ujazdowski Castle, the museum shows a Polish and international collection of works including pieces by marquee artists like Jenny Holzer and Nan Goldin.

ABOVE Late night partying at Platinium, a club in the city center. Champagne, live music, and D. J.'s fuel an exuberant post-Communist Warsaw night life.

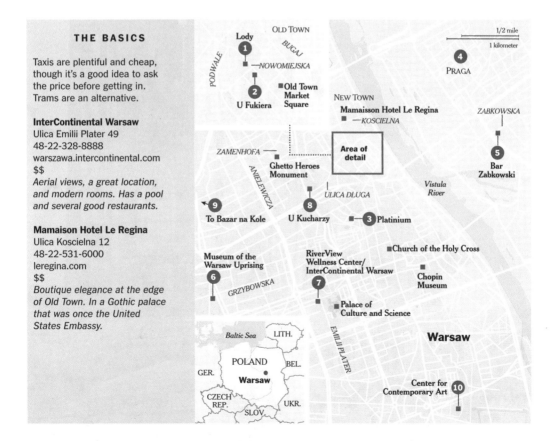

THE BASICS

Taxis are plentiful and cheap, though it's a good idea to ask the price before getting in. Trams are an alternative.

InterContinental Warsaw
Ulica Emilii Plater 49
48-22-328-8888
warszawa.intercontinental.com
$$
Aerial views, a great location, and modern rooms. Has a pool and several good restaurants.

Mamaison Hotel Le Regina
Ulica Koscielna 12
48-22-531-6000
leregina.com
$$
Boutique elegance at the edge of Old Town. In a Gothic palace that was once the United States Embassy.

OLD TOWN
Lody
1
BUGAJ
PODWALE
NOWOMIEJSKA
2
U Fukiera
Old Town
Market
Square
NEW TOWN
Mamaison Hotel Le Regina
KOSCIELNA
ZAMENHOFA
ANIELEWICZA
Ghetto Heroes
Monument
Area of
detail
ULICA DLUGA
Vistula
River
9
To Bazar na Kole
8
U Kucharzy
3 Platinium
Museum of the
Warsaw Uprising
6
GRZYBOWSKA
RiverView
Wellness Center/
InterContinental Warsaw
7
Church of the Holy Cross
Chopin
Museum
Palace of
Culture and Science
EMILII PLATER
4
PRAGA
ZABKOWSKA
5
Bar
Zabkowski
Warsaw
Baltic Sea
LITH.
POLAND
GER.
Warsaw
BEL.
CZECH
REP.
SLOV.
UKR.
Center for
Contemporary Art
10
1/2 mile
1 kilometer

Krakow

In Krakow, Poland's second city, comparisons are unavoidable. The Old Town's stately main square, ringed by outdoor cafes and dominated by the twin spires of a magnificent church? Like Prague's, but larger. The hilltop castle lording over a languorous river? Like Budapest's, but older. The rollicking night-life scene thumping in grimy tenements? Like Berlin's, but tamer. But this rejuvenated city now also packs some original surprises. Museums have sprouted in formerly dilapidated factories, and off-beat art galleries show works from the city's creative class. Shiny new restaurants are claiming space among their bohemian brethren, infusing the once-staid local food scene with fresh, modern fare. All this means that Krakow could soon be the cool, post-Communist enclave with which Europe's next crop of emerging cities is compared. — BY INGRID K. WILLIAMS

FRIDAY

1 *Walk in the Park* 4 p.m.

Krakow's compact historic districts are eminently walkable, so start with a stroll through **Planty Park**, an attractive arboreal arcade that encircles the Old Town. Follow this leafy two-mile loop toward Wawel Hill, where the majestic royal castle and cathedral are perched above the Vistula River. Weave through the hilltop courtyard and then down the back side of the hill to the manicured promenade that hugs the river's green banks. Then continue along the waterfront until you reach the new steel-arched **Laetus Bernatek Footbridge**, a pedestrian- and bike-friendly river crossing that links the Kazimierz and Podgorze districts.

2 *Free Your Mind* 6 p.m.

Kunst Macht Frei — art sets you free. So claimed a sculpture, modeled after the haunting entrance to nearby Auschwitz, that welcomed visitors to the premier exhibition at the Museum of Contemporary

Art in Krakow, or **MOCAK** (Ulica Lipowa 4; 48-12-263-4001; mocak.com.pl), in the industrial Podgorze district, when it opened in 2011. The permanent collection inside the sleek glass-and-concrete galleries features similarly provocative pieces, like a full-scale reproduction of a Guantánamo Bay prison cell by the Polish artist Tomasz Bajer.

3 *Taste of Poland* 8:30 p.m.

At **Restauracja Pod Baranem** (Ulica Swietej Gertrudy 21; 48-12-429-4022; podbaranem.com; $$), the hokey furnishings and moody oil paintings border on kitsch, but the kitchen cranks out reliably solid Polish classics. Start with a steaming bowl of shockingly purple beetroot soup or the hearty cream of mushroom soup served in a bread bowl. Then move on to pierogi ruskie — dumplings stuffed with cottage cheese — or sliced duck swimming in sweet apple cinnamon sauce. Cap off the meal with gooey gingerbread for dessert.

4 *Wodka, 100 Ways* 11 p.m.

The Old Town is peppered with bars and outdoor cafes, but to sample the local tipple of choice, head to the **Wodka Cafe Bar** (Ulica Mikolajska 5; 48-12-422-3214; wodkabar.pl). Forget sampling the entire vodka menu — there are around 100 types — and start with a chilled glass of hazelnut vodka that you'll want to sip and savor rather than shoot and scowl. Then settle in with a tatanka, an apple juice and vodka mixture, at one of the three tiny tables downstairs or in the cozy alcove above the bar.

OPPOSITE The Old Town in Krakow, the city on the Vistula River that was Poland's medieval capital and still carries the marks of its grand royal past.

RIGHT An accordionist playing for tourists' coins on Wawel Hill, the setting of the royal castle and cathedral.

SATURDAY

5 *Art Crawl* 10 a.m.

Start the day with a tour of Polish art through the centuries. Begin at the **Cloth Hall**, the enormous market building in the middle of the main square, where the Gallery of 19th-Century Polish Art is upstairs (Rynek Glowny 3; 48-12-433-5400; muzeum.krakow.pl) inside four color-coded exhibition rooms. Next visit the **Galeria Plakatu Krakow** (Ulica Stolarska 8-10; 48-12-421-2640; cracowpostergallery.com), a shop stocked with thousands of the rare 20th-century graphic-art posters that emerged as a major art form in Poland after World War II; keep an eye out for trippy pieces by Wieslaw Walkuski. Conclude the tour in the 21st century at the **Bunkier Sztuki Contemporary Art Gallery** (Plac Szczepanski 3a; 48-12-422-1052; bunkier.art.pl), a multistory space that hosts experimental, large-scale exhibitions.

6 *Boar and Cupcakes* 1:30 p.m.

Order steamed mussels or a salad with smoked goose breast for lunch at **Guliwer** (Ulica Bracka 6; 48-12-430-2466; guliwer-restauracja.pl; $), a bright and cheerful cafe a few steps from the main square. For a heartier meal, try the burger with goat cheese that comes with French fries in a deep wooden tray, or perhaps the wild boar stew. For dessert, pop in next door at **Cupcake Corner** (Ulica Bracka 4; cupcakecorner.pl), a bakery run by a cupcake-loving expat from Chicago. Flavors change daily, so cross your fingers that the moist red velvet cupcakes are on the menu when you go.

7 *History Lesson* 4 p.m.

One of the most popular attractions in town is also the most sobering. The former enamel factory of Oskar Schindler, which was portrayed in Steven Spielberg's film *Schindler's List*, is now a haunting

ABOVE Planty Park encircles the Old Town and loops for a couple of miles toward Wawel Hill.

branch of the **Historical Museum of the City of Krakow** (Ulica Lipowa 4; 48-12-257-1017; mhk.pl). The museum's impressive permanent exhibition "Krakow Under Nazi Occupation 1939-1945" traces life (and death) in the city from the outbreak of World War II through the liquidation of the Jewish ghetto with exhibits that are both informative and unforgettably moving.

8 *The Pierogi Eaters* 8 p.m.

Please your palate with a pierogi "palette" — a sampler of dumplings stuffed with various fruit, meat, or vegetarian fillings — at **Pierozki u Vincenta** (Ulica Bozego Ciala 12; 48-506-806-304; $), a sunny pierogi restaurant with van Gogh-inspired décor and a Starry Night mural swirling across the ceiling. Or mix-and-match one of three dozen pierogi varieties on the menu — cottage cheese with walnuts is a winner — with a free topping, like butter, onions, or a generous dollop of sour cream.

9 *Jewish Quarter Nights* 10 p.m.

These days, Krakow's liveliest drinking dens are packed into the dingy streets of Kazimierz, the historical Jewish quarter. On warm nights, pay a visit to the convivial beer garden at the bohemian cafe **Mleczarnia** (Ulica Meiselsa 20; 48-12-421-8532; mle.pl), opposite its brick-and-mortar location. Then saunter over to the bar **Singer** (Ulica Estery 20; 48-12-292-0622) near Plac Nowy, Kazimierz's main square, where the ersatz tables lining the sidewalk are actually antiquated sewing machines. When the temperature dips, step indoors at **Alchemia** (Ulica Estery 5; 48-12-421-2200; alchemia.com.pl), a shadowy, candlelit lair with glass beakers strung from the ceiling and a stuffed crocodile hovering above the bar.

10 *Blue Van Special* Midnight

In Krakow, the most popular street food is the zapiekanka, a toasted open-faced baguette topped with mushrooms and cheese (or any number of optional add-ons). Conveniently, the rotunda in the middle of Plac Nowy is packed with zapiekanka vendors, and one of the best is **Endzior** (Plac Nowy; 48-12-429-3754). If you're willing to walk for your midnight snack, instead seek out the blue van parked just past the elevated railroad tracks beside Hala Targowa (Market Hall) at the intersection

of Blich and Grzegorzecka. Until 3 a.m., a white-jacketed duo quietly cooks foot-long kielbasa over an open flame in a makeshift wood-burning grill beside the van. Served with a crusty bun and a pool of mustard, these sausages have earned a cult following, so be prepared to wait in line.

SUNDAY

11 *Salt Rock City* 11 a.m.

On nearly every street corner in the Old Town, there's a blue-and-white cart selling obwarzanek (Polish bagels). Grab a couple and hop on the train to Wieliczka, a quiet town about eight miles away that is home to the **Wieliczka Salt Mine** (Ulica Danilowicza 10, Wieliczka; 48-12-278-7302; kopalnia. pl), one of the very first Unesco World Heritage

sites. The three-hour guided tour of the site begins with a descent 210 feet into a 17th-century mine shaft and then snakes through a sprawling maze of underground chambers, including one fantastically grand chapel complete with an altar, chandeliers, sculptures, and bas-relief works made from salt. Don't believe it's all salt? Lick it to see for yourself.

ABOVE Mleczarnia, a bohemian cafe in Kazimierz, the historical Jewish quarter that's now home to a lively bar scene.

THE BASICS

The Krakow Airport is served by several European airlines. In town, plan to do a lot of walking.

Hotel Unicus
Ulica Swietego Marka 20
48-12-433-7111
hotelunicus.pl
$$
Spacious modern rooms in the heart of Old Town and its boisterous night spots.

Hotel Copernicus
Ulica Kanonicza 16
48-12-424-3400
copernicus.hotel.com.pl
$$$
Luxe and elegance on a cobblestone side street near Wawel Hill.

Krakow

Planty Park ①

Bunkier Sztuki
Contemporary Art
Gallery ■

OLD TOWN
RYNEK
GLOWNY

Hotel Unicus ■

ULICA
MIKOLAJSKA

Cloth Hall ⑤
Cupcake Corner ■

Wodka ■
④ Cafe Bar

ULICA BRACKA —

— ULICA STOLARSKA

⑥
Guliwer

Galeria
Plakatu Krakow

Hala
Targowa ■

GRZEGORZECKA

Hotel Copernicus ■

ULICA SWIETEJ
GERTRUDY

WAWEL
HILL

③ Restauracja Pod Baranem

Pierozki u Vincenta ⑧

Alchemia ■
PLAC NOWY

⑩ Endzior

Singer ■

2 miles

3 kilometers

ULICA JOZEFA ⏌

⑨ Mleczarnia

Vistula River

Krakow

Vistula River

Area of
detail   POLAND

KAZIMIERZ
DISTRICT

ULICA LIPOWA

LAETUS
BERNATEK
FOOTBRIDGE

MOCAK ②

⑦

PODGORZE
DISTRICT

Schindler Factory/
Historical
Museum of the
City of Krakow

Wieliczka/ ⑪
Wieliczka Salt Mine

Baltic Sea   KALININGRAD   LITH.
(RUSSIA)

Vistula —
River

GER.

Warsaw ●

BEL.

POLAND

Krakow ●

CZECH
REPUBLIC

UKRAINE

SLOVAKIA

Gdansk & Sopot

The Gdansk of many an outsider's imagination, informed by memories of the shipyard Solidarity movement that brought down Polish communism in the 1980s, is a postindustrial nightmare wrought in concrete and steel. The Gdansk of reality is a much brighter place, with a lovingly re-created 16th-century Old Town, a system of canals connected to the Motlawa River, and a hip, cosmopolitan devotion to the arts. In the summer, the city hosts a succession of festivals devoted to everything from Shakespeare and organ music to street theater and regattas. And Gdansk, it turns out, is also a tourist haven, the anchor of three Baltic Sea towns — Sopot and Gdynia are the others — that make up what might well be termed the Polish Riviera. — BY MATT GROSS

FRIDAY

1 *Arches and Amber* 2:30 p.m.

Gdansk is centered on the Main Town, a neighborhood of arched passageways, gilded ornamentation, and stately brick buildings that testify to the city's wealth in the 16th and 17th centuries. Church bells ring out the hours, buskers embark on indie-folk careers in the cobblestone streets, and children slurp ice cream cones and clutch helium balloons along the waterfront promenade. Make a first stop at the **Amber Museum** (Targ Weglowy 26; 48-58-301-4733; mhmg.gda.pl), inside a medieval fortification. The Baltic Sea holds the world's largest amber deposits, and people have been harvesting it and making jewelry from it for millenniums — not to mention marveling at 40-million-year-old ancient insects preserved inside it.

2 *Historical Craft* 4 p.m.

In your personal walking tour around the compact Main Town, don't miss the 14th-century **St. Mary's Church**, towering over everything else and said to be the largest brick Gothic church in the world; **Artus Court** (Dlugi Targ 43/44), a merchants' hall dating

OPPOSITE Gdansk, a city of placid canals linked to the Motlawa River, has become a center for festivals and the arts.

RIGHT Neptune's Fountain dates to 1633, when Gdansk was a prosperous landmark of Baltic Sea trade.

to Gdansk's days in the Hanseatic League; and the 1633 **Neptune's Fountain**. Even among the throngs of souvenir-seeking tourists, it's easy to be amazed that all these glories have survived centuries of change and turbulence. Except that they haven't. Ninety percent of the Main Town was rubble after World War II, and it took decades to achieve the historic-looking neighborhood visitors see today. In the **Historical Museum of Gdansk** in the Gothic **Town Hall**, photos show the city as it looked in 1945.

3 *Out of Town (or Not)* 7 p.m.

If the busy Main Town has left you yearning for bucolic quiet, find your way to Oliwski Park for a quick look around and then have dinner at **Dwor Oliwski** (Bytowska 4; 48-58-554-7070; dworoliwski. pl; $$), a hotel restaurant in a rustic-looking restored 17th-century building. The fare runs to foie gras and roast duck. For a different experience, dine in town at **Filharmonia** (Olowianka 1; 48-58-323-8358; restauracjafilharmonia.pl; $$), a hip contemporary place that shares a neo-Gothic waterfront building (originally a power plant) with the performance hall of the Polish Baltic Philharmonic orchestra. While you're in the neighborhood, take a look at the towering Gdansk Crane, a massive medieval structure that allowed 15th-century stevedores to hoist loads weighing more than two tons.

4 *A Bit of Brandy* 10 p.m.

History and high culture aside, Gdansk is a fine place to eat, drink, and make merry. One good, informal spot is the cozy **Café Kamienica** (Ulica

Mariacka 37/39; www.cafekamienica.com), a coffee-house and bar (try a brandy-spiked latte) in the Main Town.

SATURDAY

5 *Paddle Your Own* 9 a.m.

Pick up coffee and a paczek, a local favorite that resembles a jelly doughnut and is sold by multiple cukiernias, or bakeries, and rent a kayak at the **Zabi Kruk Harbor and Yacht Club** (Ulica Zabi Kruk 15; 48-58-305-7310; kajakiempogdansku.pl). Paddle past the promenade, viewing its restored facades from below, much as an ancient Baltic trader might have. Farther downstream, the canal opens wide, and across the wind-rippled waters you will see the famous ship-yards where the Solidarity movement was born. After falling on hard times in the 1990s, the shipyard has had a revival — though on a smaller scale than in the heyday when it employed 40,000 people — as an industrial complex turning out oil rig supply ships and other steel structures. Turn southeast, back into narrower channels, and explore canals shrouded in reeds, paved with lily pads, and populated with waterfowl.

6 *Solidarity* 11:30 a.m.

The **European Solidarity Center** (Plac Solidarnosci 1; 48-58-772-4112: ecs.gda.pl) covers modern Gdansk history in a well-designed exhibition, with special emphasis on the shipyard protests of the 1980s. They began after an electrician by the name of Lech Walesa led workers in a strike that created the Solidarity movement. After absorbing the story, find lunch in the Main Town.

ABOVE Molo, the impossibly long seaside pier (at 1,690 feet) in Sopot. Tourists arrive for the festive summer atmosphere and wide, white sand beach.

RIGHT The medieval Gdansk Crane, built in the 15th century to handle cargo.

7 *The First Battle* 2 p.m.

One more monumental thing happened in Gdansk. World War II started here. The first engage-ment of the war took place on Sept. 1, 1939, when a German battleship opened fire on Polish forces at the harbor of Gdansk, then the Free City of Danzig, and the 200 Polish soldiers there fired back. They held out for a week, fighting a brave, hopeless battle that Poles still regard as an inspiration. To see the **World War II Memorial** and ruins on the site of the battle, Westerplatte, take a bus from the main train station or an excursion boat from the Main Town.

8 *A Summer Place* 4 p.m.

Ride an SKM (skm.trojmiasto.pl) train about 20 minutes north from Gdansk to the beach town of Sopot, a thriving hot spot where Poles — and an increasing number of international vacationers — sun themselves during the day by the Baltic and then indulge in beer, vodka, and fried fish when it gets dark. Sopot has been a summer resort since the 19th century, fell on hard times in the Communist era, and like Gdansk, is now resurgent. Take a walk out onto the impossibly long pier, the 1,690-foot **Molo**. The newly refurbished domed building domi-nating the waterfront is the Grand Hotel (recently reborn as a Sofitel). Among the guests who have stayed at the Grand since it opened in the 1920s are

Charles de Gaulle, Greta Garbo, Vladimir Putin, and Adolf Hitler.

9 *Goose Dumplings* 7 p.m.

Along with its new hotels, inviting upscale shops, and refurbished Forest Opera amphitheater, Sopot has acquired a number of good restaurants. One is **Morska** (Morska 9; 48-58-351-3555; $), a stylish beachfront place that offers fish like turbot, halibut, and sea bass in various preparations, along with land-based dishes like goose dumplings and black Angus steaks. Accompany your dinner with a selection from the mostly Italian wine list. Later, you can stroll along a lively cafe- and club-lined boulevard packed with young party hoppers from all over Poland and Scandinavia. Join them, if you like, dancing at flashy venues like the **Dream Club** (Monte Cassino 53; 48-60-550-0800; dreamclub.pl).

SUNDAY

10 *Hit the Beach* 11 a.m.

Sopot's beach is clean, white, and wide, with plenty of room to sunbathe or take a swim, so find a spot, do some people-watching, and join in. Failing that, at least have a beer at a waterfront cafe. If someone suggests getting a lody, go for it. It means ice cream, and the Poles are good at it.

ABOVE Amber, a traditional harvest from the Baltic Sea, is still for sale in Gdansk.

CENTRAL

THE BASICS

Trams, buses, and a metro operate in Gdansk; trains connect Gdansk to Sopot.

Hilton Gdansk
Targ Rybny 1, Gdansk
48-58-778-7100
hiltongdansk.pl
$$
In the historic center. Pool, spa, and rooftop bar.

Hotel Hanza
Ulica Tokarska 6, Gdansk
48-58-305-3427
hotelhanza.pl
$
Attractive waterfront hotel.

Sofitel Grand Sopot Hotel
Powstancow Warszawy Street 12/14, Sopot
48-58-520-6000
sofitel.com
$$
Artfully renovated seaside resort hotel built in 1927.

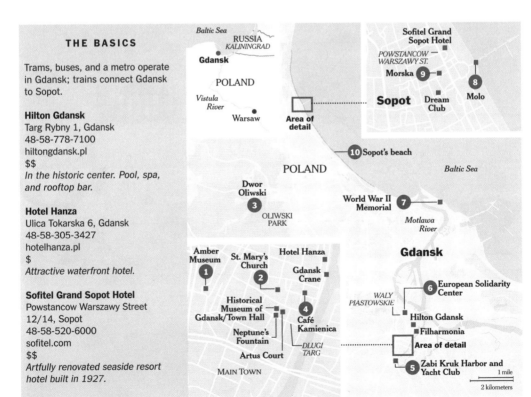

MILAN 488

Lake Como 494

VENICE 498

trieste 502

Ljubljana 506

Piran 510

Zagreb 524

Bologna 474

Genoa 484

the Cinque terre 480

Perugia 462

the Dalmatian Coast 518

FLORENCE 468

ROME

Rome 432

Naples 448

Ancient Rome 442

Capri 452

Contemporary Rome 438

458

PALERMO

SOUTH EAST

Bucharest 532 ●

...jevo 528

Sofia 536 ●

tbilisi 576 ●

DUBROVNIK
514

thrace 548 ●

ISTANBUL 562 ●

Salonika 556 ●

Cappadocia 570 ●

ATHENS 542 ●

MyKonos 552 ●

Bodrum 566 ●

Rome

The explanation about to be offered isn't the conventional one, but it's plausible: Rome is called the Eternal City because you would need an eternity to do it justice. What you have is a weekend, and that's not such a good thing. The expansion of budget airlines in Europe has created legions of two-day trippers and a mob scene around the Trevi Fountain on a Saturday at 3 p.m. that's scarier than spoiled ricotta. So you'll visit the fountain after midnight. You'll adjust, mix it up, and manage to get a taste of Rome without having your time and patience swallowed by long lines and a constant crush of bodies. You'll be clever and fleet, and by the time you pull up stakes, you'll be satisfied. Maybe even eternally.

— BY FRANK BRUNI

FRIDAY

1 *Dome, Sweet Dome* 4 p.m.

Marble and more marble, papal corpses, a lofty dome that tickles the clouds, and a little piece of statuary by Michelangelo called the *Pietà* — **St. Peter's Basilica** can't be missed. You're prepared for a mammoth church, but not for this much majesty, this much history. It's a primer for the rest of Rome. So hit it first, beating the rush on Saturday and avoiding the throngs who gather to hear the pope on Sunday.

2 *Even Closer to Heaven* 6 p.m.

To save time and breath, splurge on a taxi to **Piazzale Garibaldi** on the Janiculum Hill. The view is the loftiest and best in Rome. You can see the layout of most of the historic center and appreciate a skyline of a different, aged sort: cupolas and domes that go back many centuries. You can giggle at what in Rome passes for a newcomer: the Vittoriano, that unthinkably ostentatious white typewriter of a building, built a century ago. Stroll south along the

hilltop to the showy 17th-century fountain popularly called Il Fontanone, then walk down the staircase into Trastevere, a good example of a Roman neighborhood with narrow cobbled streets and the feel of a crumbling labyrinth.

3 *Cold Never Felt So Warm* 8:30 p.m.

There are regular enotecas and then there's **Casa Bleve** (Via del Teatro Valle 48-49; 39-06-686-5970; casableve.com; $$$), which is the enoteca as sumptuous nod to — and even sendup of — Roman grandeur. It spreads through the ground floor of a 16th-century palazzo, where retail wine is artfully displayed and dozens of dining tables have yards of space between them. Some nestle up against a stone fountain along a back wall. And below those tables, in the first-century foundations of the building, is a wine storage vault. At the end of a meal, if servers aren't too busy, they may be willing to show you. About the meal: there's an antipasti spread, but probably unlike any antipasti spread you've had: platters of vitello tonnato; beef roll-ups stuffed with herbs; turkey roll-ups showered with black truffle; roasted red and yellow peppers; mozzarella with porcini mushrooms. You point to what you want and an enormous plate is composed before you. Drink, linger, and congratulate yourself for doing Friday dinner here.

OPPOSITE With its majestic scale and artworks, and its wealth of history visible at every turn, St. Peter's Basilica is a primer for the rest of Rome.

RIGHT The Foro Italico, a series of arenas and sports-related artwork along the Tiber, was commissioned by Mussolini and still reveals his grandiosity.

4 *So Many Masters* 9 a.m.

The **Galleria Borghese**, in the Villa Borghese, which is like the Central Park of Rome, is as manageable and relaxing as the Vatican Museums can be sprawling and agitating. One reason is that it requires reservations (39-06-328-10; galleriaborghese.it) — make one about four days before your visit — so the size of the crowd at any given moment is capped. This museum's ratio of user-friendliness to artistic significance may be the most optimal in the world. On the first floor, a series of rooms largely devoted to sculpture, the attention-getting masterpiece is always in a room's center, so you can head straight to it. The Bernini sculptures are distributed so that they trace an arc of growing complexity: first his solitary *David*, then the joined figures of *Apollo and Daphne*, and finally his *Rape of Persephone*, an entire violent scene in marble. Elsewhere in the museum are paintings by Titian, Rubens, Raphael, and Caravaggio, whose work is especially well represented here and particularly riveting.

5 *Bernini Turns Up the Heat* 11:30 a.m.

Your Bernini appetite whetted, you need to see his most provocative work: *The Ecstasy of St. Teresa*, a woman in a swoon that blurs all boundaries between the spiritual and, shall we say, corporal. It's in a classic Baroque church, **Santa Maria della Vittoria** (chiesasantamariavittoriaroma.it), that's slightly off the beaten track on Via XX Settembre — and is relatively uncrowded. Be sure to get there before noon, when the church closes for several hours.

6 *Dough on the Go* 1:30 p.m.

Committed lovers of pizza bianca — which is to say, anyone who's ever eaten pizza bianca — get it at **Antico Forno Roscioli** near Campo de' Fiori (Via dei Chiavari 34; 39-06-686-4045). Pizza bianca means white pizza and is really denuded pizza — like a firm, crispy focaccia gently kissed with oil, herbs, and salt. Take yours into the **Piazza Farnese**, just a block from the hubbub of Campo de' Fiori but a world away in serenity. Sit on a stone bench outside the Palazzo Farnese, a Renaissance building made of yellow brick and partially designed by Michelangelo. Then, on the opposite side of that building, find Via Giulia, perhaps the historic center's most beautiful residential street, and take a stroll.

7 *Mussolini on the March* 4:30 p.m.

Most tourists don't take excursions into Italy's Fascist past, but you do precisely that along a pretty stretch of the Tiber that's the setting for the **Foro Italico**, a series of sports arenas and sports-related artwork commissioned by Mussolini. A handsome marble stadium, the Stadio dei Marmi, is ringed by statues of hyper-muscular athletes in poses of exaggerated physical vigor. Along with tens of thousands of square feet of pavement mosaic depicting both athletes and soldiers, they manage to provide a fascinating glimpse into Mussolini's grandiosity.

8 *All in the Family* 9 p.m.

Rome is a city where the most pleasurable, satisfying eating isn't at the high end; it's in restaurants with equal measures of sophistication and hominess. In other words, it's at **Trattoria Monti** (Via San Vito 13; 39-06-446-6573; $$$), far enough from the center of the city to feel like a discovery but close enough to be easily accessible by taxi. Walk inside and see the Camerucci family, who run the place and do the cooking. Expect terrific pasta dishes and an amazing Parmesan custard of sorts, which the restaurant vaguely labels a tortino.

9 *La Dolce Fountain* 1:15 a.m.

There are people who dismiss and deride the **Trevi Fountain** as the emblem of the most garish, touristy dimension of Rome. These people are kill-joys, and they probably didn't have the good sense to see the fountain late at night, even though Anita Ekberg and Marcello Mastroianni pointed the way. The fountain suddenly appears around a corner, in a cramped crossroads, without any kind of

OPPOSITE ABOVE The serene and inviting Piazza Farnese.

OPPOSITE BELOW Bernini's *Apollo and Daphne* in the quiet, user-friendly Galleria Borghese.

ABOVE Antico Forno Roscioli, a good spot for pizza bianca.

drum roll. It is lighted, and the light creates sparkles in all that cascading water, which you can hear, because the hordes are gone. Just don't make like Ekberg in *La Dolce Vita* and take a dip. It's outlawed.

SUNDAY

10 *Kitties and Columns* 11 a.m.

To understand how promiscuously blessed with ancient relics Rome is and to appreciate how antiquity pops up in unexpected crannies, visit **Largo Argentina**. Fluted stone columns more than 2,000 years old rise from a patch of weeds and crumbling travertine pavement in the middle of a busy transportation nexus. They'd be a prime tourist draw in a lesser city; in Rome they're the central props in a stray-cat sanctuary. You'll notice scores of cats: napping, sunning, grooming. You may also catch one of the women who care for them dropping off some food.

ABOVE The Galleria Borghese, built as a private palace by a wealthy cardinal, is located in the Villa Borghese, Rome's answer to New York's Central Park.

OPPOSITE Outdoor tables in the Piazza Farnese, a zone of relaxation just a block from the hubbub of Campo de' Fiori.

THE BASICS

Walking is the best way to get around central Rome. The Metro is inexpensive but has limited coverage.

Fortyseven Hotel
Via Petroselli 47
39-06-678-7816
fortysevenhotel.com
$$$$
Near the Tiber, which provides a verdant buffer from crowds.

Raphael Hotel
Largo Febo 2
39-06-682-831
raphaelhotel.com
$$$$
Covered in vines and loaded with Old World charm.

Hotel Santa Maria
Vicolo del Piede 2
39-06-589-4626
htlsantamaria.com
$$$
In a 16th-century cloister in Trastevere.

Stadio dei Marmi
7
Foro Italico
Rome

Raphael Hotel ■
Casa
Bleve
PIAZZA
NAVONA
3
VIA DEL
TEATRO VALLE — Largo
— VIA GIULIA Argentina
Antico **10**
CAMPO Forno
DE' FIORI — Roscioli
Piazza **6**
Farnese

VATICAN
CITY

Tiber

1
St. Peter's
Basilica

JANICULUM
HILL

Piazzale Garibaldi **2** ■ ■Hotel
Santa
TRASTEVERE Maria

Area of
detail

Vittoriano

Venice
Milan
Florence
Adriatic
ITALY Sea
CORSICA ● **Rome**

SARDINIA Tyrrhenian
Sea

Galleria **4**
Borghese ■
VILLA BORGHESE
Santa Maria
della Vittoria
5
Trevi
Fountain
9
VIA XX SETTEMBRE

Trattoria Monti **8**
■

VIA SAN VITO

Fortyseven Hotel
■

1/2 mile

1 kilometer

Contemporary Rome

Rome, a glorious jumble of history and art, changes slowly. But against its extraordinary backdrop of monuments and masterworks, these days it is offering new scenes and sights as well. A futuristic museum has opened not far from a 21st-century arts complex, adding a splash of color and complexity to the city's store of architecture. Around town, young chefs are experimenting with local ingredients to create new tastes. Venerable palazzos have been given make-overs. Rome excels at the old, but it can also welcome the new. — BY RACHEL DONADIO

FRIDAY

1 *Modern Curves* 4 p.m.

When the **Maxxi** (Via Guido Reni 4; 39-06-320-1954; fondazionemaxxi.it) opened in 2010, it was the talk of Rome. Designed by Zaha Hadid, it is the city's most ambitious contemporary art museum. The building itself is an artwork in flamboyant contemporary style, offering playful views with its odd-angled ramps, hidden corners, and oblique windows. It's a fluid space where Italian artists like Michelangelo Pistoletto meet stars of the international art scene like William Kentridge and Gerhard Richter. The museum is close to Pier Luigi Nervi's spidery dome, the Palazzetto dello Sport, which made a similarly forthright statement when it was built for the 1960 Olympics, and Renzo Piano's Auditorium Parco della Musica. In 2011, a boldly designed new footbridge over the Tiber, the **Ponte della Musica – Armando Trovajoli**, opened to link this zone of modern architecture to the Foro Italico area on the other side.

2 *Architectural Aperitivo* 7 p.m.

For a modern aperitivo, glide over a few blocks to **ReD** (Viale Pietro de Coubertin 12/16; 39-06-8069-1630; redrestaurant.roma.it), a trendy restaurant with a lively lounge bar that draws concertgoers and musicians alike. The lounge is situated on the sidewalk outside Piano's **Auditorium Parco della Musica**

(auditorium.com), a multifunctional arts complex, with the emphasis on performing arts. The Auditorium has become a cultural hub for Rome since its opening in 2002. If you are visiting in the fall, check out the Roma Europa Festival (romaeuropa.net), which brings music, dance, and theater from around the world.

3 *Pasta Nouvelle* 8:30 p.m.

For a change from the usual spaghetti all'amatriciana that dominate Roman menus, head to the residential neighborhood of Prati, where the chic **Settembrini Ristorante e Café** (Via Luigi Settembrini 21-27; 39-06-323-2617; viasettembrini.it; $$) uses classic ingredients in novel ways. Look for standouts like mullet on a bed of vegetables, tender rabbit, or a risotto with the deconstructed ingredients of eggplant Parmesan. Décor is minimal but warm, and the outside tables are roomy.

4 *Fruit Scoops* 11 p.m.

Skip dessert and grab a cone at the **Gelateria dei Gracchi** (Via dei Gracchi 272; 39-06-321-6668; gelateriadeigracchi.it) or **Al Settimo Gelo** (Via Vodice 21a; 39-06-372-5567; alsettimogelo.it), two of the best gelaterias in a city full of them. At Gracchi, the fruit and nut flavors taste fresh off the tree, and might just be worth the price of the plane ticket.

SATURDAY

5 *Resting Places* 10 a.m.

Like Père Lachaise in Paris, the **Non-Catholic Cemetery** (Via Caio Cestio 6; 39-06-574-1900;

OPPOSITE The Maxxi contemporary art museum, a symbol of Rome's growing acceptance of innovative architecture.

RIGHT Giant tulips, an installation at the Maxxi.

cemeteryrome.it) is a meditative and overlooked spot. The final resting place of non-Catholics for three centuries, the cemetery counts John Keats among its permanent residents — his tomb reads "Here lies one whose name was writ in water." Besides romantics, there's often a steady stream of graying lefties who pay tribute to Antonio Gramsci, the founder of the Italian Communist Party.

6 *Not Quite Pizza* 1 p.m.

It's not just the triangular shape. It's the sandwich-like structure of "pizza" at **Trapizzino** (Via Giovanni Branca 88; 39-06-4341-9624; $) that first catches your attention. Using yeast that owner Stefano Callegari says has been nurtured for more than a century, pockets of pizza bread are created and filled with meatballs, tripe, and other savory stuffings. The finished product is really a street food, served in a paper cone; it's crunchy on the outside and soft inside. Have wine or beer with your lunch and then stroll the surrounding and increasingly hip Testaccio neighborhood.

7 *Made in Rome* 4:30 p.m.

Not all of Rome is set in stone. For a dose of neo-realism, stroll around lively San Lorenzo (madeinsanlorenzo.blogspot.com), a former working-class district near the Termini station

ABOVE Renzo Piano's Auditorium Parco della Musica, in the Flaminio neighborhood north of the city center, has become a cultural hub for Rome.

RIGHT Aperitivo time at ReD, on the sidewalk outside the Auditorium Parco della Musica. A trendy restaurant with alively lounge bar, ReD draws a cultured crowd of concert-goers and musicians.

that has come alive with chic boutiques and workshops. A shopping trip here will turn up handmade women's clothing and jewelry at **Myriam B.** (Via degli Ausoni 7; 39-06-4436-1305; myriamb.it), as well as designed and crafted wearables and items for the home at various other shops. There's good vintage shopping here, too.

8 *Creative Kitchen* 8:30 p.m.

A handful of restaurants specialize in what Italians call "creative cuisine," new takes on old standards. One is **Pastificio San Lorenzo** (Via Tiburtina 196; 39-06-9727-3519; pastificiosanlorenzo.com; $$), an upscale yet informal restaurant and wine bar in a former pasta factory. The menu has dishes like a breaded poached egg in a delicate Mornay sauce, grilled tuna with a yogurt sauce, and roasted suckling pig with sugar-coated figs and blanched French beans.

9 *Street Life* 11 p.m.

No night on the town would be complete without a stop in the once gritty, now hopping neighborhood

of Trastevere. Its many cool bars include **Freni e Frizioni** (Via del Politeama 4-6; 39-06-4549-7499; freniefrizioni.com), where you can drink wine or a cocktail while looking out on the Tiber. Or you can grab an artisanal beer at the pub around the corner, **Ma Che Siete Venuti a Fà** (Via di Benedetta 25; 39-06-6456-2046; football-pub.com).

SUNDAY

10 *Charm of the Bourgeoisie* 9 a.m.

From the Galleria Borghese to the Palazzo Massimo, Rome has a daunting array of boutique museums in varying degrees of repair. Some are shiny and well adapted to a modern audience, others sadly faded. One of those that have been thoroughly renovated is the **National Gallery of Ancient Art of Barberini Palace** (Via delle Quattro Fontane 13; 39-06-481-4591; galleriaborghese.it). Its formidable collection, reorganized for a new millennium and a new audience, includes Caravaggio's *Judith and Holofernes*, in which the biblical heroine winces slightly as she draws her blade.

11 *Key to the City* 11 a.m.

Amid the general chaos, the city has wonderful pockets of calm. Stroll up the quiet Aventine Hill to find two little known sights. One is Rome's best Baroque joke: look through a keyhole at the headquarters of the **Sovereign Order of the Knights of Malta** (Piazza dei Cavalieri di Malta 3) to see that it perfectly frames a view of St. Peter's Basilica. The other is from the orange garden down the street; the view of the city stretching out beneath you is breathtaking. That is, after all, why you came.

THE BASICS

The Leonardo Express train runs every 30 minutes from the airport to the Termini train station.

Hotel Donna Camilla Savelli
Via Garibaldi 27
39-06-588-861
hoteldonnacamillasavelli.com
$$$$
Quiet hotel in a 17th-century convent.

Leon's Place Hotel
Via XX Settembre 90/94
39-06-890-871
leonsplacehotel.it
$$$
Sleekly modern rooms near the Termini station.

Babuino 181
Via del Babuino 181
39-06-3229-5295
romeluxurysuites.com/babuino
$$$$
Boutique hotel in a recently renovated 19th-century building.

Rome map showing locations:
Palazzetto dello Sport · Auditorium Parco della Musica · Maxxi **1** · **2** ReD · VIA GUIDO RENI · VIALE PIETRO DE COUBERTIN · Ponte della Musica - Armando Trovajoli · Al Settimo Gelo — VIA VODICE · Settembrini **3** · VIA LUIGI SETTEMBRINI · VILLA BORGHESE · Leon's Place Hotel · Gelateria dei Gracchi **4** · Babuino 181 · Pastificio San Lorenzo **8** · VIA DEI GRACCHI · VATICAN CITY · National Gallery of Ancient Art of Barberini Palace **10** · VIA XX SETTEMBRE · VIA TIBURTINA · Tiber · VIA DELLE QUATTRO FONTANE · Termini Station · Myriam B. **7** · Ma Che Siete Venuti a Fà · VIA DEI CAMPANI · Hotel Donna Camilla Savelli · Freni e Frizioni **9** · AVENTINE HILL · TRASTEVERE · **11** Sovereign Order of the Knights of Malta · Trapizzino **6** · VIA GIOVANNI BRANCA · TESTACCIO · VIA CAIO CESTIO · **5** Non-Catholic Cemetery · 1/2 mile · 1 kilometer

Ancient Rome

If you overlook a couple of aberrations, like shopping in slave markets and feeding people to lions for entertainment, the capable, swaggering ancient Romans can seem closer to our own world than most of the cowed, struggling generations that came in between. Scraps of their organized, carefully engineered universe are all over modern Rome, soaring at the monuments, shaping the cityscape, bridging the Tiber. You can't quite vacation in their city, but with a little imagination and some targeted exploring, you can time-travel far enough for a glimpse of their lives. — BY BARBARA IRELAND

FRIDAY

1 *Want Fries With That?* 4 p.m.

For an example of modern Romans' nonchalance about living with their history, look inside the McDonald's in the **Termini Station**, the city's main train station. A few yards from the counter, a section of the hulking **Servian Wall** sits right where it has since about 400 B.C. It's hard to say which is more incongruous: the pile of massive stones surrounded by plastic tables, or the complete indifference of the burger-munching customers. The Servian Wall was ancient even to Julius Caesar — imperial Rome built its own brick wall much later — and this is one of the few fragments that remain. It was uncovered in excavations for the station in the 1930s, and the architects built around it. You can see a larger section outside.

2 *The Dome and the Stadium* 6 p.m.

Pop into the **Pantheon** (rome.info/pantheon), completed in 125 A.D. by the emperor Hadrian and in continuous use ever since, as a temple and then a church. The columned front is impressive, but the dome, viewed from inside, is wondrous: an airy and artful poured-concrete structure so far ahead of its time that it seems impossible. Outside again, stroll to the **Piazza Navona** for people-watching and gelato. The piazza's strange oblong shape has a simple explanation. It's on the footprint of a sports stadium built by the emperor Domitian.

3 *Domitian's Fish* 8 p.m.

Cuisine has changed in Italy — the ancients lacked both pasta and tomatoes. But they did have oysters, bread, olives, lettuce, and arugula. And fish.

A particularly regal fish was turbot; in a satire by Juvenal, Domitian calls a meeting of his council after a fisherman presents him with an especially weighty one. For a serving of the imperial fish — perhaps in saffron and rosemary sauce — try **La Rosetta** (Via della Rosetta 9; 39-06-686-1002; larosetta.com; $$$$), a highly regarded seafood restaurant.

4 *Bacchus Was Here* 10 p.m.

If you want to do as the Romans did, you can drink all the wine you want. (But not beer — that's for barbarians.) One of the many wine bars in the lively Campo de' Fiori area is **Il Goccetto** (Via dei Banchi Vecchi 14; 39-06-686-4268; ilgoccetto.com), a cozy spot for sampling Italian wines. If the night still feels young, walk to the **Piazza del Campidoglio**, the Michelangelo-designed square on the Capitoline Hill. Both the palazzi on the piazza and the forums visible from just behind it are illuminated dramatically at night. In Rome's earliest days, traitors were thrown off this hill onto sharp rocks below.

SATURDAY

5 *Fast Track at the Arena* 8:30 a.m.

The million people of ancient Rome probably did plenty of waiting in line. But since you don't have time for that, arrive at the **Colosseum** with

OPPOSITE The stone-paved road to the Colosseum.

BELOW Traffic still passes under the ancient Appian Gate, renamed the San Sebastiano Gate in the Christian era.

tickets purchased in advance (rome.info/colosseum). Everybody wants to see where the gladiators fought and the early Christians were martyred, so for the least crowding, try to be in the first group allowed inside for the day. Later, follow the footsteps of the Caesars down the Via Sacra into the Roman Forum. Even if you have seen these ruined columns and arches before, standing in the epicenter of the Roman Empire inspires awe.

6 *Bath Break* 11 a.m.

After the tourist-choked imperial center, the **Baths of Caracalla** (rome.info/ancient/baths-of-caracalla) are an oasis of serenity. This is a place that many tourists skip, but besides being a lovely park

with green lawns, benches, and umbrella pines, it is a window into one of the favorite routines of Roman life. The scale is huge, and signs guide you through rooms where hundreds at a time could sweat in steam rooms, soak in hot and cold pools, work out in a gym, and even go to a library. In summer, the Caracalla ruins are transformed into an open-air opera house (operaroma.it/en/caracalla).

7 *Amphora Hill* 1 p.m.

For lunch in a classic Roman restaurant, take a table at **Perilli** (Via Marmorata 39; 39-06-575-5100; trattoria-romana.it/da/perilli; $$), in the Testaccio neighborhood. Roman cooks have always used the whole animal, and here you can see what they do with ingredients like lamb intestines, pork liver, and lamb sweetbreads. (The menu also has more familiar choices.) Just outside is **Monte Testaccio**, a hill constructed a couple of thousand years ago out of broken amphorae — essentially a very orderly ancient Roman trash heap. It's a park now, with trails on the shards.

8 *Nero's Hot Tub* 3 p.m.

Head to the Vatican, but skip the *Pietà* and the Sistine Chapel. Your mission here today is strictly

ABOVE A rare quiet moment in the Colosseum.

LEFT Nero's tub in the Vatican Museum.

pagan. Focus on the Greek and Roman art in the **Vatican Museum** (mv.vatican.va), and the stories that go with it. In one room, a giant hollowed-out chunk of pink marble turns out to be Nero's hot tub, large enough for many to share. Along a nearby wall is a statue of Antinous, Hadrian's extremely good-looking young lover. Its beauty and sensuousness can be admired by both genders and all orientations. Hadrian was wildly in love with Antinous, who died at the age of 19, and erected an obelisk in his memory on the Pincio Hill. You can still see it today, in the Pincio Gardens.

9 *Appian Menu* 8 p.m.

Ask your taxi driver to take you south on the Appian Way through the gate of San Sebastiano — originally the Appian Gate — where traffic now

ABOVE The still-perfect dome of the Pantheon.

BELOW The Piazza Navona, originally Domitian's arena.

squeezes through a structure that was sized for donkey carts. Alight for dinner at **Hostaria Antica Roma** (Via Appia Antica 87; 39-06-513-2888; anticaroma.it; $$-$$$), built into imperial ruins, and order from a menu featuring recipes credited to a first-century gourmet named Apicius. You might choose pollo oxizomum (chicken in fish sauce) or ham in a cake of bread.

SUNDAY

10 *The Old Neighborhood* 9 a.m.

Take a half-hour train ride from the Ostiense commuter station to **Ostia Antica** (Viale dei Romagnoli 717; 39-06-5635-8099; archeoroma.beniculturali.it),

a long-buried city that was once the seaport of imperial Rome. Before it was entombed under silt, dust, and its own collapsed buildings, old Ostia had 50,000 people. Signs in Italian and English will help you explore the ruins of elegant homes, multistory apartment buildings, a fire department barracks, temples and a synagogue, restaurants, warehouses,

ABOVE Tomb art at Ostia Antica, Rome's ancient port at the mouth of the Tiber. Long buried under silt and dust, it is now excavated and open to the public.

OPPOSITE Visitors roam over Ostia Antica's stone streets and ruins of baths, homes, and even a wine bar.

baths. At a public latrine, an orderly line of ancient toilets is laid out along a concrete bench. Bakeries have millstones and ovens. Laundries have tubs where workers jumped on wet clothes, acting as human agitators. As you roam, you're seeing not just how life unfolded in Ostia, but how most people lived in Rome, too.

11 *Lunch With Aeneas* 1 p.m.

Allo Sbarco di Enea (Viale dei Romagnoli 675; 39-06-565-0034; $$), just outside the excavations, is a restaurant with a pleasant outdoor garden. The name means "Aeneas's Landing Place," and presumably it was not far from here that Aeneas, a son of Aphrodite, left his ship and settled down to become the ancestor of Romulus and Remus (and also of Julius and Augustus Caesar—or so they claimed). As you lunch, reflect that for ancient Rome, history didn't get much more ancient than that.

THE BASICS

The ancient city center was built for walking, but buses and the metro can be helpful.

Hotel Indigo Rome – St. George
Via Giulia 62
39-06-686-611
hotelindigorome.com
$$$$
Relax like an emperor in a spa with warm pool and sauna.

Hotel Capo d'Africa
Via Capo d'Africa 54
39-06-772-801
hotelcapodafrica.com
$$$$
Steps from the Colosseum.

Hotel Trastevere
Via Luciano Manara 24a/25
39-06-581-4713
hoteltrastevere.net
$$
In Trastevere, the neighborhood known to Augustus as Transtiberina.

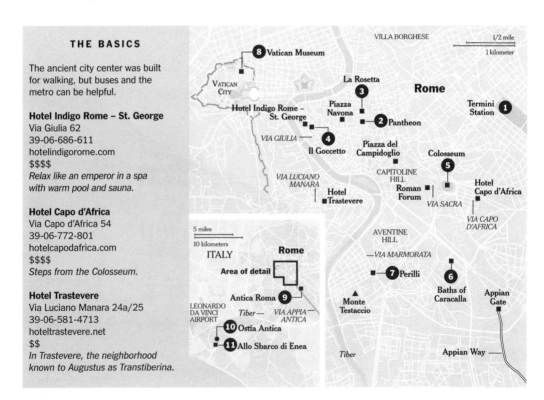

Naples

Frenetic and congested, with its share of negative press and a looming Mount Vesuvius, the Italian port city of Naples feels like it might erupt at any second. For many travelers, it serves mostly as a transit stop to the Amalfi Coast. But what a shame to pass this city by. Amid all that chaos, there's real vibrancy and a lot of color. Stunning architecture and monumental piazzas add an aristocratic touch to the Vespa-choked streets. And then there's pizza. That savory pie that calls this ancient city home is reason enough to visit.
— BY JILL SANTOPIETRO

FRIDAY

1 *Get Your Buzz On* 3:30 p.m.

Espresso may not have been invented in Naples, but the city takes its caffeine very seriously. Get into the local groove with a steamy shot of fragrant espresso at the **Gran Caffè Gambrinus** (Via Chiaia 1-2; 39-081-417-582; grancaffegambrinus.com), a marbled cafe from the late 19th century that has hosted the rich and famous, including Oscar Wilde. Sit outdoors to view the Piazza del Plebiscito, among the most impressive squares in Italy, as well as the parade of well-dressed Neapolitans going about their day.

2 *Fit for a Queen* 4:30 p.m.

If you think coral is just for fish tanks and costume jewelry, glide into **Ascione** (Piazzetta Matilde Serao 19; 39-081-42-1111; ascione.it), a high-end jeweler on the second floor at the Galleria Umberto I, across from the elegant Teatro San Carlo opera house. Ascione's lustrous coral rings, bracelets, and other baubles are made in the nearby town of Torre del Greco. Call ahead for an appointment. Small groups can also tour the museum next door, filled with cameos and other coral jewelry from 1805 to the present.

3 *Pizza Pizza* 8:30 p.m.

Naples is synonymous with pizza, and every resident has a favorite. Many swear by the legendary **Da Michele** (Via Sersale 1/3; 39-081-553-9204; damichele.net; $), claiming that its elastic dough makes the pizzas easier to digest. Others are loyal to **Mattozzi Europeo** (Via Marchese Campodisola 4; 39-081-552-1323; mattozzieuropeo.com; $), where

colorful pies are topped with silky mozzarella and blood-red cherry tomatoes. But for a truly unforgettable pizza, take the funicular to the historic heights of Vomero, and then a short cab ride to **Pizzaria la Notizia** (Via Michelangelo da Caravaggio 53; 39-081-714-2155; pizzarialanotizia.com; $). The crowds don't come for the modest décor; they come for the pizza, which is crisp, light, and a perfect blend of sauce and cheese. The secret? "We do not use a lot of ingredients, but the few we use are of the highest quality," said the owner, Enzo Coccia. Another secret: the dough rises for 10 hours.

SATURDAY

4 *Ancient Naples* 10 a.m.

Pompeii is certainly worth a visit, but to get the real feel for what that lost city looked like before its destruction by Mount Vesuvius, go to the **Museo Archeologico Nazionale** (Piazza Museo Nazionale 19; 39-081-442-2149; cir.campania.beniculturali.it/museoarcheologiconazionale). A gigantic replica of Pompeii brings the buried civilization to life, and a trove of artifacts found on the site includes objects like medical scalpels, coins, and etched horn dice. There is even a room devoted to Pompeii pornography, with risqué frescoes and phallic sculptures.

OPPOSITE Naples: Congested, frenetic, and fully alive.

BELOW The Gran Caffè Gambrinus has been been serving coffee since the 19th century, a fixture in a city that takes its caffeine very seriously.

5 *Street Snacks* 1 p.m.

Locals here love their street food, and they love it fried. For irresistible bites like pizza fritta (fried dough stuffed with cheese and ham), arancini (fried rice balls with meat and cheese), and crocchette di patate (fried mashed potato), head to the Centro Storico, the city's historical center, where you'll find them for a euro or two each. Some of the tastiest are served by **Di Matteo** (Via dei Tribunali 94; 39-081-455-262) or its archenemy, **Dal Presidente** (Via dei Tribunali 120; 39-081-210-903), run by a rival relative. Feeling guilty after yielding to this oil-encrusted temptation? Visit one of the many churches in this neighborhood to confess your gustatory sins.

6 *Veiled in Marble* 2 p.m.

The most compelling reason to visit the **Cappella Sansevero** (Via Francesco De Sanctis 19/21; 39-081-551-8470; museosansevero.it), an 18th-century prince's family chapel, is Giuseppe Sanmartino's astonishing *Veiled Christ*, carved in 1753. The sculpture proves the unlikely premise that marble can be made to look like a diaphanous veil. The museum's other attractions include more veil sculptures and two eerily preserved human bodies, embalmed 250 years ago. Outside again, walk to the Via San Gregorio Armeno for another unusual sight: shop after shop selling intricate handmade Nativity scenes, a Naples tradition, year-round.

7 *Go Underground* 4 p.m.

Built on top of easily carved rock composed of volcanic ash, Naples has a honeycombed underground of catacombs, buried ancient Roman streets,

ABOVE For a truly unforgettable pizza, take the funicular to the historic heights of Vomero, and then a short cab ride to Pizzaria la Notizia.

RIGHT Napoli Sotterranea runs underground tours into Neapolitan history. Some ancient tunnels served as World War II bomb shelters.

and early Christian hiding places. The English-language tours given by **Napoli Sotterranea** (Piazza San Gaetano 68; 39-081-296-944; napolisotterranea.org) will take you through layers of history as you descend ever deeper. Far down in the depths, Neapolitans used ancient tunnels and aqueducts as bomb shelters during World War II, leaving behind wall drawings of bombs and planes, as well as artifacts like toys, beds, and radios.

8 *Dinner With Dora* 8:30 p.m.

For some of the freshest seafood in town, reserve a table at **Da Dora** (Via Ferdinando Palasciano 30; 39-081-680-519; ristorantedora.it; $$$). Tucked away on a deserted street, Dora looks like another run-of-the-mill trattoria, with its bright lighting, old paintings, and blue-and-white checkered tiles. But this unassuming restaurant is always packed with local fish lovers. Try the catch of the day, gently roasted with olive oil, salt, and lemon and served with potatoes. The spaghetti alle vongole offers a delicious contrast of tender clams and al dente pasta. Pair your seafood with a crisp falanghina.

9 *Egg Castle* 11 p.m.

Follow the fashionable locals to Borgo Marinari, the birthplace of ancient Naples in the sixth century B.C. and home to the 15th-century **Castel dell'Ovo**, or Egg Castle. According to legend, the poet Virgil put a magical egg in the foundation of the original castle to protect it. The island lights up at night with lively bars and restaurants, though many are touristy. For a cool nightcap that feels like an insider's secret,

descend a narrow staircase to **Caffè al Barcadero** (Banchina Santa Lucia 2; 39-333-222-7023), a bohemian gem under a bridge, where a 20-something crowd gathers to chain-smoke, sip negronis, and flirt.

SUNDAY

10 *Sweet Breads* 11 a.m.

It's not breakfast in Naples unless it's sweet, so that means lots of sfogliatelle. The clam-shaped pastry comes in two varieties: riccia and frolla. The riccia is the more recognizable to Americans — a flaky pastry shell filled with sweetened ricotta. The frolla has a smooth shell. And since sfogliatelle aren't created equal, make the effort to find **Pasticceria**

Attanasio (Vico Ferrovia 1/4; 39-081-285-675; sfogliatelleattanasio.it), a small bakery that serves a heavenly sfoglia riccia hot out of the oven.

11 *The Passeggiata* 1 p.m.

Neapolitans love their rituals: stores close for the midday pausa, cappuccini are not drunk after 10 a.m., and grated cheese never goes on top of seafood pastas. And on weekends, residents take to the streets for their daily passeggiata, or stroll. If the weather holds up, everyone walks toward the Gulf of Naples, alongside the **Villa Comunale** park. It's a runway show of sorts: children lick gelati, women saunter arm-in-arm in their Sunday best, and men discuss what men in Italy always discuss: politics. It's a true slice of Naples.

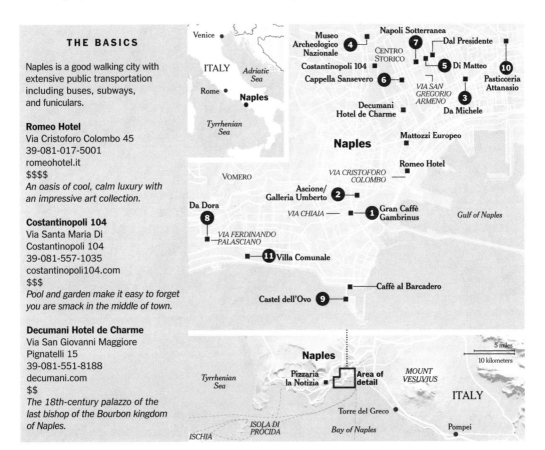

THE BASICS

Naples is a good walking city with extensive public transportation including buses, subways, and funiculars.

Romeo Hotel
Via Cristoforo Colombo 45
39-081-017-5001
romeohotel.it
$$$$
An oasis of cool, calm luxury with an impressive art collection.

Costantinopoli 104
Via Santa Maria Di
Costantinopoli 104
39-081-557-1035
costantinopoli104.com
$$$
Pool and garden make it easy to forget you are smack in the middle of town.

Decumani Hotel de Charme
Via San Giovanni Maggiore
Pignatelli 15
39-081-551-8188
decumani.com
$$
The 18th-century palazzo of the last bishop of the Bourbon kingdom of Naples.

Capri

Few specks of land yield as much romance as Capri, the fabled island in southern Italy that rises like a mirage from the Bay of Naples. It is here, some say, that Odysseus resisted the seductive but deadly song of the Sirens and the Roman emperor Tiberius indulged in debauchery in his villas. Much later, Jacqueline Kennedy Onassis used to stop by to pick up capri pants while cruising on the yacht Christina. *These days there are two Capris. One is a sun-soaked playground for the rich and famous who stay in five-star hotels; keep their own private palaces, like the Ferragamo family; or sail in on their yachts, as the Microsoft co-founder Paul Allen sometimes has. The other is filled with day trippers who come in the morning and leave with the evening tide. For a memorable and accessible weekend on Capri, there's plenty of room for a third way.* — BY ARIC CHEN

FRIDAY

1 *Fantasy Island* 3 p.m.

Most people arrive at Capri by hydrofoil or ferry, usually from Naples or Sorrento. The approach is an experience in itself. From a distance, the island, which is about four miles long and one and a half miles wide, looks like not much more than an outcrop, a sculptured rock dwarfed within a surreal panorama that spans Mount Vesuvius, Naples, and the larger island of Ischia. Capri's precipitous profile and jagged peaks are haunting and forbidding, and the hazy Mediterranean air gives it the veil of fantasy. As one nears, shades of cerulean and turquoise emerge from the water. Seagulls swarm along the steep walls of the coastal rock, where stone and stucco villas cling as nimbly as the goats that also inhabit the island. Capri begins to look real, but no less spectacular.

2 *Up Town* 4 p.m.

A funicular will whisk you up from the busy Marina Grande, where the ferries arrive, to Capri town, high above the water. Narrow streets wind along hillsides, between whitewashed facades, and among gardens scented with juniper, myrtle, and lemon trees. In the **Piazza Umberto I**, known simply as the Piazzetta, the fanny-pack crowd mixes with the well-heeled under bright cafe umbrellas. Every luxury brand and then some have colonized the area. Though

fewer and farther between, some stores continue to specialize in goods of a more local flavor. **Canfora** (Via Camerelle 3; 39-081-837-0487; canfora.com) and **Da Costanzo** (Via Roma 49; 39-081-837-8077) still make hand-tooled leather sandals. On the Piazzetta, **La Parisienne** (Piazza Umberto I; 39-081-837-0283; laparisiennecapri.it) sells clothes that are made on the island; Jackie had her capris made there.

3 *Classic Caprese* 9 p.m.

Once the flood of day-trippers has receded, Capri becomes a quieter paradise of simple pleasures derived from both its shimmering artifice and its stunning natural beauty. Find a quiet dinner in Capri town, perhaps at **Michel'angelo** (Via Sella Orta 10; 39-081-837-7220; caprimichelangelo.com; $$$$; closed November through February). Have a light meal snacking at its mozzarella bar, or a feast in the restaurant. Later, stroll back into the piazza for coffee and a grappa at one of the cafes.

OPPOSITE The rocks called the Faraglioni rise in clear waters off the shore of Capri. They mimic the island itself, which at a distance seems to emerge like a mirage from the blue Bay of Naples.

BELOW The view toward the mainland from the Villa Jovis, the home of the emperor Tiberius.

4 *Follow Graham Greene* 9 a.m.

Capri town is the larger of two towns on the island. **Anacapri**, its lower-key sister, beckons from a plateau above. Take a bus or taxi up and around Monte Solaro to get there. You will find a less chic, less tourist-driven place, with more of the feel of an everyday Italian village—utilitarian shops, children playing, a small piazza. A famous past resident was Graham Greene, who bought a house, **Il Rosaio**, and stayed there often

ABOVE The island is a favorite spot for yachts.

BELOW Boats moored in the clear water off Capri.

for 40 years. Finding the quiet of Anacapri good for concentration, he wrote parts of some of his most famous novels here. His house on the tiny Via Ceselle (No. 5) is marked by a marble plaque.

5 *Peak Panorama* 9:30 a.m.

Tourist development has not left Anacapri entirely alone. **The Capri Palace** (Via Capodimonte 14, Anacapri; 39-081-978-0111; capripalace.com; closed during the colder months), one of the island's most opulent luxury hotels, is a landmark for finding the chairlift at the nearby Piazza Vittoria. Ride the lift to the top of **Monte Solaro** (capritourism.com/en/landscape), which at 1,932 feet is the island's highest peak. The views are stupendous, and getting there, propelled on a cable up the rugged slope, is half the fun. From the top, look out over a steep cliff toward clusters of white villas, the peaked rock formations called the Faraglioni rising from the clear blue water offshore, and yachts moored in the coves.

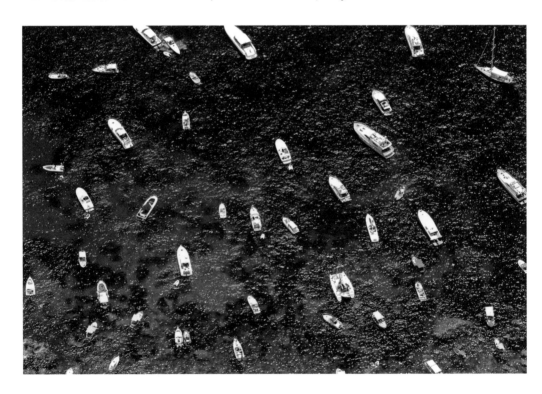

6 *Beach Bodies* Noon

Back at sea level, **La Fontelina** (39-081-837-0845; fontelina-capri.com; $$$$) is a fashionable beach club at the end of the Via Tragara, where you can have a pasta and seafood lunch and then lie among the overtanned bodies on the rocky shore, which is practically within stone-skipping range of the dramatic Faraglioni outcrops. Or if you prefer, enjoy lunch higher up and take in the vista from the poolside restaurant at the intimate **Casa Morgano** hotel (Via Tragara 6; 39-081-837-0158; casamorgano.com).

7 *Imperial Privileges* 2 p.m.

The most famous historical figure to have lived on Capri is, of course, Tiberius. Walking amid the extensive ruins of the **Villa Jovis** (end of Viale Amedeo Maturi; capritourism.com/en/archaeology), the largest of the 12 villas that the emperor is said to have built for himself here, your first observation is likely to be that he knew how to find a vista. Set high up near the island's northeastern tip, the villa overlooks the entire Bay of Naples. Nearby, a precipice called the Salto di Tiberio is where, the story goes, he had wayward subjects hurled into the sea.

ABOVE Night life in the Piazza Umberto I, usually known simply as the Piazzetta.

RIGHT The eerie beauty of the Blue Grotto.

8 *Nature's Archway* 6 p.m.

Take the easy hike to the coastal formation called the **Arco Naturale** (capritourism.com/en/landscape), the eroded remains of an ancient grotto. Stop on the way back for a glass of wine at **Grottelle** (Via Arco Naturale; 39-081-837-5719; $$$), where the terrace is yet another spot for fabulous views of the sea. Stay for dinner or return to the area near the Piazzetta for pasta and seafood at **La Capannina** (Via Le Botteghe 12 bis; 39-081-837-0732; capanninacapri.com; $$$$).

9 *Songs in the Night* 10 p.m.

Tiberius is credited with starting a tradition of hedonism and excess that endured well into the 20th century, when rich expatriates gave decadent parties

on Capri. These days, creatures of the night may wind up at **Anema e Core** (Via Sella Orta 1; 39-081-837-6461; anemaecorecapri.it), where pop stars have been known to take to the mike and modern-day revelers dance on tables. They might also head to **Pantarei** (Via Lo Palazzo 1; 39-081-837-8898; pantareicapri.it), a sleek lifestyle temple with a lounge bar and terrace. It also has a spa; you can

ABOVE The pool at the Grand Hotel Quisisana.

OPPPOSITE The main port, with Capri town perched high above. A funicular takes visitors up the cliff.

drink at night and soothe your hangover with an exfoliation the next day.

SUNDAY

10 *Circle Tour* 10 a.m.

Capri should also be explored from the water. A range of boat excursions and rentals are available, the simplest of them hourlong tours around the island from the Marina Grande. Besides going past sites like the Faraglioni outcrops and the island's many grottoes, including the famed **Blue Grotto**, they offer a rare glimpse of the Casa Malaparte, a legendary modern house with a stepped roof and Pompeiian red walls featured in Jean-Luc Godard's 1963 film *Contempt*. For a more adventurous tour, with freedom to anchor for swimming and soaking up sun, rent a small boat and circle the island on your own.

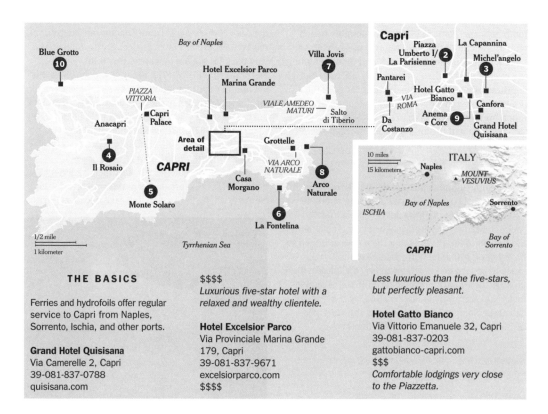

THE BASICS

Ferries and hydrofoils offer regular service to Capri from Naples, Sorrento, Ischia, and other ports.

Grand Hotel Quisisana
Via Camerelle 2, Capri
39-081-837-0788
quisisana.com

$$$$
Luxurious five-star hotel with a relaxed and wealthy clientele.

Hotel Excelsior Parco
Via Provinciale Marina Grande 179, Capri
39-081-837-9671
excelsiorparco.com
$$$$

Less luxurious than the five-stars, but perfectly pleasant.

Hotel Gatto Bianco
Via Vittorio Emanuele 32, Capri
39-081-837-0203
gattobianco-capri.com
$$$
Comfortable lodgings very close to the Piazzetta.

Palermo

In its 2,700-year history, the port city of Palermo, the capital of Sicily, has undergone three golden ages: the Carthaginians, Arabs, and Normans all found glory along its rugged shores. And now, after decades of postwar neglect and Mafia corruption, the city is poised for a fourth, or at least a well-deserved comeback. Crumbling roads have been repaved and landmarks scrubbed clean. A newfound pride can be felt, and an organization called Addiopizzo is promoting businesses that pledge not to pay Mafia protection money. Meanwhile, the essential charms of this mysterious and intoxicating city remain intact. There are still seductive old neighborhoods, a delightful patchwork of architecture (what's the word for Arab-Norman-Spanish-Baroque?), and a belching chaotic mess known as Palermo traffic. — BY ARIEL FOXMAN

FRIDAY

1 *Bread and Circus* 4 p.m.

The ancient city is studded with vibrant and raucous outdoor markets. Mix with residents shopping for weekend essentials in the **Ballarò**, the city's oldest Arab-style open market in the decrepit yet atmospheric Albergheria quarter. Join the crowds at either end (enter through Piazza Ballarò or Piazza del Carmine) and browse stalls with all types of fish still twitching on trays of ice, alongside crates of squash as long as didgeridoos and capers the size of grapes. If the vendors who perform like carnival barkers aren't entertainment enough, grab a piping-hot panella, a street-food fritter made of chickpeas.

2 *Divine Architecture* 5:30 p.m.

It wouldn't be a trip to Italy without a stop in a magnificent church. Walk north to Piazza Bellini in the old city's center and ascend the steps to a pair of famed houses of worship. The **Church of San Cataldo** (Piazza Bellini 3), a rather nondescript diminutive chapel, is best appreciated from the outside, where

OPPOSITE Via Maqueda in central Palermo and the mountains beyond. The capital of Sicily, Palermo has a history dating back to the heyday of the Carthaginians.

RIGHT A domed mosaic in the Church of Santa Maria Dell'Ammiraglio, commonly called the Martorana.

one can take in its three Saracen cardinal-red domes. But a few steps away is the **Church of Santa Maria Dell'Ammiraglio**, aka La Martorana, which offers a quintessential blend of Arab-Norman architecture, including an impressive campanile that dates back to 1143. Gorgeous, well-maintained mosaics and frescoes abound; no wonder the space is booked solid for weddings.

3 *Modern Classic* 8 p.m.

If you're hankering for a sophisticated take on classic Sicilian fare, head over to **Bellotero** (Via Giorgio Castriota 3; 39-091-582-158; $$$), a restaurant in Palermo's new town that draws discerning and lively locals. Settle into a delectable meal of spaghetti with stone bass, sea urchin, and lemon zest or lamb with oven-roasted pistachios and a vegetable caponata. Top it all off with a glass of regional Marsala (try the Donna Franca from the Florio vineyards).

SATURDAY

4 *Morning Marketing* 9:30 a.m.

Forget that espresso. Get a rush by diving into the city's most frenzied market, the souk-like **La Vucciria** (between Corso Vittorio Emanuele and Piazza San Domenico). A dizzying maze of narrow streets is filled with food stalls and illuminated with thousands

of tiny lights. Browse for a portable breakfast as you wander, and be sure not to miss the fresh-made local breads, which may be embellished with toppings and extras like sesame seeds, dried fruit, or anise seeds.

5 *Rich in Baroque* 11 a.m.

Immerse yourself in Palermo's spectacular Baroque architecture and art in the historic Loggia district. An inexpensive single pass (buy at any of the sites) gets you into the area's five architectural treasures, including the **Oratorio del Rosario di San Domenico** (Via dei Bambinai 18), a 16th-century chapel with a Van Dyck altarpiece, a Novelli frescoed ceiling, and many adorable cherubs. Grab a walking map (in front of any of the sites) and hit the other four, making sure to ponder the faces of the 15 statues representing the Virtues and the Mysteries in the resplendent rococo **Oratorio del Rosario di Santa Cita** (Via Valverde 3). They belonged to the socialites of the day.

6 *Sweet Stop* 1:30 p.m.

In a city where gelato in a sliced brioche is a legitimate meal option, get the real deal at **Pasticceria Alba** (Piazza Don Bosco 7/c-d, off Via della Libertà; 39-091-309-016; pasticceriaalba.it), a half-century-old institution with an endless takeout menu and ancient staff. Order a scoop of pistacchio bronte, take your ice-cream burger outside, and watch residents of all ages swing by for their midday delight.

7 *Dead Man Walk* 4 p.m.

File under "It Has to Be Seen to Be Believed." Take the No. 327 bus to the city's western outskirts for the exceedingly popular but no less creepy **Catacombe dei Cappuccini** (Piazza Cappuccini 1; 39-091-652-4156). The chilly passageways of this underground tomb are

ABOVE More surreal than scary, partially preserved bodies line the passageways of the Catacombe dei Cappuccini.

RIGHT Baroque style on the Piazza Vigliena.

filled with more than 8,000 corpses—fully dressed men, women, and children with frozen facial expressions—that were preserved by various methods from the 16th century until 1920. More surreal than scary, this is a memento mori on a tremendous scale.

8 *Sunset Drinks* 6:30 p.m.

Pull up a chair on the terrace bar at the **Villa Igiea** (Salita Belmonte 43; 39-091-631-2111; villa-igiea.com), a luxury hotel on the slopes of the charming Monte Pellegrino. This Art Nouveau grande dame is nestled among gardens and courtyards that offer indelible 180-degree views of the Bay of Palermo. Sip a glass of crisp and fruity Donnafugata white while sampling the wide range of tempting snacks at the Bar des Arcades.

9 *Seaside Supper* 8:30 p.m.

For a nice break from all the seafood in the city, try **Bye Bye Blues** (Via del Garofalo 23; 39-091-684-1415; byebyeblues.it; $$), an award-winning restaurant in the beachy Mondello neighborhood. Incredibly fresh ingredients conspire to create delicious plates like an appetizer of country cheeses served with walnuts and marmalade. Follow up with a delicious serving of pasta alla Norma, an island classic of rigatoni, tomato, ricotta, and fried eggplant. Pair it with one of the 350 wines on hand.

10 *Digestive Stroll* 10:30 p.m.

For dessert, stroll north a few blocks to ponder the choices and order a cone of gelato at **Le Lunette** (Viale Regina Elena 1/2; 39-091-684-1861). From there, cone in hand, head along the waterfront for

a leisurely stroll, or passeggiata, along the crystal-clear Tyrrhenian Sea. Take in legions of cabanas on white sand before fleeing the honky-tonk mix of bars, arcades, and souvenir stands at the other end.

SUNDAY

11 *Jesus on the Mount* 11 a.m.

There's a saying in Palermo that goes something like: "He who visits Palermo without visiting Monreale arrives as a donkey and leaves an ass." O.K., so it's not going on a T-shirt anytime soon, but **Monreale**, a cramped and bustling hill town a few miles west of the city center, is well worth a bus ride (No. 389). Beat a path to the 12th-century Duomo

(Piazza Guglielmo II 1) for what might be the most jaw-dropping display of Greek and Byzantine mosaic work anywhere. There are 200 intricately carved columns in the adjoining cloisters, and the 65-foot-high mosaic of Jesus glows like the sun over the central apse. The golden age of Palermo, it seems, never really ended.

ABOVE Cloisters at the cathedral in Monreale, outside the city center. In the church are Greek and Byzantine mosaics.

THE BASICS

Taxis from the airport to downtown Palermo are expensive, but much cheaper buses run every half hour.

Mercure Excelsior
Via Marchese Ugo 3
39-091-790-9001
excelsiorpalermo.it
$$
Majestic hotel in a lovely 19th-century building. Elegant rooms, restaurant, and diligent concierge.

Plaza Opera Hotel
Via Nicolò Gallo 2
39-091-381-9026
hotelplazaopera.com/it
$$
Contemporary and cosmopolitan.

Grand Hotel et Des Palmes
Via Roma 398
011-39-091-602-8111
grandhotel-et-des-palmes.com/it
$$
Old World Art Nouveau institution where the composer Richard Wagner is on the list of famous past guests.

1/4 mile
1/2 kilometer

ITALY *Adriatic Sea*
• Rome
• Naples
Tyrrhenian Sea
Palermo •
SICILY

VIA MARCHESE —UGO
Mercure Excelsior ■
—VIA CASTRIOTA
VIA DELLA LIBERTÀ
3 Bellotero ●
VIA FRANCESCO CRISPI
Bay of Palermo
Plaza Opera Hotel ■
VIA NICOLÒ GALLO —
Grand Hotel et Des Palmes ■

Tyrrhenian Sea
10 ● Le Lunette ■
MONDELLO
Bye Bye Blues **9** ●
MONTE PELLEGRINO ▲
Palermo
Villa Igiea **8** ●
Pasticceria Alba **6** ● ■
ITALY
Catacombe dei Cappuccini **7** ● ■
Area of detail

Palermo
VIA ROMA
VIA VALVERDE
Oratorio del Rosario di Santa Cita ■
Oratorio del Rosario di San Domenico **5** ●
PIAZZA SAN DOMENICO —
La Vucciria **4** ● ■
LOGGIA
VIA VITTORIO EMANUELE
2 ● Church of San Cataldo
—PIAZZA BELLINI
Church of Santa Maria Dell'Ammiraglio
PIAZZA BALLARÒ
1 ● Ballarò
VIA LINCOLN
PIAZZA DEL CARMINE

2 miles
3 kilometers
11 ● Monreale/ Duomo

Perugia

If Italy were a dartboard, Perugia would most likely be its bull's-eye. Equidistant from Florence and Rome in the bucolic region of Umbria, it is an enchanting hilltop city with a compact historic center that's a rambling maze of largely car-free medieval streets. They jam with visitors on foot during two popular annual events: a summer jazz festival that attracts the music world's biggest acts, and Eurochocolate, a huge autumnal chocolate festival.

— BY INGRID K. WILLIAMS

FRIDAY

1 *Where's Wonka?* 4 p.m.

No golden ticket is required to take a guided tour of the **Perugina** chocolate factory (Via San Sisto 207/c; 39-02-4546-7655; perugina.it) — a simple love of the sweet stuff (and an entrance fee) will suffice. The factory, now owned by Nestlé, produces the famous silver-wrapped, chocolate-and-hazelnut confections called Baci — Italian for "kisses" — at a 1,500-per-minute clip. You won't encounter any Oompa-Loompas as you wander through a test kitchen, past chocolate-themed museum displays, and above whirling conveyor belts. But you will be treated to an all-you-can-eat tasting at the end of the tour. And isn't that what you really wanted anyway?

2 *Drink In the View* 7 p.m.

Walk off the inevitable chocolate-induced belly ache with the locals as they undertake the nightly passeggiata along **Corso Vannucci,** the city's main drag. Pause for peaceful contemplation over a glass of prosecco at one of the outdoor cafes, prime people-watching locations at this hour. If you're more interested in the sinking sun than the promenading pairs, snag a table along the ledge at the outdoor bar **Il Punto di Vista** (Viale Indipendenza 2; 39-339-662-0326) to drink in a panorama of the rolling green Umbrian hills.

OPPOSITE A fresco by Raphael (top half) and his onetime teacher Perugino (bottom half), Perugia's most celebrated hometown painter, in the Cappella di San Severo.

RIGHT The pool at the Hotel Brufani Palace has a below-water view of Etruscan ruins through its glass floor.

3 *Umbria on a Plate* 8 p.m.

There's no better place to sample everything Umbria has to offer the taste buds than **Osteria a Priori** (Via dei Priori 39; 39-075-572-7098; osteriaapriori.it; $$$), a small restaurant and specialty food shop dedicated exclusively to Umbrian-sourced food and drink. You can pair a platter of charcuterie and cheese from local farms with a glass of rare Sagrantino di Montefalco, or anything else that strikes your fancy on the 270-bottle all-Umbrian wine list. Feast on hand-cut tagliatelle with ragù bianco made with chianina beef, or pork loin smothered in seasonal truffles. After dinner, linger outside on the tiny streetside patio over an artisanal Umbrian beer, like the unfiltered multigrain Birra Grifona from local craft brewery Birrificio Artigiano.

SATURDAY

4 *Master and Pupil* 10 a.m.

Perugia's most celebrated painter, Pietro Vannucci, who was also known as Perugino, once had an even more famous pupil: the Renaissance master Raphael. To see both artists' handiwork simultaneously, visit the **Cappella di San Severo** (Piazza Raffaello; 39-075-573-3864; perugiacittamuseo.it), where a fresco in the minuscule chapel is said to

have sprung from the brushes of both Raphael (top half) and Perugino (bottom half). A more extensive view of Perugino's oeuvre is in the **Galleria Nazionale dell'Umbria** (Corso Vannucci 19; 39-075-5866-8415; gallerianazionaleumbria.it). Its impressive collection of Umbrian art is housed in the Palazzo dei Priori, a grand stone building dating from the 13th century.

5 *Keep It Simple* 1 p.m.

Find a hearty, no-frills lunch not too far away at **Il Vicolo** (Via Ulisse Rocchi 13; 39-075-966-2611), up a haphazard flight of stairs and beneath an ancient brick-arched ceiling. The stone-walled dining room is simple, with paper placemats on wooden tables and glass-fronted refrigerators full of wine, beer, sodas, and water. The food is also simple, but extremely well done: antipastos, steaks, artful salads, sausages, and, of course, pasta, pasta, pasta. For dessert, chocolate creations come atop puddles of creamy sauce. For the rest of your life, when you hear anyone speak of "authentic Umbrian" cooking, you can nod knowingly.

6 *Art of Shopping* 3 p.m.

Jewelry has been big here since Etruscan times. For the latest museum-worthy creations, call ahead to visit **Anna Fornari Gioielli d'Arte** (Via Deliziosa 9; 39-075-572-1570; annafornari.com). For decades, Fornari has collaborated with museums and galleries around the world using traditional techniques as a starting point for award-winning experimental works in gold, silver, and even paper. There's more shopping, for ceramics, handicrafts, clothing, and accessories, along Via dei Priori and at Piazza Matteotti.

7 *Going Underground* 4 p.m.

Sneak away from the fountain and cathedral that dominate Piazza IV Novembre to explore Perugia's underground attractions, starting with the nearby **Pozzo Etrusco** (Piazza Danti 18; 39-075-573-3669; perugiacittamuseo.it), an eerie Etruscan well that is believed to date back to the third century B.C. Toss a coin into the enormous well's depths and then march to the other end of Corso Vannucci for another glimpse of the subterranean world upon which modern Perugia was built. In what remains of the **Rocca Paolina** fortress (Piazza Italia; 39-075-572-1009; perugiacittamuseo. it), wander through a spooky, well-preserved warren of medieval streets and squares that spreads out like a second city beneath the present-day streets above.

8 *Chilled Chocolate* 5:30 p.m.

It's a shame to abstain from chocolate for long in Perugia, so refuel with the frozen form in a gelato. Pair

a scoop of pure chocolate with the special Raffaello flavor, a rich white chocolate and coconut mixture, at **Cioccolateria Augusta Perusia** (Via Pinturicchio 2; 39-075-573-4577; cioccolatoaugustaperusia.it). For a second dose of the dark stuff, swing by **La Fonte Maggiore** (Via della Gabbia 3; 39-075-573-2939), where the rich chocolate options are distinguished by varying cocoa contents.

9 *Game for Dinner* 9 p.m.

Take a grand approach to dinner at **Gradale Ristorante** (Strada Montevile 3; 39-075-572-4214; ristorantegradale.com; $$$$), where fit-for-a-king dining seems only appropriate at a medieval storybook castle. (Castello di Monterone, now a hotel, was once a military station on the road between Perugia and Rome.) If the weather allows, choose the covered terrace, which has sparkling nighttime views of Perugia. Remembering that for centuries European kings dined mainly on game,

OPPOSITE Lessons in chocolate-making at the Perugina chocolate factory. The visitors' tour includes a taste.

ABOVE The Galleria Nazionale dell'Umbria, in the grand stone building called the Palazzo dei Priori, holds an impressive collection of Umbrian art.

RIGHT The daily passeggiata on the Corso Vannucci.

start your dinner with something like terrine of pheasant or truffle-stuffed quail, then go on to pappardelle with rabbit ragù, and maybe a wild boar main dish. For dessert, reward yourself royally with the "finding childhood" apple pie.

SUNDAY

10 *Swiss Fix* 9 a.m.

The waiters' bright red jackets and bow ties at **Pasticceria Sandri** (Corso Vannucci 32; 39-075-572-4112) are a nod to the cafe's Swiss ancestry. But since 1860, this opulent place, with chandeliers hanging from a vaulted mural-covered ceiling, has been a Perugian landmark. Admire the elegant

wood-paneled setting while enjoying a cappuccino and a slice of apple strudel laced with pine nuts, or skip right to the multilayer cakes and glistening tarts, the real breakfast of champions.

11 *Two-Wheel Cruise* 11 a.m.

Head 10 miles outside town to Lake Trasimeno, Italy's fourth largest after the popular northern threesome of Lakes Garda, Maggiore, and Como. Circumnavigation of the lake requires wheels, so in the warm months rent a shiny yellow scooter from the lakeside **Umbria in Vespa** (Via Case Sparse 42, San Savino; 39-347-463-6423; umbriainvespa. com). Brake for lunch at **Trattoria da Faliero** (Località Montebuono di Magione; 39-075-847-6341; www.hotelfaliero.it; $$), a simple roadside spot overlooking the water that is short on signage but legendary among locals for its specialty, torta al testo, a warm flatbread stuffed with various fillings, like sausage and spinach, or prosciutto and cheese.

ABOVE Rent a scooter at Lake Trasimeno.

OPPOSITE Celebrating the Etruscans, residents of long-ago Perugia who were defeated by the Romans around 300 B.C.

THE BASICS

Perugia is easily reached by air or rail. In town, an eco-friendly high-tech light rail line called the MiniMetrò zips visitors into the city center from outer areas.

Hotel Brufani Palace
Piazza Italia 12
39-075-573-2541
brufanipalace.com
$$
Elegantly styled rooms, sweeping views of the countryside, and a basement-level glass-bottomed pool exposing ancient Etruscan ruins below.

Castello di Monterone
Strada Monteville 3
39-075-572-4214
castellomonterone.com
$$
Small hotel in an ancient castle with stone terraces, rose gardens, and a pool with a view.

Cioccolateria Augusta Perusia **8**

Perugia

VIA PINTURICCHIO

Il Vicolo **5**

VIA ULISSE ROCCHI

4 Cappella di San Severo

VIA ENRICO DAL POZZO

PIAZZA IV NOVEMBRE

VIA DEI PRIORI

VIA DELLA GABBIA

Cathedral

7 Pozzo Etrusco

Fountain

La Fonte Maggiore

Galleria Nazionale dell'Umbria/Palazzo dei Priori

6 Anna Fornari Gioielli d'Arte

3 Osteria a Priori

10 Pasticceria Sandri

PIAZZA MATTEOTTI

Corso Vannucci **2**

VIA MAZZINI

VIA 14 SETTEMBRE

VIA BAGLIONI

PIAZZA ITALIA

Rocca Paolina

Hotel Brufani Palace

Il Punto di Vista

5 miles

10 kilometers

Lake Trasimeno

11 Umbria in Vespa

San Savino

Trattoria da Faliero

SWITZ. AUS.

50 miles

100 kilometers

Lake Maggiore

Lake Como

SLOVENIA

Milan

Lake Garda

Venice

LOMBARDY

ITALY

Adriatic Sea

Ligurian Sea

Florence

UMBRIA

Perugia

FRANCE CORSICA

Tyrrhenian Sea

Rome

Perugia

9 Gradale Ristorante/ Castello di Monterone

1 Perugina chocolate factory

UMBRIA

Florence

With its centuries-old art treasures and stately palazzi, Florence is still the premier place for an excursion to the Renaissance. It's little wonder that the city clings to its history. This, after all, was the home and inspiration to Dante, Michelangelo, Botticelli, and a lot of other really, really talented people. Wander around, and you get the sense that Florentines never got the memo that Italy's capital moved south 140 years ago. But the myth that Florence is a living museum is hard to sustain these days. Evidence of a more youthful and revitalized city is everywhere, with none of the old beauty sacrificed. Dilapidated piazzas have been refreshed, contemporary art galleries have sprung up to join the venerable Uffizi, and old-school palazzi have been turned into trendy restaurants.
— BY ONDINE COHANE AND DANIELLE PERGAMENT

FRIDAY

1 *Decongested Duomo* 4 p.m.

Yes, that **Duomo**, the magnificent domed cathedral that is Florence's symbolic heart. Since its piazza became pedestrian-only, without buses, taxis, and cars jamming up the street, it is a pleasant and totally new experience, even as it remains one of the city's most popular attractions. Don't miss the stunningly detailed bronze doors of the **Baptistery**. Another landmark that's received the car-free touch is the piazza of **Santa Maria Novella**. With parked vehicles replaced by strolling Italian families, the restored black-and-white marble facade of the basilica is all the more striking, as is the thriving neighborhood around it.

2 *The Other Pietà* 5 p.m.

No one packs a house like Michelangelo. To see his *Pietà* in Rome, you could wrestle the crowd and try to glimpse the top of Mary's head. Or you could visit the **Museo dell'Opera del Duomo** (Piazza del Duomo 9; 39-055-230-2885; ilgrandemuseodelduomo.it) and walk

right up to the *Pietà* that Michelangelo carved just before his death. He never finished it (the woman on the left was completed by another artist). The museum, oddly empty and under the shadow of the Duomo, also houses Donatello's masterpiece *Mary Magdalene* and the original Baptistery door panels by Ghiberti.

3 *Best in Show* 7 p.m.

Fabio Picchi's Cibrèo is to food what the Medicis were to housing — impressive, famous, and seemingly everywhere. There are four Cibrèos: the trattoria, the cafe, the restaurant, and then there's **Teatro del Sale** (Via dei Macci 118; 39-055-200-1492; edizioniteatrodelsale.it; $$), which is not only a trattoria, but also a boutique grocery, theater, and private club (membership can be bought at the door for a few euros). Snag a table close to the stage and make your way to the buffet, heaping with choices like olive tapenade, rigatoni with ricotta cheese, spaghetti with pesto, sautéed fennel, bean salad, rack of lamb and — when the time comes — chocolate mousse with whipped cream and wafer cookies. Around 9:30 p.m., the entertainment starts, and it can be anything from a poetry reading to a pianist playing Gershwin. As much as you'll enjoy it, nothing beats the bill — a full evening for the cost of the affordably priced buffet.

OPPOSITE The skyline of Florence, dominated by the Duomo, its magnificent domed cathedral. The Duomo's pedestrian-only piazza now keeps traffic from jamming in too close.

RIGHT A view of the dome, built from 1420 to 1436. Visitors can climb the cupola for a classic view over the city.

4 *Sweet Spot* 9 a.m.

A short walk outside the center, just past the reach of the tourist swarms, is the city's best pasticceria, **Dolci & Dolcezze** (Piazza Cesare Beccaria 8r; 39-055-234-5458). This tiny bakery has cases full of preciously wrapped chocolates, sweet berry tarts, and everything in between. Order a frothy cappuccino and a freshly baked cornetto (croissant) at the bar while Florentine women scurry through, picking up torta di cioccolato for the evening. Your morning in Florence is now off to a suitable start.

5 *Pretty Please* 11 a.m.

Making a bella figura (a good impression), in both appearance and behavior, is an important Italian custom. Do your part with a facial at the spa in the **Four Seasons Hotel Firenze** (Borgo Pinti 99; 39-055-26-261; fourseasons.com/florence). It's one of the only places in town that features Officina Profumo-Farmacia di Santa Maria Novella, the apothecary potions originally concocted by monks in the 13th century. And the small white marble spa also looks onto one of the city's largest private gardens, with peaceful green lawns, towering trees, and winding pathways that lead past tucked-away statues. It's a great way to experience this luxurious hotel without the price tag of a room.

6 *Pass the Panino* 1 p.m.

Custom-made panini sandwiches were once the norm in Italy, until the generic, plastic-wrapped variety took over. A deli and wine bar near the Ponte Vecchio called 'Ino (Via dei Georgofili 3r-7r; 39-055-219-208; inofirenze.com; $) is bringing that lunchtime pleasure back, one fresh focaccia at a time. Choose from 20-plus cheeses including pecorino and Gorgonzola, and add some mortadella and salami.

7 *Left Bank* 2 p.m.

Cross the Arno River to the less-traveled left bank to shop for authentic Florentine and Tuscan treasures. **L'Altrarno** (Via Borgo San Jacopo 38r; 39-055-289-268) is a small shop that carries delicate striped linens and embroidered duvets made in the Tuscan town of Anghiari by the Busatti family, which has been hand-weaving wool, cotton, linen, and hemp since 1842. **Lorenzo Villoresi** has a line of Florentine perfumes and candles that make good presents — and the view from the shop is lovely, too (Via de Bardi 14; 39-055-234-1187; lorenzovilloresi.it). Walk along the riverside at your own leisurely pace.

8 *Fashionable Florentines* 3 p.m.

Pop into the **Roberto Capucci Museum** in the 17th-century Villa Bardini, which holds the impressive fashion archive of its namesake, the Roman designer (Villa Bardini, Costa San Giorgio 2;

39-055-200-662-09; fondazionerobertocapucci.com). Afterward, join fashionable Florentines as they amble through the terraced flower and vegetable plots of the 10-acre **Villa Bardini Gardens** (Via de Bardi 1r; bardinipeyron.it). Its hilltop perspective offers spectacular views of the Duomo, Santa Croce, and Fiesole.

9 *Prized Beef* 8 p.m.

Let the rest of the world have its grass-fed organic burgers. At **Lungarno 23** (Lungarno Torrigiani 23;

OPPOSITE Florence may seem to outsiders like a living museum, dominated by its past, but a youthful and revitalized city coexists alongside the traditional town.

ABOVE The river Arno, with the medieval Ponte Vecchio bridge and its enclosed shops in the distance.

BELOW At Lungarno 23, the hamburgers are made with meat from Italian Chianina cattle raised at the owners' own farm.

39-055-234-5957; lungarno23.it; $$), the owners have their own cattle farm in the Tuscan town of Sinalunga, where they raise Chianina — an ancient Italian breed known for its white hair, long limbs, and marbled meat. The Chianina burgers are served on a sesame bun with lettuce, onions, tomatoes, and ketchup. Purists may prefer the steak at **Trattoria Sostanza** (Via del Porcellana 25r; 39-055-212-691; $$$), a century-old institution known for its succulent Chianina T-bones.

10 *Lounge Fever* 10 p.m.

Summer night life in Florence centers on small aperitivo bars that come alive after dinner, spilling into the street. A hot spot is **Volume** (Piazza Santo

Spirito 5r; 39-055-238-1460), a bar in a former wood workshop. On balmy nights it is filled with a varied yet beautiful crowd, from fashion editors to exchange students, who anchor one corner of the festive Piazza Santo Spirito.

SUNDAY

11 *Paradise Found* 10 a.m.

In a town of world-renowned masterpieces surrounded by tourist crowds, it's always wise to seek out smaller, less known gems. Among the unsung works is Benozzo Gozzoli's *Procession of the Magi* at

the **Palazzo Medici-Riccardi** (Via Camillo Cavour 1; 39-055-276-0340; palazzo-medici.it). Commissioned by Cosimo de' Medici in 1459 and now restored to its Technicolor glory, the fresco turned the chapel into a vision of paradise, with cheetahs and birds, as imagined by the newly emerging merchant class of the Florentine Renaissance. Book ahead—the palazzo's intimate space can hold only small groups.

ABOVE The cases at tiny Dolci & Dolcezze, a bakery just beyond the city center, are full of chocolates and other sweets.

OPPOSITE Florence, home of Dante, Michelangelo, and Botticelli, is still the place to experience the environment and the spirit of the Italian Renaissance.

THE BASICS

From Rome, fly to Florence or take the Eurostar (raileurope.com). Make your way around town by foot or cab.

J.K. Place Firenze
Piazza di Santa Maria Novella 7
39-055-264-5181
jkplace.com
$$$$
Small but stylish rooms on Santa Maria Novella piazza, with the Duomo and the Ponte Vecchio five minutes away on foot.

Il Salviatino
Via del Salviatino 21, Fiesole
39-055-904-1111
salviatino.com
$$$$
A restored villa with an 11-acre garden, a spa, and a terrace overlooking the city.

1/4 mile
1/2 kilometer

Florence

To Il Salviatino →

Train Station

VIA SAN GALLO
VIA CAMILLO CAVOUR
VIA DEI SERVI
BORGO PINTI

Palazzo Medici-Riccardi **11**

Four Seasons Hotel Firenze **5**

PIAZZA DI SANTA MARIA NOVELLA

Baptistery

J.K. Place Firenze

Trattoria Sostanza

Museo dell'Opera del Duomo **2**

PIAZZA DEL DUOMO

1

Duomo

Teatro del Sale **3**

PIAZZA CESARE BECCARIA

VIA DEI MACCI

'Ino **6**

VIA DEI GEORGOFILI

Dolci & Dolcezze **4**

Arno River

■Uffizi

L'Altrarno **7**

PONTE VECCHIO

VIA BORGO SAN JACOPO

PIAZZA SANTO SPIRITO

Lungarno 23 **9**

Lorenzo Villoresi

VIA DE BARDI

10
Volume

Palazzo Pitti

8

Roberto Capucci Museum

Villa Bardini Gardens

GIARDINO DI BOBOLI

SWITZ.

AUS.

Venice

Milan

FRANCE
CORSICA

Florence
●

Adriatic Sea

ITALY

●Rome

SARDINIA

Tyrrhenian Sea

Bologna

Vibrant, independent, and home to one of Europe's oldest universities, Bologna is a dynamic counterpoint to more popular, touristy cities like Rome and Florence. About 50 miles north of Florence, the city is as famous for its cuisine as it is for its fiery left-leaning politics. Market stalls brimming with asparagus and fava beans, specialty shops selling cured meats, and osterias serving fresh pasta with the city's signature ragù (known as Bolognese in the rest of the world) offer compelling reasons to linger. And then there are architectural masterpieces like the church of Santo Stefano and the iconic Due Torri (Two Towers).
— BY ONDINE COHANE

FRIDAY

1 *Upward Spiral* 4 p.m.

Bologna is known for its miles of portici, or covered terra cotta arcades, and the 666 arches that lead up to the **Santuario della Madonna di San Luca** (www.sanlucabo.org), a basilica that sits perched above the metropolis, are a great introduction. Start at the Meloncello gateway and wind up the hill. The half-hour trek is like a StairMaster session with views of city and rolling countryside. At the top, the payoff is the grand basilica and its painting of St. Mary allegedly by Luke the Evangelist. Not in the mood for the uphill climb? Then check out the much-photographed portici of the **Piazza Cavour**, and while you're there, have a gelato at **Cremeria Funivia** (39-051-656-9365; cremeriafunivia.com).

2 *Inspired Interiors* 6 p.m.

The contemporary art scene in the Saragozza neighborhood is especially notable for the inspired refurbishment of the spaces that galleries have taken over. The **Otto Gallery** (Via D'Azeglio 55; 39-051-644-9845; otto-gallery.it), for example, has reinvented a part of the **Collegio di San Luigi dei Barnabiti** (a school dating back to the 1700s) with airy, light-filled rooms perfect for displaying contemporary works by artists like the Italian abstract expressionist

Luigi Carboni and the Norwegian photographer Per Barclay, known for his evocative installations. Nearby, **Galleria d'Arte Maggiore** (Via D'Azeglio 15; 39-051-235-843; maggioregam.com) exhibits works by international figures like Andy Warhol as well as by some of today's most interesting artists. The gallery tries to show relationships between the modern art of the 20th century and what's going on in the art world now.

3 *Bite the Brodo* 8 p.m.

A classic Bologna dish is tortellini in brodo, delicate parcels of pasta filled with a pinch of minced pork and swimming in a fragrant chicken broth. A culinary temple devoted to this staple and other traditional dishes is **All'Osteria Bottega** (Via Santa Caterina 51; 39-051-585-111; $$$), a cozy space with wood floors and painted furniture overseen by its jovial owner, Daniele Minarelli. Plates of mortadella and cheese are followed by dishes like freshly made tagliatelle con culatello (considered the most delicate part of a pork haunch), eggplant Parmesan, and house specialties like grilled pigeon.

SATURDAY

4 *Gastronomy Bolognese* 10 a.m.

Consider the area around the **Mercato di Mezzo** a gastronomic must. In addition to the storefronts devoted to all manner of food, there is a new outpost of **Eataly** (Via degli Orefici 19; 39-051-095-2820; www.eataly.it), with its emporium of books and Italian gourmet products plus a wine bar and

OPPOSITE Bologna from the medieval Asinelli Tower, one of the landmark Due Torri. Atop the hill is Madonna di San Luca.

RIGHT The Bruno e Franco deli in the Via Oberdan area.

restaurant; **Tamburini** (Via Caprarie 1; 39-051-234-726; tamburini.com), a deli that also serves more than 200 wines by the glass; **Atti Panificio** (Via Drapperie 6; 39-051-233-349; paoloatti.com), a bakery that dates from 1880; and **Simoni**, a salumeria (Via Drapperie 5/2a; 39-051-231-880; salumeriasimoni.it).

5 *Snack in the Middle* Noon

Just off the charming Via Pescherie Vecchie is **Osteria del Sole** (Vicolo Ranocchi 1D; 39-347-968-0171; osteriadelsole.it), which looks like an old social club with its wooden bar and faded framed photos. The place doesn't serve food, just wines by the glass, so pick up your own gems from the market and create an impromptu picnic on one of the long tables. It is

not unusual to see a group of elderly men at the bar snacking on fava beans or a carton of fresh strawberries while catching up on gossip.

6 *Choose Your Beans* 3 p.m.

At **Terzi** (Via Oberdan 10/D; 39-051-034-4819; caffeterzibologna.com), coffee making is an art, and the owner, Manuel Terzi, is a master in making the perfect cup. Among the exotic beans on offer are a wild grown Kopi Luwak from Indonesia, and a Congo "robusta." Stand at the bar or sit at one of the four tables in the small candy-striped back room.

7 *Retail Path* 4 p.m.

Once part of the Jewish ghetto, the bustling neighborhood around Via Oberdan is home to some of the city's most charming shops. **Hoffmann** (Via Altabella 23; 39-051-223-066; hoffmann.it), a toy store, doesn't do justice to the inventiveness of its space with its installation-like windows and displays, but it has custom-made toys including wooden rocking horses and elephant lamps. Across the street, **Jacqueline** (Via Altabella 14/E; 39-051-268-190) has pretty dresses, bikinis, and flats (not to mention great lingerie). **SEMM Music Store & More** (Via Oberdan 24/f; 39-051-225-425) offers a local take on popular music with new and vintage CDs and vinyl. And even if you aren't in the market for a whole prosciutto, don't miss **Bruno e Franco** (Via

Oberdan 16; 39-051-233-692; la-salumeria.it), a deli where men in red bow ties cut cured meats into paper-thin slices. The spot also includes a fresh pasta station. If you are lucky, you might be invited to the laboratory on an upper floor across the street where ladies in pressed uniforms roll out the dough.

8 *Mamma's Cooking* 6 p.m.

At **Swine Bar** (Via A. Righi 24A; 39-051-232-631) students and fashionable types convene for an Aperol spritz (orange liqueur, prosecco, and a splash of soda) and buffet in the snug wood-beamed space in winter or at an outdoor table in balmy months. After work, businessmen and neighborhood insiders stop by **Enoteca Italiana** (Via Marsala 2/b; 39-051-235-989; www.enotecaitaliana.it), for a glass of sparkling Franciacorta or Gaja accompanied by a plate of meat and cheese. Serving only 28 people a night, **Serghei** (Via Piella 12; 39-051-233-533; $$) is one of the most sought-after reservations in town, excelling in the

"mamma-style" honest cooking that Bologna is known for. In fact, the owner here has relied on his mother to make the excellent fresh pasta like ravioli filled with arugula and topped with Gorgonzola. The entrees are also simple and traditional, like veal meatballs with ricotta and zucchini.

OPPOSITE ABOVE Bologna is known for its miles of portici, or terra cotta arcades. This one is on Via Santo Stefano.

OPPOSITE BELOW Inside the portico to Madonna di San Luca.

ABOVE Santuario della Madonna di San Luca.

BELOW Entertainers in the Piazza Maggiore.

SUNDAY

9 *Go to Church* 10 a.m.

On your way to the exquisite **Santo Stefano** church (a conjoined series of churches, cloisters, and courtyards that date from the fifth, eighth, and 12th centuries) stop in at **Colazione da Bianca** (Via Santo Stefano 1; 39-051-588-4425; colazionedabianca.it). With cornetti and cappuccino, along with lunch fare, it makes a good stop before church gazing. Enjoy your snack and then head for the cloisters.

10 *Hometown Painter* Noon

Giorgio Morandi, who died in 1964, was one of the city's most famous modern painters. The **Museo d'Arte Moderna di Bologna**, or **MAMbo** (Via Don Minzoni, 14; 39-051-649-6611; mambo-bologna.org), celebrates his fame with a permanent exhibition of his works, moved here from its former location in the city hall.

ABOVE For food lovers or just as a gastronomic spectacle, the area around the Mercato di Mezzo, with all kinds of fresh food for sale, is a must.

OPPOSITE The much photographed portici of the Piazza Cavour. Admire the intricate ceiling patterns at the tops of the arches and then reward yourself nearby with a gelato.

THE BASICS

Get around by bus or taxi, and plan to do a lot of walking.

Hotel Metropolitan
Via dell'Orso 6
39-051-229-393
hotelmetropolitan.com
$$
Boutique hotel with a great central location and reasonable prices.

I Portici
Via dell'Indipendenza 69
39-051-421-85
iporticihotel.com
$$
Housed in a 19th-century palazzo that exemplifies the city's Liberty style — Italy's answer to Art Nouveau.

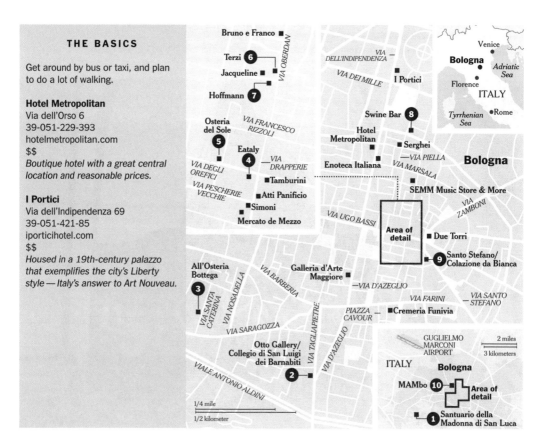

The Cinque Terre

With its miles and miles of breathtaking trails, the Cinque Terre along northern Italy's Riviera has long been a magnet for hikers. And while trekking through the five villages is certainly a backpacker's dream — each town is a unique destination carved rather amazingly into the steep terraced-vineyard coastline — that shouldn't preclude lesser athletes from heading to this wildly charming region. In fact, the only way to truly experience the sensory overload that this small area offers is to get off those well-trodden paths. It's almost unfair how many gifts — intense beauty, great cuisine, amazing aromas — are jam-packed into such a compact space. — BY ARIEL FOXMAN

FRIDAY

1 *Gain Some Perspective* 4 p.m.

Before you start connecting your Cinque Terre dots, bouncing from one village to the next, trek 15 minutes uphill near Riomaggiore through gorgeous vineyards to the **Santuario di Nostra Signora di Montenero** (the entrance is a five-minute drive west of Due Gemelli, a hotel at Via Litoranea 1; 39-0187-920-678; santuariodimontenero.org). It's a storybook climb, replete with fragrant wildflowers and colorful butterflies, and the views at the top, 1,100 feet above sea level, take in the region's entire 11-mile coastline. The sanctuary, an active church with a pink and yellow bell tower, is a spectacular example of the 14th-century buildings that put these small towns on the map.

2 *Lovers' Detour?* 5:30 p.m.

Drive down to Riomaggiore proper, park your car, and head downhill to explore its marina. Then double back to the main drag and look for signs pointing to the village's biggest attraction: the **Via dell'Amore**, the first segment of the Sentiero Azzurro or the Blue Trail — a five-hour trail that usually connects all five hamlets. A landslide closed parts of it, and full reopening is scheduled for 2017. Size up the situation; walking might put you on public roads. With the right company, though, it can still be a walk of love. Or take the train (trenitalia.com) to your next stop.

3 *Taste Test* 7 p.m.

The tiny town of **Manarola** is a sight to behold: a confection of pastel houses that climb up the side of a black cliff next to the region's most productive vineyards. This small area is known for two specialty wines: Cinque Terre white, a dry, tangy blend of three different grapes, and sciacchetrà, a super-sweet late-harvest dessert wine. Grab a table at the lovely **Marina Piccola** (Via Lo Scalo 16; 39-0187-920-923; hotelmarinapiccola.com). Ask to sample a Manarola Cinque Terre and then compare it to one that's made from grapes blended from all five villages. While you're at it, order the Cinque Terre sciacchetrà, too.

4 *Family-Style Dining* 8:30 p.m.

Find a taste of home cooking at **Trattoria dal Billy** (Via Rollandi 122; 39-0187-920-628; trattoriabilly.com; $), a quaint three-story restaurant tucked into Manarola's lush mountainside. An enchanting climb through the village's mazelike alleyways leads to a set of garden terraces where you can sample local specialties like anchovies with salt or lemon, and taglierini with tomato, pecorino, pine nuts, baby shrimp, pepper, and olive oil. Sweeping vineyard and sea views abound.

SATURDAY

5 *Secret Beach* 10 a.m.

With three towns to hit in one day, take the quick regional train via the Spezia line (trenitalia.com) to

OPPOSITE Trails connect the villages of the Cinque Terre.

RIGHT An old train tunnel leads to Guvano beach.

Corniglia, the smallest and most remote of the five villages. Forgo the 377-step climb to its tourist-filled center. Instead take the road much less traveled, to the clothing-optional private beach **Guvano**, which only locals seem to know about. It's not easy to find: above and to the right of the train platform head down a narrow flight of stairs, follow a brick coastal wall, and turn right. When you come to an industrial tunnel, you are heading in the right direction. You will need a flashlight to get through the darkness — be sure to come prepared (bring snacks and water, too). If you are lucky, by now you will have met some local people who can help you make it the rest of the way. A private vineyard overlooks two phenomenal beaches. Pay the gatekeeper a few euros for your little slice of sunbathing heaven.

6 *Square Meal* 1:30 p.m.

Vernazza, the next village over, could nab Miss Congeniality in a Cinque Terre pageant. Everything from its historical attractions and manageable size to its somewhat chic vibe make it especially agreeable. From the train station, walk along Via Visconti, the bustling main street, until you reach the adorable main square. Have a leisurely lunch at **Trattoria Gianni Franzi** (Piazza Marconi 5; 39-0187-821-003; www.giannifranzi.it; $$$$), a 50-year-old institution that still serves scrumptious dishes like ravioli with fish sauce and baked fish with potatoes. Finish things off with a glass of limoncino, northern Italy's answer to limoncello, the lemon liqueur popular in the south.

7 *Highs and Buys* 3 p.m.

With a full belly and a slight buzz, you'll want to check out these sights in this order: **Santa Margherita d'Antiochia**, a 1318 church built on sea rock with an odd facade that seems to turn its back on the piazza; the lookout towers of the 11th-century **Castello Doria**, where you'll be rewarded with magnificent aerial views of the entire region; and **La Cantina del Molo** (Via Visconti 27; 39-0187-812-302), a high-end wine shop that sells divine delicacies along with wines from the owner's vineyards.

8 *Sail Away* 5:50 p.m.

You've been stealing glimpses of the Mediterranean since you've arrived; now it's time to seize it. Board the last ferry (navigazionegolfodeipoeti.it) to the westernmost and largest village, **Monterosso al Mare**, the sandiest and most resortlike of them all. Upon disembarking, hang a left toward **Fegina** beach and join the locals enjoying sunset aperitivos. Top-notch wines and terrific bruschettas, as well as fantastic promenade people-watching, can be had at the outdoor wine shop and bar **Enoteca 5 Terre di Sassarini Giancarlo** (Via Fegina 94; 39-0187-818-063).

9 *A Modern Fish Tale* 8:30 p.m.

Traditional Ligurian cuisine, while delectable, can also get repetitive. For something regional yet refreshing, head to **L'Ancora della Tortuga** (Salita Cappuccini 6; 39-0187-800-065; $$), housed in a converted bunker that was used during World War II. The contemporary kitchen specializes in fish dishes, including a seafood carpaccio with country vegetables and the daily catch served on grapevine leaves. Be sure to reserve one of the few tables that overlook the sea, or a spot on the upstairs terrace.

ABOVE A watch tower overlooks the village of Vernazza, which has a pretty main square and a somewhat chic vibe.

BELOW Reserve a table overlooking the sea at L'Ancora della Tortuga, a restaurant in a converted World War II bunker. The contemporary kitchen specializes in fish dishes.

10 *Beach Parties* 10:30 p.m.

    You didn't come to the Cinque Terre to party, but if you're looking to keep the torch burning in Monterosso al Mare, you might be in luck. During the warmer months, day trippers and locals alike will stage beach parties along the **Via Fegina.** All are welcome. Or mix with the congenial crowds at one of the mellow, pub-style bars on **Via Roma** in the historical district.

SUNDAY

11 *Get Your Glam On* 8:30 a.m.

    The sweet and savory goodness at **Il Frantoio** (Via Gioberti 1; 39-0187-818-333) should be enough to get you up before your alarm clock rings. Take your euro coins to this unassuming alleyway shop and make a breakfast of its dolci castagnina—warm circular pastries baked with chestnuts, salt, milk, pine nuts,

and raisins. Grab a selection of the superior focacce for lunch. Then head out to soak up the town's biggest selling point: its Riviera-ness! Not far from the entrance up to Convento dei Cappuccini monastery, you'll find the **Bagni Eden** beach club (Via Fegina 7-11; 39-0187-818-256), a postcardlike world of colorful chaise longues (with matching umbrellas), turquoise water, and bronzed beauties playing Kadima paddle ball. Pellegrino, focaccia, and salty air never tasted so jet set, especially after all that hiking.

ABOVE Vernazza and its terraced hillside.

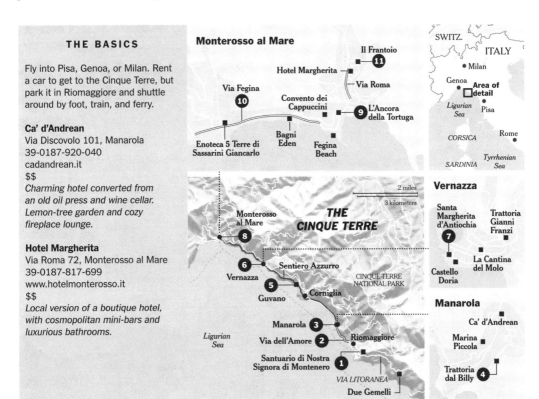

THE BASICS

Fly into Pisa, Genoa, or Milan. Rent a car to get to the Cinque Terre, but park it in Riomaggiore and shuttle around by foot, train, and ferry.

Ca' d'Andrean
Via Discovolo 101, Manarola
39-0187-920-040
cadandrean.it
$$
Charming hotel converted from an old oil press and wine cellar. Lemon-tree garden and cozy fireplace lounge.

Hotel Margherita
Via Roma 72, Monterosso al Mare
39-0187-817-699
www.hotelmonterosso.it
$$
Local version of a boutique hotel, with cosmopolitan mini-bars and luxurious bathrooms.

Genoa

Not so long ago, Genoa was far more grit than glamour — a way station to more fabulous places like Cinque Terre. And its industrial port was among the more forgettable spots along the Italian Riviera. But a complete scrub-down and restoration of its once-seedy waterfront, combined with an influx of young, well-funded entrepreneurs, transformed it into a city of inviting public spaces and cosmopolitan wine bars, shops, and restaurants. And beneath its modern veneer, a much older city of venerable history and rich medieval architecture calls out to be explored.

— BY JEREMY W. PETERS

FRIDAY

1 *Not So Square* 6 p.m.

For a sense of how Genoa teems with unpretentious night life, head to **Piazza delle Erbe**. A small square hidden amid the labyrinthine alleys that snake through the city's medieval quarter, it is home to no fewer than a half-dozen bars, two restaurants, a pizzeria, and a gelateria. Tables from the nearby establishments spill out onto the square, providing prime real estate for gazing at the hipper-than-thou young crowd, which might just give you a look that says, "Don't spoil this for us, tourist." Forgo a glass of wine (you'll probably have plenty in Genoa before you leave) and stop in **Bar Berto** (Piazza delle Erbe 6R; 39-010-275-8157), which brews its own beer.

2 *Showroom Dining* 9 p.m.

Anyone who thinks Genoa is still a grimy port town hasn't set foot inside **Muà** (Via San Sebastiano 13; 39-010-532-191; mua-ge.com; $$). It is a place where Genoa's beautiful people gather, with décor taken straight from some chic Italian design store: walls awash in gleaming white, high-backed brown leather chairs, tables propped up by thin stem-like legs. The menu has Ligurian specialties like scallops brushed with bread crumbs and olive oil. For a pasta course, try the testaroli, a kind of pasta with a soft,

OPPOSITE A restored waterfront and an influx of entrepreneurial cash have given Genoa a new polish.

RIGHT A fountain in Piazza Raffaele de Ferrari.

chewy texture more like a crepe than a noodle, in a cheese sauce.

3 *Digestif* 11 p.m.

For late evening, discos can certainly be found, but you are better off parking yourself at **La Lepre** (Piazza della Lepre 5R), a cozy bar with soothing green walls, and ordering an after-dinner grappa. It's a bit hard to find (the tiny square is not on many maps), but that only adds to the appeal.

SATURDAY

4 *Harbor Walk* 10 a.m.

With a little help from Renzo Piano, native son and star architect, the wharves along Genoa's old port, known as the Porto Antico, have been transformed into bustling, palm-lined promenades full of cafes, restaurants, and a biosphere suspended over the water. There's also an aquarium that bills itself as one of Europe's largest, but it can get mobbed. Instead, head to the **Galata Museo del Mare** (Calata De Mari 1; 39-010-234-5655; www.galatamuseodelmare.it), a maritime museum with strategic views. Don't miss the views from the roof, which overlooks the waterfront and the city. Small viewfinders identify the city's major attractions, helping you plot out the rest of your day.

5 *Littlest Sandwich Shop* 1 p.m.

Blink and you might miss **Gran Ristoro** (Via di Sottoripa 27 R; 39-010-247-3127; $), a tiny closet of a sandwich shop just off the harbor. It is so small,

in fact, that you would walk right past it if not for the line of Genoese of all stripes — cops, students, dock workers — extending out the door. The printed menu is minimal; there's just no way to list that much meat. So ask for a toasted sandwich, served on a soft, fresh roll with your choice of one of the dozens of meats — prosciutto, capicola, pancetta, spianata — hanging in the window. You won't find a more satisfying lunch bargain.

6 *(Very) Old Town* 2 p.m.

Parts of Genoa's old city still look and feel like the Middle Ages. The cobblestone alleyways are so narrow that you can stretch out your arms and touch buildings on either side of the street. Spend some time getting lost — it's easy to do — and check the small shops scattered along the narrow streets. But don't miss the **San Lorenzo Cathedral** (Piazza San Lorenzo; 39-010-246-8869), which dates back to the ninth century, in the heart of the old city. Its distinctive zebra-striped facade is one of Genoa's most recognizable landmarks, repeated on buildings throughout the city. San Lorenzo's smaller architectural twin, the **Church of San Matteo** (Piazza San Matteo), is a short walk away and has an ornate marble crypt where the explorer Andrea Doria is entombed.

7 *Salumi e Vino* 7 p.m.

Wine bars are not difficult to stumble across in Genoa. But a place that is guaranteed to whet your palate with a wide variety of whites and reds and a heaping plate of salami and cheese is **Taggiou** (Vico Superiore del Ferro 8; 39-010-275-9225; taggiou.it). If there are no seats inside the intimate, brick-ceilinged dining room, you can stand outside over one of the wine barrels that double as patio furniture.

8 *Carnivore's Paradise* 9 p.m.

Fresh fish is a staple in Genoa. But for something a little more carnivorous, try **Maxela** (Vico Inferiore del Ferro 9; 39-010-247-4209; maxela.it; $$), a steakhouse so proud to be beef-only that its meat locker opens onto the main dining room and cooks can be seen (and heard) hammering away as they tenderize cuts of beef. Favorites include the beef heifer tagliata, served with a variety of sauces like balsamic vinegar-caramelized pear and rosemary-garlic. For a first course, don't skip the

ABOVE Maxela, a steakhouse in a town whose usual staple is fresh fish. Dishes may include pesto, a Genoese invention.

RIGHT San Lorenzo Cathedral, with its distinctive zebra-striped facade, dates back to the ninth century.

OPPOSITE Wine in the afternoon at Taggiou.

handmade gnocchi with pesto. It is so soft that practically no chewing is required. And you can't leave Genoa without having pesto. As you will undoubtedly hear many times over from proud Genoese, it is said to have been invented here.

SUNDAY

9 *Light Breakfast* 9 a.m.

Genoese aren't big on brunch. So forget about having eggs and go instead to **Tagliafico** (Via Galata 31 R; 39-010-565-714; pasticceriatagliafico.it), one of the city's best pasticcerias. Its display cases are meticulously arranged, showing off perfectly crafted homemade croissants, bignés (cream puffs), and chocolates. Have an espresso and a pastry.

10 *Frescoes and Gelato* 11 a.m.

Genoa was once a sea power with its own empire, and you'll find the symbols of its grandeur on Via Garibaldi. Old palaces have been converted into museums and granted protective status by the United Nations. Tour the **Palazzo Rosso** (Via Garibaldi 18; 39-010-557-4972; museidigenova.it/it/museo/palazzo-rosso), a stately confection of frescoed ballrooms, gilded halls, and Renaissance paintings. Then stop at **Profumo di Rosa** (Via Cairoli 13R; profumodirosagenova.com) for gelato.

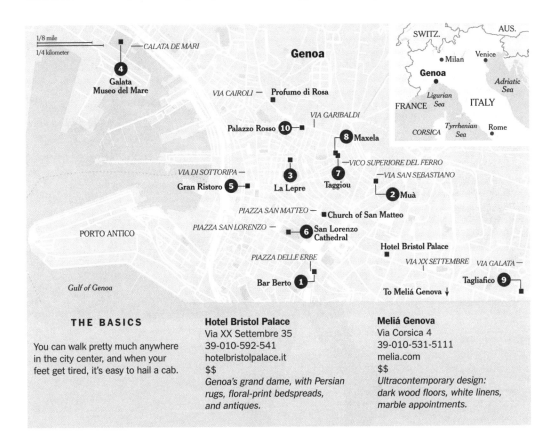

THE BASICS

You can walk pretty much anywhere in the city center, and when your feet get tired, it's easy to hail a cab.

Hotel Bristol Palace
Via XX Settembre 35
39-010-592-541
hotelbristolpalace.it
$$
Genoa's grand dame, with Persian rugs, floral-print bedspreads, and antiques.

Meliá Genova
Via Corsica 4
39-010-531-5111
melia.com
$$
Ultracontemporary design: dark wood floors, white linens, marble appointments.

Milan

Appearances matter in Milan. For proof, just stroll past the sights: the majestic Gothic cathedral, the stately Teatro alla Scala opera house, the smartly dressed Milanese (yes, they're an attraction, too). But the true charm of Italy's most cosmopolitan city is its refusal to coast on these beautiful treasures. A few blocks from Leonardo da Vinci's The Last Supper in the church of Santa Maria delle Grazie, an ambitious project is transforming the skyline: CityLife, a new center-city neighborhood featuring three dazzling, futuristic skyscrapers. And, with extra prompting from its hosting of the World Expo in 2015, the city has blossomed with new museums and restaurants. In Milan, Italy's future is already on display. — BY INGRID K. WILLIAMS

FRIDAY

1 *Design Shrine* 4:30 p.m.

Design is a religion in Milan, so start by paying your respects at the high altar that is the **Triennale Design Museum** (Viale Alemagna 6; 39-02-724-341; triennale.org). The museum, on the edge of Parco Sempione, is the first dedicated solely to Italian design. Where else could you expect to find a super-size Campari bottle beside a Brobdingnagian replica of a rainbow-hued Ferragamo sandal? Prepare for your visit with a quick aperitivo at the ground-floor DesignCafé, which closes at 5.

2 *The First Supper* 8:30 p.m.

Leave the museum in time to enjoy Parco Sempione, the city's largest park, and admire Castello Sforzesco and the Arch of Peace, on your way to dinner at **Il Solferino** (Via Castelfidardo 2; 39-02-2900-5748; ilsolferino.com; $$$), which has been serving traditional Milanese food for more than a century. If truffles are in season, your server with send shavings fluttering onto your plate. Start with something like "Arnaud's lardo" (lard) with croutons and honey, and move on to a savory dish like Il Solferino's own pappardelle with boar.

OPPOSITE Design is religion in Milan, fashion included.

RIGHT The cafe at HangarBicocca, a cavernous space bursting with mesmerizing large-scale art installations.

3 *A Man, a Plan, Navigli* 11 p.m.

Take a postprandial passeggiata — it's required — past Porta Ticinese to the glowing canals and waterside drinking dens of the Navigli neighborhood. Designed in part by Leonardo da Vinci, the narrow canals were neglected for decades, but recent preservation efforts have spurred the area's emergence as one of the city's hottest night-life destinations. Seek out **Spritz** (Ripa di Porta Ticinese 9; 39-02-8339-0192; spritz-navigli.it) for the lounge's namesake drink, an Italian classic. Then hop over to **El Brellin** (Alzaia Naviglio Grande 14; 39-02-5810-1351; brellin.it) for a glass of vino in the garden, or to the cozy beer pub **Al Coccio** (Alzaia Naviglio Pavese 2) for a Baladin beer. After that, it's your call.

SATURDAY

4 *New Kid on the Piazza* 10 a.m.

After years of restoration, the resplendent white marble facade of Milan's soaring Gothic cathedral, the Duomo, gleams anew. It also has a contemporary neighbor on the piazza, the **Museo del Novecento** (Via Marconi 1; 39-02-8844-4061; museodelnovecento.org) in the renovated Palazzo dell'Arengario. A strikingly modern interior features a spiral ramp that whisks visitors up to the galleries, where an extensive collection of 20th-century Italian art includes works by Umberto Boccioni, Carlo Carrà, and many others. The museum's showpiece, however, is the view from the top floor, where floor-to-ceiling windows frame a stunning panorama of the Piazza Duomo.

5 *A Sicilian Lunch Hit* 12:30 p.m.

The views are also superb from the museum's buzzy third-floor restaurant, **Giacomo Arengario** (Via Marconi 1; 39-02-7209-3814; giacomomilano. com)—provided you can score a table on the terrace. If not, console yourself with a cannolo at nearby **Antica Focacceria San Francesco** (Via San Paolo 15; 39-02-875-411; afsf.it), a family-friendly cafeteria-style spot that serves up Sicilian specialties like ragù-stuffed arancini, caper-dotted caponata, and thick slices of sfincione. This location, which opened in 2009, was the first outpost of the 176-year-old original in Palermo, an establishment famous for its refusal to pay pizzo (Mafia protection money).

6 *Designer Gelato* 2 p.m.

You may not be in the mood to try on couture after lunch, but Via Montenapoleone, the main avenue of Milan's haute fashion district, is worth a walk-through. A recent and particularly flamboyant addition is the designer **Roberto Cavalli's** five-story, 160,000-square-foot boutique (Via Montenapoleone 6; 39-02-763-0771; robertocavalli.com). Other, long-famed designer stores have been refurbished to stay competitive in the retail arms race. When you tire of the scenery, swing by **Officine del Gelato** (Viale Montenero 46; 39-02-5990-4118; officinedelgelato. com), a bright little shop serving gelati made with natural ingredients.

7 *Art and Design* 4:30 p.m.

Ikea this is not. At **Spazio Rossana Orlandi** (Via Matteo Bandello 14/16; 39-02-467-4471; rossanaorlandi.com), every nook is packed with fantastical pieces of designy art and arty design, an eclectic mix from emerging designers around the world. Fancy an electric-blue pig statue for the front lawn? Or an embroidered deer head to hang above the fireplace?

8 *Risotto Roulette* 8 p.m.

If you came to Milan partly for an evening at the most fabled opera house in the world, you should be formally dressed and drinking in the glamour about now as the curtain opens at **La Scala** (Piazza della

Scala; 39-02-7200-3744; teatroallascala.org). For a more casual evening, take the M1 (red) Metro line to the Pasteur stop and head to **Da Abele** (Via Temperanza 5; 39-02-261-3855; trattoriadaabele.it; $$), an unassuming trattoria northeast of the city center. In the Lombardy region, of which Milan is the capital, locally produced rice has traditionally trumped pasta as the more popular primo, and risotto is the sumptuous specialty. Only three risotti are offered at this restaurant each night, but with the options changing daily, this local favorite stays crowded.

9 *Liquid Arts* 10:30 p.m.

Since you're already out of the city center, make an evening of it and head to **Birrificio Lambrate** (Via Adelchi 5; 39-02-7063-8678; birrificiolambrate. com), Milan's first craft brewery. You'll know you've arrived when you spot an inked and pierced crowd on a narrow side street using parked cars as ersatz coasters. If you can (politely) elbow your

way to the bar, order a pint of Domm, a Bavarian-style weizen, or a pale, hoppy Montestella. Prefer not to struggle for your tipple? Abandon the search for beer and find a quiet wine bar instead. Milan has plenty, many of them pleasingly chic and relaxing. This is Italy, after all.

SUNDAY

10 *Body Polish* 9 a.m.

Immerse yourself in emerald and gold at the serene subterranean spa in the **Bulgari Hotel**, on a private street beside a garden (Via Privata Fratelli Gabba 7b; 39-02-805-8051; bulgarihotels.com). Arrive

OPPOSITE ABOVE Milan's massive cathedral, the Duomo.

OPPOSITE BELOW The Triennale Design Museum.

BELOW A box at La Scala, Milan's famous opera house.

early for a solitary dip in the shimmering pool and an undisturbed steam in the sultry hammam before submitting to an aromatherapy massage. You will emerge refreshed and as polished as one of the haute jeweler's precious gems.

ABOVE The Navigli canals, designed in part by Leonardo da Vinci, have become a center for night life.

OPPOSITE The Museo del Novecento shows modern art.

11 *Spacey Space* Noon

Head north to the city limits where a former factory has become **HangarBicocca** (Via Chiese 2; 39-02-6611-1573; hangarbicocca.org), a cavernous space bursting with large-scale art installations. It's a bit of a trek, but one worth making. The main exhibition area is a dark, lunarlike scene dominated by Anselm Kiefer's *The Seven Heavenly Palaces.* Around Mr. Kiefer's seven colossal, spotlighted towers are works like a melting wax sculpture, inverted scaffolding, or an enormous image of an old woman made of photosensitive grass. When you've reached your daily quota for wide-eyed wonderment, rehash the experience over brunch at **Dopolavoro Bicocca** ($$$), the on-site cafe.

THE BASICS

Take the 45-minute train ride from Malpensa airport to Milan's Cadorna rail station. Once in town, buy a 10-ride pass for the efficient Metro and bus system.

Hotel Spadari al Duomo
Via Spadari 11
39-02-7200-2371
spadarihotel.com
$$$
May have the best location in town, near the Duomo and next door to the food-and-wine emporium Peck.

Hotel Milano Scala
Via dell'Orso 7
39-02-870-961
hotelmilanoscala.it
$$$
Riffs on an opera theme, but its eco-conscious efforts are no act.

Bulgari Hotel Milan
Via Privata Fratelli Gabba 7b
39-02-805-8051
bulgarihotels.com
$$$$
Understated luxury on a private street beside a botanical garden.

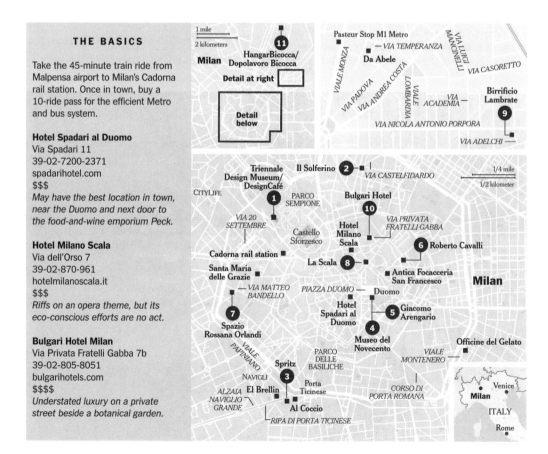

Lake Como

In the foothills of the Alps in northern Italy, Lake Como deserves its reputation as a playground for the wealthy. Virtually deserted during the winter, the wishbone-shaped lake awakens from its slumber in mid-March when glamorous crowds begin flocking to the pretty towns clustered around its midsection: Bellagio, Menaggio, Tremezzo, Varenna. But in recent years, the city of Como, on the lake's southwestern tip, has quietly blossomed into the most interesting spot for visitors of all bank account sizes. A raft of openings has infused new life there, transforming the oft-overlooked transit hub into the lake's new place to be seen. — BY INGRID K. WILLIAMS

FRIDAY

1 *View From the Peak* 3:30 p.m.

Who's afraid of heights? In Como, join the crowds clambering aboard the **funicular** that ascends the mountain to Brunate, a small town perched about 1,600 feet above the lake (funicolarecomo.it). Upon arrival, continue on foot up the treacherously steep rocky trail — less than a mile long, but what feels like the same in elevation gain — that ends at **Faro Voltiano**, a remote lighthouse with blissful solitude and an unsurpassed panorama across the city and lake to neighboring Switzerland.

2 *Off the Wall* 6 p.m.

In late 2013, Banksy's Como doppelgänger stepped out of the shadows by opening a street-art gallery named after his pseudonym, **Mr. Savethewall** (Via Giovio 5, Como; 39-031-2433-25; savethewall. it). The unusual name belongs to Pierpaolo Perretta, whose art uses cardboard or similar materials that can be affixed without defacing walls. Among the provocative paintings on display is an incisive image of a young girl praying to a tablet, Please, Holy iPad, give me back my Dad.

OPPOSITE A narrow view of Lake Como, renowned in Italy and beyond for its beauty, framed by old buildings in the tiny village of Varenna. The charming towns on the lake's shores are an integral part of its allure.

RIGHT The gardens of Villa Monastero, a former monastery in Varenna, invite strolling and relaxation.

3 *Supper in Season* 8 p.m.

The Market Place (Via Borsieri 21A, Como; 39-031-2707-12; themarketplace.it; $$$$) is a small but sophisticated farm-to-table restaurant where one evening's menu included cuttlefish-ink tagliolini with tender shrimp and fava beans. A divine dessert was an airy millefoglie with orange-scented Chantilly cream drizzled with toffee and fleur de sel. After dinner, have a drink at the cozy **Fresco Cocktail Shop** (Viale Lecco 23, Como; 39-393-7315-649; frescococktailshop.it) where the drinks are heavy on unusual spirits and seasonal fruit.

SATURDAY

4 *Cups and Cupolas* 9 a.m.

The cafe **Cremeria Bolla** (Via Pietro Boldoni 6, Como; 39-031-2642-56; cremeriabolla.it), opened in 1893, is a local favorite for a morning caffeine fix in Como. Savor a cappuccino at an outdoor table and watch the city streets spring to life. Then head to the nearby **Duomo di Como** (Piazza Duomo 6, Como; 39-031-3312-275; cattedraledicomo.it) the city's green-domed Gothic cathedral dating to the late 1300s. Among its treasures are a collection of ancient tapestries and paintings by the Renaissance-era artist Gaudenzio Ferrari.

5 *Wardrobe Wins* 11 a.m.

Should a modish Milanese man arrive in Como without a warm sweater or dapper dinner jacket, he can find what he needs at **A.Gi.Emme** (Via Vittorio Emanuele II 91, Como; 39-031-2640-96; agiemme.

com). This exquisitely stylish store began as a small shoe shop but has since expanded into four shops around town, including locations for women and children. At the men's shop, splurge on classics like cashmere cardigans, tailored wool blazers, and cozy scarves that are chic antidotes to chilly lake breezes.

6 *Dockside Dining* 1 p.m.

Hop aboard a bus or a boat bound for Bellagio, a picturesque (and very popular) mid-lake village about 18 miles north of Como. For lunch, skip the touristy tables in town and seek out **Ristorante alle Darsene di Loppia** (Via Melzi d'Eril 1, Loppia di Bellagio; 39-031-9520-69; ristorantedarsenediloppia. com; $$$), a sunny restaurant nearby. Whether seated inside the bright dining room or beneath the leafy pergola on the veranda, take a cue from the dockside location and focus on fresh fish. Recent highlights included swordfish crudo with chicory salad and lardo di Colonnata and a light seafood soup with mussels and homemade cavatelli. Afterward, stroll through the gardens of the neo-Classical **Villa Melzi** (Via Lungolario Manzoni, Bellagio; 39-339-4573-838; giardinidivillamelzi.it), a shortcut to the lakeside promenade that leads back to the ferry pier in Bellagio.

7 *It Takes a Villa* 4 p.m.

Many of Lake Como's lovely waterfront villas remain the private domain of privileged residents, but a few are open to the visiting public. One of the most magnificent is the stately **Villa Carlotta** (Via Regina 2, Tremezzo; 39-0344-40405; villacarlotta.it), a former marquis's mansion dating from the late 17th century that today functions as a museum. Located across the lake in Tremezzo, a 20-minute ferry ride west from Bellagio, the grand villa today houses artworks, including sculptures by Antonio Canova. But most captivating are the romantic Italian gardens surrounding the villa where roughly 20 cultivated acres bloom with camellias, azaleas, roses, and citrus trees.

8 *Aristocratic Aperitivo* 7 p.m.

Lake Como may not have sandy shores, but at the nearby Grand Hotel Tremezzo, the hulking luxury hotel has installed **T Beach** (Grand Hotel Tremezzo, Via Provinciale Regina 8, Tremezzo; 39-0344-42491; grandhoteltremezzo.com), a full-service beach club complete with trucked-in sand, sun beds, umbrellas, and a full-size pool floating in the lake. Go around sunset for a Campari aperitivo served with golden views of Bellagio across the lake. Or if the beach party atmosphere seems too artificial, head south to **Villa d'Este** (Via Regina 40, Cernobbio; 39-031-3481; villadeste. com) in the charming town of Cernobbio. Generations of guests have sipped aperitivi at the storied hotel's **Bar Terrazza**, nibbling on olives in the shade of ancient chestnut trees while watching boats cruise past.

9 *Night at the Palazzo* 9:30 p.m.

Take your evening meal inside another gorgeous edifice, a renovated two-story palazzo near the waterfront in Como. **Theoria** (Via Bianchi Giovini 41, Como; 39-031-305-272; theoriagallery.it) is a tearoom, lounge, and restaurant (I Tigli in Theoria; $$$$) set around a lovely courtyard garden. The first-floor dining room is an elegant space with large arched windows, coffered wooden ceilings and servers dressed in traditional Trentino folk attire. On the tables are French-inflected dishes like sea-bass quenelles and foie gras with raspberries. After dinner, head upstairs to the handsome lounge, which serves impressive platters during aperitivo hour and later pours well-mixed nightcaps like the Hugo, with mint, lime, elderflower syrup, prosecco, and soda.

SUNDAY

10 *Charged Morning* 10 a.m.

There's no finer way to greet the day than a walk along Como's sparkling waterfront. From Piazza Cavour, follow the lakeside promenade westward past **Tempio Voltiano** (Viale Guglielmo Marconi 1, Como; 031-574-705; cultura.comune. como.it/tempio-voltiano), a neo-Classical museum dedicated to Alessandro Volta, the local physicist who invented the electric battery. Double back upon reaching the palatial Villa Olmo for a round-trip stroll of just under two miles — enough exercise to warrant a reward from **Gelateria Lariana** (Lungo Lario Trento 5, Como; 39-031-266-388), an artisanal shop scooping its own gelato in flavors like fresh fig and pistacchio di Bronte.

11 *On the Water* Noon

Lazy Sunday afternoons are best spent aboard a slow ferry that floats past villas and small villages clinging to the water's edge. After a couple of hours of cruising, alight in tiny Varenna on the lake's eastern shore. Stroll south along winding cobblestone lanes to **Villa Monastero** (Viale Giovanni Polvani 4, Varenna; 034-1830-129; villamonastero.eu), a former monastery and noble's residence that today draws visitors to its lakeside gardens. Promenade beneath cypress and citrus trees and through the beautiful waterfront loggia while savoring views that have lured admirers to Lake Como for centuries.

OPPOSITE ABOVE Courtyard dining at Theoria.

OPPOSITE BELOW A sitting room at Grand Hotel Tremezzo.

THE BASICS

Ferries connect lakeside towns.

B&B Convento Sant'Antonio
Via Rezzonico 23, Como
39-335-2057-20
bblakecomo.it
$$
A restored 17th-century convent transformed into a bed-and-breakfast. Rooms are adorned with artworks and antiques.

CastaDiva Resort & Spa
Via Caronti 69, Blevio
39-031-3251-3035
castadivaresort.com
$$$$
Lavish lakeside estate, now a hotel with a subterranean spa and a swimming pool floating in the lake.

Grand Hotel Tremezzo
Via Regina 8, Tremezzina
39-0344-42491
grandhoteltremezzo.com
$$$$
Landmark Art Nouveau hotel with pools, spa, and yoga studio.

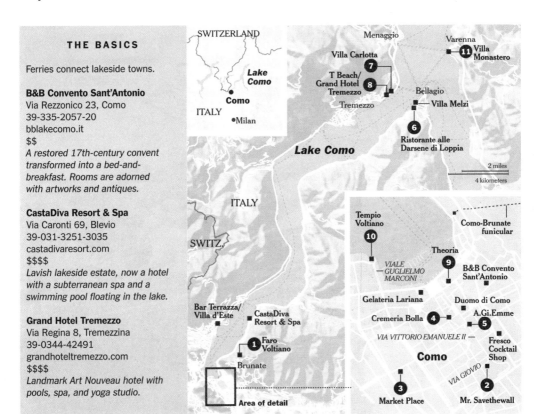

Venice

With its picture-perfect canals and waterside palazzi, Venice is a romantic idyll. No wonder 18 million tourists pile onto the floating city each year. But what is surprising is that the embattled residents still manage to carve out a hometown for themselves — a pastiche of in-the-know restaurants, underground bars, quiet piazzas, and calmer, outlying islands. And that's not counting all the cultural offerings that Venetians take full advantage of. The cool art scene now goes beyond the Biennale. And instead of sinking, architectural icons have re-emerged as new landmarks.
— BY ONDINE COHANE

FRIDAY

1 *New Perspective* 4 p.m.

Venice's artsy side is on display at the **Punta della Dogana** (Dorsoduro 2; 39-041-523-1680; palazzograssi.it), the city's former customs house that was transformed into a museum to hold part of the sizable art collection of the luxury goods magnate François Pinault. The Japanese architect Tadao Ando left the bones of the stunning landmark intact but created light and airy galleries for the heavyweight contemporary work. The view from the sidewalk is just as impressive, looking back onto the Grand Canal and across to Giudecca. Keep an eye out for Charles Ray's sculpture *Boy With Frog*, his first outdoor installation.

2 *Lagoon to Table* 8 p.m.

Dismayed by the city's reputation for high prices and mediocre food, a consortium of restaurants formed Ristoranti della Buona Accoglienza (veneziaristoranti.it), or the Restaurants of Good Welcome, with a pledge to offer transparent pricing, full disclosure of ingredients, and a commitment to culinary traditions. Among the outstanding members is **Alle Testiere** (Calle del Mondo Novo 5801; 39-041-522-7220; www.osterialletestiere.it; $$$$), a small establishment owned by a group of young Venetians that serves seasonal and local seafood like gnocchi with calamaretti and fresh grilled sea bass. Pair with a regional wine like Orto, a grassy white made on

OPPOSITE Venice, the city of palazzi and canals.

Sant'Erasmo, an island in the Venetian Lagoon. Be sure to make a reservation.

3 *Bar Scene* 10 p.m.

New hotel bars have awakened the city's once-sleepy night life. One spot is the **PG**, a restaurant and bar at the **Palazzina Grassi** (San Marco 3247; 39-041-528-4644; palazzinag.it), a 16th-century palazzo that was transformed by Philippe Starck into a design hotel. Johnny Depp held court there when filming *The Tourist*.

SATURDAY

4 *Modernist Nook* 10 a.m.

Carlo Scarpa, the architectural godfather of Venetian modernists, is back in vogue. See why at the **Fondazione Querini Stampalia** (Castello 5252; 39-041-271-1411; querinistampalia.org), where he transformed the garden and ground floor into a modernist haven in the early 1960s. Upstairs, a quiet library is a great spot to read a newspaper with locals on the weekends or to see the painting *Presentation of Jesus in the Temple* by Giovanni Bellini. It's one of the city's underappreciated masterpieces.

5 *Set in Stone* 11:30 a.m.

The **Ca' Pesaro International Gallery of Modern Art** (Santa Croce 2076; 39-041-72-1127; visitmuve.it/en/museums) shows modern works in a white marble palazzo from the 17th century. The contrast between the contemporary exhibitions and the Baroque interiors is striking. Intriguing juxtapositions have included steel, glass, and stone works by Tony Cragg, the sculptor from Liverpool, alongside sculptures by Rodin. After seeing the museum, take a walk on the winding streets behind it, a residential enclave away from the tourist fray.

6 *Lunch Pursuit* Noon

Start your lunch hour with a stroll past the stalls of the **Rialto Market**, the ancient but still thriving food market near the landmark Rialto Bridge. Then join Venetians at the counter in bacari, traditional bars that serve hors-d'oeuvre-size snacks called cicchetti. In the alleys behind the market you'll discover bacari where everything from meatballs to crab

claws to stuffed squash blossoms is tossed into the fryer. One good example is **Cantina do Spade** (San Polo 859/860; 39-041-521-0583; cantinadospade.com). Wander a bit to discover more, and find a perch at a piazza as you relish lunch and the city. Or for a more stylish lunch, take a table at **Naranzaria** (San Polo 130; 39-041-724-1035; naranzaria.it), where you can look out over the Grand Canal.

7 *Selective Shopping* 4 p.m.

Forget kitschy masks and imitation Murano glass. The streets radiating off bustling Campo Santo Stefano as far as the Grand Canal are lined with one-of-a-kind galleries and small boutiques. **Galleria Marina Barovier** (San Marco 3216; 39-041-523-6748; barovier.it; by appointment) carries hard-to-find vintage glass pieces and items by contemporary artists that end up in museum collections. **Chiarastella Cattana** (San Marco 3357; 39-041-522-4369; chiarastellacattana.it) makes tablecloths, cushion covers, and duvets from luscious fabrics of her own design. Nearby, **Cristina Linassi** (San Marco 2434; 39-041-522-8107; cristinalinassi.it) has silk lingerie and gossamer nighties that look straight out of Sophia Loren's closet circa 1955.

8 *Spritz Before Seafood* 8 p.m.

Whet your appetite with a Venetian spritz and some cicchetti at **Al Timon** (Cannaregio 2754, Fondamenta dei Ormesini; 39-041-524-6066;

Facebook: Altimon), a canalside bacaro in Cannaregio where regulars spill out along the sidewalk nightly. Then settle in for a seafood-centric dinner at **Anice Stellato** (Cannaregio 3272, Fondamenta de la Sensa; 39-041-720-744; osterianicestellato.com), a rustic osteria nearby. Most tables order the frittura mista— a tangle of fried squid, whole shrimp, small fish and vegetables (19 euros) — but don't skip the starters, like stuffed calamari in a rich tomato sauce with grilled polenta (11 euros).

9 *Party Alfresco* 10 p.m.

After dinner, the large Campo Santa Margherita becomes the city's meeting point. Students grab a spritz or beer at **Il Caffè**, known to locals as the "red cafe," or Caffè Rosso (Dorsoduro 2963; 39-041-528-7998). An older, fashionable crowd meets at **Osteria alla Bifora** (Dorsoduro 2930; 39-041-523-6119). On warm nights the piazza becomes one big multi-generational party.

SUNDAY

10 *Italian Dough* 10 a.m.

Join residents at **Pasticceria Tonolo** (Dorsoduro 2930, Calle San Pantalon; 39-041-523-7209) for the cream-filled fresh doughnuts known as krapfen. You may have to jostle Italian-style for the beloved pastry, which sells out by noon, but it's worth the effort.

11 *Island Idyll* 1 p.m.

Do as the Venetians do and head to the outlying islands that dot the lagoon. Among the gems is Mazzorbo and its six-room inn and restaurant, **Venissa** (Fondamenta di Santa Caterina 3; 39-041-527-2281; venissa.it; $$$$), which is open from March to November. Opened in 2010 by Bisol, an Italian prosecco company, the resort has given new life to a walled vineyard dating from the 1400s. Relax over a leisurely Sunday lunch at the restaurant. Dishes may include figs from a nearby tree and snapper caught in the lagoon that morning. Later, wander the main pathway along the waterfront, where a bridge connects to the more-visited island of Burano, with its vibrant pastel-colored buildings. The two islands capture what Venetians know well: you can escape the crowds in the blink of an eye if you are willing to cross the water.

OPPOSITE The Piazza San Marco in a winter dawn. The winged *Lion of Venice*, symbol of Saint Mark (San Marco) the patron saint of Venice, is silhouetted against the sky.

ABOVE Cocktails at the sleek Naranzaria.

THE BASICS

Make your way around town by foot or vaporetto.

Ca' Sagredo
Campo Santa Sofia 4198
39-041-241-3111
casagredohotel.com
$$$$
Near the Rialto Bridge, in a restored 15th-century palazzo.

Novecento
San Marco 2683
39-041-241-3765
novecento.biz
$$$
Fine staff, charming garden, and excellent breakfast.

Centurion Palace
Dorsoduro 173
39-041-342-81
centurionpalacevenezia.com
$$$$
High-end modern design inside a Gothic palazzo on the Grand Canal.

2 miles
3 kilometers

MARCO POLO AIRPORT

Venissa **11**

ITALY

MAZZORBO

BURANO

MURANO

Venice Lagoon

Venice detail

GIUDECCA

Adriatic Sea

Milan **Venice**

ITALY

Adriatic Sea

Rome

•Naples

Tyrrhenian Sea

SARDINIA

1/4 mile
1/2 kilometer

Anice Stellato

8 Al Timon

Canale delle Navi

FONDAMENTA DEI ORMESINI

CANNAREGIO

Ca' Pesaro International Gallery of Modern Art

5

Ca' Sagredo Hotel

Rialto Market

Cantina do Spade **6**

RIALTO BRIDGE

Naranzaria

Pasticceria Tonolo

10

SAN POLO

Venice

Alle Testiere **2**

Fondazione Querini Stampalia **4**

Il Caffè **9**

CALLE SAN PANTALON

Grand Canal

SAN MARCO

CASTELLO

Chiarastella Cattana

PIAZZA SAN MARCO

CAMPO SANTA MARGHERITA

Osteria alla Bifora

7 Galleria Marina Barovier

3

—CAMPO SANTO STEFANO

Cristina Linassi

PG/ Palazzina Grassi

Novecento Hotel

Canale di San Marco

DORSODURO

Centurion Palace

1

Punta della Dogana

Canale della Giudecca

GIUDECCA

Trieste

A medium-size seaport teetering on the edge of what we recognize as Italy, Trieste is a mysterious and puzzling place. Its convoluted history of serial conquest culminated in a century-long tug-of-war between Italy and Austria. It has a melting-pot population, a street plan that ranges from serenely rational to bewilderingly crooked and steep, and a forbidding limestone plateau crowding it down to the waterfront. Like a modernist novel, Trieste is complex, layered, ambiguous. It makes you dig for significance. But don't worry, the story has a happy ending: the patient visitor will go away well satisfied (and wonderfully well fed), rewarded by an experience unavailable to those looking for a traveler's quick and easy fix. — BY ADAM BEGLEY

FRIDAY

1 *Piazza by the Sea* 4 p.m.

The **Piazza dell'Unità d'Italia**, bounded on three sides by comically pompous 18th- and 19th-century buildings, most of them decorated like big, boxy wedding cakes, is wide open to the Adriatic, as though the ever-changing seascape were an entertainment staged for the city's benefit. Spend some time in this iconic piazza, a vast, glorious space.

2 *Life According to Zeno* 5 p.m.

Trieste may be overshadowed by other Adriatic cities (notably Venice, just 70 miles away), but it has a cult following. Its greatest native writer, Italo Svevo, has one, too. His *Zeno's Conscience* is a tender, devastating, hilarious portrait of modern man's absurd delusions, described by the critic Paul Bailey as "arguably the greatest comic novel of the 20th century." Zeno Cosini, the charmingly unreliable hero, blurts out, "Life is neither ugly nor beautiful, but it's original!" In the leafy **Piazza Hortis**, inspect the life-size statue of Svevo, an immobilized bronze pedestrian mingling with the passersby. When he was born in 1861, Trieste was a teeming international port of the Austro-Hungarian Empire, populated by

Italians with a mix of Slavs, Greeks, and Jews thrown in. The resulting city is — as Zeno would say — original. Jan Morris, who devoted a 2001 book to Trieste, called it an "enclave sui generis."

3 *Italy's Dubliner* 6 p.m.

A gentle stroll through the pedestrianized streets of the **Borgo Teresiano**, a calming symmetrical arrangement of city blocks bequeathed by the 18th-century Austrians, will take you past dozens of proud neo-Classical facades, some of them tarted up in the 19th century with touches borrowed from the Baroque. The setting combines Italian flair with a Germanic regard for well-ordered urban space. On a bridge midway along the abbreviated channel called the Canal Grande is a companion statue to Svevo's, a similarly lifelike bronze of James Joyce. Trieste stakes its claim to Joyce with justification. He lived here for 10 years and during that time wrote most of *Dubliners*, all of *Portrait of the Artist as a Young Man*, and portions of *Ulysses*.

4 *Trieste on Parade* 7 p.m.

It's the hour of the passeggiata, the unmistakably Italian moment when the streets are crowded with locals coolly eyeing one another or exchanging effusive greetings in Triestino, the local dialect. Sit for a while at one of the cafes in the Borgo Teresiano

OPPOSITE The pier at Castle Miramare, a Trieste landmark a few miles from the city center.

RIGHT The ornate bed of the unfortunate Maximilian I.

and soak up the daily drama. On a pleasant evening it will seem as though the entire population is passing in front of your cafe. The elderly make slow, halting progress, as do the proud young couples pushing baby carriages, while the busy professionals hurry along, overtaking the dog walkers and the last-minute shoppers. Order a glass of prosecco and marvel at the preposterously generous assortment of nibbles that comes with your drink.

5 *Try the Refosco* 8:30 p.m.

You will find it a challenge to get a bad meal in Trieste. For simplicity and authenticity, it is impossible to beat **La Tavernetta** (Via della Madonna del Mare 2; 39-040-308-594; $$$), a small wonder on a back street. A bowl of steaming pasta followed by sliced steak on a bed of arugula — bliss. The wines of the Friuli-Venezia Giulia region, of which Trieste is the capital, are well worth exploring. Try a refosco if you're drinking red, a ribolla gialla if you're drinking white.

SATURDAY

6 *Mansion District* 10 a.m.

Trieste has no great gallery — no Uffizi, no Accademia. Instead, you'll find grand mansions where the trappings of an opulent 19th-century lifestyle are on display alongside the art. At the **Museo Revoltella** (Via Diaz 27; 39-040-675-4350; museorevoltella.it), a dining room seems to have been spray-painted with 24-karat gold and the art includes canny, meticulously realistic portraits by Giuseppe Tominz (1790-1866). At the **Museo Sartorio** (Largo Papa Giovanni XXIII 1; 39-040-301-479; museosartoriotrieste.it), look for a fabulous 14th-century altarpiece, a stunning collection of drawings by Giovanni Battista Tiepolo (1696-1770), and

ABOVE Piazza dell'Unità d'Italia, seen from the seaside.

OPPOSITE Joyce and Svevo met at the Caffè San Marco.

paintings from the Byzantine to the Baroque plucked from churches in the countryside.

7 *Novel Lunch* 1 p.m.

The **Caffè San Marco** (Via Cesare Battisti 18; 39-040-064-1724; caffesanmarcotrieste.eu; $$), still a pleasant place for lunch, is famous as a haunt of Italo Svevo and James Joyce. Order a sandwich and imagine them at the next table. Svevo, a business-man who wrote novels on the side, found literary success elusive and encouragement scarce until 1907, when he met Joyce, then a penniless writer supple-menting his income by teaching English in Trieste. They liked each other right away, read each other's books, and soon settled into a waltz of sincere mutual admiration. As Joyce began to achieve success, he encouraged his friend's efforts and intervened to help him find publishers. Svevo, at age 65, found acclaim at last, experiencing what he called the literary equivalent of "the resurrection of Lazarus."

8 *The Old Neighborhood* 3 p.m.

Perched up above the old town, next to a large, taciturn fortified castle, is the 14th-century **Cathedral of San Giusto** (Piazza della Cattedrale), with a sweetly simple facade, a squat Romanesque campanile, and views of the city and out over the Adriatic. Inside the church are pretty Byzantine mosaics carefully restored. Nearby are the scattered remains of the town's Roman forum. On the way back down the hill — the colle di San Giusto — find Trieste's old Roman theater.

9 *Chocolate Soup* 5 p.m.

The coffee is delightful nearly everywhere — Trieste, after all, is the home of the Illy brand — but the Austrian influence means that the hot chocolate is heavenly, too. Stop into **Chocolat** (Via Cavana 15; 39-040-300-524) and ask for a small cup; it's ladled from the pot like a thick, dark soup. If the weather is too warm for that, sample one of the tasty variations on chocolate ice cream.

10 *Daily Fish* 8:30 p.m.

You are on the Adriatic coast, so concentrate tonight on the seafood. **Al Bagatto** (Via L. Cadorna 7; 39-040-301-771; albagatto.it; $$$$) is a Trieste classic, nearly half a century old, that serves the day's catch from the Gulf of Trieste. You might find red pappardelle with clams and asparagus, zuppa di pesce with tiny shrimp, or a fried seafood sampler platter.

SUNDAY

11 *Maximilian's Castle* 11 a.m.

The most satisfactory tourist attraction in Trieste, other than the Piazza Unità, is the brilliantly situated **Castle Miramare** (39-040-224-143; castellomiramare.it). Completed in 1860, it was the princely residence of the Archduke Maximilian, younger brother of the Hapsburg emperor. A gleaming white fairy tale vision, it floats just above the waves on a promontory five miles from the city center — you can see it from the waterfront, looking impossibly romantic, if you're that way inclined. (Skeptics might mistake it for a pile of crenellated sugar cubes.) The interior is sumptuously appointed. Miramare has a melancholy history that its brave white dazzle can't erase: the archduke had barely finished building it when he was shipped across the ocean to become Maximilian I of Mexico, a brief adventure that was not welcomed by all Mexicans. It ended in his execution by firing squad.

THE BASICS

An inexpensive bus runs from the airport into town. In the city center, explore on foot.

Hotel Residence L'Albero Nascosto
Via Felice Venezian 18
39-040-300-188
alberonascosto.it
$$
A five-minute stroll from the Piazza Unità. Friendly, helpful staff.

Grand Hotel Duchi d'Aosta
Piazza dell'Unità d'Italia 2/1
39-040-760-0011
duchi.eu
$$
In a wedding-cake building on the Piazza Unità.

Savoia Excelsior Palace
Riva del Mandracchio 4
39-040-77-941
savoiaexcelsiorpalace.starhotels.com
$$
Views of the waterfront promenade and the Adriatic Sea.

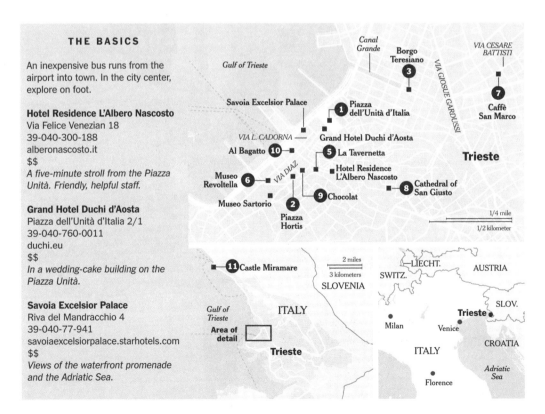

Ljubljana

The land of the Slovenes was repeatedly absorbed by empires and dictatorships — the Venetians, who imprinted an Italian influence; the Austrian (and later Austro-Hungarian) Empire; and finally Yugoslavia, from which the Slovenes separated themselves in 1991 after a 10-day war. Now Slovenia, with two million people spread over an area about the size of Wales, relishes its independence and carries off its marriage of Slavic, Austrian, and Italian cultures with an easy grace. Ljubljana, the cosmopolitan capital, brims with faded Hapsburg glory in Baroque churches, stately 19th-century edifices, and whimsical pockets of Art Nouveau. Alongside are cobbled lanes lined with medieval town houses and concrete eyesores left over from Yugoslav Socialism. New shops, restaurants, and business enterprises are buzzing, and everywhere, well-dressed people stream past on bicycles. Ljubljana has only 280,000 people — including 50,000 students — but it hums with urban energy. — BY SETH SHERWOOD

FRIDAY

1 *Ramparts With a View* 6 p.m.

Catch the funicular (lower stop at Krekov Square, or Krekov Trg) to climb the steep, forested hill to **Ljubljana Castle** (386-1-232-9994; ljubljanskigrad.si), which looks down on the rooftops and spires of the city from its highest crest. Take in the gorgeous view from the 16th-century fortifications. Below, the city wraps around Castle Hill in an orderly mass of curving cobblestone streets, red-tiled roofs, and domes, with bridges spanning the green, encircling Ljubljanica River. Out in the distance, the hills rise to rocky peaks of the Alps.

2 *Lordly Repast* 7 p.m.

Gostilna na Gradu (Grajska Planota 1; 386-8-205-1930; nagradu.si; $$), one of Ljubljana's best and more adventurous restaurants, serves its neo-Slovenian fare in the courtyard of Ljubljana Castle. Its owners take pride in using organic products and elevating old world recipes rather than dishing out a predictable mix of Italian, Austrian, and Serbian

fare as most local restaurants do. One winter menu included wild boar in juniper and cranberry sauce, Slovenian sea bass, and kranjska sausage with potato and turnips. Relax over dessert as darkness falls and the lights twinkle on in the city below.

3 *Wine and Song* 9 p.m.

Ride the funicular back down and take the short walk past St. Nicholas Cathedral to **Vinoteka Movia** (Mestni Square 2; 386-1-425-5448; movia.si), a wine bar and shop where you can taste Slovenian wines and nibble on prosciutto and cheese. Then cross the river on the landmark **Triple Bridge**, designed by the early 20th-century Ljubljana architect Joze Plecnik, to **Presernov Square**, the city's bustling social hub by night and day. The bistros and open-air cafes here and in the surrounding streets and squares, spilling down to the river and across it, are where Ljubljanans meet for lively nights of bar-hopping and music from blues to hip-hop and Slovenian pop. You might even find an open-air concert.

SATURDAY

4 *Designing Women* 10 a.m.

Two excellent representatives of Ljubljana's impressive art and design scene are **Galerija Equrna** (Gregorciceva 3a; 386-1-252-7123; equrna.si), a

OPPOSITE Presernov Square, Ljubljana's social hub.

RIGHT Repurposed military structures in Metelkova City.

pioneering private gallery of avant-garde art dating back to the former Yugoslavia, and **Tanja Pak Design** (Precna 6; 386-41-70-6760; tanjapak.com), where Pak, the artist-designer, showcases her award-winning glass creations. For fashion, seek out the minuscule boutique just off Slovenska Cesta boulevard where **Marjeta Groselj** (Tavcarjeva 4; 386-1-231-8984), the grande dame of local fashion, sells her designs on weekdays and Saturday mornings. "I'm hidden a little, but people always find me," she told one visitor. Her shelves are filled with leather handbags, many brightly colored and each hand-constructed in the on-site studio where she has worked for decades.

5 *Bridge of Glass* Noon

Take some time to wander around the old streets and squares hugging the river in the Old City. Return to Presernov Square for a daylight look at the rosy-colored 17th-century **Church of the Annunciation** and the statue of France Preseren, a beloved 19th-century Slovenian poet who greatly influenced Slovene literature and wrote what is now the national anthem. Walk along the river to the **Butcher's Bridge** (Mesarski Most), a footbridge planned in the 1930s by Plecnik (the fondly remembered local architect) and finally built in 2010, with glass and granite flooring for a contemporary spin. On the other side, you will emerge in the **Central Market** laid out along the river embankment—its colonnades are another Plecnik design—and stretching into Vodnikov Square. Things should be in full swing, a crush of shoppers, musicians, crafts vendors, bakers, and farmers selling heaps of fresh vegetables.

6 *Courtyard Lunch* 2 p.m.

Consult the day's offerings on the blackboard by the door at **Taverna Tatjana** (Gorji Trg 38; 386-1-421-0087; taverna-tatjana.si) or simply let your server guide you through choices that might include brodet, a fish stew with polenta. Tatjana spreads from charming little room to charming little room in an old house in the center of town and has tables in a pretty courtyard.

7 *Art in Creation* 4 p.m.

Ljubljana's enthusiasm for contemporary art has its formal expression at the **Museum of Contemporary Art**, or MSUM (386-1-241-6800; Maistrova 3; mg-lj.si), where the exhibits cover works from the 1960s onward, with a special focus on Eastern Europe's postwar avant-garde. Its opening in 2011, near the newly refurbished **Slovene Ethnographic Museum** and a branch of the **National Museum of Slovenia**, completed a new Museum Quarter. Just to the north is the decidedly less formal **Metelkova City**, a compound of former military barracks, now decorated with graffiti and sculptures, where galleries, nonprofit organizations, and studios for more than 50 artists have set up shop. Its partisans call it an "autonomous culture zone," and it's the place to go for alternative culture by day and youthful partying by night. A converted jail in the complex has a new life as **Celica** (Metelkova 8; 386-1-230-9700; hostelcelica.com), a spare but attractive hostel with rooms in former cells.

8 *Nouveau Goulash* 8 p.m.

A high, mirrored bar dominates the front room at **Julija** (Stari trg 9; 386-1-425-6463; $), creating a cozy dining area. This is a casual, checked-table-cloth kind of place for sampling the local food—dishes like a fresh take on traditional goulash and bread dumplings or house-made Istrian-style pasta with cèpes and asparagus.

9 *Choose Your Scene* 10 p.m.

To join students and 20-somethings at play, return to Metelkova City, where the nightclubs are just opening up. Bands from as far away as New York appear in some of these spots. If your idea of a good time is a little less frenetic, consider that Ljubljana is a terrific city for the arts. The **Slovenian Philharmonic Orchestra** (Congress Square 10; 386-1-241-0800; filharmonija.si), which traces its history back to 1701, plays in the same hall where Gustav

ABOVE Clubbing and art studios coexist in comfort at Metelkova City, with a youthful vibe the common denominator.

OPPOSITE Walking the slack line at Tivoli Park, an idyllic getaway within the city limits.

Mahler was once resident conductor. The **National Opera and Ballet** (Zupanciceva 1; 386-1-241-1766; opera.si) has a busy schedule of performances. There's a national theater and plenty of cinema, and the city is awash in cultural festivals, including the Ljubljana Festival (ljubljanafestival.si/en), which runs all summer.

SUNDAY

10 *Alpine Idyll* 7:30 a.m.

Take an early train (about 45 minutes) to **Lake Bled**, a spectacularly beautiful aquamarine teardrop of a lake that demands to be on your schedule. Tito, the longtime 20th-century ruler of Yugoslavia, spent summers here, and you will soon see why. Surrounded by the Julian Alps and ringed with forested parkland, the lake is overlooked by a romantic castle and cradles tiny Bled Island in its center. The lake is popular with rowers and hosted the World Rowing Championships in 2011, but motorboats are not allowed. From the shore, the Baroque Church of the Assumption, which sits on Bled Island, seems to float in the clean blue water. A gondola-like boat will take you there.

THE BASICS

The city center is compact and good for walking.

Antiq Palace Hotel & Spa
Gosposka 10
386-8-389-6700
antiqpalace.com
$$
Housed in a 16th-century mansion, with guest suites, a patio bar, and a spa.

Grand Hotel Union Executive
Miklosiceva 1
386-1-308-1877
gh-union.si/executive
$$$
Gorgeous Art Nouveau building amid a cluster of similar architectural masterpieces.

Vila Bled Hotel
Cesta svobode 26
4260 Bled, Slovenia
386-4-575-3710
vila-bled.si
$$$
Tito's summer home, converted into a hotel. Woods, gardens, and deck for access to lake swimming.

Piran

Only about 30 miles long, Slovenia's coast is scarcely a crumb between the Adriatic seaside expanses of Italy above and Croatia below. And that's precisely its allure. While foreign tourists flood Trieste and Dubrovnik, only cognoscenti frequent Slovenia's rustic seaside villages. The best of them is Piran, set on a slender finger of land pointing into the sea. During the centuries when the Austrians were occupying the rest of Slovenia, the wily Venetians were running a lucrative salt trade here, using the profits to build one of the loveliest settlements on the Adriatic. Houses with orange tile roofs pack a web of tiny lanes. Town houses radiate sherbet colors — peach, lime, strawberry — and a Venetian-style campanile rises high above the town, looking out at the Adriatic's boundless blue. — BY SETH SHERWOOD

FRIDAY

1 *Lazy Adriatic* 3 p.m.

Slovenia is known as an industrious country, but you wouldn't guess it on a summer afternoon at Piran's cobblestone promenade. Bodies in swimsuits lie splayed along the bulkheads as if they had staggered over from a lotus eaters' binge. Old men play chess on benches, and a sightseeing boat or two coasts lazily offshore. Walk around the edge of the small, arrowhead-shaped peninsula where most of Piran is planted, and listen to the lapping of the waves. It's a short walk farther to **Fiesa Beach**, the rocky stretch of shoreline that serves as a local swimming beach. (Reach it from a footpath next to St. George's Church — the one with the campanile — on Ulica IX Korpusa). There's not much sand at this northeastern corner of the Adriatic, but the water is clear, balmy, and inviting.

2 *Toasts in the Town* 5 p.m.

The heart of town is the vast, marble-paved **Tartini Square** (Tartinijev trg), named for Giuseppe Tartini, a Baroque-era Italian violinist and composer who was born in Piran — that's his statue in the

center of the square. The outdoor cafes here fill with a mix of laid-back tourists in sunglasses, young couples peering into their smartphones, and, as the evening wears on, boisterous groups of Slovenians who devour Balkan sausages and toast one another "Na zdravje!" ("To your health!") with the local pivo (beer). You can't miss the tall tower of St. George's Church, or **Chiesa di San Giorgio** (386-5-673-3440), built 400 years ago as a smaller replica of the campanile of St. Mark's in Venice. Walk over to it, buy a ticket, and climb the stairs to the top for an unforgettable view. If the climb is too forbidding, you can still see far out over the town from outside the church.

3 *Which Pivo?* 7 p.m.

The hardest-working people in Piran may be the ones grilling sardines and Serbian-style pljeskavica sa sirom — ground beef topped with cheese — at **Restaurant Riva** (Presernovo Nabrezje 6; 386-5-673-2180; riva.si; $-$$), one of many terrace restaurants along the seafront. Order some of each and then face the tourist's only pressing decision in Piran: whether to drink Union pivo or Lasko pivo. Forgettable touristy restaurants line the town's seaside walks, but Riva is one of the better ones, serving everything from pizzas to fresh seafood.

4 *Local Culture* 8 p.m.

Back at Tartini Square, summer weekends bring outdoor theater, dance, and chamber music. There are often concerts at Tartini's birthplace on the square, the **Casa Tartini** (Kajuhova 12;

OPPOSITE The Saturday market in Piran's Old Town.

RIGHT The Venetians used profits from the salt trade to build the medieval houses, churches, and streets of Piran.

386-5-673-3090), which under its neo-Classical facade is thought to date to the 14th century. The mansion also contains a small museum dedicated to Tartini, who bedeviled other violinists by writing music so difficult that he was one of the few who could perform it. There's a different scene down by the water at **Cafe Teater** (Dantejeva 31; 386-30-200-000), an Irish-themed pub where a mixed crowd drinks Guinness and Slovenian merlot, drifting on warm nights onto the outdoor terrace.

SATURDAY

5 *Salt Seller* 10 a.m.

Lose yourself in the shady alleyways of the Old Town, wandering through narrow streets and small squares and stopping to peek into medieval churches or browse the occasional shop or gallery; you may even find a street market. In the 15th-century red **Venetian House** on Tartini Square, stop in at **Piranske Soline** (386-5-673-3110; soline.si) and choose from the neat rows of small, plump canvas bags, stamped with a bold red logo and tied with a piece of twine, that are filled with salt harvested just a few miles away. Prized by epicures and deemed a national treasure, the salts are gathered from salt pans in what is now a national nature park, using techniques dating from the 14th century. The shop also sells salted chocolate, bath salts, and accessories like salt keepers and pestles.

6 *Slovenian Glitz* 2 p.m.

So what if nature has to have some help to create a sand beach on the Slovenian coast? It's the

Adriatic, and you might as well take advantage of the long stretch of engineer-assisted sand in neighboring **Portoroz**. (After all, Miami Beach was created by the hand of man, too.) This is Slovenia's official seaside resort, with giant hotels, casinos, yachts, spas, and attendant attractions. The popular **Pizzeria Figarola** (Obala 18, Portoroz; 386-3-131-3415; $) serves lunch on an outdoor terrace.

7 *Salt Park* 5 p.m.

With the worst heat of the day behind you, this is a good time to see where the salt that you bought in Tartini Square originally came from. At **Secovlje Salina Nature Park** (Seca 115, Portoroz; 386-5-123-3000; kpss.si) the salt flats that originally built Piran are preserved as both a gourmet, limited-edition salt works and a nature refuge with walking trails and habitat for shore birds. A museum explains the traditional methods for making the salt (basically a matter of evaporating away sea water to leave the salt behind), and you can see the wide area of grids where the process is going on. In case you missed any salt souvenirs back in town, there's another shop here, too.

8 *It Tastes Like Italy* 8 p.m.

You have noticed by now that although Piran is officially bilingual, using both Slovenian and Italian, the restaurant cuisine emphasizes Italian, based on fresh seafood and pasta. Have another taste of it at **Restaurant Pavel** (Kosovelova 1; 386-5-674-7102; $-$$), a family-style place that serves classical dishes like sea bass and battered grilled squid. This is also a good spot for people-watching over your glass of wine.

SUNDAY

9 *Sink to the Depths* 9 a.m.

Drive east into Slovenia's rugged karst region, a landscape where the underlying limestone rock is eroded by water and pocked with fissures and caves. The village of Postojna is the access point for the 13-mile system known as **Postojna Cave** (386-5-700-0100; postojnska-jama.si). Next to a tunnel bored into

LEFT The blue Adriatic and the coast of Piran. The city is set on a slender finger of land pointing into the sea.

a hillside, board a narrow-gauge train that shoots off into the cave. Forests of stalactites, sharp and menacing, hang above. Stalagmites, some as high as flagpoles, jut from the cave floor. Continuing on foot, you snake downward through claustrophobic channels and cathedral-like chambers as the strange shapes become ever more surreal: piles of gargantuan jellyfish; seas of brain coral; oversize mushroom clusters. Before you emerge, guides will show you caged examples of Proteus anguinus, pale salamander-like creatures that cling to rock in the darkest depths.

10 *Rise to the Heights* Noon

Predjama Castle (Postojnska jama; 386-5-751-6015; postojnska-jama.eu/en/other-sites/predjama-castle), near Postojna, is as dramatically situated as any castle you have ever seen — a white 16th-century fortress literally clinging to the side of a perfectly vertical cliff high in the mountains. Behind it is an older refuge, a cave "castle" where a local knight is said to have taken up residence 700 years ago. Take the tour or just sit outside, listen to the birdsong, and enjoy the view.

ABOVE An art gallery in the Old Town. Although tourism has reached Piran, it retains its feeling of workaday authenticity and its Slovenian personality.

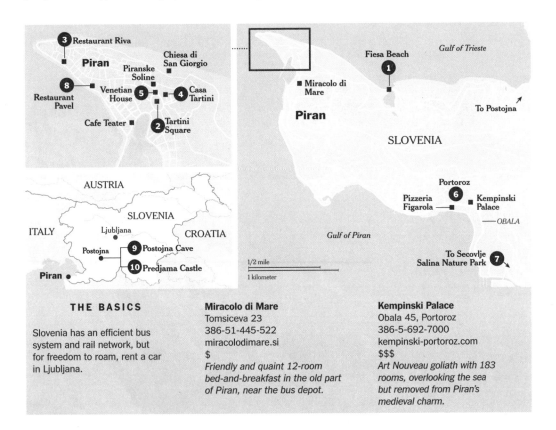

THE BASICS

Slovenia has an efficient bus system and rail network, but for freedom to roam, rent a car in Ljubljana.

Miracolo di Mare
Tomsiceva 23
386-51-445-522
miracolodimare.si
$
Friendly and quaint 12-room bed-and-breakfast in the old part of Piran, near the bus depot.

Kempinski Palace
Obala 45, Portoroz
386-5-692-7000
kempinski-portoroz.com
$$$
Art Nouveau goliath with 183 rooms, overlooking the sea but removed from Piran's medieval charm.

Dubrovnik

After a half-century in relative obscurity, the walled city of Dubrovnik has quickly made up for lost time, transforming the Croatian coast from a ragged backwater into a posh seaside resort. Celebrities and mere mortals alike have started flocking to its quiet stone streets (including one of the largest pedestrian zones in Europe) and ogling its purity of Gothic, Renaissance, and Baroque architecture, before partying on its pristine beaches. Despite the big spenders, there are still many inexpensive pleasures, not the least of which is a soothing dip in the emerald Adriatic, where summer water temperatures average 77 degrees. But more and more, hotels and restaurants are setting their prices in euros, not the local kuna, a sure sign of what's to come. — BY EVAN RAIL

FRIDAY

1 *Climbing the Walls* 5 p.m.

Get a sense of where you are with a walk in warm weather on the old city walls, which offers picture-perfect panoramas over the water, beaches, rooftops, churches, squares, and sometimes a good deal more, as the circular trail also passes within arm's reach of several apartment windows. Early evening is the best, when pale light falls on the city's ochre rooftops and swifts perform aerobatics over the shimmering Adriatic. Be sure to give yourself enough time, preferably about an hour: the ticket office next to the town's **Pile Gate** will take your money as late as 7 p.m., despite a summer closing time of 7:30.

2 *Local Favorites* 7 p.m.

With the Adriatic lapping at the city walls, it's easy to understand why Dubrovnik is awash in fresh seafood. Sample local favorites at **Lokanda Peskarija** (Na Ponti bb; 385-20-324-750; mea-culpa. hr; $$), a moody tavern with outdoor tables on the fishing dock, just a few steps from the Cathedral of the Assumption of the Virgin Mary. Dishes include garlicky grilled shrimp and seafood risotto, squid, and octopus. Be careful not to order too much; many dishes here can easily be shared.

OPPOSITE Dubrovnik enjoys being called the "pearl of the Adriatic," and few visitors are likely to dispute the nickname.

3 *Club House* 10 p.m.

Perhaps because everyone's exhausted from swimming and sunning all day, night life in Dubrovnik can be relatively sedate — and sometimes a bit sandy, with two of the best options located on or near Banje Beach. After sunset, the beach's **Banje Beach** cabana (385-20-412-220; banjebeach.eu) fills with clubgoers, who dance to Europop and disco until 4 a.m. The club was recently renovated with new décor and fluffier cushions — not that anyone's sitting down. For a quieter evening, try **Malvasija Wine Bar** (Dropceva 4; 385-20-794-557), where the owner is a winemaker who preaches the gospel of Croatian wine. Nibble on cheese and olives as he sets up a flight for you.

SATURDAY

4 *Get Your War On* 10 a.m.

The world's only exhibition space completely devoted to war photography, **War Photo Limited** depicts the reality and horror of actual combat through the lenses of accomplished war photographers. Housed in a historic building in Old Town, the space includes a permanent exhibit on the 1990s Balkan conflict, as well as compelling, if harrowing, temporary shows (Antuninska 6; 385-20-322-166; warphotoltd.com).

5 *In Vino Veritas* Noon

Wine aficionados know that Croatia has been proved to be the true home of zinfandel, America's only "indigenous" wine-worthy grape, though it stopped off in Italy as primitivo for a millennium or so before reaching the New World. Many of the country's other wines are equally remarkable, if less renowned than plavac mali, the zinfandel forebear. Find a bottle for an afternoon picnic on the beach at the **Vina Milicic** wine shop (Od Sigurate 2, enter on Stradun; 385-20-321-777), where the knowledgeable, English-speaking staff offer wonderful bottles of plavac mali, full-bodied and showing many of the berry, pepper, and oak notes of a great Sonoma Valley zin. Enjoy a stroll through narrow streets of the Old Town as you wend your way to the beach. Once there, open, pour, and drink.

6 *Beach Blanket Bingo* 2 p.m.

Beaches here are a major attraction for good reason: the shoreline ranges from pebbles to rocks and sand, while the shockingly clear Adriatic can be balmy even very early in the season. The main beach, **Banje**, just east of Old Town, is especially popular with foreigners, while locals tend to dive into the water from the rocks near the old city walls or visit the many smaller, quieter beaches on the **Lapad** peninsula. To get to the public beaches at Sumratin Bay, take the No. 4 bus on a scenic 20-minute ride from the stop just outside the Pile Gate. Whatever beach you choose, don't be afraid to go cheap: comfy lounge chairs can be rented; but there's no charge to lie down on the sand, unfurl your towel, and relax.

7 *Iconic Shopping* 4:30 p.m.

There are souvenir shops of every stripe in Old Town, but for something unusual, pore over the bric-a-brac at **Moje Tezoro** (Izmedu polaca 13; 385-20-323-523; moje-tezoro.hr), one of the city's best antiques bazaars, where elegant Matisse lithographs and vintage gold jewelry adorned with Adriatic coral

ABOVE Beaches range from pebbles to rocks and sand, and the shockingly clear Adriatic is soothingly warm.

OPPOSITE Outdoor dining in the Old Town. Fresh seafood, including squid and octopus, is on many menus.

compete for space with somber Byzantine icons from across Eastern Europe.

8 *Shell Game* 6:30 p.m.

France's fines de claire and belon oysters are far more famous — and the excellent (but uncelebrated) shellfish of the Adriatic probably prefer to keep it that way. For fresh, flavorful should-be-famous oysters from the nearby town of Ston and the traditional (and heartwarming) "Buzara" style mussels — with wine, garlic, and tomatoes — try **Kamenice** (Gunduliceva poljana 8; 385-20-323-682; $), a family-run restaurant with plenty of parasol-shaded seats on the square overlooking the Church of St. Ignatius and the ancient Jesuit College. Don't miss the huge plates of popcorn-size fish and fried calamari or the good grasevina white wine by the carafe.

9 *Stradun Strut* 10 p.m.

Make like a local and get the majority of your entertainment, socializing, and people-watching through the nightly promenade up and down Stradun, the Old Town's marble-lined main strip. Afterward, stop by what everyone still calls the Hemingway Bar, now known as **Nonenina** (Pred dvorum 4; 385-98-825-844; nonenina.com), with strong cocktails, fresh draft beer, and cozy wicker chairs. Around the corner, the outdoor **Jazz Caffe Trubadur** (Buniceva poljana 2) has great live

music and outdoor seating, drawing an international crowd to chairs and tables spread out under the stars.

SUNDAY

10 *Cool Culture* 11 a.m.

Soak up some morning rays, then soak up some culture at the **Museum of Modern Art** (Put Frana Supila 23; 385-20-426-590; ugdubrovnik.hr), which offers a cool, shady spot to unwind just a few steps from Banje beach. The 2,620-piece permanent collection includes impressionistic fin de siècle oil paintings from Vlaho Bukovac and other major Croatian artists, though the building remains a draw of its own: a vast neo-Renaissance villa originally built for one of the city's wealthiest residents.

11 *Make Room* Noon

Get some fresh air with **Adria Adventure Kayaking** (385-20-332-567; adriaadventure.hr), which offers sea kayaking, cycling, and snorkeling trips throughout the region. If that sounds too involved, take a boat out to Lokrum island, located a quick 10-minute ferry ride from the Old Port, with boats leaving every 30 minutes during the day. The lush nature reserve features an arboretum of subtropical plants, Mexican cacti, and the largest collection of unusual eucalypti outside of Oz. If you're inspired to go au naturel, the island is also home to a popular nude beach.

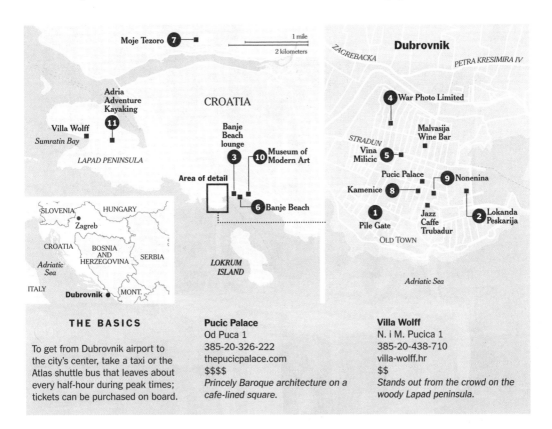

THE BASICS

To get from Dubrovnik airport to the city's center, take a taxi or the Atlas shuttle bus that leaves about every half-hour during peak times; tickets can be purchased on board.

Pucic Palace
Od Puca 1
385-20-326-222
thepucicpalace.com
$$$$
Princely Baroque architecture on a cafe-lined square.

Villa Wolff
N. i M. Pucica 1
385-20-438-710
villa-wolff.hr
$$
Stands out from the crowd on the woody Lapad peninsula.

The Dalmatian Coast

The historic region of Dalmatia, the long, slender Adriatic strip and hundreds of islands that make up much of southern Croatia, is rich in olive groves, vineyards, and some of the most beautiful coastline in the world. Most tourist attention goes to the stretch from Dubrovnik to the party island of Hvar. But the cities of Split and Zadar have their own turquoise sea vistas, rich architectural legacies, and compelling stories. Begin a Dalmatian weekend in Split, where a modern city occupies the 10-acre dream home of the Roman emperor Diocletian. Drive north, catching Adriatic glimpses along the way, and explore Zadar, an ancient town with an intriguing harbor installation that crosses the boundaries of art, music, and hydraulics.
— BY ALEX CREVAR

FRIDAY

1 *Palace Life* 4 p.m.

The foundations of **Split**, now a city of 180,000 people, were built about 1,700 years ago when the Roman Emperor Diocletian completed his city-size palace. But no one here thinks of the palace as some roped-off dig. Since the seventh century, when settlers began moving in, it has been the epicenter of the city. Now the palace is a pedestrian-only tangle of streets, home to some 3,000 residents, bounded by the old palace walls and crowded with cafes, shops, hotels, and apartments. Enter through the southern Bronze Gate, once Diocletian's service entrance, and you will find yourself in the basement, a vaulted netherworld now lined with entrepreneurs selling local arts and crafts.

2 *No More Diocletian* 5 p.m.

Climb the steep stone stairs that lead onto the Peristil, the palace's central piazza, where the emperor received visitors. Surrounded by columns on three sides, it is still a meeting point, but a rendezvous today usually includes multiple cups of kava (espresso) at one of the cafes. Make your first stop the **Cathedral of Saint Domnius** on the east side of the square. It was Diocletian's mausoleum until its seventh-century conversion to a church—a fitting historical comeuppance given Diocletian's notoriety for persecution of Christians. (No one knows where the emperor's body is now.) Inside the church is

a swirl of silver and gold, reliefs, and intricately worked sculptures, including the detailed wood carvings of a 13th-century choir stall. Climb the bell tower for commanding views.

3 *Pasticada by the Sea* 8 p.m.

For inexpensive and authentic Dalmatian food, have dinner at **Buffet Fife** (pronounced FEE-fay; Trumbiceva Obala 11; 385-21-345-223; $), a busy, very informal restaurant in Matejuska, a seaside area of town. Locals occupy many of the tables, and the dishes include lightly fried fish, fish goulash, and pasticada, a Dalmatian version of pot roast marinated with plums and served with gnocchi. Afterward, stroll along the water or head back to the palace to find live music at the cafes and bars.

SATURDAY

4 *Saturday in Town* 9 a.m.

Saturday in Split is part festival and part runway show. Shoppers crowd the palace area, where vendors sell fresh vegetables and square-jawed, tattooed men sell fresh fish, cleaning them for the buyers with a surgeon's precision. At the water's edge, take a stroll on the promenade called the **Riva**, where leggy Mediterranean girls strike instinctive poses beneath palm trees and colorful Croatian flags flap merrily beside crowded cafes.

OPPOSITE Laundry on the sunny coast at Split.

BELOW On the steps of the Sea Organ at Zadar.

5 *Beach Break* 11 a.m.

The crystal clear waters of the Adriatic demand a dip. Split's main beach, **Bacvice**, a five-minute walk east of town, is surrounded by cafes, bars, and restaurants. After you've dried off, have an early lunch of oyster soup and seafood pasta at **Bota Sare** (Obala Hrvatskog Narodnog preporoda 6; 385-21-488-648; bota-sare.hr; $$).

6 *On the Road to Zadar* 1 p.m.

The efficient inland road heading north is the A-1. The old coast road, Highway 8, is much more scenic, passing through small towns of orange-tile-roofed houses, over bridges spanning inlets, and along some stretches of scenic coast, but it would take too much of your day to drive it all the way to Zadar.

Compromise by taking the coast road to the city of Sibenik and then picking up the expressway for the rest of the trip. Stop briefly in the pretty town of Trogir, but don't linger.

7 *Survivor City* 4:30 p.m.

The Romans were smitten with Zadar, built on a 100-acre peninsula framed by Adriatic islands. Today the peninsula is the Old Town, and most of the population of about 75,000 lives on the newer, mainland side. Pedestrians can cross from one to the other on a footbridge or by waving down one of the boatmen who carry on a centuries-old tradition of rowing people across the harbor. Walk along the Old Town's stone-tiled main drag, **Kalelarga**, amid Renaissance, Baroque, and medieval buildings, past shops and cafe-bars where patrons sip coffee, grappa, and wine. Nonchalantly tucked in back of a cafe on **Narodni Trg** (People's Square) are the remains of the Romanesque 11th-century St. Lawrence Church. Zadar is a hardy survivor, having endured oppressive rule by the kingdom of Venice, constant threat of Turkish attack, 65 percent obliteration in World War II, and heavy shelling during the war of 1991-95.

ABOVE The Old Town occupies the peninsula framed by Adriatic islands that was the original Zadar.

LEFT A flower seller at Zadar's market.

8 *Glittering Treasures* 6 p.m.

Encircling the **Roman Forum,** a square designed in the first century B.C., are ancient churches. Inside the 11th-century St. Mary's convent, visit the exhibition called **Gold and Silver of Zadar** (Trg Opatice Cike 1). Hidden by resident Benedictine nuns during wartime (including the war of the 1990s), the collection is awash in Byzantine-era gold and silver and includes paintings, reliquaries, crosses, and embroidery spanning 1,000 years.

9 *Played by the Waves* 7:30 p.m.

Join the crowd at the northwest tip of the peninsula to enjoy the sunset with a 21st-century twist. Nikola Basic, a local architect, designed the **Sea Organ**, a musical instrument that is played not by human beings, but by the sea. Under stone steps, which disappear into the water, 35 pipes continually blow the notes of an unpredictable concert based on the undulations of the water and the ensuing air

pressure—and yes, it sounds like an otherworldly pipe organ. Nearby is another Basic creation, **Greeting to the Sun**, in which a representation of the solar system is futuristically illuminated by photovoltaic cells inlaid into and stretched out along the Riva, the waterfront promenade. Both installations sit below ground level, seamless with their surroundings.

10 *Zadar at Night* 9 p.m.

For a leisurely dinner, there are plenty of choices in the Old Town. **Konoba Skoblar** (Trg Petra Zoranica

ABOVE Byzantine relics in the Gold and Silver of Zadar.

BELOW The emperor Diocletian's palace in Split.

bb; 385-23-213-236; $$$) is a popular trattoria specializing in grilled fish and seafood. Enjoy your choice of entree with a Croatian wine. As the evening wears on, cafes and bars begin to fill with students from the University of Zadar, which was founded in 1396. The **Arsenal** (Trg tri bunara 1; arsenalzadar.com) is a converted 18th-century Venetian military warehouse where restaurants, a cafe, a nightclub, and boutiques intersect. The **Brazil Bar** (Prilaz hrvatske citaonice 1) is a tranquil bar open day and night, with a terrace near the Riva and the Sea Organ.

SUNDAY

11 *Isle View* 9 a.m.

For a view from the water and an excursion into the Adriatic, take the ferry to **Preko**, the port town on Ugljan, a quiet, lightly developed island a few miles out to sea. You'll find a beach, restaurants, walking and biking trails, and a few small towns. It's close enough so that you can take a look around and return by early afternoon.

ABOVE Students at lunch amid the ruins of the first-century Roman Forum in Zadar.

OPPOSITE The Zadar gate, showing the Venetian lion. In the days when Venice was a powerful mercantile republic, Zadar was one of the Adriatic cities under its rule.

THE BASICS

Drive to Split from Dubrovnik on the A-1 expressway or the slower, much more scenic coast road, the Adriatic Highway.

Hotel Vestibul Palace
Iza Vestibula 4, Split
385-21-329-329
vestibulpalace.com
$$$-$$$$
In the heart of Diocletian's palace. Sleek design against 1,700-year-old exposed stone walls.

Hotel Luxe
A. Kralja Zvonimira 6, Split
385-21-314-444
hotelluxesplit.com
$$
Boutique hotel in Split, between palace and beach.

Hotel Bastion
Bedemi zadarskih pobuna 13, Zadar
385-23-494-950
hotel-bastion.hr
$$$
Within the medieval walls of Zadar's Old Town.

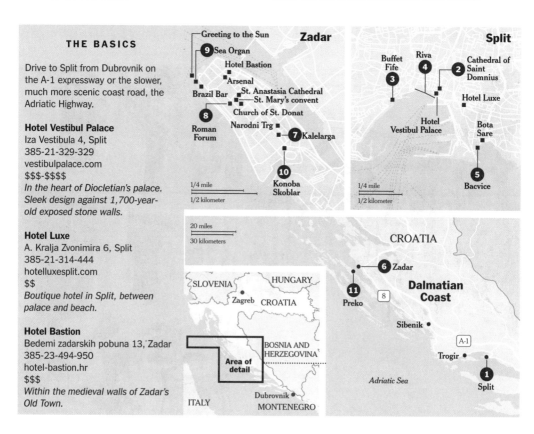

Zagreb

Something is bubbling just below the surface in Zagreb, the Croatian capital of more than a million people, and most visitors sense it instantly. It's a well-worn, East-meets-West passion that equally embraces a consumer's desire to visit a newly opened fragrance shop and the restaurant next door where an entire goat turns slowly on a spit. Zagreb is haggling with thick-fingered green-market farmers and wee-hour clubbing with boisterous Slavs—both beneath the mammoth spires of the city's cathedral. It's a leggy, high-heeled blonde visiting a bloody-aproned fishmonger. And it's mountain hiking and a slick Museum of Contemporary Art. — BY ALEX CREVAR

FRIDAY

1 *History Lesson* 3 p.m.

Get a taste of Zagreb's 11th-century roots on the cobbled streets of the area known collectively as Upper Town, where the city began as two townships: Kaptol, with its largely clerical population, and Gradec, where artisans and merchants settled. United in 1850 after centuries of feuding, the districts still have distinct personalities fueled by their origins. Kaptol still holds the city's visual calling card: the neo-Gothic **Cathedral of the Assumption of the Blessed Virgin Mary** (Kaptol 31; 385-1-481-4727), which originally dates from the 13th century, though it has gone through multiple reconstructions in the centuries since. Beneath tandem 344-foot steeples, a marble-heavy interior shelters an 800-year-old treasury and the tomb of the controversial Cardinal Alojzije Stepinac, who challenged Communist leaders in the 1950s. In Gradec, a 10-minute walk west of the cathedral, the **Zagreb City Museum** (Opaticka 20; 385-1-485-1361; mgz.hr) is a visitor's window into the city's political, architectural, and artistic history. Most fascinating: the room-sized miniature Lower Town street plan.

2 *Museum of Love Lost* 6 p.m.

Walk across Gradec, past St. Mark's Church, with its patterned tile roof depicting the Croatian and Zagreb coats of arms, to one of the town's quirkiest attractions: the **Museum of Broken Relationships** (Cirilometodska 2; 385-1-485-1021; brokenships.com). The brainchild of Olinka Vistica and Drazen Grubisic,

a former couple, answers the question: what to do with all those tokens of love collected during a relationship? The museum started with a temporary exhibition in 2006 with items like 100 discarded roses, airsickness bags, and a head-massaging "tingle." The exhibition toured 21 countries, collecting more items along the way, before getting a permanent home here. Now you can see it all: fur-lined handcuffs, a toaster stolen out of spite, and an ax used to destroy a former lover's furniture, each noting the length of the lost relationship.

3 *Carnivore Heaven* 8 p.m.

Vinodol (Teslina 10; 385-1-481-1427; vinodol-zg. hr; $), like many traditional restaurants here, pays homage to meat. Where this place, a mainstay since Tito-era Yugoslavia, differs is in presentation and technique. In the vaulted-brick dining room and in the ivy-clad courtyard, where a grill chef turns steaks and forearm-length kebabs, the service is impeccable. The lamb and grilled trout are surefire.

SATURDAY

4 *Fashion Forward* 10 a.m.

"Spica" is the Saturday-morning ritual when trendy Purgers (as Zagrebians call themselves)

OPPOSITE Zagreb is on the border of traditional and hip.

BELOW The cafe at Zagreb's Hotel Dubrovnik on Jelacic Square, the central point of town.

pack cafe patios near the central **Jelacic Square**. The result: a fashion smackdown with Yorkie-inhabited handbags, Croatian paparazzi, plenty of sideways glances, and, oh yeah, kava (coffee). Foreigners — that is, anyone wearing a money belt and sneakers — have little chance in the impromptu competition. Best just to grab a chair at an outdoor table, order a large macchiato, and enjoy the free show. Later, head to the **Millennium** sweet shop (Bogoviceva 7; 385-1-481-0850; slasticarnica-millennium.hr) for any of several extremely decadent ice creams or other desserts — and prove your figure is of no concern.

5 *At, and From, the Market* 11 a.m.

At **Dolac**, Zagreb's main fresh market just off Jelacic Square, an army of red umbrellas shades stalls brimming with lavender, nuts, honey, flowers, and cheeses, as well as plenty of local, seasonal fruits and vegetables. "What you call organic," one vendor said, "we call food." After you build up an appetite, head to lunch at **Restaurant Kerempuh** (Kaptol 3; 385-1-481-9000; $), which overlooks a corner of Dolac. There's a clutch of outdoor tables next to a chalkboard advertising daily specials, or you can watch the hubbub through big bay windows. Order a bottle of excellent grasevina, a domestic white wine, and Croatian fare concocted from market goodies, like the grilled sea bass served with Swiss chard and potatoes.

6 *Framed in Green* 2 p.m.

Lower Town, which offers a more everyday vibe than its Upper Town sibling, has a 19th-century Hapsburgesque layout dominated by a "Green Horseshoe" of urban parks. Surrounding those oases, where kaleidoscopic blooms frame spring-to-autumn concerts, is a hodgepodge of grand architecture and cultural venues. The city's main art venue is **Mimara Museum** (Rooseveltov Trg 5; 385-1-482-8100), a neo-Renaissance palace with a 3,000-plus-piece collection that runs the gamut from Persian tapestries to works by Renoir, Rubens, and Degas.

7 *Light and Art* 4 p.m.

To see a more recent Zagreb investment in culture, cross the Sava River to the **Museum of Contemporary Art** (Avenue Dubrovnik 17; 385-1-605-2700; msu.hr/#/en/), designed by the local architect Igor Franic and opened in 2010. Besides hosting rotating exhibits and running a program of film, concerts, and performance art, the museum is an artwork in its own right, with a changing play of color, light, and video images set against a horizontal glass and concrete structure.

8 *Dalmatian Flavor* 8 p.m.

Zagreb is filled with immigrants from around Croatia, so the country's diverse gastronomy is well represented. **Didov san** — Grandfather's Dream — (Mletacka 11; 385-1-485-1154; konoba-didovsan.com; $$) is a konoba, or Dalmatian-style tavern, serving specialties from the Neretva River delta. Though Grandpa has passed on, he'd be proud of his kinfolk, who dish up frog and eel stew and sautéed lamb with veggies on red-checked tablecloths under rough-sawn ceiling beams and black-and-whites of donkeys toting grapes. Of interest to the particularly ravenous is the didova tava, a huge stew.

9 *Musical Mass* Midnight

Zagreb offers late-night live music in a tangle of clubs near the cathedral and around Ribnjak Park. You might hear funk, disco, punk, ska, blues, or even rockabilly. Stop in at the offbeat **Melin Café Jazz Bar** (Kozarska 16; 385-1-488-0298; melin.hr) for live jazz and its signature Blakey's coffee, which honors the drummer Art Blakey with a combination of espresso, amaretto, Kahlúa, cherry liqueur, Jameson, brown sugar, and milk.

SUNDAY

10 *Yugo-Nostalgic* 10 a.m.

The outdoor antique market on **British Square** (Britanski Trg) proves there's value yet in Yugoslavia-era trinkets. Haggle for portraits of Tito, filigree cigarette boxes, medals, coins, and

other old-school items. Treasures in hand, look for a sign that reads "Simply Luxury Coffee" and cross to **Eli's Caffe** (Ilica 63; 385-91-455-5608; eliscaffe.com). The owner, Nik Orosi, a celebrated barista, roasts his own beans and serves, saucers down, the town's tastiest java.

11 *Nature for Nurture* 11 a.m.

Get a little perspective at the sprawling **Medvednica Nature Park** (pp-medvednica.hr; take the No. 14 tram or the 8 to the 15), 56,000 acres of mountain trails towering above Zagreb, filled with deer and foxes, chestnuts and oaks. A medium-effort hike leads to Puntijarka hut (385-1-458-0384), which houses an inexpensive restaurant perched

at the 3,200-foot mark. Reward yourself with rib-sticking bean-and-sausage stew and a half-liter of domestic beer.

OPPOSITE Spires and rooftops of Zagreb. The city's 11th-century roots are most obvious amid the cobbled streets and towering steeples of the Upper Town.

ABOVE The tomb of Cardinal Alojzije Stepinac in the Cathedral of the Assumption of the Blessed Virgin Mary.

THE BASICS

Nearly everything you'll do is a 20-minute walk from Jelacic Square. To go farther, take the trams.

Esplanade Zagreb Hotel
Mihanoviceva ulica 1
385-1-456-6666
esplanade.hr
$$
A grand swirl of marble and crystal that has hosted Queen Elizabeth II and Louis Armstrong. Opened in 1925 for passengers on the Orient Express.

Palace Hotel
Strossmayerov trg 10
385-1-489-9600
palace.hr
$
The city's oldest hotel. Its plush cafe is a vantage point for watching fashionable Croats in Strossmayer Square.

Hotel Dubrovnik
Ljudevita Gaja 1
385-1-486-3555
hotel-dubrovnik.hr
$
A straightforward affair with sleek contemporary design and an excellent location.

Zagreb

1/4 mile
1/2 kilometer

Zagreb City Museum
GRADEC
OPATICKA
KOZARSKA
KAPTOL
Didov san 8
Melin Café Jazz Bar 9
KAPTOL
St. Mark's Church
RIBNJAK PARK
UPPER TOWN
Museum of Broken Relationships 2
Restaurant Kerempuh
British Square 10
Dolac 5
Cathedral of the Assumption of the Blessed Virgin Mary 1
ILICA
Jelacic Square 4
BRITANSKI TRG
Eli's Caffe
Millennium
Hotel Dubrovnik
TESLINA
3
ROOSEVELTOV TRG
Vinodol
Palace Hotel
Mimara Museum 6
LOWER TOWN
STROSSMAYEROV TRG
TRG BRACE MAZURANIC
MIHANOVICEVA
Esplanade Zagreb Hotel

4 miles
5 kilometers

Medvednica Nature Park 11

CROATIA

Zagreb

Sava River

Area of detail

Museum of Contemporary Art 7

SLOV.
HUN.
Zagreb
CROATIA
BOS. AND HERZEG.
Sarajevo
Adriatic Sea
ITALY

Sarajevo

At midday in Sarajevo, muezzins call from minarets as church bells echo through the Dinaric Alps. Street cars rumble past hookah smokers and cafegoers. Chic women click-clack down cobbled alleyways. The charisma of this city, Bosnia-Herzegovina's capital, is intoxicating, but the hustle and bustle belie a tragic past. In 1992, Sarajevo changed from a beacon of diversity, with Yugoslav Muslims, Christians, and Jews worshiping within feet of one other, to the site of a siege that lasted nearly four years and claimed more than 11,000 lives. But much has changed since then. The creative spirit that Sarajevans fought to preserve is very much in evidence these days. Neighborhoods, cradled in this valley and ringing the foothills, are fertile entrepreneurial grounds and a testament to the epochs that came before. Cafes, theaters, boutiques, and restaurants have sprouted among buildings in myriad styles, including Ottoman, Vienna Secessionist, Communist, and modern. And locals and visitors alike are rediscovering the surrounding mountains and the slopes that hosted the 1984 Winter Olympic Games. — BY ALEX CREVAR

FRIDAY

1 *Secessionist Seduction* 6 p.m.

Sarajevo's circuitous history lesson begins with dinner at **4 Sobe Gospode Safije** (Cekalusa 61; 387-62-622-822; 4sgs.net; $$).The name means the Four Rooms of Mrs. Safija, and the restaurant occupies a house built in 1910, during the city's 40-year Hapsburg Empire epoch, by an Austrian count for a local woman named Safija. Their cross-cultural love was taboo, but this Bosnian-European restaurant, restored to early-20th-century splendor and filled with period pieces, is routinely shortlisted among the city's best. Pair the grilled veal with rosemary and anchovy sauce, or the sea bass and ginger, with a bottle of local red blatina or white zilavka.

2 *Theater of the Soul* 8 p.m.

In the same neighborhood, below the former Olympic stadium, get in before the lights dim at **Sarajevski Ratni Teatar** (Gabelina 16; 387-33-664-070; sartr.ba) — the Sarajevo War Theater, or Sartr. Established a month after the siege began, Sartr put on hundreds of shows during the war and became a symbol of defiance. "Being creative was the only way to survive during the war," said Nihad Kresevljakovic, the theater's director. "In that way, Sarajevans know that culture and art are really basic human needs, like food and water." Sartr, a black-box repertory theater, still channels those exposed-nerve instincts into empathetic works — musicals, dance, documentary theater, and dramas — on the city's most creatively free stage. One past production was *The Secret of Raspberry Jam*, which provides an intimate look at Sarajevo.

3 *Fish Kitsch* 10 p.m.

For a nightcap, head to **Caffe Zlatna Ribica** (Kaptol 5; 387-33-836-348). Cater-corner to the Eternal Flame honoring World War II victims, this cafe and bar is Sarajevo's kitschiest drinking hole. A wall of mirrors reflects a softly lighted tangle of refitted candelabra, decanters, overstuffed armchairs, musical instruments, Christmas lights, tiny TVs flickering black-and-white images, and goldfish swimming in a bowl. In the background, jazz plays. During winter, try the secret-recipe mulled red wine; in summer, order the house-made sangria with oranges and cherries.

OPPOSITE The 16th-century Gazi Husref-bey Mosque in downtown Sarajevo. A traditional haven of diversity, the city is reclaiming its spirit after recovering from the devastating war of the 1990s.

BELOW A burek, pastry dough filled with beef, at Buregdzinica Bosna. Have a slice with a glass of yogurt.

4 *Coffee Talk* 9:30 a.m.

For Sarajevans, drinking coffee is a ritual for relaxing, not quickening the pulse. Inside the rustic, wood-planked **Cajdzinica Dzirlo** (Kovaci 16; 387-61-159-965; $), on Bascarsija's eastern edge, you can unwind and imbibe thick, frothy, slow-brewed Bosnian coffee served in copper pots. For a more modern take on this intrinsic custom, visit **Rahatlook** (Ferhadija 41; 387-33-921-461), on Bascarsija's west end, and enjoy your kafa (coffee) with pastries like the walnut-strewn, sconelike orasnica.

5 *Tunnel of Love* 11 a.m.

The Times of Misfortune tour run by **Sarajevo Insider** (Zelenih Beretki 30; 387-33-534-353; sarajevoinsider.com) helps decode the complex layers of a city where new national flags have been hoisted seven times in the last 150 years. The guides do a masterly job explaining the tempestuous transitions, focusing on the war from 1992 to 1995. You'll take in panoramas of the valley from the ancient White Fortress before returning to town to the site of Archduke Franz Ferdinand's assassination in 1914, and the cemetery-surrounded Olympic stadium. The highlight is the **Tunnel Museum** (Tuneli 1; 387-33-684-032), at the start of a 2,600-foot passageway dug by citizens in 1993. The tunnel became the besieged city's sole supply line from the outside world.

6 *Dining in the 'Hood* 1 p.m.

Take a taxi into the foothills through Sarajevo's oldest, Ottoman-era mahalas (neighborhoods) for lunch at **Restaurant Kibe** (Vrbanjusa 164; 387-33-441-936; restaurantkibe.com; $). When you get to the house, ring the doorbell (reservations are a must) and climb the stairs to a fireplace-anchored dining room surrounded by panoramic views of town. You'll find some of the city's best traditional dishes here. For a starter, try the sour-cream-smothered klepe: meat-filled Bosnian ravioli. To guarantee that you can

order the spit-roasted lamb, a specialty, place your order when you make a reservation.

7 *Vintage Foraging* 3 p.m.

Along Sarajevo's main shopping promenade —which changes names from Saraci in the Ottoman quarter to Ferhadija in the Secessionist-era zone— artisans sculpt, stitch, and solder in hidden-away shops. Visit **Kazandzijska Radnja** (Kovaci 28; 387-61-144-771) for hammer-shaped copper coffee sets. Near the 16th-century multi-domed Gazi Husref-bey Mosque, **Becart** (Gazi Husref-begova 30; 387-33-534-240; becart.ba) specializes in site-crafted silver jewelry, including filigree bracelets. On Ferhadija, **Edo** (Ferhadija 16; 387-33-223-268; edocipele.ba) will take your footprint and create leather shoes and boots uniquely for you.

8 *Eat Your Veggies* 7 p.m.

In a town deficient in vegetarian options, **Karuzo Restaurant** (Dzenetica Cikma bb; 387-33-444-647; karuzorestaurant.com; $) is a blessing. It's behind the green market, and rubbing elbows with neighbors is part of the charm. The baked pumpkin gratin with chickpeas and goat cheese is rich, lasagna-like, and perfect with a glass of white wine from the international list. For nonvegetarians, there are seafood choices and even sushi.

9 *Rakija Rampage* 10 p.m.

Generations of Bosnians have grown up drinking family-made moonshine called rakija. In recent years, this fruit- or herb-flavored grappalike elixir has become the hipster spirit of choice. At the multi-level **Barhana Restaurant and Grapperia** (Dzulagina Cikma 8; 387-33-447-727; barhana.ba), you'll find 25 varieties, along with a stone oven for late-night pizzas and a hidden summer garden. Choices include plum, cherry, and honey, but try the travarica, an herbal tincture good for digestion and mood.

10 *Bosnian Brunch* 10:30 a.m.

No one is ambivalent about Sarajevo's rich street food. For many, cevapcici—beef sausages served with flatbread, onions, and a creamy cheese called

kajmak — reigns supreme; try it at **Cevabdzinica Zeljo 2** (Kundurdziluk 19; 387-33-447-000; $). A close second is burek: pastry dough filled with beef — potato, cheese, and spinach versions are called pita. At **Buregdzinica Bosna** (Bravadziluk 11; 387-33-538-426; $), pair these savory pie portions with a glass of yogurt. Complete your tour at **Cafe Slasticarna Ramis** (Saraci 1; 387-33-535-947; $), a 100-year-old sweet shop with traditional tufahija, poached apple filled with whipped cream and walnuts.

11 *Above It All* Noon
Tucked into a river-cut valley surrounded by peaks, Sarajevo has a natural beauty often forgotten amid artificial contrivances. **Green Visions** (Trg

Barcelone 3; 387-33-717-290; greenvisions.ba) runs ecotours and will pick you up anywhere in town. Tighten your boot laces and take a three- to four-hour hike through spruce forests before reaching the summit of Trebevic, a 5,338-foot mountain.

OPPOSITE Pondering pastries at Cafe Slasticarna Ramis.

ABOVE Restaurant Kibe serves some of Sarajevo's best-prepared versions of traditional dishes.

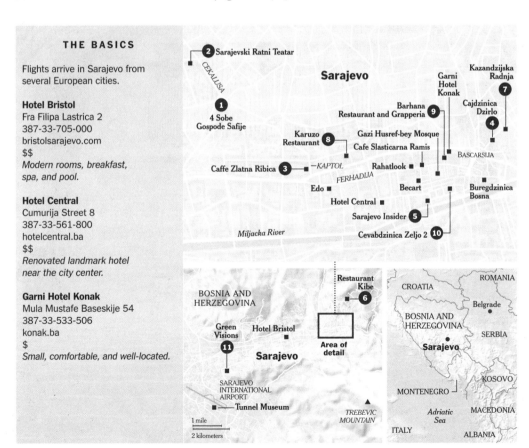

THE BASICS

Flights arrive in Sarajevo from several European cities.

Hotel Bristol
Fra Filipa Lastrica 2
387-33-705-000
bristolsarajevo.com
$$
Modern rooms, breakfast, spa, and pool.

Hotel Central
Cumurija Street 8
387-33-561-800
hotelcentral.ba
$$
Renovated landmark hotel near the city center.

Garni Hotel Konak
Mula Mustafe Baseskije 54
387-33-533-506
konak.ba
$
Small, comfortable, and well-located.

Bucharest

Bucharest, Romania's capital city, offers much of the same culture as Prague or Budapest for far less expense and without the crowds. Dinner at a revered restaurant costs a fraction of what it would in most European capitals, and seats at the opera are shockingly affordable. Not that opera is the only option. The music scene starts with the great 20th-century composer George Enescu, but quickly branches out to house D.J.'s and rollicking Gypsy bands. The cityscape is vibrant, with Byzantine churches next to palatial Beaux-Arts town houses and minimalist International-style blocks. Especially in Lipscani, the traditional heart of town, many of the old buildings now hold cafes, restaurants, boutiques, and bars. Romania is far along in its recovery from Communism and the destructive reign of the dictator Nicolae Ceausescu. In Bucharest, the energy of revitalization is in the air. — BY EVAN RAIL

FRIDAY

1 *Where Old Is New* 2 p.m.

Crossing the street is an extreme sport in Bucharest — drivers treat pedestrians like pylons on a slalom. Still, getting around by foot is the fastest way in **Lipscani**, the once-gritty old area around Lipscani Street that is now home to shiny new enterprises and serves at night as party central. Several architectural monuments house banks; step inside the lobbies you find open. The courtyard of the **Hanul cu Tei**, or Linden Tree Inn (Lipscani 63-65; berariahanulcutei. ro/en), houses hip art galleries and shops. Check out antiques stores for bargain finds, and look for stalls selling the Romanian pretzels called covrigi. Of course, it wouldn't be Romania without Dracula, and Lipscani is also home to **Curtea Veche**, or Old Court (Franceza 21-23; 40-21-314-0375; romaniatourism. com/bucharest.html), the ruins of a fortress built in 1459 by the man otherwise known as Vlad the Impaler. His statue, circa 2003, is out front.

2 *Find Brancusi* 4 p.m.

Detour to the **National Art Museum of Romania** (Victoriei 49-53; 40-21-313-3030; mnar.arts.ro). The building is the Royal Palace, which dates to the 19th

century and has a checkered history featuring royal excess, fires, and World War II bombs. The impressive permanent collection includes works by El Greco, Rembrandt, Rubens, and Sisley as well as by local heroes like Gheorghe Patrascu. Look for *The Prayer*, an early bronze work by Constantin Brancusi, who was Romanian. After you leave the museum, head back to Lipscani and stop for a glass of wine at **Bruno** (Strada Covaci 3; 40-21-317-1741; brunowine.ro), where patrons sip on a peaceful terrace.

3 *Flaunt It* 7 p.m.

A key to grasping contemporary Romanian culture is fite (FEET-sah), which roughly translates as "flaunting it." One place to do that is **Casa di David** in the Herastrau Park (Parc Herastrau, Soseaua Nordului, 7-9; 40-21-232-4715; casadidavid.ro; $$$), where some of the diners look as if they had just come from St.-Tropez. Large windows look out over a lake. Dishes that have appeared on the menu include beef fillet with morels and truffles; turbot with steamed spinach, red peppers, curry and rice; and a chocolate tart with mango sorbet.

4 *All That Glitters* 8 p.m.

Classical music reigns supreme in Bucharest, and the premier venue is still the **Romanian Athenaeum** (Benjamin Franklin 1-3; 40-21-315-2567; fge.org.ro), a magnificent red and gold neo-Classical concert hall, built in 1888, that is home to the George Enescu Philharmonic. A few blocks away, the **Bucharest National Opera** (Mihail Kogalniceanu 70-72; 40-21-314-6980; operanb.ro) has a reputation for a strong ensemble cast and performs in an elegant opera house. It's a later and different scene at **Control Club** (Constantin Mille 4; 40-73-392-7861; control-club.ro), which draws a very diverse crowd. D.J.'s keep the electronic music going as late as 4 a.m.

SATURDAY

5 *Parisian Stroll* 9 a.m.

Bucharest used to be called Micul Paris (Little Paris) because of its affection for everything French — food, fashion, and architecture. Its long boulevards like Victoriei and Dacia offer photo-worthy sights on every corner. Walk north of the city center along

OPPOSITE The Romanian Athenaeum concert hall.

tranquil, tree-lined Soseaua Kiseleff, a grand avenue reminiscent of Paris and home to the city's mansion district. You will soon pass under the **Arcul de Triumf**, an 85-foot version of the Arc de Triomphe. It was built in 1936, successor to a couple of temporary arches that had stood in the same place. If you turned to the right you would come to Charles de Gaulle Square, but keep going straight, with parkland on your right.

6 *Rustic Romania* 10 a.m.

For a glimpse of the country's rustic past, stop at the **Village Museum** (Soseaua Kiseleff 28-30; 40-21-317-9110; muzeul-satului.ro). One of the world's older museums of its kind, it was established in 1936 by royal decree to preserve a record of Romania's village life. Dozens of old houses, churches, barns, windmills, and other buildings, dating back to 1775, were brought here from all over Romania and transplanted in a wooded park along the shore of Lake Herastrau. Together, they offer insight not only into rural life in Romania—a country where most of the population still lives in the countryside—but into its history and traditions.

7 *Lunch at the Bank* 12:30 p.m.

Back in Lipscani, have lunch amid the graceful arches, pillars, and chandeliers of **Grand Cafe Van Gogh** (Strada Smardan 9; 40-31-107-6371; vangogh.ro; $), in a 1920s bank building. Sandwiches, salads, and quesadillas are on the menu along with a few meat-and-potatoes plates. The coffee is good, but you can also opt for various forms of alcohol.

8 *Megalomania* 2 p.m.

It's impossible to overstate the pomposity of the **Palace of Parliament** (Strada Izvor 2-4; 40-21-311-3611; www.cdep.ro), which is also still known by its Ceausescu-era name, Casa Poporului (or House of the People). Guides claim that it is the second-largest administrative building in the world, after the Pentagon. It is certainly among the world's weightiest, with 1 million cubic meters of marble, 900,000 cubic meters of wood, and a crystal chandelier clocking in at five tons. It was all part of Ceausescu's self-glorifying plans for Bucharest: he tore down old neighborhoods, churches, and synagogues to build this structure and a grand boulevard leading to it. A tour is essential (they're available in several languages), if only to grasp the building's megalomaniac scale: Ceausescu wanted one of the reception halls to have an open roof so helicopters could land inside. On the plus side, tucked into a corner of the building is the **National Museum of Contemporary Art** (www.mnac.ro).

9 *Gothic Beer* 8 p.m.

Caru' cu Bere (Strada Stavropoleos 5; 40-21-313-7560; carucubere.ro; $), a local favorite, is a Belle Époque beer hall with stained-glass windows, servers in peasant costumes, and entertainment that

may include ballroom dancers who offer diners a dance. Try a plate of pork shank and stewed cabbage with house-crafted beer. Desserts include strudel, profiterole, and chocolate torte. Plan to stay a while and soak up the conviviality. It's open until 2 a.m.

SUNDAY

10 *Tunics to Go* 11 a.m.

The **Museum of the Romanian Peasant** (Soseaua Kiseleff 3; 40-21-317-9660; muzeultaranuluiroman.ro) displays hand-crafted items, farm implements, and other objects answering the question of what used to be inside all of those rustic buildings you saw yesterday at the Village Museum. It also has a gift

shop filled with handicrafts. The embroidered cotton tunics for women could belong in a modern spring collection, and urban bachelors will dig the traditional wool-lined vests. Other great souvenirs include intricate woven rugs and elaborately painted eggshells.

OPPOSITE The Arcul de Triumf pays homage to Paris.

ABOVE Bucharest's city museum in the Sutu Palace.

THE BASICS

From the airport, take a taxi or express bus. In town, walk and take the metro or hire taxis from companies recommended as reliable and trustworthy.

Athénée Palace Hilton
Episcopiei 1-3
40-21-303-3777
hiltonbucharest.com
$$
Built in 1914, renovated but still preserving elements like an opulent ballroom.

Novotel Bucharest City Center
Victoriei 37b
40-21-308-8500
novotel.com
$$
Plush rooms and light and airy décor in a modern tower.

Hotel Unique Bucharest
Caderea Bastiliei 35
40-21-319-4591
hotelunique.ro
$
Small boutique hotel with sleek modern styling.

UKRAINE
HUNGARY   MOLDOVA
ROMANIA
SERBIA   **Bucharest**
BULGARIA   Black Sea

1/2 mile
1 kilometer

HERASTRAU PARK
Lake Herastrau
3 Casa di David
Colentina
6 Village Museum
5 Arcul de Triumf
SOSEAUA KISELEFF

Bucharest

Museum of the Romanian Peasant
BLVD. ION MIHALACHE — **10**   BLVD. LANCU DE HUNEDOARA   SOSEAUA STEFAN CEL MARE

BLVD. LASCAR CATARGIU   Hotel Unique Bucharest

Athénée Palace Hilton   **4** Romanian Athenaeum
National Art Museum of Romania **2**   BENJAMIN FRANKLIN
Novotel Bucharest City Center
Control Club VICTORIEI
Bucharest National Opera
Area of detail   **1** Lipscani

Lipscani
SMARDAN ST.   **7** Grand Cafe Van Gogh
Hanul cu Tei
LIPSCANI ST.
9   Bruno
Caru' cu Bere   COVACI ST.
FRANCEZA ST.
Curtea Veche
Dambovita

8 Palace of Parliament
National Museum of Contemporary Art
CALEA 13 SEPTEMBRIE

Sofia

The depth of the history is palpable in Sofia, Bulgaria's compact, bustling capital city of 1.3 million people. There has been a settlement here near the Iskar River for at least 4,000 years, and empire after empire — Roman, Ottoman, Czarist, Soviet — has left its mark. The resulting blend of architecture seems somehow the perfect backdrop for the remarkable sense of self-assurance and cosmopolitan elegance the city displays today. Spring, summer, and fall, stylish Bulgarians fill the leafy boulevards and parks, and since Bulgaria joined the European Union in 2007, Sofia has become a delightful gateway to an undeservedly little-known country. — BY GREGORY DICUM

FRIDAY

1 *Shop the Centuries* 2 p.m.

In one spot you can actually pick up and handle Sofia history. In front of the golden domes of the huge **Alexander Nevsky Cathedral** (1 Aleksandr Nevsky), antiques dealers line the plaza with the bric-a-brac of millenniums (although provenance can be hard to establish). Byzantine coins lie in piles next to Lenin busts; Howdy Doody toys rest alongside Roman lamps; German martial instruments perch atop old Turkish encyclopedias. After making your purchases, go into the cathedral, a 19th-century monument to the ouster of the Ottoman Empire, to see its collection of glowingly colored Orthodox icon paintings, some a thousand years old. Out front is a much older church, the sixth-century **St. Sofia**, with a Romanesque facade of layered brick.

2 *Banitsa Break* 3:30 p.m.

Time for a snack? Seek out a traditional Bulgarian bakery — they are everywhere in Sofia — for a banitsa: phyllo pie stuffed with eggs and sirene (the cheese known to Greeks as feta, but don't call it that in Bulgaria) and occasionally meat or vegetables. Hot out of the oven, banitsa is a great way to refuel. Wash it down with boza, a millet-based fermented drink whose sweet tartness is an ideal counterpoint to the salty, melted cheese.

3 *A City's Long Story* 4 p.m.

The Romans knew this part of Europe as Thrace, and after they'd finished conquering it, dignitaries

liked to visit Serdica, as Sofia was then known. The city's oldest building, the squat, domed brick **Rotunda of St. George** church (Rotonda Sveti Georgi; Saborna Street), dates from the fourth century, when one visitor was Constantine, the first Christian emperor. Find it — an almost exotically ancient structure looking both Roman and Byzantine — behind the Sofia Hotel Balkan (5 Sveta Nedelya Square; sofiabalkan.com), in a small archaeological park that also includes more recognizably Roman ruins. Frescoes inside St. George were plastered over by the Ottoman Turks, who made the building a mosque, and not uncovered until the 20th century. For more treasures of antiquity, tour the adjacent **Museum of Archaeology** (2 Saborna Street; 359-2-988-2406; naim.bg).

4 *Sofia Specials* 8 p.m.

Bulgarian cuisine — a hearty blend of European and central Asian — underscores the country's diversity: sirene and yogurt share the table with grilled meats and, especially in summertime, salads of juicy

OPPOSITE An umbrella makes a style statement in a city park. Sofia is a city of parks, enjoyed from spring to fall.

BELOW A golden cup in the National History Museum dates from the pre-Roman days when Bulgaria was known as Thrace.

tomatoes, cucumbers, and olives. These salads are traditionally eaten at the start of a meal, accompanied by chilled rakia, the local white brandy, a distinctive firewater similar to grappa. One good restaurant for traditional Bulgarian food is **Manastirska Magernitsa** (67 Khan Asparuh Street; 359-2-980-3883; magernitsa.com; $), where the menu includes recipes collected from Bulgarian monasteries and villages.

5 *Cocktail Challenge* 9:30 p.m.

If the rakia hasn't sapped you of your motor skills, you can continue the evening at **Oscar Club** (1 Dobrudzha Street; 359-2-981-1707; theoscarclub.com) where D.J.'s create a pleasant vibe and the bartenders can make almost any cocktail, including

some that involve bacon. It gets crowded, so if being able to sit is important, you should call head for a reservation.

SATURDAY

6 *Sacred Diversity* 9:30 a.m.

Religious tolerance is especially important in a country with such a multicultural history, and Bulgaria, which refused to turn over its Jews to the Nazis in World War II, has a good recent record. A short walk from the Nevsky Cathedral, which is Bulgarian Orthodox, is the Moorish-inflected **Sofia Synagogue** (16 Ekzarh Iosif), still a landmark although postwar emigration to Israel greatly reduced the Jewish population. To see its open space, complete with massive chandelier, in action, attend Shabbat Shacharit at 9:45. Around the corner is the **Banya Bashi Mosque** (Maria Louiza Boulevard at Triyaditsa Street), built over thermal springs by the Ottomans in the 16th

ABOVE Catching up on the Bulgarian news.

LEFT The Museum of Socialist Art honors Bulgaria's Soviet-era artists while remaining skeptical about their message.

OPPOSITE Watch the locals shopping to fill their dinner tables at the market on Graf Ignatiev, a boulevard of cobblestones, trees, and trolley cars.

century. Near all of this is a surprisingly elegant complex of godless Communist-era buildings.

7 *Market Picnic* Noon

Get a taste of the local bounty at the farmers' market extending along **Graf Ignatiev**, a verdant boulevard of cobblestones and trolley cars, where vendors' tables groan with piles of figs, melons, plums, peaches, and grapes. Put together a picnic and head to any of the nearby parks. You'll find them filled with Bulgarians strolling near the fountains, exploring the sculptures (it seems that every park features a bronze sculpture of a friendly deer, its back worn golden by generations of children), or lingering at the plentiful cafes. The parks are also great places to hear Bulgarian music—like the local food, a lively cross of East and West.

8 *Some Liked It 'Totalitarian'* 3 p.m.

The giant steel-and-glass star that once topped Sofia's Communist Party headquarters building. A towering statue of Lenin and brooding images of Stalin. Huge oil paintings of workers eagerly earning collectivist medals. All are among the 150 or so works at the **Museum of Socialist Art** (7 Lachezar Stanchev Street in the Izgrev district, near the Dimitrov subway stop; nationalartgallerybg.org). The museum is Bulgaria's solution to its glut of leftover art from the Communist era, and its backers say it is intended to

recognize artistic value even though the message has become unpopular. The subject is so sensitive that before the museum opened late in 2011, its name was toned down from the one originally intended: the Museum of Totalitarian Art. To Western eyes, it may look less like an art gallery than a cabinet of 20th-century curiosities.

9 *Traditional Sounds* 7 p.m.

Catch a show at the **National Palace of Culture** (359-2-916-6300; ndk.bg). A Communist-era entertainment complex, it often features concerts of rollicking Bulgarian folkloric music, including at times the haunting Mystère des Voix Bulgares (themysteryofthebulgarianvoices.com), a women's choir that has attained an international following. Performances are usually at 7 or 8 p.m.

10 *Kebapche With Bourgas* 9 p.m.

Throughout the summer, all across the country, families gather at tables under grape arbors or fruit-laden trees for their evening meals. You can enjoy warm nights under shady lindens at any of the innumerable restaurants with outdoor seating. At **Victoria** (7 Tzar Osvoboditel Boulevard, near the Alexander Nevsky Cathedral; 359-2-986-3200; victoria.bg; $), the food is a stylish blend of traditional and modern. Try the shepherd's salad and the kebapche—sausage-shaped spiced meatballs. This is also a perfect

place to sample the new generation of excellent—and amazingly affordable—wines that Bulgaria's reawakening industry is beginning to turn out. An entree like kebapche and kultzanitza (a lamb and veal dish) pairs well with a glass from the Bourgas region along the Black Sea coast.

SUNDAY

11 *Head for the Hills* 10 a.m.

Sofia sits in a valley ringed with mountains, so spend Sunday the way the locals do: hiking the trails of nearby Mount Vitosha in **Vitosha National Park**

(359-2-988-5841; bulgariatravel.org/en/object/237/Vitosha). Lakes, waterfalls, woods, and lovely vistas of Sofia in the valley below are all accessible by a network of relatively easy trails. The park also contains an arboretum and a museum dedicated to bears. The simplest way to get there is by taxi from the center of Sofia to the gondolas in Simeonovo or to the Aleko chalet. From there, walk down to Boyana, passing a famous waterfall, or take the popular trail to Zlatnite Mostove (the Golden Bridges), a "river" of boulders wending down the wooded flanks of the mountain.

ABOVE Alexander Nevsky Cathedral is a landmark not only for religion, but also for informal commerce. Dealers hawk antiques and bric-a-brac in its shadow.

OPPOSITE Vitosha National Park, with its abundant natural wonders, is reachable by taxi from Sofia.

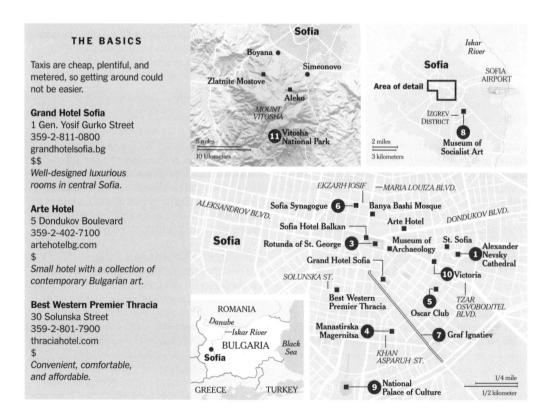

THE BASICS

Taxis are cheap, plentiful, and metered, so getting around could not be easier.

Grand Hotel Sofia
1 Gen. Yosif Gurko Street
359-2-811-0800
grandhotelsofia.bg
$$
Well-designed luxurious rooms in central Sofia.

Arte Hotel
5 Dondukov Boulevard
359-2-402-7100
artehotelbg.com
$
Small hotel with a collection of contemporary Bulgarian art.

Best Western Premier Thracia
30 Solunska Street
359-2-801-7900
thraciahotel.com
$
Convenient, comfortable, and affordable.

Athens

The Acropolis in Athens, with its glorious temples and sculpture, has been a must-see tourist destination since the ancient Romans were taking package tours— it was ancient even to them. The crown jewel is still the Parthenon, but now the new Acropolis Museum, built to complement the ancient citadel while giving a safe home to its threatened artifacts, is equally unmissable. After you have seen these essentials, the modern city has more to offer. Aside from more cultural heritage sites, there are eclectic restaurants, shopping streets, and youthful neighborhoods with galleries, clubs, and cafes. — BY JOANNA KAKISSIS

FRIDAY

1 *Tour de Force* 5 p.m.

Designed by the New York-based Swiss architect Bernard Tschumi, the $200 million **Acropolis Museum** (15 Dionysiou Areopagitou Street; 30-210-900-0900; theacropolismuseum.gr) opened to much acclaim in 2009, and the superlatives haven't stopped. The building itself is stunning, and through a glass floor, you can see an archaeological site underneath. The Parthenon Gallery, on the top floor, is the center-piece. Portions of the Parthenon frieze, carved by the ancient sculptor Phidias, are displayed on a rectangular cement core with the same dimensions as their original location. Much of the frieze was spirited away to England in the 19th century and is now at the British Museum. Spaces are left in hope that the British will give it back.

2 *Haute Home Cooking* 9 p.m.

Foodies often ignore the Peloponnese, despite its excellent olive oil, because the region is known for its stick-to-your-ribs home cooking. (Think generous cheese pies and simmered casseroles made from the thick noodles called chylopittes.) **ManiMani** (10 Falirou Street, Koukaki; 30-210-921-8180; manimani. com.gr; $$), in a restored Neoclassical house, offers inspired takes on the comfort food of the southern Peloponnese. Try tsouhtes, a carbonara from the

Mani region in the southern Peloponnese, or the pork tenderloin with creamy manouri cheese in a honey-thyme sauce.

3 *The Other Hill* 11 p.m.

Take the funicular from the corner of Aristippou and Ploutarchou in the Kolonaki neighborhood up to **Lycabettus Hill**. Greek myth has it that an enraged Athena created this "other hill" when she dropped an uprooted mountain that she had intended to use for construction of the Acropolis. The hill is now a sunset hangout for tourists photographing the whitewashed 19th-century **Chapel of St. George** and the urban panorama below. But late night is what really electri-fies that sweeping view. Darkness hides the city's modern architectural chaos, and the Parthenon glows like a crown jewel. Peaceful and secluded, this spot is a good after-midnight alternative to the smoky bars, raunchy clubs, and howling bouzouki singers in the packed and motley world below. Leave before the funicular stops running at 2:30 a.m. Walking back down is not a good idea at night.

SATURDAY

4 *Acropolis Now* 8 a.m.

The temples on the **Acropolis** (30-210-923-8175; odysseus.culture.gr/h/3/eh355.jsp), the Parthenon,

OPPOSITE The caryatids of the Erechtheion temple.

RIGHT At Cape Sounion, on the tip of the Attic Peninsula, visitors relax over an open-air taverna meal.

the smaller Temple of Athena Nike, and the caryatid-adorned Erechtheion, were built in the fifth century B.C., under the leadership of Pericles, and are considered the greatest architectural accomplishment of classical Greece. Enjoy them before the Mediterranean sun reaches its heated zenith. You will enter the Acropolis through the Propylaeum, a giant gate designed by the ancient architect Mnesicles, and can wander close to the temples.

5 *Island Life* 11 a.m.

On your way back down the hill, stop in **Anafiotika**, a tiny reproduction of a whitewashed Cycladic village chiseled into the rocks by homesick stonemasons in the early 19th century. From Stratonos Street, after passing the whitewashed **St. George of the Rock** chapel, you will see a plaque commemorating Konstantinos Koukidis, who wrapped himself in the Greek flag and jumped to his death from the Acropolis during the Nazi occupation. Steps carved in the rock there will take you into Anafiotika's alleyways. The minuscule lanes are lined with courtyards and balconies blooming with

ABOVE The temples on the Acropolis are best seen early or late, not in the heat of the day.

OPPOSITE The Parthenon Gallery, the centerpiece of the new Acropolis Museum.

jasmine and roses. Later, descend into the **Plaka** neighborhood at the foot of the hill and walk through its streets, packed with churches, Neoclassical houses, and shops, to the area around **Syntagma (Constitution) Square**.

6 *A Freddo and Mastiha* 1 p.m.

Have a sandwich and a freddo — cappuccino or espresso blended with crushed ice — at **Clemente VIII** (City Link, Voukourestiou 3; 30-210-321-9340), a packed cafe on an elegant pedestrianized street. Afterward, stroll into the square, where tourists try to distract the photogenic young evzones, elite military guards wearing the skirt-like foustanella. Nearby are the Attica department store, designer boutiques, high-end jewelers, and patisseries including baklava-crazy **Karavan** (Voukourestiou 11). **Mastihashop** (Panepistimiou and Kriezotou Streets; 30-210-363-2750; www.mastihashop.com) sells products made from the resin of the mastiha, or lentisk, tree on the island of Chios. Mastiha has flavored potions, sweets, and cosmetics for thousands of years.

7 *Walk Through History* 4 p.m.

Opposite the **Temple of the Olympian Zeus**, pedestrianized Dionysou Areopagitou Street leads to a walkway around the Acropolis and past some of the old city's most notable sites, including the Theater of Dionysus and the Odeon of Herodes

Atticus, the sophist and Roman senator. In the summer, the Irodio, as the Greeks call it, hosts concerts, plays, and dance performances during the Hellenic Festival.

8 *Souvlaki, Updated* 9 p.m.

Souvlaki is grilled meat, tomatoes, onions, and the yogurt-cucumber dip called tzatziki wrapped in a round of pita bread. It's been the favorite street food in Athens for years. Recognizing its popularity, two enterprising Athenian businessmen opened **Souvlaki Bar** (Adrianou and Thisseion 15; 30-210-515-0550; $), a sit-down restaurant in the Thisseion neighborhood that soon gained a following. Try the "sfinakia" (shots), miniature souvlaki rolls filled with chicken or pork and stuffed in shot glasses; the dakosalata, a Cretan salad with barley rusks, tomato, feta, and capers; the patates fournistes, baby potatoes served with a creamy feta sauce; and a little bottle of the pomace brandy called tsipouro.

9 *Modern Dynamism* 11 p.m.

Two popular establishments in the Monastiraki neighborhood are drawing Athenians into the art, music, dance, and theater of today. The **Art Foundation**, known as taf, (5 Normanou Street; 30-210-323-8757; theartfoundation.gr/en/arxikh), in a 19th-century complex, has galleries, a performance space, and a courtyard bar. **Six d.o.g.s.** (6-8 Avramiotou Street; 30-210-321-0510; sixdogs.gr) houses a cafe and bar as well as visual art, performances, and movie screenings.

SUNDAY

10 *Olympian Footsteps* 9 a.m.

For your morning workout, join the runners and power walkers on the track at the **Panathenaic Stadium**, the ancient Olympic stadium on the Ardittos Hill that was rebuilt from its ruins to host the first modern Olympics in 1896. Or take a walk on the winding paths of the **National Gardens**, created in 1839 by Greece's

first queen, Amalia, who arranged for the cultivation of more than 15,000 domestic and exotic plants from the coastal town of Sounio and the island of Evia.

11 *A Cape to Remember* Noon

It's a short, beautiful drive to windy and wild **Cape Sounion**, a rocky promontory on the southern tip of the Attica peninsula. At the **Temple of Poseidon**, built of white marble here around 440 B.C., look for "Byron" carved into a wall by Lord Byron, an enthusiastic tourist in Greece. The views from the temple are panoramic, and it's a good place to imagine ancient sailors venturing out in their small ships to challenge the sea. Have a seafood lunch at one of the tavernas nearby, and ask to accompany it with a bottle of the organic ouzo called Matarelli, which is smooth and slightly honeyed.

ABOVE Walk the winding paths of the National Gardens.

OPPOSITE The beach and pier on Cape Sounion.

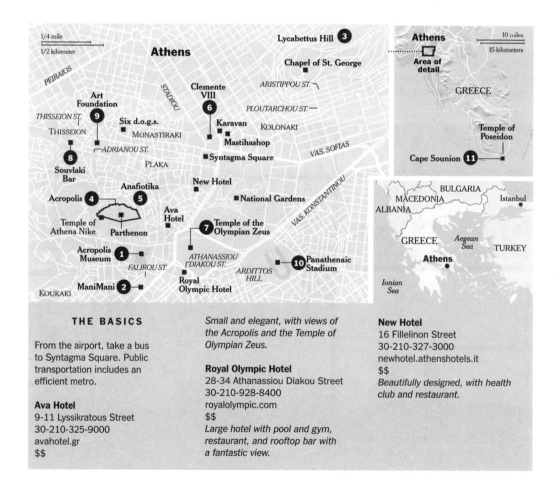

THE BASICS

From the airport, take a bus to Syntagma Square. Public transportation includes an efficient metro.

Ava Hotel
9-11 Lyssikratous Street
30-210-325-9000
avahotel.gr
$$

Small and elegant, with views of the Acropolis and the Temple of Olympian Zeus.

Royal Olympic Hotel
28-34 Athanassiou Diakou Street
30-210-928-8400
royalolympic.com
$$
Large hotel with pool and gym, restaurant, and rooftop bar with a fantastic view.

New Hotel
16 Fillelinon Street
30-210-327-3000
newhotel.athenshotels.it
$$
Beautifully designed, with health club and restaurant.

Thrace

Surrounded by two rivers, the thickly forested Rhodope Mountains, and the Aegean Sea, the Thrace region in northeastern Greece has its roots in the ancient kingdom of the same name, which also extended into Bulgaria, Turkey, eastern portions of Serbia, and the former Yugoslav Republic of Macedonia. Two or three decades ago, Thrace was known mainly as an outpost for soldiers guarding Greece from a hostile Turkey and Communist Bulgaria. Today, thanks to much-improved relations with both countries — as well as much-improved roads — travelers are heading to Thrace's homespun inns and eco-tourism centers and to late-Ottoman landmarks like Imaret, a former Muslim administrative and school complex in the city of Kavala that's now one of the top luxury hotels in Greece.
— BY JOANNA KAKISSIS

FRIDAY

1 *Portside Views* 6 p.m.

Take a walk along the seaside promenade in **Kavala**. This town is an active port on the Aegean Sea, and fishermen from countries around the Mediterranean often stop in to rest at its seafront. One man in a group mending nets near the promenade on a summer evening said that although he was Egyptian, his boat had been docking in Kavala for years. This a good spot for both gazing out to sea and looking back at the city itself, with its terra cotta roofs and concrete apartment blocks lining the steep slope. A 16th-century aqueduct cuts through town, crossing city streets, and a Byzantine fortress crowns the hill. You can also see the domes of the Imaret of Mohamed Ali Pasha, now the Imaret hotel. Built in 1817, it is a rare surviving landmark in Thrace from the days of the Ottoman Empire.

2 *Dining at the Pasha's* 8 p.m.

Even if you are not staying at **Imaret of Ali Pasha**, try to make a reservation anyway for dinner at its restaurant (Theodorou Poulidou Street 30-32; call 30-251-062-0151 before 6 p.m.; imaret.gr; $$$-$$$$). Imaret grows much of its own produce for the meals served here, which emphasize regional ingredients. Entrees have included rack of lamb with sesame and dried nuts in a honey and mustard dressing, pasta with squid ink and fish roe, and fresh fish with lime sauce. Enclosed in glass and overlooking the city and harbor, the restaurant has a lovely view, especially at night. If Imaret is booked, or you prefer something less expensive, explore the tavernas at the port or in the city center. Kavala is known for its seafood, so the fish taverns are especially good. Ask the waiter to let you see the catch of the day, and then pick out the freshest fish.

SATURDAY

3 *Roman Route* 10 a.m.

Drive inland and northeast on the **Egnatia Odos**, a new highway through northern Greece. It was inspired by the Roman-era Via Egnatia, which crossed the Balkan peninsula to reach Constantinople. In Thrace the new road parallels the Roman one, speeding you through fertile farmland with mountains in the distance. Stop when you reach the vibrant town of Xanthi. A center of fine tobacco in the 18th century, Xanthi is now known for its lively

OPPOSITE AND BELOW Two views of the Aegean Sea port of Kavala, the largest city in the northeastern Greek region of Thrace. The region's name comes from the ancient kingdom of Thrace, which also extended into Bulgaria, Turkey, and parts of what was once Yugoslavia.

pre-Easter Carnival, its music and arts scene, and its East-meets-West identity.

4 *Ethnic Blend* 11 a.m.

Explore Xanthi's old town, with its neo-Classical-style buildings and restored tobacco warehouses. Notice the minarets — this is one Greek town where the muezzin's cry sounds as clearly as the Orthodox church bells. Poke into shops, have coffee at a cafe and lunch in a taverna, but don't neglect the people-watching. Old men in skullcaps hike up the cobblestone steps, Gypsy merchants are draped in rugs for sale, engineering students stroll along, and children chatter in an acrobatic blend of Greek, Turkish, and the Slavic language of the Pomak people.

5 *Mountain Enclave* 1 p.m.

Drive out into the countryside toward the remote villages of the **Pomaks**, deep in the southern Rhodope Mountains. Border disputes with Bulgaria imposed a long isolation on these villages, which are built into some of the most stunning mountainous land in Greece. The Pomaks, Muslim Slavs who speak a language called Pomakci, were victims of politics; Greece, Turkey, and Bulgaria all claimed their territory. Greece put up a cold war-era military barrier blocking the only road to reach them, and they had to show identity cards to cross it. The barrier, or barra, came down in the 1990s, but visitors are still rare enough to remain a novelty. If you stop to explore the tiny alleys of a hamlet, perhaps Pachni or Glafki, you are likely to receive a warm welcome. On one outsider's trip to Glafki, an old man ran up to offer handshakes and hugs, children offered ice cream, and curious grandmothers waved from kitchen windows.

6 *Fish and Brandy* 8 p.m.

The city of Xanthi has some of the best food in northeastern Greece. In the old town, **Kivotos** (Plateia Antika; 30-693-727-7872; $$) serves outstanding seafood and tsipouro, a strong pomace brandy that is a favorite drink in Thrace. At **Palia Polis** (Hasirtzoglou Street 7;

30-254-106-8685; $$), try the soutzoukakia, cumin-spiced Smyrnean meatballs in tomato sauce, and hanoum bourek, pastry filled with pastourma and cheese.

7 *Xanthi Crawl* 10 p.m.

When you emerge into the streets of the old town after dinner, you will find the streets filled with young Greeks moving from cafes to tavernas to bars. Many end up at **Dili Dili** (Pigmalionos Christidi 2; 30-694-470-5005), which looks like a Seattle grunge bar transplanted to a provincial Greek town. Dili Dili is named for a Greek children's story, and it attracts young artists, college students, and musicians who like its attention to nostalgia. If you're in luck, a Greek band will be playing folk-jazz that riffs off traditional Thracian songs.

SUNDAY

8 *Urban Polyglot* 10 a.m.

Back on the Egnatia Odos, it's a short drive to the raucous city of **Komotini**, the regional capital, where market traders, students from Democritus University of Thrace, and a multicultural and multilingual population (Greek, Turkish, Pomak, Armenian, Roma) all keep things lively. Find your way to the pedestrian-only commercial area of the city center, where shops sell the creations of traditional craftsmen

ABOVE The Imaret of Mohamed Ali Pasha hotel.

BELOW Modern Kavala rests on its Ottoman and Byzantine past. Its origins are older, dating to the seventh century B.C.

and bakers offer the fresh custard-filled pastries called boughatsas. A famous and energetic pazari, or market, operates here on Saturdays.

9 *Beloved Sweets* Noon

Don't miss **Nedim** (Kriton 15-17 at Orfeos; 30-253-102-2036; nedim.gr), the toast of the city for more than 50 years, which specializes in Eastern Mediterranean sweets like dondurma, the ice cream made from sheep's milk, and ekmek kataifi, a syrupy pastry.

10 *Into the Wild* 1 p.m.

If you have some extra time, drive on to the largely undeveloped prefecture of **Evros**, named for the river that largely marks Greece's border with Turkey. The Evros Delta is an eco-traveler's paradise, especially attractive to birders and ornithologists because of its hundreds of species of migrating birds. Wild horses gallop in the nearby tamarisk forest. The well-known forest reserve near the village of Dadia is among the last refuges for European raptors, many of which are endangered.

ABOVE A winding street in old town Xanthi.

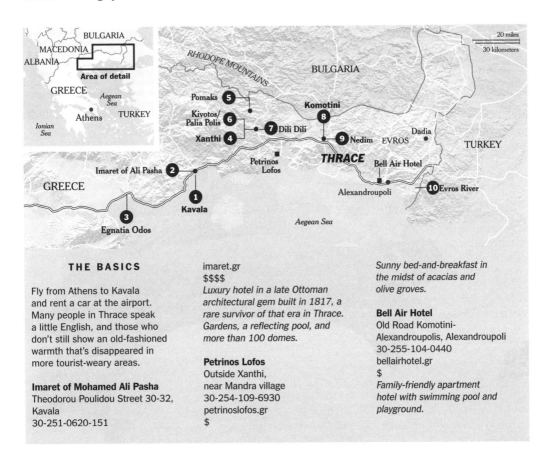

THE BASICS

Fly from Athens to Kavala and rent a car at the airport. Many people in Thrace speak a little English, and those who don't still show an old-fashioned warmth that's disappeared in more tourist-weary areas.

Imaret of Mohamed Ali Pasha
Theodorou Poulidou Street 30-32, Kavala
30-251-0620-151

imaret.gr
$$$$
Luxury hotel in a late Ottoman architectural gem built in 1817, a rare survivor of that era in Thrace. Gardens, a reflecting pool, and more than 100 domes.

Petrinos Lofos
Outside Xanthi,
near Mandra village
30-254-109-6930
petrinoslofos.gr
$

Sunny bed-and-breakfast in the midst of acacias and olive groves.

Bell Air Hotel
Old Road Komotini-Alexandroupolis, Alexandroupoli
30-255-104-0440
bellairhotel.gr
$
Family-friendly apartment hotel with swimming pool and playground.

Mykonos

Not so long ago Mykonos, Greece, one of the Aegean's most popular islands, onto which jumbo cruise ships daily deposit thousands of warm-weather day-trippers, was awash in just about everything but glamour. The island was easily dismissed as too crowded, too expensive, too much of a cliché. But it bounced back as one of Europe's jet-set playgrounds, rivaling the days when its cachet could be evoked with just two words: Jackie Onassis. Its hoteliers and restaurateurs have learned to create the magic by mixing a healthy dose of the island's hedonistic past with a new reality of luxury accommodations, fusion gastronomy, and notions of proper service. — BY ANDREW FERREN

FRIDAY

1 *Go West* 7 p.m.

Head for sunset drinks at **Hippie Fish** (Ai Yianni Beach; 30-22890-23547; hippiefish-mykonos.com), on the beach at Agios Ioannis, the island's westernmost area. It may be too early for dinner, but not for some delectably crispy saganaki and a glass of Peloponnesian chardonnay beneath the grapevine-shaded pergola.

2 *Rustic Chic* 10 p.m.

Fighting the current trend toward white-on-white minimalism, the family-owned taverna **To Maereio** (Kalogera Street, Mykonos Town; 30-22890-28825; $$$) serves straightforward fare amid charmingly simple décor. Model ships and braided loaves of bread adorn the walls, and the standout nibbles include bites like crispy zucchini fritters, rich tzatziki crunchy with cucumber, and savory keftedes.

3 *Take to the Streets* Midnight

For gay visitors (heavily represented on Mykonos), the scene gets going at **Porta** (Paraportiani, Mykonos Town; 30-22890-27087), which reaches its peak crowd around 1 a.m., and in the streets around **Pierro's Bar** (Matoyanni Street, Mykonos Town; 30-228-902-2177). The crowd is mixed — and devoted

OPPOSITE Surveying Mykonos from a sun bed at the Belvedere Hotel. Luxury has reasserted itself on this resort island.

RIGHT Uno con Carne, a steakhouse and oyster bar.

to the club scene — at the open-air **Cavo Paradiso** (Paradise Beach; 30-22890-27205; cavoparadiso.gr), among the world's mythic dance clubs, with a singular perch 100 feet above the sea.

SATURDAY

4 *Refuel* 10 a.m.

Restore yourself with a Greek coffee and a spinach-and-feta omelet at **Raya** (Old Port, Mykonos Town; 30-22890-28223; $$), where covered terraces overlook the harbor. For beach reading, pick up a selection from the glossy fashion, travel, and gossip magazines at the International Press shop.

5 *Beach Bound* Noon

Mykonos has enough gorgeous white-sand beaches lapped by crystalline turquoise water to have allowed for a bit of market specialization in terms of atmosphere and amenities. These range from simple family-style tavernas to ultra-chic lounges pumping out dance music and potent cocktails at all hours. The latter is the case in many of the coves in the south, where **Elia** is a prime gay beach. A more tranquil version of paradise can be found in the north, at **Agios Sostis**, a semi-remote stretch of sand free of crowds, lounge chairs, and disco beats at the mouth of Panormos Bay.

6 *Follow Your Nose* 2 p.m.

Just above Agios Sostis is one of the island's best-known secrets. A restaurant with no sign, no phone, and open only for lunch, **Kiki's** (Facebook: Kiki's Restaurant Agios Sostis; $$$) is well worth seeking out — just follow the smell of barbecue — and waiting as long as it takes for a seat at what could be one of the world's most idyllic seaside restaurants. The sweeping sea view is matched by the simple, rustic fare: salads of lentils and artichokes or pasta with tuna and cherry tomatoes, to be followed by grilled octopus or a succulent chicken breast stuffed with feta and sun-dried tomatoes.

7 *Above the Fray* 10 p.m.

Nestled on a hill overlooking Mykonos Town is the **Belvedere Hotel** (School of Fine Arts District; 30-22890-25122; belvederehotel.com), the gold standard of Mykonian chic and now a nexus of international gastronomy. While the sushi is slung at Nobu Matsuhisa's restaurant on one side of the Belvedere's romantically lantern-lit pool deck, the well-known Greek chef Nikos Zervos operates at **Thea Restaurant** on a terrace overlooking the pool and with sea and sunset views. Named for one of the Titans who preceded the ancient Greek gods, it's a festive environment for Zervos's light-hearted and innovative cooking, which is showcased in a tasting menu ($$$$) that plays with Greek and Mediterranean traditions:

perhaps beef marinated in espresso tinged with orange and cardamom, or yellowfin tuna with lentil sprouts, yogurt mousse, citrus oil, and salty ice plant. The dessert menu might offer walnut pie with Cognac cream, cacao syrup, and honey ice cream.

8 *Hit the Meat Market* Midnight

Check the scene at **Uno con Carne** (Panachra, Mykonos Town; 30-22890-24020; unoconcarne.gr), a steak and sushi place with an oyster bar set in the spectacular Art Deco space of Mykonos's former open-air cinema. Aside from the restaurant, there's a long bar with well-mixed cocktails.

9 *Star Search* 1 a.m.

If driving out to the clubs or finding a taxi at this hour seems like too much, don't worry. Just stroll instead to **Astra** (Tria Pigadia Street, Mykonos Town; 30-22890-24767; astra-mykonos.com), a boîte designed in the late 1980s by the local jeweler Minas, who incorporated a fiber-optic "starlight" ceiling that pulses to the music. This gem has lost none of its luster and still packs in models, magnates, rock stars, Formula One drivers, and even a recent Miss Greece or two. The party can go until dawn.

ABOVE Agios Sostis, a quiet, uncrowded beach. Mykonos has enough sand to serve a varied clientele, including gay travelers, hedonists of various stripes, and families.

SUNDAY

10 *Rehab* Noon

Recuperate on the beach, this time at **Psarou**, followed by a decidedly over-the-top lunch at **Nammos** (Psarou Beach; 30-22890-22440; nammos.gr; $$$$), purveyor of four-figure bottles of Cristal and 100-euro-plus-per-kilo grilled lobster. You might also choose something far less expensive like an amazing homemade tagliatelle with scorpion fish, but this is kind of missing the point of Nammos. Ostentation is right at home amid summer's wildly see-and-be-seen crowd, many of whom arrive by yacht and are shuttled ashore in vintage mahogany skiffs. The restaurant's whitewashed beach shack décor provides a crisp backdrop for the display of deeply suntanned skin, vividly colored pareos, and important jewelry. Psarou also features such vital amenities as a day spa, a hair salon, and an outpost of the chic boutique Luisa called **Luisa Beach** (30-22890-22015), just in case someone left her Missoni gown in the plane's overhead compartment.

ABOVE View from Nammos at Psarou Beach.

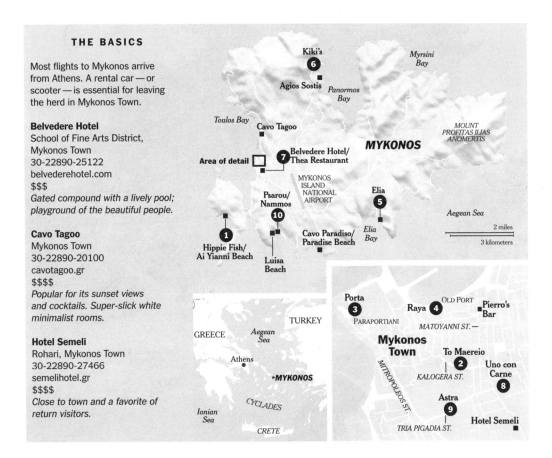

THE BASICS

Most flights to Mykonos arrive from Athens. A rental car — or scooter — is essential for leaving the herd in Mykonos Town.

Belvedere Hotel
School of Fine Arts District,
Mykonos Town
30-22890-25122
belvederehotel.com
$$$
Gated compound with a lively pool; playground of the beautiful people.

Cavo Tagoo
Mykonos Town
30-22890-20100
cavotagoo.gr
$$$$
Popular for its sunset views and cocktails. Super-slick white minimalist rooms.

Hotel Semeli
Rohari, Mykonos Town
30-22890-27466
semelihotel.gr
$$$$
Close to town and a favorite of return visitors.

Kiki's **6**
Myrsini Bay
Agios Sostis
Panormos Bay
Toulos Bay
Cavo Tagoo
MOUNT PROFITAS ILIAS ANOMERTIS
Area of detail
Belvedere Hotel/ Thea Restaurant **7**
MYKONOS
MYKONOS ISLAND NATIONAL AIRPORT
Elia **5**
Aegean Sea
Psarou/ Nammos **10**
2 miles
3 kilometers
Hippie Fish/ Ai Yianni Beach **1**
Cavo Paradiso/ Paradise Beach
Elia Bay
Luisa Beach

TURKEY
GREECE
Aegean Sea
Athens
MYKONOS
CYCLADES
Ionian Sea
CRETE

Porta **3**
PARAPORTIANI
Raya **4**
OLD PORT
Pierro's Bar
MATOYANNI ST.—
Mykonos Town
To Maereio **2**
KALOGERA ST.
Uno con Carne **8**
Astra **9**
Hotel Semeli
METROPOLEOS ST.
TRIA PIGADIA ST.

Salonika

Punctuated by palm trees and relics of antiquity, the mazelike streets of Salonika, the second city of Greece, open to century-old marketplaces or lead down to a harbor on the Thermaic Gulf, an arm of the Aegean Sea. Young ramblers are everywhere in this city of one million people: on the seafront promenade, near the 14th-century White Tower, at the crowded cafes and bars. Most are among the 150,000 or so students at local universities; many others are young artists and professionals. All contribute to the youthful, culturally lively vibe of modern Salonika (called Thessaloniki in Greece), a counterpoint to a rich history dating back to the days of its namesake Thessaloniki, wife of the city's founder and half-sister to Alexander the Great.
— BY CHARLY WILDER AND JOANNA KAKISSIS

FRIDAY

1 *Russian Inspiration* 4 p.m.

Already a southeastern European center for cinema because of its film festivals, Salonika is enjoying a resurgence in its eclectic visual arts and music scenes. The **State Museum of Contemporary Art** (Kolokotroni 21, Moni Lazariston; 30-2310-589-143; greekstatemuseum.com), housed in a former monastery in the suburb of Stavroupolis, has played a central role. Its own surprising core is a stirring group of 1,275 works by the Russian avant-garde — from the years before Stalin crushed Russian modernism — amassed by the Greek collector George Costakis. A waterfront spinoff, the **Center of Contemporary Art** (Warehouse B1, Port of Salonika; 30-2310-546-683; cact.gr) houses eclectic presenta-tions of video and new-media art. A past exhibition featured works inspired by the spiritual writings of Nikos Kazantzakis, the author of *Zorba the Greek*.

2 *Photographic Memory* 6 p.m.

If you've made it to the port, linger to visit the **Museum of Photography Thessaloniki** (Warehouse A, Port of Salonika; 30-2310-566-716; thmphoto.gr),

which describes itself as "a place of memory" and mounts intriguing exhibitions in a two-story century-old structure. One popular exhibition used still photographs and video from 22 artists representing 11 countries in southeastern Europe to explore how the past influences the present. There's also a third museum in the neighborhood, devoted to cinema.

3 *Thessalonian Fare* 8 p.m.

Salonika's ouzeris, establishments devoted to purveying ouzo, the potent anise-seed liquor that many consider the Greek national drink, offer the national foods, too. Try **Agora** (5 Kapodistriou; 30-2310-532-428; ouzeriagora.gr; $), located on a quiet side street a few blocks from the excavated actual agora of ancient Thessalonica. Select from the traditional dishes — fava beans with octopus in a red sauce, perhaps, or a fish soup called kakavia.

4 *The Coo Crowd* 10 p.m.

Coo (Vasileos Irakliou 4; 30-2311-274-752) a cafe, bar, music space, and gallery that also has its own radio station and record label, is home to quirky experimental acts from ambient pop to electronica. Run by a collective, Coo opened its doors late in 2011 and quickly became a go-to spot for Salonika's artistic set. Another favorite is **Fragile** (Valaoritou 29; 30-2310–547-443), where T-shirt-clad art students

OPPOSITE The White Tower in Salonika.

RIGHT Old fortifications along the Gulf of Thermaikos. Salonika, called Thessaloniki in Greece, has had many rulers.

shout over a mix of vintage doo-wop and '90s alt-rock, or duck into a covered bar area that evokes a vaguely postal theme with corkboard-lined walls cross-hatched with packing tape.

SATURDAY

5 *Aristotelian Wake-Up* 10 a.m.

Order your morning coffee at a cafe on **Aristotelous Square**, a busy central plaza where curved, columned facades open to the waterfront. Its name may be ancient (yes, that Aristotle), but the square's buildings date back less than a century. They were designed by an international group of architects after much of the city center was lost

to fire in 1917. (Earthquakes in 1978 also damaged parts of town.) Once home to five open-air cinemas, the square today has the Olympion, a theater built in 1948 and now the headquarters for the Salonika International Film Festival, which draws thousands every November. Salonika hosts three more cinematic festivals in the spring, devoted to documentaries, short films, and videos of dance and other motion. Still in the square, turn your back on the sea to look up toward Ano Poli, the Upper Town, a district of Byzantine fortifications, narrow residential streets, and lovely small gardens.

6 *How Much for the Cloves?* Noon

Salonika is an old trading town, and a stroll through its markets is a kaleidoscopic journey into scent, sound, and color: cumin and sage, broad spreads of fresh meat and fish, Pontic cheeses, even the odd village medicinal potion, all wrapped in an aural force field of greengrocers promoting their eggplant in booming rhymes. (Cafes and food stalls will also provide your lunch.) The Louloudadika is a

ABOVE Aristotelous Square, a plaza where curved facades open to the waterfront. The name comes from Aristotle, but the buildings were not constructed until after a fire in 1917.

LEFT Coo, a cafe, bar, music space, and gallery, also has its own radio station and record label.

flower market; the Kapani has everything for dinner and more. The **Modiano** market, founded in the early 1920s by the architect Eli Modiano, a member of a Sephardic merchant family, was once a hub for Salonika's Jews. They thrived here and were at one point a majority, but Nazi occupiers virtually eliminated them. Their story is told in the nearby **Jewish Museum** (13 Agiou Mina Street; 30-2310-250-406; jmth.gr).

7 *Sail Through Byzantium* 3 p.m.

Salonika is strategically located between the Mediterranean and the Balkans, and a walk around the city reveals a mosaic of cultural influences: Greek and Roman ruins; Byzantine churches; Ottoman-era hammams and mosques; the pink house where Ataturk, founder of the Turkish republic, was born in 1881. One interesting trove of relics and priceless artwork, spanning the centuries when Roman influences gradually melted into the medieval, is well displayed at the **Museum of Byzantine Culture** (2 Leoforos Stratou; 30-2313-306-400; mbp.gr). A quick trip through the exhibits is well worth your time.

8 *Something Fishy?* 8 p.m.

Bistros, some quite chic, are well established in a once rundown, now trendy Ottoman-era neighborhood that includes some of the old Mondiano marketplaces. At **Xontro Alati** (Ermou 26; 30-2310-281-566;

xontro-alati.gr), you forgo a bit of style in exchange for a meal that's likely to delight any seafood enthusiast: smoked mackerel, grilled sardines, grilled octopus, or seafood paella.

9 *Urban Rock* 11 p.m.

On the popular night-life stretch of Zefxidos Street, near the seventh-century Church of Aghia Sophia, prides of revelers fill spots like **Urban Bar** (30-2310-272-821; facebook.com/Urban.Bar.Cafe), a onetime gallery that is now one of Salonika's best-loved rock bars. Students bob to the music, dominating the crowd, but a few aging hipsters may be sipping drinks, too.

SUNDAY

10 *On Promenade* 11 a.m.

Catch some Mediterranean sea breeze with a stroll on the waterfront promenade along the harbor, between the port and the 14th-century fortress known as the **White Tower** (30-2310-267-832; lpth. gr), the city's best-known landmark. An infamous prison in the days of Turkish rule, it is now a tame

ABOVE Salonika is largely a city of the young. Of its one million people, 150,000 or so are university students. Many others are young artists and professionals.

exhibition space, displaying artifacts from the city's history. To gain perspective on the city in more ways than one, climb up through the six-story exhibit and emerge on the top of the tower for commanding views. Near the tower, that bronze figure on the rearing horse is Alexander the Great, who hailed from these parts. (Salonika is the capital of the Greek region of Macedonia, not to be confused with the Republic of Macedonia.) Not enough sun and sea? If you have a car and some extra time, drive out to the beaches on the **Chalkidiki** (also spelled Chalcidice)

peninsula, a three-pronged projection into the Aegean that's also home to fields, pines, and the ancient monasteries of Mount Athos that have never allowed a woman on their turf.

ABOVE Seafront buildings face the roadway and promenade along the gulf. The White Tower is in the distance.

OPPOSITE Wine at a table inside the covered Modiano food market. Salonika is an old trading town, and a stroll through its markets is a journey into scent, sound, and color.

THE BASICS

Taxis and buses serve the city, with a metro under construction. To explore out of town, rent a car.

Met Hotel
Eikostis Ektis Oktovriou 48
30-2310-017-000
themethotel.gr
$$
On the harbor, with stylish rooms, restaurants, and spa.

Electra Palace
9 Aristotelous Square
30-2310-294-000
electrahotels.gr
$$
Salonika's traditional main central hotel. Sea view rooms at a premium.

Hyatt Regency Thessaloniki
13th Km Thessaloniki Perea
30-2310–401-234
thessaloniki.regency.hyatt.com
$$
About eight miles from the city center, near the airport.

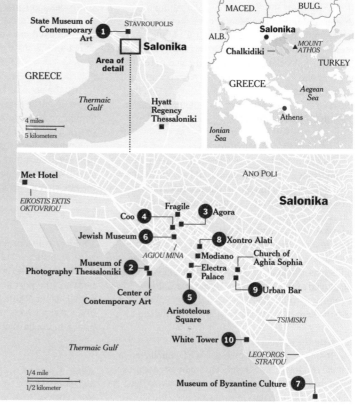

Istanbul

From a skyline featuring both minarets and church spires to the call to prayer competing with lounge music in a hip cafe, Istanbul is the only major city to span two continents. While it is known for sights dating back thousands of years, it also has a fascinating, and often ignored, contemporary scene that is finally receiving international attention. Whatever the point of view, Istanbul is among the world's most visually stimulating cities.
— BY JENNIFER CONLIN AND SUSANNE FOWLER

FRIDAY

1 *Strait and Narrow* 2 p.m.

With too little time to indulge in the six-hour ferry ride up and down the Bosporus, a trip recommended by most guidebooks, try **TurYol** (turyol.com; call the TurYol information bureau for details: 90-212-512-1287), a company that operates smaller, faster boats every half hour for both locals and tourists. It offers a 90-minute ride from the Eminonu ferry dock, at the foot of the Galata Bridge, Golden Horn side, up to Rumelihisari, the site of an Ottoman fortress at the narrowest part of the Bosporus, before returning to Eminonu. The captain tries to stay close to the shore so you can check out the charming old wooden Ottoman houses, new luxury villas, and many upscale restaurants, clubs, and fancy hotels that line both sides of the strait. Afterward, visit (or revisit) the **Hagia Sophia** (hagiasophia.com), the great Byzantine and Ottoman monument, or the **Grand Bazaar** (grandbazaaristanbul.org). Both are nearby.

2 *On the Avenue* 5 p.m.

Take a walk down Istanbul's famous **Istiklal Caddesi**, a pedestrian avenue in the Beyoglu district that is filled with boutiques, restaurants, and galleries. Stop at **Ficcin** (Kallavi Sokak, Beyoglu; 90-212-243-8353; ficcin.com) on a small side street, order a Turkish coffee, and watch modern Turkey pass by: teens dressed like pop stars and women in head scarves. When you're ready for something stronger to drink, seek out **360 Istanbul** (Istiklal Caddesi 163, Beyoglu; 90-212-251-1042; 360istanbul.com), a rooftop bar and restaurant with a view that matches its name. Order a martini and look out over the Bosporus, the Hagia Sophia, even the Sea of Marmara. Enjoy the

view indoors, too, as this glass-and-steel bar is a favorite place to see and be seen for both jet-setters and Istanbul's own glamorous denizens.

3 *A Feast (for the Eyes, Too)* 8 p.m.

Mikla, atop the Marmara Pera Hotel (Mesrutiyet Caddesi 15, Beyoglu; 90-212-293-5656; miklarestaurant.com; $$$$), is known for its stunning views as well as its modern, elegant décor. Designed as a "multidimensional outdoor living space," it has an indoor restaurant and bar, outdoor dining areas on two terraces, and a third terrace with an open-air bar and swimming pool. No matter where you end up sitting, you will feel that you're part of the skyline. You can take a selfie with the Topkapi Palace, the Hagia Sophia and the Blue Mosque all in the background. Be sure to call ahead for restaurant reservations. The hard part is deciding which of the "new Anatolian" dishes to order.

SATURDAY

4 *The Other Side* 9 a.m.

Take a ferry and cross the Bosporus to the less-harried Asian side of Istanbul, a greener, cleaner,

OPPOSITE The Hagia Sophia, a symbol of Istanbul.

BELOW A TurYol boat tour on the Bosporus. Ottoman houses and new villas, restaurants, and hotels line the strait.

and often more conservative swath of the city that offers its own multicultural mix. Make your first stop at the 19th-century **Beylerbeyi Palace** (Abdullahaga Caddesi 29; 90-216-321-9320; www.millisaraylar.gov. tr/portalmain-en/default.aspx). It's not Topkapi, despite being nearly as lavishly decorated, but it is an impressive Imperial Ottoman edifice with Baccarat crystal chandeliers, grand staircases, Yildiz porcelain, Hereke carpets, and a decorative indoor marble pool and fountain. It was once host to visiting European royalty, and its last official overnight guest is said to have been Mustafa Kemal Ataturk, founder of the Turkish Republic. Tours are available in English.

5 *A Blend of Beliefs* 11 a.m.

The arts colony of Kuzguncuk was once a melting pot of cultures and boasts a mosque and a synagogue, plus Greek Orthodox and Armenian churches, along with a crop of cute cafes. Rows of colorful wooden townhouses with carved-gingerbread balconies have made this zone a destination for new brides with photographers in tow. Souvenirs by local designers line the shelves at **Bir Kuzguncuk Dukkani** (Icadiye Caddesi 40A; 90-216-532-9691; birkuzguncukdukkani. com). Look for painted Popsicle-stick bookmarks by Ayse Durukan or small purses of recycled materials from the Cop Madam cooperative, which employs, and empowers, Turkish housewives.

6 *Far Pavilions* Noon

Grab a cab to **Buyuk Camlica** (Turistik Çamlıca Caddesi, Uskudar), a hilltop park favored by conservatively dressed Turks and Gulf Arab tourists and near where a new mosque dominates the Asian-side skyline. Here at one of the highest points in Istanbul, more than 850 feet above sea level, the view, which shows nearly every twist in the Bosporus, has inspired writers like Lord Byron and Lady Mary Wortley Montagu. Inside a renovated Ottoman coffeehouse surrounded by rosebushes, settle in for a slice of hazelnut cake or a cup of thick black coffee, served on an etched-brass tray.

7 *Savory and Anatolian* 2 p.m.

It's hard to find a better, or more intriguing, lunch than at the sidewalk tables at any branch of **Ciya** (www.ciya.com.tr/index_en.php), the popular outpost of what was nearly forgotten Anatolian cuisine. At the one at Gunesli Bahce Sokak (48B, Kadikoy; 90-216-336-3013; $), for example, the kebab choices include meats and vegetables prepared with ingredients and seasonings like sour cherries, pomegranate sauce, mint, and sumac. (The fruit flavors and scents also go into Turkey's famous candies.)

8 *Matinee Idyll* 4 p.m.

At the tiny **Sureyya Opera House** (Bahariye Caddesi 29, Kadikoy; 90-216-346-1531), where seats can be had at low prices, the Istanbul State Opera and Ballet (https://secure.dobgm.gov.tr/opera2013/devopera. aspx?Mud=2) performs European classics from the likes of Verdi and Rossini on Saturday afternoons and has also presented Turkish works like the two-act *Hurrem Sultan* ballet about Suleiman the Magnificent and his scheming bride. The space also is host to concerts as part of the annual Istanbul Music Festival.

9 *Spoon With a View* 8 p.m.

The man-made and natural light shows don't get much better than from the terrace of **Tapasuma** (Kuleli Caddesi 43, Cengelkoy; 90-216-401-1333; $$$), a restaurant on the grounds of the Sumahan on the

ABOVE A candy maker fashions Turkish sweets.

BELOW A street on the city's Anatolian side.

Water hotel. As the moonlight on the water intensifies, the sparkling lights on the First Bosporus Bridge change from white or yellow to pink or blue and even turquoise. The seasonal menu is international with a Turkish twist. The available dishes one night included sea bass stew and a dessert of three Turkish milk puddings: rosewater, berries, and mastic.

SUNDAY

10 *The Modern* 10 a.m.

The **Istanbul Modern** (Meclis-i Mebusan Caddesi, Karakoy; 90-212-334-7300; www.istanbulmodern.org/en) has not only two floors of contemporary artworks by local artists, but also a sculpture garden, library, and restaurant. Look for the work of Mubin Orhon and Fahrelnissa Zeid. Whatever you choose to see, don't miss out on lunch on the stylish terrace overlooking the Bosporus, where the view rivals the art. Amazingly, the food, a mixture of Turkish and European dishes, is great, too. One day's menu included manti, a lamb ravioli served with a garlic yogurt, and for dessert, tiramisu with coffee sauce.

ABOVE A book stand, complete with mascot, on Istanbul's quieter, slower-paced Anatolian side, across the Bosporus from the main tourist sites and technically in Asia.

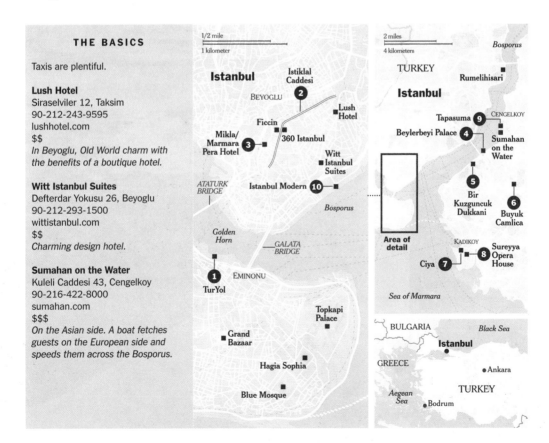

THE BASICS

Taxis are plentiful.

Lush Hotel
Siraselviler 12, Taksim
90-212-243-9595
lushhotel.com
$$
In Beyoglu, Old World charm with the benefits of a boutique hotel.

Witt Istanbul Suites
Defterdar Yokusu 26, Beyoglu
90-212-293-1500
wittistanbul.com
$$
Charming design hotel.

Sumahan on the Water
Kuleli Caddesi 43, Cengelkoy
90-216-422-8000
sumahan.com
$$$
On the Asian side. A boat fetches guests on the European side and speeds them across the Bosporus.

Bodrum

With its balmy shore and shop-lined streets, the city of Bodrum on the Aegean has long been a favorite seaside retreat in Turkey. Ancient travelers knew it as the site of one of the Seven Wonders of their world, a rich king's monument to himself. But sometime around the year 2000, this old fishing village and the smaller towns nearby on the Bodrum peninsula emerged as stops on the global party circuit. A glance at the yachts lined up in its harbors hints at its new identity. In summer, Bodrum feels a bit like St.-Tropez, except perhaps for the belly dancers. What are the attractions? Gorgeous scenery, for one. The peninsula is a painterly tableau of whitewashed stucco homes, purple bougainvillea, and olive-green hillsides. And Bodrum's night life beckons partiers like a siren's song. — BY SETH SHERWOOD

FRIDAY

1 *Alexander's Nemesis* 3 p.m.

Like leitmotifs, icons of the region's history infuse all parts of modern Bodrum. There's an amphitheater built by the ancient Greeks, a medieval fortress, the traditional wooden boats called gulets. When Alexander the Great tried to seize Bodrum, then named Halicarnassus, he found it so well defended that he was forced to ask for the only truce of his conquering campaign. For Antony and Cleopatra, the peninsula was a stop on a voyage to Rome. For Brutus and Cassius, it was a place to plot the murder of Caesar — and to hide out afterward. Bodrum even keeps the memory of ancient Ephesus alive with a beer named for it, called Efes. Duck into a waterfront bar and sample one.

2 *Bodrum Bazaar* 4 p.m.

Plunge into the Bodrum street scene with some shopping. Bodrum is known for handmade sandals crafted of leather dyed with crushed acorns. Ali Guven, the craftsman who established Bodrum's san-

OPPOSITE Bodrum, called Halicarnassus by the ancient Greeks, now beckons with sunbathing, shopping, and night life.

RIGHT Turkbuku, on the northern end of the Bodrum peninsula, attracts a moneyed and glamorous crowd.

dal making reputation, and whose customers included Mick Jagger, died a few years ago; but others turn out similar footwear. Try **Bodrum Sandalet** (Cumhuriyet Caddesi Hilmi Uran Meydani No. 2; 90-252-316-8497; bodrumsandalet.com). For carpets, one place to look is **Gallery Mustafa** (Dr. Alim Ekinci Caddesi 48; 90-252-313-1043; gallerymustafa.com). Check out the shops for more — ceramics, curios, and jewelry.

3 *Dinner in the Hills* 8 p.m.

In the wooded hills a few kilometers from town you'll find **Ent** (Selahattin Pinar Farm, Kayirli Kume Elveri 12, Kizilagac; 90-252-369-2426; entrestaurant. com; $$$$), a chef-owned restaurant that's limited to 30 guests each evening. They choose between two fixed-price menus, one short and one longer, which may offer dishes like borek, a triangular pastry filled with seafood and mushrooms, and a sour yogurt panna cotta. Either way, you select wines from a list that seems to have almost every wine made in Turkey. In warm weather, guests dine at tables scattered in a garden.

4 *Liquid Refreshment* 11 p.m.

Cumhuriyet Caddesi, known to everyone as Bar Street, teems with bars and clubs for every persuasion, from British-style pubs to sleek designer dens. One of the most decadent spots is the **Catamaran Club** (Dr. Alim Bey Caddesi 1025 Sokak 10; 90-252-313-3600; clubcatamaran.com), a large boat with a glass dance floor that sails every night. Another is the gargantuan **Halikarnas** (178 Cumhuriyet Caddesi; 90-252-316-8000; www.halikarnas.com.tr),

a playful pastiche of classicism with marble floors, Ionic columns, and amphitheater-style seating. The hedonism, however, is genuine.

SATURDAY

5 *Village Color* 10 a.m.

The public minibus to **Gumusluk**, a town on the farthest tip of the peninsula, will take you on a winding, swerving voyage through traditional Turkey. Dipping along country roads, it passes ruined stone farmhouses, herds of cows, ramshackle stands selling melons, rural mosques, and fields of lavender. The town here in the days of the Roman Empire was called Myndos, but an earthquake long ago crumbled it into the sea, earning it the nickname the Sunken City; the tops of the ancient ramparts still poke above the waters. Have lunch at one of the cafes, and shop in the small crafts market, where stalls brim with gourds, spices, and circular amulets painted like the pupil and blue iris of an eyeball.

6 *Beach Party* 2 p.m.

On the buzzing boardwalk in the town of **Turkbuku**, a rustic past collides with a glamorous present. Moneyed couples in Chanel sunglasses and young women in gold bikinis poke into swimwear and jewelry boutiques, pausing occasionally to eat boiled mussels bought from scruffy fellows operating make-shift sidewalk stands. Fishermen hustle through the crowd carrying dripping plastic bags of freshly caught sea bass to restaurants where white-haired men rattle backgammon dice and sip milky-hued raki, the lightning-strong, anise-flavored national drink. Join the scene at one of the beach clubs, which provide ranks of plush white mattresses, fluttering white canopy beds, gauzy Arabesque tents, and

ABOVE Soft breezes, Mediterranean sun, and blue Aegean waters define Bodrum's beach scene.

RIGHT Carpets at Gallery Mustafa in Bodrum.

amply stocked bars. You will probably not be charged a fee to use the club, but you will be expected to buy drinks. One favorite spot is the **Maçakizi** (90-252-311-2400; macakizi.com).

7 *Dinner at the Dock* 8 p.m.

Relax over dinner at **Fidele** (Yali Mevkii, Turkbuku; 90-252-377-5081; fideleotel.com; $$$), a candle-lit dockside spot in the heart of the Turkbuku boardwalk. As yachts float past, diners partake of Mediterranean and Continental specialties, including grilled jumbo shrimp, pasta, chops, and a highly sought-after cheesecake.

8 *Be Seen* 10 p.m.

Compared to its counterpart in Bodrum, night life in Turkbuku is more stylish, more see-and-be-seen, and so more haughty. Make your first port of call **Ship Ahoy** (Yali Mevkii, 90-252-377-5070), a nautical-themed outdoor restaurant and bar that bursts at the seams on summer nights with the Istanbul elite and periodic Turkish celebrities.

SUNDAY

9 *Ancient Wonder* 10 a.m.

The **Mausoleum of Halicarnassus** in Bodrum (bodrumturkeytravel.com) may be reduced to some toppled columns and a bare foundation, but it is one of only two remaining Wonders of the Ancient World (with the Pyramids of Giza). During his reign here in the fourth century B.C., the ruler Mausolus hired a classical-era dream team of sculptors and

architects to build him a massive, 150-foot-high funeral monument. He died inconveniently early, and the project was taken over by his widow, Artemisia. Somehow she managed to oversee the monument (by now you have guessed where the word "mausoleum" comes from) despite her daily guzzlings of wine, which legend says she mixed with her late husband's ashes. In her grieving and dedication, Artemisia showed a devotion that went beyond that of even the most bereaved wives — perhaps because she was also Mausolus's sister.

10 *Sunken Treasure* 11 a.m.

The answer to the riddle of the Mausoleum's disappearance lurks inside the massive towers and crenellated walls of majestic **Bodrum Castle** (Bodrum Harbor; 90-252-316-2516). Literally. When the Knights of St. John (the Hospitalers) rode into town early in the 15th century, they found the Mausoleum in ruins, apparently the result of an earthquake. So the crusaders finished the job, pillaging every stone they could carry to build their fortress. Now it shelters the **Bodrum Museum of Underwater Archaeology** (90-252-316-2516; bodrum-museum.com). Filled with once-sunken ships and the remains of their gear and cargoes, the galleries unfold the physical record of vanished peoples who traveled by sail and oar, navigated by sun and star, and ultimately put their safety in the hands of the gods and the elements.

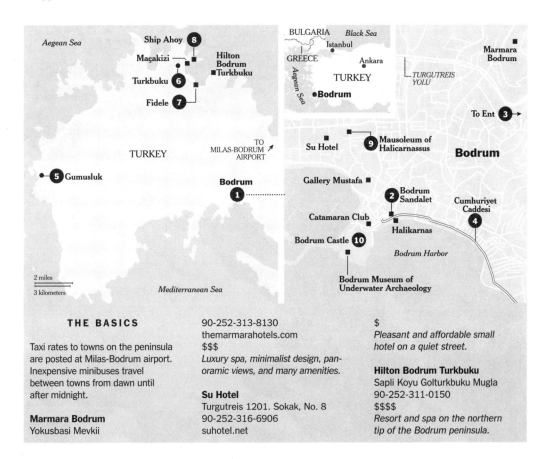

THE BASICS

Taxi rates to towns on the peninsula are posted at Milas-Bodrum airport. Inexpensive minibuses travel between towns from dawn until after midnight.

Marmara Bodrum
Yokusbasi Mevkii
90-252-313-8130
themarmarahotels.com
$$$
Luxury spa, minimalist design, panoramic views, and many amenities.

Su Hotel
Turgutreis 1201. Sokak, No. 8
90-252-316-6906
suhotel.net

$
Pleasant and affordable small hotel on a quiet street.

Hilton Bodrum Turkbuku
Sapli Koyu Golturkbuku Mugla
90-252-311-0150
$$$$
Resort and spa on the northern tip of the Bodrum peninsula.

Cappadocia

Spread across the middle of Turkey like a lunar landscape, Cappadocia is a bizarre field that stretches across 50 square miles of sun-baked hills and valleys riddled with giant anthill-shaped cones, rock-hewn churches, and underground cities. It is a spectacular sight that has captivated travelers for centuries. As recently as 20 years ago, most of the cave dwellings were empty—abandoned for more modern, concrete homes. In the last several years, though, affluent Turks and foreigners have started turning them into second homes and, in a few cases, boutique hotels. While several of them offer dramatic views, one should make an effort to experience this landscape on foot. Of course there is even a better option: gliding overhead in a hot-air balloon. — BY GISELA WILLIAMS

FRIDAY

1 *Bird's Eye View* 4 p.m.

Pigeon Valley, near the village of Uchisar, is named for the thousands of pigeon houses carved into the rock. (For generations farmers raised pigeons for food and used their droppings as fertilizers. Now most of them use modern fertilizers but some of the pigeon lofts are still occupied.) Looking out over this ravine from one of several viewpoints is a surreal scene: an outrageously phallic landscape straight out of a Salvador Dalí painting. The conical formations are the result of volcanic eruptions that took place millions of years ago. Wind, rain, and other forces of nature have eaten away at the volcanic rock, creating tufa, a soft and malleable stone, and mushroom-capped towers, some the height of apartment buildings.

2 *Sunset Hike* 5 p.m.

Cappadocia's seemingly impenetrable landscape is surprisingly friendly on foot. What appears to be a desert-like valley often reveals orchards, rivers, and vineyards. One of the most popular hikes is through the astonishing red-banded pillars and chimneys of **Rose Valley**, named for the rock found there, which is stained light pink by mineral deposits. Along a hike

OPPOSITE Ballooning over the village of Uchisar.

RIGHT Cappadocia is 50 square miles riddled with giant anthill-shaped cones, rock-hewn churches, and underground cities.

of two or three hours, you might wave to farmers and explore the White Church, a cave with towering ceilings and soaring columns that look as though they are carved from ivory. At sunset the valley turns dramatic shades of red and orange.

3 *Drinks on the Rocks* 8:30 p.m.

Head to the intimate and upscale town of Urgup, nestled under sandy yellow cliffs, and reward yourself with a fresh watermelon cocktail and a mountain of mezes (small, tapas-like dishes) at **Ziggy's** (90-384-341-7107; ziggycafe.com; $$), a popular cafe in an ancient yellowed stone house that has been renovated and polished with faultless care by its stylish young owners, Nuray and Selim Yuksel. At night Ziggy's is at its most atmospheric: candles flicker across the faces of a well-dressed crowd that cozies up in banquettes and tables clustered on three open-air terraces. If you're really hungry, try the set 12-course menu—but don't forget to leave room for the Sweet Ziggy dessert: tiny boreks (mille-feuille pastry) dusted with powdered sugar and cinnamon.

SATURDAY

4 *Open-Air Museum* 10 a.m.

The **Goreme Museum** (90-384-271-2167) dates back to A.D. 900–1200 and is now a Unesco World

Heritage site. There are several churches and refectories within this extraordinary rock-hewn monastic complex, an early religious education center that dates to between 900 and 1200 B.C. Wander counterclockwise, starting from the Church of St. Basil and ending at the Girls' Tower, a six-story convent that once housed up to 300 nuns. Throughout the churches you will come across two types of paintings: child-like

ABOVE Alaturca serves big portions of traditional Anatolian cuisine like kayseri mantisi, the Turkish version of ravioli, served with garlic and yogurt and pepper sauce.

BELOW For generations, local people dug into the tufa rock to build homes. This array is at the Anatolian Houses hotel.

geometrical patterns painted directly on the rock and frescoes painted on plaster that depict scenes from the life of Christ and his followers.

5 *Anatolian Lunch* Noon

Alaturca in Goreme (90-384-271-2882; alaturca.com.tr; $), a sprawling two-story restaurant with plenty of terrace seating, serves up big portions of traditional Anatolian cuisine like kayseri mantisi, the Turkish version of ravioli, served with garlic and yogurt and pepper sauce. For the less adventurous, the menu also lists Turkish-style burgers, salads, and sandwiches.

6 *The Weaver's Art* 2 p.m.

It's almost impossible to avoid visiting a carpet sales room anywhere in Turkey, and that's true in Goreme. After lunch, take a five-minute walk to **Sultan Carpet** (32 Muze caddesi, Goreme; 90-384-271-2003), where your visit is likely to include a cursory education in wool and silk production and carpet weaving.

Practice your sales resistance as tempting examples of hand-woven Turkish rugs and kilims are spread at your feet.

7 *Duck Underground* 4:30 p.m.

Take a drive to the underground city of **Kaymakli**, a large historical subterranean settlement. Be prepared to duck. The first four of its eight floors are open to the public and consist of a maze of narrow tunnels that lead from stables to churches, kitchens, and several wineries. Wine, for these underground dwellers, was one of the few luxuries. Who can blame the thousands of persecuted Christians who hid out here for needing an occasional buzz? During the three centuries after the birth of Christ, large numbers of Christians migrated here to escape the Romans. They dug deep into the area's soft rock and created Kaymakli and as many as 150 other underground settlements. Some of the cities used hollowed-out spaces already in existence, built by the Hittites as far back as 1900 B.C. They were used again as recently as 1839, when locals hid from the invading Egyptian army.

ABOVE The Rose Valley, named for its pinkish rock, turns red and orange at sunset.

RIGHT Camels wait in Goreme for tourists to hire them for riding through the Cappadocian landsape.

8 *Home Cooking* 7:30 p.m.

A meal at **Aravan Evi** (Ayvali; 90-384-354-5838; aravan.com; $$), a welcoming intimate restaurant within a charming family house, is the closest you may come to being invited for a meal inside someone's home, though here you're required to make a reservation. Guests are led through an arched stone entry and into a central courtyard sprouting with fig trees and flowers, and then given the choice of sitting indoors on pillows or outdoors under a grapevine-covered pergola. The cooking here is what a Turkish grandmother might prepare for a visiting family member: bulgur "wedding soup," freshly baked flat breads served with mezes, and lamb stews baked in a tandir, a traditional earthen oven.

SUNDAY

9 *Up and Away* Dawn

If there was ever the absolute right place to take a ride on a hot air balloon, Cappadocia is it. The perfect meeting point of outstanding landscape, consistent and dry weather conditions, and a long season, the region is on every balloonist's top ten list; and on any given morning, it's possible to spot as many as 20 balloons in the sky. Make your reservation, haul yourself out of bed as the sun is just thinking about coming up, and join in. Seeing the surreal peaks and valleys from the air — at the crack of dawn — adds a new and profound dimension to your trip. The silence soon after takeoff, as everyone in the basket is struck speechless by flight, is as dramatic as what rolls by underneath you: narrow canyons carved with dovecotes or pigeon nests sandwiching green small gardens, Cappadocian villages like Uchisar and Ortahisar, and apricot trees so close that sometimes you can pick fruit as you go by. There are multiple ballooning companies in Cappadocia, but a reliably good selection is **Kapadokya Balloons** (90-384-271-2442; kapadokyaballoons.com).

ABOVE Weather and landscape make for good ballooning.

OPPOSITE The fairy chimneys and their basalt caps.

THE BASICS

Planes arrive at Kayseri from Istanbul; car rentals are available there. If you want to use guides, one reputable service is Argeus (90-384-341-4688; argeus.com.tr).

Serinn House
Esbelli Sokak 36, Urgup
90-384-341-6076
serinnhouse.com
$$
Chic six-room property offering cave rooms, glass-walled showers, and Wi-Fi.

Anatolian Houses
Gaferli Mah, Goreme
90-384-271-2463
anatolianhouses.com.tr
$$$$
Rooms with whirlpool tubs and Anatolian antiques. Several suites in the fairy chimneys.

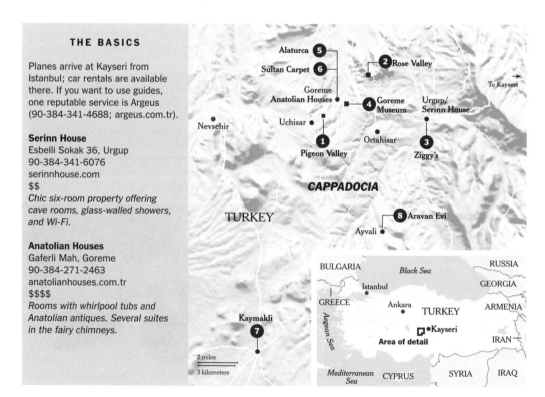

Tbilisi

The speck of Caucasian turf known as Georgia has survived invasions by Mongols, Persians, Turks, and Russians while keeping its language and culture intact. More than a quarter of its four million people live in their frenetically lively capital, Tbilisi, built along the steep banks of the Kura River (also called the Mtkvari) and encircled by snowcapped mountains. Some of its cobblestoned old streets are barely wide enough for a Mini Cooper, while skyscrapers, shopping malls, and new hotels have moved in on main avenues. Short hops lead to beautiful Black Sea shoreline and open-bowl skiing. Now that a new generation favors English over Russian as the second language of choice, it seems only a matter of time before Tbilisi becomes a tourist draw on par if not with Paris or Prague, then with St. Petersburg or Moscow. — BY LIONEL BEEHNER

FRIDAY

1 *Starter Walk* 3 p.m.

Begin at **Rose Revolution Square** (formerly Republic Square), near the Rustaveli metro stop and McDonald's, and take a stroll down **Rustaveli Avenue**, an elegant thoroughfare lined with trees, expensive perfume shops, and architectural oddities like a Moorish-style opera house. Ignore the drivers of taxis and marshrutkas (van-sized buses) leaning on their horns. The boulevard empties into **Freedom Square**, where the former City Hall and its clock tower provided a theatrical backdrop to the Rose Revolution of 2003. Stop in at the tourism office on the south side of the square for a free map. Then follow the street to Old Town, a cluster of buildings both shabby and refurbished, religious iconography shops burning incense, artisan studios, and sloping guesthouses with twisted chimneys and ornate flower-patterned balconies. Within a few blocks, you can light a candle in an Orthodox basilica, pray in a synagogue, or meet an imam at a mosque—a testament to Georgia's history of multi-faith hospitality.

2 *A Closer Look* 4 p.m.

Search the Old Town for sights and shops. Find hand-crafted cloisonné enamel jewelry as well as wall art at **Ornament** (7 King Erekle II Street; enamelart. ge). Shardeni Street is lined with inviting cafes and galleries. (To find work by contemporary Georgian artists, check online at facebook.com/tiflisavenue.) Inside the Georgian Orthodox **Sioni Cathedral**, an aged riverside church with a round tower, is a venerated relic, a cross made of grape vines entwined with the hair of St. Nino, a Cappadocian woman who brought Christianity to Georgia. Cross the Kura River on the fanciful **Bridge of Peace**, an undulating glass and steel footbridge designed by the Italian architect Michele De Lucchi.

3 *New Georgian* 8 p.m.

Have dinner in a peaceful garden in the summer or a cozy dining room in winter at **Café Littera** (13 Machabeli Street; 995-59-50-31-112; $$), tucked behind the Writers' House of Georgia, a leading cultural institution. Chef Tekuna Gachechiladze, who studied psychology in Germany and food in New York, is known for her "new Georgian" fusion cooking, for example, pairing badrijani (fried eggplant stuffed with walnut paste) with foie gras.

OPPOSITE Tbilisi, encircled by mountains, wraps itself around the steep banks of the Kura (or Mtkvari) River. This view is from the fortress hill of Narikala.

BELOW Traditional Georgian dress at a folk music festival. Tbilisi has a full schedule of cultural events.

4 *Vintage Soviet* 10 a.m.

Artists, craftsmen, junk dealers, collectors, and various opportunists spread out their goods on blankets at the sprawling **Mshrali Khidi (Dry Bridge) Flea Market** (Deda Ena Park), a Saturday morning institution. Look for ceramics, paintings, jewelry, embroidery, all kinds of vintage items, and — of special interest to Westerners — memorabilia of the Soviet era, including medals that the owners presum-

ABOVE Orthodox cathedral towers of Tbilisi.

BELOW Baths fed by Tbilisi's natural hot springs.

ably no longer cared to wear. (Flea market regulars will caution you to watch for fakes.) For lunch, walk back toward the Old Town and find one of the many cafes where you can order khinkali, Georgian dumplings embedded with spicy meat. Or drop in at 26 Leselidze Street, one of the outlets of **Machakhela** (995-322-102-119; $), a local chain specializing in khachapuri, a cheese pie, and other meat-filled pastries baked in a traditional wood-fired oven.

5 *Fortress View* 2 p.m.

Mother Georgia, which overlooks the city much as *Christ the Redeemer* gazes down on Rio de Janeiro, was erected in 1958, Tbilisi's 1500th anniversary. For nice views of the huge statue, take the steep hike up the hill to **Narikala**, a 17th-century fortress. Not much remains but for a church and some ruins, but the view is commanding, and it's adjacent to a **botanical garden** that was originally a royal project in the 1600s.

6 *Into the Sulfur* 5 p.m.

Tbilisi is named for its natural hot springs ("tbili" means "warm"), and about a half-dozen underground blue-marble-tiled banyas can be found at the base of the Narikala hill, identifiable by the sweet smell of sulfur and their beehive domes. They were favorite resting spots of Pushkin and Alexander Dumas. It's a long way from a luxury spa, but it's relaxing and inexpensive. Try the elaborately tiled **Orbeliani Baths** or the **Royal Baths**, where you can rent a private room.

7 *Fare That Sizzles* 8 p.m.

If you are not invited to a supra — a multi-course meal of endless rounds of drinking, toasting, and dancing — with Georgian friends, then make your way along the river to **Puris Sakhli**, or the Bread House (7 Gorgasali Street; 995-322-303-030; mgroup.ge; $$$), where you can sample locally expensive Georgian cuisine and watch your cuts of lamb deep-smoked in outdoor pits.

8 *Wine of the Ancients* 10 p.m.

Irakli Abashidze Street, a fashionable tree-lined thoroughfare, bustles with upscale wine bars and restaurants, some featuring live jazz. Seek one out, ask for some expert advice, and sample Georgian wines. Georgia has 500 traditional varieties of wine grapes, and everyone here firmly believes that it was

the first place in the world where wine was made. The National Museum of Georgia cites archaeological evidence suggesting that winemaking here may go back 8,000 years, and local connoisseurs cite references to the region's wines in the works of Homer and Apollonius. In the Soviet period, old vines were torn out and clueless managers added sugar and alcohol to the mix, but since then the vintners have revived their ancient craft.

TOP Elegant Rustaveli Avenue is lined with tall trees and fine old buildings that hold expensive shops.

ABOVE Grape stomping at a Tbilisi festival. Georgians have made wine for thousands of years.

SUNDAY

9 *Tempest Teapot* 10 a.m.

For coffee, pastry, and a large selection of teas—plus books in English—take the metro to the Rustaveli stop and walk to **Prospero's Bookstore and Caliban's Coffeehouse**, 34 Rustaveli Avenue; 995-322-923-592; prosperosbookshop.com). If some things about Georgia seem a bit puzzling, this is a good place to get tips and answers from English-speaking expats.

10 *Old Gold* 11 a.m.

The **Simon Janashia Museum of Georgia** (3 Rustaveli Avenue; 995-322-997-176; museum.ge) tells the story of the people of the Caucasus region far back into prehistory. A large and unusual collection of ancient jewelry and other objects crafted in gold comes from archaeological finds dating to well before the Christian era. Even more impressive are fossils of Homo erectus georgicus, a relative of modern humans who lived 1.8 million years ago.

ABOVE Puris Sakhli, or the House of Bread, serves classic Georgian food, including lamb dishes.

OPPOSITE Bread baking over the flames of a traditional clay oven at Puris Sakhli.

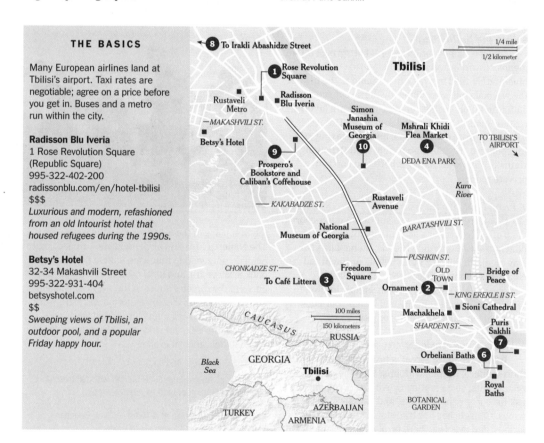

THE BASICS

Many European airlines land at Tbilisi's airport. Taxi rates are negotiable; agree on a price before you get in. Buses and a metro run within the city.

Radisson Blu Iveria
1 Rose Revolution Square
(Republic Square)
995-322-402-200
radissonblu.com/en/hotel-tbilisi
$$$
Luxurious and modern, refashioned from an old Intourist hotel that housed refugees during the 1990s.

Betsy's Hotel
32-34 Makashvili Street
995-322-931-404
betsyshotel.com
$$
Sweeping views of Tbilisi, an outdoor pool, and a popular Friday happy hour.

NORTHERN

Oslo 602

STOCKHOLM 584

Reykjavik
608

Goteborg
598

594

Lund & the
Swedish Riviera

Gotland
& Faro
590

COPENHAGEN
612

Turku 622

HELSINKI 616

St. Petersburg's White Nights 648

tallinn 626

St. Petersburg in Winter 654

Riga 632

MOSCOW 642

Vilnius 638

Stockholm

Stockholmers revel in the long days of summer, when the sun rises as early as 3:30 a.m. and doesn't set until after 10 p.m. Many depart for their country houses, but those who remain spend as much time as possible outdoors — easy enough, since water and parkland make up almost two-thirds of the city. Situated on the Baltic at the mouth of Lake Malaren, Stockholm is built on 14 islands connected by bridges. On sunny days, waterside bars and cafes are packed with people tucking into summer favorites like herring (served in a variety of ways) and toast Skagen (shrimp in mayonnaise with lemon and dill served on bread). Everywhere, visitors will find establishments, new and venerable, celebrating Nordic design, cuisine, and culture. — BY STEPHEN WHITLOCK

FRIDAY

1 *Walk in a Circle* 4 p.m.

Get your bearings and work up an appetite with a bracing five-mile walk that loops around Riddarfjarden, Stockholm's main body of water. Start at Stadshuset, the City Hall, where each year's Nobel laureates join Swedish royalty at the Nobel Banquet, and cross to Riddarholmen, visiting the church where generations of Sweden's monarchs are interred. Carry on to Sodermalm, the large southern island, taking beautiful cobbled Bastugatan. Fortify yourself at **Kaffebar** (Hornsgatan 78; 46-76-875-2992), one of the city's best coffee bars (and the old haunt of Stieg Larsson, author of the Lisbeth Salander novels). Continue over the high bridge called Vasterbron, which offers amazing views, and then descend to return to the island of Kungsholmen. Reward your-self with waterside drinks at **Malarpaviljongen** (Norr Malarstrand 64; 46-8-650-8701; malarpaviljongen.se), an open-air cafe-lounge with three floating decks, one of Stockholm's most popular summer hangouts.

2 *Local Heroes* 7:30 p.m.

Stockholmers often seem to take a magpie approach to food, importing their favorite trends from abroad. Fortunately, there are several places that are committed to serving locally sourced food that takes Swedish cuisine to the next level. One of the most enjoyable is **Restaurang Volt** (Kommendorsgatan 16; 46-8-662-3400; restaurangvolt.se; $$$$). Opened by four young men who have worked at many of Sweden's top restaurants, the small space includes just one sparsely furnished room — all the excitement is on the plate. You can order à la carte, but it's far better to opt for the three-, five-, or seven-course menu, featuring dishes like rabbit with carrots and dandelion, or, for dessert, fennel with white chocolate and licorice.

3 *Straight Up* 10 p.m.

There are a couple of places where you can get a drink with a panoramic view of the city. **Gondolen** (Stadsgarden 6; 46-8-641-7090; eriks.se) is part of a viewing platform on the edge of the Sodermalm neighborhood, which overlooks the Old Town (Gamla Stan) and harbor. For even more dramatic views, visit **Och Himlen Dartill** (Gotgatan 78; 46-8-660-6068; www.restauranghimlen.se), a bar and restaurant atop a Sodermalm skyscraper.

SATURDAY

4 *Story Time* 11 a.m.

When it comes to iconic Swedish writers, not even Stieg Larsson can match Astrid Lindgren, the creator of Pippi Longstocking. **Junibacken** (Galarvarvsvägen; 46-8-5872-3000; junibacken.se) is a sort of indoor amusement park where you can

OPPOSITE Stadshuset, Stockholm's City Hall.

RIGHT Stylish lighting at the Nobis hotel.

visit Pippi's house and take the Storybook Train, which will carry you through a series of tableaux drawn from Lindgren's books. Even for an adult with no knowledge of Lindgren's work, it's great fun; for children, it's thrilling. Afterward go for a rhubarb tart or a slice of mango-cardamom cheesecake at nearby **Helin & Voltaire** (Rosendalsvagen 14; 46-8-664-5108; helinvoltaire.com), a cafe that looks as if it came straight out of a fairy tale.

5 *Island Lunch* 1:30 p.m.

Any visit to Stockholm should include an exploration of one or more of the thousands of islands that make up the Stockholm Archipelago. It takes several hours' sailing to reach the heart of the

archipelago, but you can get a quick fix by taking a ferry to Fjaderholmarna, a group of islands just 20 minutes from downtown. Book ahead for lunch on the deck beside the water at **Fjaderholmarnas Krog** (46-8-718-3355; fjaderholmarnaskrog.se; $$$$). The midsummer menu includes plenty of herring, dill-smoked salmon, and oysters.

6 *Main Street* 3 p.m.

On Hamngatan, one of the city's main shopping streets, two retail titans are squaring off, and national pride is at stake: on one side stands **NK** (Hamngatan 18-20; 46-8-762-8000; nk.se), the venerable Swedish department store that opened in 1902. Almost directly opposite is the challenger, the Danish design store **Illums Bolighus** (Hamngatan 27; 46-8-718-5500; illumsbolighus.dk), first established in Copenhagen in 1925. NK has the edge in food and fashion, but when it comes to cool Scandinavian design, Illums is

ABOVE NK, the venerable Swedish department store. Many shoppers in Stockholm seek out cool Scandinavian design in furniture and all sorts of home décor.

LEFT Riche, a restaurant-bar open since 1893, attracts an affluent, sometimes glamorous crowd.

OPPOSITE Fotografiska, in a former tollhouse, is worth visiting just for the views from the top-floor cafe.

unbeatable. Here you will find pieces by all the big names of Danish design—Finn Juhl, Hans Wegner, Verner Panton—as well as international brands at all prices.

7 *Nordic by Nature* 4 p.m.

Book a treatment at the **Nordic Spa & Fitness** inside the **Grand Hôtel** (Sodra Blasieholmshamnen 8; 46-8-679-3575; grandhotel.se), the landmark 19th-century hotel where Nobel laureates stay when they come to receive their awards. The spa feels thoroughly Nordic, with blocks of granite underfoot in the shower and murals with pixilated views of the archipelago. Of course, treatments include classic Swedish massage.

8 *Animal Instinct* 5:30 p.m.

The Old Town, in the heart of the city, has no end of restaurants targeting tourists; it also has some of the best places to eat. **Djuret** (Lilla Nygatan 5; 46-8-5064-0084; djuret.se; $$$$), whose name means "the animal," offers a meat-heavy menu that focuses on one meat-and-wine pairing at a time: lamb with Bordeaux, for instance, or veal with Barolo and Barbaresco. In summer, Djuret closes the main restaurant for two months and instead offers a top-notch pork barbecue in the courtyard behind the building, weather permitting. Its name? Svinet, which means "the pig." No reservations, so arrive soon after it opens at 5 p.m.

9 *Vintage Drinks* 10 p.m.

The restaurant-bar **Riche** (Birger Jarlsgatan 4; 46-8-5450-3560; riche.se) has been going strong since 1893 and attracts a glamorous, affluent crowd. You'll most likely hear more Champagne bottles being popped open here than anywhere else in town. If the crush is too much, cross the road to **KB** (Smalandsgatan 7; 46-8-679-6032; konstnarsbaren.se), a classic Stockholm restaurant that has a charming

bar with murals dating from the 1930s of ale-swilling Vikings and tipsy monks sipping Chartreuse.

SUNDAY

10 *The Art of Brunch* 11:30 a.m.

Stockholm can be a sleepy town on a Sunday, and few restaurants serve brunch. The restaurant at the **Moderna Museet** (Skeppsholmen; 46-8-5202-3660; modernamuseet.se) has a lavish weekend buffet brunch serving Asian, African, American, and European dishes ($$$) between 11 a.m. and 4:30 p.m. Reservations are required. If you don't have a brunch reservation, visit the cafe and enjoy a simpler meal alfresco on the large terrace.

11 *Picture Perfect* 1 p.m.

Fotografiska (Stadsgardshamnen 22; 46-8-5090-0500; fotografiska.eu), in a former tollhouse on the quayside of Sodermalm, has photographic exhibitions of varying quality, but it's worth visiting the top-floor cafe to gaze out its enormous windows overlooking the Old Town. The view is so spectacular that even if you don't like the photos on the gallery walls you're bound to end up snapping a few yourself.

ABOVE Malarpaviljongen, a cafe-lounge with three floating decks, is one of Stockholm's most popular summer hangouts.

OPPOSITE A quiet, cobbled street in the old town.

THE BASICS

Trams, subways, and buses take visitors around the city and across its many bridges. Ferries cross to outer islands.

Nobis
Norrmalmstorg 2-4
46-8-614-1000
nobishotel.se
$$$
Great service, a perfect location, and rooms that manage to be stylish without sacrificing comfort.

The Rival
Mariatorget 3
46-8-5457-8900
rival.se
$$
A project of Benny Andersson of Abba. Movie stills on guestroom walls range from Garbo in Queen Christina *to, of course, Abba:* The Movie.

Map labels:
1/2 mile
1 kilometer

Stockholm

Restaurang Volt **2**
HUMLEGARDEN
KOMMENDORSGATAN
Nobis
KB
9 Riche
NK **6**
NARVAVAGEN
OSTERMALM
Illums Bolighus
Central Station
HAMNGATAN
STRANDVAGEN
KUNGSHOLMEN
Malarpaviljongen
Nordic Spa & Fitness/ Grand Hôtel **7**
SKEPPS-HOLMEN
4 Junibacken
Stadshuset
Helin & Voltaire
VASTERBRON
Djuret **8**
RIDDARHOLMEN
10
DJURGARDEN
Riddarfjarden
Moderna Museet
LANGHOLMEN
Kaffebar **1**
Gondolen **3**
Fjaderholmarnas Krog **5**
HORNSGATAN
The Rival
SODERLEDEN
GOTGATAN
11 Fotografiska
NORWAY
FINLAND
Lake Malaren
SODERMALM
BONDEGATAN
Och Himlen Dartill
RINGVAGEN
Skagerrak
Stockholm
SWEDEN
DENMARK
Baltic Sea

Gotland & Faro

Gotland, the largest island in the Baltic Sea, lies about 60 miles off the southeastern coast of mainland Sweden and has a year-round population of less than 60,000. Outside of its only sizable town—the protected medieval city of Visby—an idyllic landscape unfolds, dotted with rustic cottages and rural farmhouses. Not so long ago, Gotland was a placid place even in summer, attracting vacationers prone to bike trips and cobblestone strolls. Now those travelers have been joined by an exuberant young crowd that fills nightclubs in Visby and fuels a freewheeling "after beach" scene. The rest of Gotland—along with the tiny neighboring island of Faro—has caught the eye of well-heeled Stockholmers who buy summer houses or unwind at expensive small hotels. Fortunately, Gotland is large enough to please everyone. — BY INGRID K. WILLIAMS

FRIDAY

1 *Afternoon Exploration* 3 p.m.

You could fly to Gotland, but arriving by ferry lets you watch the intimidating watchtowers and steep tile roofs of Visby emerge from the horizon. Inside the two-mile-long city wall that rings Visby, the cobblestone streetscape demands exploring. Spend some time poking into shops and venturing down alleyways where the stone walls are softened by climbing roses. After your orientation stroll, check out **Kallbadhuset** beach club (Strandvagen; no phone; kallisvisby.se) overlooking the sapphire sea right next to Gotland University. The open-air lounge is packed with young city dwellers who take the 35-minute flight from Stockholm in search of sun, sand, throbbing music, alcohol, and each other. First drawn by an annual weeklong, Champagne-soaked dance party called Stockholmsveckan, the revelers now come and go all summer.

2 *Pleasures of the Sea* 7:30 p.m.

After taking in the hedonistic scene, rent a bicycle from **Gotlands Cykeluthyrning** (Skeppsbron 2;

OPPOSITE The medieval wall of Visby, a city that mixes cobblestone charm with a throbbing club scene.

RIGHT Faro, a fishing island gone upscale, is best known as a setting for films by Ingmar Bergman.

46-498-21-41-33; gotlandscykeluthyrning.com) and pedal along the shore outside Visby's walls to more peaceful environs. But don't overdress. A warm sea current makes Gotland much warmer than its northern latitude would suggest. Time your return ride to coincide with the sunset: a glowing orb slowly sinking into the water over the horizon. Back in town, **Bakfickan** (Stora Torget 1; 46-498-27-18-07; bakfickanvisby.se; $$-$$$) serves the best seafood in a simple, casual setting. This is a popular place, so make a reservation well in advance.

3 *The Party Crowd* 11 p.m.

To sample the twilight version of the youthful party scene, check out the string of clubs on Stora Torget and the bars along Sodra Kyrkogatan; two of the most popular are **Gutekallaren** (Lilla Torggrand 3; 46-498-210-043; gutekallaren.com) and **Munkkallaren** (Sankt Hansgatan 40; 46-498-27-14-00; munkkallaren. se). If you prefer a less frenetic dusk, this can be a magical time to see the ruins of St. Nicholas Church (St. Nicolaigatan), which was largely destroyed by German invaders in 1525 and was never rebuilt. On many summer evenings it becomes a memorable stage for plays or chamber music.

SATURDAY

4 *Sheep Two Ways* 10 a.m.

Drive into the haunting beauty of the Gotland countryside. The ribbon of road unfurls across a flat green landscape. There are no billboards, no guardrails, just country churches and the occasional

squat old windmill or sleek modern wind turbine twirling slowly. You'll also pass grazing herds of the indigenous gray, curly-haired sheep that Gotland is known for. To take home some of the ultra-soft lambskin stop at **Risungs Gard** (Rute; 46-498-22-33-85; risungsgard.com), a boutique that sells products from its adjacent working farm. Here, the lambskins get second lives as pillows, slippers, and rugs — and all at prices far lower than in Visby.

5 *Lunch With a View* Noon

Down a desolate stretch of dirt road on the northern tip of Gotland sits the top-notch restaurant (and tranquil small luxury hotel) **Farosunds Fastning** (Farosund; 46-498-22-10-22; farosundsfastning.com). The long, low, almost bunkerlike complex is situated in a converted stone fortress with views across the water to Faro, a 10-minute ferry ride away. Enjoy the surroundings while feasting on an artfully prepared lunch of Swedish summertime classics, like gravad lax with a creamy side salad of new potatoes, on the deck.

6 *Enigmatic Spin* 2:30 p.m.

Head southeast and cross an isthmus that leads to the islet Furillen and **Fabriken Furillen** (Larbro; 46-498-22-30-40; www.furillen.com), a luxury hotel at the site of a former limestone factory. It is a mystifying, postapocalyptic dreamscape cluttered with incongruous objects: a shiny silver camper parked at the base of a high mound of stones, a rusted crane hanging motionless at the end of a cement pier, old railroad ties leading to the door of a small wooden

house. Poke around the sprawling property — the hotel has bicycles available — and afterward ponder your findings over a coffee or local Wisby pils beer at the hotel's afternoon fika session.

7 *Cool Fire* 5 p.m.

Continue driving south along Gotland's east coast to **Narsholmen**, a nature reserve on a sandy peninsula. A dusty road plunges through a scene like a savannah to the edge of a rocky coast emblazoned by waves of indigo wildflowers, fittingly called blaeld, or blue fire. Hike to the red-and-white lighthouse, and see if you can resist taking a picture.

8 *Peace of the Beach* 6:30 p.m.

A few miles back toward the north, in the small town of **Ljugarn**, the beach is a snapshot of calm, untrammeled nature: a long stretch of fine sand fringed by tall grass and cold, clear water lapping gently at the shore. This was a seaside resort around the turn of the last century, favored by the Swedish royal family. Only a few of the old structures are still standing, but this is a good place for a beach walk.

9 *Gotland Gourmet* 8 p.m.

Taste the very best of Gotland, from lamb to seasonal white asparagus, at **Krakas Krog** (Kraklings 223, Katthammarsvik; 46-498-530-62; krakas.se; $$$-$$$$), an elegant restaurant in the countryside with exceedingly warm, friendly service. The sophisticated fare is made with ingredients sourced from local producers, often including vegetables and herbs from the restaurant's own garden. The extensive wine list is also excellent.

SUNDAY

10 *Bergman's Island* 10 a.m.

At Farosund on the northern tip of Gotland, board the ferry that crosses to the sparsely populated island of Faro. Head first to **Langhammers** beach to see the most impressive raukar, odd limestone formations found along the coasts of Gotland and Faro. Molded by erosion over millenniums, the strangely shaped, hulking gray stones contribute to the spooky, dramatically cinematic landscapes that

inspired the director Ingmar Bergman, who lived and filmed on Faro. It's easy to imagine Bergman's famous image of Death personified lurking behind one of the eerie stones.

11 *Full-Service Crepes* 12:30 p.m.

For a strange scene of a different sort, check out **Kutens Bensin** (Broskogs; 46-498-22-68-18; kuten.se). On the surface, it's a run-down old gas station surrounded by a graveyard of vintage cars and other rusted curios. But by day, it's actually a creperie, called Creperie Tati, serving delicious crepes. Patrons dine in two rooms packed with memorabilia from the 1950s and 1960s and at tables in the grassy front and back yards. At night, it

serves as a bar (likely the only one on the island) with live rockabilly music or old Elvis tunes playing, and chrome car parts adorning the walls.

OPPOSITE Cycling on the island of Faro. Gotland and Faro, islands that were once isolated, now attract affluent Stockholmers looking for summer homes and quiet hotels.

ABOVE Hotel umbrellas near one of Gotland's nature reserves. The reserves protect untrammeled seaside landscapes.

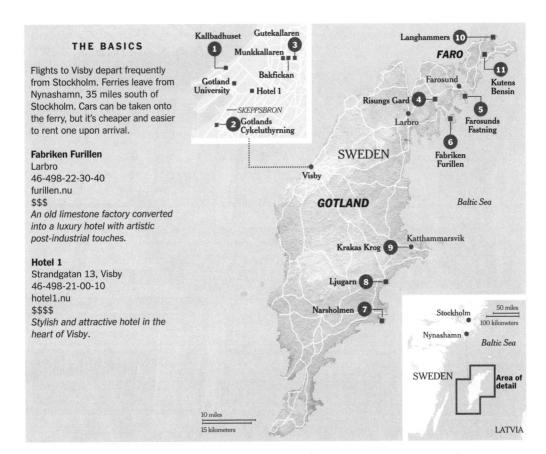

THE BASICS

Flights to Visby depart frequently from Stockholm. Ferries leave from Nynashamn, 35 miles south of Stockholm. Cars can be taken onto the ferry, but it's cheaper and easier to rent one upon arrival.

Fabriken Furillen
Larbro
46-498-22-30-40
furillen.nu
$$$
An old limestone factory converted into a luxury hotel with artistic post-industrial touches.

Hotel 1
Strandgatan 13, Visby
46-498-21-00-10
hotel1.nu
$$$$
Stylish and attractive hotel in the heart of Visby.

Kallbadhuset   Gutekallaren
1   Munkkallaren   **3**
Bakfickan
Gotland   ■ Hotel 1
University
—SKEPPSBRON
2 Gotlands
Cykeluthyrning

Langhammars **10** ■
FARO
11
Farosund   Kutens
Bensin
Risungs Gard **4**
Larbro   Farosunds
Fastning
6
SWEDEN   Fabriken
Furillen
Visby
GOTLAND   *Baltic Sea*

Katthammarsvik
Krakas Krog **9** ●

Ljugarn **8** ■

Narsholmen **7** ■

Stockholm ●   50 miles
100 kilometers
Nynashamn ●
Baltic Sea

SWEDEN   Area of detail

10 miles
15 kilometers

LATVIA

Lund & the Swedish Riviera

With its cobblestone streets, vibrant intellectual community, and relaxed ambience, Lund, in Sweden's southernmost county, Skane (pronounced SKOH-nah), is an archetypal college town, surrounded by farmland and rolling fields. It is also just a few miles inland from the summer playground unofficially known as the Swedish Riviera. A country with a considerable chunk of its real estate above the Arctic Circle may not suggest miles of white sand baking in the sun, but in the long days of the Nordic summer, Skane's seashore provides just that. The whole region was once part of Denmark, and Copenhagen is less than 40 minutes from Lund by way of the rail and highway bridge over the Oresund strait. Once you've explored Lund, it's another easy reach to some of Sweden's loveliest beach towns. — BY RUSS JUSKALIAN AND ANDREW FERREN

FRIDAY

1 *Stone Giants* 3 p.m.

To find Lund's most prominent building, the 12th-century Romanesque-style Lund Cathedral, or **Domkyrkan** (46-46-35-87-00; lundsdomkyrka.org), all you have to do is walk toward its 180-foot towers. Inside is a magnificent astronomical clock, standing over 20 feet tall and built before Christopher Columbus was born, that charts the positions of the sun, the moon, and other celestial bodies. In the dark medieval crypt, a granite statue of the bearded giant Finn wraps its arms around a support column. Legend says that Finn challenged the man overseeing the construction of the cathedral to guess his name before the job was finished. If he couldn't, Finn said, "you will owe me your eyes." Luckily, one day the man overheard the giant's wife calling him by name. Finn, enraged by the way things turned out, grabbed a pillar to pull down the building and was immediately turned to stone.

2 *Spiral Up* 4 p.m.

Students are everywhere in Lund — 30,000 of them study at Lund University, founded in 1666 — so you may as well visit their leafy habitat, with its paths shaded by stately chestnut trees. Campus buildings, like the majestic university library, are built of brick and stone, and you can stop at two art museums, the **Museum of Sketches** (Finngatan 2; www.adk.lu.se) and the **Konsthall** (Martenstorget 3;

46-46-35-52-95; lundskonsthall.se). Spare a few minutes to peek inside the **Kungshuset**, or King's House (on the northeast end of Lundagard Park), a looming brick building with a circular tower and fantastic oak spiral staircase. Frederick II, a 16th-century Danish king, built the Kungshuset for the bishop of Lund. It is now home to the university's philosophy department.

3 *Evening Shade* 6:30 p.m.

There are hours of daylight left, so as you stroll in the 20-acre **Botanical Garden** (Ostra Vallgatan 20; 46-46-222-73-20; botaniskatradgarden.se), you may be happy to find a quiet slice of shade. Others will have the same idea — young families having picnics and students lounging on blankets. But this is more than a quiet park. A resource for university botanists, it contains thousands of kinds of plants, including hundreds in greenhouses divided into seven climate zones.

4 *Nouveau Bistro* 8 p.m.

The **Grand Hotel Lund** first opened in 1899. Its castlelike building, designed by the prominent

OPPOSITE Blue sky over Lund, a sun-kissed college town.

BELOW Old streets in Lund are virtually free of cars.

19th-century Swedish architect Alfred Hellerstrom, still retains some of its original Art Nouveau style. Its first-floor bistro, **Gambrinus** (Bantorget 1; 46-46-280-6100; grandilund.com; $$$), offers food and drinks in a relaxed atmosphere. The restaurant features locally produced and organic ingredients in menu items like pickled herring, Skane ham, and fish from nearby waters.

SATURDAY

5 *Thank Forkbeard* 10 a.m.

Explore **Adelgatan**, **Tomegapsgatan**, and the smaller streets on the east side of town. Here, the old roads are narrow and almost completely free of cars; roses and other flowering plants frame 18th-century homes. You will see plenty of bikes. Nearly half of Lund's 83,000 residents are bicycle commuters, and the city has lighted paths and even a multistory bike parking garage. If you talk to a local — and you will, since everyone from the aproned woman behind the bakery counter to the spiky-haired philosophy student is eager to explain the town's history in flawless English — you'll hear that Lund was founded (in 990) by the Viking Sweyn Forkbeard, who by some accounts also founded Copenhagen.

6 *The Sausage Faction* Noon

If you talk to a local butcher, you'll get a different history: Lund was built on sausage, sometime around 1960. That sausage is lundaknake, a pungent pork and beef knackwurst made only here. The story goes that when industry was blossoming in the mid-20th century, owners and laborers alike more or less survived on the stuff, which has a gamey, smoked flavor and makes an audible snap when you bite into it. At the food market, **Saluhallen** (Martenstorget 1; lundssaluhall.se), you can try lundaknake—warm, plain, and wrapped in paper for a proper grip. Have

ABOVE A beach on the Falsterbo peninsula.

some strong-flavored local cheese, too, with rye knackebrod, a hard flatbread. For a sit-down lunch at one of the restaurants in the market, try to get a table at the often-crowded **Terrin & Vin** (46-70-275-75-11). The menu is short and limited by what ingredients can be found fresh at the market. Expect offerings like salmon soup, lamb cutlets, and dishes incorporating wild boar.

7 *Skulls in the Shire* 1 p.m.

Even those who have grown weary of museum visits will enjoy **Kulturen** (Tegnersplatsen; 46-46-35-04-01; kulturen.com), billed as the second-oldest open-air museum in the world. Once beyond the main building, with its ominously arranged skulls from Lund's violent periods, there are more than two dozen constructions set on a few green acres in a sort of chronological mash-up of traditional rural life. The cluster of peasants' homes in particular—built of wide planks covered in moss and tall grass, and with doorways low enough that a modern human needs to bow to enter—are a sort of a real-world version of the Shire, minus the Hobbits.

8 *On to Falsterbo* 4 p.m.

The **Falsterbo** peninsula is Sweden's gloriously balmy far southwestern corner, a hooked sandy spit with miles of gorgeous beach, seaside golf courses, and prime spots for birding. The town of Falsterbo and its adjoining neighbor, Skanor, take up much of the peninsula and are top contenders for the "Swedish Hamptons" title. You could rent a car to get there from Lund, but there's no need to. The trip by train and bus takes only an hour and a quarter.

9 *Viking Chic* 6 p.m.

Towns farther east on Sweden's southern coast can be congested, with rocky coast and the Swedish version of beach honky-tonk. But **Skanor** and Falsterbo are quite simply what beaches and beach towns are supposed to be. The tree-shaded lanes have just the right mix of lively cafes, art galleries, and ice cream parlors, perfect for a predinner walk. With their steeply pitched roofs and eyebrow dormer windows, the unpretentious 18th-century houses look like descendants of the traditional Viking longhouses. Fully rigged model schooners and clipper ships can be seen in many parlor windows. Once important links to the Danish market for herring, today these idyllic towns sell understated Swedish chic to summer visitors.

10 *Lingering Sun* 8 p.m.

For dinner, stop in at one of the cafes or at **Skanors Fiskrogeri** (Skanors Hamn; 46-40-47-40-50; rogeriet.se; $$$), a harborside spot for smoked fish and other Skane dishes. Linger a while, and when you emerge, dusk may finally be approaching. Head toward the sea to watch the tranquil transition to the Swedish summer night, when darkness is a long time coming.

SUNDAY

11 *Full Sun* 10 a.m.

Time to get into the water. The miles of broad white sand beaches on the Falsterbo peninsula are dotted with tiny pastel-painted beach huts, holdovers from the days when changing clothes in public was a punishable offense. The gentle slope of the beach means you can walk "almost over to Copenhagen without getting your hair wet," one local resident said.

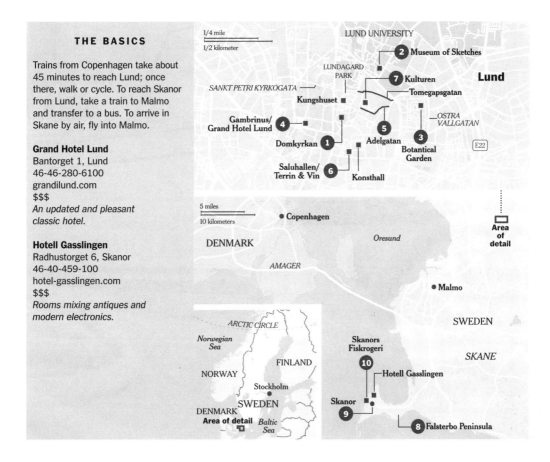

THE BASICS

Trains from Copenhagen take about 45 minutes to reach Lund; once there, walk or cycle. To reach Skanor from Lund, take a train to Malmo and transfer to a bus. To arrive in Skane by air, fly into Malmo.

Grand Hotel Lund
Bantorget 1, Lund
46-46-280-6100
grandilund.com
$$$
An updated and pleasant classic hotel.

Hotell Gasslingen
Radhustorget 6, Skanor
46-40-459-100
hotel-gasslingen.com
$$$
Rooms mixing antiques and modern electronics.

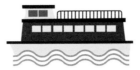

Goteborg

Like its big sister Stockholm, Goteborg, Sweden's second city, is as much about boats and water as it is about bricks and mortar. Built on the broad estuary of the Gota River, greater Goteborg stretches for miles before fanning out into the North Sea across an archipelago of some 1,000 islands. This is a young city by European standards, founded in 1621 when King Gustav II Adolf, looking to keep the Danes away from the Swedish coast, hired Dutch engineers to put a fortified town on the marshy riverbank. The Baroque old city remains, inside a later city built on trade and industry and spreading out to include the headquarters of Volvo and Hasselblad. Today's Goteborg (often called Gothenburg by English speakers) has added contemporary art and fashion, Swedish Modern antique shopping, and notable gastronomy: several of its restaurants rate stars in the Michelin Guide.
— BY ANDREW FERREN

FRIDAY

1 *Poseidon's Hilltop* 3 p.m.

When the old city walls came down in the 19th century, replaced by the verdant curving park called the Kungsparken, a grandiose new city spread out to the south. To catch its spirit, look no farther than the broodingly massive **Goteborg Konstmuseum** (Gotaplatsen; 46-31-368-35-00; konstmuseum.goteborg.se), built in 1923 and set prominently on the crown of a hill. Its grand plaza has theaters for concerts and the ballet and a colossal yet oddly spritelike bronze Poseidon gazing down to the harbor. The museum has a superb collection, from Impressionists to 20th-century Scandinavian masters whose work can seem like a revelation to visitors who have never seen it before.

2 *Dinner Discovery* 7 p.m.

Few travelers come to Sweden for the food, but more places like the cozy Michelin-starred **28+** (Gotabergsgatan 28; 46-31-20-21-61; 28plus.se; $$$$)

OPPOSITE Boats are a big part of life in Goteborg, a town founded as a North Sea fortress.

RIGHT The moat, now a waterway for tour boats, borders the oldest part of Goteborg, built in the 1600s.

could change that. Although it dates to 1985, 28+ seems fresh and of the moment with its focus on seasonal, local and mostly organic ingredients. You'll notice that a lot of Swedes dine here, some dressed more casually than the tourist patrons. The service is relaxed but professional, and waiters are happy to explain the menu, which may have as few as four starters and four main courses. Though servings can seem small, dishes like beef tartar with caviar and foie gras with pork cheek give the lie to any idea that Swedish dining involves deprivation, as do the extensive wine list and the well-chosen wine pairings for the two tasting menus.

3 *A Stylish Sip* 9 p.m.

For drinks in an urbane setting, try the cocktail lounge at **Locatelli** (Kungsportsavenyn 36-38; 46-31-727-1089; locatelligoteburg.se), a chic, lively Italian restaurant in the Elite Park Avenue Hotel. Have one of the vodka drinks made with homemade juices and observe the stylish Swedes who meet over them.

SATURDAY

4 *On the Avenyn* 9 a.m.

The main boulevard crossing the middle of the city and the Kungspark is the grand Kungsportsavenyn, better known as the Avenyn, and it is the axis on which most of Goteborg's prominent shops and restaurants, not to mention theaters and nightclubs, can be found. Take an easy, pleasant walk from the art museum, at one end, across the park to the wedding-cake-like Stora Theater, and into the old

city. For shopping, detour to flagship stores for two wildly successful Goteborg-based streetwear fashion brands, **Nudie Jeans** (Vallgatan 15; 46-31-609-360; nudiejeans.com) and **Velour** (Magasinsgatan 19; 46-31-701-0080; velour.se). Long winters seem to have made the Swedes excellent nest featherers, and you'll find some of their well-designed home décor at two retail outlets that have stood the test of time: the century-old **Josephssons** (Korsgatan 12; 46-31-17-56-15; josephssons.se) and **NK** (Ostra Hamngatan 42; 46-31-710-1000; nk.se), Sweden's venerable department store.

5 *Urban Evolution* 11 a.m.

Luxury retail is nothing new in Goteborg: for 80 years until 1810, the East India Company had 36 clipper ships making the trip to East Asia and returning here with porcelains, silks, and spices. The company's former headquarters on the central canal is now the **Goteborg Stadsmuseum** (Norra Hamngatan 12; 46-31-368-3600; goteborgsstadsmuseum.se). Stop in for a quick overview of local history from the Vikings to Sweden's neutrality during World War II.

6 *Inside the Moat* 12:30 p.m.

Join the locals at the central city market, the **Stora Saluhallen** (Kungstorget), a large indoor hall with stalls selling all the ingredients Swedish foodies need to lay a good table: fresh meat, fish, vegetables, cheeses, produce, baked goods, and more. For lunch, belly up to one of the counters selling prepared food at bargain prices, and then find a place to

sit and enjoy it. One midday visitor scored a plate of baseball-size Swedish meatballs in rich brown gravy with the standard boiled potatoes, lingonberry preserves, and green salad. Expect to share the market-stall ambience with business types, shoppers, and students—Goteborg's large university and smaller technical institute together have about 30,000 students. The market sits just inside the old city, which is bordered by the Kungsparken and the pretty Dutch-built moat.

7 *Swedish Modern* 2 p.m.

If you're looking for the vintage version of Swedish design, head to Haga, the city's oldest suburb, where the rows of beautifully restored 17th-century wooden houses now shelter cozy cafes and antiques stores. Look for the colorful and graphic 1950s and '60s Swedish ceramics—teapots, chafing dishes, casseroles—that are hugely popular among Japanese collectors. Find 20th-century furniture at **Bebop Antik** (Kaponjargatan 4; 46-31-13-91-63; bebop.se). For something contemporary, pop in at **Mors Mossa** (Husargatan 11; 46-31-13-22-82), a well-curated commercial art gallery.

8 *Goteborg Bohemia* 5 p.m.

Drift west to the **Langgatan**, or Long Streets, for a younger, more adventurous scene of galleries and artists' studios, junk shops, recording labs, and record stores. Late at night teenagers and 20-somethings flow into some of these streets, notably **Andra Langgatan**, as shuttered storefronts open to become the kinds of clubs where indie bands get their start. In the daytime, hit the cafes and do some people-watching.

9 *Surf and Turf* 8 p.m.

Sjomagasinet (Adolf Edelsvards Gata 5; 46-31-775-5920; sjomagasinet.se; $$$$) was already a renowned Goteborg institution, regarded as one of the world's great seafood restaurants, before

LEFT Get around Goteborg with a City Card, which covers trams, buses, archipelago boats, and museums.

OPPOSITE See what the Swedish foodies are buying, and buy your own lunch, at Stora Saluhallen, the city market.

it was taken over by Ulf Wagner, a Goteborg chef with a history of earning Michelin stars. Suitably located in a former East India Company Warehouse on the harbor, Sjomagasinet mixes seafood with ingredients from terra firma in dishes like cod with ox marrow jus and duck liver or sashimi of elk calf filet with bleak roe and crayfish mayonnaise.

SUNDAY

10 *The Ferry or the Fish Church* 10 a.m.

While most of the 1,000 islands of the Goteborg archipelago are no more than bare rocks that turn into popular perches for sunbathing Swedes in the heat of summer, others have small villages and are served by ferries. Take a picnic and set out to explore quaint harbors and rocky shores. Two of the most popular islands are **Vinga** and **Styrso**. For a less ambitious voyage, hop on one of the tour boats that float along Goteborg's canals and moat, past 18th-century row houses, Baroque churches, and the Feskekorka, the "Fish Church," which looks convincingly like a house of worship but is really a fish market.

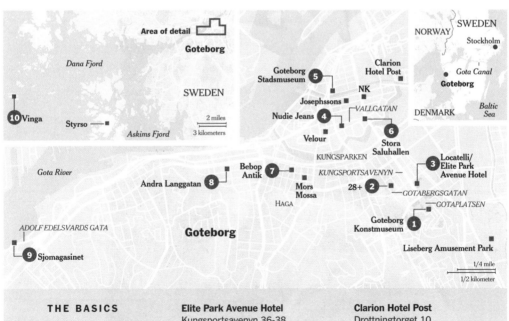

THE BASICS

From Stockholm, fly into Goteborg or, if you have abundant time, take a boat on the scenic Gota Canal. In Goteborg, buy a City Card for admission to trams, buses, archipelago boats, museums, and the Liseberg Amusement Park.

Elite Park Avenue Hotel
Kungsportsavenyn 36-38
46-31-727-1000
elite.se
$$$
Rooms with an urbane touch; situated handily for museums and night life.

Clarion Hotel Post
Drottningtorget 10
46-31-61-9000
clarionhotelpost.com
$$$
Ambitious member of the Clarion chain, housed in an old post office building.

Oslo

The first thing anyone who knows Oslo says when you mention that you are headed there is, "It's really expensive." The second thing they say is, "No, I'm not kidding. It's really expensive." And, indeed, a visit to Oslo brings with it immediate sticker shock: a bottle of wine at dinner can practically equal a month's mortgage payment back home. But you quickly, if grudgingly, accept the damage done to your wallet after a few hours strolling around this beguiling city — particularly in summer, when the sun's last rays still haven't faded by 11 p.m. and the locals, unshackled from the oppressiveness of Norway's winter, seem to be in a nonstop party mode. — BY STUART EMMRICH

FRIDAY

1 *Royalties* 4 p.m.

If you walk down Karl Johans Gate, a tree-lined promenade bordered by restaurants, cafes, and upscale stores, you'll eventually be face-to-face with the **Royal Palace**, the mammoth cream-colored home of the Norwegian royal family. It's open to the public only a few hours each day (Slottsplassen 1; 47-22-04-87-00; kongehuset.no). In summer, one of those times is 4 p.m. on Friday, when an English-language tour is given to visitors. You'll get a CliffsNotes version of Norwegian history from the informative guides as well as a spectacular view of the city from the windows that open to the royal balcony.

2 *Cocktail Hours* 5:30 p.m.

Sample Oslo's hipsterish Grunerlokka neighborhood with a stroll up Thorvald Meyers Gate amid groups of young people dressed with deliberately casual flair. Stop at **Bar Boca** (Thorvald Meyers Gate 36; visitoslo.com/en/product/?TLp=16393) a tiny and crowded bar with a menu of creative cocktails. Sip one as you watch the bartenders labor intensely over sprigs and twists and juices.

OPPOSITE The Vigeland Sculpture Park, the work of the sculptor Gustav Vigeland, gave Oslo not only 200 sculptures to view, but a popular place to stroll and sunbathe.

RIGHT The pedestrian promenade at Aker Brygge, a lively waterfront development of bars, restaurants, and a huge indoor shopping center.

3 *Fruit of the Sea* 8:30 p.m.

Solsiden (Akershusstranda 13; 47-22-33-36-30; solsiden.no; $$$$), in a converted warehouse on the waterfront, offers an ideal setting for dinner, particularly when staff members roll up the huge canvas window shades and patrons can watch the sun as it begins its slow descent across the Oslo Fjord. Local seafood is the specialty at this spot, and the restaurant makes the most of a short season — it is open only from May to September. Many diners start off their meal with a huge platter of fruits de mer.

4 *On the House* 10 p.m.

When the **Oslo Opera House** (Kirsten Flagstads Plass 1; 47-21-42-21-21; operaen.no), designed by the hot Norwegian firm Snohetta, opened in 2008, the Norwegian capital got more than a world-class performing arts center. It also got an unlikely playground. At almost any time of the day or night, hundreds of visitors scramble all over the building's sleek, gently angled Italian marble surface, inching their way up to the plaza-like rooftop. Think of it as a cultural institution that doubles as a jungle gym.

SATURDAY

5 *On the Fjord* 10:30 a.m.

The sun's been up for hours by now, so stir yourself and enjoy its rays while taking a boat trip around the **Oslo Fjord**, gliding past bucolic islands dotted with the colorful summer homes of the city's well-to-do residents. Boats (Radhusbrygge 3; 47-23-35-68-90; nyc.no) leave from a dock opposite the Oslo City Hall.

in white wine and baked sea pike. Reservations are essential. Afterward, stroll around the area, popping into the Nobel Peace Center, City Hall, and perhaps the shopping center. If you're looking for Scandinavian housewares, walk a few more blocks to **Kitch'n** (Bryggegata 8; 47-22-83-45-20; kitchn.no), which sells everything from elegant salad bowls to rolls of brightly colored toilet paper.

6 *On the Table* 1 p.m.

After returning to land, head over to nearby **Aker Brygge**, a lively waterfront development of bars, restaurants, and a huge indoor shopping center. There are plenty of dining options here, but probably the best place for lunch is **Lofoten Fiskerestaurant** (Stranden 75; 47-22-83-08-08; lofoten-fiskerestaurant. no; $$$), particularly if you can snag an outdoor table. Summer offerings are likely to include mussels

7 *A Playwright's House* 4 p.m.

Yes, behind every great man is said to be a woman. But how many women all but chained their elderly husbands to their desks for two and a half hours each morning, demanding that they put in a full quota of work before letting them escape down the street for a leisurely lunch and a welcome drink? That seems to be the legacy of Suzannah Thoresen, the wife of the Norwegian playwright Henrik Ibsen, as entertainingly recounted by the English-language guides at the **Ibsen Museum**. (They also let you

know that she was so penurious that Ibsen had to go behind her back and secretly order the expensive French fabric he coveted for the drawing room windows.) There's more here than the retelling of domestic squabbles, however, as you walk through the painstakingly restored home where Ibsen, who had been self-exiled from his home country, wrote his last two plays, *John Gabriel Borkman* and *When We Dead Awaken* (Henrik Ibsens Gate 26; 47-40-02-36-30; norskfolkemuseum.no/ibsenmuseet). Don't miss the short black-and-white film about Ibsen's life and career, which includes newsreel footage of his funeral. It's shown in alternating Norwegian and English versions. (The Norwegian one is oddly compelling, even if you don't speak a word of the language.)

8 *Try the Reindeer* 8 p.m.

For a sampling of traditional Norwegian cuisine, like medallions of reindeer in a sauce of port and raisins, head over to **Engebret Café** (Bankplassen 1; 47-22-82-25-25; engebret-cafe.no; $$$$), a quietly

OPPOSITE ABOVE Karl Johans Gate, the main central street.

OPPOSITE BELOW The Ibsen Museum tells a domestic story.

ABOVE The Oslo Opera House, a performance center designed by the Norwegian architectural firm Snøhetta.

elegant restaurant set in a low-slung 17th-century building. If the weather is nice, grab one of the outdoor tables, where the voices of the other patrons are softened by the sound of the bubbling fountain in the adjoining courtyard.

9 *Nightcap or Night Starter* 10:30 p.m.

After dinner, walk down to the waterfront until you encounter the park surrounding the famed **Akershus Castle**, a cannon-protected fortress that offers romantic views of the Oslo Fjord. Following the winding path will eventually lead you down to the bars of the Aker Brygge promenade, like the barge-like **Lekter'n** (Stranden 3; 47-21-52-32-31), where many of the city's youth are getting ready for their night to shift into high gear.

SUNDAY

10 *We All Scream* 11 a.m.

Two words: *The Scream*. You can't visit Oslo without seeing this masterwork by Edvard Munch, which is on view at the **National Gallery** (Universitetsgata 13; 47-21-98-20-00; nasjonalmuseet.no), with helpful signs leading you along the way. But take a few moments to check out other, lesser-known works, like several pieces by the painting duo of Adolph Tidemand and Hans Gude, whose *Bridal Voyage on the Hardanger Fjord* is described as

"one of the most important in Norwegian art." A total immersion in Edvard Munch, both of his own work and of the art he collected, can be found across town at the **Munch Museum** (Toyengata 53; 47-23-49-35-00; munchmuseet.no).

11 *Writing in Granite* 1 p.m.

The **Vigeland Sculpture Park** (vigeland.museum.no) is the work of the sculptor Gustav Vigeland (1869-1943), who not only designed the park itself but also created the more than 200 sculptures that dot its

grounds, including the massive Tower-of-Babel-like centerpiece known as the monolith, with its collection of writhing, naked bodies carved out of a single granite block. The park, which you can reach either via a short ride on the No. 12 tram or with a pleasant walk through a lovely residential neighborhood, is extremely popular with the locals. On one warm afternoon, the crowd included picnickers, sunbathers, families out for a stroll, and even two groups of rival cheerleading squads practicing their routines. (Was *Bring It On* a big hit in Norway?)

ABOVE Quotations in the pavement on Karl Johans Gate.

OPPOSITE The 173-room Royal Palace, still the home of Norway's kings, is open for partial tour on a limited schedule.

THE BASICS

Oslo Airport Gardermoen is served by multiple international carriers, and the city is also easily accessible by train, highway, and boat. In town, the subway, buses, trams, and ferries share a ticket system.

First Hotel Grims Grenka
Kongens Gate 5
47-23-10-72-00
firsthotels.com/en
$$$
Sleek modern hotel in the city center, next to the National Museum of Architecture.

Thon Hotel Opera
Dronning Eufamias Gate 4
47-24-10-30-00
thonhotels.com
$$
Part of a popular midrange Norwegian chain. Views of the Opera House.

Map

NORWAY

11 Vigeland Sculpture Park
Bar Boca **2**
FROGNER-PARKEN
BYGDOY-FROGNER
SLOTTS-PARKEN
Oslo
TOYEN-PARKEN
TOYENGATA
Area of detail
Munch Museum
Oslofjorden

1/2 mile
1 kilometer

PARKVEIEN
SLOTTSPARKEN
Royal Palace 1
National Gallery
10
UNIVERSITETSGATA

7 Ibsen Museum
KARL JOHANS GATE
City Hall
Oslo
CHRISTIAN FREDERIKS PLASS
Nobel Peace Center
Lekter'n
RADHUSBRYGGE
KONGENS GATE
Thon Hotel Opera
Kitch'n
AKER BRYGGE
5 Oslo Fjord boat dock
First Hotel Grims Grenka
6 Lofoten Fiskerestaurant
3 Solsiden
8 Engebret Café
AKERSHUSSTRANDA
4
Oslo Opera House

Norwegian Sea
9 Akershus Castle
NORWAY
FIN.
Bergen
Gulf of Bothnia
Oslo
Oslofjorden
SWEDEN
LAT.
DEN.
Baltic Sea
LITH.
GER.
POL.

Reykjavik

A chattering woman swirls her screwdriver as if it were cabernet sauvignon, not seeming to notice the waves of orange liquid crashing over the rim. A cackling woman in a strapless black dress whirls by, glancing over her shoulder to make sure her three beer-toting, leer-throwing suitors are still there. When I get up and start to walk toward the door, a woozy man heading in the same direction falls onto my back to use me as transport. He mumbles something in Icelandic. It's midnight on a Saturday, which means Reykjavik's runtur, or pub crawl, is under way. Many bars stay open past 4 a.m. on both Friday and Saturday, and partiers come from around northern Europe and around town. The runtur goes on even in the Icelandic winter, which is surprisingly mild for a country that nudges the Arctic Circle, and it stayed lively even after Iceland's financial collapse in 2008. It's a spectacle you won't want to miss, but try to stay awake for a while in the daytime, too, because there's more to do in Iceland than drink. — BY FRANK BRUNI

FRIDAY

1 *Walking Before Crawling* 3:30 p.m.

Don't dally! If it's January or February, you don't have much sunlight left, and you want to get your Reykjavik bearings well in advance of the overnight pub crawl, when the number and unruliness of the locals in the downtown streets, coupled with your own possible inebriation, could make navigating (or even perambulating) slightly difficult. Start on the northeastern edge of **Tjornin**, the pond in the center of this city of only about 120,000, which feels more like an overgrown village. Walk northeast, past the Hotel Borg and the lovely square it faces, and turn right on Austurstraeti street. Follow it as it rises uphill and becomes Laugavegur. You'll get tantalizing peeks of the stunning harbor and the modern Harpa concert hall.

2 *Reindeer on a Fork* 9 p.m.

If you're smart you've planned a late dinner and taken a little nap beforehand, so you don't have to bow out of the night's pub crawl before you've made a decent go of it. If you're even smarter, you've thought to make a reservation at **Fish Market** (Adalstraeti 12; 354-578-8877; fishmarket.is; $$$$),

which fills up quickly. It spreads over two handsome floors and, most important, has a menu that lets you know you're in Iceland. You can sample smoked puffin, which has an appealing livery quality like that of many game birds. Grilled whale meat is even more compelling: it has the appearance, texture, and heft of beef, but faintly saline nuances that suggest its source was the sea. Drink frigidly cold, excellent martinis made with Icelandic vodka as you move on to reindeer (predictably like venison), goose, or Arctic char.

3 *Round One* 11 p.m.

Ready…set…runtur! You're seeing only the beginnings of the pub crawl at this hour, as you walk through the barely marked entrance to **Boston** (Laugavegur 28b). Its main room, up a narrow staircase, is part Victorian bordello, part hunting lodge, with both candles and taxidermy among its adornments. Observe how quickly your fellow drinkers—beer is the libation of choice—proceed from one round to the next. Take note of their faces,

OPPOSITE Ghostly bliss in the geothermally heated open-air Blue Lagoon, outside Reykjavik.

BELOW A stop on the runtur, the famous Icelandic pub crawl that goes on well into the night.

because the comforting smallness of Reykjavik means that you'll come to recognize people teetering down the sidewalk at 2 a.m. without coats, their cosmetic concerns trumping any desire for insulation from winter temperatures that seem slightly colder than New York's.

4 *Color Me Tipsy* 1 a.m.

The shelves of liquor behind the bar at **B5** (Bankastraeti 5; 354-552-9600; B5.is) are bathed in glowing lights of different hues: orange, yellow, pink. And the big front window provides a great view of a street scene that still hasn't reached its peak. Cars cruise back and forth, windows down, as young Icelanders partake of the runtur on wheels. It's *American Graffiti*, only with snow and a soundtrack that favors Bjork.

SATURDAY

5 *Comes a Horseman* 10:30 a.m.

Assuming your hangover is manageable, you should get out of Reykjavik, because Iceland is a topographical marvel: craggy, desolate, the way you imagine the surface of the moon. Through Reykjavik Excursions (re.is) you can arrange hiking and snowmobiling day trips. For something less time-consuming and with more freedom, rent a car to head to the stables at **Eldhestar** (Vollum, Hveragerdi; 354-480-4800; eldhestar.is), for a short ride on a short horse. Icelandic horses are famously squat and agreeable, and your guide will help you manage yours.

6 *From Turf to Surf* 12:45 p.m.

An additional reason for a late-morning ride at Eldhestar is that it puts you in position for lunch at

Fjorubordid (Eyrarbraut 3a, Stokkseyri; 354-483-1550; fjorubordid.is; $$$) on a windswept stretch of the Icelandic coastline. You can have a creamy langoustine bisque then a big pan of peel-and-eat langoustine tails, with drinks, without using up your entire vacation budget. The restaurant's sure hand with these delicacies lures celebrities: photographs on the walls chronicle the visits of Bette Midler and Martha Stewart.

7 *Harborside Bargains* 4 p.m.

Back in Reykjavik after a drive of about 90 minutes in good weather, you can choose to shop in pretty boutiques with designer labels. Or you can rummage through an amusing hodgepodge of goods — bulk seafood, vintage record albums, wool mittens — at the bustling **Kolaportid** (Tryggvagata 19; 354-562-5030). This shaggy Wal-Mart of sorts is open from 11 a.m. to 5 p.m., weekends only, in a hangar-style building right on the harbor.

8 *Pub Crawl II* 11 p.m.

Big nightclubs aren't the whole nighttime scene. Life bubbles in smaller spots. At Reykjavik's oldest cafe, a 1950s throwback called **Prikid** (Bankastraeti 12; prikid.is), one winter night, a D.J. with dreadlocks spun LPs as white lights from a mirrored ball skittered across the room. Patrons in stylish knit hoodies

ABOVE The Northern Lights, bright at Iceland's high latitude. If you are in Iceland in the right season, and skies are clear, join a tour to see them.

OPPOSITE Even in winter, it's essential to see some of Iceland's marvelous volcanic landscape outside the city. Many tours are available; this one goes on horseback.

swayed to the rhythm of a saxophone. At **Olstofa** (Vegamotastigur 4) writers, journalists, artists, and other locals cozied up in wooden booths drinking beer, and as the evening went on, more people arrived in a steady stream.

SUNDAY

9 *Not Like the Movie* 10 a.m.

The final item on your must-do list: an outdoor bath. It's a local tradition. There are geothermal pools and tubs scattered throughout the city, each promising the heady sensation of a body enveloped in warm water but a head exposed to bitingly cold air. The mother of all baths is the **Blue Lagoon** (Grindavik; 354-420-8800; bluelagoon.com; reservations often required), about 40 minutes southwest of the city, where you can float through a sulfurous, misshapen lake of sorts. The mist over the water is thick, and there are currents so hot you may recoil from them. A bus will take you there, and the scalding-freezing splash is all the hangover remedy anyone could need.

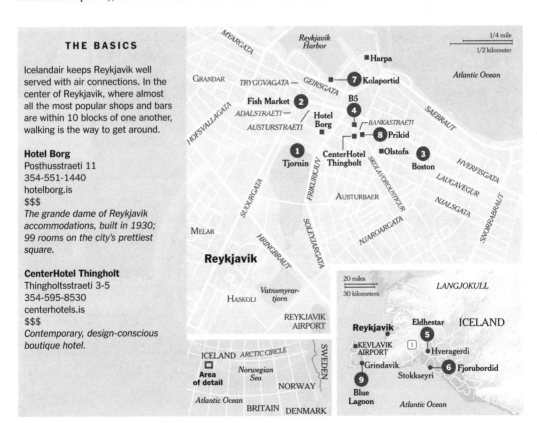

THE BASICS

Icelandair keeps Reykjavik well served with air connections. In the center of Reykjavik, where almost all the most popular shops and bars are within 10 blocks of one another, walking is the way to get around.

Hotel Borg
Posthusstraeti 11
354-551-1440
hotelborg.is
$$$
The grande dame of Reykjavik accommodations, built in 1930; 99 rooms on the city's prettiest square.

CenterHotel Thingholt
Thingholtsstraeti 3-5
354-595-8530
centerhotels.is
$$$
Contemporary, design-conscious boutique hotel.

Copenhagen

Copenhagen still charms visitors with its maritime setting and copper-domed landmarks, but a youthful, creative new energy has spilled over its storybook lanes. Contemporary art is proliferating, and young designers are reinvigorating Danish furniture and home décor, carrying the torch passed down by Arne Jacobsen and other towering figures. Upstart jazz and world music clubs are creating a night life without borders, and the revelers can get home at any hour on the futuristic, driverless Metro. Most impressively, fresh-faced chefs have elevated a national cuisine traditionally dominated by pork and sausages. The renowned Noma is widely considered one of the world's top restaurants and even Tivoli, the beloved amusement park that opened in 1843, has become a dining destination. Like Denmark's most famous export, Lego, Copenhagen is colorful, accessible, and effortlessly cool. — BY SETH SHERWOOD

FRIDAY

1 *A Danish Dubai* 5 p.m.

No neighborhood shows off Copenhagen's new spirit more impressively than **Orestad**. A few years ago, it was basically a barren flatland on the route to the airport. Today the district is a futuristic, master-planned community of state-of-the-art architecture. The elevated Metro whisks you past the soaring blue tower of the Cabinn Metro Hotel, designed by Daniel Libeskind; the solar-panel-clad Crowne Plaza Copenhagen Towers; and, perhaps most notable, the **Copenhagen Concert Hall** (Emil Holms Kanal 20; 45-35-20-30-40; dr.dk/koncerthuset), designed by Jean Nouvel. The glowing blue, cubelike exterior contains several concert spaces, including an auditorium with a jagged orange interior that looks carved from desert rock.

2 *Beetroot for Dessert* 7 p.m.

Not many Michelin-starred restaurants have featured musk ox as a cornerstone of their menus. But then again, not many restaurants are so passionately

OPPOSITE A cargo bike, a variation on a familiar theme in Denmark, where nine out of 10 adults own a bicycle.

RIGHT The glowing blue Copenhagen Concert Hall.

dedicated to glorifying the obscure fare of the Nordic climes as **Noma** (Strandgade 93; 45-32-96-32-97, noma.dk; $$$$). Its chef, René Redzepi, creates artful collages from ingredients like Greenland shrimp, Faroe Islands shellfish, Icelandic seaweed, rhubarb, and wood sorrel. Reservations must be made months in advance. If you can't get one, try for another Michelin-starred restaurant, **A.O.C.** (2 Dronningens Tvaergade; 45-33-11-11-45; restaurantaoc.dk; $$$$), a curvy, cavernous white complex of rooms filled with black-clad couples and suited businessmen. The red beetroot ice cream on one evening's dessert menu came on a bed of black licorice pellets.

3 *Rebirth of Cool* 10 p.m.

During the 1960s and early '70s, the **Jazzhus Montmartre** club was one of the high temples of the European jazz scene, drawing legendary talents like Miles Davis and Dexter Gordon. It closed in 1976, made a few struggling efforts to reopen, and finally went silent in the 1990s. It's now back in its original location (Store Regnegade 19A; 45-70-26-32-67; jazzhusmontmartre.dk) and has attracted marquee names like the drummer Jeff (Tain) Watts and the pianist Abdullah Ibrahim.

SATURDAY

4 *Tap Into the Past* 10 a.m.

Two liters of beer for breakfast. No, that's not a suggestion. That's the amount of suds Danish Royal Navy sailors used to consume daily, as tour guides happily announce during the one-hour boat

voyage and history lesson offered by **Strömma Tours** (45-32-66-00-00; stromma.dk). Departing from Nyhavn, Copenhagen's touristy but highly picturesque 17th-century harbor, the sightseeing trips glide past Renaissance-era icons and modern architectural feats.

5 *Easy Riding* 11:30 a.m.

Nine out of 10 Danish adults own bikes. (The ubiquitous bicycle paths are a good fit with the windmills on the horizon and other signs of serious eco-mindedness.) If you arrived without your two wheels, **Baisikeli** (Ingerslevsgade 80; 45-26-70-02-29; baisikeli.dk) has rentals. In summer you could join multitudes pedaling to the beach, but cycling is also one of the best ways to sightsee in Copenhagen's city center. Cruise to the stately **Amalienborg Palace** (Amalienborg Slotsplads; kongernessamling.dk/amalienborg), where the Danish monarch lives, and then over to the **Rosenborg Palace** (Ostervoldgade 4A; 45-33-15-32-86; rosenborgslot.dk), where you can stroll the gardens and tour rooms bedecked in frescoes. Glide by the Dutch Renaissance-style stock exchange, the **Borsen** (Borsgade 1). For a knockout view, climb up the gilded candy-twist spire of **Vor Frelsers Kirke** (Sankt Annae Gade 29; vorfrelserskirke.dk/english) in the historical Christianshavn district.

6 *Smorrebrod Supreme* 2 p.m.

The fried herring may taste like something from an old-school Copenhagen tavern, but **Aamanns Etablissement** (Oster Farimagsgade 12; 45-35-55-33-10; aamanns.dk; $$$) has a modern take on it, complete with minimalist décor, homemade akvavit, and microbrew beers. The frequently changing menu may include smorrebrod, traditional open-face sandwiches made with meats and vegetable trimmings.

7 *Designing Danes* 4 p.m.

Stroget, the pedestrian-only retail strip that threads through centuries-old town houses and majestic squares, is your yellow-brick road to Danish design. **Georg Jensen** (Amagertorv 4; 45-33-11-40-80) is devoted to Jensen, the silversmith, and other legendary Danish designers. **Stilleben** (Niels Hemmingsensgade 3; 45-33-91-11-31; stilleben.dk) sells ceramics, porcelain, and glassware from young creators. Updating the famed minimalism of Danish designers like Arne Jacobsen, Finn Juhl, and Jacob Jensen, the furniture designers for **Hay** (Pilestraede 29-31; 45-42-82-08-20; hay.dk) favor bright colors and soft forms. For fashion, shop at **Bllack Noir** (Ostergade 52, Illum department store; 45-33-14-40-02; noir.dk/bllack-noir.php), which leaves Scandinavian white and lightness far behind, or its opposite, **Baum und Pferdgarten** (Vognmagergade 2; 45-35-30-10-90; baumundpferdgarten.com), where the clothes are romantic and very feminine. For something that makes a statement, visit **Henrik Vibskov** (Krystalgade 6; 45-33-14-61-00; henrikvibskovboutique.com), known for avant-garde wear.

8 *Jackets Not Required* 7 p.m.

Danish hospitality comes to the fore at **Madklubben** (Store Kongensgade 66; 45-33-32-32-34; madklubben.dk; $$). It says so on the menu: "The staff has been selected for their cheerful spirits and contagious laughter, not their intense studies of all the wine and cheeses of the world." The kitchen is similarly unpretentious, whipping up affordable Nordic-modern dishes for 30-somethings who pack into the low-ceilinged, minimalist white space.

9 *Norrebro by Night* 10 p.m.

Working-class Norrebro, an ethnically mixed neighborhood, is becoming a diverse party spot as well. **Underwood Ink** (Ryesgade 30A; 45-35-35-55-53;underwood-ink.dk) feels like the living room of an eclectic intellectual, with bookshelves packed with international literature (for sale), paintings by obscure European artists (ditto), and tables piled with bottles of Danish beers. A few blocks away, the stage at **Global** (Norre Alle 7; 45-50-58-08-41;globalcph.dk) showcases wide-ranging

ABOVE Part of the tourist crush at the harbor. Walk a short distance away for good shopping on the Stroget.

acts like Mali's Bassekou Kouyate and the Serbian Gypsy trumpet legend Boban Markovic.

SUNDAY

10 *Nature Beckons* 10 a.m.

There's no better cure for too much pork and beer than a vigorous walk in the crisp Nordic air. Copenhagen's three adjacent lakes are a favorite of cyclists, joggers, and strollers, with picturesque trails lined with shady trees and reeds. For a copious brunch buffet, **Den Franske Café** (Sortedam Dossering 101; 45-35-42-48-45; denfranskecafe.dk; $$) has tables inside and out overlooking a pleasant spot where swans and ducks gather.

11 *Paters* Noon

The **Statens Museum for Kunst** (Solvgade 48-50; 45-33-74-84-94; smk.dk) displays European masters and also offers a vivid introduction to Danish modern art, including paintings by Vilhelm Hammershoi and a surrealist statue by Peter Land of a seated man with outlandishly overlong legs.

ABOVE Touring by boat in the picturesque harbor.

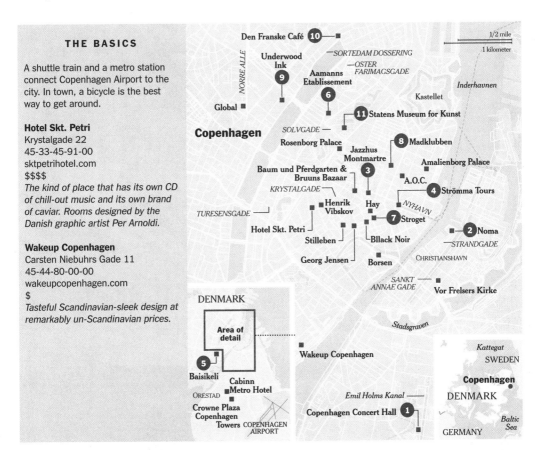

THE BASICS

A shuttle train and a metro station connect Copenhagen Airport to the city. In town, a bicycle is the best way to get around.

Hotel Skt. Petri
Krystalgade 22
45-33-45-91-00
sktpetrihotel.com
$$$$
The kind of place that has its own CD of chill-out music and its own brand of caviar. Rooms designed by the Danish graphic artist Per Arnoldi.

Wakeup Copenhagen
Carsten Niebuhrs Gade 11
45-44-80-00-00
wakeupcopenhagen.com
$
Tasteful Scandinavian-sleek design at remarkably un-Scandinavian prices.

Helsinki

It's easy to feel transported to some gorgeously surreal interzone while strolling the streets of Helsinki, Finland's capital and metropolis. Neoclassical domes, 1930s futuristic architecture, and languid Baltic light seem stuck in limbo between Russia and Scandinavia. While the locals' famous stoic attitude, "sisu" as the Finns call it, seems colored by the old era of Russian domination, the quirky functionalist design, newly evolved national haute cuisine, and sense of fun are distinctly Scandinavian. One of the first modern planned cities, rebuilt on a grid pattern under Czar Alexander I, Helsinki sits atop a verdant archipelago jutting into the Gulf of Finland. It is surrounded on three sides by water and seemingly endless numbers of hidden coves, beaches, and inlets. Perhaps this setting helps explain the fluid sense of design, the perpetually pink-cheeked nature-loving inhabitants, and the fresh berries that seem to find their way into every restaurant meal. — BY FINN-OLAF JONES

FRIDAY

1 *Hot Cultural Immersion* 3 p.m.

Ready to get rid of that jet lag? Saunas are a regular part of Finns' lives, and Helsinki has some of the country's best-designed spots to sweat with the locals. Although you are expected to strip down to your birthday suit, males and females customarily take saunas separately. Locals will argue incessantly about which is the city's best sauna, but aficionados swear by **Kotiharjun Sauna** (Harjutorinkatu 1; 358-9-753-1535; kotiharjunsauna.fi), built in 1928. Students and their professors from the nearby University of Helsinki can sometimes be found seated on the street in front of the Kotiharju in heated debate while cooling off in their towels.

2 *North Star* 8 p.m.

Just two decades ago, Finnish cuisine often meant boiled fish and vegetables, but now a team of youthful, internationally educated chefs have set about a gastronomic revolution, chief among them Teemu Aura and Tommi Tuominen of **Demo** (Uudenmaankatu 9-11; 358-9-2289-0840; restaurantdemo.fi; $$$$), who take native seasonal products and cook them up with Gallic flair — for which they were awarded a Michelin star. Settle into the cozy yet minimalist setting for their seasonal prix fixe multi-course menu, which can include versions of anything picked, hunted, or fished locally, from pickled herring to berry soufflé.

3 *Top of the Town* 10 p.m.

Climb the narrow stairway on top of the Hotel Torni to find the **Ateljee Bar** (Yrjonkatu 26; 358-10-784-2080; raflaamo.fi/fi/helsinki/atelje-bar), one of the highest spots in the city and a favorite of a glamorous clientele. The bar has a shifting exhibit of local artists' work and can get quite crowded, but the two terraces are great late-night spots to enjoy the sea air and — if you are very lucky — see the Northern Lights merging into the Gulf of Finland.

SATURDAY

4 *Outside With Sibelius* 10 a.m.

Join the locals for a stroll or jog at the tranquil **Sibelius Park & Monument** on the western edge of the city center. Appropriately, given the epic, landscape-inspired compositions of Jean Sibelius, the famous and beloved 19th-century Finnish composer, the park is kept in a natural, semiwild condition. In the monument, his stern stainless steel visage keeps sentinel over a giant sculptural pipe organ that seems to float amid the park's ancient birches.

OPPOSITE The Lutheran Cathedral at the neo-Classical Senate Square. Russian rulers built the square in the 1800s.

RIGHT A portrait of Alvar Aalto, the influential architect. Home décor designed by Aalto and his wife is still sold.

5 *Heroic Meal* 1 p.m.

Located in the shadow of the magnificent onion-topped spire of the Orthodox Uspenski Cathedral, the **Bellevue** (Rahapajankatu 3; 358-9-179-560; restaurantbellevue.com; $$$) is a maze of cozy, candlelit dining rooms where you will be served the czarist-era dishes that have become Helsinki institutions. Even Baron Carl Gustaf Mannerheim, who became Finland's national hero for battling the Russians, dined here—perhaps because this is one of the few establishments that serves up bear.

6 *Book Smart* 3 p.m.

Step into what appears to be a bland office building at the top of the Esplanade, Helsinki's grand boulevard and park, and emerge in a white geometric explosion of lightning-like skylights, marble balconies, and books—lots of them. The **Academic Bookshop** (Pohjoisesplanadi 39; 358-20-760-8999; akateeminenkirjakauppa.fi), built in 1969

and designed by the great Finnish architect Alvar Aalto, might well be Europe's biggest bookstore, with many titles in English. In a magnificent setting like this, browsing is practically a performance art.

7 *Designer Street* 4 p.m.

The blocks immediately east of the Academic Bookshop are Helsinki's main shopping drag, an intimate version of Fifth Avenue with many of Finland's top designer stores, including **Marimekko** (Mikonkatu 1; 358-50-572-5632; marimekko.com), whose bold and colorful fabric designs are still chic all these years after Jacqueline Kennedy sported its simple dresses. For cutting-edge glassworks,

BELOW Limber entertainers on the Esplanade.

OPPOSITE ABOVE The memorial to the composer Jean Sibelius.

OPPOSITE BELOW The Museum of Contemporary Art Kiasma.

ceramics, and other household objects, check out the international favorite **Iittala** (Pohjoisesplanadi 25; 358-20-439-3501; iittala.com). **Artek** (Keskuskatu 1b; 358-10-617-3480; artek.fi), founded in 1935 to market the interior designs of Aalto and his wife, Aino, still celebrates the Finns' love for furniture with clean lines and natural materials.

8 *The Temple of Aalto* 8 p.m.

Eight floors above the Esplanade, the airy **Ravintola Savoy** (Etelaesplanadi 14; 358-9-6128-5300; ravintolasavoy.fi; $$$$) is Finland's design and food Valhalla. Virtually unchanged since the Aaltos put together its elegantly functional appearance in 1937, this is a popular spot for Helsinki's power elite to nibble sumptuously prepared local game and fish. It's pricey, but what else would you expect from one of Finland's most distinct sensory experiences?

SUNDAY

9 *Russian Outpost* 10 a.m.

Grab an espresso, a fresh-baked pastry, and a front-row seat to the human theater that takes place every weekend in the neo-Classical Senate Square. The venerable **Café Engel** (Aleksanterinkatu 26; 358-9-652-776; cafeengel.fi; $-$$), located in one of Helsinki's oldest buildings, is the prime spot to watch the action. The square has been the city's focal point ever since

the Russians constructed it in the 1800s when Finland was part of their empire. Czar Alexander II's statue still looms over the setting as a reminder of who used to run things here, and indeed the square has been the stand-in for St. Petersburg in several Hollywood movies. During the winter, snowboarders can sometimes be seen making furtive swoops off the steep steps leading up to the domed, gleaming white Lutheran Cathedral.

10 *Edgy Iceberg* Noon

The **Museum of Contemporary Art Kiasma** (Mannerheiminaukio 2; 358-29-450-0501; kiasma.fi), which appears like a sleek iceberg floating toward Helsinki's sumptuous Art Nouveau main railroad station, looks quintessentially Finnish but was actually

designed by the American architect Steven Holl.
A hyper-innovative display center for modern art,
electrical performance pieces, and new gizmos,
the Kiasma is in the vanguard for futuristic trends.
A visit through its dramatically angled galleries provides a stimulating look at Helsinki's contemporary

ABOVE Finlandia Hall, designed by Alvar Aalto.

OPPOSITE Hanging out on the grassy Esplanade.

role as a major crossroads for design and high tech.
Its cafe has chairs by the Finnish designer Vesa
Honkonen, and high chairs by Stefan Lindfors.

11 *Art Deco Dip* 2 p.m.
    After a weekend in Helsinki you might be feeling
native enough to take a dip at **Yrjonkatu Swimming
Hall** (Yrjonkatu 21 b; 358-9-3108-7401; hel.fi/hki/liv/en/
Sports+facilities), a 1928 Art Deco fantasy of marble
arches and mosaics. You won't have to pack a wet
bathing suit for the trip home, as most locals swim
in the nude. Check the website for the separate swim
times for men and women. There's probably no better
way to finish your weekend in Helsinki than with a
Finnish purification in one of the pool's five saunas.

THE BASICS

Fly into Helsinki-Vantaa International
Airport and take a taxi to Helsinki. Or
arrive by ferry from Stockholm.

Hotel Kamp
Pohjoisesplanadi 29
358-9-576-111
www.hotelkamp.fi
$$$
*Turn-of-the-century grand hotel.
Some higher-priced suites
have saunas.*

Klaus K Hotel
Bulevardi 2-4
358-20-770-4700
klauskhotel.com
$$$
*Cool design and themed rooms;
located in Helsinki's design district.*

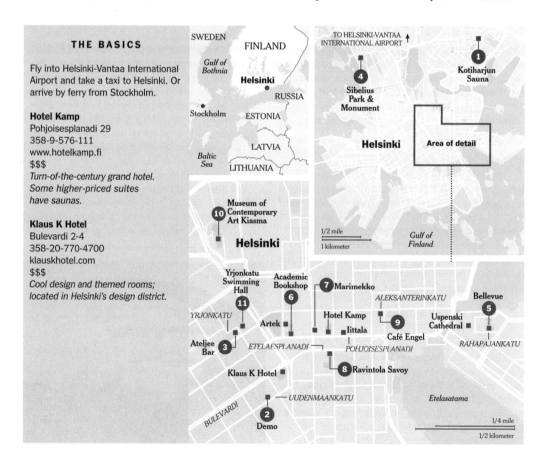

Turku

A free-spirited, artistically inclined city of about 185,000 people at the mouth of the Aura River, Turku has a rich history and a vibrant cultural life. It has produced some of Finland's leading artists, among them the performance artist Meiju Niskala, the sculptor Kim Simonsson, and the composer Ulf Langbacka. It boasts one of Finland's best art academies, and its events and performances have drawn crowds from across the Nordic countries. Turku was once Finland's largest city, and although today it has fallen to sixth-largest, it is one of the most inviting: a laid-back town that is the gateway to the Archipelago Sea, a latticework of perhaps 20,000 pristine islands in the Baltic. — BY JOSHUA HAMMER

FRIDAY

1 *Fortress Finland* 2 p.m.

This tidy, strategically placed coastal town was Finland's most important city for five centuries, and the center of its cultural, religious, and commercial life. Turku's prominence faded after the Finland War of 1808 and 1809, however, when Russia seized the Grand Duchy of Finland from the Swedish Empire and established a new capital in Helsinki. The **Turku Castle**, or Turun Linna (Linnankatu 80; 358-2-262-0300; turunlinna.fi), is a relic of those long centuries of Turku's dominance. It's a massive medieval fortress, dating from around 1300, at the spot where an invader coming from the Baltic Sea would enter the Aura River. Behind the castle's thick stone walls, interlocking corridors and courtyards offer hints of its glory days in the mid-16th century, when it served as the sumptuous court of the Duke of Finland. It's now a popular exhibition space and banquet hall as well as a museum.

2 *Hero With a Chisel* 4 p.m.

Waino Aaltonen Museum of Art (Itäinen Rantakatu 38; 358-2-262-0850; wam.fi), a boxy modernist building in a leafy riverside setting, displays modern and contemporary art with particular empha-

sis on works of Waino Aaltonen, a sculptor and painter from Turku. Aaltonen captured the country's nationalistic spirit after its declaration of independence from Russia in 1917, creating monuments to Finnish heroes — a marble bust of the composer Jean Sibelius, a bronze of the 1920s Olympic runner Paavo Nurmi in motion, even a granite monument to Finnish settlers in Crozer Park in Chester, Pennsylvania.

3 *Beer Class* 7 p.m.

Finns were making beer in the Middle Ages, and **Brewery Restaurant Koulu** (Eerikinkatu 18; 358-2-274-5757; panimoravintolakoulu.fi; $$-$$$), downtown, capitalizes on the tradition, billing itself Finland's largest brewery restaurant. You can sample the house beers or the wines at Koulu's Winestube, with 80 different labels, and get a glimpse of the brewery in the basement. The dinner menu runs to hearty entrées like beef tenderloin and roasted pike. The building was once a school, and the restaurant riffs a bit on the classroom theme with school desks as decorations and a "school lunch" menu earlier in the day.

SATURDAY

4 *Around the Square* 9 a.m.

Market Square was designed by the German-born architect Carl Ludvig Engel after a fire destroyed almost all of the city in 1827. Now it's the place where people gather, shop in open-air stalls, and visit such architectural jewels as the domed Russian Orthodox church and the neo-Classical Swedish Theater,

OPPOSITE A market in inviting, laid-back Turku. The city was once a Baltic Sea fortress.

RIGHT Turku Castle, dating from around 1300, is a relic of the centuries when Turku was Finland's powerful capital.

Finland's oldest, built in 1839. (The theater caters to the 5 percent of the city's population who speak Swedish as their first language—a legacy of Turku's days as a strategic fortress town of the Swedish empire.) Just off the square is the indoor **Old Turku Market Hall** (Eerikinkatu 16; 358-2-262-4126; kauppahalli.fi), eye candy for foodies and a good place to seek out a simple brunch.

5 *Old Town* 11 a.m.

Walk a couple of blocks toward the river to the renovated Old Library Square and the **Turku City Main Library** (Linnankatu 2), a gleaming glass construction with airy, wood-paneled interior spaces that are inviting whether or not you want to stay inside and read. Amble over the bridge across the Aura River to Old Great Square and relax for a while at the **Turku Bookcafé** (Vanha Suurtori 3; 358-2-469-1396; kirjakahvila.org; $), a charming little cafe and bookshop that serves vegan cakes and pies and hosts live music, readings, and other cultural events. You're a few steps away here from the 280-foot-high **Cathedral of Turku** (Eerikinkatu 3A; turuntuomiokirkko.fi), Finland's most important church, an impressive cross between Westminster Abbey and St.-Germain-des-Prés. And a short walk from there is the **Sibelius Museum** (Pisspankatu 17; 358-2-215-4494; sibeliusmuseum.fi), where musical instruments and Sibelius memorabilia are displayed.

6 *Even Older Town* 1 p.m.

To see a medieval settlement—the remains of a real one, not a romantic reconstruction—walk back

about three blocks to **Aboa Vetus & Ars Nova** (Itäinen Rantakatu 4-6; 358-20-718-1640; aboavetusarsnova.fi), twin museums devoted to archaeology (Aboa Vetus) and contemporary art (Ars Nova). The rough stone walls of the settlement are in the basement, an archaeological excavation that remains where it was found.

7 *The Sea Route* 2 p.m.

During the warm months, get out onto the labyrinth of islands and inlets guarding Turku's Baltic seafront with a cruise to **Naantali**, a resort town a couple of sea inlets north of Turku that has yet another inviting Old Town, shops, and an amusement park. It's only a 20-minute drive away if you take the land route, but the **Steamship Ukkopekka** (Linnankatu 38; 358-2-515-3300; ukkopekka.fi/en) takes you on a leisurely trip that offers a taste of the beauty of Finland's Baltic islands. The cruise takes about an hour and a half, and offers a lunch buffet. Return by bus or taxi to Turku.

8 *South to North* 5 p.m.

Have dinner at **Blanko** (Aurakatu 1; 358-2-233-3966; blanko.net; $$-$$$), a riverside cafe that is one of Turku's most popular and stylish restaurants. Expect a varied menu, including Asian dishes like Thai pork belly, some Italian-style pastas and risottos, and distinctly Nordic additions like elk pastrami and Finnish salmon.

9 *Find a Stage* 7 p.m.

You're in a Finnish culture capital. Find a performance. There may be a concert at the attractive **Turku Concert Hall** (Aninkaistenkatu 9; tfo.fi/en), a play at one of the theaters, or a show at **Logomo** (Köydenpunojankatu 14; 358-29-123-4800; logomo.fi), an ambitious cultural and event center. Many of the city's hopes for a future as a cultural hub

LEFT The Brinkkala Mansion on Old Great Square. Turku is one of Finland's most inviting cities, a cultural capital and gateway to the 20,000 islands of the Archipelago Sea.

OPPOSITE Turku Cathedral, Finland's most important church. The cathedral is reminiscent of both Westminster Abbey in London and St.-Germain-des-Prés in Paris.

and Baltic meeting place are vested in this daring project in a cavernous former warehouse and railway maintenance shed that dates back to the era of the czars. In addition to its concert hall and a large restaurant, it will have exhibition space and a collection of artists' studios.

SUNDAY

10 *Lawns and Lindens* 10 a.m.

Stroll along the **Aura**, a narrow waterway that winds through the heart of Turku, on a promenade lined with linden trees that is the city's most popular gathering spot. Bicyclists pedal leisurely along the waterway path, university students read on verdant lawns, and smartly dressed couples sip cappuccinos in sidewalk cafes. The spiffiness of central Turku gives way to a slightly rougher edge if you follow the Aura farther toward the Baltic

Sea. A three-masted schooner has turned maritime museum. Patrons gather at riverboat restaurants, popular places to sit on a deck and drink beer or hard cider while listening to music and, at night, enjoying the sight of the city lights reflected on the river. Old tobacco factories and warehouses have been reborn in recent years as condominiums and cultural centers.

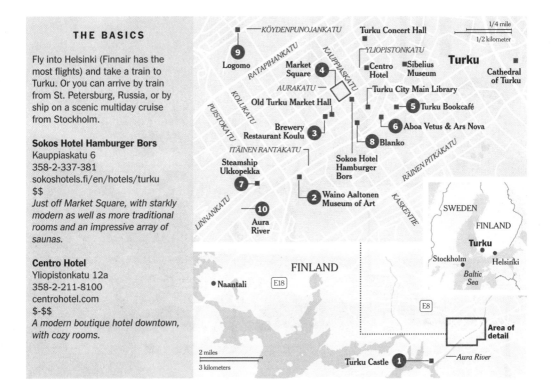

THE BASICS

Fly into Helsinki (Finnair has the most flights) and take a train to Turku. Or you can arrive by train from St. Petersburg, Russia, or by ship on a scenic multiday cruise from Stockholm.

Sokos Hotel Hamburger Bors
Kauppiaskatu 6
358-2-337-381
sokoshotels.fi/en/hotels/turku
$$
Just off Market Square, with starkly modern as well as more traditional rooms and an impressive array of saunas.

Centro Hotel
Yliopistonkatu 12a
358-2-211-8100
centrohotel.com
$-$$
A modern boutique hotel downtown, with cozy rooms.

Tallinn

Estonia may be one of the smallest countries in Europe, but its 1.3 million citizens know how to stay in the cultural vanguard. Tech-savvy companies like Skype have main offices here. A full schedule of cultural events includes many music festivals — this is, after all, the country that paved the way to independence with a Singing Revolution. Remnants of the Soviet era are repackaged as tourist attractions, while many of the city's chefs, inspired by the "new Nordic" movement, are busily creating a Baltic cuisine that takes traditional ingredients — from beetroot to wild boar — and uses them in inventive ways. The Old Town still trades heavily on its medieval past but, throughout the city, a 21st-century vibe is apparent.
— BY STEPHEN WHITLOCK

FRIDAY

1 *Along the Watchtower* 3 p.m.

Start your visit by walking a section of the medieval wall that encircles the Old Town. A Danish king began building the defenses in 1310, and by the 16th century the wall was more than a mile long, with 46 towers. Of these, 26 remain. You can reach three of them and a section of wall via the gate on **Suur-Kloostri**. Clamber up the 45 steps to the wall, and from there you can ascend into the towers. A word of warning: the stairways are steep, dark, and narrow. This is not advised for infants, claustrophobes, or anyone in heels.

2 *In Town, Out of Town* 7 p.m.

If you're staying in town, visit the city's coolest restaurant-bar, **Sfaar** (Mere puiestee 6E; 372-5699-2200; sfaar.ee; $$), which also has a chic clothing shop. The menu adheres to traditional Estonian flavors, perhaps wild boar patty with potatoes and a sauce of mushroom and thyme; lamb's liver as a starter. Don't skip dessert. The pastry with curd cheese, an Estonian favorite, is delicious. If you're here in

winter, **Neh** (Lootsi 4; 372-602-2222; neh.ee) is the incentive you need to venture beyond the Old Town. An outstanding restaurant spread over two floors of a small stone house, it's open only in the cold months. The rest of the year the staff moves back to Padaste Manor, a luxurious gastro-lodge on the island of Muhu, about 100 miles away. Expect dishes like salted ostrich served with a shot of pine vodka, or a quince posset with rose hip ice cream and hay ash.

3 *Float In for a Drink* 10 p.m.

If you want a mug of beer served by someone dressed as a medieval wench while lute music plays in the background, you're spoiled for choice in Tallinn. At **Butterfly Lounge** (Vana-Viru 13/Aia 4; 372-5690-3703; kokteilibaar.ee), you can avoid that tourist hoopla and get a well-mixed martini from a waiter in a bright pink shirt while 1980s electro-pop provides the soundtrack. They take their cocktails seriously here, and trophies from various mixology competitions fill a glass cabinet. Order a plate of the extremely tasty duck spring rolls.

SATURDAY

4 *Nothing Here! Really!* 11 a.m.

The elevator in the **Sokos Hotel Viru** (Viru Valjak 4; 372-680-9300; sokoshotels.fi) doesn't go to

OPPOSITE The Alexander Nevsky Cathedral, an Estonian Orthodox church built in the 1890s. The cathedral dates from the days when Estonia was part of the Russian Empire.

RIGHT The pink facade of the Riigikogu, Estonia's parliament building, on the Toompea hill overlooking the Old Town.

the top floor. That's because for years it housed a secret K.G.B. office, now open as a small museum with regular English-language tours. The Russians' subterfuge seems amateurish now (the door bears a notice that reads, in Russian and Estonian, "There is nothing here"), but their surveillance techniques were sophisticated. There were bugs in the hotel rooms, the phones, and even the sauna, as well as bugged ashtrays and bread plates that were used to keep an ear on restaurant chatter.

5 *Church and State* 1 p.m.

Make your way up Pikk Jalg to Toompea, the hill overlooking the Old Town. There you can visit the onion-domed Estonian Orthodox Cathedral, **St. Alexander Nevsky** (Pikk 64-4; 372-641-1301; orthodox.ee), and see the pale pink parliament building, the **Riigikogu** (Lossi plats 1a; 372-631-6331; riigikogu.ee). Return via the Danish King's Garden, a vantage point with great views of the Old Town.

6 *Something Sweet* 3 p.m.

The name of Tallinn's oldest cafe still in use, **Maiasmokk** (Pikk 16; 372-646-4079; kalev.ee), means "person with a sweet tooth," which is a neat description of your average Estonian. Since 1864 people have been coming here to enjoy traditional cakes. Just next door, and owned by the same company, is the **Kalev Marzipan Museum Room**, where you can watch marzipan figures made from Californian almonds being hand-painted with colored food dyes. They are particularly popular at Christmas and remain edible for up to four months. For a more modern indulgence, cross the street to **Anneli Viik** (Pikk 30; 372-644-4530; anneliviik.ee), a cozy cafe selling handmade chocolate truffles and hot chocolate so dark and dense the spoon almost stands up in the cup.

7 *Sound of Music* 7:30 p.m.

Considering that Tallinn's population is less than 500,000, the range and quality of music on offer most

nights at the **Estonia Concert Hall** (372-614-7771; concert.ee) and the **Estonian National Opera** (372-683-1201; opera.ee) is staggering. Audiences span all generations. Both venues are at Estonia puiestee 4, just outside the Old Town, but they have separate box offices. For a pre- or post-theater drink, head upstairs at the bar-lounge **Wabadus** (Vabaduse Valjak 10; 372-660-4019; wabadus.ee). It takes its name from the Estonian word for freedom, which is significant as it was formerly named Moskva, after the Russian capital.

8 *Heavenly Repast* 9:30 p.m.

Enjoy a late supper at **O** (Mere puiestee 6E; 372-661-6150; restoran-o.ee; $$$$), next door to Sfaar. Its name, which is pronounced "ur," is the Swedish word for island. With lots of gauzy fabrics hanging from the ceiling and little angels' wings on the lighting fixtures, the dining room looks ethereal, and in the open kitchen local ingredients take flight. Meals might start with a beetroot consommé or wonderful pieces

of eel poached in apple wine. The simplest choice, one of several tasting menus offered each evening, is the six-course tasting menu.

SUNDAY

9 *Smart Souvenirs* 10:30 a.m.

Everywhere you turn in Tallinn there are stores and street vendors selling amber and linen. Not

OPPOSITE Sfaar, a restaurant with a sales floor.

ABOVE A preserved structure in the Old Town.

BELOW The interior of Alexander Nevsky Cathedral.

everyone on your gift list back home will love amber, but who doesn't appreciate a new tea towel? Most of the designs are supertraditional, but **Zizi** (Vene 12; 372-644-1222; zizi.ee) in the Old Town sells linens with

ABOVE The K.G.B. Museum. The guides' anecdotes about life during the Soviet era are both chilling and ludicrous.

OPPOSITE A deceptively quiet stroll in the Old Town. Tallinn may look medieval, but it is well known around Europe as a capital of technology by day and partying at night.

bold, modern patterns that call to mind the Finnish company Marimekko. There's everything from napkins and tablecloths to duvet covers and cushions, all made from Estonian linen and at excellent prices.

10 *A Final Treat* 1 p.m.

For one last treat before you depart, drop into **Bonaparte Deli** (Pikk 47; 373-646-4024; bonaparte.ee), which sells a wonderful collection of international foods, from Japanese teas to New Zealand wine and loaves of Irish soda bread. One of its excellent Estonian pastries with smoked bacon and minced meat is just what you need when you've been wandering the cobbled streets. They're called toorsuitsupeekoni-hakklihapirukas and taste every bit as good as they sound.

THE BASICS

The cobblestone streets of Old Town are made for walking. Taxis are plentiful and cheap.

Three Sisters Hotel
Pikk 71/Tolli 2
372-630-6300
threesistershotel.com
$$$
In three 14th-century buildings. Counts the queen of England and emperor of Japan among its past guests.

Hotel Telegraaf
Vene 9
372-600-0600
telegraafhotel.com
$$
A former post office with suites named after Samuel Morse and Alexander Graham Bell.

Savoy Boutique Hotel
Suur-Karja 17/19
372-680-6688
tallinnhotels.ee
$$
Art Deco styling, hand-plastered walls, and marble bathrooms.

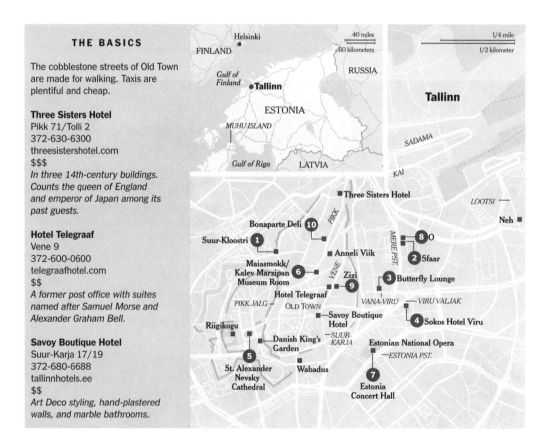

Riga

Riga, Latvia's capital and its major city since the 1200s, has been through a lot — a parade of rulers including Poles, Germans, and Swedes; World War II destruction; Nazi and Soviet occupation; and, in the 21st century, a jarring economic boom and bust tied to international financial trends. But nothing has quenched the spirit of this Baltic city for long, and certainly no conqueror has defeated its beauty. Riga's architecture is some of the richest in Europe, from reconstructed medieval treasures to Europe's largest collection of Art Nouveau buildings. Its new restaurants have brought its cuisine into the present, and its night life is vibrant. And while it is one of the most sophisticated outposts of Eastern Europe, it also holds onto beloved traditions, from autumn mushroom foraging to winter warm-ups with a super-potent beverage called Riga Black Balsam.
— BY JON FASMAN

FRIDAY

1 *A Violent Century* 3 p.m.

Understanding a bit of recent Latvian history will greatly enhance your time in Riga, and there is a perfect place to start. In the mid-1960s, the Soviets built a Museum of the Revolution in the southwestern corner of the Old Town; in one of the more delicious strokes of post-independence revenge, Latvia turned it into the **Museum of the Occupation** (Strelnieku Laukums 1; 371-6-721-2715; occupationmuseum.lv). With clear English explanations, this is among the most thoughtfully designed and well-curated historical museums in Europe. Its comprehensiveness is extraordinary, taking in everything from Nazi and Soviet uniforms to propaganda posters, from chess sets carved from scrap and wood in the gulags to heartbreaking, hastily scribbled notes thrown from trains by deportees to Siberia.

2 *The Heart of the Country* 6 p.m.

Vecriga, Riga's Old Town, is a cabinet of wonders best explored aimlessly, guided just by eye and fancy, but if you had to pick a place to start, it would be **Doma Laukums** (Cathedral Square), just across from the Occupation Museum. At its center is the enormous medieval cathedral, begun in 1211 by Albert von Buxhoeveden, the German missionary-warrior who sailed north to convert the Livonian heathens. The more interesting building, though, is the **House of the Blackheads** (Ratslaukums 7; melngalvjunams.lv), on the southern side of the square. Built to house bachelor Hanseatic traders and sailors, it derives its name from their patron saint, Mauritius, or Maurice, traditionally depicted as an armed Moor. The Soviets completed the destruction of this magnificent Gothic-Dutch Renaissance building that World War II had begun — its Teutonic architecture was too decadent — but after independence, it was one of the first structures to be rebuilt. Being very close to Rigans' hearts, the work was financed by individual donations.

3 *Caucasian Feast* 8 p.m.

Riga's days in the Soviet sphere did have a culinary benefit: exposure to the well-spiced, hearty cuisines of countries of the Caucasus: Azerbaijan, Georgia, or, in the case of **Akhtamar** (Merkela Iela 9; 371-6-721-5032; akhtamar.lv/par-restoranu; $$), Armenia. The shashliks (kebabs, so named for the shashki, or sabers, on which they were once cooked) are full-flavored and perfectly cooked, and Akhtamar's Caucasian cuisine shines especially in the deeply flavored stews, particularly the tomato- and herb-based chakhokhbili.

OPPOSITE Riga's collection of Art Nouveau buildings is Europe's largest, and only part of its architectural heritage.

BELOW Taka Spa, one of the more glamorous of Riga's saunas. The hot-to-cold sauna ritual is a serious custom here.

4 *Drinks and Conversation* 11 p.m.

Riga's thriving bachelor party trade means it abounds in bars featuring scantily clad women, music that rattles dental fillings, and vodka served by the gallon. Give these the widest possible berth. Better to cap off your night at **Galerija Istaba** (Krisjana Barona Iela 31a; 371-6-728-1141), just north of the elegant Vermanes Park district. Its first floor is an art gallery, filled with knickknacks designed by local artists; the second floor is a cozy, friendly bar that nightly attracts a wide swath of bohemian Riga. The bar is well stocked, the service friendly.

SATURDAY

5 *Purify Yourself* 10 a.m.

Like its neighbors, Latvia takes its saunas seriously: most people prefer to get their hearts racing by dashing between a steam room and a cold pool rather than on a Stairmaster, and a few hours enrobed in eucalyptus steam is an ideal way to sweat out the excesses of a late night. Riga's saunas run the gamut, from unrepentantly grimy Soviet sweat shacks to the beautiful **Taka Spa** (Kronvalda bulvaris 3a; 371-6-732-3150; takaspa.lv). In its stylish surroundings, move from the sauna to the steam, get as hot as you possibly can, and then dive into the cold water. The sensation is truly exhilarating, and you will leave feeling rejuvenated.

6 *Going Green* 1 p.m.

Osiris (Krisjana Barona Iela 31; 371-6-724-3002; cafeosiris.lv; $$) opened in 1994, which makes it a Riga institution. It was the first Rigan restaurant to address the grim effects of Soviet crimes against salad: Osiris's salads are large, leafy, and based around fresh vegetables, a welcome contrast to the once-standard quivering bowls of mayonnaise and carrot cubes. Osiris draws a mixture of urban professionals, artists, writers, and politicians and was among the first gay-friendly spots in Riga. The menu honors today's international culinary trends: it is eclectic and changes frequently. You might follow a traditional herring-and-potato salad with kung pao chicken or excellent pelmeni (small Russian dumplings served with sour cream and vinegar). A specialty dessert — pancakes folded over enormous wedges of homemade sweet cheese — will fill you up for days.

7 *Street Art* 3 p.m.

Riga boomed in the late 19th and early 20th centuries, both in population and wealth. The most visible remnant of that boom can be seen in its collection of 750 Art Nouveau buildings. **Alberta Iela**, just north of the Esplanade and Kronvalda Park, is the best single street for viewing these ornate, quirky, and always eye-catching treasures. Mikhail Eisenstein, father of the film director Sergei, designed several of the most striking examples.

8 *Jewels and Antiques* 5 p.m.

For a city so steeped in history, it seems only fitting that the jewel of choice is amber, which has been washing up on Baltic seacoasts for millenniums. For convenience's sake, you can get your amber at any souvenir or jewelry shop; for local color, though, visit the stalls behind St. Peter's Church or along **Valnu Iela** behind the Hotel Riga. Riga's antiques shops also hold treasures of the more earthly kind: everything from old artwork to church artifacts to Soviet knickknacks. Small stores dot the city; sample their variety, depth, and cheerful disorganization.

9 *Starry Night* 8 p.m.

Vincents (Elizabetes Iela 19; 371-6-733-2830; restorans.lv; $$$) is widely recognized as a standout among restaurants in Riga. Martins Ritins, the chef and owner, pioneered the local-organic approach in Latvia; his restaurants almost single-handedly enabled the survival of dozens of small farmers. More important, he makes extraordinary food. His style could be described as Franco-Baltic-Scandinavian—such as yellowfin tuna tartare served on ice. He also has a showman's touch: one dinner featured as a palate cleanser an instant sorbet, composed tableside from Riga Black Balsam (a local bitter spirit, like Fernet-Branca with heavier caramel notes), black currant juice, brown sugar, club soda, and liquid nitrogen.

SUNDAY

10 *Capitalism in Action* 11 a.m.

Find the sprawling **Central Market** in the fascinating, grimy area of town known as Maskvas

OPPOSITE The reconstructed House of the Blackheads.

BELOW Wet weather in the cobblestoned Old Town.

Forstate (the Moscow Suburb). More than 1,000 vendors are spread across five enormous zeppelin hangars, as well as a secondary, more informal network of stalls outside the market proper. Vendors are arranged more or less by wares, and even if you buy nothing (though it would be a shame to go home without a loaf of Latvia's glorious rupjmaize black bread), simply strolling through the market provides a carnival of delights. You can find everything from fresh farmer's cheese to lemongrass to pig snouts;

outside the market, the stall holders sell leather goods, DVDs of dubious provenance, and freshly foraged mushrooms.

ABOVE Situated on the Gulf of Riga at the mouth of the Daugava River, Riga has always been an important Baltic city.

OPPOSITE Amber, harvested in the Baltic Sea, takes the form of necklaces, bracelets, rings, and other jewelry pieces for sale at a stall in Vecriga, Riga's old town.

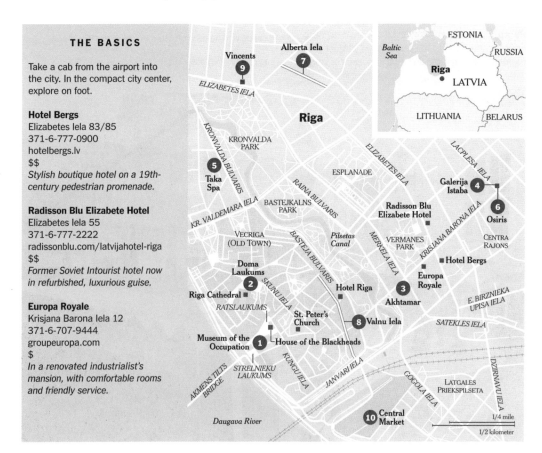

THE BASICS

Take a cab from the airport into the city. In the compact city center, explore on foot.

Hotel Bergs
Elizabetes Iela 83/85
371-6-777-0900
hotelbergs.lv
$$
Stylish boutique hotel on a 19th-century pedestrian promenade.

Radisson Blu Elizabete Hotel
Elizabetes Iela 55
371-6-777-2222
radissonblu.com/latvijahotel-riga
$$
Former Soviet Intourist hotel now in refurbished, luxurious guise.

Europa Royale
Krisjana Barona Iela 12
371-6-707-9444
groupeuropa.com
$
In a renovated industrialist's mansion, with comfortable rooms and friendly service.

Vilnius

Maybe it is the cobblestone byways that meander through Vilnius and appear more suited for horses than horsepower. Perhaps it is the unexpectedly historic architecture or the hulking castles that whisper of medieval derring-do. While modernity certainly intrudes — and Lithuania, in the post-Communist boom and financial-crisis bust of the early 21st century, underwent many changes — somehow or other, this capital city often has the feel of an old-world diorama sprung to life. — BY CLIFFORD J. LEVY

FRIDAY

1 *Get Lost* 4 p.m.

In the **Old Town**, it is not difficult to get lost among the crazy-quilt streets, and you may be thankful that you do. This Old Town is one of Europe's most beautiful and one of its largest, spreading in a web of alleys lined with elegant, straight-backed buildings. There's an alluring mishmash of architecture — from Gothic to neo-Classical and more — and one of the world's largest assortments of Baroque buildings. Whatever the style, the place sure is nice to gaze upon, whether you are lugging around an architectural tome or simply enjoying going astray among the narrow streets.

2 *Sour Cream, Not on the Side* 7 p.m.

Food culture has blossomed, and you can sample everything from Greek to Chinese, but first, go Lithuanian. At **Forto Dvaras** (Pilies Street 16; 370-5-261-1070; fortodvaras.lt; $), you'll find something of a Lithuanian culinary theme park: rustic furniture, staff in national costumes, and a menu laden with blini, pancakes, and giant dumplings called zeppelin. California spa cuisine it is not. (If you have a sour cream addiction, you won't be disappointed.) But portions are tasty and sizable, and the bill is light on the wallet.

3 *Make New Friends* 9 p.m.

All over Vilnius, night life is lively and unpretentious. You can follow the party all the way from the

bars or sidewalk cafes where you drink beers and munch sliced pig's ear (a traditional Lithuanian beer snack) to the more refined **Cozy** (Dominikonu Street 10; 370-5-261-1137; cozy.lt), a popular restaurant that brings in D.J.'s on weekends.

SATURDAY

4 *Towers and Spires* 10 a.m.

The Old Town has dozens of centuries-old churches. Modern-day pilgrims flock to the **Vilnius Cathedral** in the heart of the Old Town, not just to pray on Sunday but to hang out the rest of the time in the broad piazza. The cathedral itself is a frequently altered landmark with an 18th-century neo-Classical facade but an interior that dates in part to the 15th century. Next to it is an imposing detached bell tower 180 feet high. For a sharp contrast, there's **St. Anne's Church**, as curious and enthralling a Gothic edifice as you will find. Go ahead, squint. The facade truly is made of exposed bricks of numerous shapes, even the spires, as if someone turned loose a master builder with a masonry Lego set. Impressive in a different way is the **Gates of Dawn**, a bulwark that blocks a narrow road. Once part of the city's original fortifications, it was later transformed into a small chapel containing a venerated icon that has long drawn pilgrims, including Pope John Paul II.

OPPOSITE AND RIGHT Vilnius Cathedral. The city's Old Town is an alluring mishmash of buildings from Gothic to Baroque to neo-Classical.

5 *Street Shopping* 11 a.m.

Chat your way from peddler to peddler on cobble-stoned **Pilies Street**. Many of these vendors are craftsmen and folk artists. Some sell jewelry made from amber; others offer items like hand-crafted wooden bowls. Around them is a buzzing scene of stores and cafes, shoppers and street musicians. You are not far here from the elegant campus of **Vilnius University** (Universiteto Street). Founded in 1579, it is based in a complex of buildings dating back even farther, some with frescoes and lavish decoration.

6 *Hometown Lunch* 1 p.m.

For a lunch that's even less expensive than last night's dinner, take your midday meal at **Busi Trecias**

(Totoriu Street 18; 370-5-231-2698; busitrecias.lt; $), a cozy brewpub that serves a Lithuanian fry-up of potatoes, bacon, mushrooms, and cream. It could double as a good hangover remedy for those who indulge in too much of this place's excellent dark beer.

7 *The Context* 2 p.m.

Lithuania documents its sometimes glorious, sometimes troubled history, as told through its culture and art, at the **National Museum** (Arsenalo Street 1; 370-5-262-9426; lnm.lt). A statue of Lithuania's only king stands outside. Inside, both permanent displays and temporary exhibitions are interesting and well done.

8 *Fortified View* 4 p.m.

Hike up a cobblestone path to the **Upper Castle Museum** (Arsenalo Street 5; 370-5-261-7453; lnm. lt), in the Gediminas Tower (it's also a part of the National Museum). First constructed in the 13th century, the castle offers lovely views of the city

ABOVE Towers old and new: a television tower high above the city and the bell tower at Vilnius Cathedral.

LEFT On Pilies Street, not far from Vilnius University.

OPPOSITE Inside the Gates of Dawn, an old fortification transformed into a small chapel containing a venerated icon.

from its open-air roof, as well as exhibits of medieval weaponry. If you don't want to walk up the hill, you can ride a funicular.

9 *Fine Dining* 8 p.m.

La Pergola, in the Grotthuss Hotel (Ligonines 7; 370-5-266-0322; grotthusshotel.com; $$$), is a tablecloth-and-candlelight restaurant serving high-quality meals. The menu sprinkles in Lithuanian favorites amid more internationally inspired dishes.

SUNDAY

10 *The Dark Past* 10 a.m.

Shards of the nation's mournful past remain in Vilnius, and it is worth acknowledging them. The **Museum of Genocide Victims** (Auku Street 2A; 370-5-249-8156; genocid.lt), known as the K.G.B. museum, is in a former prison where the Soviet secret police

once imprisoned, tortured, and killed Lithuanian nationalists and dissidents. The cells are intact, and you can walk into them. The **Holocaust Museum** (Pamenkalnio Street 12; 370-5-262-0730; jmuseum.lt) relies extensively on witness testimony and original documents to build a time line of the Jewish community's ascent and destruction in Vilnius. Maps and photographs of the two ghettos where Jews were detained by the Nazis show how little the footprint of the city has changed. In some places, what now look like quaint gates were once covered with barbed wire. Larger Holocaust museums may present comparable exhibits, but to gaze upon them here, after walking those very same streets, is especially affecting.

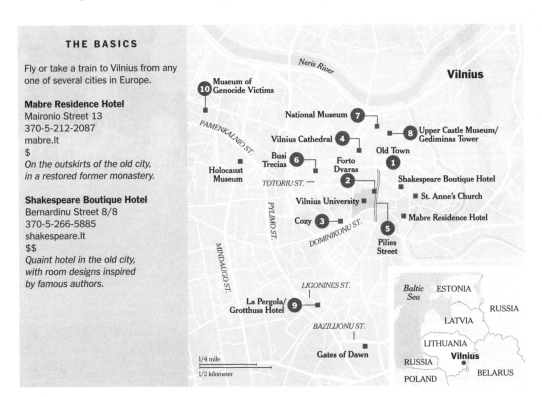

THE BASICS

Fly or take a train to Vilnius from any one of several cities in Europe.

Mabre Residence Hotel
Maironio Street 13
370-5-212-2087
mabre.lt
$
On the outskirts of the old city, in a restored former monastery.

Shakespeare Boutique Hotel
Bernardinu Street 8/8
370-5-266-5885
shakespeare.lt
$$
Quaint hotel in the old city, with room designs inspired by famous authors.

Moscow

Post-perestroika, Moscow evoked a giant college dormitory gone wild. Free from oppressive and overbearing Soviet leaders, Muscovites set upon their city with freshman-like zeal, indulging in the fruits of capitalism, hangovers be damned. But the global slowdown after 2008 knocked some of the sparkle out of Russia's economic growth and injected a bit of maturity — and perhaps even some sobriety — into a city where subtlety once seemed taboo. You can still safely bring your tight leather trousers or leopard-print hot pants, if that's your thing. But those with more refined tastes will also find a more subdued sense of chic, not to mention the enduring survival of the classic Russian love of the arts.

— BY MICHAEL SCHWIRTZ AND STEVEN LEE MYERS

FRIDAY

1 *Chocolate Factory* 4 p.m.

One of the city's cooler scenes was once its sweetest. On an island across from the Kremlin, the **Krasny Oktyabr**, a red-brick chocolate factory from the 19th century, is now a modish cultural complex with galleries, lecture halls, and cafes. Top galleries include the **Lumiere Brothers Center of Photography** (3 Bolotnaya Naberezhnaya, building 1; 7-495-228-9878; lumiere.ru), one of the few places dedicated to the preservation and study of Soviet and Russian photography.

2 *Old Moscow* 6 p.m.

If it's not too cold, walk across the **Patriarchs Bridge**, a footbridge where newlyweds affix padlocks in a Russian marriage tradition. Offering spectacular views of the Kremlin, the bridge links the chocolate factory to the gold-domed **Cathedral of Christ the Savior**, which was built in the 1990s as a replica of the original demolished under Stalin. For a glimpse of pre-revolutionary Moscow, continue to Bolshaya Nikitskaya Street and stop into **Kvartira 44** (22/2

Bolshaya Nikitskaya; 7-495-691-7503; kv44.ru/bolshaya-nikitskaya.html). Popular with the artistic intelligentsia, it offers inexpensive drinks (and food). The piano bar on the top floor turns raucous around midnight. If there's no room, head across the street to **Mayak** (19/13 Bolshaya Nikitskaya; 7-495-691-7449; clubmayak.ru), which is owned by the same family.

3 *Grunge and Glam* 9 p.m.

Back on the island, the Strelka Institute's **Strelka Bar** (Strelka; 14 Bersenevskaya Naberezhnaya, building 5A; 7-495-771-7416; strelkainstitute.com; $$$-$$$$) is a hangout where the city's glitterati deign to mingle with the grungy bohemian crowd that pours into the bar after film viewings and art lectures given on the premises. The food is eclectic: cream of lentil soup, lasagna with spinach, and desserts like lemon meringue pie.

4 *Please, Mr. Doorman* Midnight

Moscow night life doesn't really get going until well after midnight, and becomes interesting only much later. For a low-key evening, stay at Strelka, where D.J.'s spin till morning and well-dressed partiers drift in and out. Strelka has made its neighborhood a new place to see and be seen well after darkness falls as clubs, bars, and high-end restaurants have sprung up in its increasingly glamorous

OPPOSITE St. Basil's Cathedral on Red Square, one of the world's most photographed, and photogenic, buildings. It was a project of Ivan the Terrible in the 16th century.

RIGHT The Patriarchs Bridge and the Cathedral of Christ the Savior, a replica of a church destroyed by Stalin.

daughters, wives, girlfriends, or mistresses with galleries to keep them occupied. **Garage** (7-495-645-0520; garageccc.com), a nonprofit center in Gorky Park, is one of the few devoted to modern art, and one of the coolest. For more established art, don't miss the **Pushkin State Museum of Fine Arts** and its **Gallery of European and American Art** (14 Volkhonka Street; 7-495-697-1546; arts-museum.ru). This is the place to find the Pushkin's famous collection of Impressionist and Post-Impressionist paintings, with heavy representation of Monet, Cézanne, Picasso, Matisse, and the other marquee-name Impressionists.

shadow. For a more intense experience, stroll over to the other side of the island and **Club Icon** (9 Bolotnaya Naberezhnaya; 7-495-256-4944; iconclub.ru), and hope that you pass muster at the door. (Hint: Ask the desk at your hotel to make a reservation for you.) Inside, you'll have to purchase a bar deposit card that you can use to buy drinks. You'll join up to 2,500 partiers in various halls, some of them in the 36 V.I.P. lounges, all of them writhing to dance music.

SATURDAY

5 *Oligarchs and Impressionists* 11:30 a.m.
Luckily for artsy Muscovites, it has become fashionable for Russia's billionaires to set up their

6 *Skates in Red Square* 3 p.m.
When it's warm, follow the sound of singers rehearsing at the New Opera to the **Hermitage Gardens** (entrance at 3 Karetny Ryad; mosgorsad.ru), a charming park with cast-iron gazebos and cafes, where locals like to lounge when not at their country houses. There are also frequent outdoor concerts. As the weather gets colder, the terraces come down and ice skating rinks go up. Try the rink on **Red Square** for

TOP A culinary map of Georgia at Khachapuri, a relaxed cafe that caters to Muscovites' love for Georgian food. Try the full Georgian feast, and pair it with a Georgian wine.

ABOVE The Ritz-Carlton, a high-end choice in a city of expensive hotels. This luxury suite has a view of Red Square.

a unique view of Russia's most famous landmark. Warm up with a drink at the **O2 Lounge** (3 Tverskaya Street; 7-495-225-8888; ritzcarlton.com/moscow), a chic rooftop bar atop the Ritz-Carlton, with stunning Kremlin views. As darkness falls, Red Square is dramatically lighted.

7 *Georgian Menu* 6 p.m.

Despite Russia's hostilities with Georgia a few years ago, Muscovites still love Georgian food. With its assortment of cheese-filled pastries, grilled meats, and spicy soups, Georgian cuisine is for Russians what Mexican food is for Americans. Try the perfectly grilled shashlik or shish kebabs at **Dzhondzholi** (20/1 Tverskaya Street; 7-495-730-1013; $$$), a cavernous restaurant with a large trellised veranda in summer. Or, for the cheesy pies known as khachapuri, head to aptly named **Khachapuri** (10 Bolshoi Gnezdnikovsky Side Street; 7-985-764-3118; hacha.ru; $$$), a relaxed cafe with a mostly Georgian staff and a white-haired piano player with a penchant for jazz standards. Or choose the full Georgian feast at either restaurant, accompanied with Georgian wine.

8 *The New Old Bolshoi* 8 p.m.

If you like ballet, you are in the right city. Even if you think you don't, after you've seen one at the **Bolshoi Theater** (1 Teatralnaya Square; 7-495-455-5555; bolshoi.ru), you may change your mind. The performances are impeccable, the dancers are superbly athletic artists, and the newly refurbished red and gold leaf interior is dazzling. The six-year restoration completed in 2011 brought back the old 19th-century Bolshoi, when the czars were the chief fans, erasing alterations made in the Communist era and replacing hammer-and-sickle signs with the old imperial eagles. Don't expect to walk up and get a ticket; you should reserve in advance.

ABOVE Part social club, part spa, the Russian banya rejuvenates the bather. This steamy pool is at Sandunovskiye Baths.

BELOW Rustic Russian antiques, a hint of the old peasant life, on display at Izmailovsky Market.

SUNDAY

9 *Bathhouse Therapy* 8 a.m.

A Russian tradition is the banya, or bathhouse. Part spa, part social club, the banya exposes the body to extremes of hot (in the steam room) and cold (in dunking pools of various degrees of frigidity). The city's most famous banya is the **Sandunovskiye Baths**, or Sanduny (Neglinnaya 14, 7-495-782-1808; sanduny.ru). There are separate sections for men and women; the men's "high," or elite, hall has a fin-de-siècle décor of columns, carved wood, and brass.

10 *Flea Market Capitalists* 10:30 a.m.

Izmailovsky Market, near the estate where Peter the Great played war games as a boy, is a sprawling open-air market that evolved out of the first Soviet experiments in capitalism: the flea market. One area has been refashioned into a souvenir paradise, with stalls offering nesting dolls, lacquer boxes, art, antiques, carpets, and things you cannot imagine. The market is at 73 Izmaylovskoye Shosse, but don't expect to see any sign. Follow the crowds from the Partizanskaya metro station.

ABOVE Matryoshka, the beloved Russian nesting dolls, for sale at Izmailovsky Market.

OPPOSITE Impersonators hoping to attract tourist rubles mimic Leonid Brezhnev, Joseph Stalin, and Vladimir Putin.

THE BASICS

The city's amazing metro system can take you within walking distance of almost every major attraction.

Ritz-Carlton
3 Tverskaya Street
7-495-225-8888
ritzcarlton.com/moscow
$$$$
On the high end in a city with some of the most expensive hotels in the world. Steps from the Kremlin.

Golden Apple Boutique Hotel
11 Malaya Dmitrovka
7-495-980-7000
goldenapple.ru
$$$
Well-located and one of Moscow's few boutique hotels.

Godzillas Hostel
6 Bolshaya Karetnaya Street
7-495-699-4223
godzillashostel.com
$
One of few options for frugal travelers.

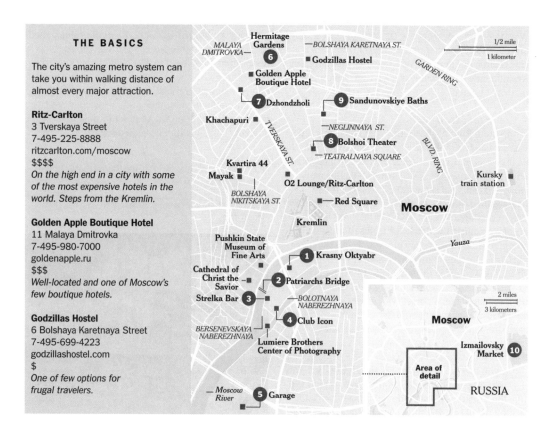

St. Petersburg's
White Nights

In St. Petersburg, the grand city of the czars, they call them the "White Nights": those 80 or so evenings, running from May to the end of July, when the city celebrates nearly round-the-clock daylight. Residents have gloried in their brief, bright midsummer ever since Peter the Great founded the city in the early 1700s, but for most of the 20th century, the joy was muted by wars, revolution, and the grim imperatives of the Soviet state. Once again a time of festive events and giddy pleasures, the White Nights have now become an intrinsic part of St. Petersburg's identity, drawing partiers from abroad along with well-heeled Russian tourists — their wallets fat with petrodollars — and members of the increasingly mobile Russian middle class.

— BY JOSHUA HAMMER AND CLIFFORD J. LEVY

FRIDAY

1 *Where the Czars Reside* 3 p.m.

St. Petersburg was constructed on what originally were more than 100 islands formed by a latticework of rivers, creeks, streams, and canals that flow into the Baltic Sea at the mouth of the Neva River. The wide Neva itself basically divides the city in half. On the southern side, most reminiscent of Venice or Amsterdam, are many of the most familiar landmarks. The northern side is made up of a cluster of islands. There are bridges, but take your first trip to the islands by subway. Exit at the Petrogradskaya stop and head for the **Peter and Paul Fortress** (7-812-230-6431; spbmuseum.ru) on Zayachy Island. This is the city's oldest section, filled with museums and the gorgeous, not to mention slightly eerie, **Cathedral of Saints Peter and Paul**. Stone vaults inside are the crypts of the czars, including the last one, Nicholas II.

2 *Dinner With Dostoyevsky* 5:30 p.m.

Amble back to the city center, crossing the Neva on the Troitsky Bridge, with its vistas of the city. Pass through the Field of Mars, a park with an eternal flame and war memorial that is often visited by brides and grooms on their wedding days. Look up and you will see the colorful onion domes of the **Church of the Savior on Spilled Blood** (Konyushennaya Square, 7-812-315-1636; eng.cathedral.ru/spasa_na_krovi/). Have a pre-theater dinner with vodka shots at

The Idiot (82 Moika Canal; 7-812-946-5173; $$), a popular cafe that pays homage to Dostoyevsky with a design intended to resemble an apartment of his era as well as with its name (the title of one of his gloomiest novels). The menu features excellent Russian and vegetarian cuisine.

3 *Mad for the Mariinsky* 7 p.m.

The **Mariinsky Theater** (Teatralnaya Ploshad 1; 7-812-326-4141; www.mariinsky.ru) is the kind of place where an opera or ballet can draw crowds of young people who act as if they're at an American rock show, talking excitedly about the performance during intermission and thronging around concession kiosks buying cards and photos of their favorite stars. The performances are of the highest quality (this used to be called the Kirov), and the theater is an important part of the White Nights Festival, an international arts extravaganza that runs from May to July. Buy tickets in advance.

OPPOSITE The Griboyedov Canal from a bridge with statuary-supported cables. Late-evening boat rides are a diversion in the White Nights, when the sun never quite disappears.

BELOW Visit Kuznechny market to see Russian abundance: produce, spices, honey in the comb. These bins hold dried fruit.

4 *Late-Night Gleam* Midnight

It's midnight, and it's not dark yet. What better time to go out on the water? Thread your way through the revelers on Nevsky Prospekt, St. Petersburg's main street, and board a tour boat at the **Fontanka Canal** or **Moika Canal**. Pass under low arched canal bridges and out into the vast Neva River, and all of St. Petersburg spreads before you, with pink,

ABOVE Crowds gather at 2 a.m. in the dim glow of the White Nights to watch a spectacle on the wide Neva River. Four drawbridges open slowly in turn, letting ships into the city.

BELOW Crossing Nevsky Prospekt, the grand boulevard that hums during the day, after 2 a.m. on a summer night.

peach, and violet clouds streaking the horizon. The golden spires of the Peter and Paul Cathedral glint in the fading sun, and the maritime air greets you with a pungent mix of gasoline and ripe river smells.

SATURDAY

5 *Hydrofoil to the Fountains* 11 a.m.

Now for a glimpse of the glories, or depravities (depending on your point of view), of the czars. French royalty had an out-of-town pleasure zone at Versailles; the Russians had **Peterhof** (2 Razvodnaya; 7-812-450-5287; peterhofmuseum.ru), an 18th-century complex of palaces and gardens west of the city center. The estate is famous for its cascading fountains. The easiest and most enjoyable way to get to Peterhof is by hydrofoil. Boats depart frequently in summer from the jetties near the Hermitage, the University embankment, and the Senate Square.

6 *Yes, That Museum* 3 p.m.

Perhaps you've heard of the neat little museum near the hydrofoil berth. Of course, you could spend the entire weekend in the **Hermitage** (2 Dvortso-vaya Ploshchad, or Palace Square; 7-812-710-9079; hermitagemuseum.org), but even a few hours can give you a scrumptious taste. It all started with Catherine the Great's monumental art collection, and the acquisitions continued right through World War II, when the Red Army brought home a trove of looted art (reversing the energetic Nazi looting that had gone in the other direction). The Impressionist paintings are among the most popular works in this storehouse of masterpieces, but the collection spans eras from the time of the ancient Egyptians to the 20th century.

7 *Russian Italian* 9 p.m.

The sun is still bright outside, so fortify yourself for the long night ahead with a leisurely casual dinner at **Probka/Il Grappolo** (6 Prospekt Dobrolyubova; 7-812-918-6910; probka.org; $$), a modern wine bar and restaurant. The wine list includes top-flight reds and whites from a dozen countries, and the menu features Italian and other European food. Try one of the pizzas or a pasta dish like tagliatelle with rabbit or black taglioline with red caviar.

ABOVE Practicing at the classic Mariinsky Theater.

8 *Out With the Crowd* 11 p.m.

Join in a White Nights ritual, the downtown walkabout through the area around the **Moika Canal**. Stroll amid the crowds on Nevsky Prospekt, passing curio shops, theaters, and ethnic restaurants. Walk through Palace Square to a plaza beside the river, facing Vasilyevsky Island. On the plaza and along the riverbank, the energetic scene includes teeming crowds, stands selling ice cream and American-style hot dogs, street theater, jam sessions, and sightseers dodging splashes from sightseeing boats while sitting on steps leading down to the river. As the sun lingers (on the longest days here, the sunset nearly merges with the sunrise), celebrations are going on not just at riverside, but in every corner of St. Petersburg. Dance clubs and private beach clubs stay open until at least 6 a.m.

9 *Bridge Party* 2 a.m.

Every night at 2 a.m., the four big drawbridges that cross the Neva, all illuminated, rise to a 90-degree angle to allow barges and other big vessels to pass. This happens throughout the year, of course, but the warm weather and the still-bright skies of the White Nights make it a popular midsummer spectacle. There's a celebratory feeling as the hour approaches, and the multitudes watch from both sides of the river. One by one, at 15-minute intervals, each of the spans goes up in turn. Their graceful upward movement, each following another with what seems like perfect

synchronicity; the anticipation and the interplay of lights and water convey a magical effect. Traffic grinds to a halt, people gape from both sides of the river, and barges from the Gulf of Finland sweep into view.

Market (3 Kuznechny Pereulok; 7-812-312-4161), where there is an abundance of fruit, vegetables, and spices from former colonies in Central Asia and the Caucasus region. A stop here will convince you that the storied food shortages of the Russian past are well past. And once you nibble the fresh honey proffered on the comb or from vats, it may be difficult for you to settle for the stuff from a jar back home.

SUNDAY

10 *Honey and Spice* Noon

Russia used to be an empire, and you'll sense this history in a wake-up visit to the **Kuznechny**

ABOVE Part of the payback for the long Russian winter is the opportunity to relax by the Neva in the summer twilight.

OPPOSITE The Cathedral of Saints Peter and Paul inside the walls of the Peter and Paul Fortress.

THE BASICS

Arrive at Pulkovo Airport or travel four hours from Moscow on the new high-speed train.

Grand Hotel Europe
Nevsky Prospekt, 1/7
Mikhailovskaya
7-812-329-6000
grandhoteleurope.com
$$$$
Guests have included European monarchs, Tchaikovsky, and Luciano Pavarotti.

Renaissance St. Petersburg Baltic Hotel
4 Pochtamtskaya
7-812-380-4011
marriott.com
$$$$
Next to St. Isaac's Cathedral.

Petro Palace
14 Malaya Morskaya
7-812-571-3006
petropalacehotel.com
$$$
Well regarded mid-priced hotel.

St. Petersburg

Cathedral of Saints Peter and Paul

1/2 mile
1 kilometer

ZAYACHY ISLAND

Malaya Neva

9 Neva River

TROITSKY BRIDGE

PROSPEKT DOBROLYUBOVA

Probka/ Il Grappolo **7**

1 Peter and Paul Fortress

VASILYEVSKY ISLAND

Hermitage **6**

FIELD OF MARS

PALACE SQUARE

2 Church of the Savior on Spilled Blood

Renaissance St. Petersburg Baltic Hotel

Petro Palace

Grand Hotel Europe

NEVSKY PROSPEKT

The Idiot

Fontanka Canal **4**

8 Moika Canal

3 Mariinsky Theater

TEATRALNAYA PLOSHAD

10 Kuznechny Market

FIN.

KRESTOVSKY — ISLAND

Baltic Sea

EST.

St. Petersburg

LAT.

RUSSIA

VASILYEVSKY — ISLAND

LITH.

Moscow

BEL.

Area of detail

Neva River —

RUSSIA

2 miles
3 kilometers

5 Peterhof

Gulf of Finland

TO PULKOVO AIRPORT ↓

St. Petersburg in Winter

It made wimps of earlier invaders, but the dread Russian winter — which defeated both Napoleon and Hitler — need not intimidate the traveler. Hardy souls who visit then, especially in the Russian holiday season, discover a city aglow, its broad boulevards, graceful bridges, glittering palaces, winding canals, and beautiful, snow-blanketed parks illuminated throughout the long, dark nights. St. Petersburg boasts cultural treasures that rival those of Paris, Vienna, London, and Rome, but perhaps its greatest attraction in any season is its history. Vibrant and ever present, St. Petersburg's bloody, tumultuous past is as inescapable as the mists that rise from the ice-glazed streets with the winter sun at midmorning.
— BY STEVE DOUGHERTY

FRIDAY

1 *Street Caviar* 2:30 p.m.

Avoiding the high prices of the city's elegant hotel dining rooms, you can nonetheless boast back home that you lived on caviar all weekend. Just buy it in blini — the thin Russian pancakes that are a ubiquitous St. Petersburg snack, often purchased as take-out and eaten on the street. The blini are spread with sour cream and a forkful or two of red caviar, then folded into bite-size envelopes. **Teremok** ($) a popular Russian chain, has several locations around town, including one at 93 Nevsky Prospekt, where you can get blini with caviar or a variety of other ingredients, including mushrooms, cheese, and salmon.

2 *Czarist Decorating* 3 p.m.

It's winter, so tour the **Winter Palace** (7-812-710-9079; hermitagemuseum.org). In this massive building on Palace Square, covering a full block, you will glimpse not only some of the fabulous Hermitage museum's art collection, but also the lavish lifestyle

OPPOSITE The Catherine Palace, one of the huge homes maintained around St. Petersburg by the Russian czars and empresses, is about 12 miles south of the city center.

RIGHT Hardy tourists who arrive in winter discover St. Petersburg as its residents know it day to day: a stately and livable city with deep cultural and historic roots.

of the czars. Rooms are furnished with thrones and gold carvings, grand staircases curve up to marble-pillared colonnades, ballrooms and reception halls await. History buffs and Tolstoy fans should not miss the 1812 War Gallery, with portraits of heroes from the victory over Napoleon.

3 *Armenian Specialties* 8 p.m.

It's been dark for four or five hours, and the cold is deepening, so have a meal in a cozy spot. **Kilikia** (26/40 Gorokhovaya; 7-812-327-2208; $) is a local favorite, a Caucasian-Mediterranean restaurant with emphasis on the Armenian. (Kilikia, or Cilicia, was an Armenian kingdom.) Warmed by brick ovens, it serves kebabs, a delicious potato dish called khauma, and spicy tava stew.

4 *Bands and Bunny Suits* 10 p.m.

Winter gets a hedonistic spin at **Purga** (11 Fontanka Embankment; purga-club.ru), a wildly raucous basement club whose name means "snowstorm." Expect scenes like servers (male and female) in fuzzy bunny suits, "New Year's Eve" revelers in Father Frost Santa hats regardless of the date on the calendar, shirtless bartenders, and conga lines of carousers singing drinking songs. For a less riotous scene, go to the **Griboedov Club** (2A Voronezhskaya; 7-812-764-4355; griboedovclub.ru), which features

popular D. J.'s and alternative bands. Or relax at the **JFC Jazz Club** (33 Shpalernaya; 7-812-272-9850; jfc-club.spb.ru), said by some to be St. Petersburg's best spot for live jazz.

SATURDAY

5 *Blood and Poetry* 10:15 a.m.

In Palace Square at this hour, throngs of schoolchildren await the opening of the Hermitage, and if it's holiday season, cobblestones sparkle and glisten from winking Christmas lights. But in 1905 this was a place of carnage, when Czar Nicholas II's royal guards opened fire on citizens petitioning for democratic reform. The ensuing public anger helped fuel the Russian Revolution. Walk about five minutes to the **Pushkin Museum** (12 Moika Embankment; 7-812-571-3531; museumpushkin.ru), where you can ask yourself how many countries would make a national idol out of a poet. Pushkin's image greets you here in grand public squares, museums, and street-corner posters. This location is an apartment where he lived — and where he died after being shot in a duel in 1837, at the age of 37. Displays include thousands of books and his dueling pistols.

6 *Northern Connection* 11:30 a.m.

At the **Russian Ethnographic Museum** (4/1 Inzhenernaya; 7-812-570-5421; ethnomuseum.ru),

the Siberian exhibit is a must-see for Americans raised on the story of the Indians' arrival in North America via a land bridge from Russia. Tableaus depict indigenous people in far eastern Russia who until very recently lived in teepees, wore beaded buckskin clothing, hunted with bows and arrows, and plied rivers in canoes. (They also rode reindeer.) Next door at the **Russian Museum** (7-812-595-4248; rusmuseum.ru), a vast collection of Russian art ranges from medieval icons to works by Kandinsky. A statue of Pushkin stands in the small park out front.

7 *Main Street* 1 p.m.

Take a stroll on **Nevsky Prospekt**, a broad boulevard lined with stores, boutiques, office buildings, and palaces. Check out the shops, and choose a restaurant for lunch. Then walk toward the Neva River. At the winding Griboyedov Canal, which snakes south through the heart of the old Haymarket District made famous by Dostoyevsky, is the **Cathedral of Our Lady of Kazan**, modeled after St. Peter's at the Vatican. The city's holiest shrine, it was converted into the Historical Museum of Religion and Atheism during the Soviet era. In front of it is a far-larger-than-life-size statue of Mikhail Kutuzov, the Russian general who defeated Napoleon. In *War and Peace*, Tolstoy

ABOVE The richly decorated interior of the rococo Catherine Palace, in Pushkin city.

depicted him as a sleepy, sly, one-eyed old fox under-estimated by friends and foe; here Kutuzov looks like a Roman emperor in heroic pose.

8 *Remembering Nabokov* 4 p.m.

Walk along the riverfront to the **Bronze Horseman**. That is the name Pushkin gave to the famous statue of Peter the Great — and it stuck. It's a short walk from there to the **Nabokov Museum** (47 Bolshaya Morskaya; nabokov.museums.spbu.ru), where Vladimir Nabokov was born in 1899 and lived until his family left the city in 1917, part of the tide of aristocrats fleeing the revolution. He describes the house in his autobiography, *Speak Memory*. Inside are artifacts gathered from his relatives, including books and part of his butterfly collection. Besides writing his novels, Nabokov made his mark as the translator, into English, of Pushkin's masterpiece, the verse-novel *Eugene Onegin*.

9 *Join the Audience* 7 p.m.

It's the high season for performances, and you are in one of the world's great capitals of classical music, opera, and ballet. Take in a concert at **Shostakovich Philharmonic Hall** (2 Mikhailovskaya; 7-812-312-9871; philharmonia.spb.ru), where during the Nazi siege in World War II, an orchestra premiered Symphony No. 7 by Dmitri Shostakovich. He had remained in the city and had written part of the symphony there

as the shells were falling. Or choose opera or ballet at one of several theaters: the **Mariinsky**, the renamed Kirov; the **Mikhailovsky**, formerly the Mussorgsky; or the **Hermitage Theater**. If you are comfortable watching a play in Russian, you can probably find one at the **Pushkin Theater**, where Chekhov's *The Seagull* bombed at its 1896 premiere.

10 *Après Theater* 10 p.m.

1913 (13/2 Voznesensky Prospekt; 7-812-315-5148; en.restaurant-1913.spb.ru; $$-$$$) is a tablecloth and

ABOVE The Hermitage, one of the world's greatest museums.

BELOW St. Michael's Castle, part of the Russian Museum.

candlelight kind of restaurant. You can choose either international standards or distinctly Russian favorites like sturgeon, beef Stroganoff, or the Siberian ravioli called pelmeni. The wine list is extensive and varied.

SUNDAY

11 *Three-Horse Glide* 11 a.m.

For the ultimate Russian winter experience, head about 12 miles south of the city to the Catherine Palace and **Pavlovsk Park** and take a sleigh ride (sometimes the rides are in the classic three-horse troika sledge, sometimes pulled by a single horse) through the English garden commissioned by Catherine the Great. Tucked into a wool blanket at the back of a colorfully painted sleigh with a driver whipping a long green stick, you will feel you have died and gone to Tolstoy heaven.

ABOVE A celebration of Orthodox Christmas at the Russian Ethnographic Museum. The museum documents Russia's many native cultures and their traditional lives and customs.

OPPOSITE The angel atop the Alexander Column, on Palace Square, looks out over the Winter Palace.

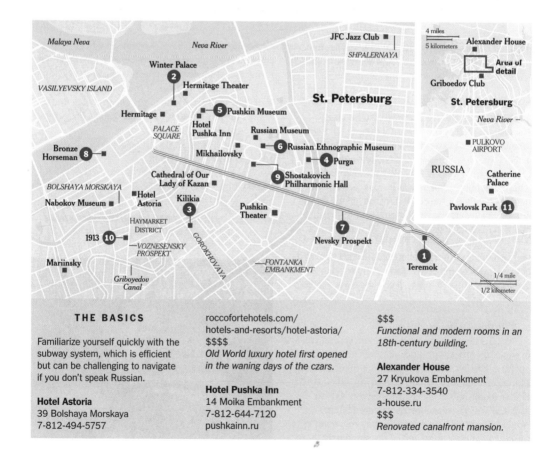

THE BASICS

Familiarize yourself quickly with the subway system, which is efficient but can be challenging to navigate if you don't speak Russian.

Hotel Astoria
39 Bolshaya Morskaya
7-812-494-5757

roccofortehotels.com/
hotels-and-resorts/hotel-astoria/
$$$$
Old World luxury hotel first opened in the waning days of the czars.

Hotel Pushka Inn
14 Moika Embankment
7-812-644-7120
pushkainn.ru

$$$
Functional and modern rooms in an 18th-century building.

Alexander House
27 Kryukova Embankment
7-812-334-3540
a-house.ru
$$$
Renovated canalfront mansion.

Indexes

AFTER DARK

ARCHITECTURE

ART

Contributors

Yoder, Dave 324, 471 below, 480, 481, 482 above, 482 below, 483, 484, 485, 486 above, 486 below, 487, 491, 498, 500, 524, 526, 527

ADDITIONAL PHOTO CREDITS

Aranda, Samuel/Getty Images 252 below
Azumendi, Gonzalo/Getty Images 287
Bally, Gaetan/European Press Photo Agency 356
Barbier, Bruno/Getty Images 88
Blumberg, Caroline/European Press Photo Agency 154
Bolton, Mark/Getty Images 255
Buena Vista Images/Getty Images 204
Chicurel, Arnaud/Getty Images 135
Daniau, Mychele/Getty Images 144
De Hogues, Bruno/Getty Images 124
Dilkoff, Dimitar/Getty Images 536, 538 above
Dolzhenko, Sergey/European Press Photo Agency 411
DONEV/European Press Photo Agency 541
Doychinov, Nikolay/Getty Images 538 below
Durand, Francois/Getty Images 143
Dyachyshyn, Yuriy/Getty Images 414, 415
Eurasia/Getty Images 250
Faint, Grant/Getty Images 432
Fell, Frank/Getty Images 474
Finney, Julian/Getty Images 6
Foto Polska 426, 427, 428 above, 428 below, 429
Gallup, Sean/Getty Images 292, 293, 296, 298
Getty Images 548
Glowimages/Getty Images 268
Gouliamaki, Louisa/Getty Images 544

Hache, Valery/Getty Images 190
Hansen, Catherine/Getty Images 168
Harvey, Philip Lee /Getty Images 253 above
Hellier, Gavin/Getty Images 412
Herrmann, Falk/Getty Images 310
Holmes, Peter/Getty Images 251 above
Juinen, Jasper/Getty Images 252 above
Lackner, Christof, Fotograf www. christoflackner.at 382, 383
Layda, Siegfried/Getty Images 330
Libera, Pawel/Getty Images 12
Lightfoot, Jeremy/Getty Images 17
Long, Dave/Getty Images 448
Messinis, Aris/Getty Images 542, 545
Muenter, Beate/Getty Images 300 above
Olive, Albert/European Press Photo Agency 261
Oliviero Olivieri/Getty Images 84
Oll, Robert/German National Tourism Board 312 above
Paul Photography/Getty Images 256
Petrova, Valentina/Getty Images 537
Photoservice Electa/Getty Images 440 above
Plattform/Getty Images 584
Richter, Juergen/Getty Images 270 below
Romanian National Tourist Office Romanian National Tourist Office 532
Schlenker, Jochen/Getty Images 286
Secchi, Marco/Getty Images 488
Shalvatis, Matthew – Roads Less Traveled Photography/Getty Images 410
Studio Vizualis/Esko Keski-Oja/www. vizualis.fi/Finland Tourism Board 622
Thompson, Paul/Getty Images 590
Tomlinson, Ruth/Getty Images 180
Travel Pix/Getty Images 198
van de Graaff, Tao (flickr.com/ taovdg)/Getty Images 605
Van Houts, NILS/Getty Images 120 above
Vanderelst, Guy/Getty Images 2, 318
Villalobos, Horacio/European Press Photo Agency 127
Vision/Cordelli/Getty Images 283
Weatherly, Karl/Getty Images 4

Weihrauch, Roland/European Press Photo Agency 657 above
West, Ian/Getty Images 289
White, Tim/Getty Images 576
Willnow, Sebastian/Getty Images 315, 317
Wilson, Patrick Jude 443, 444 below, 445 above, 446, 447
Wothe, Konrad/Getty Images 334
Yeowell, Gary/Getty Images 130
Zunino Celotto, Vittorio/Getty Images 222

Acknowledgments

We would like to thank everyone at *The New York Times* and at TASCHEN who contributed to the creation of this book.

Special recognition must go to Nazire Ergun and to Nina Wiener, Eric Schwartau, and Anne Sauvadet, the dedicated editors behind the scenes at TASCHEN; to Natasha Perkel, the *Times* artist whose clear and elegantly crafted itinerary maps make the traveler's pathway comprehensible; to *Times* photo editors Phyllis Collazo and Evan Sklar; and to Olimpia Zagnoli, whose illustrations enliven every article and each regional introduction.

Guiding the transformation of newspaper material to book form at TASCHEN were Josh Baker and Marco Zivny, art directors, and Philipp Sendner, production manager, as well as Doug Adrianson, Craig B. Gaines, Rick Landers, Jennifer Patrick, Susan Tudor, Sarah Wrigley, and Misty Zhou. Steve Bailey copy-edited and updated the manuscript. Fact-checkers and translators for the European-language editions included Juliette Blanchot, Nazire Ergun, George Filias, Tina Flecken, Evelyn Hartmann, Locteam of Barcelona, Chiara Mattioli, Halina Risse, Aija Soininen, Petra Sparrer, Somnur Vardar, and Ekaterina Werzeiser. At *The Times*, Heidi Giovine helped keep production on track at critical moments.

But the indebtedness goes much further back. This book grew out of the work of all of the editors, writers, photographers, and *Times* staff people whose contributions and support for the weekly *36 Hours* column built a rich European archive over many years.

Great thanks must go to all of the writers and photographers whose work appears in the book, both *Times* staffers and freelancers. And a legion of *Times* editors behind the scenes made it all happen, and still do.

Stuart Emmrich created *36 Hours* in 2002 and then refined the concept, first as the *Times* Escapes editor and then as Travel editor. Without his vision, this book would not exist. His successors in the role of Travel editor, Danielle Mattoon and then Monica Drake, have brought steady leadership to the column and support to the *36 Hours* books.

Suzanne MacNeille, now the column's direct editor, and her predecessor Denny Lee have guided *36 Hours* superbly through Europe by finding and working with writers, choosing and assigning destinations, and assuring that the weekly product would entertain and inform readers while upholding *Times* journalistic standards.

The talented *Times* photo editors who have overseen images and directed the work of the column's photographers on European assignments include Phaedra Brown, Lindsay Blatt, Lonnie Schlein, Jessica De Witt, and Gina Privitere.

Among the many editors on the *Times* Travel and Escapes copy desks who have kept *36 Hours* at its best over the years, three who stand out are Florence Stickney, Steve Bailey, and Carl Sommers. Fact-checkers for the weekly column have included John Dorman, Emily Brennan, and Rachel Lee Harris.

And a special acknowledgment must go to Benedikt Taschen, whose longtime readership and interest in the *36 Hours* column led to the partnership of our two companies to produce this book.

— BARBARA IRELAND AND ALEX WARD

Editor Barbara Ireland
Project management Alex Ward
Photo editor Phyllis Collazo and Evan Sklar
Itinerary maps Natasha Perkel
Illustrations Olimpia Zagnoli
Editorial coordination Nazire Ergun, Nina Wiener and Anne Sauvadet
Art direction Marco Zivny and Josh Baker
Design and layout Marco Zivny and Rick Landers
Production Philipp Sendner

EACH AND EVERY TASCHEN BOOK PLANTS A SEED!
TASCHEN is a carbon neutral publisher. Each year, we offset our annual carbon emissions with carbon credits at the Instituto Terra, a reforestation program in Minas Gerais, Brazil, founded by Lélia and Sebastião Salgado. To find out more about this ecological partnership, please check: www.taschen.com/zerocarbon
Inspiration: unlimited. Carbon footprint: zero.

© 2016 TASCHEN GmbH
Hohenzollernring 53, D–50672 Köln
www.taschen.com

ISBN 978-3-8365-4048-3   Printed in Latvia

YOU CAN FIND TASCHEN STORES IN

Amsterdam
P.C. Hooftstraat 44

Berlin
Schlüterstraße 39

Brussels
Rue Lebeaustraat 18

Cologne
Neumarkt 3

Hamburg
Bleichenbrücke 1-7

London
12 Duke of York Square

London Claridge's
49 Brook Street

Milan
Via Meravigli 17

Paris
2 rue de Buci

REYKJAVIK

NORTH ATLANTIC

LONDON

AMSTERDAM

PARIS

SOUTH WEST

MADRID